Dear George & Jim

Hope you enjoy dipping
into this!

Love
Robert & Sandra
x

EX CORDE CARITAS

GEORGE WATSON'S
— COLLEGE —

An Illustrated History

Preface

I have wanted to create this long overdue and necessary history for over thirty years, so it is a joy to see it ready for public inspection. It does not pretend to be an academic work, but is, nevertheless, a sound illustrated story easily consulted by all adults and youngsters alike. If it is not interesting then it has failed.

"It is astonishing how little we know of the old Hospital days and still more astonishing to think that Watson's alone (or almost alone) of the great Scottish schools has found no Homer to sing its epic. Surely there must be somewhere some loyal son of the school with a flair for historical research who might be inspired by filial piety to undertake the task. One can imagine how such a history would be welcomed by thousands of Watsonians all over the World." (*Watsonian* Editor, Robert Dunlop, 1951)

Well, not a Homer, but instead a Howie, a mere humble Broughtonian who in 1971 on board a Corporation bus spied Watson's and asked the question 'Why?' Roy Mack, Fiona Hooper and Graham Gibb – the early birds of the staffroom – were inspirational in getting me going on this project. There were so many unanswered questions regarding Watson's history from the Founder to modern uniform. It really was exhilarating to connect each new piece of the jigsaw. An investigation of Watson's in WW1 as part of the History Department's Battlefield Tours unearthed a huge amount of material as did subsequent research into our move to Colinton Road in 1932 and then Watson's in WW2. A great joy was the discovery of contemporaries who were more than willing to communicate and felt that they had been neglected in previous years. The success of booklets on those topics among Watsonians of all ages, plus renewed interest in Remembrance Day, convinced me that a school history was long overdue. Also convinced were the Principal (Gareth Edwards) and the Governors, especially the one who anonymously financed a term's full-time research without which this book would have been impossible. I researched and wrote *Part 1: George Watson's Hospital, 1741–1870* and *Part 2: George Watson's College, 1871–1974*.

The Ladies' College, meanwhile, found a Smith to forge and hammer its tale, namely Liz, its proud and loyal standard-bearer. Unfortunately, the history of GWLC has been much neglected, ignored even, thus this is our attempt to rectify matters. I just could not think of anyone else I would trust to write its history better than Liz whose love for all things Watson's has been proven time and time again. Her enthusiasm and joy are wonderfully infectious; her total honesty too. Liz is extremely grateful for the support given by The Watsonian Club.

Meanwhile, the post-merger period has been lovingly covered by the best person for the job, a small chap, namely Robert, who as Head of Watson's History Department lived through that eventful period, survived, flourished and only recently retired. His deep knowledge, understanding and feeling for the place shine through everything he does. We should feel honoured that Robert has taken the time and trouble to become associated with this work.

The final section is an evocation and celebration of Watson's by individuals, plus representatives of clubs and societies. If there are sins, they are sins of omission. It was simply impossible to include everyone and everything. Please feel free to write to me at the school or to the *Watsonian* with any information you think should have been included, errors, etc. I am hoping to bring out a supplement based on that, so don't hesitate to write, email, visit or telephone. Watson's is a friendly zone for FPs and friends! As Editor of the *Watsonian* I am also hoping to keep memories of the school alive in its pages, so, don't sit there and grumble, but, instead, start writing!

I feel proud not only to have inherited the mantle of school historian from the gentle Hector Waugh, but also the post of Editor of the *Watsonian*. I trust Hector would approve.

So, there it is. I hope you will find something of interest, something to inspire, something which intrigues, something to contemplate or something on which to base future plans. Who knows what will spring from all of this? If there is any blame then lay it at my door. I did my best!

Les Howie

Les Howie

Liz Smith

Robert Small

AUTHORS
Mr Les Howie
Miss Liz Smith
Mr Robert Small

EDITORS
Miss Elizabeth White
Mr Graham Gibb

PUBLISHER
Mrs Karen Tumblety

DESIGN & TYPESETING
Mr David Brown

PRINTED BY
Butler and Tanner

© Copyright 2006 George Watson's College
Colinton Road, Edinburgh, EH10 5EG

SOFTCOVER VERSION
ISBN 0-9501838-2-2
ISBN 978-0-9501838-2-4

HARDCOVER VERSION
ISBN 0-9501838-1-4
ISBN 978-09501838-1-7

www.gwc.org.uk

Childhood

- Born Edinburgh 23 November 1654 to John Watson and Marion Ewing. Had a young brother James.
- Father died when George was very young.
- Mother married Mr Symmer. George had a stepbrother, John.
- His family had become impoverished, so George and James went to live with their father's sister, Elizabeth Davidson of Curriehill.
- Probably attended Currie Parish School.

Youth

- Apprenticed on 2 April 1669 at age of 14 to James Cleland (Edinburgh Merchant) for five years.
- Stopped early – sent to Holland for training.
- Learned arithmetic, accounting and bookkeeping.
- Returned to Scotland, 1676.

The only known portrait of George Watson, painted in Edinburgh in 1720 by William Aikman.

Early Manhood

- Became secretary and accountant to Sir James Dick of Priestfield (Prestonfield), a rich merchant.
- Started Watson's financial activities with a free loan of £200 sterling.
- Stopped working for Dick in 1696.
- Became an accountant with the new Bank of Scotland. Wouldn't accept cutbacks, so was dismissed.

Life Begins at Forty

- Started to make lots of money, but also to help good causes.
- Donated money to Merchant Maiden Hospital founded by Mary Erskine in 1694. Became Treasurer and Governor.
- Encouraged Presbyterian education in Highlands and Islands.
- Died 3 April 1723 aged 68. Buried in Greyfriars' Churchyard.

Involved in financing New Mills woollen manufacturing in East Lothian.

Lent money to eminent people such as the Duke of Argyll and made sure he was repaid with interest.

Bought £300 Scots worth stock in the new Bank of Scotland.

Local agent for a London bookseller.

How did he make £189,239 Scots? Some examples.

Shipping deals, eg 1697, bought one-eighth share (£3,876 Scots) in *Sun Galley* sailing from Leith to Venice.

Part of a consortium who bought, at auction, the right to collect Edinburgh's local tax on beer. He became its Treasurer & Cashier.

Unlike George Heriot who gained most of his money acting as a pawnbroker to the rapacious James VI & I, and his shopaholic wife Anne, Watson got most of his by acting as a merchant banker and money-lender. He encouraged small businesses, but sometimes also enforced foreclosure.

Auditor of Bank of Scotland's accounts.

By *not* investing in the disastrous Darien Company which collapsed in 1700.

Bought houses to rent in Parliament and Fishmarket Closes.

In 1694, bought shares in linen manufacturing.

A staunch Presbyterian who studied theology as a hobby. Probably sympathetic to the Covenanting wing who stood steadfast unto death in the face of a violently repressive English Episcopalian dictatorship imposed after 1660 by Charles II. However, Watson did not let religious politics get in the way of making money. His first employer, Dick, was a Catholic and a friend of anti-Presbyterian and brazen Catholic James VII & II. Watson emerged squeaky clean from Dick's criminal activities.

Fiercely loyal to the aunt who brought him up and gave him a chance in life.

Not a hint of scandal eg James Gillespie was also a bachelor, but he has direct descendants. Gillespie left a lot of money to his maid.

His personality? This is how writers have described Watson.

Frugal, patient, systematic, hard-working and exacting.

Modest, quiet and retiring. Not physically strong.

Bore no malice to the mother who gave him away as a child. Supported her with money, credit and advice. Mum died in July 1697. George went to live with the Symmer family and stayed there all his life at a rent of £28 sterling a year.

Stubbornly pursued all who owed him money. Ruthlessly pursued financial gain

No jealousy towards his step-brother. Included John in business activities and appointed him the first accountant of Watson's Hospital.

Watson is described in the Bank of Scotland Minute Book of 1697 as, "... *a debonair and well-groomed bachelor.*"

So, Why a Hospital?

'Hospital' was used in Scotland to mean a boarding school, coming from 'hospitality' which involves giving bed and/or board with schooling tagged on. It was brought into use by George Heriot whose institution was modelled on Christ's Hospital in London. A place for sick people in Scotland was an 'Infirmary'.

- Given his childhood circumstances it is hardly surprising that Watson looked favourably on Heriot's Hospital (for poor, fatherless children) and the Merchant Maiden (for the daughters of merchants who had fallen on hard times). He intended to found the male equivalent of that institution (ie for sons and grandsons of 'decayed merchants', but with a preference for the names of 'Davidson' and 'Watson'). There was a gap in educational provision in Edinburgh and he intended filling it.
- It was to be for Protestant children with Protestant teachers.
- As a bachelor with no children, but plenty money (£15,769), he was buying a kind of immortality.

TOP: The Original plaque from George Watson's grave in Greyfriars' Kirkyard.
CENTRE: In 1991 a new Commemorative Plaque designed and executed by Mr Gill and Mr McVitie of the Art Department. Mr McVitie modelled the carving from the William Aikman portrait. After a service in Greyfriars' Kirk the Plaque was mounted on the Flodden Wall.
BOTTOM: G McVitie (left), M Gill (right).

Why Did the Merchant Company Become Involved?

It is odd considering that the purpose of the Company was to create and maintain a lucrative monopoly as regards those who could sell cloth in and around Edinburgh. Anyone who dared challenge it was vigorously pursued. Similar guild organisations run by the craftsmen combined with the Merchant Company to run Edinburgh politically as well as economically. They were the Freemen whilst the rest of the people were the Unfree. This clash resulted in a divided city with the reputation as one of the most violent in Europe. However, the Merchant Company had been set up in 1681 as a perpetual company by royal grant thus ensuring permanency and stability. To Watson this was necessary to ensure that the terms of his Will were implemented over the years to come.

In addition, the Company had run Merchant Maiden to Watson's great satisfaction, especially its devolved management by Governors. It was a model which Watson wanted to copy as regards his own proposed Hospital. Others were also impressed. In 1801, James Gillespie followed Watson's example as did Daniel Stewart in 1860.

George Watson was never a member of the Merchant Company.

Watson's Will Disputed

Watson's niece, Bessie Watson, ratified the Will on 10 April 1723. Almost immediately it was challenged by two of Watson's relatives, John Shaw (great-great-grandson of George Watson's grandfather) and Margaret Durie (great-granddaughter of the same). They claimed that unmarried, 47 year old Bessie was not in her right mind and the Will was, therefore, invalid. On 3 May, the sheriffs decided...

"That the said Elizabeth, alias Bessie Watson, is of a composed mind and rational Person; and neither is nor has been furious, fatuous nor a natural Idiot."

The Merchant Company arms: 'By Land and Sea'.

With all that money at stake, however, the issue was not dropped, but instead taken to the Court of Session where nits were picked and straws clutched at with all the desperation one might expect from those about to see a fortune sail away across the horizon. On 13 November 1723, the case was settled in favour of the defendants. Watson's Hospital would go ahead.

[The case was] taken to the Court of Session.

---

1 May 1724, the Statutes drawn up in 20 Chapters. The 3 Trustees named by Watson could change these, but, after their death, that right would pass to the Merchant Company.

→

Edinburgh Council approve the Statutes and takes the Hospital into its protection

→

The first Governors' Meeting in the Council House on 18 May 1724. The Minutes are begun.

↓

Governors begin to act like a finance and investment group, eg purchasing debts, making loans and then buying land (Merchiston and Cockburn in 1729).

←

Governors begin the long and difficult process of recovering the £12,000 sterling owed to Watson's estate.

←

Trustees buy Thomson's Yards for £420 on which to build the Hospital.

↓

Governors thoroughly enjoy making money. Building a Hospital suggested in 1726, but nothing comes of it. 1735, adverse comments by members of the public spur the Governors into action.

→

1734–6, furious debate over the suitability of Thomson's Yards. Heriot's offering to sell land while the Infirmary offer to purchase Thomson's Yards.

→

Governors buy Heriot's Croft. 1 February 1738 a committee appointed to meet with Trustees and an architect to discuss plans for a Hospital.

The Pros

- A beautiful site with a fine view of Hope Park (The Meadows) and also spacious for future expansion.
- The price was the same as got from selling Thomson's Yards
- Heriot's had no problem getting teachers, or with Governors' meetings.
- Greyfriars' Church was very close.
- The City Wall had not stopped Heriot's boys from going AWOL. Be vigilant.
- Away from nasty students with all their vices. Also, away from city centre ruffians.

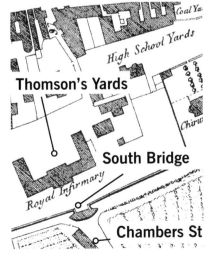

The Cons

- The new site was far away from the centre of town.
- Difficulty of getting teachers who would have to walk too far.
- Also too far for the Governors.
- New site was outside the City Wall. Boys would break out easily and 'stray'.
- Cost of Heriot's Croft would be too much.
- Heriot's Croft was also too big.

After considerable debate the Trustees eventually agreed to go along with the new proposal.

The Death of George Watson: A Mystery

But first, the above is a copy of Watson's birth entry in the Canongate Register.

"23 November 1654. John Watsone Merchant Marione Ewing a s(on) n(amed) George witn(esses) James Durie Merch(ant) Johne Bello (?) Samuel Denham Merch(ant) James Cowan Merch(ant) George Ramsay Merchant."

Translated by Olive Geddes, Senior Curator, Manuscripts, National Library of Scotland. Note the 'e' in 'Watsone'.

The Doctor's Report

"On the 3rd April 1723 the great man died. The exact cause of his death is a mystery. He died at a time when modern medicine had not begun, even in Edinburgh. Medical records and death certification were not made. However, there were many medicinal treatments given by doctors and patients were charged accordingly. The school still has the original invoices for the medicines given to George Watson and for the health carers who looked after him.

The first invoice is dated January 26th. 1723 when a form of cough mixture was prescribed. The frequency of prescribing increases to almost daily in late March. Laxatives and diuretics (to promote urine discharge) were prescribed throughout the illness. From March 13th. painkilling creams and emollients to one of his arms are invoiced. An abscess on his arm is now logged. Between March 20th and the fateful beginning of April stryptic plasters (to arrest bleeding) to treat his back are included. Gangrene on his back is mentioned. The last invoice was the day after his death for the use of 'dead powders' and 'aromatick oils' to apply to his corpse.

Further clues to the progression of his fatal illness are given in the accounts relating to Sarah Grindley and a nurse. Sarah was employed between February 7th and March 12th to provide meat and drink … and, on one occasion, breast milk. From 6th March to the 5th April a nurse was employed.

It would seem highly likely that George died of an infectious disease. Like the Third World today 18th Century Edinburgh's main killer diseases were infectious. However, it is not clear exactly which particular nasty one George caught.

George's considerable wealth could not overcome the poverty of medical knowledge and skills of the time. No doubt his wealth gave him a lifestyle that included non-cramped housing, good food and drink. He did not have to endure the appalling working conditions of so many of his fellow Edinburgh citizens. He died aged 70 years – well beyond the life expectancy of the day."

Dr Mike Hewitt

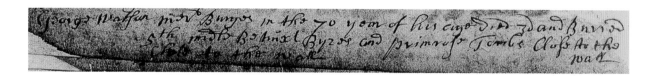

"George Watson mer(chant) Burges(s) in the 70 year of his age died 3rd and Buried 5th middle Betwixt Byres and Primrose Tombs Close to the wall"
Translated from the Greyfriars' Burial Register by Olive Geddes.

George Watson died in, or near, Conn's Close in the High Street. In 1824, unfortunately, the entire Close was destroyed in the Great Fire which obliterated most of the area between St Giles' Cathedral and the Tron Kirk. The site of Watson's house was near the present-day Old Assembly Close.

> George Watson, Treasurer to the Society for Propagating Christian Knowledge, died about the Middle of last Week, he has left about 12000 L. for Building and endowing a Hospital, to be called *Watson's Hospital.*

From *The Caledonian Mercury.* This is the first public intimation that a Hospital was intended.

1738   A Hospital Rises   1741

Governors buy Heriot's Croft. 1 February 1738 a committee appointed to meet with Trustees and an architect to discuss plans for a Hospital.

→

By January 1741 the building is about completed, including a marble chimney in the Governors' Room

→

9 March 1738 The architect, William Adam, hands in two plans the smaller of which is accepted. Estimates received and one chosen: £4,168 11s 4d.

→

Watson's Hospital is opened at Whitsun 1741.

The Foundation Stone

Facta sunt cum bono
Deo harum aedium fundamenta
22 Maij AD MDCCXXXVIII.

Helped by God's bounty the foundations of this building were laid 22 May 1738.

A coat of arms was envisaged above the main door, but Watson didn't have one. The Trustees then set about putting something together. It was matriculated on 29 February 1740 with the motto *'Ex Corde Charitas'*. Made from Craigleith sandstone for £18 18s

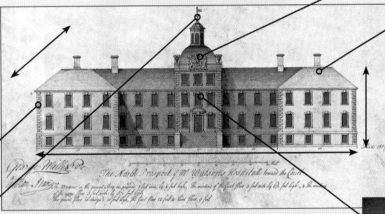

Foundation Stone, NE corner

42 feet wide

Rustic corners

Stone cornice around whole house

33 feet high

185 feet long

"As a Spire Bell and some other ornament is to be put on top of the Cupiloe to point out the airths for which the Wind blows, shall this be a ship?"

(16 September 1740) A ship, resting on a globe, was eventually produced costing £5 10s to cover the huge amount of gilt and *"troublesome work"*.

Agreed on 29 February 1740 to have a 'Character Stone', in marble, inscribed in Latin and set above the marble chimney piece in the Governors' Room. The letters were blacked in July 1745. An English translation was painted above the outside of the door leading into the Governors' Room.

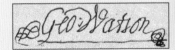

An expensive brass and steel, eight-day clock costing £40 was installed in the Cupiloe. Above is its only known depiction from Maitland's *Edinburgh*, published in 1753.

The globe seems to have disappeared by that time while the unreliable timepiece was removed by 1813. But when were the dolphins made?

GEORGE WATSON,

MERCHANT AND CITIZEN OF EDINBURGH,

SPRUNG FROM A LONG LINE OF ANCESTORS, CITIZENS, AND MERCHANTS COMMANDED THIS BUILDING TO BE ERECTED, AND THE GREAT WEALTH WHICH HE HAD NOT INHERITED FROM HIS PARENTS BUT HAD WON, THROUGH THE GRACE OF GOD, BY HIS OWN INTEGRITY AND PERSEVERANCE, HE DIRECTED TO BE GIVEN BACK TO GOD, THE BENEFACTOR OF ALL, AND TO BE ADMINISTERED PERPETUALLY BY THE WORTHY MERCHANT COMPANY OF EDINBURGH FOR THE BENEFIT OF THE NEEDY SONS OF THE AFORESAID MERCHANT COMPANY WHOM HE, A BACHELOR AND WITHOUT OFFSPRING, WISHED TO BE ADOPTED AS HIS OWN. HE FURTHER DESIRED THAT THEY SHOULD BE RECEIVED INTO THIS HOUSE AND THERE BROUGHT UP AND INSTRUCTED IN TRUE PIETY, IN THE LIBERAL ARTS, AND PARTICULARLY IN ARITHMETIC AND ACCOUNTS (TO WHICH, THROUGH HIS GOOD FORTUNE, HE PARTICULARLY ATTRIBUTED THE INCREASE IN HIS WEALTH). THIS HE ORDERED IN HIS LAST WILL AND TESTAMENT, 7TH FEBRUARY, A.D. 1723.

1689   The Universal Architect   1748

Adam's Tomb

Heriot's

Photograph taken in the 1840s by Watson's first Drawing Teacher, David Octavius Hill, a pioneer of modern photography.

William Adam, who designed Watson's Hospital, was the son of a stonemason from near Kirkcaldy and educated at its High School. He was a fine-featured, good-looking chap, small but full of energy, who combined being an intellectual with practical ability. His confidence, charm and straightforward manner made him friends easily. He married Mary Robertson, his partner's daughter.

Apart from architecture, Adam had an astonishing variety of money-making schemes: coal, salt, land, farming, forestry, milling, brewing, bricks, tiles, stone and iron, *"... whereby he acquired a handsome fortune* *with an unspotted character."* (Sir R Douglas, 1753.)

By the 1720s he was undoubtedly Scotland's leading architect pioneering a rebirth of Greek and Roman architecture which his more famous sons (John, Robert and James) developed further into the 'Adam style'. John Clerk of Eldin declared him as, *"... the universal architect of his country."*

He moved to Edinburgh in the 1720s staying at first in the Cowgate then at a villa in north Merchiston before finally moving to an estate now known as Blair Adam.

Adam died on 24 June 1748 and is buried in Greyfriars' Churchyard.

¶*¶ That the Governors of *GEORGE WATSON's* HOSPITAL, Edinburgh, being resolved to take into the Hospital against Whitsunday next 12 Boys, the Children or Grandchildren of decayed Merchants of Edinburgh, and of the Ministers of the Old Church thereof, for whose Maintenance and Education the said Hospital is designed, (now that the Hospital is finished and fit for their Reception and Accommodation;) and that in order thereto it will be necessary that the Hospital be provided with a sufficient Master or Governor, and Schoolmaster, who shall have suitable Encouragement: Have therefore thought fit to give this publick Notice thereof, that all Boys who are duly intitled by the Statutes of the said Hospital may apply for the Benefit thereof, by lodging their Applications in the hands of the Clerk or Treasurer of the Hospital betwixt and the 3d of April next, that being the Day appointed for their Election; and that such as intend to offer themselves for Master and Schoolmaster, may likewise lodge their Applications as aforesaid, together with proper Certificates of their Qualifications.

The first advertisement for pupils and staff placed in the Caledonian Mercury *on Friday 6 March 1741 and repeated on four further occasions between 10–19 March. (By kind permission of the Signet Library, Edinburgh.)*

The Building

It may have been of a fine and simple neoclassical design, but parts were poorly built whilst initial cost-efficiency measures resulted in an ever recurring problem of dampness. The roof leaked from the start, but it took 12 years for a drastic solution to be accepted, namely taking the slates off and putting them down afresh. John Watson, the chosen slater, soon found the cause of constant leaks: the slates did not overlap! Indeed, the work was *"so gross"* that even the architect, William Adam, agreed that the Governors had a claim against the original slater, John Mein, who should be taken *"before the Sheriffs"*.

Far more serious was dampness caused partly by inadequate drainage on a very wet site and partly by initial cost-cutting. However, nearly 100 years went by before the problem was tackled. In 1834, an investigation revealed the main cause was that the external walls had not been lathed and plastered on the inside. The solution was to line the rooms and passages with wood to a height of about 5 feet and then lath from the top of the wood to the ceiling. The work took two months, cost £260 and the boys got an extra few weeks' summer holiday. Nevertheless, ventilation problems persisted.

Parsimony was the guiding principle which had resulted in a rather plain building both externally and internally. From time to time Governors made suggestions as to improving its external appearance (eg a blocking course along the top front of the Hospital, new windows and rough casting), but these invariably fell through either due to a lack of money, or a reluctance to part with it. Internally, as late as 1834, the Governors noted, *"... many parts... particularly the Dining and School Rooms... are finished in the very plainest manner and in winter more especially exhibit a most cold and comfortless appearance."*

On 15 July 1742 the Governors decided to install a bell at a total cost of £18 5s 9d. It is clearly dated 1742 and still in use, but has the time come for its sheltered retirement?

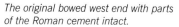
The original bowed west end with parts of the Roman cement intact.

1857 extension, Chapel exterior.

Some Governors now wondered if it *"... be worth considering whether it might not be better to have an entirely new building rather than to expend so very large a sum in enlarging the old one..."* The plan was dropped, but cheap internal rearrangements costing £200 resulted in more bed space. It was, however, decided to be very cautious about actually taking more boys in. There the matter rested until 1842 when the issue of admitting Day Scholars was raised.

The Governors decided against extending the building, or building a separate one, partly because a loan would have been required, but also because it wasn't needed as only 35 boys had been refused entrance in 10 years either because they were too old, or were in bad health. Again, cheaper internal rearrangements costing only £300 increased the maximum numbers to a possible 86.

Two decisions forced change 14 years later: firstly, the admission of Day Scholars from 1852 and, secondly, the decision to appoint a married House Governor (with family) which would require extra accommodation. John Lessels's plans were first considered in 1857.

Two new wings extending southwards to the Meadows would provide a workshop, a large playroom, four classrooms, book cupboards, a library, two reading rooms, a clothes store, toilets, a drawing classroom *"lighted from the roof"*, apartments for

Chapel interior.

the House Governor, four bedrooms and a new Chapel. Lessels also produced a plan for a new building at a cost of £22,000 which was rejected in favour of the additional wings costing £9,190. The Governors, however, rejected the Chapel which would save £1,500.

Occasionally the Governors had no choice but to spend money as, for example, in 1850 when the steps to the Main Entrance began to wear out. Happily, this coincided with a period of financial prosperity which the improvers used as an opportunity to decorate the original work with a circular balustrade (designed by John Lessels) on each side of the stairs using best-quality Craigleith stone. Suitable material was unavailable, so Humbie rock was used instead. About the same time a revolutionary new material – Roman cement (a form of concrete) – was used on the external walls with six coats of white lead and oil used to cover it. Thus very little was done to

alter the original fabric of the building by its centenary.

The only major addition was made in 1857. It was recognised as early as 1819 that about 70 pupils was the maximum the existing arrangements could cater for. In 1820, a bold plan was proposed to radically extend the Hospital at the enormous cost of £4,000, soon hiked by the builders to nearer £9,000.

Lessels was less than impressed arguing that the Chapel was an integral part of his plan, the absence of which would result in *"confusion and trouble"*, but he did amend his scheme, saving £500. Only one Governor thought the whole thing was a complete waste of money, but the boys must have been delighted with the resulting two-month vacation while the work was carried out. Even Victorian builders, however, couldn't keep to schedule and no return to the Hospital building was possible until April 1858!

Extensive internal decoration followed and the Chapel was painted in 1861: the cornice was to be cream, the walls pale green. Woodwork was varnished with the shutters, doors and window arches made to match the resultant colour, while the crowning glory, the ceiling, would have its ornament picked out in gold, and both the circular and triangular areas decorated.

So the building stood until the boys left in 1870 and demolition took place in 2004.

The Boys

On Whitsunday 17 May 1741 11 boys aged 9–10 years were the first to enter Watson's Hospital.

Alphabetically first was Archibald Borthwick. As with all other applicants his parents had to prove that he belonged to a group that Watson intended to help. His father, Patrick, was a merchant burgess and guild brother (ie he had undergone an apprenticeship successfully and was a member of the Merchant Company) and produced the correct documents to prove it. Indeed, he also produced proof that his father held the same qualifications too. In addition, a certificate of Archie's age was shown which stated he had been born on 13 May 1732.

In this instance there was no need to have evidence of the family's poverty (indigency) as it was well known to several Governors and members of the church to which the Borthwick family belonged. A medical examination showed Archie to be healthy. The Governors voted to accept his application and he was then said to have been 'elected' to join the institution.

The Governors were responsible for ex-Hospital boys up to the age of 25. They helped a boy get an apprenticeship, gave him an allowance each year and paid a substantial bounty provided he didn't marry before the age of 25 without the consent of the Governors. The sums involved were kept in line with changing circumstances and inflation. If used wisely these combined privileges amounted to a huge advantage to a boy whose family was down on its luck, enabling him to even consider the possibility of opening a potentially prosperous business at a young age. Although Watson was mainly interested in giving boys a chance to become skilled workers, businessmen and merchants, the Governors were always sympathetic to boys who showed ability in academic work, or an interest in medicine.

The Governors enforced these regulations and followed up any reports of abuse. The most infamous case which emerged was that of the Hill family conspiracy. In August 1823

Two frescos adorned the walls of the Governors' Room painted sometime before 1785 by Alexander Runciman. After Watson's moved away in 1870 these frescos were copied (in 1874) as oil paintings by Walter B Smith. The one depicted here hangs outside the Principal's Office. The other is similar, but painted as an autumn or winter scene. The little chap in the foreground is standing, not, as here, fishing. Where has this other painting gone? It is thought to have been destroyed in the London Blitz.

The Governors were always sympathetic to boys who showed ability in academic work, or an interest in medicine.

William Hill, the father, claimed that he was so ill he had been confined to bed for three years. Although he had been in business for 20 years he had very little savings and had a wife and nine children to support. The Governors had admitted one child who had already gained six years, free clothing and maintenance, plus £100 support for each year of his five-year apprenticeship and a £50 bounty. Another son was still in the Hospital.

But when William died in 1818 he left property valued at an astonishing £8,000! The Governors were furious that they had been hoodwinked, "... *by Mr Hill and his friends.*" The Governors, even although their legal advice was "... *to be more careful in future*", decided to pursue the Hills for compensation.

In 1823, Hill's trustees offered 150 guineas, but the Governors argued that it cost £34 10d per year to keep a boy in the Hospital, thus the two boys had cost about £400 and there was still the allowances and bounty to consider. The money, however, was not the main issue, "... *but the improper means that had been practised to obtain the admission.*" It was decided to settle as best they could which turned out to be for a mere 200 guineas.

By 1749, numbers had risen, but there were still only 30 boys in the Hospital. With such small numbers discipline problems must have been minimal, but within 70 years the number more than doubled to 70. The limit was reached in 1842 with 86 boys on the roll and this was maintained until the end of the Hospital system in 1870. A very small number of Day Scholars came in from the 1850s.

Wards

A ward was a dormitory and each one contained boys of all ages. The problems may be imagined. In 1827, an examination by the Governors' Education Committee recommended that the boys should be divided into three teaching groups (the youngest, the more advanced and older boys) which should then be reflected in the sleeping arrangements. The youngest boys were to be separated from the older ones not only during school hours, *"but at all times"*. They would occupy a room the key to which was to be left with the maid servant in charge of looking after the young ones. The middle section would occupy the middle and westernmost wards whilst the oldest would sleep in the eastern wards with only two keys to be held by definite named members of staff. The door between the middle and eastern wards was to be locked while only the English teacher would hold the key to the east ward where the oldest slept. The beds on the north side of each ward were to be made up by the same house servant and those on the southside by another. The boys would sleep on the side maintained by the servant who was in charge of their linens.

The past bad influence of young girl servants, often from the poorest parts of town, forced the Governors to specify that those linens had to placed on each bed *before* the boys entered their wards in the evening. In the morning boys were required to leave their neatly folded shirts at the bottom of the bed to be collected *after* the boys left the wards. All these proposals were agreed and implemented. Nevertheless, behavioural problems remained and the Governors alternated between having a porter, teacher or special hired help sleeping either in a ward, or close by. Boy ward monitors were introduced in 1855 who had to report each morning to the Head.

Boys slept two to a bed. Sharing with a bed wetter hardly bears thinking about. In 1860 it was agreed that *"… separate beds should be provided for each of the boys as they [the Governors] believed that such an arrangement would greatly conduce both to the health and the morals of the Boys …"*. Gray &

Son, George Street, offered to supply 30 new simple beds for 17s 6d each, or 'superior ones' for 23s 6d. A double bed could be converted for 6s 8d. The Governors agreed to buy the superior ones at a total cost of about £300 and also entirely new bedding. Feather beds, with a worsted coverlet, had been used from the start, but mattresses were gradually introduced.

Boys did die in the Hospital, the first being John Coutts in May 1749. The Heriot's Governors, in October 1853, whilst investigating overcrowding in their Hospital claimed that the death rate in Watson's was far higher even although the space was much the same, ie about 325 cubic feet per ward. Watson's furiously rejected this claim arguing that during the preceding eight years only six boys had died, a 1 in 114 mortality rate, which included the recent scarlet fever epidemic. There had been no deaths in the previous 2–3 years and when everything was taken into account the death rate had been 1 in 215, very similar to that in Heriot's.

Health

The first serious health disorder erupted in May 1768 when James Allan and William Ker became, *"… distrest with scropluous disorders."* What the Clerk was attempting to spell was 'scrofulous' meant as a medical condition, not figuratively, which was tuberculosis affecting the lymph nodes of the neck and spread via the respiratory route. Untreated it led to ulcers and sores. Children needed to be isolated, but Watson's didn't have a special sickroom, so the pair were sent for treatment to St Bernard's Well in Stockbridge. Only in 1812 did the Governors consider *"… a detached Ward…"*. The result was the purchase of a substantial tenement house and grounds opposite the west boundary wall (Lauriston Lane) which could also be used if numbers increased as well as providing more classrooms. Eventually this proved a worthwhile investment once a special sickroom had been created in the Hospital.

That room was ready in January 1832 when the dreaded cholera reached Edinburgh. Watson's decided to isolate itself, but boys still went to

Church on Sundays. Luckily no-one caught the disease. However, they were not so fortunate three years later when smallpox rampaged through the city. Many of the boys who had not been given cowpox ended up in the Sick Ward. George Merry died in agony, followed soon by the Second Master, David Hastings. The boys were sent on an early summer vacation.

In November 1836, John Menzies died of Scarletina and in June the following year another boy (Crawford) died of *"… inflamation of the wind-pipe consequent of an attack of measles."* Two boys died of consumption: Robert Gulane (1840) and George McNaughton (1845). Alex Wallace was paid the handsome amount of £6 in 1844 for spending what must have been a wonderful four months curing the boys of ringworm. In 1849, the Hospital surgeon warned teachers not to overtax the boys with work because *"… the last two deaths in this Institution have been caused by water in the head (a stroke)… I remember at least two other similar cases… during the past ten or twelve years."* The boys needed recreation, *"… and poor Gardner who died a few days ago, although a very willing boy, told his friends more than once, that he felt he had too many lessons."* This resulted in more 'Play Hours'.

There were also some very sad incidents. In 1831, Erskine Allan had an accident on ice within the Hospital grounds. For *three years* he lay in his room being looked after by the Hospital staff because his own family had moved to New South Wales, effectively deserting him. The boy was *"… in a state of utmost destitution"* and the Governors agreed to give him £50 to buy clothes and a ticket to Australia. Unfortunately, poor Erskine became even more ill and died alone.

Scarlet fever struck on 12 February 1851 with both Heriot's and the Trades Maiden Hospital also being badly hit. Francis Dick died in April. The surgeon advised the early installation of a boiler and bathroom near the Sick Ward as all the hot water had to be carried up from the kitchen. It was agreed. The highly contagious fever continued and 18 boys were isolated. James Kerr died on 5 May. The boys attended his funeral. Two boys were boarded out to help stop contagion. By 8 May 25 boys were isolated and an early vacation was agreed. It took until June 1851 for the fever to disappear entirely.

On a lighter note, from April 1854, cod liver oil started to be administered on a regular basis, *"When any of the boys shows a tendency to droop."*

Cleanliness is Next...

It took 87 years before a bath was introduced into the Hospital, the boys making do with metal basins in a washroom with no piped water. Baths were agreed on in 1828, but showers together with piped hot and cold water *"... would be quite unnecessary."* In 1830, the original copper basins were badly in need of repair, but instead it was decided to replace them with delft-ware. The issue of hot and cold piped water was raised again in 1831 and the Governors were advised that it *"... should be no longer delayed."* Finally, a shower bath – one only – was installed in 1835 just when they were becoming fashionable elsewhere.

A barber was employed as early as 1742. One hundred years later barber James Hogg was charging £4 6s for four cuts per year, £5 5s for five cuts and, *"... for shaving the heads of each boy"* a mere £3! From August 1840, the boys were supplied with hairbrushes and toothbrushes. The lucky lads had their shoes cleaned from 1741 onwards either by a porter or house servant, but all that came to an end in October 1856.

Let There Be Light...

Candles, oil lamps and coal fires are either cosy or gloomy depending upon one's perception, but that was all the light available to the boys and staff from 1741 to 1828. Newfangled gas lighting was suggested in 1826 and estimates requested. The expensive sticking points were that the Hospital needed a connecting pipe to the gas company's main line either in George Square or at Lauriston, plus a gasometer. The Hospital doctor was asked whether gas would be a medical danger to the boys and he replied in the negative. There was a lack of unanimity among the Governors which was not resolved until 1828, when a compromise was

The engraving produced in 1819 by R Scott from a drawing by Andrew Scott Mason and hand-coloured. This is the north front of the Hospital which faced Lauriston Place and George Heriot's Hospital.

The building was lit up with candles and lamps in a spectacular display ending with fireworks.

reached to the effect that not all of the Hospital should be lighted by gas, but only the school rooms, the dining room, kitchen, laundry and corridors. The deciding factor, however, was that a new main gas pipe had been laid along Lauriston Lane which made connection much cheaper. Savings would also be made on oil and candles. Indeed, gas would produce *"... a more efficient quantity of light the want of which is very much felt and complained of by the Masters..."* Gas was installed by John Weil at a cost of £65.

Gradually gas lighting was extended throughout the building. The Council Room was connected in 1841 and 10 years later the Masters' Rooms, the Matron's Rooms and the Infirmary (new name for the Sick Ward), but on the strict understanding that lights would only be used after all the boys

had gone to bed at 10pm. Gas was first used outside the Hospital when a lamp was erected at the East Gate in 1843, but it had to be put out at 10pm. That was a great pity as, in 1851, it must have made it more difficult to see the infestation of rats!

One stunning event was the 'illumination' of the Hospital for the marriage of the Duke of Rothesay to Alexandra of Denmark on 10 March 1863. Virtually every major Edinburgh building was lit up with candles and lamps in a spectacular display ending with fireworks.

"5 October 1817. A letter was read from Andrew Mason, Drawing Master in Edinburgh, accompanying a Drawing of the Hospital House and ground about it by his own son one of the Boys of the Hospital, executed when he was 12 years of age and which his father had got neatly framed and now presented to the Governors. The Governors agreed to accept of this present indicating a genius in this Boy and authorised the Treasurer to pay the father £5/5/– to defray the expenses of the Drawing and its Frame." (Hospital Minutes) The subsequent engraving has become probably the best known depiction of the Hospital. In 1817 there was an avenue of trees leading down from Lauriston Place, but by the 1860s this had gone which led some to conclude that the trees pictured had been 'fanciful'.

Mason's picture re-worked in the 1860s by a Hospital boy, Robert Gibson. On 4 April 1864 the Governors decided, "... that in future each boy be photographed at his departure from the Hospital... the expense would be trifling."

The Hospital as painted in 1871 by Sam Bough, RSA.

Luckily some of these superb photographs survive, including one of Robert Gibson himself.

Runaways

Some boys just couldn't take any more and simply 'did a runner'. The first of many were James Hutton and Sam Stewart who, in April 1747, "... *made ane elopement from this Hospital for some days.*" Boys invariably had no specific reason and the Governors, with a remarkably enlightened attitude which continued throughout the years, simply ordered them to be 'publicly rebuked' when they were warned that if it happened again then they would be 'extruded' (expelled).

Sometimes that approach was sorely tested such as when Alex Day, in February 1773, had "... *frequently deserted the Hospital.*" Four times he was allowed back, "... *but had again left... for several weeks past and had been endeavouring to seduce the other Boys.*" In fact, he had actually been gone for an astonishing eight months. Alex showed no sign whatsoever of being sorry. He was expelled, but his family got up a petition. The Governors, however, were in no mood to have him back as "... *it would be of dangerous consequence to the other Boys to restore him to the Hospital.*"

And so it went on and on. In 1775, for example, Alex Tod just disappeared and was eventually discovered working in Glasgow. He forfeited all his Hospital privileges. Four years later Alex Davidson had deserted so often that he was expelled without any fuss. In 1786, nine–year-old James Stuart kept hopping over the wall,

but because of his age he was also continually allowed back. In 1800, James Bowie was such a nuisance runner that, when finally caught, he was put in solitary confinement for a week, confined to the Hospital for a month, publicly reprimanded and his relatives told to get him a job!

Alex Davidson had deserted so often that he was expelled without any fuss.

In January 1858, Alex Fleming ran off because he had been caught cheating and lying. True to their liberal approach the Governors allowed him back when they discovered he was a poor orphan and only 10 years old. Almost exactly a year later two aspiring sailors, Tom Sime and Peter Glover, were discovered in South Shields having walked all the way there. Because both were of a "*wandering disposition*" they were allowed back! On only one occasion were deserters belted (October 1852: Antony Hay – 15 years and Charles Forrest – 13 years) because the Headmaster didn't consult the Governors. It never happened again.

If you are wondering why anyone would want to run away from the Hospital you could do worse than read the next section.

Boys Will Be Boys

Heriot's always had behavioural problems amongst its inmates which is hardly a surprise considering the conditions of the Hospital system, lack of suitable staff and its closeness to the less than salubrious Grassmarket, but this reached new depths between 1764 and 1825, probably due to a relaxation of Hospital discipline. Theft, violence, drunkenness, mass riots, bullying and desertions on a vast scale plagued the Hospital. Its infamous FP organisation, quaintly known as 'The Decorating Club', openly challenged the Head and Governors, freely invaded the precincts, abused youngsters and encouraged the institutionalised system of bullying known as the Garring or Garren Law. Given the unsavoury nature of that institution Watson's was the very model of civilised behaviour, but it did have its moments.

Robert Arthur Robertson, in 1753, has the dubious honour of being the first boy expelled from Watson's because he *"… either by accident or design, wounded Hamilton Lithgow, another of the boys, in the wrist with a knife."* Right throughout the Hospital's history one group of Governors after another displayed an amazingly enlightened and liberal attitude to behavioural problems in a genuine attempt to create a civilised atmosphere. Indeed, right from the start those in the Hospital were always referred to as 'the Family'.

Nevertheless, there was one notable exception in June 1779 when six boys were accused of *"… pilfering money from the servants in the house."* The boys were confined, but two, John Mein and John Wilson had broken out and run off. An inquiry proved that five boys were indeed guilty and their parents were recommended *"… to get them disposed of in His Majestie's Navy…"* Thomas Rhind, John Pringle and John Mein had been *"… engaged in a Combination to screan and conceal each others faults on all occasions. And having considered the evil tendency of such Combinations, the Governors ordain these three boys to be publicly whipt in the school and continue in the House on trial of future good behaviour."*

This is the only surviving Hospital group photograph. It was taken between 1864 and 1868. The boys, unfortunately, cannot be identified, but the others can.
FROM THE LEFT: 1. 'Beardie' Sinclair, an Edinburgh 'character' and frequent visitor 2. Eckford, lodge-keeper, Lauriston Lodge 3. James Clark, English Master. 4. Thomas Reid, Classical Master 5. Thomas Knox, Governor 6. James Miller, Headmaster 7. Mrs Milligan, Matron 8. Friend of Mrs Milligan. 9. Son of Mrs Milligan. The faces at the upper windows are servants. Missing: Second English Master William Jolly and old-established teacher, Alexander Gilmour.

Theft, violence, drunkenness, mass riots, bullying and desertions on a vast scale plagued [Heriot's] Hospital.

About four weeks later two boys, John Muirhead and William Steven, were found guilty of stealing 2s 6d from the till in a candlemaker's shop in Potter-row after coming in on the pretence of buying gunpowder. Steven was caught in the shop, gave a fictitious name and was confined in a room. A teacher was called who had him taken back to the Hospital where he was locked up with Muirhead. The latter confessed to the Governors, but Steven ran away. Both were expelled and forbidden from *"… haunting or frequenting the said Hospital or precincts thereof."* If they did both would be handed to the civil magistrates, *"… to be punished as Law will."* The House Governor was sacked.

The feud with Heriot's usually amounted to little more than adolescent enthusiasm called 'bickers' in Edinburgh. At times, however, it did become serious.

On 18 May 1822, a 'Play Day', a Watson's boy called Alex Deuchar had gone to visit his father in North Bridge Street. Early in the evening he left with a hard biscuit in his hand and was cutting it with his penknife when he met a boy called Gray and his brother, both from Heriot's. Gray attacked him *"… and gave him a blow upon the breast… a fight commenced between them in the course of which Deuchar gave Gray some wounds with the penknife."* Gray was found to have four stab wounds, *"… one of them in the Belly… and another in the side towards the back."*

If they had been deeper wounds Gray could have died. Deuchar was put on solitary confinement for four weeks and if he showed himself to be truly sorry after two, the remainder of the sentence would be remitted. An attempt by the Governors to co-operate with Heriot's in order to end such incidents came to nothing.

Of greater importance was the Gibson case in August 1825 when an enraged parent, John Gibson, an auctioneer in Edinburgh, submitted a printed letter to the Governors, *"… containing a string of very grave and serious charges against the boys of the Hospital implying of course some heavy reflections against the individuals who have the superintendence of the education and the names of the boys."* The charges rose in seriousness. First that a combination of two young and two older boys *"… abstracted money from their parents…"* which was used to buy sweets, *"…and partly in the purchase of pistols and some small cannons and gunpowder for their amusement."* They also stole lead to make the pistol balls. Secondly, there was profane swearing with the use of gross and obscene language among the boys which had been going on for years and just taken for granted by the staff. Thirdly, that the infamous 'Garring (or Garren) Law' was embedded in Watson's. 'Gar' is the Scots word meaning 'to cause to compel' and in this case meant older boys forcing younger ones to do whatever the older ones wanted and to keep absolutely silent about their activities to the authorities. Such older boys were known as 'gars' or 'garrers'. In England, this system was known as 'fagging' and shamelessly used by staff in many of its public schools to help keep order. Nothing like that happened in Watson's. An inquiry by the Governors fully supported the first two allegations, but could find no evidence of the Garring Law. But they were worried, and needed to be, for it was notoriously difficult to uncover. The Governors stated that *"This would seem to be the first enormous transgression that has taken place in this Hospital."* Nevertheless, their response was enlightened and sympathetic to nearly all involved. The older boys left immediately, but kept all their financial privileges. The younger ones were also required to leave, but had their schooling paid for by the Hospital and also kept their financial privileges. As in nearly all such cases a lot of heart-searching ensued and ways found to improve the situation. In this case, masters' salaries were raised, a young man was appointed to supervise the boys, while the curriculum and hours of teaching were reformed. The Second Master, Mr Gibson, was sacked.

Another incident with huge consequences occurred in 1845. It started as just another case of pilfering, in this case books from the school library which were then sold to Joe Miller, a bookseller in Bank Street. An inquiry soon revealed that at least fifteen boys had been involved and that they had stolen not only 33 volumes from the library, but also 19 volumes from Mr McMorine, the Head Master. McMorine didn't check his books at the end of each period, he had no idea what books the library had in stock and had no system for checking books out and in.

The ringleaders were two 15 year-olds, James Baird and William Adam who had been in Watson's for five and six years respectively and described as bad characters. Baird sold books to Miller on fifteen occasions, but then stole four books from him! He also admitted a string of offences including stealing a silver watch from Hodge's Shop in Victoria Street as well as a music box, scent bottle, a match box and sand glass from a shop on the Bridges. He persuaded two younger boys to take all the blame for stealing the books by offering one the music box and the other 9s (45p). Baird also induced his little brother and another boy to lie in his defence. Both Baird and Adam also admitted bringing wine and whisky into the Hospital. Adam even stole a pistol. Both boys denied their guilt until the bitter end. What was alarming was that the Garren Law seemed to be operating with a Fagin-type gang of younger boys (the youngest being 10) acting as lookouts and carriers. Baird and Adam were expelled, but Baird was most definitely the school bully of whom the younger boys were terrified. The parents of the other boys involved were asked to remove their sons who either lost some or all of their privileges. The Head resigned, a huge inquiry was held into the working of the Hospital and progressive improvements in all spheres resulted. Nevertheless, opponents of the Hospital system always cited this case as the one which proved the system caused moral delinquency.

In December 1844, the Hospital doctor informed the horrified Governors that one boy, William Wilson, had contracted a disease of a sexual nature. Wilson was 15 years old,

clever, but not well behaved and always blamed others if he got into any little scrape. Wilson was a friend of an FP, George Gibson, who visited his little brother in the Hospital. Gibson used *"… very improper and even obscene language and to have spoken of matters which ought never to have formed the subject of conversation among such young boys."* Gibson got the blame for inciting Wilson, but it was Wilson who asked a pal, Charles Wemyss, to meet him one Saturday evening (after returning from his parents) at the head of the Meadows to *"… see some females of loose characters."* Wilson spoke to one, took her to a nearby lane and *"… a very improper intimacy took place."* This was the cause of Wilson's little problem, although when first seen by other boys in the washing area he claimed he had been kicked. Only when Matron's ointment failed to work was the truth uncovered! Both Wilson and Wemyss were expelled, Gibson was banned from the Hospital and a letter was written to the Police Superintendent, *"… calling his attention to the state of the Meadow Walk after Dusk…"* Some things never change.

The most bizarre case of the lot occurred on Friday 28 April 1854. The only reason this case appears in the Minutes is because the Editor of the *Evening News* made contact and the Governors wanted to make a clean breast of things, so to say. Apparently the boys were changing to go out of the Hospital when one, William Watt, was attacked by three boys: James Leechman, John Kirkwood and William Syme. Watt ended up with a long cut at the base of an intimate part of his anatomy. *"The wound was said to have been caused accidentally by a fall during some frolic…. It afterwards came out, however, on the confession of one or more of the boys, that the laceration had been caused by forcible traction by one individual of their number, while others held the sufferer and prevented his escape."* Amazing leniency occurred. The boys promised not to do it again, were publicly belted once Watt had recovered sufficiently to see it done and the incident was described as a result of *"… the thoughtless levity of youth."* However, boy monitors were then appointed for all sleeping wards. But what were these little monsters really up to?

Clothes and Uniform

The Statutes specified that the boys had to be *"... decently apparelled in cinnamon coloured clothes"*, but it is not known if this colour was strictly adhered to. The first mention in the Governors' Minutes occurs in October 1779 when a Committee investigating another matter discovered that the boys' clothes were *"very much broken down"* and made of *"improper fabrick"*, two-thirds of the shoes were falling apart with one-third having the *"feet through the soles"* all as a result of being *"deceitfully made and improperly soled"*. As a consequence the socks were also severely holed. Shirts which were meant to last two years were in tatters because the *"linen was of an improper fabrick and quality for the boys' wear."* All this reflected badly on the House Governor and, of course, the Governors. From then on the latter took a greater interest in the matter insisting on tighter controls, but that didn't stop the run-down, dishevelled state of the boys being noticed both in 1823 and 1854.

Uniform existed from the beginning in the sense that the jackets, waistcoats, breeches, shirts and caps were made from the same materials just as all boys were provided with the same footwear, but there does not appear to have been any long-term insistence upon a particular colour or design. In 1821, leather caps replaced the cloth ones and in 1822 grey corduroy replaced wool for trouser material. In 1824, toilinette used for waistcoats was replaced by cloth the same colour as the jackets, with the addition of smart gilt buttons.

The following year, for the first time, a wardrobe was introduced in an attempt to keep the sleeping wards tidier and the clothes cleaner. Two other innovations followed in 1827 when cloaks were provided made in 'camlet' (wool and goats' hair) and elder boys could wear black socks made of cotton or kid leather. In addition, by 1832, all boys received clean linen shirts three times a week, stockings twice weekly and a nightshirt plus nightcap once a week. Underwear was a cotton

The pictures on this page come from an unpublished book of 'Old Edinburgh Characters and Costumes' illustrated by Edinburgh photographer and artist, James Howie sometime during the late nineteenth century and collated for Lord Provost John Boyd in 1890. Although not contemporary the illustration of the GWH boy (top left) accords with the written evidence (1830–65) and was produced when GWH boys were still alive. This source has eluded previous Watson's historians as it was wrongly catalogued as 'John Watson's'.

The boy, bottom left, shows the Heriot's uniform c.1860. The strange device in his hand was used to measure the diameter of the famous 'scudding balls' made by boys for Founder's Day each June. The figure, top right, illustrates the uniform of Cauvin's Hospital, the building of which remains standing at Duddingston crossroads and is now used as a home for the elderly.

During the nineteenth century a uniform such as those above increasingly became regarded as a mark of shameful charity and the crushing of individuality.

(Reproduced by kind permission of Edinburgh City Archive)

lining attached to the breeches, but, in 1827, another first was the introduction of cotton and woollen drawers issued once a fortnight whether needed or not.

A recognised Hospital uniform appears to date from 1832. On 24 December of that year the colour of the cloth for jackets and waistcoats was specified as *"Dark Bottle Green"* and remained so right up to the end of the Hospital system in 1870. (After 1906 the Cadet Corps opted for the same colour for its doublets until forced to change to khaki during WW2 after which only the Pipe Band continued wearing dark green into the 1950s.) The jacket style changed in 1833 when, *"… instead of short coats at present worn by the Boys they shall be allowed to wear round jackets for the ensuing year as being less expensive and a more suitable dress for Boys of their age."* The colour of the trousers continued to be drab (grey) corduroy. It is quite clear that this is regarded as a uniform, so much so that the Governors, in 1842, complained that boys were in the habit of changing their clothes when outside "on leave". The boys were told in no uncertain manner that if caught they would be "renouncing the benefits of the institution." The uniform had to be worn during the holidays as well!

Subsequent changes were really quite minimal. The wearing of *"neck handkerchiefs"* in winter (1842), glengarries (1849), flannel undershirts (1857), cotton shirts with starched linen collars and wristbands (1858), cloth caps (1861), capes instead of cloaks (1862), umbrellas (1863) and boots replaced shoes (1858) with each boy receiving three pairs instead of four pairs of shoes at a saving of 1s 6d per boy. In 1864, as part of a cost-cutting exercise, boys had to wear their clothes for a longer period, eight to nine months instead of six. The cast-off clothes were usually sold, but, from 1845, they were given *"… to the poorer class of children attending the Free School attached to James Gillespie's Hospital."* Incidentally, Heriot's uniform by the 1860s was a brown cloth jacket

and vest with dark tweed trousers, a brown cloth cap for Sunday and a Kilmarnock bonnet for weekdays.

The biggest change, however, was the introduction of hard-wearing tweed (from Leeds), first, in 1854 for greatcoats, then, in 1856, for trousers and vests and finally, in 1857, for the jacket. Indeed, in 1857, two tweed jackets were introduced as an experiment. One had simple black buttons for use in the Hospital, but the other, in an obvious attempt to make the uniform more attractive to the boys, was a rather swish *"… jacket of green cloth with brass buttons to be worn with the Tweed vest and trousers when out of the Hospital."* In 1862, grey tweed trousers were introduced thus establishing some link with the corduroy of the past. This was obviously successful as, in October 1865, both jacket and waistcoat were to be *"… made of Grey Tweed instead of Green Cloth, the former being more durable and better suited for boys".*

Just before the demise of the Hospital its distinctive uniform, however, was seen as being part of the problem of 'monasticism': *"… the same faces, with the same expression, the same clothes, the very tie of the neckerchief and of the shoe always the same are themselves influences hard to re-act against."* (*The Laurie Report, 1868*).

Simon Laurie suggested that *"… the boys themselves might be allowed to choose the colour of their jackets from materials sent to the Hospital. This will encourage individuality and independence."* The Governors did not go that far, but the 40 boys sent to the High School in 1868 (see p39) did have new clothes. Unfortunately, no details were given. The youngest boys who remained in the Hospital to be taught continued to wear the grey uniform.

A new Watson's after 1870 had to create a different image and that included ditching a 'charity school' outfit reminiscent of both prison and workhouse. Only when times and attitudes had changed considerably by the 1920s did the concept of a school uniform become once more acceptable. By that time, however, the colours of dark green or grey belonged to a past, largely forgotten age.

Alexander Adam

Engraved by Samuel Freeman after Sir Henry Raeburn.

In 1760, Alexander Adam began his professional life in Watson's Hospital where he taught as 'Schoolmaster' (First Master) for three years. For over forty years (1764–1809), however, he was the foremost influence in the transformation of the High School into an engine of creative excellence churning out the Scottish intellectual elite in huge numbers. He was said to be a vocational teacher, an inspiration to those taught with a deep and genuine love of learning and an appealing dash of eccentricity. Robert Burns appears to have been in the minority when he described Adam as a *"… puritanic, rotten-hearted, hell-commissioned scoundrel …."*

Adam was also a very Scottish dominie working within the Scottish Presbyterian tradition which meant that even as Rector he was simply *primus inter pares* among other teaching professionals, a system which unfortunately Watson's helped destroy after 1870 with its more dictatorial and authoritarian administrative structure rooted in the Hospital system and akin to that of elitist English so-called 'public' schools.

However, there was not even a pretence of democracy in the classroom where discipline of the most violent sort reigned. Classroom experience in both Watson's and the High School was thus very similar, but Adam believed in a more humane approach which was encouraged more often than not by Watson's governing body rather than practised by its teachers.

Incidentally, his descendants, Marcus and Adam Roberts, attended GWC during the 1990s.

Founder's Day

There was no celebration of George Watson until after the Governors secured his only known portrait painted by William Aikman in 1720. This painting was in the hands of George Watson's relatives who first offered to sell it in April 1755. This was investigated, but no purchase was made.

In November 1767, the picture was again offered for sale with a similar result. Only on 11 August 1777 were fuller details of the situation recorded. The picture *"… was in the hands of Susanna and Janet Dalgleish as Daughters of the deceast Mr Robert Dalgleish late Minister of the Gospel at Linlithgow and of Susanna Symmer his Wife, who was daughter of John Symmer, Merchant in Edinburgh, Brother to George Watson…"*. The sisters were quite happy to part with it, *"… but being in low worldly circumstances expected some gratification…"* The picture was produced and the Governors agreed to pay 25 Guineas. Two months later it was hung in the Governors' Room.

Within weeks, on 10 November 1777, *"… the Governors on a motion of the Preses (the Chairman, Alex Hunter), agreed that the Second Monday of June be allowed to be kept annually by the Boys of the Hospital as a Play Day in commemoration of the Founder of the Hospital."*

There seems to be no logical reason for this date except that it was conveniently close to Heriot's Founder's Day so that a joint service could be held at Greyfriars'.

On 10 May 1825, this appeared in the Governors' Minutes:

"An application on behalf of the Boys of the Hospital stating their desire to observe an Anniversary in grateful remembrance of Mr Watson the generous founder of the Institution and craving that this may take place on the Second Monday of June yearly. The Governors agreed to this and directed the Treasurer and the Masters to allow them this annual day as a play day to the Boys and to give them an addition of Fruit or Pastry to their Dinner upon that day as it comes around."

It is not clear why this statement was made. Perhaps the celebration had

The original portrait is in Merchants' Hall and two copies are held in the College.

fallen into abeyance, or that its survival was somehow threatened.

Whatever, in the following year some of the more unruly boys became a little over-enthusiastic as *"… they had been supplied with a quantity of ardent spirits by a shopkeeper in Bristo Street."* Despite this hiccup the celebrations seem to have continued. Even the Centenary Meeting of the Governors (3 April 1841) was remembered by teachers and boys being *"… entertained by the Governors at Dinner in the Hospital."* Three days later the Governors opted for more adult entertainment at Barry's Hotel in Queen Street to which all past Chairmen were invited.

The next mention of Founder's Day in November 1859 comes, however, as a bombshell because the *"usual celebrations"* are now on 23 November! There is no explanation for this in the Governors' Minutes, but it may be connected with the 'Anthem dispute' of the early 1840s. Although both Heriot's and Watson's shared the annual Founder's Day service at Greyfriars', it was Heriot's who clearly dominated the show. From 1773, Heriot's had produced a special anthem to be sung which, although changed every year, was clearly a Heriot's Hospital song and Watson's boys were obliged to sing along.

By May 1840, the Watson's Governors were obviously getting fed up with this and loftily suggested that the Heriot's Governors consider *"… the propriety of confining the services of the above mentioned Day in future to those ordinarily observed on the Lord's Day and that the Music on that occasion shall be such as that the whole Congregation may join in and that the Boys shall not be required to take any prominent part in the same …"*.

Heriot's refused to budge and the dispute continued until 1842 when the Watson's Governors decided that their boys would not sing the anthem after that year.

Watson's boys continued to attend the June celebration, but it was quite clear that a separate Founder's Day was necessary and November was chosen because the 23rd was George Watson's birthday.

The original concept of a simple 'Play Day' soon came under attack by the more serious minded. In 1860, *"… a lecture on chemistry had been delivered …"*. However, at least some of the Governors had the good sense to state, *"… that in future an entertainment more adapted for the amusement of young boys should be arranged for the Anniversary."*

After the demise of the Hospital in 1870 Founder's Day was downplayed as it was a reminder of Watson's lowly beginning as a charity school.

In future an entertainment more adapted for the amusement of young boys should be arranged for the Anniversary.

The Grumpy Governor Game – What Would You Do?

This is a real incident from 1863. It is the only time in the Governors' Minutes that what people actually said was written down verbatim. Also, by sheer luck, we have photographs of two of the boys involved taken within a year of the incident.

On Wednesday 30 September 1863 three boys ran off from the Hospital. They were back after a few hours and kindly treated. Then on Saturday 3 October they were off again, taking Hospital property (their cloaks) with them. One returned that night, but the others didn't appear until Sunday.

The Head punished and put them into isolation. It is now 6 October. The boys and teachers have been summoned to the Education Committee who have the right to expel *"vicious, turbulent and disobedient"* boys. Imagine you are a Governor. What would you do? Read the evidence….

William Kerr, July 1864

*William K. Kerr.
July 1864.*

WILLIAM KIRKLAND KERR

Born 29 December 1849. Son of the late James Kerr, a planter in Jamaica. Elected to GWH 3 April 1857. Now 13 years old. Nearest living relative is a brother in Glasgow. Only adult is an uncle in Jamaica.

"I have been seven years in the Hospital. On Wednesday last I ran away from it. I never did so before. Up till Wednesday I received kind treatment, but on that day, when I was acting as a Carver, I ate a bit of bread which I knew to be against the Rules as I should have waited until the other Boys had their dinner. I repeated this fault immediately afterwards and for breaking the Rule Mr Munro deprived me of my dinner. He was also about to punish me, but I refused to hold up my hand. Mr Munro said he would tell the House Governor, but he did not do so. It was for being deprived of my dinner that I ran away. After the Boys' dinner that Wednesday I went to classes, but left the Hospital in company with Wemyss and Arnott about half-past five on that Wednesday. I proposed to them to run away. They said they would if they were punished badly. They intended to wait and see if they were punished. When we left we intended to go to Glasgow, but went only to Hailes Quarry to Mr Burns. We told Mr Burns we had run away, and he brought us back on the Wednesday evening. The House Governor did not punish us. This was about nine o'clock. We were offered bread and butter.

On Saturday morning we again ran away having arranged this on Friday night. We left before breakfast and took our cloaks with us. We went up to the Canal. Wemyss and Arnott had bread with them part of which I got. After going up the Canal I parted with them as they wanted to go on and I did not as I thought I was doing wrong.

I am not often whipped and never except when I do what is wrong. The two others intended to go to Glasgow. We went beyond Burns and I returned alone to Hailes Quarry and one of the Burns brought me back to the Hospital. When escaping we went over the Wall. I have a brother in Glasgow who is an engineer."

Mr Munro (Teacher)

He admitted that he had been too lenient when he started teaching and had, therefore, more trouble than other teachers.

"As regards Kerr, he was a Carver and was told not to eat during the dinner. I told the Carvers that they should lose their dinner if they did eat bread then. Accordingly when I saw Kerr was doing so I told him he should get no dinner. He thereupon flung away the bread in a disrespectful manner. I took him to my room and spoke of the impropriety of his conduct asking him whether he had any objection to punishment on account of his disrespectful conduct, but he said he would not submit to punishment. He cried and seemed in a discontented mood and owing to this unsatisfactory state of disposition I thought it better not to punish him then. I expect he may have suggested running away.

Kerr is a slow boy, but there is nothing bad about him."

Mr Millar (House Governor)

"Kerr is a weak silly boy with no brain, but wonderful influence in the playground."

Mr Jolly (Teacher)

"Kerr is a boy of very weak intellect, but I never had any difficulty with him. He was not disobedient to me. He could not be the leader in any mischief as he would not have the spirit."

He is a troublesome boy and speaks to me when he should not. When I punish him he does not submit to his punishment properly.

DAVID OGILVIE ARNOTT

Born 18 February 1852. Son of the late David Arnott. Elected GWH 3 April 1860. Mother in Liverpool.

"I was twelve years of age last February and have been in the Hospital four years in April. On Wednesday I ran away with Kerr and Wemyss. I did so because I got cold porridge a day or two before for washing my hands in the well and not having my hair combed. I know this was a fault and that I was liable to be punished for it, as other boys guilty of similar faults have been so punished. My getting cold porridge was my only reason for leaving.

We were to go to Glasgow. Both Wemyss and Kerr came and told me they would run away and asked me to join them. I think it was Wemyss who proposed first. I agreed. We went over the Wall at the bottom of the green. We went up to Hailes Quarry to Burns. Mr Burns was not in, but we saw the servant. When Mr Burns came home we told him we had run away and he said he would take us back to the Hospital. He did bring us back. On our arrival the House Governor spoke kindly to us, but said we had done wrong. He did not threaten to punish us. He offered us supper, but we did not want it. He said he would settle the matter on the Thursday, but I was not punished for running away on the Wednesday.

On Saturday we ran away again. We arranged this on the Friday. I think it was I who proposed to run away as also to take the cloaks as they cover us at night. I had bread in my pocket which some of the boys had given to Kerr to enable us to run away. These boys knew we intended to do so. Their names I don't know. I think I told some of the boys that I was going to run away. I told Peter Wood I think on Friday.

Prior to Saturday I was punished for saying the boy Bryce was short-sighted. He was saying his Latin lesson at the time and made a mistake. I thought that Mr Munro did not know that he was short-sighted and therefore I told him. He gave me twelve stripes (of the tawse). He frequently whips me, but only when I do wrong."

Mr Munro

"I think as regards Arnott there is nothing very bad about him only he is a troublesome boy and speaks to me when he should not. When I punish him he does not submit to his punishment properly. Arnott was punished for speaking at dinner."

Mr Millar

"For two or three years before last year, he was very troublesome and never out of mischief, but he has been improving latterly and I think trying to do better. I understand, however, that he has not been so towards the Masters and from his recent conduct I think he must be getting bad again. He is not a good boy, but there are others in the Hospital worse than he."

Mr Jolly

"Arnott is quite a difficult boy. He is stubborn if contradicted, especially if he thinks himself unjustly treated. His general behaviour is not good. Perhaps he is one of the worst boys. He is headstrong though I make him submissive. I had at one time cause often to punish him. I must keep power over him. He likes to be thought a hero. Between the first and second running away he was very bumptious in his conduct."

ALEXANDER GALL WEMYSS

Born 18 December 1850. Son of Alex Wemyss, upholsterer, Edinburgh. Elected GWH 3 April 1860.

"I am going on 13 years of age and have been four years in the Hospital. I ran away from the Hospital on Wednesday. I never did so before. I then left because I got cold porridge. I got cold porridge because I was late for dinner on Wednesday and my hands were not washed nor my hair combed. I knew that I had done wrong and that I would be punished. I was never late for dinner before.

It was Kerr who proposed to run away. This was after dinner between two and three. At first I said, "I don't know", but afterwards said I would go. I never thought of running away before. We were to go to Glasgow. We had no money except for Kerr who had ten and a half pence. We went to Hailes Quarry to Burns' House. Saw at first Burns' brother and servant, remained an hour and Mr Burns came in and said he would take us back. We arrived at the Hospital with him about ten. We saw Mr Miller who asked us why we left. I told him. He spoke kindly to us, but said we had done wrong, but that he would try and not speak about it. I was not punished for running away.

On Saturday, we again left the Hospital. This was arranged on Friday. Waddell and Lamb were in the secret. I said, and Kerr said, that we were going to Haddington. We had bread which some boys had pocketed for us, but I did not pocket bread. Lamb, Bryce and others gave me bread. Kerr still had ten and a half pence. I had no friends in Haddington. We went towards Glasgow. Kerr left us at the head of the Edinburgh–Glasgow road. He said he was going back. He gave no reason. We were as far as Ratho then. After Kerr left us we also returned, but we first went to my father's house. We saw my mother. She kept Arnott and I till Sunday when we were brought back.

On Monday I was punished. I am not often punished. I was never whipped when I did not deserve it. The Masters were always kind to me. I think we did wrong."

Alex Wemyss, April 1864.

Mr Munro

"As regards Wemyss he is provoking in his manner and endeavours to incite laughter and make himself a little 'hero'. He is looked up to by other boys owing to his taking his punishment so bravely. He is turbulent and disobedient, or nearly so. Wemyss was punished for coming in late to dinner."

Mr Millar

"For myself I have had no occasion to find fault with Wemyss, but latterly the other Masters have found him a turbulent boy though not a wicked one."

Mr Jolly

"Wemyss is much the same kind of boy as Arnott, but 'dour'. He is strong-willed and puts it to a wrong purpose. He is getting worse and is a great plague. He keeps us in a ferment. He has more sway than Arnott. He knocks the other boys about. Punishment does not affect him. He never cries."

What the Grumpy Governors Decided

The Education Committee recommended that *"all three boys be expelled and lose all privileges"* (ie all financial help if they went into further education or an apprenticeship, plus a generous bonus at the age of 25).

After hearing the boys and staff members, the Governors were divided, but decided not to expel the boys and deprive them of all privileges. *But what punishment should they get?* Two Governors proposed corporal punishment (the belt) plus losing holidays and school treats. Two Governors thought this was too severe and proposed depriving them of holidays, treats and isolating them from the other boys. After some discussion it went to the vote and a majority agreed that the boys should be belted in front of the entire Hospital and Governors at 4pm the next day. The boys were called in and told their fate.

> ## The Governors had a change of heart and suspended the public "flogging".

Next day, just before 4pm, the Governors had a change of heart and suspended the public "flogging" to see if the boys would show any remorse. The assembled boys got a lecture and the ex-runaways a reprimand.

On 12 November the miscreants were *"... now conducting themselves well."* The Governors then decided that if they behaved themselves for another four weeks then there would be no corporal punishment.

Well, were the Governors so grumpy? Did they make the right decision?

Andrew Jack, July 1867.

George Darling, May 1867.

Andrew Laurie, July 1867.

Alex Cowie, July 1866.

Clever Laddies

In 1866, ten boys entered the Edinburgh University local examinations. David Dickson, Convenor of the Education Committee, stated:

"It had been an impression that somehow education in Hospitals must necessarily be of a less thorough and effective kind than that in other schools and there was an impression very common in the minds of the community that if boys trained in Hospitals were to compete with those trained in other schools they must be found deficient. The results of the late University local Examination were well fitted to dispel these impressions. In the first place, the boy who gained the highest honours over all Competitors was a boy from Stewart's Hospital (an institution especially under the management of the Merchant Company). The appearance of the competitors from George Watson's Hospital was in the highest degree gratifying …".

Mr Millar (Head Master)

"Of the ten boys who went up for examination eight passed, one having failed in Latin and one in English., but ten passed in Mathematics being all the boys in the Senior Section who were of age to enter as candidates, excepting one who was but two months past thirteen years of age. One of the boys obtained … first class honours in Classics. Three other boys took first class honours in Mathematics, one of these taking similar honours in English also. … the two Hospitals for boys … under the care of the Merchant Company … carried off more honours for junior candidates than any institution in Scotland, each having four honours."

The Chairman of the Governors presented the successful boys with their certificates.

It was this group of pupils ably led by the multi-talented George Stronach who created the first school magazine, *Our Bark,* under the guidance of English teacher William Jolly. George took the original hand-written magazine when he left the Hospital, but his grandson returned it many years later. George was Dux in 1866 and his brother Gordon also achieved this honour in 1868. George became a journalist and a senior Librarian in the Advocates' Library. The one sister in this talented family, Alice, attended the Ladies' College and became the first great woman journalist in Britain and a friend of literary giants such as Shaw, Barrie and Kipling.

The Merchant Company deliberately tried to give preference to intelligent boys in the 1860s. Given the uncertainties of the age one possibility was the creation of a boarding school on the English so-called 'Public School' model with boys selected on academic merit. See Chapter 4 for a more detailed examination of this period.

George Stronach, July 1866.

Mathew Aitkan, July 1866.

William Smith, July 1866.

John McDowall.

WATSON'S HOSPITAL 3rd APRIL 1827
NEW ARRANGEMENT OF THE TEACHING HOURS & FOR THE EMPLOYMENT OF THE BOYS THROUGHOUT THE DAY

	7 A.M.	8.	9.	10.	11.	12.	1 P.M.	2.	3.	4.	5.	6.
Section 1st containing 23 or 24	English with Eng. Master	Latin with Latin Master		Preparing or Rehearsing Tasks under Monitors while English Master is employed with History or Geography				Writing	English with Eng. Master			Tasks and Amusements under Superintendence of English Master. Beds at ½ past 8
Section 2nd containing 36	Latin with Latin Master	English with Eng. Master		Farthest advanced Division Geography and Histy. with Eng. Master. Remr. Latin with Latin Master	Farthest advanced Divn. Latin with Latin Master. Remr. Geogy. & Histy. with Eng. Master			Farthest advanced Divn. Antiquities & Classical Geogy. with Latin Master. Remr. Latin with do.	Writing and Arithmetic		Writing and Arithc.	Preparing Tasks for next day under superintendence of Latin Master. Beds at 9
Section 3rd containing 22	Latin 3 days of the week English Composition 2 days with Head Master	Latin and Greek with Head Master		Geometry with Head Master	Geography and History with Eng. Master			Writing, Arithmetic and Bookkeeping	French with Head Master		Writing, Arithmetic and Bookkeeping	Preparing Tasks for next day under superintendence of Head Master. Beds at 10 or ½ past 10

Timetable for the new arrangements made in 1827. Reproduced in The Watsonian, April 1939.

The Curriculum

At first this was an unrelenting stodgy diet dictated by the Statutes: English, Writing, Reading, Arithmetic, Latin (plus Greek for some), Bookkeeping (accounts) and vocal church music. The inclusion of Classics from an early age thus kept open the possibility of a university education for, without Latin, it would have been impossible to gain entrance. English, however, was becoming increasingly important and, in 1805, the Governors insisted *"… the new method of English be strictly enforced."*

By 1811, other subjects had been introduced such as Geography and History, but the majority of time was spent on Reading, Latin and Bookkeeping. Some Governors wanted more time spent on more modern subjects and so the discussions, or arguments, began. A major inquiry was launched in May 1818, the result being a broadening of the curriculum to include Geometry and Civil History as well as the employment of more specialist teachers and assistants. More emphasis began to be placed on actively raising the interest of the boys and keeping them *"… in a state of active exertion."* In order to create a more manageable system of classes where boys would be more or less at the same stage of progress the Statutes were altered in 1820 to allow younger

boys in (7 to 10 instead of 8 to 11) and older boys to leave after the age of 14 (instead of 16). The latter had a lot to do with behaviour problems associated with bored, non-academic boys.

Nevertheless, there were still problems. In 1823, another inquiry was held into *"… the depressed and labouring state of the education … and the means of restoring it to its efficiency"*. The main problem was that far too many boys still entered the Hospital inadequately prepared with the result that teachers were hard pressed to cope with so many individuals at so many different stages. The proposed solution was to 'set' the boys, concentrating on the basics of English for the junior ones. The other problem was the dominance of Latin which, like Maths today, was said to be good for you whether you understood it or not and despite the fact that most people never use it after leaving school. Enforced Latin caused a lot of unnecessary hostility among the boys. The problem was not resolved by 1870, but a specialist English teacher was employed who would also promote History and Geography. Serious Latin was beginning to be seen as a subject for seniors only. Greek was temporarily dropped and a specialist French teacher employed in order to allow the Head more time to concentrate on teaching the senior classes.

Several university professors were invited to give their solutions, but there was absolutely no agreement whatsoever on either causes or solutions. Professor Dunbar for example, said the boys should enter earlier at six years and that Latin was not a problem, but wonderful for all whilst Professor Pillans said the main problem was Latin because most Watson's boys didn't go to university. He proposed that English be the main subject, that promotion from class to class be by ability not age and that public annual examinations be held. The problems were never resolved, despite resorting to a drastic solution in the 1860s by sending pupils to the Royal High School.

Both Governors and teachers were well aware of the limited horizons and experiences that many of the boys had and did a great deal to improve these as best they could. The introduction of gymnastics was proposed in 1827, 1830 and 1831. On each occasion it was rejected, as was an alternative, dancing. In 1834, however, the Governors at last agreed to a trial period of a few hours per week for *"… some lessons in Dancing and the Callisthenic exercises …"*. Both proved very popular. Short excursions into the countryside during the summer began in 1827, a weekly Tea Table where boys and staff could discuss anything began in the same year, a weekly walk in 1828, drawing was introduced in 1828, dining at the same table as staff in 1849, practical technical in 1851, military drill in 1853 and Physical Sciences in 1855. In March 1850 the Drawing Master's brother invited the boys to his print shop to see the exciting new painting by David Roberts entitled *The Fall of Jerusalem.* In the same year the Governors encouraged the youngsters to visit the zoo as often as they wanted by paying the entrance charges and groups were taken to the Royal Academy exhibitions at the Mound. The annual excursions were still taking place in the 1860s with 'omnibuses' whisking them away to Hopetoun House. Of huge importance was the steady improvement of the Hospital Library which, by 1856, was a well-ordered department with a printed catalogue for each boy and a weekly issue on Friday afternoons. From July to December 1856 it had issued 670 books for 65 readers (the youngest boys were excluded). Most boys had taken 10 books out, but the older ones were taking 15 and more.

Rewards

The first prizes for academic attainment were awarded in October 1763 in order *"... to encourage emulation amongst the boys, books to the value of 30/- should be distributed amongst the most deserving."* Thus a long tradition was begun. Indeed, it was so successful that the amount spent was doubled in two years. The first annual prize giving was established in October 1802 when the prizes were to be given out *"... in presence of the Governors and School...".*

In November 1827, it was proposed that *"... a silver medal should be worn by the Dux of each class throughout the year and this both during school and play hours."* This accompanied a radical change in the Hospital education system. (See section 'The Curriculum'). Previously, *"... boys did not give or take places in their classes."* Now every boy would change his seat in class according to his marks achieved.

"The Committee hope to find the Boys of the institution as eager to secure, and as anxious to retain, an honourable

place among their class fellows as the Boys in any of the Public School of this City."

In February 1828, the medal scheme was debated and rejected. Instead, books were to be given as prizes. Three more 'firsts' then followed. Prizes for good behaviour were begun which depended on the votes of the boys in each class, but, far more lasting, was the introduction of a medal to the Dux of the whole school combined with the honour of having *"... the name of the boy who receives the medal to be annually painted on a Board to be placed in the large school room or common hall."* In August of the same year it was agreed to present a Silver Medal upon which was to be engraved a suitable design and inscription.

All boys leaving the Hospital had received a Bible, but in 1842, given the high religious excitement in the Church of Scotland which preceded the Disruption, each boy was also given a copy of *The Confession of Faith.* In October 1856, another Hospital first was begun: 'House Prizes' for those who achieved *"... neatness and cleanliness in their dress and have kept their books in the best condition and generally have conformed most attentively to the House Regulation."*

By 1857, the prize system was getting out of hand and the Governors insisted that in future there be no more than 90! That even included the new 'Prize for Arithmetic' which consisted of an entire case of mathematical instruments. By 1860, the annual prize-giving was turning into a big Hospital event. The Governors even agreed that each boy should celebrate by being given *"... a pie and bread and cheese."* Perhaps a modern equivalent could be reintroduced!

The first prize donated to the Hospital came from John Dudgeon, the Tenant of Spylaw farm, who, in September 1859, donated £20 towards a prize which would encourage boys in their studies. The Governors agreed to buy a medal, call it 'The Dudgeon Medal' and award it to the best writer of dictation.

Thus by the time the Hospital system was destroyed much of our modern award system was already in place. The myth that Watson's Hospital was an academic 'sink' really comes from those who wanted to destroy the system.

Dux Medal, 1861.

Dudgeon Medal 1860/61.

Note the ribbons on these medals. Dark green was the Hospital 'colour', not maroon.

A Healthy Body ...

Sport, so important to the future Watson's, played little part in organised Hospital life. Cricket was the first game to be recognised by the staff and games were organised against other Hospitals, certainly in the 1860s, if not earlier. Indeed, the boys refer to the 'Watsonian Cricket Club'. The Annual Games, started as a part of the annual excursions, included (in 1864) such events as the Long Jump, High Leap, Hop Step and Leap, Putting the Stone, Small Long Race, Middle Race, Long Race Sweepstakes and Swimming (50yds). These were, surprisingly, 'professional' games as each place had a money prize. The Middle Race, for example, had a top prize of 2s 6d while the boy placed sixth won 4d. The talented all-rounder George Stronach won the Swimming Race and collected 9d presented by the Head Master. The boys clearly enjoyed these as witnessed in the first Watson's school magazine *Our Bark, 1864–65*

edited by much-loved English teacher William Jolly and hand-written by the boys. He wrote:

"It would be a pity if any of our excellent outdoor sports, good for us both mentally and bodily, should require to be prohibited, as last year, on account of laziness in work, which, at all times and in everything, must stand first...."

Other entries also make it clear that the demand for sport is coming from the boys and is not being imposed on them. One boy wrote that it was a pity that there was no training for the Excursion Sports which is a plea for some form of PE.

Andrew W. Jack.
July 1867.

"Secondly, it is about time we were trying our hand, or rather our feet, at football ... As for golf and shinty we are all adepts at them and only long for Mr Editor using his influence with the reigning power to let us have a holiday as a regular beginning."

Mathew Aitkan.

"It would be a very admirable thing if at the annual excursion it was a regular custom to have games and that the Governors would have stated prizes like the High School and Merchiston Castle."

John W Johnson, Day Scholar.

> *Just set out on her —*
> *First Voyage*
> *The A.1. ship "Our Bark"*
>
> *This vessel has just been launched from the celebrated dockyard of the "G. W. H. Coy", registered, and entered as A.1. at the literary Lloyd's. She is to be employed in the Merchant service and has the most ample accommodation for every article of freight. She is intended to trade between this port and the city of Criticism and has just set out with a full cargo from food houses in town. A rapid and successful voyage is anticipated.*

Five years later the Hospital system came to an end, but the demand for games and sport rolled on into the new school and a new age.

Food Glorious Food

Just as the subjects taught followed a rigid timetable, so did meals, including the size of the portions. The Governors also insisted on quality, and changes were regularly made to improve the variety of what can only be described as hearty and healthy. Right up to the 1850s breakfast consisted of porridge, butter, milk and, in the earlier days, ale instead of milk. For dinner, variations were made from lamb or mutton with bread and milk. On Sunday was the much-looked-forward-to beef and broth.

"Note: It has been the practice to give the Boys ale for their Dinners, tho' there was no such Allowance in the former Appointment and, therefore for the future they are to have no Ale to Dinner except when they get roast beef." (1752)

By 1868 a greater variety of vegetables had been introduced, potatoes were on the menu at least three times a week along with eggs, rice (very unpopular), fish, eggs, rice puddings (popular) and boiled raw sugar. The potatoes were steamed in nets so that they didn't break up. During the 1860s, hoping to create a more homely atmosphere, a group of eight senior boys took charge of the eight tables and acted as 'Mum' to the others. At the end they then dined quietly as a group.

All Work and No Play ...

The hours set aside for various activities were rigidly set, but progressively liberalised over the years. The first regime was unremitting schoolwork, but this was liberalised in April 1772 when the summer school hours (ie from 1 April to 1 October) were fixed. In the forenoon of each day (except Sunday) school would be from 7 to 9am and then from 10am to 12 noon. On Monday, Wednesday and Friday afternoons school would run from 2 to 4pm, while on Tuesday and Thursday afternoons it would last one hour longer until 5pm. An exception was that there would be a 'play afternoon' every second Wednesday. Saturdays remained the same, ie school in the morning, out to see friends or relatives in the

CONTRACTORS WANTED.

THE GOVERNORS of GEORGE WATSON'S HOSPITAL wish to Contract for supplying the Hospital with the following Articles :—
1st, 500 Stones BUTCHER MEAT, or thereby, of the best quality ; to consist of rumps of beef, free from the great bone, and hind quarters of very best mutton, to be furnished in the course of twelve months, as the consumption may require.——Likewise, 15 Stones of Hind Legs of Lamb, furnished from beginning of July to middle of August, and these legs of lamb to be weighed with the beef and mutton. Also a quantity of Houghs.
2d, 12,000 TWENTY-OUNCE LOAVES, and 24,000 FIVE-OUNCE ROLLS, more or less, of the best quality.
3d, 240 Gallons of good TABLE BEER.
4th, 6000 Pints of SWEET MILK, or more.
5th, 2000 Pints of best BUTTER MILK.
6th, 200 Cart-loads of best SCOTS COALS, 12 cwt. each cart.
7th, 80 Good LEATHER CAPS, according to pattern.
8th, 320 PAIRS of SHOES, as per pattern, being four pairs for each boy, and upholding the same sufficiently by mending, per specimen, during twelve months—three pairs of old shoes to be returned to the contractor at the expiry of the contract, and one pair of the best to be kept.
9th, 360 Yards DARK BOTTLE GREEN WOOLLEN CLOTH, wool-dyed, stout make to pattern.
10th, 400 Yards DRAB 8-SHAFT CORDUROY, to pattern.
11th, MAKING about 160 Suits of CLOTHES, agreeable to pattern, or
160 Suits of Clothes ready made, a pattern to be seen at the Hospital.
12th, 600 Yards 7-8ths wide LINENS, full bleached, of a stout fabric for shirts or bolster slips ; and 360 yards 4-4th wide strong white CALICO, for night shirts.
13th, 80 Bolls Mid Lothian OATMEAL.
14th, STATIONERY and BOOKS, conform to list.
The Contracts to be twelve months from the 1st of January next; and the several articles, less or more, to be furnished as occasion may require. The persons wishing to contract, to lodge their offers, sealed, with a sufficient person surety for the faithful performance of the contract, with ARCHIBALD MACKINLAY, Esq. Treasurer to the Hospital, betwixt and the 27th curt. who will give every information that may be required by intending contractors.
Contractors must observe, that every Contractor will be held to the strict fulfilment of his engagement, either as to the quality or price, &c.
December 6, 1824.

Edinburgh Advertiser
8 December 1824.

afternoon and back to the Hospital in the evening. On Sundays the entire school went to the morning service at Greyfriars' which was followed by religious activities in the afternoon and an evening service in the Hospital. In-between times boys ate and played. During the darker winter months the format was much the same except that morning school ran from 9am to 12 noon and did not go beyond 4 in the afternoon. It was also specified for the first time that each boy had to have 'a task' (homework) to help occupy the evening hours. The boys rose at 6am in summer and 7am in winter whilst 'lights out' was always at 10pm.

This remained much the same until the end except that little breaks and 'play hours' were introduced. By 1849, the Governors were agreed that confining boys to classrooms for many hours each day was not an efficient aid to learning, indeed *"… the very reverse tendency."* Thus school hours were reduced for all, especially the younger ones.

However, what to do with them otherwise? Sport, for example, was never considered, but had the Hospital survived beyond 1870 it is very likely that it would have been introduced. The Governors, with typical liberalism, also recommended that Sunday *"should be a day of Holy Joy rather than a day of Gloom."* Boys should feel *"refreshed"* at its end. A pious sentiment, at least.

It was also specified for the first time that each boy had to have 'a task' (homework) to help occupy the evening hours.

Holidays

The Hospital was a substitute for family life. The boys lived there all year, day in and day out, allowed out on a Saturday to visit relatives or friends (if any lived nearby), but initially with no long holidays as we know them. 'Play Days' could be given, but the first extended holiday was granted as a reward, in August 1768, for success in the Annual Examination: *"…give them a vacation … for any space not exceeding a month."* So began a summer holiday tradition which usually began in late July and ended at the beginning of September.

The first Christmas holiday was granted in 1849: *"… the Boys shall have a vacation at Christmas commencing with the morning of Christmas Day and ending with the morning after New Year's Day."* This was an enlightened and progressive act at a time when most Scots did not celebrate Christmas with a holiday. It was a normal working day right up to the 1950s.

The first Easter holiday began on 17 April 1863 and lasted until the 28th. Thus the annual pattern of modern vacations had been created.

Day Scholars

The first proposal to consider allowing day boys into the Hospital was at a Governors' meeting on 4 October 1830. The main criticism of the Hospital system was that a huge amount of money was being spent on a small number of youngsters, but there was also a growing feeling that the attitudes created by life within a closed system were injurious to the educational and social development of the boys and, finally, it was encouraging a wider dependency culture. In 1830, the argument was that day scholars would be an inexpensive way of extending the benefits of the foundation, involving fees of no more than 10s 6d per quarter from Merchant Company members and causing little trouble to the system (eg election of day boys could take place at the same time as Hospital entrance and day boys would provide their own books and paper). In addition, fees could be used to extend the school or masters' salaries. However, a Committee to inquire into this stated that it doubted the Statutes could be changed and grandly announced that Britain was famous for keeping strictly to the intentions laid down in wills!

The issue continued to be discussed into 1831. For the first time those in favour of reform used the argument that the 'spirit' of the Statutes should be considered so that changes could be introduced which would fulfil the benefits which the Founder undoubtedly intended if he were alive. This 'spirit of the Founder's will' would be a much-used argument in the late 1860s. It was proposed that day scholars be between 7 and 10 and each would have to have had two years of schooling. The Governors, however, voted against the proposal in March. The subject went into abeyance for 10 years. In 1841, it was raised again, which is hardly surprising as Heriot's had been given during the intervening period such as parliamentary approval to extend the benefits of its foundation by building a series of 'Free Schools' throughout Edinburgh serving thousands of children, especially those of skilled workers. But there was no agreement amongst the Governors and the issue drifted into 1842.

Five years later in 1847 a much more robust campaign was begun by some Governors to include day scholars. They argued that change was imperative especially as the whole issue of Hospital funds was now a public one and that the injurious effects of the Hospital system had become much clearer since 1830. The 'moral delinquency' was, they argued, amply shown by recent notorious incidents (see 'Boys Will Be Boys'). Watson's should either create one or more separate schools, or simply allow day scholars into the existing building, the latter being the cheapest option. If it was necessary to go to Parliament, then so be it. The defence was equally robust arguing that no change was necessary. Watson's was a useful institution to families in distress and the problems of behaviour and attitude stemmed not from the Hospital system as such, but from the dysfunctional families from which the boys came and the attitudes of the teaching staff towards them. The 'day boy' issue was just the thin edge of the wedge and disguised the real intention of their opponents which was to destroy the Hospital. And so the debate continued and very hotly at times. The Merchant Company, however, would have to decide whether to back an approach to Parliament. In October 1847 the Company voted 64 to 19 to obtain an Act of Parliament. The Watson's Governors went along with it.

By February 1848, a printed proof of the proposed Bill (to admit day scholars and erect day schools) was shown to the Governors who voted overwhelmingly in favour. Indeed, only two dissented. The Bill was, however, thrown out by the Chairman of the Committee of the House of Lords on Private Bills, the now ancient Lord Shaftesbury who argued that there should be no deviation from the will of the Founder, namely education plus board and lodging. That during the 1830s it had been Shaftesbury who had supported the Heriot's scheme for 'Free Schools' was not lost upon anyone. Shaftesbury had become too old, befuddled and just 'lost the plot'! The Governors received a letter of sympathy from Lord Dunfermline.

Three years later, in June 1851, another attempt was made to gain parliamentary approval as Lord Redesdale had replaced Shaftesbury as Chairman of the Committee. However, before engaging in all the trouble and expenses Merchant Company representatives showed their proposals to Redesdale. He saw no objections to day scholars, extending the building, fees, allowances (called 'scholarships') or bursaries to boys going to university, but 'Out Schools' would be *"... too great and too marked a departure from the intentions of the Founder."* Thus a proposed Bill was built around Redesdale's comments, and – what a surprise – received the Royal Assent in June 1852. The Statutes were thus not written in stone and could be changed if there was a political will to do so. The cost of change? £785 11s 8d.

So the work went ahead to introduce day scholars, eight being welcomed in October 1852, the first being James Hamilton Inches. After all the fuss, work, money and effort the effect was minimal. Between 1852 and 1867 only 44 day scholars had been admitted and not many more had applied. There was no noticeable effect on the institution whatsoever, except that some of them disrupted the discipline of the place by continually arriving late in the morning.

The First Band

"9 June 1859: The Preses having called the attention of the meeting to the establishment of Bands of Music amongst the Boys of several institutions throughout the kingdom which have formed a source of cheerful and rational recreation, and a letter from the surgeon strongly recommending that a band should be formed among the boys of this Hospital. the meeting unanimously approved of the suggestion and remitted to the Education Committee to make the necessary arrangements, the cost not to exceed £15 in the meantime."

So a brass band was born. This was undoubtedly one of the first juvenile bands in Edinburgh, if not the first. The one usually credited as such was 'The British League Cadets' (a Temperance and anti-Catholic organisation begun by John Hope), but it only started a band in January 1860. Nevertheless, it was resplendent in its red Garibaldi shirts and blue trousers. Watson's never went quite that far.

Life in the Old Hospital

Written by Robert Gibson from Paxton, Berwickshire, who entered the Hospital in 1863 at the age of seven. It was published in the July 1930 edition of *The Watsonian*. The photograph below is of Robert and his sister in 1866 and the one (left) was taken when he was about to leave the Hospital several years later.

Entering School (1864).

EACH boy was stripped naked and examined by Dr Joseph Bell, a kindly old soul, and if found sound in wind and limb, was taken away by the janitor to the bathroom, where

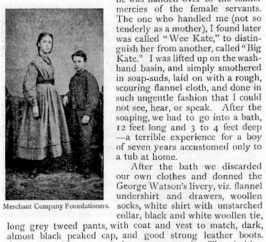

Merchant Company Foundationers.

he was handed over to the tender mercies of the female servants. The one who handled me (not so tenderly as a mother), I found later was called "Wee Kate," to distinguish her from another, called "Big Kate." I was lifted up on the wash-hand basin, and simply smothered in soap-suds, laid on with a rough, scouring flannel cloth, and done in such ungentle fashion that I could not see, hear, or speak. After the soaping, we had to go into a bath, 12 feet long and 3 to 4 feet deep —a terrible experience for a boy of seven years accustomed only to a tub at home.

After the bath we discarded our own clothes and donned the George Watson's livery, viz. flannel undershirt and drawers, woollen socks, white shirt with unstarched collar, black and white woollen tie, long grey tweed pants, with coat and vest to match, dark, almost black peaked cap, and good strong leather boots. On each article your number was stamped. The clothing contractors brought the goods in bulk, and each boy picked out a size suitable for him. Any little alteration was done by the tailors, who came on Saturdays to mend and alter: but we were all supposed to sew our own buttons on, while the servants darned our socks when necessary.

Daily Routine.

We rose at 6 a.m. and made for the wash-basins, one of the janitors being in attendance to maintain law and order. After washing we made for the shoe-room, where there was a general scramble for blacking (No. 2) and polishing (No. 3) brushes. Then there came an hour's drill out in the play-ground, under Sgt.-Major Coghill, an old Crimean veteran, after which we assembled in the hall and marched to breakfast in the dining-room. Before partaking of porridge and milk (and plenty of both!), we chanted our grace, "Blessed God, what shall we render to Thee for all Thy mercies, etc." After breakfast there came prayers in the Chapel, which everyone had to attend. Then Mr Miller inspected the School, and woe betide the hapless monitor if any of his seven or eight younger charges was found untidy! Then to the class-rooms from 9 to 12. After that came dinner, a short play-time, and the afternoon session.

"Hospital" Sundays.

After breakfast and prayers on Sundays we were all dressed in our best and marched to the big class-room, where the Headmaster gave out sheets of paper to the VI Form to take down the "heads" of the sermon. We marched two abreast to Old Greyfriars' Church, where old Dr Robertson was the minister. We used to amuse ourselves by carving on the pews our names, dogs, ships, men. The pews were cut and hacked in every conceivable way. After service we had dinner, then back to church again for the afternoon service, followed by Catechism and Bible studies, then supper and prayers, and so to bed!

The Heriot Feud.

The Heriot boys attended the same church, and were our deadly enemies. Whenever we met there were fights. Whatever the reason of this enmity, and how it originated, I cannot tell. In my time I fought twenty times with them, sometimes two at a time. We went so far in our feud as to invade Heriot's grounds. Eight or ten Watson's braves on the Heriot June Day went there purposely to make trouble, and the honours, as a rule, lay on our side, unless we were outnumbered.

Amusements.

We had always a good Cricket 1st and 2nd XI. Our pitch was in the back green, and we had matches with Stewart's and other schools on Saturdays, but never with Heriot's. We played "rugger" too—rough work, too often ending in free fights! Marbles ("bools"), skipping, "papes," hounds and hares, base-ball; paper-chases also took up our spare time. Then we had our theatrical performances, and performed (I remember) *William Tell* and *Rob Roy* with great éclat before the Governors and outside friends.

"The Band."

We had a brass band, taught by Herr Longbach, who had a musical instrument shop at the foot of Leith Walk—a great boy and a good teacher! I tell you we could kick up a terrible row, if nothing else, but really we played very creditably on holidays, or marching out for a walk in the country. Our annual holiday was a grand event. I remember going to Aberdour, Falls of Clyde, St Andrews, and Abbotsford. On the Aberdour excursion we all got on board a tug-boat at Leith and sailed merrily away with the band playing. When we got within a mile or so of the Fife shore, the boat ran aground owing to the ebbing tide, and we boys had a great time running *en masse* from side to side trying to get her off. Finally the captain went overboard, swam part of the way, waded the rest, and got boats to land us safely. Then the woods for one or two of us, after pheasants' eggs! We got three, and had two keepers after us, but we out-ran them and got safe to camp.

Revels by Night.

The dormitories held from 12 to 20 beds. These were in rows with about eighteen inches between. After prayers we went to bed at 8 p.m., winter and summer. On winter nights we used to tell stories made up by ourselves about travels in the Pacific. Then on the long light summer nights we usually had pillow-fights. Graham was King of England and I was Wallace or Bruce. Each King gathered his troops to his end of the ward. Each boy stuffed his pillows hard into the bolster, twisting it hard to get a good hold. Then we marched over the top of the beds till we met in mortal combat. There was of course an awful row; but beforehand we placed a boy at the keyhole. When he saw

anyone coming upstairs he gave the alarm, and in an instant all was quiet and every boy in bed fast asleep! One night after a battle in which the beaten army had to run the gauntlet a boy, Benny Gunn, got knocked down, cutting his nose almost in half on a corner of an iron bed. He fainted, so the alarm bell had to be rung, and up came masters, nurses, and janitors, and carried him to the sick-room. Gloom, bitter and dark, hung over us all that night. No questions were asked until morning, but we got off. Excuse —— running to toilet, tripped, fell on bed!

An Escapade.

I remember Mr Reid, the classics teacher in the old School had a good way of making us remember the Latin prepositions, etc., by putting them into a song: a, ab, absque, cum, clam, coram, de, e, ex, pro, pre, palam, sine, tenus, etc. to the tune of "Not for Joe." Another lot was, arcus, acus portus, quercus, ficus, artus, tribus, etc. etc. Poor old Reid! when we annoyed him his punishment was always— "Gibson, you take no beef to-day," and if you still contradicted, "Take no beef for two days." One day I got into grips with him and in the scuffle his wig fell off. Oh! what a scene it caused. No one knew he had one, but still he and I were good friends. After running away once, I was brought back and put up in the attic with corduroy pants and coat as punishment. I piled up old furniture and, getting out through a skylight on the top of the School, climbed up to the ship and captured young jackdaws. Then I went round the parapet and threw down lost balls to a lot of boys below. Suddenly the boys edged off, I saw, and I was just in time to duck, but saw Miller's face peering up from the stone steps leading to front entrance. I down into the garret, closed the skylight, and put a chest of drawers in place, lay on my bed or mattress on floor, and pretended innocence. Up come Miller and "Weelum" the janitor. Of course I had not left the garret, etc., etc. I was hauled downstairs and thereby hangs a long story which I have not time now to write!

I enclose photo of myself in the full dress of Watson's, taken with my sister, who was in the Merchant Maidens' Hospital, in the year 1866-67.   R. GIBSON.

James Craig's entry in the George Watson's Hospital Register. It shows that he was apprenticed to Patrick Jamieson, a Mason. Also, James' Apprentice Allowances had been paid as well as his £50 Bounty.

No Watson's – No New Town

The winner of Edinburgh's competition in 1766 to design a New Town was James Craig. He was born to elderly parents in October 1739 and his father was sufficiently 'decayed' by 1748 to have the application accepted for his son to enter Watson's Hospital as its 44th Boy.

James had no training as an architect, was not related to any and did not have enough money to study privately, especially abroad. After seven years at Watson's he was apprenticed for six years as a mason, part of the building industry elite. At that time builders tended to combine the jobs of architect and contractor in order to save money, so James' training was restricted to that. Thus it is absolutely astonishing that he won the competition to design Edinburgh's New Town. Indeed, he was still in his twenties and had barely begun his trade. After receiving that accolade, however, James' career stuttered, stumbled and tumbled. The only contact James milked for all it was worth was a dead poet, his Uncle James Thomson (1700–48). Uncle Jim was a likeable, dreamy and lazy, but talented Border poet who moved to London, never returned, and helped shape the future of English literature. James was forever using his famous relative to gain contracts, big or small. By 1782, however, James was out of luck. He had been unemployed for 18 months with an elderly mother and aunt to support. To survive, James pawned the Gold Medal and Silver Box which he won in the New Town Competition. He failed to repay the loan and the prizes subsequently disappeared.

James lived in a small flat, filled with broken furniture, at the foot of the West Port. There he died in 1795, forgotten and in debt. For James, it had been a hard life. He is buried in Greyfriars' Churchyard not far from George Watson and William Adam.

James Craig.

The Curious Case of John Wright Collins

John entered Watson's at the age of eight in 1861. He wrote two articles for the first magazine *Our Bark*. In 1868, in common with most others, he was apprenticed, his employers being Brodie, Hamilton & Co, Tea Merchants of 9 Picardy Place, Edinburgh. His eyes were opened to a world of opportunities in the Empire.

Towards the end of his apprenticeship John applied for the Colonial Office, claiming he had passed, with honours, Edinburgh University's local examinations in mathematics and history while still at Watson's. He also claimed to have won the Merchant Company award for an essay on direct and indirect taxation and then studied at King's College London. Impressed, the Colonial Office appointed him in December 1874 as schoolmaster in the capital of the Falkland Islands, Stanley.

John then entered the colonial administration where his career dazzled like lightning in the miniature world of Stanley. In May 1878 he was appointed *Justice of the Peace*, followed by *Treasurer, Collector of Customs, Registrar* and, finally, *acting Colonial Secretary*. John was a rising star.

Or he was until 1881 when HMS *Dwarf* arrived in Stanley and Governor Kerr asked the ship's Paymaster to check the island's accounts.

On 29 December serious errors were found, John was arrested and a locked cupboard broken into in his home which produced a wealth of incriminating evidence. John had suppressed despatches and registered letters, stolen cash from the mail, sold prized mint Falklands stamps to Stanley Gibbons and other collectors in England. The *Dwarf's* Captain noted that *"The Governor is so good-hearted he wants to let this man off, which would be utterly useless as he is a drunkard too."*

John was tried by the Falkland Islands Supreme Court with the Governor as judge. John pleaded guilty and was sentenced on 13 January 1882 to seven years' penal servitude. After a year in Stanley gaol he was shipped to Malta as the Falklands had no facilities for long-term prisoners.

Was John a corrupt villain, or a chancer who got caught when his ambition ran ahead of his abilities?

Does anyone know what happened to him? After Malta he disappeared, probably to another colony where he could bury his past. John represents those GWH scholars whose Hospital training set them in good store for other institutions less salubrious and even more confining.

John W. Collins.
July 1867.

George Watson's Hospital Staff, 1741–1870

Master/House Governor

George Anderson	1741–1752
Alexander Duning	1755–1779
Rev James Richardson	1779–1785
? Little	1785–1811

Superintendent of the Family

George Burel	1813–1815
(Too young to take	
the post in 1811)	

Headmaster

John Lyon	1815–1826
Rev Robert Cunningham[1]	1826–1832
John F Brown	1832–1836
Rev Thomas Munro	1836–1841
Adam Thorburn	1841–1843
David Middleton	1843–1843
Samuel McMorine	1843–1846
Rev John Johnston	1846–1856
James Millar	1856–1868

House Governor

William King	1868–1870

The Schoolmaster

John Penman	1741–1742
James Watson	1742–1746
John McKay	1746–1756
David Lindsay	1756–1757
James Hastie	1757–1760
Alexander Adam	1760–1763
William Rob	1763–1768
? Balfour	1768–1771
James Davidson	1771–1773
William Blackie	1773–1775
John Frazer	1775–1778
Alex Christieson	1778–1781
Richard Buchanan	1781–1791
John Christison	1791–1800
David Smith	1800–1808
Thomas Little	1808–1811

As the House Governor became far more of a teacher around 1815 and classes were reorganised, the situation as regards teachers becomes a little confused. 'The Schoolmaster' became known as 'The Second Master'.

The Second Master

John Dow	1814–1818
Patrick Douglas	1818–1823
Robert Gibson	1824–1825
Thomas Bell	1825–1827
John MacMillan	1827–1831
John F Brown	1831–1832
William Carmichael	1832–1833
David Hastings	1833–1835
Rev William Whyte	1835–1843
John McLaren	1843–1847
James Browning	1847–1849
Robert Drummond	1849–1852

Differences of status and salary between 2nd and 3rd teachers abolished, 1852.

John Stark	1852–1855
Alexander Leslie	1855–1856
Alexander Anderson	1857–1861
David Pryde	1861–1862
William Jolly	1862–1868

1868: 40 boys attend the High School. Only 3 teachers required in GWH.

Junior Master

Archibald Murray	
John Inglis [2]	1771–1773
David Grant	1774–1777
John Stewart	1777–1781
William Brown	1781–1785
John Christison	1785–1788
? Sangster	1788–1791
David Ballingall	1791–1792
Robert Burton	1792–1794
David Smith	1794–1799
Adam Robertson	1799–1800
Peter Smith	1801–1803
? Gardner	1803–1805
George Burel	1805–1809
	1809–1813

Confusion reigns as regards the Junior Master until the mid-1820s when an extra teacher is employed. Three now reside in the Hospital.

Junior Master Cntd

? Robertson	1818–1824
John Dalgleish	1825–1829
William Dickson	1829–1849
Alexander Gilmour	1849–1855
John Andrew	1855–1870
(Post suspended)	1823–1826
John MacMillan	1827–1827
John F Brown	1827–1831
William Carmichael	1831–1832
David Hastings	1832–1833
Thomas Monro	1833–1836
Adam Thorburn	1836–1840
Edward Smith	1840–1843
Andrew Gordon	1843–1846
Robert Stewart	1846–1848
Robert Drummond	1848–1849
Frederick Crombie	1849–1852

Two Day Teachers now appointed

Alexander Leslie	1852–1855
Mrs Francis Braidwood	1855–1862
John Munro	1862–1864
James Clark	1864–1868
John Rogersson	1852–1856
John Hogg	1856–1856
James Gibson	1856–1862
Thomas Reid	1862–1868

Specialist Teachers

French

Mr Espinasse	1823
Mr Cornillon	1823–1827
John Monnard	1836–1838
Mr Cornillon	1838–1852
Mr C H Schneider	1852–1855
Louis V Chemery	1855–1857
Francis Brown	1857–1865
Mons F Chaumont	1865–1868

Drawing

David Octavius Hill	1828–1856
Gourlay Steele	1863–1863
William Fergusson	1863–1868

Drill

Serjeant Webster	1853–1864
Serjeant Coghill	1864–1870
Captain Roland	1870

(1) The founder of The Edinburgh Institution (Melville College).
(2) The first GWH FP to become a GWH teacher.

The Men

Teachers were men. That simply reflected the entire Scottish system of Parochial and Burgh Schools.

One of the perennial problems appeared very soon after the Hospital opened: men who started as teachers, but aimed to become Ministers in the Church of Scotland and then left teaching as fast as they could. In this respect teachers at Watson's were no different than in any other Presbyterian school in Scotland. James Watson, appointed in 1842, soon got *"the Call to the Kirk of Newbattle"*. His successor, John McKay, lasted a good 10 years, but, in November 1755, he simply abandoned his class to the House Governor and disappeared for five weeks! That the Governors were not told until those five weeks had passed says something about the management style of those days. On his return McKay informed the House Governor that he was now the Minister in the north of Scotland and refused to contact the Governors. Understandably peeved the Governors stated that never again would they appoint a *"Student of Divinity"*. However, all that candidates did was keep quiet about their intentions. It is almost laughable that their next appointee, David Lindsay, lasted a year before owning up as a crypto student. He was sacked on the spot. A series of jolly wheezes were tried over the years such as six months, probation (1760), three months' notice, or forfeit one-quarter annual salary (1775 and 1863) and an attempt to be reasonable (1794) by allowing

attendance at divinity classes for one week per session. The fact remained, however, that teachers didn't stay long. If it wasn't the 'Minister issue', then it was the unrelenting nature of the job in a boarding school. The two teachers with the longest service were David Octavius Hill and John Dalgleish, both with about 21 years of service. Hill was, however, a part-time teacher. Dalgleish was sacked in 1849 for criticising the Governors. So much for loyalty.

In the first few years the other major problem was the relationship between the House Governor and the Schoolmaster as regards who was in charge of what. It blew up almost immediately in 1741 between Anderson and Penman. The Governors tried to clarify the matter by stating that the Schoolmaster had to obey the House Governor *"... in the order and economy of the House."* Penman, who was doing most of the daily teaching work, was having none of it. Anderson complained about Penman's *"disobedience"* and Penman was sacked. There was a gradual realisation that a House Governor was an expensive luxury and, by itself, an unattractive job. Alexander Duning replaced Anderson in 1755, but he soon proved a lazy liability and was there on sufferance. Two attempts to get someone else (1771, 1779) received no applications. Duning staggered on, a cross between a pensioner and porter. His successor became a Minister within six years! By 1785, the House Governor was becoming more of a teacher, being required to teach all subjects and requiring a *"...vigour and activity of mind."* By 1826, the

job became that of a *"Head Master"* in charge of the school and Hospital. This was a new departure in Scotland as a Head Master was usually *primus inter pares* in the Burgh Schools. His post was dignified by a new gown, *"... which he should wear in the exercise of his duties and ordered by the Statutes which had very recently fallen into disuse."*

Complaints about teachers give an interesting insight into the Watson's world. In November 1783, a parent, Mrs Hepburn, complained about the poor teaching her son was receiving from Mr Buchanan and requested that he be placed in Mr Stewart's class. Stewart supported Buchanan stating that one cannot give in to parents *"who entirely mistake"* how clever their children are, or who don't realise how lucky they are being taught at Watson's. Stewart added, *"... the boy is naturally so dull that I am afraid he will never make great progress in his education under any Master ..."*. The Governors happily supported Buchanan as this complaint was *"... a method of retaliation ... which in the end would destroy all discipline and good order."*

In December 1815, John Gib ran off claiming that he had received severe treatment by a teacher His family encouraged him to run away. When his father came to meet the Governors he told them that *"... he did not approve of his son being taught Latin."* Further, if disciplined as a result of doing none he told his son to run away. The Governors said this was *"... totally subversive of the discipline and good order of the Hospital."* Gib was expelled.

---

q*q That the Committee appointed for taking Trial of the Qualifications of such as have applied or shall apply to be Schoolmaster of *GEORGE WATSON's* Hospital, are to meet upon Teurfday the 23d April inst. in the Hospital-house, at 3 o'clock Afternoon; and they are defired to bring with them proper Certificates of their Characters and Qualifications for the faid Office.

The second GWH advertisement placed in the Caledonian Mercury *on Thursday 16 April 1741 and repeated on 20 April. (With the permission of the Signet Library, Edinburgh.)*

One bizarre incident occurred in November 1799 when a boy ran off after being threatened with punishment by Mr Burton for not doing an exercise. The boy's father brought him back, but complained to the Governors "... *that Mr Burton was so often absent from the school, and paid them [the boys] so little of the attention he ought to do, that it was not to be wondered at that he and the other boys should be incapable of getting the lessons presented to them.*" A subsequent inquiry proved the father to be quite correct. According to another teacher, John Christison, Burton averaged one hour per day attendance for a year, usually arriving in the late morning. The Matron, Mrs Rennie, stated that Burton just stayed in bed and she even brought him breakfast at the start. Burton didn't bother going to breakfast after a while as his relatives brought him food. He refused to go to church and so was locked in after all the staff and boys had left. Burton then just went out through a window. Christison put Burton's behaviour down to "... *extreme indolence and want of relish, or dislike to, his profession as a teacher.*" Mrs Rennie said that all the staff were averse to speaking out as "... *Mr Burton was sober and inoffensive and blameable as far as he knew for nothing but great indolence and inattention.*" Burton, amazingly, denied everything and when it was suggested he should resign (to protect his character) he refused and demanded a meeting with all the Governors who were not in the slightest impressed by his defence that he had been busy writing an essay! The Governors insisted he went quietly and quickly, hastened with "*compensation*" of half a year's salary. The reputation of the Governors would suffer if this story were ever to be made public.

If the Governors were enlightened as regards corporal punishment, then the teachers were less so. In 1825 Robert Gibson was sacked and immediately ordered from the Hospital after "... *several acts of great severity, bordering indeed, in some cases, upon cruelty upon the Boys after repeated reprimands from the members of the Committee to abstain from such acts.*"

In late 1849, however, the Governors got a little more than they bargained for. The incident started on 3 October when one boy (Macdowall) claimed he had been belted over his clothed backside so severely by Mr Browning that the skin was broken and discoloured. Apparently it was not the first complaint. Invited to meet the Governors, Browning chose instead to resign. End of story? Not quite. Browning immediately went to Glasgow and contacted *The Witness* newspaper to tell his story and, unbelievably brave or stupid, John Dalgleish, Watson's longest-serving teacher, supported him. The Governors split, some arguing Dalgleish was only acting as a friend and had a perfect right to make public statements. Others accused Dalgleish of meddling in matters of no concern to him. A heated debate ensued, but the Governors voted 13–2 to censure Dalgleish. Browning's defence was that there were only three cases and in each the Governors had believed the boy

Extreme indolence and want of relish, or dislike to, his profession as a teacher.

concerned. The first involved a boy (GC) who feigned illness to avoid work and punishment. The second involved (EJ), a "*notoriously deceitful and vindictive*" boy according to Browning, who claimed that Browning had kicked him violently on the shin when, in fact, another boy had owned up to it. Browning did admit severity in the third case when he belted Macdowall with "... *three stripes with the tawse over the trousers on a fleshy part of the Body...*". Browning claimed it had been the start of the session when boys were "*refractory and indolent*", that "... *the prevalence of the prejudice against the study of Greek and Latin*" supported by parents made the boys restless and lazy plus the fact that Macdowall (deceitful and stubborn) was after "... *gaining a victory over the teacher.*" Explaining his sudden resignation Browning claimed a vendetta by some Governors who were Established Church whilst he

was a strong Free Church member (the Disruption had occurred less than six years before) and that other Governors ousted him "... *from a mistaken but well known disapproval of corporal punishment in all cases...*". He then launched into a tirade against the Governors using similar arguments as a later group would in order to destroy the Hospital system, but he blamed the Governors' enlightened regime.

"*It would indeed be strange, if, in a large institution in which boys are confined night and day, from week to week, of all classes, and ages, and tempers, who have been subjected to all kinds of training prior to admission, who are of necessity mixed together in classes without consideration of their fitness, or unfitness, whom the teacher must retain in a class which they were introduced without his approval and who not infrequently have inducements to resist authority presented to them in various ways by well meaning, doubtless, but highly injudicious parents, friends and Governors ....*"

The surprising thing is that John Dalgleish, the longest-serving teacher, agreed with Browning, supported him publicly and rounded on the Governors that he had the right to question their activities in a "*free country*", stating that some of them treated teachers "... *after the fashion of mere under-beings.*" Not surprisingly the Governors voted 14–4 to sack him!

Another issue which caused a storm was that of celibacy which was required by the Statutes. On 12 May 1840 the Governors received a petition from the Headmaster (Rev Munro), the Second Master (Rev Whyte) and a teacher, Adam Thorburn, arguing for an end to celibacy on the grounds that enlightened public sentiment was against it, they were debarred from a normal married life, it led to a high staff turnover, it created an unhealthy male monastic society within the Hospital, Heriot's had already abandoned it and the Watson's janitor was married anyway! The Governors were unimpressed arguing for example, that salaries were to blame for high staff turnover, that staff would neglect the boys in favour of their own families and that it would never work in Heriot's. Staff comfort might be greater, but there was no advantage to the Hospital. In response, Mr Thorburn resigned for the easier life of a missionary in darkest Stockbridge.

Seven months later a bombshell landed, or to be more exact a letter from the Treasurer of Heriot's. It is scarcely believable, but the Rev William Whyte had written a bitter letter about Watson's to the Treasurer complaining that *"... we are all much dissatisfied"* with salaries, conditions and treatment by the Governors. The Treasurer handed the letter over to the Governors of Watson's who understandably were vexed. The Headmaster, Munro, was carpeted and asked whether he agreed with Whyte. Munro became as shifty as any guilty pupil and evaded a direct answer. Three days later a letter was received from Whyte expressing regret about his *"improper expression ... made on the spur of the moment."* The Governors accepted this and intended to rebuke him for his use of *"...offensive terms"*, but to do it quietly in order to calm the situation. Whyte was then sent a copy of the relevant Minutes detailing what the Governors had discussed. Obviously Whyte felt he was taking all the blame here for he promptly offered to resign, but stated that it had been Munro who had dictated the original letter to the Treasurer of Heriot's! Munro was again carpeted. His defence was so long and convoluted that few understood it, even fewer were impressed and nobody believed it. Nevertheless, the Governors calmed the situation, nobody resigned and peace reigned ... or rather it did not as Whyte and Munro then went to war against each other.

Munro, showing the same sense of tact and wisdom as previously, then declared war on the Governors by supporting Merchant Company objections to the Governors' attempts to change the Statute which allowed the Head to be present at Governors' meetings. Whyte, showing his usual restraint, wrote to the Watson's Treasurer that Munro *"... habitually and systematically sacrifices the comfort of everyone in the Hospital to his own"* and then went off on summer holiday without telling anyone.

The Governors were getting mightily fed up. Whyte had to be censured, but Munro needed to be more tactful in dealing with staff especially avoiding his haughty and distant manner, *"... which makes it difficult, as well as unpleasant, for those to approach him."* On his return from unofficial holiday Whyte was willing to compromise, but Munro protested his innocence and set about getting witness statements as regards his wonderfully co-operative and sweet nature. The Governors had just about had enough when Munro, out of the blue, announced he had been 'called' to be Minister of Fala! And so it ended.

But harmony reigned most of the time and, to be just, the Governors were fair and supportive to staff who they believed had served the boys well. Staff are on record as having appreciated that and also as having a great affection for the Hospital despite the daily problems encountered.

The Old Boys

One consequence of the Hospital system, for many but certainly not for all, was male bonding, the strength of reinforced concrete. The first mention of former pupils banding together comes in June 1847:

"... former inmates of the institution have annual meetings for the purpose of keeping alive the friendships formed within the walls of this Hospital."

In April 1864, such informal gatherings flowered into something much grander:

"The Treasurer having reported that some of the former inmates of the Hospital had formed themselves into an association to be called 'George Watson's Club' of which Mr Millar the House Governor was to be President for the purpose of keeping up of mutual intercourse and of holding occasional meetings for literary purposes resolved to record their approbation of the Club having been formed and authorised the Treasurer and House Governor to give such facilities and encouragement to it as they saw proper."

Thus 'GWC' enters our history even before the demise of the Hospital and, in March 1868, it is even referred to as 'The Watsonian Association'.

Former inmates of the institution have annual meetings for the purpose of keeping alive the friendships formed within the walls of this Hospital.

The Steward or Janitor

Although the Statutes specified the use of the title 'Janitor', the first was dubbed a 'Steward' perhaps because he, George Robertson, had served the Earl of Moray in a similar function. It was obviously not the job Robertson expected and he resigned within a year. The second Steward was an ex-merchant, Kenneth Bisset who served an astonishing 27 years, longer than any teacher in the entire history of the Hospital,. He died in service on 8 May 1769. In the years following, the job title changed to that of '1st Porter' and, in 1826, he *"... should assume the title of Janitor which seems to be the title given him in the Statutes."* The Governors were looking for a person of middle age, in sound health, of good appearance, either married or unmarried (but no children with him), who would live in the lodge at the gate, eat at the servants' table, get coal and candles free, and also supervise the boys at play, all for an annual salary of £20.

In 1827, the two Janitors were provided each with a suit of clothes at the expense of the Hospital so they would look smart *"... when they accompany the Masters and Boys to Church."* The following year the duties were clarified. They had to keep the gravel walk around the Hospital clean, *"... keep out all sturdy beggars and*

The above illustration comes from James Howie's unpublished Old Edinburgh Characters and Costumes *collated in 1890. There is no documentary evidence to support this uniform style and Howie gives no indication as to the period in which it may have been worn. Nevertheless, Howie is accurate as regards other drawings which can be checked.*

vagrant persons…", stop boys leaving the grounds, report damage, lock the gates when required, cut the bread into portions, shut the shutters at nightfall, open them in the morning, lay tablecloths, clean tables, carry up meals, remove dishes, swab the school rooms daily, carry up coals, put on fires, remove ashes, light candles, clean candlesticks and snuffers, trim and light the lamps in the lobbies and passages, weigh goods entering, see shoes were mended, darn clothes, supervise senior boys, ring the bell for meals and prayers and ensure the boys' wardrobes were neat. In their spare time they were asked to be *"useful"*.

Sometimes the Janitors could be just a trifle difficult. On 18 August 1828, William Reid, James Currie and two female servants, plus their male acquaintances, got wildly drunk and forgot to lock the gates. John MacMillan, acting as Deputy Headmaster, reported *"great difficulty"* in getting the male acquaintances removed between 10 and 11 at night. Eight days later Reid was drunk again and when MacMillan asked him to lock the gates he was told to go away in *"very insulting"* language. Reid was sacked, James Currie rebuked and the servants *"warned"*! Drink reared its head again in 1844 when James Currie was sacked for having *"some irregular habits"*.

The Janitors will have, however, the last laugh as the only part of the old Hospital building to survive demolition in 2004 was the old Janitor's Lodge opposite the main entrance to Heriot's.

Mistress and Servants

The Mistress was in charge of all food, linen, the servants and the sick. The female servants – whose number varied – cleaned the Hospital, took care of all brushes, combs and shirts, looked after the junior boys (combing and brushing hair, washing them and their clothes), made the beds, removed dirty linens, opened windows, served at mealtimes, cleaned shoes, cut meat into portions and carried plates and meals. Keeping them apart from the elder boys was a recurring problem. If any servants were found receiving gifts from boys, parents or friends the result was instant dismissal.

"In these days a kiss meant expulsion! A foundationer, James Miller, one day risked his all for stolen sweets; as the boys were marching in line from room to room he left the ranks to steal a kiss from a pretty housemaid who happened to be working in the vaulted corridor. For his bravery he was hauled before the authorities, expelled and sent back to his parents in far New Zealand, where he prospered exceedingly."

(The Oldest Watsonian: Charles R Somerville. *The Watsonian*, December 1937)

If any servants were found receiving gifts from boys, parents or friends the result was instant dismissal.

The Janitor's Lodge was erected as part of the 1857 building programme.

Lauriston Lodge (Hospital Janitor).

Heriot's Railings. Line of old Town Wall.

Approx site of Wall Turret.

GW Hospital Railings.

Lauriston Place

In February 1764, the Trust attempted to get a Bill through Parliament. Both the Governors and the Merchant Company were against it as they wanted one daily toll to be payable which would allow a traveller entry through all tolls within a six-mile distance from the toll bars erected next to the City. A few weeks later the Trust was successful in getting its Act of Parliament.

Three years later, however, the road had yet to be built owing to a dispute between Watson's and the Trust as regards the nature of the new dyke. The Trust wanted an inexpensive sunken fence whilst Watson's wanted *"… a parapet wall of three feet high with an iron rail."* This was not resolved, but a narrow version of the road was built by 1769.

In June 1786 the Council was pressing for the town wall to be taken down and requesting the removal of Watson's dyke. In February 1787, the Governors agreed. Both wall and dyke were removed. Nevertheless, the narrow road was not immediately widened. Indeed, it still had not been done by November 1791. Only in the summer of 1792 was it intimated that Lauriston Place was going to be widened to a breadth of 60ft. Thus the north boundary of Watson's was set well back from the line of the current road and down a slope which allowed the boys to see out and everyone else to see in. A new boundary wall was needed quickly and decided upon within weeks. The broad road, however, was never actually built.

When a pavement was begun to be constructed along the narrow road in August 1845 the Governors decided to move the entire wall northwards to meet it in order to ensure privacy. In 1846 an iron railing was put on top of the wall. It is that wall and railings which run today along Lauriston Place opposite Heriot's. The space between the old and new walls was landscaped with a sloping bank, shrubs and trees.

On 4 October 1762 the 'Turnpike Road Trust of the County of Midlothian' proposed laying a toll road from Bristo Street westwards to *"… the two penny custom (Tollcross)."* Edinburgh's town wall, with towers and parapets, lay along the present-day Heriot's side of

Playground game of 'Soldiers' described in Our Bark *by W Cruickshank writing under the pseudonym, 'Mr Couts'.*

Lauriston Place. The space between the town wall and Watson's Hospital was too narrow *"… for making a proper road"*, so the Trust asked the Governors to remove the dyke upon the north of Watson's Hospital and the Council to pull down the wall. The Governors agreed provided the Trust paid for the dyke's demolition plus its rebuilding further back. The issue was then the toll road, and a fair number of Governors were not happy about *"… several Toll bars … hurtful to the interest of the Hospital."* By February, the opposition elsewhere was so strong that the Trust didn't apply to Parliament for an Act to allow the road to be created.

1.4   Why Did Watson's Become a Day School in 1870?

Why Watson's changed from a Hospital to a Day School is a major, but often misunderstood and troublesome issue, yet frequently asked by both parents and students. An explanation may be found in the following four interlocked reasons:

- Hospital life became to be regarded as an evil which had to be eradicated for the benefit of the children.
- The Hospital system began to be seen as an inefficient use of scarce resources desperately needed for other purposes.
- The Merchant Company feared government intervention and the loss of control over its Hospital funds.
- The Company was in terminal decline. Hospital reform was a means of self-preservation and regeneration.

A small group of dedicated Progressives within the Company then succeeded in gaining Government support for an Act of Parliament which would allow internal reform. The nature of those reforms resulted in a storm of protest which made further Hospital reform a major issue in Edinburgh, and Scotland, for the next 30 years.

Evil Monasticism

Since about 1830 there had been a rising tide of public criticism against the 'evils of monasticism' as practised in a Hospital education. In the 1873 Royal Commission into Scottish Endowed Schools and Hospitals those alleged evils were clearly set forth in evidence given by William Jolly, an Inspector of Schools, but once a teacher at Watson's Hospital for six years, residing there for two.

Jolly's criticisms were threefold: educational, intellectual and moral. 'Monasticism' produced an inertness of mind, work and aspiration resulting from a want of emulation in a closed community. That unnatural life gave a limited and contracted knowledge of the world with little real-life experience, or even the ersatz experience given by parental conversation. Intellectually, there was a dullness of perception and understanding combined with a short memory and attention span. More energy was needed by Hospital teachers as the inmates were not self-motivated and lacked intellectual self-reliance. Intellectual eminence was, therefore, very rare. Hospital boys seemed distant from the rest of the world and antagonistic to it. Jolly noted the sharp contrast in his view between the Day Scholars and the indoor boys. Above all, the moral evils were the greatest. 'Monasticism' bred exceptionally good liars and utter selfishness. As regards emotional development domestic feelings were stunted whilst moral habits were "... *bad in ways that one would require to speak about with reserve.*" He agreed

it was ever thus when boys bandied together, but Hospital life perpetuated a lower moral tone.

If the above criticisms were not sufficiently damning Jolly introduced a further reason to destroy 'monasticism': the Garring Law. If a boy, for example, does better in class than another, stronger boy, "... *I have known him give his successful companion a severe thrashing.*" This, he said, was one cause of the dead level of intelligence, tone and work which the system produced. The Garring Law, although not officially recognised by the governors, was, "... *the traditional moral code of the hospital.*" Staff could raise the tone, but never eradicate the evils altogether. His conclusion was that the Hospital system had to be abolished with the rights of foundationers protected.

The Laurie Report
In the summer of 1868, the Merchant Company invited Simon S Laurie, Secretary to the Education Committee of the Church of Scotland, to inspect all the Hospitals it managed (ie Watson's, Stewart's, the Merchant Maiden and Gillespie's). This was meant to be an impartial inspection, but Laurie was a well-known progressive educationalist, later to become Professor of Education at Edinburgh University, with well known views as regards 'Monasticism'.

As regards Watson's his inspection *of the school* resulted in a good report, despite the fact that the Head, Mr Millar, was suffering from "*nervous exhaustion*" and had lost his grip somewhat. Laurie liked the idea, for example, that progress from one class to another depended on merit

Professor Simon S Laurie.

and found the teaching to be of a high standard: "... *the opinion which prevails in many quarters, that they are Institutions characterised by inefficient work and filled with half-idle officers, is utterly without foundation.*" Indeed, Mathematics was taught by the Head with "... *great vigour, clearness and precision.*" Mr Jolly was described as being of a "*rare efficiency ... and aptitude.*" Laurie disliked other parts: Geography was "*dry and unattractive*" and Latin might as well "... *disappear from this school with positive advantage to the boys.*" More written exams were needed to stimulate the boys and there was "... *too free use of the strap.*" Nevertheless, it was not a damning report.

Even the main inspection of *the Hospital* was reasonable. The domestic arrangements were described as *"good"* with the boys being well clothed and fed, despite a lack of butter. He didn't like the Sleeping Wards: *"If it were possible to divide them, so as to have fewer in a room it would prevent the immorality or rebellious spirit of one ill-conditioned boy infecting many at a time."* He recommended wooden partitions, more time for play, no uniform (for some *"a badge of inferiority"*), with more organised games and music. None of his Report so far indicated any profound change.

Laurie, however, then produced his bombshell, a separate report entitled, *General Remarks on Hospital Training* which utterly condemned the 'monastic' system in similar terms as described by William Jolly above. He even went so far as to describe the boys as *"aliens"*. His remedy was to turn the Hospital into a boarding house with plenty holidays (free weekends, more free time, three weeks at Christmas, two in Spring, six in Summer) and send the senior boys to the Royal High School for their education.

A Revolution Begins

It was this separate report that the Merchant Company and Watson's Governors pounced on. Laurie's Report was approved on 3 July 1868. Events moved fast. All senior boys would go to the Royal High School as from September, the uniform for those boys was abolished, the Hospital would become a boarding house, long weekends were introduced and all the Hospital staff were sacked! Even Laurie was surprised at how quickly events unfolded as his main recommendation was merely reform. Laurie really did not expect the Merchant Company to adopt his radical solution, what even he described as a "bold" move. If Laurie's milder reforms had been adopted then Watson's could have developed into what we would describe as an English-type 'public' school. Given the prestige and superiority accorded to the English Public Schools during the same period the arguments in Scotland against 'monasticism' look pretty unconvincing, but perhaps Scottish opinion was less than enamoured of boarding schools, or perhaps it can be viewed as just blinkered, or even hypocritical.

Whatever, destroying 'monasticism' was not the main motivating factor behind the Merchant Company's actions. It merely acted as a moral smokescreen behind which lay some far more genuine and selfish motives.

Hospitals: an inefficient use of resources

"The traditional English traveller is reported to have said that the people of Edinburgh must be very sickly, they had so many hospitals about their town."
(Sir A Grant: *Recess Studies.* 1870)

In 1868, of the 11 major Scottish Hospitals, nine were in Edinburgh and three were under the management of the Merchant Company. Gillespie's, also under Company trusteeship, was regarded as a minor institution. Capital stocks of the Company Hospitals had reached £500,000, producing an annual income upwards of £20,000. However, they catered for only a small number of children: 67 boys in Stewart's, 83 in Watson's, 75 girls in the Merchant Maiden and 200 in Gillespie's Day School. There had been increasing public criticism over the years that more could be done with such vast funds. As early as 1836, Heriot's, the richest Hospital in Scotland, had begun a vast expansion of its activities by providing Free Day Schools of which there were 13 by 1868 serving 3,000 pupils. In 1847, Dr Guthrie, the founder of the Ragged School movement, had suggested turning all Edinburgh's Hospitals into schools for the poor and destitute. In 1852, Watson's admitted Day Scholars, but to no great effect. In 1855, the Lord Advocate was being petitioned to create 'Free or Day or Industrial Schools' from Hospital funds. In 1868, Heriot's turned 60 of its 180 foundationers into day boys. Other influential people such as Sir Alexander Grant, Principal of Edinburgh University, were beginning to think of a grand design which would involve using Hospital funds to create a graded system of schooling from 'ragged', industrial and primary through to classical, commercial, technical, adult and up to university education. The Merchant Company was sensitive to such criticism, but this, by itself, did not trigger the reforms of 1868–70.

Fear of Government Intervention

By the 1860s all principal European nations, the USA and Canada taxed the community to provide public education because religious and charitable institutions could not maintain the high costs involved and failed to provide uniform provision. The first British public grants to schooling began in 1839, but every attempt of Government from 1847 to 1857 to extend provision had run into a wall of denominational dissent, the only united front being to oppose secularism. In Scotland, unlike England, there was a long-standing parochial system rooted in Presbyterianism, but it had severe problems adapting to both industrialisation and urbanisation. Whether an independent Scottish Government could have supplied a catalyst for change is open to debate, but the fact remained that Scotland was a junior partner in a union dominated by English interests represented in the Westminster Government. The Merchant Company was acting within this complicated framework. The 1860s witnessed probably the most intensive investigation of educational provision ever seen in this country. One consequence was the destruction of the entire Scottish Hospital system, begun by the Merchant Company in 1870 and completed by others within thirty years.

The Newcastle Commission

The first major investigation in England was the Newcastle Commission which reported in 1861 on the state of popular education and the means to provide sound and cheap elementary instruction to all classes. This was the first comprehensive survey of English elementary education and included comparisons with other countries. Two and a half million children were being schooled, most left at 11 and the average time spent at school was 4–6 years. It proposed state capitation grants, based on payment by results, supported by local rates, but rejected free education and compulsion. The only recommendation accepted by Government, however, was payment by results (The Revised Code, 1862) which set the tone for all governments throughout the 1860s, especially that of Gladstone's Liberals post-1868. Teacher training and pupil certification were devalued and class sizes increased. As Robert Lowe stated: *"If it is not cheap it shall be efficient; if it is not efficient it shall be cheap."*

Alarm Bells Ring

Meanwhile, in 1861–2, the Lord Advocate was struggling to push through a Bill to extend educational provision in Scotland and meeting the usual denominational opposition. It was Clause 38 that set the first alarm bells ringing throughout Scotland's endowed institutions as that would give the government *"power to revise all foundations …"*. On 25 April 1862 a joint meeting was held of representatives from all the Merchant Company Hospitals plus Heriot's and Schaw's. The Merchant Company had written to the Lord Advocate asking whether Clause 38 would apply to Hospitals and the answer was in the affirmative. The meeting voted to meet the Lord Advocate for some discussion on the issue. If they opposed the Clause there would be a sizeable group in Parliament against them and the public would think they had something to hide. The result would be *"… more rigorous powers to a Board of supervision"*. Four days later the Lord Advocate agreed to alter the Clause so that any reform would be with the Governors' consent. The Merchant Company saw this as merely a reprieve and its future policy became quite clear and consistent from that moment: there was going to be an inquiry into Scottish educational provision and it couldn't escape that, but what was desired was a 'permissive clause' in any future Bill which would give substantial freedom of action without the need to apply to Parliament for specific changes. The Merchant Company, it declared, would act for the benefit of its members alone and not those of the general public.

The Clarendon Commission

The next investigation applied only to England, but it was hitting a target closer to home as far as the Merchant Company was concerned. Following criticism during the Newcastle Commission concerning the nature

and application of educational endowments the Government decided to inquire into those of the nine English so-called major 'public' schools. The subsequent Clarendon Commission reported in 1864 and, although favourable to the schools themselves, it recommended a drastic revision of the statutes as well as the powers of both governing bodies and headmasters. This led to the 1868 Public Schools Act which *forcibly* reformed the governing bodies and statutes.

The Taunton Commission

What followed was perfectly logical: to inquire into the hundreds of other endowed institutions throughout England. Indeed, many of those felt quite insulted that they had been left out of the Clarendon inquiry and made to look second-rate. (That, incidentally, led to the Headmasters' Conference, the main aim of which was to preserve funds and management from state intervention.) Part of the fact-finding exercise was to see if any concerted attempt was needed to improve English *secondary* education. Thus the Taunton Commission was established in 1864 to investigate 10,000 private and 3,000 endowed schools involving one million children from the middle and upper classes. After a Herculean evidence-gathering exercise the Commission reported in 1868 proposing a radical secondary school system supported by endowments and presided over by a new central authority responsible to the Minister of Education. The schools would be graded: Third to age 14, Second to age 16, First to 18–19. The Government ignored all recommendations, but targeted the endowed schools by appointing three Commissioners to supervise and reorganise the existing management bodies with very little freedom allowed the trustees. The main reason was that in 1867 the millions of urban skilled workers had gained the vote. The priority was now universal elementary education which culminated in the English 1870 Education Act.

The Argyll Commission

Scotttish educational provision could not be ignored and so the Argyll

Commission was established in 1864 which corresponded to the Newcastle, Clarendon and Taunton Commissions all rolled into one. This massive Inquiry produced three Reports by 1867. The first contained evidence given by the 136 convenors of the religious education committees plus others dealing with elementary education, such as the 'ragged' schools, HMIs and individual teachers. The second was a detailed examination of the elementary schools while the third concentrated on burgh and middle-class schools. Its overall conclusion was that the old parochial school system worked well in the countryside (although buildings tended to be in poor shape), but less so in the towns. Literacy levels were very much higher than in England as was the degree of social mobility through education. However, there were two great problems. The first was that one-third of Scottish children did not attend school and that was mostly an urban problem. The second was that middle-class needs were met by private schools with variable standards and high fees. In France and Germany, for

The private Edinburgh Academy was regarded as one of the best schools in Britain.

example, powerful state secondaries prepared pupils for stringent exams and were cheap, efficient and open to all classes. Scottish burgh schools could have developed in a like manner. Unlike similar schools in England they had the advantages of antiquity and public status and were not overshadowed by prestigious boarding schools. This awakened the Scottish public to the possibility of rescuing the burgh schools from neglect and creating a national system open to all through a system of scholarships. Already 1 in 205 youngsters were receiving secondary education in Scotland compared to 1 in 249 for progressive Prussia and 1 in 1,300 for England. The Commissioners were hugely impressed by the burgh schools even although their teaching hours were twice as long as those at Eton or Winchester. The private Edinburgh Academy was regarded as one of the best schools in Britain. However, there was a variety of provision which could be reformed: *"All these evils are due to want of organisation and suggest the necessity of some central authority to regulate the education of the country."* The biggest problem was that of money and alarm bells sounded even louder for the Merchant Company. Referring to endowed Hospitals it stated: *"Could any considerable proportion of these be made available for the encouragement of the higher or secondary education, the question of funds would be very much simplified and the demands on local rates or the public purse would be greatly reduced."* Bursaries and scholarships to allow poorer pupils to attend university were vital, but *"Funds for this purpose could hardly be expected from Government. But there are great educational mortifications in the country which do comparatively little good. It is estimated that in and around Edinburgh there is nearly £60,000 a year from funds of this description."*

A Threat to Hospital Funds

The Merchant Company was deeply concerned. Even although the Government ignored most of the Reports and concentrated on elementary provision (which led to the ill-fated 1869 Bill followed by the successful 1872 one) the Company could sense that a climate of opinion was being created within which a future government would find it remarkably easy to redirect Hospital funds to benefit the Scottish public. To forestall that is a major reason why the Company acted so quickly.

The Merchant Company in Decline

By the 1850s the Merchant Company was in serious decline. Industrialisation, changing trading patterns, liberalism and the growth of democracy had destroyed the necessity of belonging to the Merchant Company in order to trade and weakened its political

influence both locally and nationally. At the same time the professions (especially lawyers) expanded in numbers and increased their status. By the 1850s why would anyone want to spend upwards of £145 to join the Company?

- To join a long-established and respectable fraternity with established status.
- Meeting business contacts.
- The chance to influence political affairs through an organised and recognised body.
- A chance to help manage a few Hospitals.
- The prospect of free boarding and education for any children if the father's business hit the rocks.
- From 1827, the Widows' Fund.

Indeed, the latter proved to be the biggest attraction. The entrance fee to the Company took that into account so an older applicant might have to pay well over £200 for admission. However, there were other methods of providing financial security. The Company was in trouble. From 1800 to 1830, new members numbered 474, but from 1831 to 1861 this had dropped to only 261. The Merchant Company needed the mercantile community, but the latter did not need the Company.

Within the Company, however, was a far-sighted, committed and determined group, sometimes dubbed the Progressives, who took it upon themselves, sometimes without official Company backing, to drag the Merchant Company into the nineteenth century and improve the status of the mercantile community in Edinburgh. The five leading characters were Thomas Boyd, James Duncan, Thomas Knox, Thomas Strong and Alexander Kirk Mackie.

The attractive option would be to open the Hospitals as schools for the middle class with moderate fees, especially if one could retain preference for the children of Merchant Company members, but without any poverty restriction. A virtual educational monopoly could be created, above all in secondary education, which would help make the Company a far more attractive

organisation and ensure its survival. It worked. In 1875, during evidence given by Thomas Boyd to the Endowed Schools Commission, he was asked by Sir Edward Colebrooke how many members the Merchant Company had. Boyd answered that it had more than 300 merchants, bankers and traders of Edinburgh and Leith.

Colebrooke: *There have been great additions recently to its Numbers from persons connected with the City?*
Boyd: *Yes; very numerous additions…*
Colebrooke: *And it is now in a very prosperous State?*
Boyd: *Very much so indeed.*

Boyd also defended Company preference because its reforms had done so much public good that there was no need to deprive its members of their *"vested interests"*.

Self-preservation was the Merchant Company's main motivating factor in transforming Hospitals into schools and explains why it was galvanised into a ferociously determined action, during 1868–70.

James Duncan: Master of the Merchant Company, 1865–8.

Thomas Boyd: 1868–70

Thomas Knox: Convenor, Watson's Education Committee, 1868
Merchant Company Treasurer, 1869
Master of the Merchant Company, 1871

Thomas Strong: Merchant Company Secretary, 1859–69

A Kirk Mackie: 1869–89

Desperately Seeking a Permissive Clause

The Merchant Company was looking for a 'permissive clause' to slip into any education measure, but this looked unlikely when the third Report recommended that the Scotch Education Board *"… examine the statutes of their [the Hospitals'] foundation, and, subject when necessary to the approval of Parliament, to make alterations therein, with a view to the extension of education."* In an attempt to pre-empt criticism, the Company brought in Simon Laurie in April 1868 to inspect the Hospitals. He had finished his inquiry by June, but, for maximum effect, it was made known just after the third Report had been published in July. To show that the Company was serious about self-reform, Watson's senior boys would be educated in the Royal High School only using the Hospital as a boarding establishment. It was of dubious legality, of course, and depended upon a clause in the 1852 Act which allowed Watson's to use *"adjacent classrooms"*. The Roayl High School was two miles away! Even progressive reformers like Thomas Boyd, the Treasurer, were aghast, but, nevertheless, a determined James Duncan drove it through so that the Company would be seen as *"… pioneers in opening up the Hospitals and extending the benefit of education so far as in their power."* Seen as being responsible here would then lead, it was hoped, to a 'permissive clause'.

Unfortunately for the Company the Government had introduced a Parochial Schools Bill in 1868 which had one clause copied from the English Public Schools Act allowing a central authority to investigate endowed schools and forcibly take any necessary action. This had to be stopped, but the Company went much further by preparing a draft bill of its own which would allow it to reform its endowments. In truth, it was not the Company at this stage, but a private initiative by Knox, Duncan and Boyd who, if successful, then hoped to persuade the Company to go along with them. In February 1869, both Knox and Boyd went to meet MPs in London, persuaded the Lord Advocate to ditch the offending clause in the Parochial Schools Bill and gained support for a separate 'permissive bill', not only from him, but also the Home Secretary, Henry Bruce, and Forster, responsible for education in England. All in all, quite a successful little sortie!

"Every suggestion we have made has been most freely conceded by the Government – the Bill I framed containing the provisional Orders has been put in the hands of Government officials and ordered to be printed and will be introduced by the Home Secretary who entirely approves and the Vice-President."
(Strong in London to Boyd, Edinburgh, 26 February 1869)

The Merchant Company reforms were going to be used as a model for England.

The Endowed Hospitals (Scotland) Act was introduced in the Commons on 14 April 1869 and sailed along beside the Endowed Schools Bill for England. The two could hardly have been more different. The English measure dictated that *"… absolute power is given to a Board of three persons appointed by the Crown to overrule, by new schemes, the founder's intentions."* The Scottish Bill had no such central authority, being completely permissive except for a supervisory role given to the Home Secretary. Indeed, it is hard not to draw the conclusion that the Merchant Company reforms were going to be used as a model for England. There was hardly any debate and only minimal change. Only Sir Edward Colebrooke demanded an immediate inquiry, but he was ignored. Irish Disestablishment overshadowed the Bill and most English MPs apparently thought it was about Scottish medical provision! It received Royal Assent on 26 July. Knox called it *"…one of the neatest little Parliamentary weapons that perhaps ever was forged."* So, how would the Company reform its institutions?

SIR THOMAS J. BOYD

Sheriff R Orr, *The Watsonian*, December 1930.

"The picture would not be complete were I to omit Sir Thomas Boyd, the shrewd and sagacious Master of the Merchant Company, whom I can see smiling as he puts the medals and bundles of book prizes into the hands of the happy winners …"
(Sheriff R Orr, *The Watsonian*, Dec 1913)

Thomas Knox, *The Watsonian*, April 1925.

" … the leonine head of Thomas Knox, who succeeded Thomas Boyd in the chair."
(Sheriff R Orr, *The Watsonian*, Dec 1913)

A Kirk Mackie (Picture courtesy of the Edinburgh Room, Edinburgh Central Library).

The Merchant Company Reforms

Not surprisingly the Merchant Company was the first to act. It unanimously endorsed a scheme of reform proposed by Thomas Boyd on 28 February 1870 and within six months its Hospitals had been transformed and thrown open as Day Schools. The speed of action was astonishing. The determination of its leadership was equally so as it not only sold the old Watson's building to the Royal Infirmary, but also contemplated opening a completely new school for girls with all the work, trouble and expense involved in both ventures. For example, a serious delay was caused by traditionalists within the Company taking out an interdict against the sale to the Infirmary. Nevertheless, the work went on despite all obstacles and on all fronts.

The scheme proposed by Boyd included recommendations made by all the various Commissions to ensure that there would be swift progress in Parliament. His 'General Scheme' proposed a graded system by making the education in Watson's higher than Stewart's which in turn would be higher than Gillespie's. The Merchant Maiden would have the same status as Watson's as would a brand-new school for girls founded from Watson's funds. A specially endowed Chair at Edinburgh University would be funded from Stewart's and Watson's for the 'Teaching of the Theory and Practice of Commerce, Finance and Mercantile Law' while at the other end of the scale an Industrial School would be founded for *"neglected Boys and Girls".*

From the latter school upwards scholars of *"merit and promise"* would

be advanced by means of scholarships, bursaries and allowances. 'Moderate fees' were promised which would benefit the entire community. Existing foundationers would be boarded with parents, or in a special boarding house which would also be open to fee-paying pupils from beyond Edinburgh. The numbers of foundationers would be reduced and, in future, open to competitive examination amongst pupils. Again, school bursaries and travelling scholarships would follow the same principle. But Boyd was very vague about the scale of operation thus leaving his options open. The Scheme retained the discretionary right of the Company to use its Hospitals *"wholly or partly"* as day schools and *"to establish additional Day Schools ... where they are most needed."* Despite this massive attack on 'privilege' and the concentration on 'merit', the whole issue concerning the rights of Merchant Company members to access these schools without the bar of poverty or merit was downplayed.

All this came across very well indeed to the Edinburgh community – or those that bothered to read the press – and there was remarkably little criticism. The Collegiate School, for example, objected to ex-charity school Watson's taking the name Collegiate which "*... would give a handle to the Boys of the school to taunt the pupils of the Edinburgh Collegiate School*". The Merchant Company then agreed to 'College Schools' whilst the proposed change of the Merchant Maiden to 'The Collegiate Institution' was altered to 'The Edinburgh Educational Institution for Young Ladies'. The attitude of the Progressives was totally positive and confident. When the name of the university Chair was altered, Knox rejoiced: "*Glorious success. Fortune favours the brave. The Chair like the rose smells by any name.*" In May and June 1870 Boyd, Knox and Duncan were all in London pressing their case for an opening of the schools by September. They met the right people once again including Lord Advocate George Young, Henry Bruce (Home Secretary) and William Forster (Vice-President of the Committee of Council on Education). Being economical with the truth was one strategy when, for example, the politicians were assured that all the other Edinburgh institutions agreed with the Company reforms when, in fact, there was no such agreement. Buttering up the Lord Advocate by wining and dining his son was another, as was paying the Lord Advocate's Secretary £20 for his 'trouble'! But the politicians were mostly impressed by the charm, knowledge, preparedness, thoroughness and determination of Company leadership.

There was no public inquiry and the Provisional Orders became law in July 1870. By the end of September the Company schools had enrolled an impressive 3,300 pupils.

Reaction to the New Schools

The Prospectuses were ready by July, but it was not until pupils had been enrolled in late September that the full extent of the Merchant Company actions became revealed. There were no 'additional schools' established where they might be needed, no 'Graded Scheme' to aid social mobility, no 'Industrial School' for the poor, no purely secondary school system but, instead, five Hospital buildings crammed with 3,300 middle-class pupils aged from five to sixteen years. What was new? Where was the public benefit? A storm of protest hit the Company, the press and the Government.

Edinburgh's small army of private schools was the hardest hit as fees for the new Company schools were not 'moderate' as promised, but downright low. To be more exact they were high enough to exclude working-class people, but were low enough to entice middle-class customers. As good businessmen the Company had simply undercut its competitors. An enraged Edinburgh teacher commented ...

"*None of us ever dreamt when their schemes were before Parliament, that the Company meant virtually to take charge of education in Edinburgh. The Merchant Company ... has acted in the manner of a coup d'etat, as if the existing state of things had been powerful and dangerous, only to be overturned by stratagem... They do not add one feature of novelty or excellence to the apparatus of instruction in Edinburgh. All their peculiarity is their cheapness.*" (St Jus, 1870, p14)

Another critic commented: "*The Scheme is nothing less than a gigantic system of outdoor relief for the sons and daughters of the middle class.*" ('Fair Field and No Favour', *The Scotsman*, 20 October 1870)

The highest fee at a Company girls' school was one-third of that usually charged by private schools while the highest fee for a boy was half that of the Royal High. Private schools in the southern districts, above all Newington, were devastated, schools on the north side suffered considerably and the Royal High by 1872 had lost about 100 pupils. Principal Alexander Grant of Edinburgh University had previously endorsed Boyd's graded scheme, but was furious at what had actually happened, especially when he had been away on holiday. He argued that the Company had simply substituted its schools for existing ones, when their funds "*.. are urgently wanted for other purposes.*" He wrote to the Home Secretary, "*It was a great pity that a Permissive Bill was ever allowed to these misapplied endowments*" and demanded "*a general inquiry ... as regards the wants of the community.*"

The Company couldn't deny that private schools had been hurt, but argued that either they rapidly recovered, or that only the owners suffered as teachers got jobs in the Company schools. This latter argument was preposterous. In November 1870, 300 Edinburgh teachers petitioned the Lord Advocate against the Company actions. Even more debatable was the argument by the Company that it had improved teachers' salaries. Dr W Graham of 'The Edinburgh Institution' argued that Company salaries had been reduced to the point that "*... they lower the tone of education in Edinburgh very much. ... no lad of talent would enter upon the teaching profession with such a view before them.*" The truth is uncertain.

The only other institution to be allowed to reform was Bathgate Academy. Other applicants were Stirling Academy, the Trades Maiden and Hutcheson's. In addition, Heriot's also applied with a ready-made scheme, but the damage had been done. A storm of protest forced the Government to grant an inquiry which had been proposed by Colebrooke back in 1869. That inquiry (the Colebrooke Commission) eventually gave support to the Company reforms. For the next 30 years the biggest battle would be over the future of Heriot's: to continue as a preserve of the Edinburgh artisans, or be forced to provide even more middle-class education.

Some would draw the conclusion that the interests of the Edinburgh public might have been better served had an inquiry been held first and a co-ordinated scheme of Hospital reform been carried out by a central authority ultimately responsible to the electorate. Others would argue that the subsequent history of the Company schools shows that at least large sections of the Edinburgh public benefited from a stringent educational system which provided the model for secondary schooling publicly funded from 1892 onwards.

Sale of Watson's Hospital Building to the Infirmary

Two Myths

- Thomas Boyd and Councillor Colston were both involved with raising money for the new Infirmary. There is absolutely no evidence of any impropriety here. Both openly declared their interest. Both kept out of discussions and voting.

- There was no 'plot' against the Merchant Maiden. When the Hospital was sold the Watson's Governors and the Merchant Company had in mind no specific site for the new school. What gave them some freedom of movement was "… *the Estate of Merchiston on which they could build at any time.*"

The view that 'the girls were sacrificed' in the interests of Watson's is absolute nonsense. In financial terms the situation was that Watson's was sold for £43,000, the Merchant Maiden was bought for c.£18,000 and the British Hotel in Queen Street (the new home for the MM, now called Erskine House) purchased for £14,000. Everyone made a handsome profit. Also, the girls moved to a far more salubrious site, the centre of middle-class Edinburgh packed with flats in those days, not offices.

> *The view that 'the girls were sacrificed' in the interests of Watson's is absolute nonsense.*

Three Facts

- The Infirmary was built on the site intended for the first Hospital at Thomson's Yards. Watson's sold it in 1736.
- The Infirmary was built on a site occupied by Watson's. It was sold to the Infirmary in 1869.
- In 1932, Watson's moved out of the old Merchant Maiden building it had occupied since 1871. The Infirmary bought it in 1926 and it was subsequently demolished

The print below comes from the Prospectus for 1870. It would never be repeated as the boys moved in the following year to their new home in Archibald Place and the Infirmary occupied the Hospital site. Note that the name was never 'George Watson's *Boys* College'. Also, the intention was to build more than one school in areas of the city where they were needed, but that never happened.

GEORGE WATSON'S COLLEGE-SCHOOLS
FOR BOYS.

Old Hospital, New School (1870–1):The First Days

A new Headmaster, George Ogilvie who had been Head at Daniel Stewart's, was appointed on 26 July 1870, and 29 new teachers followed. The new school was opened in the old Hospital building on 26 September. After four days the roll was closed at 800 boys aged from 5½ to 16 chosen from 964 applicants.

"… I should say we were herded – a strange and awkward squad – into the field behind the school, and there sorted out, according I suppose, to age and size, into lots which formed the nuclei of the future classes."

Sheriff R Orr,
The Watsonian, December 1913

"The boys were a tough lot. Gathered from all parts of the city and country, owning no common tradition, and animated by no esprit de corps … their hand literally against everyone. Free fights were the order of the day… The venue was George Square Lane – a secluded spot of sanguinary memory where neither policeman nor master was likely to appear to bring the combat to an abrupt and abortive close."

GC Ligertwood,
The Watsonian, July 1920

"Herr Fischer was supposed to teach German, but … he did not control the class … The whole thing is a blurred memory-picture of noise, confusion, disorder, with Herr Fischer vainly gesticulating and appealing in somewhat broken English to a crowd of boys who scarcely heard or heeded him. …"

Sheriff R Orr, op cit

"So strong was the feeling against the School that no other school would join ours in games."

George Ogilvie

"Dr Ogilvie was to us an object of distant veneration … Dr Ogilvie's secretary appeared occasionally … He was a short, quiet, parchment-faced young man. … He became afterwards Professor of Philosophy at Aberdeen and Glasgow Universities."

Sheriff R Orr, op cit

David Leitch, Janitor from 1870 to 1903.

"We had with us the old George Watson Hospital boys, some still dressed in their old uniform … they were not popular with us, as their Hospital training, with its strictness and seclusion, had tended to make them sly, and low in their tastes and ideas."

AG Fortune,
The Watsonian, July 1936

The Foundationers

"These … gave some trouble as they were under the impression that they were being deprived of their rights and privileges by outsiders … I endeavoured to conciliate them and gain their confidence … I scattered them throughout the classes, placing as few as possible in the same class. Their power of combination was thus prevented, but they continued restless and somewhat troublesome."

George Ogilvie

The Janitors

"Bustling about here, there and everywhere are Davie and Weelum, without whom it was not possible that the George Watson's of the seventies could exist for a day. They were familiar friends of every boy and they never failed a boy in any time of need."

Sheriff R Orr, op cit

"Discipline in the playground … Davie, big and burly, was the man for the job. … He had a commanding presence, a voice to command and well developed biceps."

GC Ligertwood op, cit:

The Franco-Prussian War, 1870–1

"…play during the short intervals usually took the form of battles on the rough ground – the weapons were glengarries, bonnets and twisted cravats – between those who favoured the Germans and those who supported the French … the majority of the Scots were on the side of the 'Prooshians' … the Prussians were religious, with the same beliefs and obligations as the Scots possessed."

Duncan Cameron,
The Watsonian, July 1941

"It was all but impossible to secure, on such short notice, a thoroughly efficient staff. While we had some weak men, we had some strong men. …I was glad when we got to the end of the first session without a breakdown."

George Ogilvie

George Ogilvie.

Demolition

In late 2004, the last William Adam building in Edinburgh, George Watson's Hospital, was demolished by a consortium calling itself *Quartermile*. This group has included the following:

- The Gladedale Group (Bett Homes, Furlong Homes and Furlong City)
- Bank of Scotland Corporate (part of HBOS)
- Southside Capital
- Kilmartin Property
- Taylor Woodrow
- Hurd Rolland Architects
- Masterplanner Foster & Partners (London architects led by Norman Foster). In partnership with Page & Park (Glasgow) and Richard Murphy (Edinburgh).

Quartermile boasts that it will invest £400 in the development of the site and the annual return for Edinburgh would be £135 million.

Although the vast majority of the Hospital building was still standing and initial plans were for it to be developed as a hotel, neither the City of Edinburgh Council nor the Scottish Parliament opposed demolition. Indeed, even Historic Scotland did not contest the issue. A sad end for a great building.

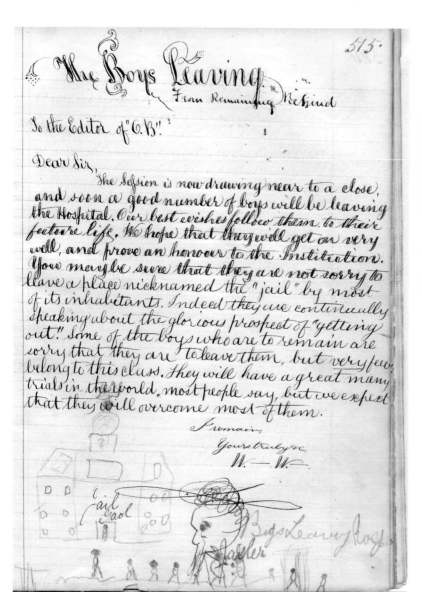

Andrew Jack

The page to the left was written and drawn by Andrew Jack (under the pseudonym 'WW'). Note his depiction of the Hospital crowned by the ship. His photograph was taken in July 1867.

Archibald Place, 1871–92

The Main Entrance

The main entrance was via the gate to Archibald Place. The other gates were at the far end of the playground leading onto the Meadows.

The Head Janitor's House

David Leitch's house for 33 years. Rebuilt 1878–9 with a Luncheon Room adjoining under Davie's supervision. Class photos were often taken against the wall of this house – look for the curtains on the windows. The last building to be demolished in the 1930s.

The Main Hall

Building approved on 19 July 1872. Designed by Macgibbon and built by W & D Macgregor of Grindlay Street for £4,867 11s 5d. Completed by 15 May1873. Lit by gas and excellent for exams as it stopped boys, *"copying from each other."* Used for drawing classes and occasional science lectures, *"but the acoustics are so bad that the Lecturer has great difficulty in making himself heard."* Used for lots of fund-raising events, eg January 1887, Minstrel Entertainment for Athletic Club funds. Electric light installed in 1900. Note the ship on top of the cupola.

The Wee or Little School (The Elementary School)

Described as, *"a gaunt, unlovely building of 4 storeys high, reached by an opening in the wall on the east side of the large playground and had its own diminutive playground and sheds."* It was separated from the Infirmary by very high walls. Ogilvie tried to expand it in 1875 and 1880 by building on decayed outhouses and a toilet. This is the only known illustration taken from the Prospectus of 1884/5.

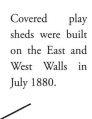

Covered play sheds were built on the East and West Walls in July 1880.

The New West Extension

Completed on 24 April 1883 at a cost of about £2,000. It included a fine new gymnasium. On 16 July planning began for an East Extension.

1884: Would it be easier to rebuild the Elementary Department rather than repair and alter it? No action taken.

1876: Name Change

George Watson's College Schools becomes George Watson's College for Boys as no further schools, promised in 1870, were intended.

1883: Crumbling Main Stair rebuilt using stone from White Hailes Quarry.

October 1890: Parallel bars to be put into the playground to encourage healthy activity.

The old Merchant Maiden building before alterations.

The New East Extension

Completed in 1884 at a cost of about £2,400. Ground-floor classrooms of old building were too small, dark and airless. This wing gave six extra classrooms. Hoped to clear the ground floor of old building, then lower it and create a play area 70 x 50 ft, a swimming pool and toilets. Head not happy about a pool as it would require a lot of maintenance and supervision, but only benefit a few boys. Entire plan scrapped and the area turned into cloakrooms for hats and coats.

Archibald Place, 1893–1932

1905: A huge flagpole (3 storeys high) was erected after the old one blew down in a storm. The new one also blew down in 1915 and went right through the roof!

In April 1916, a German airship (a Zeppelin) bombed Watson's. A brass Prussian eagle was set into the playground and a heavy metal plaque made from the bomb casing was set into the wall above the spot where the bomb landed.

1891: Edinburgh Royal Infirmary offered to buy the Elementary School as more accommodation and a clinical teaching area were required as well as rooms for new women students. In April 1892, Watson's agreed to sell, but where was the Elementary School to go? Purchasing a big house was suggested as was a move to Falconhall, but the Head suggested building two new wings and the Governors agreed. The Wings, complete with towers, cost £8,271 and were opened on Wednesday 25 October 1893 by Lord Elgin, Viceroy of India, and direct descendant of Robert Bruce.

In April 1893 the Sick Children's Hospital sent a bill for 14s 6d for window glass broken by boys throwing stones. The school paid. A friendlier pastime was waving to the nurses.

In January 1894, the muddy holes in the playground were filled up yet again and filled this time with Musselburgh gravel. It looked great, but, when boys played football, it wrecked even the toughest boots.

Classrooms were heated by open fires, but a new central heating system for the corridors was installed in 1893. Gas-fired fans aided ventilation as did Tobin's tubes in each room which led to an extractor fan in the roof. Electricity was already in place by 1890, but, in 1892, the school was undecided about introducing speaking tubes or telephones. Telephones won.

Head Janitor's House

1912: In 1912 a Miniature Rifle Range was built beside the Gym.

1893: A new Gym (70 x 45 ft) built here and connected to the main building by a covered passage. The original stone arms from the old Hospital building was cemented into the Gym's gable end. It is now in the West Quad.

1893: A swimming pool had been proposed once again, but rejected in favour of a Laboratory and Workshop.

After WWI two German howitzers were given by the War Office as war trophies. The War Memorial (The Shrine) was built later in front of the Main Stair.

"As a result of so many alterations and additions the external appearance of the College suffered. The classic simplicity of the original front has been destroyed, and it is a matter of difficulty to designate or even describe the style that has taken its place. Indeed, one regrets that the Zepp raid of 1916 which came so near to wrecking the building, did not succeed, and so have furnished the opportunity of providing a habitation really worthy of the history and reputation of the school." (George Ligertwood, July 1920)

The new Hall opened in 1873 and used for exams, lectures, assemblies, prizegivings and fund-raising activities for which 'The Christy Minstrels' were always popular.

Although 'unacceptable' these days Minstrel troupes abounded and this one (The Christy Minstrels) was formed in 1884 by Watson's boys, encouraged by singing teacher Mr T Richardson. Its first concert was given in the Hall which was crammed to overflowing. The Sand Dance was also very popular and practised on an empty piece of ground since built on by Warrender Baths.

The Old

These are the earliest known pictures of classrooms in Archibald Place and were taken by a very young pupil, FM Chrystal, for the 1898 Lit Club Magazine. You can see how these rooms compare with modern ones. Note in particular the long bench-type communal desks which were common right throughout the school. The teacher's desk below seems to have survived. Do you know what room it is in?

...The New

Geography

These new classrooms were opened on 19 November 1908 by Lord Avebury. Those desks would be definitely useful for Geographic activities.

Science

"With the new session have come several changes in the disposal of School time. Owing to changes in the curriculum it has become necessary to divide the day into seven periods. History and Geography are now taught as separate subjects, and every Classical boy now waits in the temple of Archimedes on the top flat four periods per week. In other words, Science is a compulsory subject."

Technical

Headmasters

1. Doctor Who?

If one man can be said to have stamped his mark on Watson's it was most certainly 'The Doctor', George Ogilvie, Headmaster for twenty-eight years from 1870–98. Visitors to the school often assumed that the tall, imposing and bearded figure with the gentle, charming manner and magnificent uniform who met them at the door was the Headmaster, but were astonished to discover that he was Davie Leitch, the Head Janitor. Instead, the shuffling, hen-toed wee man behind Davie in the badly fitting, old frock coat, baggy-kneed trousers, elastic sided boots and old-fashioned top hat was the top man. Indeed, Doc Ogilvie was Peter Pan in reverse, perpetually ancient with grizzled grey beard and soft, sad brown eyes.

He was a Scot, through and through: homely, unassuming with a big streak of Aberdeen pawkiness and a lack of pretentious Olympian aloofness which lesser spirits adopt to hide fear and inadequacy. The Doc was an excellent, patient listener, shrewd, practical, tactful and friendly. It was impossible to rattle him. Once or twice he experienced rudeness from visitors, but he was never ruffled. *"Oh, it doesn't signify,"* he would say, *"So long as they don't strike me."* He was never boastful either about himself, or Watson's; his was a many sided and self-respecting pride without any affectation. Once when an angry French teacher burst into his study complaining bitterly that a colleague was calling himself 'Senior French Teacher', Ogilvie calmly and simply resolved the situation by replying, *"Oh, you can just sign yourself the same."* Ogilvie gained respect, support and even love.

Youngsters really liked him and The Doc knew them – individually. He was famed for his prodigious memory of each and every pupil. Even after an absence of years Ogilvie could recognise a face and then describe the strengths and failings of its owner, sometimes resulting in extreme embarrassment, but more often in mirth plus disbelief. Partly this was a mere conjuring trick, but mostly it was the result of a genuine interest in each pupil. Every morning he visited the youngest Watsonians in the Elementary School for he believed that future appropriate behaviour and attitudes were nursed there. Names and faces stuck. Unfortunately, once he was confused with a name, it also tended to stick (eg younger brothers could be called regularly by the name of an elder sibling), but youngsters

George Ogilvie, taken with his famous old-fashioned top hat, at the opening of Myreside Pavilion on Saturday 1 May 1897.

smiled, shook their heads and forgave him. Few, if any, truanted, for Ogilvie religiously read the daily absence list, immediately sent for a brother to inquire about the health of the missing one, contacted parents and carpeted the chap on his return. Only those who travelled by train and claimed it had been 'late' continually missed his attention.

The Doc made youngsters feel he had a deep regard for them and a real interest in their progress. He had the habit of getting a finger between a boy's shirt collar and Adam's apple, or lightly gripping a collar, or taking a hand in his own. This was intimacy, always combined with humour usually beginning with a play on words (eg *Well, Lowe, I hope your marks are high today.*), progressing to a joke (eg *My mother didn't want me to study vulgar fractions because she wanted me to have a refined upbringing.*) and the interview always ended with a soft 'dunt oan the heid' with the rim of his old top hat. If a boy did well The Doc would say, *"Well, ask your Mum for a jeely piece."* On entering a class he would ask it for the Latin for 'yesterday morning' and the reply would be joyously roared back, *'Hairy Manny'!* He was never known to have inflicted the belt on anyone.

Ogilvie always kept an eye on teachers, especially new ones. If he kept out of a teacher's room, then that teacher had passed his probation. George Ligertwood started teaching in Watson's in 1878. Ogilvie was never out of his room, but there was always humour. As Ligertwood had come from Hastings, Ogilvie told the other staff in deep, ominous tones to watch him: *"He's been in England."* The Doc followed a rigid daily

pattern. One part involved catching 'late' teachers by taking the class over and then quietly depart on the teacher's arrival. On one such occasion the teacher asked the class, *"Was the Doctor long in, boys?"* They replied, *"He prayed for you, sir."*

Ogilvie was born in Aberdeen during 1825, the third son of William Ogilvie a farmer in Rothiemay, Banffshire. There were five sons and each achieved a notable place in the educational world. William, the eldest, died as Rector of Morrison's Academy, Crieff. Alexander became Headmaster of Robert Gordon's, Aberdeen. Robert, became a HM Chief Inspector of Schools while Joseph was appointed Rector of the Episcopalian (Teacher) Training College in Aberdeen. A remarkable achievement by any standard. George was schooled in Fordyce and Aberdeen Grammar, attended Aberdeen University where he gained a distinction in Mathematics, taught in Dyce, Dunnottar and Turriff before being appointed Head and House Governor at Daniel Stewart's Hospital in 1856. After fourteen years of quiet efficiency, combined with a detestation of the 'monastic system', the Governors were so impressed he was given the Watson's job in 1870. Nevertheless, the Chairman, Thomas Boyd, told him straight that he had to, " *make a success of this school or give way to a better man.*" The Doc knew what that meant: high academic success and nothing less. In that he undoubtedly succeeded and made Watson's the leading school in Scotland, so much so that the Scotch Education Department used it as a model for all other secondary schools. By 1898, when The Doc retired, he needed no other memorial than Watson's itself.

Ogilvie, a bachelor, retired to a comfortable house in Corrennie Gardens. He was also 'comfortably off'. Although his first pay rise came as late as 1883 (£400 to £450) he had, as a real canny Scot, accepted a per capita agreement in 1870 which gave him an extra payment for each boy in the school. As the Merchant Company only expected about 200 pupils at first, the continued roll of between 1,000 and 1,650 over 28 years didn't do The Doc's bank account much harm. Eventually he retired to 14, Albyn Terrace, Aberdeen and died there on 27 June 1914, just one day before the Assassination of Archduke Ferdinand of Austia-Hungary which sparked off World War One, a war which would slaughter hundreds of youngsters which he proudly regarded as his own.

2. William Carrie

William Carrie was the 21st member of Watson's College staff when he arrived in 1878 and very quickly became Head of English on the Classical Side. Born in Arbroath in 1854 Carrie had taught in the Edinburgh Provincial Training College before arriving in Archibald Place. He was an absolutely brilliant teacher, a cultured human being who got on exceedingly well not only with youngsters, but also with other members of staff and FPs. Indeed, he was President of the Athletic Club from 1895 to 1897. When The Doc retired in December 1898 after 28 years in post, Carrie, only 44 years of age, was appointed Head as from January 1899.

Carrie promised much: he was young, popular, go-ahead and put far more emphasis on sport than Ogilvie. Watson's was going to be differently shaped and moulded by a man up to the challenges of a quickly changing world. Things, however, did not quite turn out like that.

Carrie was not an administrator and he felt more and more the weight of responsibility as an increasing burden he could not manage. In June 1903, he fell out badly with his former friends in the Athletic Club when he *"unwarrantably assumed a power"* he didn't have by disqualifying a senior pupil, A F Wilson, from taking part in the Annual Sports. Acting in breach of Rule 6, *"the action of Mr Carrie was ill-timed and his decision wrong"*. Carrie had made a hasty and unthinking decision.

It was not the only one. Parents were beginning to remove their children. Principal Martin of New College who had been Dux in 1874 and President of The Watsonian Club, 1898/99, even withdrew his son Hugh and sent him to the Academy. Excuses were given, but everyone knew that Carrie was letting things slip very badly indeed. In June 1904, parents complained to the Governors about truancy on a massive scale and over a long period of time with Carrie doing nothing about it. They also complained about Carrie's 'personal habits'. On a warm summer's day he is reported to have raised the window of his room, one floor up and looking onto the playground, and bellowed to the boys playing outside, 'Take a skating holiday'. He was not eccentric, but roaring drunk. Ironically, a few months earlier, he had been made ex officio member of The Watsonian Club's Licensing Committee!

A prompt investigation by the Governors resulted in Carrie being requested to offer his resignation. In a sad letter of a few miserable sentences Carrie said, *"I have felt that the strain of administering this large school is beyond my physical powers."* The affair was hushed up, his many friends said nothing and Carrie was given a pension plus a substantial Honorarium of £500. He soon got another job teaching and apparently became like his old normal self. When he died in 1916 his 29 friends on the Watson's staff announced in The Watsonian they were raising money for a tombstone in Newington Cemetery. So much was collected that the surplus was used to fund an annual award, 'The WL Carrie English Literature Prize'.

3. John Alison

After the Carrie disaster the Governors were looking for a safe pair of hands and found them in John Alison, a dry and dusty Mathematician who obviously had undergone pioneer surgery for personality by-pass. A specialist in Maths at Edinburgh University pondering such intriguing mysteries as 'the Nine Point Conic' and 'the Dynamics of a Particle', Alison trained at Moray House, taught Maths at the Academy, came to Watson's and was soon appointed Head of Maths. Good at drilling pupils, and an even better bureaucrat, he got the job of Rector of Glasgow United Free Church Training College. Only in post two years ambitious Alison applied for the vacant Head's post at Watson's and got it.

John Alison had his work cut out trying to clear up the mess left behind by Carrie. Having enormous energy he not only managed this, but also coped with the pressures brilliantly. Alison was genuinely interested in science and sport, encouraging both as much as he could and dragged Watson's into a different era, for good or ill. He began Prefects, Houses, The Watsonian, the seven period day, the Cadet Corps and compulsory science. Privately he bowled, golfed and, sign of an ill-spent youth in Dysart, played billiards. He was founder of the Edinburgh Mathematical Society and President of the Secondary Teacher's Association, 1909/10. Sadly, he had to cope with the Great War and all that meant for the Watson's community. After a Watson's connection lasting 40 years, 22 as Head, John Alison retired in 1926, a respected figure. His farewell gift from the College was a World Tour.

William Carrie, 1898.

John Alison, 1898.

As Ithers See Us

Not everyone was entirely happy with the changes brought about since the retirement of The Doc. This article by 'CMM' appeared in *The Watsonian* of December 1910, a spoof for *The Evening Jackal* entitled 'As Ithers see us'.

The activities of the School are being extended in every direction, as is witnessed by the interesting improvements which have been carried out in various parts. Above the platform in the Hall has been placed a patent extinguisher which descends upon any speaker who so far forgets himself as to cast any aspersions upon the College; while at the same time a gramophone automatically strikes up:-

"Far North and South, far East and West,
Her sons have proved her first and best,
Until she stands by all confessed,
The great and glorious Watson's"

This, the authorities hope, will restore the equanimity of the audience.

As an earnest of the desire of the authorities to see that football is properly taught at the College, and that it is not made subservient to any other branch of study, the following rules have been decided upon:-

"That the compulsory subjects in the College be football, cricket, and mathematics: in deference to the wishes of a few old-fashioned parents facilities will be given for the pursuit of Classics after hours, but on no account must they be allowed to interfere with the serious work of the College."

Teachers

George Ogilvie tried to get the best staff possible, but he did have great difficulties at times, especially in the beginning. Following the creation of Board Schools after 1872 there was a terrific demand for teachers. Salaries were far higher in those new schools than in Watson's and Ogilvie warned the Governors that he was losing good staff, was having difficulty replacing them with quality people and those remaining were, *"restless and constantly on the outlook for the appointments daily advertised."* In 1875, he raised the salaries of three of his strongest staff, Messrs Blyth, Robson and Sellar, but the Merchant Company paid for these by sacking the Drill Masters in Watson's and Gillespie's. In 1876/77, all teachers got a salary rise, but Ogilvie continually had to fight to stop salaries falling behind other institutions.

Ogilvie was totally honest about his staff. Good ones remained, but bad ones had to go.

1874/75

"Mr McLellan is an accomplished scholar and excellent teacher, but deficient in the power of maintaining discipline, especially among the younger pupils who are less able to appreciate his tuition."

"Herr Fischart is the most unsatisfactory teacher in the school. He can teach well, but is incapable of maintaining discipline." (Next session Herr Blume takes over)

1876/77

Classics: Mr Donald: *"cold and unsympathetic".*
Classics: Mr Young: *"wanting in energy and his class is the least satisfactory in the school."*
Elementary: Miss Harrower: *"a languor and listlessness here where animation and cheerfulness in the teacher are of the utmost importance."*

In July 1877, 32 teachers out of about forty petitioned Ogilvie to have their children educated free, arguing that their salaries were below those in other schools and they could not afford to give their own children the kind of education they were offering to others. Ogilvie and the Governors were unimpressed arguing that it would amount to a salary increase for married teachers which would be totally unfair on single ones, or those couples without children.

Watson's was a very Scottish school. Even as late as 1931 it was remarked about one teacher, Mr Goddard, leaving for London: *"Consider his achievement. That an Oxford man from an English Grammar School who does not claim even one Scottish ancestor, we understand (mirabile dictu) should come into our so typically Scottish school and, in spite of these (enormous) handicaps, should in less than four years make himself not merely tolerated, but a true and welcome and representative Watson's man – the thing is scarcely believable."* However, changes which may be described as 'anglicisation' began with Carrie and Alison, including one appalling decision in 1903 to appoint staff only after they had passed a test for *"purity of accent."*

Other less delightful Scottish traditions also applied:

"The behaviour of one or two masters was hopeless and would not be tolerated today. One came round behind you and cuffed your ear; when not doing that he spat in the fireplace."
(Dr A Smart: Remembering the 1890s)

He was not alone and mothers, so it was said, could tell whether their offspring had behaved themselves that day by the redness (or not) of their lugs. All teachers also used the belt: *"Summary execution is dealt out to unruly members by means of the dreaded tawse … a long piece of leather about a quarter of an inch thick and two inches wide and cut into two tails at the end."* Its use on the hands (one to six strokes) was a normal part of schoolboy life, even in the Elementary School.

No, I fear that we were not always well-behaved boys. When on a wet day, a considerate master allowed us into the classroom during the interval, it was not fair to play cricket matches with his umbrella and a piece of chalk. Sometimes a knotted duster supplied the means for vigorous games of football, resulting in abraded shins and torn garments. When these amusements failed we indulged in the objectionable pastime of cap-throwing.

Anon, 1880s

The Notice Board was a vital part of school life in the days before modern communications. At first the window of the janitor's office on the first floor had been used, but it was then moved down to near the main entrance.

Holidays

Between 1870 and 1914, holidays did not change much. Up to session 1887/88 a new term would begin in late September or early October and finish towards the end of July. In 1876, the holidays were:

Fast Day:	October 26
Christmas:	Dec 22–Jan 3
Good Friday:	30 March
Spring:	April 2–May 7
	Queen's Birthday
(Victoria Day):	24 May

The last Fast Day holiday was 23 October 1884. An 'Edinburgh Autumn Holiday' was given in 1889/90, but dropped thereafter. A mid-term holiday in the second term was given (Meal Monday) and a 'skating' (freezing weather) holiday was possible, but rarely granted.

Dr Ogilvie favoured a summer holiday in the summer months of July/August and it was obvious that many parents agreed for, in 1887, almost 100 pupils *"had left the school for holidays previous to the close of session …."* In session 1888/89, the term was ended in mid-July and a new one begun in mid-September. This change was really to prepare parents for a more drastic one beginning in 1891 when term would close at the end of June and a new one started at the beginning of September. Many parents objected to this and a hard core of eminent ones even signed a petition to Ogilvie. Under pressure this supposedly permanent change became 'an experiment' which continued until 1892 after which the original '1870–88' structure was reinstated.

Who Was Where in 1913?

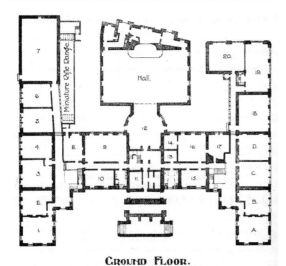

GROUND FLOOR.

Scale of Feet

Plan of the School.

ABOVE is the ground-plan of the School mentioned in Mr McCrae's interesting communication. For the benefit of former pupils we give below a key to the plan.

(1) Mr Currall—*French.*
(2) ,, Albert—*History.*
(3) ,, Cooper— ,,
(4) ,, Dallas—*German.*
(5) ,, M'Innes—*English.*
(6) ,, Mitchell—*French.*
(7) Messrs Seymour and Anderson, *Gymnasium.*
(8) Kitchen, Miss Panton.
(9) Lunch Room.
(10) Staff Lunch Room.
(11) Furnace.
(12) Physical Exercises Room.
(13) Janitor's Store Room.
(14) Kitchen Store.
(15) Cloak Room.
(16) Lunch Room.
(17) ,, ,,
(18) Manual Instruction Room, Messrs Hay and Murray.
(19) Art Room, Messrs Hay.
(20) Art Room, Mr Dandie.
A. Miss Seggie—*Elementary.*
B. Miss Robertson— ,,
C. Miss Cormack— ,,
D. Miss Smith— ,,

MAIN FLOOR.

Scale of Feet.

Plan of the School.

IN last number a plan of the Ground Floor of the College was published. It has been suggested that by way of illustration in this, the contemporary history of the School, complete plans of the building might be reproduced. Above is a plan of the main floor, and below a key to the same.

(21) Prefects' Room.
(22) Mr Driver—*Mathematics.*
(23) Mr Allan—*Classics.*
(24) Mr Stephen—*English.*
(25) Dr Pinkerton—*Mathematics.*
(26) Mr Philip— ,,
(27) Mr Ramsay— ,,
(28) Cloak Room.
P. Mr Alison—*Headmaster.*
S. Miss M'Ritchie—*Secretary.*
W.R. Waiting Room.
J. Janitors.

(29) Library.
K Keyroom.
(30) Mr Mill—*English.*
(31) Stationery Room.
(32) M. Naulet—*French.*
(33) Mr A. R. Anderson—*German.*
(34) Mr Munro—*Mathematics.*
(35) Ladies' Staff Room.
E. Miss Milne—*Elementary.*
F. Miss W. Smith— ,,
G. Miss Martin— ,,
H. Miss Davidson— ,,

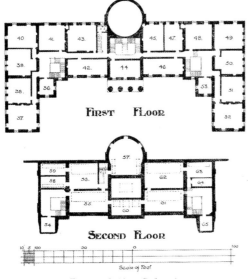

FIRST FLOOR

SECOND FLOOR

Scale of Feet

Plan of the School.

ABOVE are the plans of the second and third floors of the College buildings. Our readers will recall that in previous numbers we have published plans of the ground and main floors. As a matter of contemporary history alone these plans—for which we are indebted to Mr Macrae, the Company's Superintendent of Works—are very valuable. Below is a key showing the present occupant of each room.

FIRST FLOOR

36 Staff Room—*Masters*
37 Mr Mansion—*French*
38 Mr Shepherd—*Classics*
39 Mr Adams—*Classics*
40 Mr Shaw—*Classics*
41 Mr Ligertwood—*English*
42 Mr Maybin—*Classics*
43 Mr Doig—*Mathematics*
44 Mr Paske—*Juniors*
45 Mr Westwood—*Juniors*
46 Mr Williams ,,
47 Mr M'Alister ,,
48 Mr Miller ,,
49 Mr Gilchrist ,,
50 Mr Lennie ,,
51 Mr W. W. Anderson ,,
52 Mr Davidson ,,
53 Staff Room—*Ladies*

The Library drawn by R Lim (IVB), 1913. Spot the one piece of furniture which is now in Colinton Road.

The Elementary Department

ABOVE: *Jean Rosie Davidson, 1898.*
BELOW: *Miss Martin, 1898.*

The Wee School

ABOVE: *Mary Cormak, 1998.*
BELOW: *Caroline Seggie, 1898.*

Gardener George

If Senior School pupils were blooms in George Ogilvie's examination hothouse, then the seeds were sown in the Elementary Department. Ogilvie recognised – as did a much later Head, Roger Young – that appropriate attitudes and habits were inculcated at a very early age. The Doc visited that Department every day, his loyalty and enthusiasm being returned by a staff who tended to remain and give valuable service over many years.

The Department at first consisted of four classes, the highest taught by a male and the rest by three female teachers, who were, said Ogilvie, *"better adapted for training younger pupils than the male."* One, Miss Souter, was given the highest praise by The Doc: *"She has the means of making the Elementary Department the most popular Department in the school."* Indeed, parents were soon clamouring to enrol their children and Ogilvie was clamouring to expand its facilities. By 1890, it had doubled its teachers and in 1893 moved into bright, modern rooms in the New Extension

As in many other areas The Doc used his brothers to gain the services of the best students and teachers they knew of. Most came from Aberdeenshire. Caroline Seggie was recommended by HMI brother Robert as she was the top student two years running at Moray House. Miss Seggie – they were all 'Miss' – mothered them all and, according to her farewell eulogy in the Watsonian of 1915, *"You had seen love, sympathy, cheerfulness, compassionate patience and many other good things at work. Her pupils glowed with happiness …".* Miss Seggie also studied part-time for a law degree.

Another star was Jean Rosie Davidson, an Aberdonian spotted by Joseph Ogilvie at the Church of Scotland teacher training college there and recommended to his brother George. Jean had gained the equivalent of an MA degree – a remarkable achievement in the days before women were allowed to enter university – by private study and lecture courses. She became Head of the Elementary Department and even Senior boys continued to visit right up to her retirement in July 1919.

Then there was Miss Martin, straight from College in Stirling who used sweets and kindness, but always had 'Tickle Tom' tucked in the drawer just in case. She was the only teacher who insisted that her class sing 'Scots Wha Hae' with great gusto and was known for having a 'down' on English history. She retired in 1927. Miss Mary Cormack from Fyvie was recommended by both Joseph and Robert Ogilvie. She joined Watson's in October 1885 and soon gained a serious reputation for being, *"gentle, kind, courteous and motherly."*

The Elementary Department was a remarkable success story. The Doc summed it up in 1879: *"The solid foundation they are laying in what may be called the nursery of the school will contribute much to the attainment of a high standard in the future senior classes."*

The Longest Serving Teacher: Mr Yes, Yes

William Stephen, 1898.

The longest serving member of Watson's Staff – William Stephen – began his career in the Elementary Department in 1873. Like Miss Seggie he studied part-time for a degree, graduating MA in 1882. He then taught English for fourteen years, was appointed Head of the Commercial Side in 1896 and then three years later as Head of English which he retained until his retirement, and death, in 1914. He spent an incredible 41 years – almost the entire stretch of this chapter – as a teacher in Watson's. *The Watsonian* dubbed him, *"the Father of the staff."* His record has never been equalled.

Stephen was born in Lanarkshire in 1849, schooled in Carnwath, trained as a teacher in Glasgow and taught in Cambusnethan before coming to Watson's. He said once that, *"it is better to serve in Watson's than reign elsewhere."* His energy was unbounded as he also taught evening classes at Heriot-Watt College, served as an officer in the Forth Submarine Engineers, supported his local church and never had an absence at school for a single day through ill health until that started to break down in 1910. An enthusiastic golfer, Stephen joined the Baberton Golf Club and then Mortonhall. He was also Captain of the Watsonian Golf Club when its team won the 1913 Dispatch Trophy. A kind and gentle man his most memorable phrase was the double affirmative, *"Yes, yes"*.

Davie

"Scentit soap! I heard that they used it in the Leddies' Colleges, so I thocht we micht as weell be upsides wi' them."

David Leitch (Davie), 1903.

Apart from The Doc, the most revered, respected and loved figure in the school was Head Janitor, David Leitch, a friend to both staff and pupils, whose service spanned an astonishing 33 years from 1870 to 1903. The Doctor and Davie were looked upon as integral and essential parts of Watson's. Pupils came and went, teachers were passing acquaintances, but Doc and Davie seemed to go on forever.

Davie came from farming stock in Ceres, Fife. He was trained as a gardener, but, being good with horses, he doubled up as coachman-gardener coming to Edinburgh in the service of John Clapperton, one-time Convenor

of Watson's Governors. Thanks to him Davie got the job of Janitor.

As seen in the photograph, Davie was a dignified figure often mistaken for the Headmaster. He also had old world courtesy which charmed everyone and a quiet sense of humour which youngsters appreciated above all. But he was, nevertheless, a strict disciplinarian and was empowered by The Doc to keep order within and without the building. Davie's booming tones *(Gang an' play ootside)* were rarely disobeyed. Nevertheless, he always carried a wee bit of rope, or a bit of a pointer just in case, but used rarely and always half-humorously.

Physically strong Davie began doing jobs which previous janitors had simply called in workmen to perform eg tricky locks, undisciplined window blinds, cluttered gutters and dodgy desks. Indeed, it was this that endeared him to the Governors and persuaded them to give Davie one pay rise after another. He also kept the playgrounds free of litter and rang the school bell when required. He was fiercely proud of Watson's and kept the grounds scrupulously tidy

Davie was reliable and well-organised, never missing or late for an engagement. But more than that he was seen as a friend, someone to listen and help. He bound and cared for bruised fingers and cut legs, supervised the physically weak and was always 'there' when needed, even when called by lady teachers to crush a classroom mouse.

In speech he was candid and forceful, always in broad Scots and a twinkle in the eye. *(You a Minister! Ye ken far mair aboot jumpin' ower sticks than lecturin' ower a poopit.)* He could be eccentric, for example, he used a tricycle sometimes fitted with a sail on which he careered around the playground in the early hours of the morning.

With his savings Davie bought a small property at Balmalcolm, near Kingskettle, and retired there in 1903. He claimed he was cultivating a giant strawberry which would astonish the world. Unfortunately, Davie died on 1 April 1905 and was buried three days later in Newington Cemetery witnessed by an enormous grieving crowd of Watsonians, young and old.

Weelum

There were two other famous janitors during this period. One was William (Weelum) Graham, an ex-Galashiels weaver and intelligent red-hot radical. He was of average height, but he walked with a stoop and had a squint. Unlike Davie he had no uniform, but he always wore a tweed suit of pepper and salt grey with a hard felt hat. Willlie's job in the morning was collecting the names of absentees for The Doc to read and 'sort'. His general knowledge was famous and stunning. He actually owned the earliest edition of *'Chambers' Encyclopaedia'* and read it cover to cover. Youngsters liked this quaint old chap and never gave him trouble. He retired in 1894.

Willie

The other was Willie Gray who became Head Janitor after Davie retired in 1903. He had been Davie's assistant since 1894 and had served as a sergeant with the 1st Battalion Argyll and Sutherland Highlanders. He wore the medal and clasp for the 1879 Zulu War.

He was kind, cheery and helpful, always ready to listen especially to the youngsters in the Elementary School who regarded him as either Jove, or George Watson.

He superintended the army of women who dusted and scrubbed the school, personally printed all exam papers and belted boys on behalf of the Head. An accomplished curler and golfer he retired in 1924.

Founder of the After School Club
Wee Michael had to wait until 3pm when his big brother came to take him home. Until then he went to visit Willie who kept him busy with comics, errands or a saunter along the corridors.

What Shall We Learn Today?

The organisation and curriculum remained much the same throughout the period albeit with important additions around the turn of the century. The school was divided into three departments: Elementary, Junior and Senior.

The Elementary Department took boys between five and eight grouped into classes around a single teacher who taught all subjects. Reading, simple arithmetic, writing on slates, geography and grammar, without the use of textbooks, formed the core area, but some Latin and French was being taught too. Lessons were short and a lot of play was introduced throughout the day. At the end of every hour there was a break for a few minutes and the boys were allowed to play outside. At 1 pm the youngest pupils were dismissed while the older ones had an extra half-hour. Lunch for the entire school was a half-hour between noon and the sound of the Castle's one o'clock gun.

The Junior School was composed of about eight classes, four 'Upper' and four 'Lower' containing boys aged between 8 and 12 grouped around a single teacher who taught most subjects, except specialist areas such as French and Drawing. English, Grammar, History, Writing and Arithmetic constituted the core curriculum. Latin was begun at 10 years and French the following year. The younger boys ended their day at 2 pm and the older ones a half hour later.

The Senior School (composed of boys from 12 upwards) was divided into two 'Sides': 'Classical' and 'Commercial'. There were always more Classical Classes than Commercial, the latter aimed at boys who did not intend going to university, but wished instead to embark upon a business career. Classes were taught by specialist teachers in English, Maths, Arithmetic, French, German and Mechanical Drawing. The Classical Side was much the same, except that Latin was the main subject as it so dominated university entrance requirements. Greek was also taught for a similar reason. Drawing was 'free-hand' on this Side. Other subjects such as Drill, Singing and Gymnastics were tagged onto both sides as was a weekly lecture on the sciences. School ended at 3pm unless there was a specialist subject to be tackled which might go on to four o'clock. The Head, Dr Ogilvie, always favoured the Classical Side as it was his intention to build the new Watson's into a hothouse for university and college entrance. By so doing he created the Watson's version of 'snobs and yobs'. One old boy commented, *"Commercials seemed to live another life from ours."* Even the Governors complained as early as June 1875 that too much prominence was being given to the Classical Side. After all, the Founder would most likely have been a 'Commercial'!

Changes of a minor nature included the introduction of Shorthand in 1882, gymnastics in a new Gym in 1884, Singing classes in 1896, the option of taking German instead of Greek in 1899, RE classes for all in 1893, but also the abandonment of some subjects such as Dancing in 1875 and Fencing in 1884. Art rooms, *"beautifully equipped and lighted"*, were opened in 1908 as was a new room especially designed for Geography. The Library was extended into the old Chapel after 1908 and, five years earlier, *"periodic reports to parents"* had been issued for the first time at two per session and posted home, *"in a plain envelope."*

More important changes followed increasing government interest in the provision of secondary schooling from 1882 onwards and the increasing demand for more scientific subjects. Compulsory government inspection of secondary schools began in 1882 and, following the Parker Report of 1888, national 'Leaving Certificates' were introduced. A Higher Grade Certificate was a declaration that the candidate was fit to enter higher education such as a three year university 'Arts' course. A Lower Grade declared a candidate to be fit for any medical school type of training. In 1903, passes were 'grouped' (ie fail one subject and you failed the Certificate) plus the requirement that a candidate must have completed four years of secondary schooling. To stop cramming there was meant to be no prescribed syllabus and the examination questions were meant to be 'open'. Until 1908, there was also an 'Honours Grade' for those interested in Oxbridge. or the Indian Civil Service. In 1888, Watson's decided to enter all pupils for the Scotch Education Department's Certificates. Largely as a result of Merchant Company pressure an 'Intermediate Certificate' was introduced for those who did not wish to pursue their schooling beyond three years.

One new single Certificate which drastically changed the Watson's curriculum was that of 'Science' introduced in 1889 entailing much building and restructuring. By 1895, Watson's had a fully equipped science laboratory and six years later had two specialist ones: Chemistry and Physics. In the same year Elementary Science was on the curriculum of both 'Sides'. The Prospectus informed parents that the SED Science Course was being followed and that the Leaving Certificate required at least three years study of Physics and Chemistry. A major landmark occurred in 1902 when William (Bill Andy) Anderson was appointed as Head of Science and Second Mathematical Teacher. This was the beginning of the 'Science Department' when, one year later, the entire Senior School was divided into modern 'departments'. In 1908, further additions to the science labs attempted to bring them up to the standard of those of Broughton Higher Grade School, built in 1903 and the first to have custom-built

science facilities. The new labs were opened by Lord Avebury. Thus, by 1914, the modern Watson's had begun to emerge.

A Likely Tale?

From 1870, Science had been advertised as being taught, but it merely amounted to an hourly lecture per week given, in the early days, for example by Dr Davidson, Professor of Anatomy at the Vet College.

In 1883 'Natural History' and 'Natural Philosophy' changed to 'Natural and Physical Sciences', but little else did. The story goes that in 1885, AJG Barclay, a Maths teacher, was approached by a boy whose hobby was chemistry asking for special science classes to be put into the timetable. Barclay suggested that he spoke to the Head. Dr Ogilvie said that, although he was sympathetic, the time table was already packed. Nevertheless, he asked the boy to see what his peers thought about it. A few days later the boy returned with six sheets of foolscap (larger than A4) filled by the top three classes in each of the Classical and Commercial Sides. Ogilvie then approached the Governors.

The result was that the Governors challenged the boys to a real test of commitment. A science class would be held last thing on *Friday afternoon* in the warm summer term and just might stray towards 4 pm! If sufficient turned up then new facilities would be provided. As a further endurance test Ogilvie found an empty, dusty and cobweb-ridden attic room at the top of a long winding, creaky old staircase. Fitted with a desk and some basic apparatus the classes were conducted by Mr Barclay.

It really does say something for all involved that during the summer holidays a small adjoining attic room was fitted-up as a laboratory with some of the work being done by the boys themselves so that practical Chemistry could begin the following session.

This is a wonderful story, but the gloss was taken off somewhat when the records revealed that the school had already decided in 1884 to fit up rooms for chemistry and spend £150 on scientific apparatus. Indeed, in November 1885 a Magic Lantern was bought along with experimental equipment. All that was needed was a blackout facility!

Not all boys were enthusiastic about science. An anonymous chap writing in 1913 commented: *"Chemistry was a new subject then and so long as it proved interesting and was exemplified by a sufficient number of explosive experiments, so long were we content to be instructed therein. But the moment chemical equations were introduced we adjoined to the solitude of the roof ...."* Easily done as one of three ways thereto lay through the attic openings beside the labs. Lazing, sunbathing or doing homework on the roof was an old Watson's tradition kept up by class skivers right to the very end.

Prizes Galore

The old Hospital Annual Exhibition, or Prize Giving, carried on into the new Watson's. In 1872, it was held in the Music Hall, George Street, but at all other times in the school Hall. The only other exception was in 1902 when the Synod Hall was used and a special lorry had to be hired to transport the prizes.

Prize Giving was usually in the forenoon, with teachers dressed up in gowns and fine linens and, unusually, smiling at all and sundry. The boys, *"… passed the time of waiting by the familiar rhythmatic stamping of the feet, two long and three short."* The piano was always on the right hand side of the stage next to a small choir. Most of the programme consisted of comic, tragic and nondescript recitations in Greek, Latin, French and German which most parents would have understood as much as double-dutch. There was also some poetry, *"usually of a rather trying nature."* At the end, however, came the summer holidays.

Prizes were awarded with David Leitch, the resplendently attired Janitor, attending on the right of the platform to lift small boys down.

Speeches ended the proceedings. One FP remembered:

"We were always told that our schooldays were the happiest of our lives, a statement we thought was unsound and painted the future in unnecessarily dark colours."

Every year an attempt was made to reduce the myriad of prizes just as every

year the main prize winners had their names published in the Prospectus. The old Hospital Dudgeon Medal was awarded to the Dux of the Commercial Side from 1876 onwards, but the first school Dux was Sheriff RL Orr born in Glasgow in 1854

Robert Low Orr, First Dux Of the College, 1870/1.

having come to Watson's via Elgin Academy. He graduated with First Class Honours from Glasgow University, went into Law and became an Advocate in 1881. In 1908 he became a judge and died at 73, Great King Street in March 1944. His 1871 Gold Medal was presented to the school in 1949.

Prize Giving was always looked forward to, if only for the fact it heralded the long-awaited summer holidays.

Housey, Housey

In 1904, John Alison broke the school into four 'Houses' to encourage athletics, competition, promote discipline and a sense of belonging often lost in a large school. Each was named after a person or place associated with school: Ogilvie, Preston, Lauriston and Cockburn. Each was given its own colour:

Ogilvie – Black
Preston – Green
Lauriston – White
Cockburn – Red

Who should be in each House? Simple – there were three classes in each year (eg 1A, 1B, 1C) on the Classical Side, but only one on the Modern/Commercial Side. Thus Ogilvie got all the 'As', Preston the 'Bs', Lauriston

the 'Cs' and Cockburn the 'Moderns'. Unfortunately, it didn't quite work out as the poor, downtrodden Commercials refused to co-operate and Cockburn sank without trace. As in farming, rotation proved to be the answer.

Poster made by a pupil.

"The Watsonian has always striven to hold the balance fairly even between the literary and athletic sides of the School, and it has been our consistent policy to refrain from that deification of the athlete which makes our sporting papers such a mournful comment on our civilization. But there is no getting away from the fact that the demands of the modern secondary school system on the pupils' powers of mind and body are very great. Some form of recreation is an absolute necessity if the student is not to go forward to a life of physical inertia and chronic dyspepsia – to put it at its mildest. To meet that the House system was devised, and as it starts reorganized we commend it anew to the patriotic spirit of the School."

The Watsonian, April 1913

Uniform

During this period a uniform was unacceptable as it had been associated with the Hospital, a charity school. Certainly 'school' articles did appear, for example, the belt buckle *"with ship in full sail"* worn by Major Archer in the 1870s, the tiny maroon-and-white bow tie often espied strangling an odd boy in faded photographs, or the famous *"little maroon cap"* for which there may have been official sanction, but was never made obligatory.

Boys wore the fashion of the day, or invented it. Writing of the 1880s, John Paterson records: *"We wore long stockings with jolly tight garters above the knees and our short breeks were puckered with another elastic below the knee. Our jackets had one button at the neck and an Eton collar of five inches deep was the common wear. Fellows with well-off fathers appeared in Norfolk suits complete with belts and a cap to match. These caps were shaped like an inverted tuppeny pie, but a glengarry or Balmoral hat was also much used because when the ribbons, cockade and toorie had been safely lost or torn they made the ideal headgear for the game of 'hattie' in the Meadows – so suitable for kicking, especially when damp, and they took the mud beautifully. For lots of us, a navy blue jersey had to service as a jacket and vest – with a big Eton collar, and one of those tiny maroon-and-white bow ties."*

> *For lots of us, a navy blue jersey had to service as a jacket and vest – with a big Eton collar, and one of those tiny maroon-and-white bow ties.*

Although of the 1880s this description could apply to anytime in this period as countless photographs testify.

Fashions were invented as, for example, when in 1883/4 Classical VI started to wear black bowlers to school. Hung up on the palings around the trees in the Meadows while their owners played football, they provided perfect target practice for Classical V. At other times boys wore flashy ties or bright socks. Nevertheless, times were a-changing. By 1910, the now famous jacket, *"In the correct shade of Marone Flannel with School Badge embroidered on pocket, or without it ..."* was being advertised, but this was a 'sporting' jacket as was the white jacket for cricket, both authorised by the Athletic Club. Ties, belts and socks were also available *"in regulation Watson stripe"*. In October 1906, a cap badge and hatband with badge came into use both being sold by the Janitor with strict instructions not to let either fall into the hands of non-Watsonians. However, none of these articles was obligatory as part of a uniform.

The Watsonian, *April 1914.*

> *Boys wore the fashion of the day, or invented it.*

The Watsonian, *April 1912.*

Advertisement, *July 1914*

A spoof article in The Watsonian, *December 1910.*

This is the new Gymnasium opened in 1893. The school arms which is now on the wall above the door to the Dining Hall in the West Quad used to stand on the other side of the Gym gable wall.

The height of cool, 1903. Note the turned-up collar, muffler, buttoned-up jacket, cap over brow and hands in pockets. Enough to give any teacher apoplexy. The boy is JJ Murray-Macnaughton.

TROPHY CAPS
AND SENIORS' CAPS

Part of an advertisement by Forsyths placed in The Watsonian in December 1913.

Roll and Class Size

It was hoped to keep class sizes to between 25 and 35, but this proved an impossibility as the roll increased year on year. By 1887, most classes were over 40 and parents increasingly complained, as did the Inspectorate. In 1908, new government guidelines fixed maximum size in Senior Classes to 30 which needed at least two more classrooms and an enforced drop of the roll.

The roll between 1887 and 1903 was as follows:

1887: 1,568
1890: 1,604
1895: 1,654
1899: 1,722
1903: 1,640

In 1903, 408 were in the Elementary Department, 525 in the Junior Department and 707 in the Senior Department (457 Classical and 250 Commercial) with an average class size of 45. Watson's was a victim of its own success, but it was also 'Head-led' as both Ogilvie and Carrie got 5s per pupil per year plus salary.

The numbers had to come down if for no other reason than the new government regulations covering grants for secondary education stipulated that the roll had to be reduced to 1,200 by 1911 otherwise Watson's would have its grants withdrawn. One factor which undoubtedly helped was the negotiation of a fixed salary (£850) in 1904 by new Head, John Alison. From 1911 onwards Watsonians must have felt a lot less like sardines.

Fees, 1870–1909

	1870/1	1871/2	1873/4	1879/80	1889/90	1903/4	Now per term (3) not quarter 1808/9
Elem	12s 6d qtr	10s	12s 6d		12s 6d	17s 6d	£1 1s
					15s	£1	£1 8s
Junior	£1						
Lower		15s	£1			£1 7s 6d	£1 15s
Upper		£1	£1 7s 6d			£1 7s 6d	£2 9s
Senior	£1 5s						
Lower		£1 5s	£1 15s			£2 7s 6d	£2 16s
Advanced		£1 10s	£2 2s	£2 2s		£2 17s 6d	£3 10s

New School Badge, 1906

This is the official description given in December 1906 by Alex Heron who was Secretary of the Merchant Company.

The Heart (symbol of tenderness and gentleness) in Gules with flames in Or.

The Oak Tree in Vert signifies strength and endurance.

The Shield (escutcheon) in Argent.

The Roundles (bezants, the ransom money of prisoners of war, or the right to mint coin) in Or.

The Broad Band (the fess, or military waist belt) drawn horizontally across the centre of the shield in Azure.

The badge portrayed here comes from a hatband produced between 1906 and 1914, hence the faded colours. Has anyone got a maroon boy's cap with badge?

The scroll on which is placed the Motto 'Ex Corde Caritas' (changed from ex corde charitas, but still meaning 'Straight from the Heart') has been placed below instead of, as is usual, above the shield.

An *unofficial* explanation is that the Oak Tree represents learning, the Roundles represent Watson's legacy as does the Shield, the blue Broad Band represents Loch Lomond from where the Watson family stemmed and the real meaning of the Motto is '*Love from the Heart*'.

There was no school badge before Session 1906/7. What was used instead was taken from the Merchant Company coat of arms which any school managed by that organisation was entitled to use. By 1906, a special badge for Watson's (boys and girls) had been agreed upon. It was taken from the coat of arms for George Watson matriculated by the Governors on 20 January 1739. For the background the artist adopted one school colour – maroon – which set off the varied colours of the badge.

First Year, 1911

Henry as a child.

Young Henry Raeburn Dobson was fun to be with, entertaining people with magic tricks, or just making them laugh.

He was born on 29 May 1901 in Merchiston Crescent and came to Watson's on 26 September 1911. Just as today's proud parents might take a snapshot, Henry's artist father (Henry John) decided to paint a memory of his son in First Year.

Apart from the well-scrubbed face note the typical Eton Collar, maroon and white tie, plus, glued to his head, a maroon cap with brand new badge.

Henry's best subjects were Latin and French. He left in July 1917 to attend Art College. Eventually he became a portrait painter. He is described as being, "*an elegant man*".

Henry died in 1985.

Henry as an adult.

Heaven

The huge flagpole

The Ship

Archibald Place

Chirnside's

On one corner of Archibald Place as it connected with Lauriston Place stood Chirnside's Bakery of fond and glorious memory to all. Two quotes from *The Watsonian* are quite sufficient to evoke this marvellous place and even conjure the aromas:

"There were some dullish cakes provided at school, but very few paid any attention to that, for at the top of Archibald Place there was a Mecca. There was Chirnside's, a notable bakery from the pupils' view; all the goods seemed to be specially made or coming up hot from the oven just for eating."
(Smart, 1890s)

"And Chirnside's where rich chaps bought steaming-hot cranberry tarts, and positive millionaires would swank down Archibald Place deeply engrossed in a tupenny pie, to say nothing of the baker's board in the school with those shiny-topped currant bricks!"
(John Paterson, December 1928)

Chirnside's even pioneered the Lunch Ticket.

Once lunch had been bought boys would often saunter past the Infirmary (trying to avoid fights with Herioteers), down Middle Meadow Walk and then by the Meadows back to school. *"Some of the dashing youths would go via George Square School, distracting the girls from their lessons. Complaints came in and we were forbidden to go there!"* Happy days.

Mrs Currie's Gundy Shop

Turning down to the College on the right-hand corner of Archibald Place with Lauriston Place stood an institution known to thousands of Watsonians as 'Mrs Currie's Gundy Shop'. At one time this tiny structure had acted as a toll house on the pay-as-you-go road to Lauriston, but had long since become to boys of all ages a veritable Aladdin's Cave.

A tiny wee quiet woman, Mrs Currie, coped admirably with a daily mass of shoving boys, each

eager to taste one or more of its tantalising delights. Apart from the boring, but necessary notebooks, pencils and slate markers, there were divers sticky sweets, boilings for the connoisseur, jaw-jammers for the bold, sherbet pouches to mess up the jacket, jujubes to keep the dentists in business, liquorice sticks for rainbow tongues and, what else but 'Wonder Ball', called such because although it started dark brown, if it was sucked slowly enough the globe transformed into blue, red, mauve and finally, shocking pink.

The lovely wee soul also purveyed strong elastic for a cattie (catapult), copies of *The Boys' Own Paper*, garish transfers, bools (marbles), kite string, rubber balls and elastic bands. But, unfortunately for some, she stopped short of selling mice which small Watsonians occasionally used to amuse assorted teachers.

Chirnside's where rich chaps bought steaming-hot cranberry tarts.

As early as 1878/9 the College realised the necessity of providing lunch by the provision of a purpose-built Luncheon Room with lunch supplied, at first, by a baker, Edward Sawers. Some boys even had lunch supplied by local residents. (No 'Health and Safety' factor there then.) In 1893, hot lunches such as meat and potatoes were supplied for the first time. In 1894, a Committee examining food provision recommended that one room be set aside for cooked meals and another for light refreshments such as bread, cheese, cold meats, soup, milk and coffee. That is the origin of today's Bun Room. Despite all the work and thought, boys still preferred Chirnside's!

Watson's College Boys Patronise Us

Facsimile of Tickets for Lunch

Quality Recommends Itself

This Ticket is value for
2d.
Half-Ticket, 1d. | Half-Ticket, 1d.
D. CHIRNSIDE, Baker,
25 LAURISTON PLACE.

Estimates furnished for
**Socials
Marriages
and Dances**

Bunches of **10** Tickets for 1/6
or 18/- for £1 worth

D. CHIRNSIDE
Baker, Confectioner, and Purveyor
25 LAURISTON PLACE
(Corner Shop—Top of Archibald Place)

The Lit Club

Nobody is really sure when the Literary Society was formed. One of the first Watsonians, Major RS Archer, was positive there was one in 1876/7 held on Saturday evenings in either a classroom, or the Chapel. The pupils, mostly senior 'Classicals', decided to form a Society despite The Doc's lukewarm reaction.

The initial idea seems to have come from Fred Scott Oliver who was the son of radical Liberal MP for Edinburgh, Duncan McLaren, and his wife, Priscilla Bright, daughter of John Bright a co-founder of the Anti-Corn Law League. (Both are buried in St Cuthbert's graveyard at the West End.) In later life Fred became a notable political writer and intellectual. Luckily the Head's Secretary, Mr Gilray, who eventually became a Professor of English Literature in New Zealand, was very enthusiastic and encouraged the boys' efforts.

The Society's Minute Book begins on 13 November 1883 and the first recorded debate was, *'Is the present system of competitive examination injurious?'* on which the House divided. In 1885, it voted in favour of the admission of women into the learned professions. Every second week, however, there were lectures on writers such as Scott, Longfellow or Browning.

The Society failed to impress all. *"I vaguely remember some heathery-headed, spectacled boys ..."* remembered one FP about the 1880s, *"... who met from time to time to vent their immature opinions on literary matters, without, so far as I am aware, causing a ripple to appear on the surface of school life."* Nevertheless, at times those involved took it very seriously indeed. The Lit Club had a room on the ground floor where feuding factions fought each other. Once, one faction expelled another from the room, *"whereupon the excluded ones retaliated by kicking in the panels of the door."* The Doc closed down the room for a week.

Apart from such nonsense. the Lit Club did have some beneficial affects such as the creation of a School Library in 1884 formed with the aid of the Governors. A room was granted by Dr Ogilvie in December 1884 which was the origin of the modern Library. However, entry required Lit membership which then doubled in a year! It also pioneered the hugely enjoyable, but often riotous, Mock Elections, known in the 1880s as 'Parliamentary Debates'. Also, each year 'The Topic' was held, a dissection of a play with lots of essays on the plot and characters read by the boys, with much enjoyable cross-questioning.

The Lit Club also helped encourage the establishment of *The Watsonian*. TG Winning from Hawick, who wrote the School Song, also put forward a motion in 1903 in favour of a magazine, but nothing came of it until the persuasive Sandy Morrison became School Captain, John Alison was appointed Head and Henry John Findlay agreed to be Editor.

School News

The first attempt to record events in the new Watson's was Christmas 1873 when four boys (John Lambert, Alex Philip, Thomas Bickerton and David Morgan) belonging to V & VI Classical hand-wrote the *Watson's College Quarterly*

Watson's College Quarterly Magazine, *1873*.

Magazine which was then superbly illustrated by David Inglis. Two further issues were definitely produced, one in March 1874 and the next in March 1875, but it is unknown if any more saw the light of day.

Soon after another magazine appeared, but this time run as a joint venture with other Merchant Company schools. None, unfortunately, is known to have survived. Between 1881 to 1890, however, *The Merchant Company Schools Magazine* came out, but it was merely a repository of literary efforts and of very little use in investigating school history.

On 24 June 1897 The Watsonian Club received a letter from one of its members, James Muir, proposing that efforts be made to start a Watsonian Monthly Magazine. The Watsonian Club fully supported this idea and formed a sub-committee on 9 July 1897 to look into it, *"... or, alternatively, a Magazine for the combined Merchant Schools."* One year later the sub-committee reported that progress had been made, but declined to expand further. Another 12 months later on 10 July 1899 the main obstacle was revealed: the difficulty of finding a suitable Editor. The whole matter went into abeyance.

A new Head in 1904, John Alison, was much keener on the venture and persuaded the Head of English, Henry John Findlay, to become the first Editor of a new venture to be called *The Watsonian*. Findlay took to it with enthusiasm and energy. Despite *The Watsonian* occasionally transgressing into being a pupils' arts magazine, or when a new height of idiocy was reached by the publication of a full page photograph of a bird's nest, it has successfully reported school news unabated for over a century.

A Song for Watson's

The Watsonian Club began the quest to secure *"a good school song"* as early as April 1896, but nothing seems to have come of it. Nine years later the ball was set rolling again in a letter to *The Watsonian* by 'JHT': *"Why should a School which occupies such a position as ours in the realms of education not have a school song?"*

The first anonymous effort of four verses appeared in July 1905 in English and Latin. The Editor commented that it was a bit sombre and lacked a chorus.

	TRANSLATION.
En, amici, debitas Scholae quam amamus Laudes atque gratias Rite nunc agamus ! Dona iam diutius Non donata damus Qui solutis vocibus Matrem invocamus	Rightly, comrades, may we now Thankful praises render : Watson hearts to School, I trow, Beat aye true and tender. Grateful gifts to her we bring— Though in this long failing, Yet with voices clear now sing, Alma Mater hailing.
Mater neque divitum Nec venustiorum Sed dignorum omnium Scotia Scotorum	Scotia's fame through wide earth runs Not for gilded pleasures— Mother she of worthy sons, They her dearest treasures.

Col CA Edes popped up in June 1906 suggesting a *"series of songs"* and offered a mighty six verses which he put to music, then had privately printed in 1910 and sold in the school for 6d. The first verse gives us a taste of what was to follow:

A SONG OF "WATSON'S."

ONE might fare the world over, North to South, East to West,
All eager to find the true fountain of knowledge.
He would save his poor feet and succeed in his quest,
If he entered the portals of old Watson's College.
For *there* is the bright crystal stream ever flowing,
From wisdom of ages its waters distilled,
What you cannot learn *there* is not really worth knowing,
None goes empty away if he's fain to be filled.

Chorus.

So here's to the College that stands by the Meadows,
A maxim I'll give, 'tis a safe, simple rule—
In marching through life with its sunshine and shadows,
Be true to the nation, yourselves, and the School.

This certainly inspired more budding bards. In December 1907, John Douglas of Greenock submitted *A Song for Watson's*, but his real aim was to encourage others to write, *"a Watsonian anthem worthy of the Queen among schools."*

A SONG OF "WATSON'S."

OUT to the Rockies, over the Line,
Under the banyan, under the pine,
Sons of me here by the broad, green Meadows,—
Welcome, Watsonians mine !

Far in the jungle, far on the snow,
Out where the seven seas ebb and flow,
Sons of me here in the old, grey city,—
Greeting, wherever you go !

The Old School.

SOME sing of battle, some of fame,
And some of love and honour,
But there's a theme that I would name
To lay my praise upon her ;
My country first, my neighbour next,
Has been the golden rule,
But now I'll add another text
And sing—our own old School.

The School ! The School !
A song for the School !
And swell the lusty chorus ;
Come, join your lays
For the brave, bright days
That lie behind and before us !

In July 1908, Arthur Poyser produced *The Old School*: Despite the many, and often painful, efforts nothing seemed to catch on. Then, as so often happens, one stuck. In July 1910, TG Winning's effort, *Hail to the Old School*, was printed in *The Watsonian*. Mr Moonie of the school Music Department set it to the tune of *Hail to the Chief* and had the school choir sing it at the Annual Prize Giving in July 1910 as an impromptu item on the programme. The audience was bowled over and soon Watsonians everywhere had adopted it as *The School Song* which, believe it or not, it still is!

A School Song.

HAIL to the Old School that claims our allegiance !
Gladly we yield it, whole-hearted and strong,
Here we acclaim her with loyal devotion,
"Queen of the Meadows," and theme of our song.

*Chorus—*Watson's the name we sing,
Long let the echoes ring,
Dear to her sons are her praise and her fame,
'Neath home or alien skies
Loud shall the chorus rise,
"Watson's for ever," again and again.

Many her sons are, and far tho' they wander,
Each in the wide world to play well his part,
Proudly they claim her, proudly they name her
"Queen of the Meadows," and "Queen of their heart."

Chorus—

Days that are bygone have crowned her with honour,
Days that are coming fresh laurels will yield,
Let us uphold then her fame and her glory,
First in the forum, and first in the field.

Chorus—
T. G. WINNING.

Finally, a four-page *Watsonian Song Sheet* was produced as a supplement to *The Watsonian* in December 1910 ready for the next Watsonian Day on 20 January 1911. *"It is hoped that the new Watsonian songs … will find a place in the programmes of each of the many gatherings on that night."*

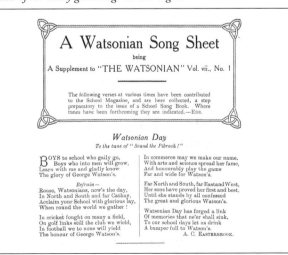

A Watsonian Song Sheet
being
A Supplement to "THE WATSONIAN" Vol. vii., No. 1

The following verses at various times have been contributed to the School Magazine, and are here collected, a step preparatory to the issue of a School Song Book. Where tunes have been forthcoming they are indicated.—EDS.

Watsonian Day
To the tune of "Sound the Pibroch !"

BOYS to school who gaily go,
Boys who into men will grow,
Learn with me and gladly know
The glory of George Watson's.

Refrain—
Rouse, Watsonians, now's the day,
In North and South and far Cathay,
Acclaim your School with glorious lay,
When round the world we gather !

In cricket fought on many a field,
On golf links still the club we wield,
In football we to none will yield
The honour of George Watson's.

In commerce may we make our name,
With arts and science spread her fame,
And honourably play the game
Far and wide for Watson's.

Far North and South, far East and West,
Her sons have proved her first and best,
Until she stands by all confessed
The great and glorious Watson's.

Watsonian Day has forged a link
Of memories that ne'er shall sink,
To our school days let us drink
A bumper full to Watson's.
A. C. EASTERBROOK.

NB *God of Our Youth* came with the girls in the 1974 merger and is the *School Hymn*.

Prefects

Before 1904 there were no prefects, ie no authority bar the staff. John Alison, a new Head, asked the senior boys in October 1904 to nominate a 'School Council' of 16 members to help with school discipline. There was no head of the Council, but it was probably dominated by Sandy Morrison, Captain of the 1st XV and a forceful personality who expected things to be done in only one way: his!

In Session 1905/6, Sandy, still 1st XV Captain, was referred to as School Captain (Head Prefect). Thereafter, the Football Captain was automatically School Captain too, until Session 1916/17 when a separate appointment of 'School Captain and Head Prefect' was made.

On 9 May 1907, on a proposal by John Alison, the Governors agreed that Prefects should be supplied with a special silver badge which they could retain after leaving school. The initial sketch showed a watch-chain fob which was a very popular article at the time, but Bailie Inches suggested instead that it be made, *"to be worn in the buttonhole."* That was agreed as was a later proposal that it could be worn on a hatband (eg straw boater in the summer). By July 1907 a die had been made and the first 25 badges struck at a cost of 4s 6d, a considerable sum for a badge at that time. If anyone desired their name engraved on the back the school would cover the cost of 6d to have it done.

A special Prefects' Room was set aside. At first it was an ante-room behind the Main Hall, but, about 1910, it moved to a room on the first floor, just at the top of the stairs in the West Wing. If a member of the 1st XV was not a Prefect, but had been awarded colours, then he was also allowed to use the room famous for its many names deeply incised into the woodwork.

The Earliest Class Photograph, 1874

This is the earliest known class photograph. It was sent to *The Watsonian* in 1909 by James H Stewart-Lockhart. The photo was taken during his last year at school in 1874, the days of, as he put it, *"Ogilvie the Great"*. It was a small extra class carved from Classical Class V (which was, claimed Stewart-Lockhart, the highest in the school) in order to do advanced reading of the classics with Mr Stewart. S-L maintained that 'Tommy' Stewart, the Senior Classical Master, had the greatest influence on him. Stewart eventually became Senior Inspector of Schools in Scotland.

- Alex Martin became a Professor of Apologetics in New College.
- Welsh became Fellow and Tutor of Jesus College, Cambridge.
- Hope died after a long illness. He had been a Presbyterian Minister in New Zealand.
- Lang described by Alex Martin: *"Lang's mathematical prowess was a never-ending source of wonder to those of us who had none of the 'low cunning' needed in order to gain distinction in that branch of human attainment …"*. He went into engineering.
- Philip was described by Martin: "For originality, humour, and the things that make the salt of life Philip was the pick of the bunch of us – his proposals for the reform of the calendar now before the country, are only a clue to one side of him."

S-L excelled at languages and sport. In 1874, he was joint Dux as well as Captain of both rugby and cricket. In 1878 he took up a Hong Kong cadetship and spent over 40 years there and on mainland China. After holding the posts of Colonial Secretary and Registrar General of Hong Kong he was appointed Governor of Wei-hei-wei province in north China. S-L fought against colonial racism, became a Confucian and strongly advocated the Chinese way of life. Indeed, his beliefs helped to shape present-day Hong Kong. Over a lifetime he amassed a huge and valuable collection of all things Chinese. He was knighted, gifted his important Chinese Collection to his old school and there had a suite of rooms named after him.

S-L died in 1937, but, 50 years later, a film was made of the life of his protégé, Reginald Johnston, who had been the last tutor to the Emperor of China. Peter O'Toole played Johnston in *The Last Emperor*.

"One boy said he would not speak to any boy who did not live in a villa, detached or semi-detached. He was thrashed till he promised to speak to any boy."
Rev Alfred Garvie, Watsonian 1941. Remembering the 1870s.

BACK ROW: (Left to Right): Hope, Hunter, Martin, Foulis, Philip, Waddell.
FRONT ROW: Valentine, Welsh, Mr Stewart, Stewart-Lockhart, Lang.

Boarding Boys

If a pupil required to board away from home then it was his parents' responsibility to find appropriate accommodation. However, the school still had to consider those on the Foundation as part of that included 'maintenance'.

In the first year of the new school, 1870/1, two boarding houses for Foundationers were taken over at 9/10 Royal Crescent, but, in July 1871, Home Lodge (on the site of the present Boroughmuir High School) was leased for six years, but eventually purchased four years later. In 1874, it was suggested that the special boarding feature for Foundationers should be ended, but the Governors split 50/50 on this and so Home Lodge continued on the Chairman's casting vote. It was agreed, however, that its internal structure should be overhauled, especially its management and supervision. The Matron, Mrs Milligan, was sacked and an *"educated person"*, Mrs Mary Annand, appointed instead.

Dr Ogilvie was asked to take charge which meant he got free accommodation as well as his salary and a capitation allowance. He really felt he should not be around the boys too much ('familiarity breeds contempt', etc) and insisted that a resident 'Tutor' be appointed to keep the boys occupied, take part in their activities and dine with them. This worked fine, but Home Lodge soon proved uneconomic and The Doc's prejudice against Foundationers soon reared its head once again. He said they lacked self-reliance and energy, appreciating the value of little as everything was provided free. In 1881, therefore, Home Lodge was given up and the boys billeted with friends or relatives.

Only in 1903 did the Education Committee of the Merchant Company suggest that supervised boarding arrangements might encourage applicants from abroad, the services and other parts of the country. However, by 1914, no action had been taken.

In 1870/1, only 1% of boys boarded. In 1871/2, this had grown to 7% and then to an enormous 16% the following year. Up to 1914, it varied between 16–20%. Most lived in ones and twos with widows or maiden aunts. JW Tullo, captain of the 1st XV in 1888/9 said that the most important part of his job was going around elderly ladies on Friday nights ensuring they would let members of his team out on the Saturday morning no matter how bad the weather!

A hand-made poster advertising The Watsonian, 1910.

Mr Munro regarded a pleasant Saturday excursion to be a twenty mile walk over the Pentlands.

London–Edinburgh, 1873

In 1873, two members of the School Staff, Mr George Munro and Mr Stephen Adam Munro (they were not related) walked from London to Edinburgh with a friend. There is no record how long they took. George Munro taught English Literature and, with a proper regard for Walter Scott, thought it would be appropriate to commemorate Jeannie Deans's walk to London by retracing her steps to Edinburgh. Of good Highland stock himself Mr Munro regarded a pleasant Saturday excursion to be a 20-mile walk over the Pentlands – and that before the days of buses to Fairmilehead.

Our statistician, during an interval when the general showers were coming down outside, had the curiosity, in pacing the corridor, to count how many people had *not* their hands in their pockets. The task was an easy one. From the lowest form up – we shall not say how far – he found only *four* shameless renegades to this most laudable practice !

The Watsonian, *December 1906.*

We have to record a gallant act of life-saving by a present pupil. A Joppa lad, Neil Stuart, was playing on Galloway's Pier, North Berwick, on 24th August last. He overbalanced and fell into deep water. His friend, W. Boak (IIв. Classical), was at hand, and without hesitation plunged in. Stuart could not swim, but his rescuer could, and brought him in safety to the pier steps. We congratulate Boak on his plucky act, and rejoice that the Royal Humane Society is going to recognise his courage. Boak has likewise been presented with a silver watch from the Carnegie Heroes' Fund.

The Watsonian, *December 1911.*

Members of the Cadet Corps will probably be pleased to know that one of their pipers has the champion chest of the School, being the proud possessor of a 5⅛ inch expansion.

The Watsonian, *April 1906.*

Rugby Comes to Watson's, 1870–6

Rugby was introduced into Scotland around 1855, but was unknown to Watson's when it opened as a day school in 1870. By 1914, however, it had become well established as the main sport virtually kicking Cricket into touch. But how did it begin?

In 1870/1, the only place in the College grounds for sport was the grass area between Lauriston Place and the Hospital building, but, apart from the Dutch rams which inhabited it and fought each other savagely (much to the delight of small boys), frequent cricket and soccer matches soon reduced that area to mud. Players joined outside clubs. The move next door to Archibald Place was not much better. The area around the old Merchant Maiden building was either gravel, or trees (soon removed) while the West Meadows was being raised by 3ft and the East Meadows was just a bit far away.

A combination of a small group of keen pupils and an equally keen teacher resulted in the first team. Most of the keen boys had entered Watson's either from Circus Place School (and had played as 'Canonmills House'), or from the Merchiston/Morningside area where rugby was already popular. They were joined by others such as CA Edes who arrived in March 1871 from another keen rugby-playing school in Royal Circus called 'Begbie's Private Classes'. Harry Armour and W Merry Macphail were among these boys. It was Edes' idea to form a Watson's team and he became the first Secretary of the School Rugby Club. Harry Armour was chosen Captain simply because he was the oldest, *"... on the strength of his growing whiskers."* Merry Macphail was elected as the unfortunate Treasurer whose difficult job it was to extricate 1s per member for a ball.

It was a few boys from the Classical side of the College who were pushing this game and much resented by 'The Commercials' who played football. Drop kicking in the playground was broken up, players attacked, verbally abused and the embryonic team driven to the Meadows to practise, using coats as goals. It was there that the first game was played against a team calling

itself the 4th Merchiston. Opposition teams were, however, a bit of a luxury then as few school teams would play a 'middle-class charity school'. Anyway, Watson's had no field, not to mention a strip of any kind. Into this scrappy situation came Frank Sellar, a new teacher at Watson's (and a relative of the Head!) who was interested not only in rugby, but also cricket (playing in a Leith cricket team under the name 'Frank Munro'). He had a ferocious reputation as, *"a man with a tremendous capacity for boxing a lazy boy's ears."* Sellar's energy undoubtedly helped forge the first team and he ran College rugby until 1886.

A field was desperately needed. In 1871, Edes and Armour went to Ogilvie who promised to ask the Merchant Company. It offered a small field on the north bank of the Union Canal, near Harrison Park, called Bainfield, or 'Baneful' as it became known. Its woeful condition was painfully described in a letter by Thomas Bickerton to the *College Quarterly Magazine* in 1873:

"First, our Park is in an out of the way part of the City, so that very few care for going that far. It has no gate, so that we require to climb the walls; it is too small ... Cattle are lodged in it so that it is a continual mess and no-one can play with pleasure. Now, how could we invite any respectable club to play in such a place? I would suggest, therefore, that the Merchant Company get us a more commodious park in a more easily reached part of town and that it be kept free of cattle and exclusively for our games, or at least, that a gate be made and cattle kept out of the present one."

Guides were needed to take newcomers, but taking girlfriends was almost impossible as most refused to climb the wall! An old gnarled oak tree was also part of the pitch which must have confused and bemused the opposition, least of all as its branches acted as Watson's first 'pavilion'. A shed came next, but that was demolished by local boys looking for wood for a boanie (bonfire). The joiner who created the goal posts had obviously never seen a rugby game as the posts above the crossbar were only about two feet high which caused endless disputes about the score. Local youths, jealous of the loss of 'their' ground,

Frank Sellar, 1884.

stole touch-line flags which then had to be guarded. Fights and chases were an inevitable part of this new rugby experience. Nevertheless, it was in those circumstances that the first games were played and Watson's rugby born.

The great historic date in Watson's rugby was 2 November 1872: the first officially recorded match against a team from Warriston (Puddocky to us locals) composed of boys from different schools. Watson's tried to look like a team. Two-thirds had jerseys which were roughly the same shade of blue, so it was decided that the remaining third should obtain similar jerseys. All conformed, except one chap who arrived wearing deep, dark blue. Long trousers were worn with socks drawn over the ends. After a tough match, Watson's emerged victorious one goal to nil. The second match was against The Collegiate School from Charlotte Square run by Dr Hamilton Bryce. Again Watson's won with a dropped goal by W Merry Macphail. However, as few schools would play them, most matches were against Stewart's whose boys had formed a team following Watson's example. During one match the ball went over the wall into an adjoining nursery and was promptly confiscated by an angry, red-faced gardener. Both teams ended up sitting on the wall in pouring rain using, *"cajolery, sarcasm, abuse and humility to obtain its restoration."* Only as the teams started to drift away did the fuming ogre return it! That ball, said Edes, *"deserved a niche in the School Museum ..."*. During the next Season (1873/4) 8 matches were played, 4 won, 1 lost and 3 drawn

By then the human dynamo – James Stewart-Lockhart – had joined the team, but the old rules still allowed the team to play the formidable Mr Sellar!

From such humble beginnings did Watson's rugby emerge, driven by boys themselves despite lack of College support and even hostility, or apathy, from amongst their peers. The Headmaster, Ogilvie, despite his own lack of enthusiasm for sport, did support youngsters if he saw they were keen enough and, when approached in 1876 for a better field, he and the Governors strongly backed an approach to the Merchant Company. The result was Old Myreside.

Invincible Ragamuffins

The very first school players just wore anything they could find by ransacking clothes cupboards at home. *"Tentative experiments were made with jerseys of hues that were fearful and wonderful …"*, said one, *"a variegated and motley appearance"* said another. A local headmaster described Watson's as *'Invincible Ragamuffins'*.

A uniform appearance was attempted in November 1872 when it was discovered that two-thirds of the team had similar blue jerseys. The other third went along with this, so a mid-blue (certainly not dark) became the first strip.

Other colours and combinations may have been tried, but the one which is recorded and memorable was orange and blue. How this came about is not clear. A cheap job lot? Frank Sellar's attempt to create a school strip? This could well be the answer as it was not just the rugby team which used these colours. They were chosen by the College for the first school games in 1876, including *"striped orange and blue stockings"*. The FP team adopted these colours which even fluttered over the corner flags at Bainfield.

But there is no doubt whatsoever that the boys loathed and detested that combination. In 1876, both the College and FPs reverted to blue. Sometime during that year the school team met in a classroom and opted for maroon and white for no other reason that they just liked the colours. The FP team followed suit and the colours just stuck.

Watsonian Rugby

Understandably, FP rugby really couldn't begin until there were some former pupils eager to play. It took five years for a few of Mr Sellar's old pupils to come together. The historic date for FP rugby is 30 January 1875 when an FP team played against St George. The result was a draw.

The second historic event was when the team met in a classroom in Archibald Place sometime during 1876 to discuss its future. Among the items to be discussed was its name. The favourite was *'George Watson's College Former Pupils' Rugby Football Club'*. Luckily this piece of Victorian verbosity was short-lived when James Aikman Smith suggested 'Watsonian Football Club'.

In 1877, it was admitted to the four-year-old Scottish Rugby Union as its eleventh member. Watsonian rugby, however, really took off when a new field was acquired at Myreside

VERY BACK: McMinn.
BACK: James Wilson, Andrew Henderson, Newbigging, A Aitken Ross, JM Johnstone, JN Stark.
MIDDLE: AH Robertson, Jackson.
FRONT: TH Manson (Full-Back), R Helm, John Tod (Qtr-Back), John Glegg (Half-Back & Capt), D Laing (Qtr-Back), WJ Laing.
VERY FRONT: Tom Robertson.

Cricket

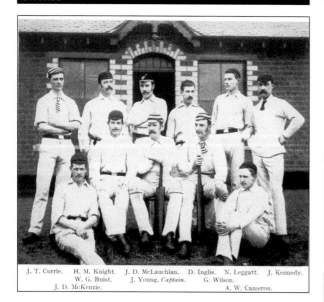

J. T. Currie.   H. M. Knight.   J. D. McLauchlan.   D. Inglis.   N. Leggatt.   J. Kennedy.
W. G. Buist.   J. Young, *Captain*.   G. Wilson.
J. D. McKenzie.   A. W. Cameron.

Cricket had been an organised activity in the old Hospital, but between 1870 and 1873 there was no official team, captain or games. Two cricket matches were played in 1872 between Watsonians and Edinburgh Moray, but it was probably a mixture of staff, pupils and FPs. The first team played at Bainfield in 1874 under the Captaincy of James Stewart-Lockhart and had been organised by Frank Sellar. Apart from Lockhart it also included W Douglas MacKenzie (Professor of Theology in Canada), AD Fairbairn (Founder of The Watsonian Club), Hugh Pillans (mighty hitter of balls into the Canal) and RW Waithe (a West Indian who scored Watson's first century against a team from Dalkeith). The team started playing 2nd XIs of the leading clubs, but it soon had two teams and gradually became accepted.

Watsonian cricket emerged in 1876 from the demise in 1875 of the Edinburgh Moray Cricket Club for which FPs had played since 1870. Again, Frank Sellar, who had played with Moray, was influential in creating a Watsonian team along with the first Watsonian Captain, John Young and the first Secretary, William Forbes. Three matches were played in 1876. The first against Burntisland Thistle was played on 3 June 1876, but was abandoned. The second against Burntisland was lost. The third, against Dalkeith 2nd XI was won – probably the first Watsonian Cricket win!

A detailed survey of Watson's cricket can be found in the excellent *Watsonian Cricket Club, 1875–1975'*

Cricket had been an organised activity in the old Hospital, but between 1870 and 1873 there was no official team.

Dub Dub

*WW (Dub Dub) Anderson
Frank Sellar, was the unofficial 'Games Master' from 1872 to 1886. He was followed by another enthusiast known affectionately as Dub Dub who continued until 1901. Both did yeoman service in promoting sport at Watson's. The photograph above was taken in 1888.*

But Not Everyone Did Sport

A Watsonian's Aeroplane.

IT will perhaps be of interest to Watsonians to know that an old Watson boy, Mr George Gibson, has built an aeroplane which is probably the first Scottish built aeroplane to leave the ground. Mr George Gibson and his father, Mr John Gibson, have been practising with Biplane No. 2 this summer. It is 28 feet span, and the chord, or breadth of the planes, is 5 feet, thus giving an aspect ratio of 5·6. From the double elevators in front to the double tail behind, it is 32 feet. The tail has double rudders. The main planes are not furnished with side curtains or screens of the box-kite type. The tail booms converge towards the tail, and so do the elevator booms in front.

The aeroplane stands 10 feet 2 inches high and weighs nearly 900 lbs. The engine is a 2-cylinder, horizontal opposed, of 30 horse-power, which drives a 6 feet 8 inches propeller of 3 feet 9 inches pitch at 1100 revolutions per minute. Mr George Gibson has been piloting the machine, but owing to engine troubles, smashes, etc., it was only in October that he managed to fly it with moderate success. It has meant many months' hard work building the machine, experimenting with it, repairing, and learning how to handle it.

During its trials the machine has been so much damaged and

The above article appeared in The Watsonian *in December 1910. The school Model Aeroplane Club began on 22 November 1909 meeting in the gym. Its first Secretary was CS Matley of Classical VI, but it was Messrs. Gibson who had inspired it.*

Old Myreside

Old Myreside

New Myreside

Bainfield

> *There is a confusing problem of nomenclature here as most youngsters today would call 'New Myreside' the area in front of the Stand beside the nursery school, ie on the east side of Myreside Road. But that would mean renaming Old Myreside as 'Old, Old Myreside' which is a bit ridiculous. Perhaps one part should be called simply 'Modern Myreside'?*

The Merchant Company was petitioned in 1876 for a better field than Bainfield and were granted an area termed 'Old Myreside' because it was near Myreside Farm. The farm stood where the big chimney now stands. An early nickname was 'Quag-Myreside' because of the mud.

Instead of getting a professional team to level and lay out the ground for both rugby and cricket at a cost of £550, the Merchant Company thought the local farmer could do it just as well for less. The Governors even advertised in the new Prospectus for parents that a Cricket Park would be available in

1877. By the summer of that year, however, the ground was still not ready at a cost of £748 and rising. Rumours abounded: the pupils petitioned against the building of what they thought was an ice-rink!

By 1878, after much grief, Old Myreside was open for cricket, rugby and other athletic activities. Amazingly the boys collected £22 10s towards the cost of a pavilion. So impressed was the Education Committee that it agreed to pay for the pavilion and put the boys' money to its fittings. It might have had second thoughts had it known that the initial estimate of £35 would rocket to £163, but the result in March 1878 was an *"ornate brick building"* with wooden shutters and two small dressing rooms, quaintly dubbed the 'Cricket House'.

Cricket

This was where school and Watsonian cricket really took off. An attempt was made in 1879 to raise standards by employing a professional coach, Mr Buchan, but it soon transpired that he could only bowl underhand. He left in the middle of the season taking with him the keys of the pavilion! As a groundsman was required it seemed sensible to combine that job with a cricket professional. Thus John Howell was appointed on 26 February 1884 at £1 5s per week plus a £10 per annum housing allowance. John gave magnificent service, but died in 1897, just a few weeks before the move to New Myreside.

John Howell.

School Spirit

John Howell's presence deterred burglars and thieves, but there was an obvious problem with alcohol by both adults and youngsters which was not so easily sorted. There was a continuing tussle between those who wanted alcoholic refreshment to be available and those who did not. At times visiting adult rugby teams, for example, would occasionally dive for the straw bounding the field to find the hidden bottle of 'Auld Reekie'!

Rugby

Watsonians pitted their strength against 2nd XVs during the first season. It was not until 1879 that they met the mighty Royal High 1st XV which was the signal that they had at last 'arrived' in Edinburgh rugby circles. Both sides scored a try, then the High scored a goal which was promptly disputed. Unable to resolve this in the days before dictatorial referees, both sides left the field headed by their respective Captains.

School rugby went from strength to strength as the main teams gradually accepted Watson's into their fold. Col CA Edes commented in 1906:

> *"For seriously, I am convinced that the introduction of Rugby Football did more for the elevation of the School than appeared then upon the surface. It brought it into line with other schools and was the means of overcoming prejudices which were actual and deep-seated. In its subsequent development it instilled an esprit-de-corps which must have worked for good. In its later stages, it brought together the 'Commercial' and 'Classical' sides of the school on common ground where antagonisms could be sunk and in time forgotten."*

Andrew Scott.

Andrew Scott started at New Myreside in 1898 and gave a remarkable 26 years of service. He cared for the ground with not a lot of backup from an impoverished Athletic Club, or the Merchant Company, neither really understanding the subsoil difficulties with which he battled nobly day after day.

Between 1905–7 he coached the school Cricket XI simply because he felt it unfair that the Watsonians had a professional coach and the boys did not. He did it gratis. Watson's Cricket usually languished at the bottom of the league, but, under Andrew's direction it won for the very first time the School Championship. Heroic stuff!

A versatile chap he could repair almost anything from fishing rods to waders and build anything from a tennis court to a curling rink. Andrew was always in good temper, cheerful and courteous. Andrew retired in July 1924.

The New Myreside Dispute

It was clear by 1888 that Old Myreside was too small for the demands made upon it. Things started to move as early as 1888 when the Athletic Club represented by its energetic Treasurer, AB Easterbrook, asked for extra ground to be allocated by the Merchant Company for *"laying down permanent Lawn Tennis Courts"*. Even the usually phlegmatic Dr Ogilvie was outraged at the possibility that one of the cricket fields might be asphalted for what he saw as a passing fad. The Merchant Company then offered another part of Myreside Farm, west of Craighouse Road, the agricultural lease of which was due to expire in 1894, provided that the Athletic Club pay the necessary costs. By 1892 the Athletic Club was busy raising funds to help pay for the levelling of the field and the building of a new pavilion. A massive annual bazaar scheme was begun which involved stalls by the dozen including one with mechanical ducks.

In June 1893, the cost of levelling New Myreside and building a pavilion was estimated at £4,905 plus £100 for furnishings. The dispute between the Athletic Club and the Merchant Company began over the extent of ground being offered. The Company was willing to give the Club an extensive and valuable area of land west of Craighouse Road amounting to 13.4 acres, but wanted to retain a strip of ground 150 feet 3 inches wide (3.65 acres) running parallel with Colinton Road in order to feu it for housing. The Club, however, wanted the entire field arguing that without that strip of ground the field would be too small for sporting purposes. Three rugby pitches would be impossible to achieve, that strip was the only area suitable for tennis courts and the space for cricket would have to be curtailed. Further, the ground was desperately needed by 16 rugby teams (12 of them school) and 13 cricket teams (11 of them school) while tennis was being stifled because of a lack of courts. The Club was an active and thriving organisation with over 1,000 members, 600 of them schoolboys, and deserved to be encouraged. Apart from the entire field, the Club also wanted some security of tenure and compensation if ousted at a future date, that the school pay half the costs involved and that the pavilion include a house for the groundsman/professional. The Company, however, felt that it was offering the Club an extremely good deal.

By 1893, the Club was convinced it had done its best as regards fund raising and again approached the Merchant Company for help. The Company replied that it was not in a position to help financially, but the Club should approach them next June when the agricultural lease of the field would have almost expired. The Club Committee had expected rather a different outcome. As one member said, *"Hope deferred maketh the heart grow sick."*

The Company was in absolutely no hurry as the lease did not actually expire until 11 November. When told by the Company merely to *"renew their application"*, the Athletic Club calmly, but firmly, requested a joint meeting at New Myreside. On 19 July the Master of the Company, Governors, Dr Ogilvie and the Committee walked over the fields. All agreed that the field west of Craighouse Road was, *"unquestionably the most suitable for the Club"*, but the Committee seemed to have gained the impression that the Company also agreed that without the strip intended for feuing the area was too small. In September, a plan of the field was prepared showing that the proposed rugby pitches would run north-south and the pavilion would be at the south corner of the field.

On 16 October 1894, the Governors saw the plan and gave their agreement. The Club then discovered that the Governors still intended to retain the feuing strip, that if the Company took the area back then any money spent by the Club would be paid back less 5% depreciation per annum, that the pavilion provision would have to be cut, but in return for accepting these conditions the Company would now be prepared to pay a substantial amount towards the project. Many on the Committee wanted to keep fighting, but were urged by others that it was better to go along with this deal than risk losing all. Reluctantly by some, but it was accepted. Some members felt that their voluntary efforts to support Watson's were not being fully reciprocated by the Merchant Company. The Company felt, however, that its loss of revenue and potential profit from a valuable area of real estate was also not being appreciated. The Club, it felt, was getting a fair and good deal.

In January 1895, the Company still considered that the revised plans for the pavilion were still too grand. The Club then shaved £400 off the pavilion provision, reducing the total cost to £4,325. During the past years the Club had raised an astonishing £2,500 and, therefore, needed £1,825. The Governors agreed to recommend to the Company that it should pay the outstanding amount. The Company agreed.

Like terriers the Club didn't give up. In May 1895, it proposed to the Company that the feuing strip could be rented by the Club until houses were built. The Company responded by requesting more savings on the pavilion! (That issue was not resolved until 1913 when the idea of feuing was given up and the strip became part of New Myreside. Why? Unclear, possibly lack of demand, or problems with drainage.) At long last, in May 1895, the levelling of the fields began and was just about ready in August. The pavilion, unfortunately, was delayed as costs had risen to £4,861 thus exceeding the amount sanctioned by the Company by £536. The Club wanted the Company to go 50/50 with that amount. The Company delayed. By November, the amount exceeded had been cut down to £386 the result of more cost-cutting plus the fact that the work done so far did not include the tennis courts. The Company then agreed that any amount up to £275 would be paid to get the job finished if the Club would agree to spend pound for pound. The Club responded that it was broke, having raised £2,700 to date for a scheme which would certainly benefit its members, but would equally benefit the College and be an incentive for parents to send their children to the school. Eventually on 10 December 1895, a sporting compromise was reached: the Company would pay £275 if the Club paid £111. The ground would be ready, but without the tennis accommodation which had sparked off the entire issue.

The opening ceremony on Saturday 1 May 1897 was a big occasion starting at 12 noon with all the razzmatazz associated with the Annual Games. At 3pm, Mrs Robertson, wife of the Master of the Merchant Company, unlocked the pavilion door and declared the park open. Thousands applauded and the band played, but no champagne glasses clinked as, after a heated debate, alcohol had been banned. Fed by some disgruntled Watsonians the local press commented unfavourably on the delay in opening the facilities and blamed the Company. This did little to restore goodwill.

By 1900, the Club was in financial trouble as the upkeep of New Myreside was forcing it into debt. Subscriptions would have to be raised. The Company bailed it out with a grant of £50 which was then repeated annually. By 1908, membership was on the slide. There were only 499 members, 343 being pupils and 156 FPs. The school was now using New Myreside far more than the FPs, but not contributing its share in a proportionate manner. The Club suggested a Matriculation Fee of 2s 6d per pupil which would encourage boys to participate, help create an *esprit de corps* and increase crowds at matches. The Governors agreed, however, that a bigger annual grant would be provided.

Nevertheless, by 1914 an excellent facility had been provided to the benefit of thousands.

Game For It?

The Annual Games had been a feature of the latter days of the old Hospital. always connected with the Annual Excursion. Youngsters competed for small cash prizes, but when the Hospital system was destroyed, so too went the Games.

The demand for a Games, however, came from the boys themselves. Instrumental in reviving them was a certain senior pupil Charles Campbell MacLeod born in North Uist on 19 June 1858 who came to Watson's in the early '70s and left in 1876. He went on to become an Indian tea, mills and mines mogul, but he helped organise an annual event which has continued to the present day.

The First 'Athletic Sports' were held on an idyllic summer's day, Saturday 13 May 1876 starting at 1pm on the school field of the Edinburgh Institution (Melville College) as Old Myreside was not yet ready. The site is now Warriston Playing Fields. Thousands turned up and the event soon became 'an occasion' as the girls turned it into a fashion parade. Indeed, each year Watson's Ladies College provided some of the prizes with echoes of a romantic medieval tournament. Spectators stood around the ropes, picnicked on the grassy slopes or packed the soft-drinks Refreshment Tent in readiness for the 100 yards, the great mile race, throwing the cricket ball, high leap, long leap and 60 yards sack race. Consolation Races for the losers and a Band Race (which continued with the Cadet Pipe Band until the Corps

May, 1876. The first Annual Games Prizewinners photographed a week later in Princes Street Gardens. Can anyone name the lucky people?

was disbanded). Music was provided by the 'Castle band of the moment, the Queen's Own Highlanders.

Charles MacLeod won the school Steeplechase, high and long jump. In 1914, he donated the 440 yard School Challenge Cup. One young winner recalled: *"Nor do I forget how proudly I held my cup as, seated on top of an old-fashioned horse tramcar, I returned home with my equally proud parents. On the following Saturday the prize winners were photographed in Princes Street Gardens …".* It was a hugely enjoyable event and brought together schoolboys, parents, staff and FPs, the latter competing as vigorously as the pupils.

So successful were the Games that the Governors always donated £25 each year to the organisers. From the 1880s that role was taken over by the Athletic Club. No striking performances occurred until 1888 when M Bowman threw the cricket ball 106 yds

2 ft which remained a record until 1920. In 1897, a new mile record was set by DG Robertson (4 mins 56 2/5th secs). In 1892, L Edmonston ran the 100yds in 1 min 10 4/5 secs which was not beaten for over thirty years. Watson's produced a galaxy of athletics stars, such as Hugh Welsh, who kept the crowds rolling in year after year.

Bicycle races were introduced in the 1890s, putting the weight in 1901, hurdles in 1902 and, in 1909, the relay race which became very popular as a House event with Preston being the first winners. The Watsonian Club of Canada adopted this event and, in 1910, presented the 'Canada Cup'. In 1899, the College Games Championship was instituted, the first winner being WE Callander who was the Scottish Amateur 100 and 200 yards Champion while still at school.

The Games was one of Watson's great success stories.

A Golden Age?

"Watson's College is one of the richest successes in Scotland, and the scholars get every encouragement to prosecute athletics, cricket, football and all kinds of outdoor sports, and their recreation grounds at Myreside are a credit to the school and the country." (Athletic Times, May 1898)

It would be a mistake to assume that there was some Golden Age of Sport before 1914. The dominant Headmaster of the age, Dr Ogilvie, *"was no friend to anything that took boys off their lessons."* Douglas Foulis, remembering the 1890s, stated that *"He had, however, no interest in Games and, like his generation, probably considered them a waste of time. I don't remember him ever attending the Annual Sports. Rugby and Cricket were fostered by a devoted master, WW Anderson (Dub Dub), who for twenty years or more gave all his spare time and paid his own travelling expenses without getting*

a penny from the Merchant Company. Even on his retirement his services were never adequately acknowledged." Not quite true as in 1896 Dub Dub was offered a £10 honorarium and thanked for his services to athletics by the Head and Governors. The £10 was never paid. Instead, his salary was increased by that amount per year. The next two Headmasters – Carrie and Alison – were, however, much keener on promoting sport.

Also, boys, at first, were not all that interested. Duncan Cameron who was at Watson's in the 1870s recalled this about organised games: *"We did not feel the want of them, because most of us had long tiring walks between school and home to cover."* Indeed, some boys walked to and from Comely Bank! Again remembering the 1870s, AG Fortune said that they *"kicked a ball about"* at break and had snowball fights on the Meadows, but *"I never saw a young man playing either Golf or Bowls all my boyhood days."* Even of the 1890s, Dr Smart said that *"No-one worried whether*

we played games or not; and if they did there was no money to spare in our family for equipment." Membership of sports' clubs bobbed up and down throughout the period and the main thrust of the new House system in 1904 was, *"… to arouse interest in athletics in a larger number of boys than hitherto".*

The pressure for sport came from a small, but keen and vocal group of boys, supported by a similar group of FPs and a very few enthusiastic members of staff. It was they who built and expanded Watson's into a centre of sporting excellence and encouraged participation at all levels. Membership of the Athletic Club rose from 200 in 1882 to over a thousand in 1895, half of whom were schoolboys. An astonishing achievement. Attitudes had certainly changed a great deal since 1870. Nevertheless, by 1914, membership was on the slide despite the new House system. Turning those great members o' the puddin' race into fine tuned athletes was never, ever going to be a pushover.

The Athletic Club

Money spent on sporting facilities by the Merchant Company combined with a rising demand for sport both from within the College and Former Pupils meant that it soon became necessary to manage that situation to the benefit of all. The Company needed to ensure that its property was maintained and cared for, teams needed to be time-tabled, the interests of College and FP players required to be amicably resolved and, above all, someone had to sanction use of existing and any future facilities.

The College, under 'The Doc', was not interested in taking on board this burden. In 1882, however, an organisation 'emerged' to co-ordinate all College and Watsonian sporting activities, called 'The Watson's College Athletic Club.' One of its founders was Forrest Lightbody. As the first records of this organisation are missing it is unclear how this body achieved that position. Nevertheless, it proved to be a huge success. Any Club claiming a right to use Watson's facilities had first to affiliate to the Athletic Club. Strict rules were laid down for team priorities and responsible financial control introduced. Neglect by the authorities had spawned a strong and independent organisation.

The origins of Watson's Rugby and Cricket Clubs have been dealt with elsewhere. Tennis became extremely popular in the 1880s and was introduced into Watson's around 1887. A court was planned for the west side of the Main Hall in Archibald Place for the use of the Ladies' College as well as the boys, but it is unclear if it was actually built. The formation of a Watsonian Golf Club was proposed in 1887 by a small group of eight FPs meeting in the Old North Bridge Hotel. At a subsequent meeting in the school James M Balsillie was elected Captain and 40 members enrolled. A few years later the Braid Hills were acquired by the Council and The Watsonian Club made that its home. It is unclear when a Cycling Club began, but it was certainly operating in the mid-1880s when Jim Inglis broke the record for the 50-mile tricycle race with a time of 3hrs 35mins 45 secs. Tricycle Races even became part of the Annual Games. High bikes were used at first, but never brought to school. It was thought great fun to ride down Colinton Road on the way to Myreside 'legs over'. The first modern 'low bike' was brought into school in 1887 by a certain Sammy Davidson and his brother, but despite the enthusiasm

out of school, the school Club never really prospered. Again it is unclear when the Gymnastic Club affiliated to the Athletic Club, but Gymnastics had been taught as part of the curriculum since 1870 and, in 1884, a new spacious and fully equipped gymnasium had been built. It would seem likely that a Club may have been formed on or around that year. Thus, in 1892, the clubs affiliated were:

School	FPs
Football	Football
Cricket	Cricket
Tennis	Tennis
Cycling	Gymnastics
	Golf

All were thriving apart from the Tennis Clubs, due to a lack of ash courts, and the Gymnastic Club due to a lack of an instructor. The tennis players were expecting a great deal from the opening of New Myreside. There was no Swimming Club mainly because there was no Watson's pool, but pupils and FPs did swim many being associated with the Warrender Club. Watson's boys, however, did take part in the annual inter-scholastic Swimming Championships. Fencing had been a curricular activity from 1870 to 1883, but it seems to have continued as a small extracurricular activity, never reaching the numbers to constitute a 'Club'. The Doc was consistently against encouraging warlike activities such as shooting, but, nevertheless, 'unofficial' groups did operate. Indeed, as early as 1879 a team encouraged by Frank Sellar had won The School Shooting Trophy and won it again in the early 1880s. The Athletics Club was also responsible for the organisation of the Annual Games. Frank Sellar left in 1886, but his place was taken by William 'Dub Dub' Anderson who was responsible for "*whole School Athletics*". His "*zeal and energy*" and "*enormous labours*" compensated for the lack of such from the Head and Governors.

In 1892/3, the FP Cross Country Club affiliated, being formed by John Bartleman and a group connected with Edinburgh Harriers, the premier club in the East of Scotland. The Club became the first Harrier Club connected to a private school. Season 1892/3 became famous as the first season when the Watsonian 1st XV gained the premier position in the Championship of Scotland. Sixteen matches were played, 12 won, 4 drawn and none lost. It retained its position in 1893/4 and also the season after that, suffering only one defeat by

Hawick. A fantastic achievement by any standard. Watson's boy swimmers were another successful group having won the inter-scholastic Swimming Championships for nine years. The Gymnastic Club was still having problems and had been banned from using the brand-new Gym in Archibald Place because its low numbers would not cover the cost of a Gym teacher being present. It was, unfortunately, caught in a vicious cycle: low numbers – no instructor – low numbers.

By 1894, the Golf Club was claiming to be, "*one of the strongest in the country*" whereas the Gym Club's attempt to resuscitate itself failed miserably. A grandstand had been erected for the first time at the Annual Sports which proved extremely popular as did the new Smoking Concert held in the evening at the Waterloo Hotel. It was "*hoped that this chance of reunion will be annual.*" Also, that year saw for the first time since 1870 the school rugby teams playing all the boarding and day schools. The days of prejudice had indeed vanished. Cross country was booming and had one of Britain's top runners as a leading member, the great Hugh Welsh. Unfortunately, the swimmers failed to make it '10' at the 1894 Championships being defeated by the Edinburgh Academy. It was noted, however, that of the successful 40 members of the Warrender Club, 35 were Watsonians!

In 1894/5, the school rugby team was emulating its older brothers and had the most successful season in its history. Hugh Welsh was not only the Club Champion, but regarded as the finest distance runner certainly in Scotland. Even the Cricket Clubs were doing well. The FPs won the new East of Scotland Championships while the school team beat Merchiston for the first time!

Sadly the luck of the Watsonian 1st XV ran out in season 1895/6 and it was beaten into second place. Hugh Welsh continued his brilliant form and was hailed now as the best distance runner in Britain. In 1897, he set up a new Scottish record in the mile: 4 mins 24 1/5th secs. In 1898, he won World Amateur Championship, shaved about another second off the Scottish mile record and beat the Irish Record. He would probably have smashed the British record had his shoe not come off!

The Watsonian Golf Club won the *Dispatch* Trophy for the first time in 1897 and again in 1900. One of the team members, Mr Allan, won the Scottish Amateur Golf Championship in 1897. On 9

November 1899, J Forbes proposed starting a Watsonian Hockey Club and was asked to prepare a report, but little seems to have come from it. A school Swimming Club was also proposed with the redoubtable Harry Easterbrook suggesting a *"boating branch"*. The Club began in 1900. The Cricket Club wanted a to hire a professional, but couldn't afford it. Cycling was losing its attraction: the school Club was doing fine, but there was a complete lack of interest by FPs and the open bicycle race was deleted from the Annual Games.

Curling came to the fore for the first time in 1900 when the groundsman laid down an artificial curling rink at the back of the pavilion which was then much used. On 26 June 1900 the formation of a Curling Club was proposed and its first meeting fixed for 9 July in the school. Robin Welsh was elected as the first President in 1901 and in the following year it was requesting a rink, 50 x 30 yds to be created parallel to Craighouse Road at the back of the pavilion. In March 1902, this energetic Club decided to go ahead by asking its 20 members for £1 each. In December, it decided to light the rink by gas from the pavilion. The ghostly figures on frosty nights soon became a remarkable feature of New Myreside. In 1904, five rinks had been authorised and membership had grown to over fifty. Matches were now being played against other teams. The success was being put down to the commitment and energy of William Inglis.

Meanwhile, back in 1900, a gold watch had been offered by US Watsonians as a prize for the School Champion in the Annual Games. The first winner was AG McCallum and, amazingly, won it again the following year. A cricket professional had been appointed (Mr Wright) and also two bowlers to coach the youngsters. Eleven teams were put out with one from the Junior School. Just to show that Club fortunes wax and wane Cross country had virtually collapsed by 1901 as had cycling.

A new-fangled telephone was installed in the pavilion in 1903, the charge being 1d per call. Cross country revived a bit in 1904, especially as John Ranken won the National Cross Country Individual Championship of Scotland and Captained the Scottish Team at an International Contest in Manchester. Ranken retained the Scottish Championship the next year. As for cricket, the Governors agreed to pay £30 for a professional while, Andrew Scott, the groundsman, agreed to coach the school teams. Shooting would have a much brighter future as the new Cadet Corps, founded in 1904, obviously had a strong reason to foster that activity. For the first time entries were down for the Annual Games and a distinct lack of interest was noted among the boys.

The cricket professional chosen for 1908 (Ashby) failed to play a straight bat. At the end of the season he purloined much of the cricket material from the pavilion and absconded without paying his rent. Luckily, the cricket stuff was found still in his room!

Rugby Club fortunes rocketed in 1908/9 when they shared Championship honours with Hawick, but hardly surprising as in the team were giants: wee Jimmy Pearson and ferocious AW Angus.

As the new Heads, Carrie and Alison, were interested in promoting sport the school began to take more and more of an organisational role. From October 1907 the College paid an Honorarium to a member of staff to act as 'Superintendent of School Athletics', the first being JA Doig who taught in the Senior Department. The Athletic Club continued its yeoman-type service unabated until a greater and far more dangerous game erupted in 1914. The disruption caused by war, however, would lead to a reassessment of its role in the post-war years.

Medals such as this were awarded by the Athletic Club.

Pioneers of Curling

This is the only known photograph of the Myreside Curling Rink. This was the first tarmac rink in Scotland – the forerunner of hundreds to come – laid in 1902, on his own initiative, by the groundsman, Andrew Scott, who had, four years earlier, laid a concrete one. Tarmac was far superior to the previous concrete rinks which tended to crack and develop bumps. It was also far cheaper: £100 for concrete and £20-30 for tarmac. It was also easier to prepare for play as a concrete rink required an inch of water and a hard frost whereas tarmac required only a light spray of water and a minimum of frost.

New lighting also improved the game immensely. Candles, lanterns and flares gave way to naphtha, paraffin, acetylene, gas and, eventually, electricity.

The first tour by a Scottish curling team in Canada took place in 1903.

The rinks are now under the groundsman's house and Myreside car park.

The first Canadian team arrived in Edinburgh on a frosty evening in 1909. A Watsonian curler went to the North British (Balmoral) Hotel and invited the Canadians to a game. Thus the first impromptu international match was held at Myreside.

Such excellent facilities helped Robin Welsh win a Gold Medal for Great Britain at the 1924 Winter Olympics.

The Watsonian Club

The Watsonian Club began on 5 March 1894 with two aims: to organise an Annual Dinner for FPs and to donate an annual prize to the school for the, *"best all round boy of the year in scholarship and athletics."* Eight stalwart Watsonians were responsible for creating this organisation: Harry Armour, AB Easterbrook, A Glegg, J Stuart Gowans, H Lawson, FS Paterson, Charles White and Alex Robertson. Armour was elected Chairman. In July, the Committee was widened to include one boy from both sides to act as Assistant Secretaries. Membership had risen to 111 and the first recipient of the new prize was Bernhard Richardson, aged 16, and a member of 6th Classical who received a Silver Medal.

The Watsonian Club Medal. The second recipient was James Lochhead.

The following year a Medal was instituted for each side of the School, but, by 1899, a real problem was becoming clear, namely that boys good at games were not necessarily good academics. Choosing winners fairly was proving impossible and very often the medals were not awarded. In 1905, the Committee considered changing the award in order to help the new Cadet Corps who wanted a prize for shooting and possibly piping. Occasionally, however, one boy stood out. In July 1906, Eric Milroy easily qualified for the award and clearly had a great future ahead. He was the Lit Club Secretary and a Prefect, Captain of the 2nd XV, a Sergeant in the Cadet Corps, a member of the Golf Club and a reserve for the Cadet shooting team. On the academic side Eric had a Honours Leaving Certificate in Maths, English and Latin plus a Higher Grade in Greek. Sadly he was killed in 1916 serving with the Black Watch on the Somme. He is commemorated on the Thiepval Memorial to the Missing.

The Club promoted things Watsonian such as a magazine and school song. In January 1904 it presented a silver salver to much-loved janitor Davie Leitch doing

it quietly as he was old and in ill health. In July 1899, the Club presented the Governors with a portrait by Sir George Reid of Dr Ogilvie costing the enormous sum of £189. Four years later it was covered in glass for safety reasons and an inscription put on the frame.

Above all the Club promoted similar organisations beyond Edinburgh. In July 1898, Arthur Hunter in Philadelphia wrote to the Committee that he had started The Watsonian Club in the USA. The Committee wrote to Charles Smith in order to encourage him to set up one in India. He replied that he didn't think it would be successful, but, nevertheless, the Committee encouraged him to at least 'have a go'. In January 1900, the Rev W Lyall Watson made contact stating that he had just started a Club in Buenos Aires called *"The Watsonian Club of the River Plate."* By 1910, largely due to the establishment of *The Watsonian* with its strongly pro-FP Editor, Henry Findlay, Clubs had been established in London, Chile, Hong-Kong, Rangoon, Calcutta, South Africa, Toronto, Winnipeg and New York.

In December 1907, it was proposed, and unanimously agreed, *"That a day be selected to be known as 'Watsonian Day' on which the Annual Dinners of The Watsonian Clubs throughout the World should be held … "*. After consulting the various branches it was decided that the third Friday in January would *"suit the greatest number"* and that the Edinburgh Club would hold its Dinner in the school Hall. In December 1908, the old toast of 'George Watson's College and its Athletes' was replaced by a simple 'The School'. Soon each branch began sending telegrams to each other's Dinners.

In March 1909, a Badge was proposed and samples were supplied by Bartleman & Sons. In July, the Badge was agreed and the design was finally selected and adopted in January 1910. Does anyone have one?

In November 1909, AJ Niven & Co (Chartered Accountants) ambitiously suggested establishing 'The Watsonian Club Ltd.' to create a social and residential club by issuing £1 shares. The Committee thought

The earliest known photograph of Eric Milroy taken in 1904 12 years before his death at the Battle of the Somme.

The Watsonian, *April 1912.*

this impractical, but decided nevertheless to investigate the matter and consult the Athletic Club. In November, it decided that such a venture would be unnecessary and no further action was taken. Interestingly, if it had not been for AJ Niven & Co the story of The Watsonian Club and the Athletic Club would have been largely lost as that firm preserved the relevant Minute Books and gifted them to the school archive.

Although owing allegiance to Watson's, each club was effectively independent. What brought them together was *The Watsonian* magazine and its ever-enthusiastic, ebullient and hard-working Editor, Henry John Findlay. In 1928, the Athletic Club and The Watsonian Club, plus all the overseas bodies and Year organisations that had survived the First World War, came together to found the modern united body known as The Watsonian Club. Its first President was the forceful AW Angus and its first Secretary was the popular and unassuming George Byres. The Club has continued to grow and flourish.

The College flag hoisted on the morning of 21st January announced the second celebration of "Watsonian Day." That celebration, as on a former occasion, was confined to the Old Boys alone. Hence, perhaps, that reflection of a College poet whose verses have been crowded out of this number :—

"Gone are the glories of Watsonian Day,
    A day on which the College part is *nil !*"

This hint may suggest to the proper authorities an extension of the ceremonies associated with our common natal day.

A comment on Founder's Day in The Watsonian, *April 1910.*

"And though our lonely graves be dug
In some far-distant land,
Our spirits, coming back again,
Will hover near at hand,
And the boys will hear us whisper,
And the boys will understand."

James (Peary) Pearson
Watsonian, Internationalist, Private Soldier, Gentleman

The Watsonian

The first number of *The Watsonian* produced during the First World War was published in December 1914. The frontispiece remained the same throughout the conflict with the exception of July 1915 when one deemed more appropriate was designed by Watson's talented art teacher, Ralph Hay. This bold design was dominated by the pagan classical goddess of wisdom (Minerva) and the god of war (Mars). No reason was given for it being discontinued, but although Minerva would certainly patronise a war of defence she would have absolutely no sympathy with Mar's savage love of violence and bloodshed. Perhaps this design just proved to be a little too controversial.

In the December 1914 number a grand memorial page appeared for those killed-in-action. This was a design for a war that would be over by Christmas. As the conflict intensified, so the number of casualties rose. By July 1915, 43 Watsonians had been killed, many in horrific engagements such as Neuve Chapelle, Aubers Ridge, Second Ypres and, of course, the disastrous Gallipoli Campaign against the Turks in which the 4th Royal Scots was heavily involved. Given the numbers involved the old-style memorial page had to be altered and Ralph Hay came up with a second, more suitable style for the July 1915 number.

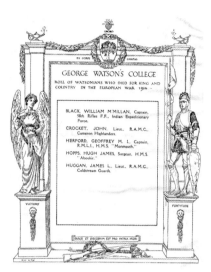

On the afternoon of 26th February a rather startling accident happened in school. A gale was raging outside, and about 2 p.m. the flagstaff snapped, and fell with a tremendous crash on the roof of the Geography and Science rooms. Classes were at work in both rooms at the time. Pieces of the flagstaff and fragments of half inch glass showered liberally down on them. The marvel is there was no serious injury inflicted. Mr Ligertwood got his shoulder bruised by a falling bit of wreckage, and one or two boys were cut by the glass, while everybody got a bad scare.

The din was so alarming as to give the impression that our Hunnish foes had at last paid us a visit. One scared youth staggered into a neighbouring room and fell into the master's arms, exclaiming "Oh, those Germans!"— or words to that effect.

In April 1905, The Watsonian recorded that an enormous flagstaff (three storeys high) had been erected on the school roof. Ten years later …

In July 1915, new categories appeared for 'POW's' (five names), 'Gassed and Missing' (one name), 'Missing' (one name) and 'Wounded' (89 names). A special graphic was designed for the latter and used in each subsequent number until the end of the conflict.

Casualties

The first photographs of those killed-in-action appeared in July 1915. These were set into another specially designed graphic by Ralph Hay inscribed, in Latin, *"How sweet and noble it is to die for one's country."* In the pages which followed an obituary would be printed. The first photograph was of Lieutenant JB Aitchison and his obituary is typical of the multitude yet to come.

LIEUT. J. B. AITCHISON.
PTE. W. G. BARTLEMAN.   LIEUT. D. CAMPBELL.
PTE. L. V. COWAN.

In April 1917, there was a significant change of format with a new inscription translated as, *"He was not afraid to die for his dear friends and country"* which reflects a change of mood since 1914. The terse and vague nature of the obituaries was due to censorship.

LIEUT. D. A. ANDERSON.   PTE. J. A. T. BLAKE.
L.-CPL. A. C. BROWN.   PTE. G. A. BROWN.
LIEUT. T. E. BRYDON.   LIEUT. A.-SCOTT CALDER.

JOHN BREBNER AITCHISON,
Second Lieutenant, 5th Royal Scots.

JOHN BREBNER AITCHISON, son of Mr Richard S. Aitchison, C.A., 61 Braid Avenue, Edinburgh, was born in Edinburgh, 28th September 1895. He entered Watson's in his eighth year and left in 1913. He was a member of the Cadet Corps, attaining the rank of sergeant, and subsequently gaining Certificate A, which qualified him for a commission. Prior to entering on his professional training as a chartered accountant, he visited Belgium and Canada. Gazetted to the 5th Royal Scots in March 1914, he was called up on the outbreak of hostilities, and at once volunteered for foreign service. He took part in the operations on the Gallipoli Peninsula, and, the battalion having been ordered to take a wood at all costs, he fell in the charge. "He was a brave boy," wrote his O.C., "and did his work fearlessly. He was well liked by his men, and is mourned by all. His name will be remembered by the regiment as that of a gallant officer who died doing his duty."

This striking graphic (above) by Ralph Hay from the December 1914 number was the earliest and longest lasting of all. It depicts a representation of the Cadet Corps Pipes and Drums proudly on the march from Lauriston Place and heading for Princes Street. The total number of Watsonians who served in the First World War? An astonishing 3,102!

Starting in April 1915 were lists of those who had won awards such as 'Mentioned in Dispatches'. The July 1916 number proudly announced that the first Watsonian to win the Victoria Cross was H Peel Ritchie, Commander of HMS *Goliath*. The other VC holder was David L McIntyre of the 6th Highland Light Infantry who won his in late 1918.

Yet another VC winner was discovered in the 1980s: David McGregor, who attended both Watson's and Heriots.

Victoria Cross	2
Distinguished Service Order	51
Military Cross	277
Distinguished Flying Cross	3
Distinguished Conduct Medal	13
Military Medal	24
Mentioned in Despatches	303
British Decorations other than above	93
Foreign Decorations	62

(H Waugh (ed), George Watson's College, *1970)*

Of particular interest are the two summaries produced in April and July 1916 which break down the numbers of those serving with particular regiments, or other branches of the armed services. Unfortunately, these summaries were abandoned in favour of a much less useful general sort. From June 1916 to November 1918, 1,165 more Watsonians either volunteered or were conscripted which means that at least 62.5% of those who served did so voluntarily. That was a huge and impressive contribution to the war effort. Luckily, a simplified summary appeared in April 1919 which helped produce the analysis on the following page.

SUMMARY OF GEORGE WATSON'S COLLEGE ROLL OF HONOUR as at 9th MARCH 1916.

Unit.	Total.	Officers.	Unit.	Total.	Officers.
Navy	66	57	Royal Scots Fusiliers	12	11
Scots Guards	6	1	King's Own Scottish		
Royal Scots Greys	8	1	Borderers	24	23
Lothians & Border Horse	76	1	Scottish Rifles	27	27
Lovat Scouts	10	...	Border Rifles	8	7
Scottish Horse	14	...	Royal Sussex Rifles	3	...
Other Cavalry Units	21	5	Black Watch	42	37
Royal Field Artillery	105	73	Durham Light Infantry	6	6
Royal Horse Artillery	3	2	Highland Light In-		
Royal Garrison Artillery	49	38	fantry	37	31
Royal Engineers	50	31	Seaforth Highlanders	34	30
Royal Scots	12	12	Gordon Highlanders	19	18
,, 3rd	3	2	Cameron Highlanders	37	29
,, 4th	113	30	Argyll and Sutherland		
,, 5th	40	13	Highlanders	77	45
,, 6th	17	14	London Scottish	20	1
,, 7th	13	10	Army Service Corps	36	16
,, 8th	16	15	Royal Army Medical		
,, 9th	122	19	Corps	187	156
,, 10th	6	6	Indian Medical Service	15	15
,, 11th	3	3	Army Veterinary Corps	9	3
,, 12th	10	9	Other Units	101	57
,, 13th	12	8			
,, 14th	17	17	Indian	92	29
,, 15th	15	11	Canadian	104	18
,, 16th	19	9	Australian	22	9
,, 17th	3	3	African	43	19
,, 18th	4	3			
Northumberland Fusiliers	11	11	Total	1799	991

Scotland's Einstein: William Gordon (Seggie) Brown

Seggie was born at 6 Great Stuart Street in 1895 and then moved to 3 Blackford Road. Seggie attended Watson's for 13 years from 1901 to 1914. He had outstanding ability, especially in Mathematics. Far from the later image of a fragile and retiring academic Seggie was promoted to Col-Sgt in the Cadets, appointed a Prefect and elected Treasurer of the Literary Club. Indeed, he was a first-class shot and range-finder.

In 1914, instead of going to Edinburgh University, Seggie enlisted as a Private in the 4th Battalion Royal Scots and served in Gallipoli where he was invalided home. Although not fully recovered Seggie insisted on being transferred to the Royal Naval Division which soon crossed to France and took part in the final phase of the Somme Battle: the attack alongside the 51st Highland Division on Beaumont Hamel on 13–18 November 1916. Seggie was killed on the 13th.

Amazingly, Seggie had continued his mathematical studies while serving in the army, even contributing to *The Philosophical Magazine* an article entitled 'Note on Reflections from a Moving Mirror' and providing the mathematical theory of a phenomenon in optics.

It was said at the time that only two other people had achieved so much as undergraduates: Clerk-Maxwell and Kelvin. Seggie also left behind him other papers some of which were placed in 1922 before the Royal Society of Edinburgh. These dealt with tubes of electrical force in a four-dimensional space. Seggie had arrived independently at the same conclusions regarding Relativity as had Albert Einstein.

Cecil Coles: Musician of a Lost Generation

Cecil Frederick Coles was born in Kirkcudbright on 7 October 1888 and came to Watson's in 1899. He entered Edinburgh University as a music student at the remarkable age of 16 and then, in 1906, won a prestigious scholarship to the London College of Music. In London he joined the Morley College Orchestra whose conductor was Gustav Holst. There began a strong, fruitful and lasting relationship. A sign of what could have been had not the War intervened was his appointment, in 1908, as assistant conductor of the Stuttgart Royal Opera – an astonishing achievement considering that he was a foreigner and only 23 years old.

In 1914, Cecil was called up immediately as he was the regimental Bandmaster of the 9th Battalion, Queen Victoria's Rifles and acted, as all musicians, as a stretcher-bearer. Despite all difficulties he continued to compose even in the trenches – as testified by his mud-bespattered and shrapnel-torn manuscripts which he sent to Holst. On 26 April 1918, Cecil heroically volunteered to bring in some wounded comrades following an attack. He was shot by a sniper. Musician to the end, he died humming Beethoven. He is buried at Crouy on the Somme.

Cecil was the musician of a doomed generation. His *Behind the Lines,* composed in 1918 amidst the thunder of the guns, has strength, depth and beauty, the last movement, 'Cortege', being the most powerful and haunting. His traumatised wife, Phoebe, refused to talk about him and no music was ever again played in her home.

"He was a genius before anything else and a hero of the first water." (On Cecil Cole's gravestone at Crouy)

The Victoria Cross

The Victoria Cross.

Lieutenant David Lowe Macintyre

Lieutenant David Lowe Macintyre was born in 1895 in Portnahaven (Islay) and attended Watson's from 1907 to 1914. His father was a minister in the United Free Church and, in Edinburgh, his family lived at 25 Downie Terrace, Corstorphine. When war broke out David joined the Argyll and Sutherland Highlanders serving in Egypt, Jerusalem and France. On 24 August 1918, while attached to the Highland Light Infantry, he was involved in the ferocious fighting required to break the mighty Hindenburg Line at Henin near Arras. His Victoria Cross was earned by coolness under heavy shell and machine-gun fire during which he pursued an enemy machine-gun team through a barrage into a pill-box, killed three, captured an officer plus ten other ranks and five machine-guns. From that pill box David and his men then raided three others and enabled his battalion to capture the entire position. Subsequently, while reconnoitring the exposed right flank, a single enemy machine-gunner opened up on him. Without hesitation he rushed it single-handed, chased the enemy away and brought back the gun. Whilst in London on 26 October recovering from a bullet wound in the thigh David heard he had been awarded the Victoria Cross. As a Gaelic-speaking Highland officer David was not only a hero, but a living embodiment of the Scottish military tradition.

Lieutenant David Lowe Macintyre.

David later achieved the rank of Major-General and after the Second World War was a senior civil servant. In 1939, the Scottish Naval and Military Museum at Edinburgh Castle had closed and its artefacts put into storage. Given post-war austerity and anti-militarism things just might have stayed that way had it not been for David who insisted that it re-open under the supervision of the Ministry of Works. Thus, twice a hero.

David died on 31 July 1967 in Edinburgh.

Without hesitation he rushed it single-handed, chased the enemy away and brought back the gun.

Commander Henry Peel Ritchie.

Lieutenant David McGregor.

Douglas Gillespie.

Commander Henry Peel Ritchie

Commander Henry Peel Ritchie was born in Edinburgh in 1876, the eldest son of Dr RP Ritchie, and attended Watson's between 1882–5. He joined the Navy and became Army and Navy Light-Weight Amateur Boxing Champion in 1900. On 28 November 1914 he was in command of HMS *Goliath* charged with a search and demolish operation at Dar es Salaam, Tanganyika (now Tanzania). *Goliath* entered the harbour unopposed, but then erupted a storm of shell and bullets from all directions. Henry was hit eight times in 20 minutes, but carried on until he fainted from loss of blood. He was awarded the Victoria Cross on 10 April 1915. Henry was later promoted to Captain. He died on 9 December 1958 in Edinburgh.

HMS *Goliath* was a 16-gun, twin-screwed battleship launched at Chatham in 1898 at a cost of £920,806. It weighed 12,950 tons, had a 13,500 horsepower engine with a top speed of 18.6 knots, a crew of 750 and had played a part in the Chinese Boxer Rebellion of 1900. In 1914, it went on escort duties in the East Indies operating against the German light cruiser *Konigsberg* on the Rufigi River, East Africa. After the attack on Dar es Salaam on 28–30 November 1914 *Goliath* took part in the ill-fated Dardanelles/Gallipoli Campaign and was sunk on 13 May 1915 with the loss of 570 men.

Lieutenant David McGregor

Watson's third VC holder is shared with Heriot's. Lieutenant David McGregor of the 6th Royal Scots, attached to the Machine Gun Corps, attended Watson's between 1900–8 and Heriot's for three years. He was the son of David and Annie of Ferragon, Craigs Road, Corstorphine. David is buried in Stasegem Communal Cemetery, Belgium. He was only 23 years old. The citation for the VC is given below:

"For most conspicuous bravery and devotion to duty near Hoogmolen on 22 of October, 1918, when in command of a section of machine guns attached to the right flank platoon of the assaulting battalion. Immediately the troops advanced they were subjected to intense enfilade machine-gun fire from Hill 66 on the right flank. Lt McGregor fearlessly went forward and located the enemy guns, and realised that it was impossible to get his guns carried forward either by pack or by hand without great delay, as the ground was absolutely bare and fire swept. Ordering his men to follow by a more covered route, he mounted the limber and galloped forward under intense fire for about 600 yards to cover. The driver, horses and limber were all hit, but Lt McGregor succeeded in getting the guns into action, effectively engaging the enemy, subduing their fire, and enabling the advance to be resumed. With the utmost gallantry he continued to expose himself in order to direct and control the fire of his guns, until, about an hour later, he was killed. His great gallantry and supreme devotion to duty

Douglas Gillespie attended Watson's between 1908–15. He became a famous RFC pilot during WW1, but was shot down on 6 April 1918 by the 'Red Baron', Manfred von Richthofen, leader of the famous Flying Circus.

Of the Coalition Government that won the First World War five members were Watsonians: RS Horne (Civil Lord of the Admiralty), Ian Macpherson (Vice-President of the Army Council), TB Morison (Lord Advocate), Eric Geddes and his brother Auckland. The Geddes brothers were undoubtedly the most famous of them all.

Eric Campbell Geddes was born in 1875 at Agra (India) to a Scots civil engineer. The family returned to Edinburgh in 1880 living at 16 Athole Crescent and Eric entered Watson's in October 1887 at the age of 12. He didn't last very long. And within a year he had been moved to Merchiston. Indeed, he didn't last long anywhere and was expelled from six of the seven schools he attended. Eric was a cheerful imp consistently at the bottom of the class. When asked by his father to explain this, Eric simply said that it was much more fun than being at the top! But Eric was bright and he excelled at games and swimming. On leaving school he appears to have had a very long 'gap' session, but eventually 'found himself' when he joined the North Eastern Railway in 1904. Within ten years he had become its General Manager, famous for his energy, organising ability, dynamic personality and use of modern innovative management techniques such as statistical analysis.

During WW1 David Lloyd George (as Minister of Munitions) was on the lookout for *"men of push and go"*, thus Eric was drafted to serve as Deputy Director of Supply. His reward for ensuring sufficient shells for the Somme offensive was a knighthood. In 1916, Eric was sent to France as Inspector General of Douglas Haig's British Expeditionary Force. As such he gained the honorary title of Major-General. Eric revolutionised the BEF's transport and supply system helping make it the equal of the German Army.

Faced with the consequences of Jutland and unrestricted U-boat warfare Lloyd George moved Eric to the Admiralty, installing him as First Lord of the Admiralty. Eric was now both a General and an Admiral! His strenuous work there helped save Britain from defeat by the U-boats. His reward this time was a seat in the House of Commons as MP for Cambridge.

Unfortunately, his post-war career was less than illustrious. He gained fame (and notoriety) for his promise to squeeze the German lemon, *"until you can hear the pips squeak."* If the Treaty of Versailles was a factor in the rise of the Nazis and a cause of WW2, then Eric Geddes bears some responsibility. He also gained a dubious and lasting renown as the author of the *Geddes Axe* in 1922, proposing savage expenditure cuts which would stifle educational opportunity for working-class children, slash spending on health and pensions, cut teachers' and police pay and savage the military. Even his right-wing government colleagues were aghast.

Eric subsequently became Chairman of Dunlop and then Imperial Airways. He died on 22 June 1937 and his ashes were scattered over the English Channel from Flying Boat *Canopus*. Had he survived to experience the Second World War there is no doubt Eric would have revolutionised aircraft production and thereby achieved the unique position of high command in each of the three services.

The Auck: Cut and Thrust

Auckland (The Auck) Campbell Geddes was born on 21 June 1879 and spent his entire school career at Watson's. Unlike his brother he was a workaholic as well as a talented swimmer and footballer. Auckland gained entrance to medical school, took part in the Boer War and then trained as a surgeon. Before the War he advanced from Assistant Professor of Anatomy at Edinburgh University to Professor at the Royal College in Ireland and then on to Canada and McGill University, Montreal.

When war broke out in 1914 Auckland was commissioned as a Major in the Northumberland Fusiliers, but then made the astonishing leap – perhaps aided by his brother – to become Director of Recruiting at the War Office between 1916 and 1917. He proved to be remarkably efficient, but attempts to conscript increasing numbers of men brought him into conflict with the trade unions as well as Irish nationalism. He became a Conservative MP for Basingstoke (1917–20) and, post-war, held a number of public posts including Ambassador Extraordinaire to the USA (1920–4) and Civil Defence Regional Commander (1929–42).

Unfortunately for his future reputation Auckland was also Chairman of the mining company Rio Tinto (1924–47) which, along with Hitler, Mussolini and the British Government, supported Franco's fascists in a civil war against the democratically elected Spanish Republican Government. Shockingly, he even told the Company's 1937 AGM in London:

"Since the mining region was occupied by General Franco's forces there have been no further labour problems. … Miners found guilty of troublemaking are court-martialled and shot."

Auckland was made a Baron in 1942 and died in 1954.

Eric Geddes.

Auckland Campbell Geddes.

Eric was a cheerful imp consistently at the bottom of the class.

Watsonian War Service, 1914–18

Highland Regiments
416 fought in Highland Regiments (ie 13.4%) which comprised the 51st Highland Division used as a 'Stormer' unit. As such it took part in some of the most ferocious battles of the First World War and, of course, suffered appalling casualties.

Officers
62.4% of Watsonians served as officers which is not unexpected given their educational and class background, as well as being from a school with an active Cadet Corps which prepared boys for military leadership. However, surprisingly, a huge number served as private soldiers. This could reflect a spirit of the times when many preferred to fight alongside friends or colleagues rather than seek or accept promotion especially in another regiment.

Which Branch?
Only 4% served with the Royal Navy. The vast majority joined the Army although 116 did transfer to the Royal Flying Corps. One who did was Douglas Gillespie who was shot down in 1918 by the 'Red Baron', the leader of the famous Flying Circus, Manfred von Richthofen. Fifteen served with the Tank Corps, 54 with the Machine Gun Service, 2 with the US Army whilst 29 acted as Chaplains.

Imperial Forces
462 fought with Indian, Canadian, African, Australian and New Zealand units, ie 14.9%.

The Royal Scots
- A total of 476 (15.3%) Watsonians served with the Royal Scots, all but 11 serving with the Territorial or New Army Battalions. This represents the highest percentage of Watsonians serving in any regiment, or other branch of the armed forces.
- To 23 June 1916, 196 served as officers, ie 45.7%.
- The two Battalions which attracted most volunteers were the 4th and 9th. To 23 June 1916, the 4th attracted 26.3% and the 9th 29%. Thus, on the eve of the Battle of the Somme, 53% of all Watsonians in the Royal Scots were serving (or had served) in just two Battalions.

RAMC
280 (9%) served with the Royal Army Medical Corps, sometimes dubbed 'Rob All My Comrades', but that, of course, would not have applied to any Watsonian.

Killed-in-Action/Died of Wounds
605 Watsonians lost their lives in the First World War. This represents about 1 in 5 (19.5%) of all Watsonians who served in the armed forces from 1914 to 1918.

Artillery or Engineers
381 served with such specialist units, ie 12.3%.

Scottish Units
To 23 June 1916, 907 served with easily identifiable Scottish infantry regiments, ie 46.8%.

"DUCKBOARD PARADE."   A. F. MACPHERSON, *The Royal Scots*

The drawing (left) 'Duckboard Parade' appeared in July 1918 and was sketched by Alexander Macpherson. He had joined the 9th Royal Scots, but, in 1919, transferred as an officer to the Highland Light Infantry. He fought on the Somme, including Beaumont-Hamel, but was wounded in April 1917 at Arras.

YPRES–1918.

As a result of government censorship no realistic account of warfare was ever published in The Watsonian, *but two drawings did appear. The sketch of 'Ypres 1918' (left) appeared in July 1919. It was drawn by Alan Ronald of the 17th Royal Scots who had won the Watson's Special Drawing Prize when at school. The devastation had been caused by artillery, not bombing. The GWC History Department takes a party of youngsters to the Western Front every three years. Ypres is always a memorable and moving occasion.*

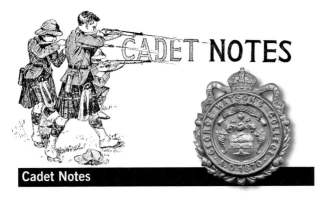

Cadet Notes

A Pacific Beginning

The militarisation of Watson's really began not in the summer of 1914, but 10 years earlier when a military Cadet unit had been established.

Military training in schools had been a hotly disputed issue ever since the days of the French invasion scare of 1859 which had sparked off the new adult Volunteer movement and its junior counterpart, the Cadets. The British community was deeply divided between enthusiastic support and fierce opposition, the latter mostly from religious groups. For about 30 years after Watson's opened as a day school the Headmaster, Dr George Ogilvie (1870–98) was totally against the introduction of any military unit.

> The Cadet Corps, which now bulks so largely in the School life had, like football, a very modest beginning. Away back in the early eighties a master might sometimes have been seen stealthily leaving School with five or six boys carrying rifles which on no account were to attract the attention of the headmaster. The Doctor had a rooted antipathy to all things military, and Mr Sellar had practically to have recourse to weekly "gun running" to let the boys get decent practice. In spite of this handicap the Rifle Club made good. One year the inter-schools trophies for swimming and for shooting were won by the College, and the boys were very proud of the double achievement. The Doctor, however, could not get over his prejudice against the rifle, and one remembers with amusement his estimate of the relative value of the trophies from his remark, "This is for saving life, that for destroying it."

| GC Ligertwood, Jubilee Number, July 1920.

An Earlier Organisation?

This letter was written to *The Watsonian* in November 1920 by a Mr J Boyd Jamieson:

> Firstly, in Mr Shepherd's account of the School Cadets he states that "there was no military organisation attached to the School before 1905." This is a mistake, for in 1885 an enthusiastic company, some sixty strong, armed with muzzle-loading Enfield rifles and sword bayonets, were wont to parade for drill in the playground of the Little School, at the grisly hour of 8 A.M., under the command of Capt. W. R. Mackersy, of the Queen's Edinburgh Rifles, of course a Watsonian. This company, which had no uniform, was greatly helped by the enthusiasm of Mr Seller, and was probably the first Cadet Company to be formed in Scotland, if not in Great Britain. When the questions of making it a permanency and of clothing it in a uniform came to be discussed, the opposition of Dr Ogilvie to all things military caused the extinction of the formation.

It has been suggested that this group also formed the first school Pipe Band. If so, that would make it the earliest civilian pipe band in Scotland. Unfortunately, the documentary evidence is 'missing'. Jamieson is quite wrong regarding the first Cadet units which were formed in the very early 1860s.

A Change of Mood

A new Headmaster, Dr John Alison (1904–26), was of a different persuasion and, supported by a new team of Governors, he introduced a Cadet Company. Merchiston School had the first school Cadet Unit in Edinburgh, but Watson's was the first day school to have one and was the first to start a Pipe Band.

The decision to start a Cadet Corps attached to the Queen's Rifle Volunteer Brigade was taken in 1903 and the Corps actively recruited in 1904. On 27 June 1905 its uniform had been agreed as:

- Glengarry bonnet with Blackcock feather and the school badge in white metal.
- Green serge jacket (service pattern) with buttons the same as the Queen's Rifle Volunteer Brigade.
- Hunting Stewart kilt with pin.
- White goat sporran with black tassels and school badge in white metal.
- Hose tops and garters to correspond with the tartan, if not too expensive.
- White spats.

On 14 December 1905, metal letters for the shoulder straps were agreed. The choice of dark green jackets is intriguing. Was a deliberate effort being made to revive the old Hospital colour, or was it a mere coincidence?

One problem was that previous Cadet organisations in Edinburgh (eg John Hope's 'British League Cadets') had targeted the poorest social groups and there was a certain stigma attached to the name. In 1908, however, that problem was overcome by Haldane's army reforms which changed the Cadets into 'The Officers' Training Corps' (OTC). Watsonians, however, usually just called it 'The Cadet Corps'. By 1913 it was a popular, efficient and successful school organisation.

This photograph of December 1912 shows the uniform which the boys provided at their own expense. The Cadet age limit was between 13 and 18, and, in 1905, the smallest Cadet was just over 4ft while the tallest was 6ft 1in. Captain FP Shepherd was the first CO ably assisted by Lieutenants Dr HJ Scougal and Sandy Morrison along with Sergeants E Milroy, JR McGlashan, W Kennedy and C Marksman, the latter acting as Colour-Sergeant.

CADET CORPS—OFFICERS AND NON-COM. OFFICERS, 1912
Front Row—Sgt. J. N. Dandie, Capt. A. M. Shaw, Sgt. F. H. Allan
Second Row—Col.-Sgt. D. M. Stewart, Lt. W. R. Cooper, Sgt. T. L. Barker
Third Row—Sgt. W. S. Morrison and Sgt.-Drummer J. Kennedy

The Corps drilled every Tuesday and Friday after school hours in the playground. The first drill instructor was Colour-Sergeant Bradford from the Royal Scots. The first Pipe Band consisted of six pipers, four side drummers and one bass drummer who wore a leopard skin presented by an FP in India. The first Pipe-Sergeant was Neil Morrison and the first tutor was Mr Stuart. All those in the photograph served in the armed forces during WW1. Dandie and Morrison were both awarded the Military Cross. Kennedy was killed on 27 May 1917. Stewart was wounded in 1917 and died in Edinburgh on 3 January 1919.

Cadet Capers

Apart from drill and military field exercises Watson's Cadets offered a variety of activities which must have seemed extremely attractive to boys brought up in a more restrictive society than ours.

- Shooting
- First Aid
- Pipe Band
- Cycling
- Signalling
- Summer Camps

Rifle shooting took place at Hunter's Bog in the Queen's Park, at a range in Malleny and also in a Morris Tube situated in the Drill Hall, Forrest Road run, by the Royal Scots. A miniature rifle range was opened in Watson's in May 1913.

Cadet Scouts

This is a Cadet Scout camp held at Taynuilt during the Easter vacation, 1908. It was organised by Sandy Morrison who is the large figure in the Watson's jersey. Inset, is Sandy Somerville in his Cadet uniform. Sandy became the first Scoutmaster of a troop independent of the Cadets which became the 9th Midlothian.

We have reserved for latest mention in this introductory paragraph what is perhaps the most noteworthy development of the term in connection with the Corps, affording pleasing proof of its robust vitality—the institution of a Scouts' Class conducted by Lieutenant Morrison, who has manifestly transmitted to his "disciples" the enthusiasm which he himself exhibits in this as in all other departments of the work of the Corps.

The Watsonian, *April 1908.*

GEORGE WATSON'S COLLEGE TROOP BOY SCOUTS (THE 9TH TROOP), FOUNDED MAY 1908.

LOOKING back it is interesting and not a little significant to notice the development of the "Scouting" idea in Watson's. There grew up in the early days of the Cadet Corps a Scout Section, or Military Reconnaissance class, under Sandy Morrison. With them the "Wanderlust"—the call of the Wild—was very strong, and gave itself expression in an Easter Camp, which was held two years at Taynuilt and one other at Aberfoyle.

About the same time *Scouting for Boys* began to come out in its original 4d. parts, and by April of 1908 a number of "Lone" patrols had been formed. Malcolm Mallace—the first Silver Wolf in Scotland—and Norman Peacock were leading amongst the Scouts. They approached Sandy Morrison and asked him to become their Scoutmaster. He being too much taken up already, turned the matter on to his then Scout Sergeant, the present Scoutmaster. Thus in May 1908 the troop became registered, and has continued through various times and circumstances ever since.

The Watsonian, *Jubilee Number, 1920.*

Cadet Soccer

Back Row.—J. Rettie, J. A. Ferguson, Mr Cooper, W. D. Morgan, R. Calder, Mr Adams.
Front Row—Mr Maclean, Mr Findlay, Mr Alison, Mr W. Anderson, Mr Doig,
Mr Welch, J. Melrose.

SCHOOL "SOCCER" TEAM.

Back Row.—Pipe-Cpl. D. Morrison, Pte. C. Robertson, Sgt. J. R. Hill, Sgt. D. Campbell,
Pte. H. M'Millan, Col.-Sgt. E. Thomson, Lce.-Cpl. Piper Butti.
Row.   Pte. N. B. Lothian, Pte. W. G. Stuart, Lieut. Morrison, Capt. Shepherd, Lieut. Sl
Col. O. Price, Sgt. J. Horne

The Cadets also encouraged football as in this Staff v Cadets match at Myreside on 11 March 1908. A hard, spirited, but fair game resulted in a 3–1 victory for the Staff.

Cadet Rivalry

FIELD EXERCISES.—On Saturday, 11th March, the Contingent, in conjunction with Heriot's O T.C., engaged in a tactical exercise on the ground of Swanston Farm, kindly placed at our disposal by Mr Jack. Heriot's took up a defensive position under the shadow of "Steep Caerketton," where they invited attack from our men. As usual, both sides won.

The Watsonian, *April 1911.*

Cadet Pipe Band

A START was made with the Tactical Exercises on 7th April, when the Corps defended Craiglockhart Hill against an attacking force consisting of the 3rd Highland Company, Q.R.V.B., R.S. (Captain Fleming). Several useful lessons were learned, and the movements were afterwards thoroughly discussed.

On that day also the Band made its first public appearance, and greatly improved the marching of the Corps.

The Watsonian, *June 1906.*

G.W.C. C.C.

The Cadet Corps, 1905/6 - What Happened to these Boys in the Great War?

In June 1906 photographs of the entire Cadet Corps were published in *The Watsonian*.

1. RP Cormack, Despatches **2.** PG Campbell, Served Mid East **3.** JG Jack, Invalided Out, 1918 **4.** E Thomson, Canada
5. HM Baikie, Engineers **6.** JS Rogerson, Canada, Killed 23.5.1917 **7.** R Ewing, Wounded, Despatches **8.** AR Ross, RAMC
9. WA Alexander, RAMC **10.** EF Ranken, Killed 5.3.1916 **11.** NB Lothian, Canada, Killed 15.5.1916 **12.** JA Ferguson, Indian Army
13. WN Wear, Unknown **14.** JH Smith, RAMC **15.** WL Morris, Wounded, 1915 **16.** L Dobbie, Unknown
17. N Morrison, Cameron H's, Wounded, 1917 **18.** AW Somerville, GWC Scout Master, Seaforth H's, Twice Wounded
19. PC Lempriere, GWC Dux and Gold Medalist, 1907. Served 1914–18 **20.** J McDonald, Served **21.** LBC Marksman, RAMC
22. F Young, Unknown **23.** HJ Scott, Killed at Loos, 1915 **24.** L McCallum, Unknown **25.** D Matheson, Served

1. O Price, Died Flu, 20.12.1918 **2.** E Pringle-Pattison, Wounded Sept 1917 **3.** JB Panton, Wounded, March 1918
4. D Stewart, Served **5.** J Gunn, Wounded 1915 **6.** A Storer, Unknown **7.** S Cranston, Military Cross **8.** R Aitken, Wounded, April 1917
9. J Wellsted, Unknown **10.** R Ritchie, Killed 20.5.1918 **11.** C Deane, School Captain, 1909/10, MC/DSC, Lieut Col 6th South Wales
Borderers (CO), Killed 29.5.1918 **12.** W Morgan, Cpt 1st XV, School Captain, MC/DSC/Croix de Guerre, 5 x Despatches
13. H Watson, Unknown **14.** JM Ewing, Unknown **15.** G Thomson, Killed 22.3.1918 **16.** J Gardiner, Unknown
17. M King, Unknown **18.** S Gibson, Unknown **19.** D Campbell, Wounded **20.** JB McGlashan, Gassed, October 1918
21. F Hird, RAMC, MC (1918), Despatches (1917) **22.** V Davis, Unknown **23.** J Gunn, Gallipoli, France, Mid East, Wounded, 1915
24. E Price, RAMC, Despatches

1. *JW Low, Transport* 2. *A Green, Navy, Despatchers* 3. *J Scougal* 4. *K MacLeod, RAMC, Killed, 1918* 5. *JR Hill, Killed, 3.6.1915*
6. *E Brown, Medical Orderly* 7. *A Sutherland, Unknown* 8. *C Stewart, Canada, Thrice Wounded* 9. *DM Murray, Wounded, 1917 &*
1918 10. *WS Stevenson, Thrice Wounded, MC/DSC, Croix de Geurre, 4 X Despatches* 11. *G Lammie, Wounded 1916, Gassed 1918,*
Despatches 12. *A McCrostie, Wounded* 13. *GS Mill, Gurkhas* 14. *J Allan, Unknown* 15. *FW Herald* 16. *J Stewart, Served*
17. *J Ross, Served, Russia* 18. *GSH Young, Killed Gallipoli, 13.7.1915* 19. *ES jackson, RFA, 1914–18*
20. *GW Cowan, Gallipoli, France, Tank Corps, MC, Despatches, Wounded, 1918* 21. *JL Geddes, Wounded, 1915*
22. *RC McCrankie, MC, Twice Wounded* 23. *E Milroy, Killed, 1916* 24. *C Anderson, Wounded, Ypres, 1916*
25. *J Wood, RAMC, Died, 14.9.1918* 26. *AC Currie, Killed, 1918* 27. *LM Wilson, Killed, 1918* 28. *JA Butti, Killed, 24.10.1918*

1. *JG Bell, Killed, 17.8.1918* 2. *PM Mcandrew, POW, 31.5.1918* 3. *AC Smith, Killed, Pozieres, 1916* 4. *W Aiton, Killed, 21.3.1918*
5. *HA McMillan, MC, Despatches, Wounded, 1917* 6. *A Christie, Unknown* 7. *F Begg, RAMC, Despatches* 8. *WJ Dey, Unknown*
9. *A Kerr, RAF* 10. *R Kennedy, Wounded, 1915* 11. *TA Torrance, Unknown* 12. *GD Fairlie, RAMC, wounded, July 1916*
13. *JS MacBeth, Saolnika, 1916–18* 14. *JB Morrison, Died/Wounds, 1918* 15. *G Lawson, Wounded, 1918* 16. *A Pole, Unknown* 17.
JWG Horne, Served, 1914–18 18. *J Black, Unknown* 19. *DJ Morrison, RAMC* 20. *RGN Young, MC, Killed, 21.3.1918*
21. *CF Allan, Killed Gallipoli, 28.6.1915* 22. *T Tucker, Unknown* 23. *AB Purves, Hong Kong, Civilian* 24. *WI Bell, MC, Croix de Guerre*
25. *W Kennedy, RAMC* 26. *W Anderson, Unknown* 27. *GG allan, RAMC, Torpedoed* 28. *MC Turiansky, (Torrance), RAMC*
29. *CW McIntosh, Served, 1914–19*

Missing From Photographs

1. W Robb – MC, 2 X Despatches, Wounded
2. EA Dale, Unkown
3. DC McGregor – Intelligence, GHQ 1917
4. AW Mather – RAMC
5. JH Weir – Invalided, April 1918
6. H Honeyman – Died of Wounds, Dec 1918
7. J Robb – Despatches, Croix de Chevalier, Legion of Honour, Wounded, 1915
8. R Stark – MC & Bar, Gassed 1917
9. J Strachan – 2 X Despatches, MC, Croix de Guerre
10. A Park – Killed 29.9.1918
11. GA Rusk – MC, Wounded April & June 1916
12. A Stewart – School Dux Killed 12.4.1918
13. J Plummer – Served RFA

Summary	
• Total (Inc. A Morrison)	120
• No Trace/Unsure	23 (18.3%)
• Served in WWI	96 (99%)*
• Killed-in-action/ Died of Wounds	25 (26%)*
• Wounded	26 (27%)*
• Military Cross	14 (14.2%)*
• Despatches	13 (13.4%)*
• Royal Army Medical Corps	14 (14.4%)*

As a % of those traced.

School Battalion, 1914

"I was one of the Spectators of the first dress parade of the Cadet Corps on a chilly afternoon late in 1905, and like many another Watson's boy from outside of Scotland, I was entranced with the pipes, so I joined the Cadet Corps to become a piper. a sergeant from the Seaforths (then stationed at the Castle) gave us lessons once a week, and after some weeks' tuition, I ventured to ask him how long it took to learn. His sardonic reply was that 'it would take the likes of you seven years and seven generation.' I put that dream away."

Former Pupil Eric Thomson from Canada, quoted in *The Watsonian*, May 1953.

A wet drill day means a lecture, the nature of which we, raw recruits, can only guess at, for it has never rained on a drill day yet, save once, when we were subjected to a gentle unbraiding of our faults. We believe great store is put by these lectures, and we may be pardoned for expressing the hope that one will come our way soon.

It is significant that in a large school such as ours no one has raised any objection to being drilled. The necessity, in this present crisis, of bearing such subsidiary evils as drill has enforced itself on the minds of all. Every one is impressed with a sense of duty, but should there be any misguided souls who may imagine that the path of glory is by way of a wilful disobedience to commands, there looms over them the grim, dread shadow of defaulters' drill.

It is not for us to speak of the progress we have made. We can, however, candidly admit that we know more about military matters than we did at the beginning of October; and that we know just enough to recognise how little we really know.

Just now the Meadows resent the appearance of having had all their grass crushed in the earth by countless human feet. For the benefit of strangers I may remark that we did drill in the Meadows. To produce such effects the drill must be strenuous. That it is. For one hour we tramp and turn and wheel, form sections, double incline and go through all manner of evolutions. At the end of the hour, you may be sure, we are not sorry to hear the whistle, sharp and shrill, summon us back to the playground.

Could you get a glimpse of the playground (perhaps I should say parade ground) at this hour you would see the Battalion at the 'Tention, you would feel the intense hush as the officers fall out, and would understand the feeling of relief when we hear,

"Battalion–Dismiss!" JSB (VI)

First Dress Parade, 1905.

In October 1914, *the entire school* was transformed by the Headmaster into a military-style 'School Battalion'. Those who were already in the OTC, or its junior training reserve, were also expected to take part. At first it was quite popular, but the boys soon realised that all it amounted to was drill, more drill and yet more drill with the added bonus of being bossed about by some members of the OTC. This was one enthusiastic response by the Headmaster which was gradually allowed to wither away.

The School Battalion idea didn't last long, but more permanent were the changes to the voluntary Cadets. The Great War saw an end to the green jacket and spats. Instead, the Corps donned khaki and hose. Before 1914, all Watson's Cadets wore blackcock feathers in their glengarries in imitation of their parent regiment, The Royal Scots, but that soon disappeared too. Only the Pipe Band still maintained an old tradition by continuing to wear the full pre-1914 uniform into the 1950s.

On the 2 October last, the Senior School, with the exception of the first year classes, assembled in the Hall. The headmaster, in a short speech, pointed out that it was the duty of one and all to join the OTC in this time of crisis. He gave in detail the conditions of joining, and concluded by ordering the whole school to parade in the playground. From that day to this we have paraded regularly every Monday and Friday.

The first year classes did not figure in the original scheme. It is because they bitterly resented such treatment that the Battalion in full strength appears in this number.

Lieutenant Gerard and a staff of competent officers control and manage the affairs of the battalion. Those who, from long service and ability, have attained a high place in the OTC are given command over their less fortunate fellows. The consequence is that the school is divided into squads, each with its own squad instructor, and each full of the belief that it is the best squad in the Battalion. The reader must not think that we have become an armed camp: for we have not yet got rifles. This is a grievance to many.

The early stages of our drill were marked by a tendency on our part to reduce the cosmos to chaos when we received the order to form fours on the march. The confusion has departed from us. We are become like unto machines. Wherefore hath drill become not a very pleasant subject, and one which we hope is but a necessary preliminary to better things.

"The land is lucky this year in having so many of last year's successful band back, and is looking forward to having another good year. There is a large number of piper recruits, and we trust that the hope that one day they may become full-fledged pipers will be some solace at least to the parents whose war-torn nerves must bear the full brunt of that fearsome din that bagpipes can produce in inexperienced hands. Piper recruits should be interned in a sound-proof garret, or marooned on some distant island – at least so think those who suffer from their practising."

A cheery note from The Watsonian, December 1917.

The School Battalion, 1914.

Raising a Watson's Pals' Battalion

This was seriously considered in the autumn of 1914 by a group, which included the redoubtable Sandy Morrison. In fact, it was probably his idea. Such battalions were extremely popular at that time and were associated with towns (eg Hull, Sheffield and Barnsley), or work (eg Commercials, Tramways, Post Office), or large organisations (eg Public Schools, Glasgow Boys' Brigade). So why not a school battalion?

The agency through which this could be achieved was created and named, *The Watson's Military Training Corps*. The aim was to be sanctioned by the War Office as a separate unit of Kitchener's New Army. Very quickly 350 Watsonians joined the Corps. However, a number somewhere around, or over, a 1,000 was the minimum required. Efforts to secure such a number within a short period failed and the War Office refused to recognise the Corps.

Having failed to create a battalion the idea then moved onto the idea of creating a Watson's Pals' battalion within an existing regiment. That also proved difficult, but large numbers joined the 4th, 9th or 15th Battalions of the Royal Scots, the parent regiment of Watson's Cadets. A warm reception in the 4th was assured as one in three of its officers were Watsonians.

The 9th was known locally as '*The Dandy Ninth*' because it was the only battalion of the Royal Scots dressed in full Highland military regalia. Indeed, the uniform of the Watson's Cadets had been modelled upon it, so it is hardly surprising that many ex-Cadets wished to enrol.

From J Ferguson's Record of the 9th, *published in 1909.*

War Work

Christmas 1914

Boys collected over £15 so that Miss Panton (the school cook) and her kitchen staff could make plum puddings for the troops. Staff collected £2 to buy tobacco. Ladies collected clothing. All sent to 2nd Royal Scots in France.

Some suggested gifting the puddings to the Germans who would then immediately surrender!

Staff

Ten had joined up by Christmas 1914, including the entire PE department. Others gave up free periods to cover. More and more women came to fill the ranks, but by 1918 even they were leaving to join the Wrens and WAAC.

The Watsonian in Trouble

In 1914 it was decided to send a copy to every serving Watsonian. Then photographs of the dead were published in each number. As the casualties mounted *The Watsonian* began to sink into debt. In 1915 the price was doubled to 6d and then doubled again in December 1918.

- Every week S3 pupils took wounded soldiers to tea in town (April 1916).

- Older boys went to summer logging or replanting camps.
- YMCA (1916) appealed for books for soldiers and got enough for 13 libraries!

The Literary Club

It held debates on several issues, eg
1. That men are mostly fools.
2. That war has been the most effective instrument of human progress.
3. That patriotism is to be condemned.
4. That Democracy and Empire are incompatible.

Watson's Scouts

Engaged in all sorts of war work, eg Red Cross, message carrying, orderlies at recruiting offices. All this counted towards a War Service Badge. In April 1917 four Scouts were praised for helping day and night with the arrival of wounded soldiers at Waverley Station. Some took part in coastguard duties.

Muscles

Teachers volunteered (1915) to work during the holidays in a munitions factory in Barrow, or local farms. Some said this would improve school discipline as it would strengthen 'belting arms'!

Fund Raising

- Oct 1914 – staff began a monthly levy. First amount went to Belgian refugees and then the Red Cross.
- April 1915 – Ladies of the College held a sale of work which raised £175 for the Waverley Station Tea Room Fund.
- Boys continually raise funds, eg the Boys College Bed in the Infirmary for wounded soldiers.

Watson's Boys.

Boys, boys, boys !
Just an avalanche of boys
With the maximum of noise
   On the stairs :
Rushing, crushing, in your hurry
To be done with school-time worry
   And its cares.

Din, din, din !
When the pipes and drums begin
After three, while we're kept in
   Here perchance.
Yet they make our sad hearts thrill
With the thought of war's stern drill
   There in France.

Watson's boys !
When man's power to you belongs
Be ye eager to right wrongs
   At life's call !
Be ye worthy of their fame
Who have fought in freedom's name,
   'Sonians all !

The Watsonian, *July 1916*

Sandy Morrison

Captain 1st XV, 1904–6
First School Captain, 1905–6
Founder of the Cadet Corps, 1904
Founder of The Watsonian, *1903*
Founder of GWC Scouts, 1908
Founder of the Training Corps, 1914

Most obituaries were terse, but, on occasion, someone's contribution to school life had been so great that much more was deemed appropriate. Captain Alexander Morrison, 5th Cameron Highlanders, rightly belonged to that select band. Sandy had been born in Oban, the third son of Mr and Mrs John Morrison, but moved to Canaan Grove, Edinburgh. Sandy entered Watson's in 1899. He was killed-in-action on 25 September 1915 leading his company during the Battle of Loos in a charge upon the infamous Hohenzollern Redoubt. With every Scottish regiment represented, Loos had the largest concentration of fighting Scots in any battle in history. The casualties were, quite simply, shocking. Sadly, like so many others, Sandy has no known grave and is commemorated on the Loos Memorial, Dud Corner Cemetery, Panels 119–124. At least 13 other Watsonians are commemorated alongside him, 11 being killed on the same day. The photograph was taken when he was School Captain.

Soldier Poets

Alexander Robertson (far left) & Arthur James (Hamish) Mann (left).

Alexander Robertson

Alexander was born on 12 January 1882, son of the Headmaster of Edinburgh Ladies' College. He entered Watson's in 1890 and gained a First Class Honours Degree at Edinburgh University in 1906. He then taught in Watson's and at the Lyce in Caen before embarking upon postgraduate studies at Oxford. In February 1914, he was appointed Lecturer in History at Sheffield University. Six months later Alexander enlisted as a Private in '*The Sheffield Pals*.' After some time in Egypt his Battalion was ordered to France in March 1916.

At 7.30am on 1 July 1916, Alexander took part in the opening attack of the Battle of the Somme at the village of Serre. The men were met with shell, rifle and machine-gun fire. Within minutes he had been hit and his body was never found. He is commemorated on the Thiepval Memorial to the Missing.

Alexander wrote two books of poems: *Comrades* and *Last Poems*.

Lines Before Going

Soon is the night of our faring to regions unknown,
There not to flinch at the challenge suddenly thrown
By the great process of Being – daily to see
The utmost that life has of horror and yet to be
Calm and the masters of fear. Aware that the soul
Lives as a part and alone for the weal of the whole,
So shall the mind be free from the pain of regret,
Vain and enfeebling, firm in each venture, and yet
Brave not as those who despair, but keen to maintain,
Though not assured, hope in beneficent pain,
Hope that the truth of the world is not what appears,
Hope in the triumph of man for the price of his tears.

Arthur James (Hamish) Mann

Hamish was born on 5 April 1896 in Broughty Ferry, near Dundee. He attended Watson's between 1904–13. His family lived at Red House in South Gillsland Road. At the beginning of the war Hamish assisted at Craigleith Military Hospital (now the Western General) and became joint editor of *The Craigleith Chronicle* submitting articles under the name of Lucas Cappe.

In August 1916, Hamish joined The Black Watch and fought in the Battle of the Somme. On his way to High Wood on 9 October 1916, he wrote *The Zenith*.

The Zenith

To-day I reached the zenith of my life!
No time more noble in my span of years
Than this, the glorious hour of splendid strife,
Of War, of cataclysmal woe, and tears.
All petty are the greatest things of yore,
All mean and sordid is my dearest lay;
I have done nothing more worth while before …
My hour, my chance, my crisis, are today!

On the opening day of the Battle of Arras, 9 April 1917, Hamish was wounded and died the following day. Three days before the attack he penned his last and most famous poem, *The Great Dead*, put to music in 2003 by one of our pupils, Kirsty Gorman.

The Great Dead

Some lie in graves beside the crowded dead
In village churchyards; others shell holes keep,
Their bodies gaping, all their splendour sped.
Peace, O my soul … A Mother's part to weep.

Say: do they watch with keen all-seeing eyes
My own endeavours in the whirling hell?
Ah, God! how great, how grand the sacrifice.
Ah, God! the manhood of yon men who fell!

And this is War … Blood and a woman's tears,
Brave memories adown the quaking years.

Peary; The Myreside Pals

James Pearson was born on 24 February 1888 and lived at 3 East Castle Road. He attended Watson's from 1896 to 1907. Although short and light Peary became a giant on the sports field playing for both the 1st XI and 1st XV school teams, winning the 1907 School Championship against formidable opposition and becoming one of the best known and loved Internationalists of his age.

Peary had the good fortune to play alongside two future great internationalists, Eric Milroy and Alex Angus, as well as the dominant Watsonian of the day, Sandy Morrison. Only Angus would survive the war as a Lt-Col in the Gordon Highlanders, winning the DSO and mentioned three times in despatches.

Those four were good friends – chums or pals to use the then fashionable words. They socialised, had a laugh and got into scrapes. The story below comes from *The Watsonian* of 1929 and gives us a rare glimpse into the social life of pre-1914 Watson's youngsters. 'Ben' was Ben Gray who emigrated to Canada, joined the Canadian Army in 1914 and was killed at Vimy Ridge in April 1917. A Lost Generation indeed.

The earliest known photograph of Peary, 1904.

A modern GWC sportsman, Jamie Woods, beside Peary's grave, 2002.

There must be many who remember pleasant Saturday (or Sunday) afternoons (or evenings) spent in Ben's flat in Bruntsfield Place. Myresiders and non-Myresiders, former pupils, younger brothers, "swots," and loafers climbed the long stair and spent an hour or two (and sometimes five or six) discussing poetry, football, religion, food, politics, or love with this prince of eccentrics. On a wet winter Sunday afternoon you might find there Sandy Morrison, the Angus brothers, Robin Law, Duncan Macgregor, Tom Bowie, Donald MacInnes, Pat Watson, and a few more. One summer evening some of us had gone up there to get a good view of one of the cyclists' processions of those days. One of the party, leaning over the window, was amusing himself with a pea-shooter and a pocketful of peas. A complaint from an onlooker brought up to the door a heavy-footed constable who was wearing very wide trousers. We stood with bowed heads in the passage and listened to his rebuke. All was going well until Jimmy Pearson in the background made some disparaging remark about "the slop's breeks." That settled it. All our names and addresses were noted down and we were instructed to report at Causewayside Police Station at such-and-such a time. Sandy Morrison was not in the flat that afternoon, but when we crept into the Inspector's room, wondering whether it would be the birch or penal servitude, we found Sandy sitting in an armchair beside the Inspector. The latter, with a twinkle in his eye, brought home to us the gravity of the offence, but "let us off." In the street outside Sandy accepted our thanks for his intercession, and gave us the good advice, "put not your trust in princes: make friends with the police." A trivial thing to remember. I forget who were all there and know not where some of them are now, but the tenant of the flat, and the friend of the police, and the critic of the constabulary trousers are in "some corner of a foreign field that is for ever" Scotland and Watson's.

Not less memorable were those suppers in Newbattle Terrace, in the little room on the ground floor, when Sandy entertained with Highland hospitality and Highland music. During supper a small boy (who is now a member of Parliament) and one (or sometimes two) of his brothers had to pace solemnly up and down the room playing the pipes. Then came the long ascent to the sanctum on the top floor and the philosophy and the poetry and the charm of Sandy.

This article was published in The Watsonian *in 1929.*

Tom Bowie.

Robin Law.

Eric Milroy.

Sandy Morrison.

Alex Angus.

David Angus.

Ben Gray.

Peary scored 103 tries and a total of 338 points for Watsonians during their golden age when the unofficial rugby football championship of Scotland was won in 1908/9, 1909/10, 1911/12 and 1913/14. Watsonians' success was based on players with football skills playing together in combination, the fulcrum being the half-backs and the centre-threequarters who were a superb mid-field quartet, including Peary. His speed as an athlete combined with his football skills made him a centre-threequarter of international standard and he played 12 matches for Scotland.

His final appearance on a rugby pitch was at the Melrose Sports in April 1914. The memorable moment happened when Peary gained possession behind the goal line and ran the length of the pitch to score a try and win the Ladies' Cup.

When war broke out on 4 August 1914 Peary joined the Watsonian Military Training Corps led by his pal Sandy Morrison. Peary needed the training as he had never joined the school Cadets. When the idea of a Pals' Battalion collapsed Peary joined the 9th Royal Scots, 'The Dandy Ninth' which became the first Edinburgh Territorial Regiment to go to the Front. Arriving on 26 February 1915 in the Ypres Salient the Ninth were caught up in the aftermath of the world's first gas attack at St Julien, helping to stem the German advance.

On 27 April the Battalion was in Sanctuary Wood digging trenches frantically under a massive artillery bombardment as the Germans attempted to hammer their way into Ypres. The Ninth held its line until the night of 22–23 May when it was eventually relieved.

It was Peary's bad luck to be hit by a sniper just hours before he was due to leave Sanctuary Wood. He was going to get water for tea. His grave was destroyed by shellfire, but miraculously found in 1930. In that year a comrade wrote this account in *The Watsonian*:

"Sanctuary Wood has many memories, but there is one which transcends all others—the sight of the wee white face with the little smile as we filed passed the little athlete lying in his last long sleep, clad not in the panoply of greatness which he deserved, but in the common tunic and kilt of a private lying like a warrior taking his rest, with a blood-stained greatcoat round him.

"His name was known and loved by thousands. Countless times he had thrilled them with his genius, and now, in the sacred cause, he had laid down his life as a humble soldier. Never again will the little round-shouldered figure, with its long arms and gloved hands, gather a ball unerringly as of yore; but there must always be one spot in Sanctuary Wood that is for ever hallowed in Scottish Rugger hearts—the resting-place of Jimmy P., peerless three-quarter, private soldier, and gentleman." J. H.

Watson's Bombed

The account below was written by a Watson's schoolboy and comes from the December 1918 number of *The Watsonian* – the first permitted account.

DORA was the 'Defence of the Realm Act' which authorised censorship. The Leaving (Leavers) Certificate was the equivalent of 'Highers'

Pace DORA

"DORA is dead, or at least dying. We are therefore in a position officially to inform our readers there was an air raid on Edinburgh and especially George Watson's College, on the morning of the 3rd of April 1916.

Why the 3rd of April? If you mark the coincidence, the Latin 'Leavings' were to be held – and were held – on that day. Now it is not for us to pry into the combined mysteries of the doings of the German High Command and the Leaving Certificate Examinations, and the relations these bear to one another. Mr Le Queux will probably tell us all about it in his revelations of the secret life of the ex-Kaiser. Till then we shall say nothing.

To descend from the general to the particular, it happened that the writer of this article was one of the unhappy wights doomed to spend that day in the torture cham— I mean the Examination Hall. The night before I had gone to bed sorrowful, for I felt I knew nothing whatsoever about the work for the exam. At 12.56 3/4 am I was awakened and informed that an air raid was in progress.

Without a moment's hesitation I arose and bolted for the cellar, snatching up a Latin Grammar en route. After some half-hour of study in that region I returned to bed, little dreaming of the happy aim that had attended one of the enemies' missiles. On my road to School in the morning I met several joyous persons who informed me that the Easter holidays had begun—compulsorily. Eager to know the worst, I hurried on and discovered that, raids notwithstanding, I had a morning of examination yet to pass through. Of that paper let us say nothing. Suffice it that we examinees were to some degree recompensed by being the only ones allowed inside the gates, with the result that both before and after the exam, a casual observer might have though that a lesson in the gentle art of digging oneself in under fire was being given, such was the number of people lying down in the dust, and excavating feverishly. A closer inspection proved, however, that the industrious grovellers were merely souvenir-

The plaque, made from the bomb's heavy iron casing, was placed on the wall after the War. Now in the History corridor.

A bronze Prussian eagle was set into the pavement. Who has it now?

hunters in search of fragments of bomb. How many pieces of commonplace lead piping are still being treasured as mementos of the Great War I do not venture to say.

The damage done, though fairly serious, was noting in comparison with the excited reports that were flying about among those who has not seen the 'ruins'. The outside wall of Room 1, beside which the bomb fell, was blown in, while all the windows in the front of the School had vanished in the night. The passages, too, were thickly carpeted with a mysterious powder, consisting apparently of crumbled plaster, broken glass, window-frames, classroom doors and such like trifes. Several enthusiastic scientists were keen to take samples for home analysis.

'It's an ill wind' etc, and there were some compensating features even about an air raid. First and foremost was the additional week's holiday obtained (though a raid appears to be much less powerful in this line than epidemic influenza); and, let it be whispered gently, some vindictive spirits seemed to find a curious pleasure in contemplating the havoc wrought in certain class-rooms belonging to masters

with ideas on the subject of tidiness. But the chief recompense was the pride we felt that, though not ourselves in the trenches, we too had experienced War. The scars still remain on the fence at the School, and the battered pillar from the steps stands in the playground as a reminder to future generations of what happened to Watson's in the War– and also forming most convenient wickets for the use of small boys' summer game of miniature cricket."

AHC (VII)

During the Zeppelin air raid on the night of 2 and 3 April 1916, a bomb fell on the playground just outside the west wing Classrooms, smashing windows and doing considerable damage. To the excitement of the boys was the added satisfaction of an additional week's holiday. A plaque was set in the wall near the point of impact, and a German eagle was set in the pavement. Both of these were offered to the Merchant Company Education Board by the demolition contractors after Watson's moved from Archibald Place to Colinton road.
H Waugh (ed),
George Watson's College, 1970

The Bomb was dropped here on 3 April 1916.

Remembering 1914–18: Family Memorials

The Ford Trophy (April 1916)

This was the first family memorial to be announced.

"Mr G Ford, Portobello, in memory of his two sons, George Turner and Charles Henry Ford, 1/4th Royal Scots, both pupils of Watson's, who fell at the Dardanelles on 28 June 1915, has endowed an athletic prize for the school to be known hereafter as the 'Ford Prize'. It will be awarded for the 220 yards race at the Sports in May. In the name of the School we tender the generous donor heartiest thanks for his gift, and trust that those who win in future years may be animated with the same heroic spirit as those whose memory it commemorates."

JOHN RANKEN,
Corporal, A Coy., 1/4th Royal Scots.
Wounded in Gallipoli 28th and
died 29th June 1915.
Mentioned in Dispatches.
School Period 1885-1898.
His first mile, W.C.A.C., 4m. 59s.   -   1898
His best mile, S.A.A.C., 4m. 30½s.   -   1903
Scottish Cross Country Champion   -   1904
And   -   -   -   -   -   1905

ERNEST FORD RANKEN,
2nd Lieut., 7th K.O.S.B.
Wounded 20th March and died at St Omer,
France, 25th March 1916.
School Period 1894-1906.
Joined Cadet Corps at Formation.
Played in Watsonian Rugby Team
1911 to 1914.
Both joined their old Battalion,
4th Royal Scots, 5th August 1914.

George Turner Ford (left) and Charles Henry Ford (right).

The Ranken Memorial Trophy.

Two of Mr Ford's four sons were killed in WW1, both on the same day, in the same Regiment and within yards of each other in Gully Ravine, Gallipoli.

The Ranken Memorial Trophy (July 1917)

John was a great runner, gaining Scottish Athletic International honours for four years. He was killed while leading a bombing party on a Turkish trench. Ernest was famous for cycling, football and rugby.

> *We tender the generous donor heartiest thanks for his gift, and trust that those who win in future years may be animated with the same heroic spirit as those whose memory it commemorates.*

The Eric Milroy Trophy (Spring 1920)

"The relatives of Eric Milroy have intimated to the Headmaster their intention of presenting an athletic trophy in his memory. It will probably be awarded for the Place and Drop Kick competition at the games. we thank the donors very sincerely for this permanent memorial of so fine a man and so loyal a Watsonian."

Eric was a brilliant rugby player and played in almost every International Match from 1910 to 1914. He toured with the British team in S Africa in 1910. Eric first joined the 9th Royal Scots, but soon gained a commission with The Black Watch. He died during the Battle of the Somme whilst engaged upon an attack on Delville Wood in July 1916. His body was never found.

College Memorials

In the July 1916 *Watsonian* a letter was published from an Arthur Hunter in New York who suggested the creation of a relief fund to aid orphans and dependants of those killed or maimed. This was eventually to lead to the establishment of the Watsonian War Memorial Fund in July 1917. This would provide a permanent memorial and financial assistance to those in need. By December 1919, the enormous sum of £9,594 had been raised. Designs were then sought for a permanent memorial and it was also decided to publish a *Watsonian War Record* to commemorate all those who served during the Great War.

By December 1920, 50 dependants were being supported by the new fund and a drawing was produced showing the proposed new permanent memorial which would cost around £3,000. During the Winter Term of 1921 the memorial was erected in front of the main school steps. On Friday 16 December at 3pm the memorial was

The unveiling of the memorial, December 1921.

unveiled after a solemn ceremony by the Chancellor of the Exchequer, Sir Robert Horne. This is the memorial which was later moved to Colinton Road. Note the OTC, Pipe Band and the ERI building in the background.

An indoor memorial in the form of a fine carved display cabinet to hold the *Watsonian War Record* was presented by Mr John Crerar and friends. Does anyone know where this is? Two new cabinets are now in the Library and pages from the Memorial books for both World Wars are still religiously turned each day by Mrs Hooper.

Other Memorials

"To record, for future generations, the insensate brutality of the Hun, the Merchant Company Education Board has placed on the wall of the College, nearest the spot where the Zepp Bomb struck, a bronze tablet with this inscription —

'THIS CITY WAS RAIDED BY GERMAN AIRSHIPS ON THE NIGHT OF 2ND APRIL 1916. NEAR THIS SPOT A BOMB EXPLODED, CAUSING SERIOUS DAMAGE TO THE COLLEGE BUILDINGS.'

The precise point of impact is marked with a Prussian eagle in bronze, let into the pavement.

Near by stands a captured German field-gun. The conjunction of the two is not without significance to the reflecting mind."
December 1919

All the 420 obituaries in *The Watsonian* had been written by the Head of English, Mr Henry John Findlay, who also spent countless hours preparing the now invaluable *Watsonian War Record, 1914–18*.

ARMA VIRUMQUE by WS Craig (VI). Two field-guns were given to Watson's by the government as war trophies. What happened to them?

In 1922 this oak Memorial was made to hold a copy of the **Watsonian War Record** *and paid for by John Crerar and friends. It was placed at the head of the central staircase facing the clock. In 1932, it was erected in the Masonic Hall (now part of the Library). Does anyone know where it rests now?*

The First Armistice Day Remembrance, 1919

"On 11 November we joined in the national Act of Remembrance by observing the two minutes' silence in our classrooms. The drums of the Corps sounded in the corridors, and the classes, suspending their work, stood to attention for the prescribed time, with a very full understanding of, and sympathy with, the meaning and significance of the act."

Steps to a New School, 1924–32

Why Move?

- The building was old-fashioned, dark and cramped despite efforts to modernise it.
- It was confined to a small area with little room to expand especially after the wings had been built.
  There was limited room for safe play or recreation. The playground was used by everyone from 5 to 18 year olds.
  A plan in 1893 to combine all the bottom level classrooms, lower the floor by 12 inches and tar it to provide a wet-weather playing area for younger pupils came to nothing.
- A swimming bath was now seen as a necessity. There was no room to build one at Lauriston. Pupils used Warrender Baths.
- The school was distant from its playing fields at Myreside. Sport, fitness and exercise became more fashionable in the 1920s.
- The Infirmary needed to expand. In 1932, it was said that 3,000 patients could not be treated unless its facilities were improved.
- It needed the Watson's site as the alternative was to build the entire Infirmary elsewhere which would be far too costly.
- Merchiston Castle School wanted to move westwards from its site around the old castle (now Napier University). As this was adjacent to Watson's land at Myreside it provided an opportunity to move and have ample room to develop.

STEP 1
28 November 1924
Merchant Company Annual Dinner

- Announced that it had been decided to sell the Archibald Place building for a 'fair' price to the Infirmary.
- The cost of the new site would be greater, so people were urged to support the new venture by contributions.
- No site was chosen, but space, especially for athletics, was important after the cramped site at Lauriston.

STEP 2
1 January 1925

The Watsonian Club offered its services to help finance the new buildings, but there was obviously a lot of hostility to the proposed sale. The President of The Watsonian Club, HJ Findley, described it as *"sentiment and conservatism"*. A lot of persuasion was, therefore, necessary to gain active support. It was announced that an anonymous donor had already given £1,000. The ball had started to roll …

STEP 3
Spring 1925–Spring 1926
Negotiations between the Merchant Company Education Board and the Infirmary continued for a year.

- £90,000 was agreed as the price of the sale of the school.
- Only a donation of £10,000 by John Finday saved the negotiations from collapse.
- The Infirmary would take possession in 1931.
- A new site for the new school was now urgent.

STEP 6
Winter 1927: A Start

- All competition plans had to be sent in by 31 March 1928. Winner was to be announced next summer. What was required was a well-proportioned, dignified, light, airy and fire-resistant building, but, above all, *"economy is imperative"*.
- Access for builders to Merchiston Playing Fields would start on 11 November 1928.
- The War Memorial would be moved to the new school.

STEP 5
Summer 1927: Site Decided

- Main School to be built on the old Merchiston School playing fields parallel to Colinton Road. The classrooms would face the sun.
- The Elementary School would be built around Merchiston Castle. The old keep would be retained as a feature. Some of the school would be built across the road around the Abbotsford Park area.

STEP 4
Winter 1926: Nothing Definite

- Negotiations were still continuing with Merchiston Castle School to buy the site around the Castle, but a deal was close.
- A competition was opened for architects to design the new school for *"… a site which in openness and outlook must surely be incomparably superior to that of any day school in the kingdom."*

STEP 7
June 1928: Competition Winner

- Judged by John Keppie of the Royal Institute of British Architects. Winner was James B Dunn, a Watsonian, whose plan was described as *"simple, direct and masterly style"*. The runners-up got 100 guineas each.
- The cost of the new building was calculated at £160,000.
- The Scottish Education Department (SED) would be consulted re the plans.

STEP 8
Winter 1928: Progress Slow

- Slower progress than expected. The SED suggested improvements, eg heightening the corridors to a minimum of 12 feet, making the Assembly Hall oblong and its floor flat instead of sloped. The extra cost would be £20,000.
- Hoped to start building in April/May 1929.
- New Merchiston Castle School building was going well.
- Speed necessary as the Infirmary wanted entry in November 1931.
- Hoping to open the new Watson's in September 1931.

STEP 9

August 1929: Building Starts
See details and photographs further on.

STEP 10

July 1930: Appeal Brochure Appears
Glossy brochure produced to help raise funds. £150,000 needed. Described as *"a venture of faith."*

STEP 11

Summer – Winter 1930: Drama
- On 25 August 1930 James Dunn, the architect, died. His son Herbert and partner, George Martin, continued with the work.
- The SED recommended that the Elementary School should not be built around Merchiston Castle because there was only a limited amount of land there for facilities, the school administration would be fragmented and the heating costs would be far greater than if supplied from the Main Building. Suggested a new site to the south of the *"Pleasure Ground at Merchiston Gardens."* Watson's agreed.
- George Martin designed new plans – for inspiration he visited some Lanarkshire schools – which helps explain why the Junior school doesn't really fit the design used elsewhere!
- All this delayed the work considerably.

STEP 12

Winter 1930 – Summer 1932: Building Continues
- Because of the delays (yet another caused by the increased depth of the foundations) the Infirmary had to wait a year to gain access to the old school.
- Although the new school impressed people, Watson's still had difficulty raising the necessary funds. Part of the problem was that of 9,000 ex-pupils only 4,700 had been found.
- The War Memorial was removed in the Spring of 1932.
- The new building was completed in the Summer.
- The Opening Ceremony was arranged for Thursday 22 September 1932.

Now used as the Head Boy's and Girl's symbol of office the torch was originally the School Captain's. Carved in 1934 by a member of staff, J Parnell, the oak was taken from the front stair rail of the old school in Archibald Place – see picture above. The silver was the work of D Stuart, an FP.

Former pupils took, or bought, souvenirs from Archibald Place. A supporting pedestal of one of the pilasters of the balustrade of the old school was sent to decorate Carl Smith's garden in Dunedin, New Zealand. Has anyone got other souvenirs?

Significant Changes

Given the enormity of the job surrounding a new school the old Headmaster, John Alison, decided that after 22 years as Head he would rather retire. In April 1926 George Robertson was appointed and he immediately began changes most of which are still with us.

Robertson had started at Watson's when he was four years old and in 1899 left with a GWC bursary. After brilliant careers at Edinburgh and Oxford Universities he became a Professor of Classics in South Africa.

George Robertson, 1926–43.

In 1913, he returned to Dulwich College and between 1914–25 was Headmaster of Eltham College, Kent. Many of his 'new' ideas were simply borrowed from his English experience. In those days Anglicisation was seen by some as being 'socially progressive."

How absurd it seems now that Scots should ape and copy the attributes of what was arguably one of the worst systems of schooling devised in the industrial world.

Robertson's aloof character seems to have been tolerated or loathed in equal measure.

Morning Registration Begins, Winter 1926

"The last strokes of the School bell in the morning no longer peal to the ears of a crowd racing at the last moment for the Hall. After the first few strokes of the bell the playground is deserted. A roll-call has been instituted in the hall before prayers."

Homework Policy Introduced, Spring 1927

"The said High Olympians have also brought into force a novel scheme whereby no boy may do more than two hours of work each night. This idea might be popular were it not also decreed that no boy may do less than two hours."

Classes into Forms, Summer 1927

"Since our return to School, our humble 'Classes' have been elevated to the status of 'Forms'. We are more conscious of our new dignity than the Staff, who still persist in sending boys up to their 'Class'-masters."

Assembly Hymn Singing Introduced, Winter 1927

"Hymn-singing has been introduced into the morning service this term and, we are glad to note, has been an immense success. Several of the older boys seem reluctant 'to make a joyful noise,' but we expect they will soon overcome this shyness. The notice board has been graced, indeed, with a song on the subject, but we believe that it has been perpetrated by one who does not take part but only looks and listens."

The 'College Blazer' was the Sports Blazer which some had worn for that purpose for several years. It was not compulsory for all from 1927, but it is clear that pressure was being applied. In 1929, the blazer was indeed made compulsory for those up to and including S4, but only during the Summer Term. Robertson hoped the older boys would wear it. Only the tie and cap were compulsory throughout the year. Shorts were still worn by boys right up to the end of S4 ("preferably" grey with maroon socks). Only boys from S5 could wear long trousers. The fact is that most chose to wear the new blazer – or rather their parents chose for them!

In 1939, school uniform was made compulsory although the colour of the shorts was changed to navy blue. The pullover was specified as "plain grey, V-necked". Robertson's last piece of absurd Anglicisation was to force all into shorts, including S6. This foolishness, unfortunately, lasted until the late 1940s.

School Uniform Begins, Summer 1927

"A welcome change for the brighter has been inaugurated this Term in the compulsory wearing of the College blazer. It has been noticed that the University are affecting to emulate this scheme. Probably as a result of the above innovation, several new summer fashions have come into being – as, for instance, the wearing of blue shorts and cricket shirts, and the pernicious habit of turning up the collar of one's blazer."

> *Farewell, thou multi-coloured tie;*
> *Farewell, thou sporting jacket;*
> *Full many a day must you and I*
> *Forego our wonted 'habit'.*
>
> *Farewell, your gorgeous reign is past.*
> *Farewell, till school is over;*
> *Till I have left behind at last*
> *That institution's cover.*
>
> *But meantime I must don attire*
> *Ordained by the Head,*
> *And under threat of penance dire*
> *Appear at the school 'a Red'.*
>   *JSW (V)*

Watson's usually closed at the end of July and started towards the end of September. A change in SED examination dates, however, meant that September was a wasted month. Robertson wanted the session to end in June, but this was not achieved until after WW2.

Rules for Everything, Spring 1931

"The edict has gone forth that all books brought to School must henceforth be surrounded by a strap. One wonders what to call some of the articles used for this purpose."

New House System, Spring 1931

The system had stagnated, so rivalry was introduced, *"... to raise standards of various activities."* There would be more House matches and teams with points so allocated that every pupil, *"... will have to be either a help or a dead-weight to the House."* Academic *"progress"* marks would also count towards the House Championship.

Building Begins

South Block. Main Corridor, looking east.

South Block. SW Corner – the lowest level.

August 1929

Building work started on the old Merchiston Castle playing fields. The War Memorial Car Park was built on Number 1 Merchiston Rugby Pitch whilst our Assembly Hall sits on top of the erstwhile Merchiston Cricket Square! The main contractor was James Miller & Sons Ltd. Colin Macandrew built the Elementary School.

The Main Entrance.

Girder for the New Hall.

Spring 1930

Work was well advanced on the Main Building. Note the light railway built to carry materials onto the site. On 19 May a giant girder 45 feet long and weighing 8 tons arrived by rail from Glasgow at Lothian Road goods yard. From there a powerful steam lorry carried it along Lothian Road, but it still took an hour to get to Colinton Road. It was to be used to take the whole weight of the roof above the stage in the Assembly Hall, but progress was delayed as two thrushes had built a nest in the bogey needed to transfer it onto the site.

The Main Entrance.

Girder for the New Hall.

Winter 1930

The Main Building had been roofed and work was beginning inside. The architect, James Dunn, died suddenly and the work was taken over by his son Herbert and partner, George Martin. The Merchiston Castle site for the Elementary School was abandoned and this caused a considerable delay.

Open-air Gymnasium, 1932.

The Gymnasium, Spring 1932.

The Elementary Block, Spring 1932.

West Quad, Spring 1932.

Winter 1931

By the summer of 1931 the plasterers and glaziers were busy in the Main Building while the playgrounds were being furrowed with trenches for drains. The PE block and the swimming bath, however, were still not roofed. The Prep School building was way behind schedule, but Tipperlinn had just been sown with grass seeds and the new embankments turfed.

Building work continued throughout the winter. It was hoped to gain entry by the Summer Term, but there were further delays. The final building – the grandstand at New Myreside – was about to be started.

LEFT: Swimming Baths, Spring 1932
RIGHT: Summer 1932.

Spring 1932

The Prep School had now been roofed and the internal work was about to begin. The swimming bath was just about finished, as was the Assembly Hall. The Quads were about to be tar-macadamed. An entry date was decided:

"Thursday 22 September will be a date of note for Watson's."

A huge amount still had to be done at New Myreside to complete the grandstand, terracing and pitch on land that had once belonged to Cluny Rugby Club. A little-known fact is that the terracing is composed of rubble from the foundations of the old school in Archibald Place.

Mr J Crawford, President SRU, opening the stand, 4 March 1933.

Features of the New School – Information and Quotes from *The Scotsman* Newspaper 1932

42 acre site, including Myreside. Total expenditure was £250,000.

Geography had special map tables supplied, plus a clay modelling table and the rooms were given special blinds for showing slides, etc..

The School Museum had special showcases now occupied by the Biology Department.

Science labs with all mod cons including a tiny window in the walls for distance telephony and telegraphy experiments

The huge chimney needed for the boiler house was objected to by local residents. The height was lowered and the residents politely told to get used to it.

A forecourt for parades. Now the front hockey pitch.

The latest 'endless band' blackboards with tray beneath to catch chalk dust.

Entrance Hall (80x32ft). *"Here we have a cool translucent atmospheric green, which suggests to some degree a shimmering submarine effect, with just a hint of mystery and illusion."* This was the staff entrance and to be used for ceremonials. The flat lights in the ceiling for daylight plus electric corner lights were novel. The terrazzo work (bits of stone set in cement and polished) was chosen for its clean smoothness. It was the first time this effect had been used

on pillars. A touch of gold was said to enhance the entire effect.

The Assembly Hall
Can seat 1,835. Oak floor, but, as elsewhere in the school, cedar panelling. The ceiling is coved and lighted by semicircular lights. *"Ornamentation and relief are provided by pilaster retrievement."* Two grilled recesses either side of the stage for the later installation of an organ (eventually built by Sandy Keith, Ron Looker, Jim Braithwaite, Roy Mack and others between October 1978 and December 1982). Seating by easily folded wooden seats of three with rubber 'suspension'. An orchestra pit with lights was provided as was an efficient lighting system for dramatic productions. Changing rooms existed behind the stage. A fireproof projection room was provided to show films.

Stone from Doddington, Northumberland, which was part of the battlefield of Flodden (1513).

Crevices avoided to make cleaning easier (eg curved edges to the corridor floors).

State-of-the-art kitchens with a special machine for making fish and chips. The cafeteria system with trays was in use even then.

"...a revolution in architectural method and purpose ... no attempt has been

made to imitate a temple or Gothic cathedral ... ornamentation which is unnecessary has been avoided."

Non-slip stone used on all stairs.

Radiators on brackets for easy floor cleaning and put beneath hooks to dry pupils' coats.

Open-air gym floored with unusual jarrah wood which is extremely hard and now very expensive.

New filter system in the Swimming Pool was so good that it turned brown Edinburgh Corporation water into blue Watson's water!

Airy classrooms facing the sunny south. Ventilation by using the hopper system operated by a worm gear turned by a key.

Master electric clock which sets the time for all the clocks, plus a device using pins for ringing period bells. An *"absolutely mechanical"* system, which was ultra-modern in 1932.

Automatic telephones installed in every department. *"This arrangement obviously increases the headmaster's power of control."*

Oak and walnut porch. First time these woods were used together.

The Golden Key

Thursday 22 September 1932

- An OTC guard of honour was drawn up on the hockey pitch with kilts, rifles and glinting bayonets. Behind them was the Pipe Band and behind that were long lines of maroon-coloured school jackets and caps. The public stood in the last few rows.

- At 2.30pm prompt HRH Prince George arrived with an entourage at the East Gate. The Master of the Merchant Company, Gilbert Archer, whose grandson kindly donated the photograph on the right, met him. Prince George is in the front on the left and Gilbert Archer is beside him.

- The School Captain, Fred Keay, gave a wreath of red poppies to Prince George who then laid it at the War Memorial.

- The party then walked to the Main Entrance. The OTC gave a general salute and the Pipe Band played 'The Garb of Old Gaul' in honour of the OTC's association with The Royal Scots.

- Prince George inspected the Corps and stopped at Angus Dow (17) who at 6ft 4in was 'the Goliath of the Guard'. The Prince asked him if he was still growing. Angus just said, *"Naw!"* The Prince smiled and moved on.

- At the main door the architect, George Martin, presented the Prince with a Golden Key to formally open the school.

- The Hall was full of guests and a large orchestra played selections.

- Speeches followed. The Prince said he was glad that at last there was *"… a recognition of the importance of physical fitness."*

- Three cheers and 'God Save the King' ended the opening ceremony.

- The Prince left just after 4pm, *"… being given a hearty send-off by the boys and others gathered outside."*

- So where is the Golden Key?

Plan of the New Watson's, 1932

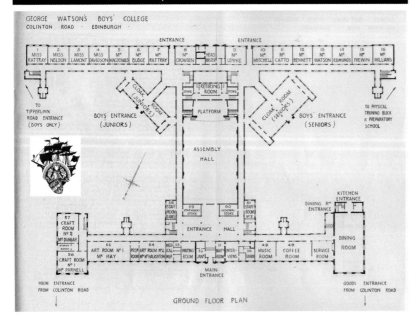

GEORGE WATSON'S BOYS COLLEGE
COLINTON ROAD · EDINBURGH

GROUND FLOOR PLAN

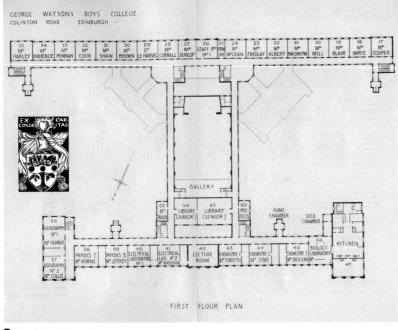

GEORGE WATSON'S BOYS COLLEGE
COLINTON ROAD · EDINBURGH ·

FIRST FLOOR PLAN

Spot the changes?

In 1934, Women Watsonians gifted the oak bench below the memorial tablet. Another gift for the new school was *The Harvest* by George Smith. Although donated by the artist for the new Hall it now hangs in the Dining Room.

The Hall Lectern

"The Hall Lectern, illustrated elsewhere in this number, is now installed and in daily use at morning prayers. In this connection we wish to thank the School Architect, Mr Martin, who, from sketches supplied by Mr Parnell, provided a full-size working drawing and offered valuable suggestions regarding constructional details, and also the late Vice-Convener of the School, Mr Stewart Morton, for so treating the oak as to bring it, in shade and finish, into harmony with the desk and chairs gifted by Mrs Dunn. The motto – St Augustine's, 'Thou hast made us for Thyself' – is part of perhaps the most memorable sentence outside the Bible."

Exceeding Expectations?

The Prep School loved the miniature desks and seats, the low-level windowsills and basins, the fountains, gym and bun room. One seven-year-old said: *"I think I will like the holidays, but I'll be sure to be back the first day."*

The new swimming pool was undoubtedly the smash hit. In 1931 only 40% of junior and senior boys could swim, but by July 1933 this had risen to an amazing 90%. Even although swimming periods were sometimes cancelled, classes still turned up!

Pupils liked the magnificent Hall, the cafeteria and the library, but Fred Keay, the School Captain, commented in July 1933 that *"Its very size … it is very easy to lose touch with one another and for the school to split into sections."* His advice was for people to join clubs and activities.

The Assembly Hall may have looked magnificent, but it had

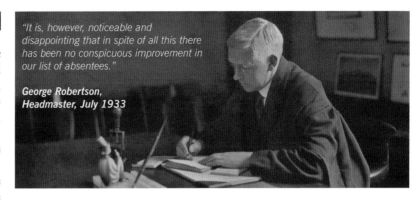

"It is, however, noticeable and disappointing that in spite of all this there has been no conspicuous improvement in our list of absentees."

George Robertson, Headmaster, July 1933

problems. In 1933, an expert in acoustics by the delightful name of Hope Bengal came from London to inspect it. He reported that although brilliant for orchestral work it was less so, if less than half-full, for the speaking voice. He recommended 3,400 sq ft of absorbent material to dampen the reverberations, including a new curtain to be hung under the gallery. Panels of *"glass silk"* were ordered from Glasgow for the walls and ceiling at a total cost of £464 12s 6d.

There were serious complaints about the swimming pool as so much vapour was being produced that staff couldn't see from one end to the next. The cause was that the bath area was cooler (52 Degrees) compared to the water (73 Degrees). The pupils also complained that the dressing areas were far too cold. The solution was for the school to spend more money on coal! Another serious problem was that water lying on the terrazzo work made it extremely slippy and thus a danger. This was not solved so easily.

The Final Reunion

On the evening of 15 July 1932 over 800 former pupils attended the final reunion in Archibald Place in order to say farewell to their old school. They explored old haunts, swopped reminiscences in the corridors and were photographed together in a historic group by Edward Reuben Yerbury. He used the curved line and moving camera technique which, when used with schools, allowed smart scallywags to get into the photo twice. Some of those in the photograph had been in George Watson's Hospital in the 1860s, others had been there on the opening day as a school in 1870 and many had fought in the Great War.

Finally, the FPs met in the old Assembly Hall for a farewell speech

by the College's first Dux, Sheriff RL Orr. *The Watsonian* then recorded *"The sight of that crowded assembly singing 'Auld Lang Syne' as the epilogue to a memorable evening was a heart-moving spectacle, and a convincing testimony of the strong spirit which knits Watsonians to their Old School."* The group then set about looting their old school, even pinching the Janitor's bell which was used to signal the end of each period.

The sight of that crowded assembly singing 'Auld Lang Syne' as the epilogue to a memorable evening, was a heart-moving spectacle.

Watson's *by John Munnoch. The boy is Lothian Taylor Wyse, a pupil from 1910 to 1920. This was before school uniform became compulsory and is here worn as a 'sports' jacket. Note the white piping which was an alternative sold by some Edinburgh shops before standardisation. This superb painting was donated in 1983 by Lothian Wyse from Toronto. Lothian's father Henry had taught art in the Ladies' College and the family lived at 106 Braid Road. The painting in the background is a copy of a Velázquez.*

Demolition Begins

The old Assembly Hall full of memories of plays, assemblies, roll-calls, concerts, dances, exams, the list of duxes, busts of 'ancients' like Homer, the stains left by the mock election and the tawny owl which flew in during the 1931 examinations and perched in the cupola. In 1903, Stewart-Lockhart had presented two Chinese hangings for the Hall. The boys were convinced that both simply read, *"To Hell with Heriot's!"* All was to be swept away forever. Most of the photographs here were taken by James Allan (an FP) who loved the old place.

1931.

The Old Building

"Leaving her dolorous mansions to the peering day."

It gives one rather a shock to go along to the Meadows these days. Instead of the stately building which we lately vacated, there is a massive ruin with gaunt walls and sightless windows looking out on the Meadows. Beauty in decay is never a pleasing spectacle, so we shall spare our readers a picture of their old Alma Mater being desecrated. When last we passed, the roof of the Hall had been stripped off, the Science rooms had disappeared, and the third storey was well on the way to demolition. It had to be of course; but one could not see it without feeling a pang of regret. One came away as one does from the dentist after having parted with a front tooth.
(*The Watsonian*, Spring 1933)

All gone by Summer 1934. The last to go was the Head Janitor's House.

Roots and Wings

Watson's is about people: memories, feelings and connections which forge strong links across the generations. For example, in 2002, the seventieth anniversary of the move to Colinton Road, Duncan Veitch was in S3. Duncan's grandfather, David, played what must have been a sad, but memorable violin solo at the very last concert in the old school in Archibald Place. He went on to become the leader of the orchestra in the new school. At the '*70 and Moving On*' Assembly Duncan played a clarinet solo in memory of his grandfather.

David's violin, unfortunately, has 'gone' for, in 1940, he was refused permission to take it on board the boat evacuating him from the beach at Dunkirk. He went on to win the Military Cross, but lost most of his teeth. After the war David became President of The Watsonian Club. His son, George (Duncan's dad) became Deputy Head Boy, 1967/8. Duncan's brother Andrew was appointed Head of S6 1998/9 and Ruth left S6 in June 2002.

By sheer chance a neighbour of the Veitch family was Alexander 'Tiger' Jamieson who started his teaching career at Watson's on the very first day the school opened in Colinton Road. He stayed teaching Maths for about 40 years. He taught David on "*the first period after the first break on the first day.*" His wife, incidentally, was Head of French at John Watson's.

" *Onward, seaward, never-failing,*
Steer the ship superbly sailing
To the unknown sea."

Drawing and text taken from the menu for a 'Dinner in Honour of Retiring Assistants (Merchant Company)' held on 25 November 1932 in the Merchants' Hall, Hanover Street, Edinburgh.

Left to Right: Jessie, Bertie, David, 1930.

David lost most of his teeth at Dunkirk.

David, 1945. The Military Cross.

David, 1934.   *Mrs Jamieson & 'Tiger', 1982.*   *Andrew, Duncan & Ruth, 1998.*

George, 1968.

William Cogman.

Serving

Unlike 1914 the mood was sombre and unenthusiastic. The glory of war had died in the mud of Flanders. A grim determination to 'get the job done' was reflected in the simple graphics used for *The Watsonian*. This first appeared in December 1939. Former Pupils were requested to send their full name, home address, date of leaving school, rank, unit and service address. First on the list was Lieutenant I Aird (Royal Army Medical Corps). Opposite the list appeared the light-hearted piece reproduced below. Little did the Editor realise he had touched upon a story which was to turn out bizarre, sad and tragic.

Little did the Editor realise he had touched upon a story which was to turn out bizarre, sad and tragic.

Si Sic Omnes!

Members of The Watsonian Club who are remiss about forwarding their Annual Subscriptions should take to heart the heroic example set by Flight-Lieutenant W. C. G. Cogman, R.A.F., who recently had the misfortune to run short of fuel in a storm and was forced down into neutral territory. From his place of internment, however, he has not forgotten his duty to the Club, and has forwarded a cheque to the Secretary in payment of his Annual Subscription.

William Cogman of 22 Barnton Gardens left Watson's in 1931 for a job in the Civil Service. In 1936, he joined the RAF. When war broke out, his squadron was the first to drop leaflets over Germany, but he ran short of fuel in a storm and was forced to land in neutral Belgium. William was taken prisoner and interned. He escaped and reached London in December 1939.

Back with his old squadron William was then shot down over Germany on 19 May 1940. He managed to bale out and walk into neutral Holland where he was taken prisoner and again interned.

Yet again he escaped, making his way to Ostend in Belgium by walking, rowing and cycling. He managed to board a British ship in the harbour which was then torpedoed in the North Sea by a German U-boat.

The Red Cross announced on 13 July that he was a prisoner, but the Air Ministry doubted the truth of that report. Then began an agonising period for his wife and parents as they waited for accurate news.

In April 1941, *The Watsonian* announced that William had been declared *'killed-in-action'*.

Casualties

The first graphic to head the list of those who died on active service appeared in the July 1940 number of *The Watsonian* shortly after the British defeats at Dunkirk and St Valery, as well as the Fall of France. Designed by Watson's Art teacher Otto Irvine, it remained unchanged until the cessation of hostilities in 1945. The total number of Watsonians known to have served in the armed forces was 1,822. The number killed-in-action, or who died on active service, was 202. Both figures are far below those in the First World War. Sandy Bathgate was the first Watsonian to be killed-in-action.

KILLED IN ACTION

"They shall not grow old, as we that are left grow old :
Age shall not weary them, nor the years condemn.
At the going down of the sun and in the morning
We will remember them."

Alexander Grant Bathgate

In Memoriam

ALEXANDER GRANT BATHGATE
(Aircraftman, First Class)
Royal Air Force

Born 3rd March 1918

Reported "Missing—Believed Killed"
6th September 1939

———————

"*Per Ardua ad Astra*"

"It was with the utmost regret that we read the name of Aircraftman (First Class) Alexander Grant Bathgate in one of the earliest Casualty Lists issued by the Royal Air Force during the present war.

The youngest son of Mr and Mrs RGM Bathgate, Ravenslea, Hawick, 'Sandy' entered Watson's in 1927 and left in 1934, when in the Third Form of the Senior School, to enter the Royal Air Force. After a bombing raid early in September he was reported 'Missing, believed killed' at the early age of 21. A comrade-in-arms writes of him:–

'It is perhaps fitting to know that his life belonged to the Air. To fly in the morning dew or to return through an evening storm was his very life-blood, and to die in that unconquerable realm was, I am sure, his wish... Should God be willing, I shall go through this conflict with the stimulating influence of a loved friend to urge me on, and, should the need arise to join him in that time, I shall have nothing to fear.'

To his sorrowing parents and brothers we tender our deepest sympathy."

DREAMS OF HOME
[Aircraftman AG Bathgate, RAF, was reported "Missing, believed killed" in Spetember 1939. His mother writes: "As poetry I don't suppose what Sandy wrote would count as very much, but it gave him a lot of pleasure to write, and now to us it is very precious. He had a great love for his country and much of what he wrote expressed that feeling." – Ed]

To sit upon the river's edge
And dream the hours away
Or rest upon a mountain top
And watch the clouds go by;
To stand upon the rock-bound shore
And hearken to the cry
Of seagulls, floating on the wing,
In the breathless sky.

Now soon, so very soon, I'll see
My Scotia, and once more
I'll cross that far-famed River Tweed,
And leave this alien shore
'Tis then, only then, I'll feel
As free as mountain air
To wander as my heart dictates
In my highland home so fair.

And so until that wondrous day
I'll live on dreams alone
And pictures in my longing mind
Of scenes in the past I've known.

A G Bathgate

Wiliam Duthie Morgan

Entered the RMA Woolwich and gazetted to the Royal Artillery in 1912. Served in France, 1914–19 and was awarded the DSO, MC and Belgian Croix de Guerre. Mentioned in despatches five times. Meteoric rise to fame in WW2. In 1939, he began as a Regimental Commander, but moved swiftly to command the 55th Division. Became Chief of the General Staff, Home Forces, in 1942. In 1944, he was in charge of Southern Command.

In 1945, he was promoted to Chief of Staff to the Supreme Allied C Med Theatre. Finally he became Supreme Allied Commander in the Med Theatre. Retired in 1950.

He was a dashing player and gave his forward line a splendid lead.

William D Morgan, 1906 (Cadet).

Mr W. D. Morgan, School Captain 1908-9.

OUR last year's captain is a son of Dr A. Morgan, Principal of the Edinburgh Provincial Training College. He was a member of the first XV. in W. G. Stuart's year, and on the departure of the latter he was made Captain. He was a dashing player and gave his forward line a splendid lead. He was Captain of the Lauriston team which carried off the honours in the first year of the School Championship. Morgan was also Sergeant of No. 1 Section of the Cadet Corps, and proved an excellent N.-C.O. His team won at Camp the Indian Watsonian Prize for general excellence. It was largely due to Sergeant Morgan's enthusiasm and gift of command that his team came out first in this Competition. Morgan is now attending the Military Classes at the University, and intends, we believe, going in for the Regular Service. He carries with him into his future career the best wishes of all his former associates.

Raymond Nisbet Valvona

In 1934, Raymond's father had co-founded the now famous Italian food shop in Elm Row, but had run into financial difficulties, so his partner took over. The Valvonas lived in the same street as David Calder. Raymond's mum was a Macpherson whose brother ran the chemist shop in Craiglockhart Road North. Raymond was at Watson's from 1928 to 1939 and then attended Leith Nautical College where he gained a First Class Certificate of Merit in June 1940. Raymond joined a tanker bound for Trinidad to make his first voyage. On the return journey his ship was torpedoed within a day's voyage from home on 25 August 1940 and only six of the crew of 39 were saved. Raymond was 16 years old.

Many of Raymond's Italian relatives and friends, although having lived here for years, were arrested as enemy aliens and concentrated in internment camps awaiting shipment to the colonies. The first ship, SS *Arandora Star*, was sunk by a U-boat in July 1940; 800 Italian and German internees were drowned among whom were Raymond's friends and relatives.

Raymond N Valvona, 1934/5.

Raymond N Valvona, 1937.

War Service & Casualties, 1939–45

THE ROYAL NAVY
Seen as being much more attractive than the army compared to WW1. Only 4% of Watsonians joined then compared with 14.7% in WW2. 10.9% were killed-in-action.

ARTILLERY/ENGINEERS
20.2% of Watsonians joined these service arms compared to 12.3% in WW1, perhaps reflecting the increased emphasis on school science and maths. 6.3% were killed-in-action. The lowest casualty rate was in the artillery (5.2%).

ROYAL ARMY MEDICAL CORPS
Exactly the same percentage served here in both World Wars (ie 9%).

THE ROYAL AIR FORCE
This was the glamour service arm of WW2, again reflecting the quality of science and maths teaching in GWC. The RAF attracted 398 Watsonians, ie 22% of all those who served in the War. Unfortunately, it also had the highest casualty rate – 21.5%

THE ARMY
During WW1 the vast majority of Watsonians joined the army. This had, understandably, lost its glamour in the bloodbath of the Western Front. In WW2 only 34.1% of Watsonians served with the army.

- *Only 3.8% served with the Royal Scots compared to 15.3% in the Great War.*
- *Even the swagger and pride of the Highland Regiments no longer pulled the recruits. Just 4.3% of Watsonians served with these regiments compared to 13.4% in WW1.*

Of those who served with the army 9.11% were killed-in-action, or died during active service.

TOTAL CASUALTIES
202 Watsonians died in WW2 compared to 605 in WW1. The WW2 figure represents 11.2% of those who served (c 1 in 10) compared to 19.5% (c 1 in 5) during the Great War. Of the 1,822 Watsonians who served in WW2, 1,808 were traced. The statistics quoted are based on that number.

David James Calder

David James Calder, 1940/1.

David came to Watson's in 1937 from Carrickfergus where his father was a minister. Stayed at 33 Lockharton Avenue. Good at tennis, rugby and singing. Also, Treasurer of the Lit Club. Spectacular wavy hair which he hated, but the girls loved. Brilliant at maths, so left school early when he gained a scholarship to Edinburgh University. Became an Officer Cadet in University Air Squadron. Although he started his flying training at Turnhouse he was sent to the USA to complete it under the 'Empire Training Scheme'. When he gained his Wings he was a Sergeant, but very shortly was appointed Pilot Officer. It was in Tuscaloosa, Alabama, when flying as an Instructor, that his pupil 'froze' at the controls and David was killed. You will not find his name in the RAF Book of Remembrance in the 'Shrine' at Edinburgh Castle because he was killed in a *"non-medal-earning area"*. He was 19 years old.

James Milne Robb

Youngest of three sons of Mr J Robb, JP, of Hexham. All three sons attended Watson's. James left in 1912 for Durham University. In 1914, joined the army as a private. Transferred to the Royal Flying Corps in 1916 and twice wounded. Awarded the DFC. Shot down seven enemy aircraft. In 1919, transported PM Lloyd George between London and Paris during the peace conferences. In Iraq, 1922–5, and won the DSO bombing the Kurds. Commanded No2 Bomber Group in 1940. In 1944, Eisenhower appointed him Deputy Chief of Staff (Air) at Supreme HQ. One of those who took the German surrender. 1948–51, he was C-in-C Air Forces in Western Europe. Died 1968.

Robb's personal aircraft as AOC-in-C Fighter Command.

OTC Notes

In Watson's the response to the Government's 'National Service Appeal' was that many joined the school OTC, or Cadets as they were usually known. By 1939, most Form Classes had over 50% membership. The First Year were too young to join, but were, nevertheless, drilled by the NCOs last period on a Friday in an effort to increase future smartness and esprit de corps. Teachers surely loved it, but the long-suffering NCOs were less than amused.

During the last term of peace the Corps embarked upon a couple of field exercises with the Royal Scots, mostly remembered for hot days and sweaty winter shirts. Cadet membership reached a high peak of 208. Watson's even introduced its own form of conscription that had been tried in 1914, ie everyone in S4–S6 was given 'an intensive course of military rudiments'. As the war crisis deepened all OTC camps were cancelled, but the Headmaster substituted an 'OTC Week' (17–21 July) which included training with the Royal Scots Fusiliers.

"One recalls with pleasure arduous efforts at trench digging, route marching in thick deepening mist, and last, but not least, hurtling through mud and water in Bren Gun Carriers."
(*The Watsonian*, December 1939)

When war was declared there was an immediate appeal for Local Defence Volunteers (The Home Guard). Thirty Cadets and three Officers volunteered to form a mobile guard. The Panzergrenadiers must have been shaking in their jackboots!

The Junior Training Corps

The War Office changed to this more egalitarian nomenclature as part of its drive to recruit more officers from outside middle-class private schools. The idea was to train NCOs capable of proceeding to an Officers' Training Unit. Despite encouragement, propaganda, pressure and an existing state of war it was clear by 1940 that becoming an infantry soldier was *not* entirely appealing to those pupils in Watson's who were within a few months of being conscripted. Most new recruits (70%) were from S3 and below. The spectre of the trenches cast a long and powerful shadow. During the Summer Term of 1941 one parade of two hours per week was held on Fridays instead of two shorter ones. Courses in Bren gun operation, the rifle, bayonet and mortar firing were regular features. One janitor was teaching bugle calls. Mortonhall was a favourite for exercises such as rounding up German parachutists whilst Merchiston Castle School offered a course in Intelligence!

By Christmas 1941, the Corps was 200 strong, holding two parades a week and a War Office inspection recorded that it was "*... now very good indeed.*" In the Spring of 1942 the armoury was being kept open at morning intervals so that Cadets could use the Aircraft Recognition Sheets. Visits were arranged to a barrage station, an aerodrome, an anti-aircraft battery and a central defence battery. The Corps had marched during 'Allies Week' and been inspected at Holyrood.

By January 1943, it was reported in *The Watsonian* that huge numbers of NCOs had left to join the forces. Also, a large party had been invited to the

Usher Hall to hear the Prime Minister, Winston Churchill. The Corps took part in a parade at St Giles' Cathedral and also one to celebrate United Nations Day. In order to aid training, a new assault course had been built in the school grounds.

In 1943, it was decided to inscribe on the beams of the school armoury the names of all senior cadets (CSMs and CQMs) since the inception of the Corps. This intricate task, lovingly carried out in gold, is now under a coat of cheap emulsion. Summer camp in 1943 was held for ten glorious days at Gosford House, Longniddry. Somehow, all the kilts had 'disappeared' during wartime and it was not until 1947 that an appeal was made for their safe return.

Despite encouragement, propaganda, pressure and an existing state of war it was clear by 1940 that becoming an infantry soldier was not entirely appealing.

The smallest Corps member in 1936. Later he became 'Sir' Donald Maitland.

Leading Drummer, Alex Slater Brown, 1937. Killed-in-action with the Royal Scots in the defence of Hong Kong, 1941.

The Air Training Corps

Early in 1941 the Headmaster arranged with the Air Ministry for the formation of a 'School Flight' which would co-operate with the 4th City of Edinburgh Squadron. Thus was created the junior version of the glamorous arm of the services.

The ATC proved extremely popular, with membership hovering around the 100 mark. Boys were taught navigation, aircraft recognition and signalling which were required for RAF entrance. The first major parade was along Princes Street on 11 October 1941. The entire Edinburgh Wing was present with the salute being taken by the Lord Provost. One of the major organisers of ATC units in the East of Scotland was none other than that famous Watsonian from WW1 and the 1932 School Appeal, Alexander Angus. By 1942, aerodrome visits were regular features as were flights in trainers and bombers. A considerable amount of supplies and equipment had been amassed, including new earphones and wireless sets. Between 1942–4 the ATC maintained its strength and programme which included summer camps and taking part in the memorable 1943 'Wings for Victory' parade. By the spring of 1945, however, there was a *"general falling-off of numbers"* with only 72 enrolled. A joint camp was held with the Royal High School in the summer, but the old enthusiasm was gone.

The Home Guard

Begun in 1940, its task was to act as a mobile guard unit. A guard was mounted on the school telephone in case of invasion and a week was spent digging weapons pits on the outskirts of the city – the perimeter defence zone. With no invasion, and no uniform except for an armband, there was a cry for some action. It came with anti-tank training with grenades and mortars at Castlelaw, plus Sten gun and gas courses usually in co-operation with regular army units such as The Royal Scots.

A guard was mounted on the school telephone in case of invasion and a week was spent digging weapons pits on the outskirts of the city.

Training Corps Cadets, 1943.

Evacuation

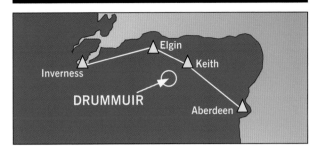

Drummuir Castle

Drummuir Village

As early as 4 February 1939, Edinburgh Education Committee, plus representatives from the Department of Health, the Scottish Education Department and the private schools, met to hear the government's proposed emergency evacuation scheme.

The Merchant Company was worried and rightly so. As far as the Government was concerned it was easier to split big private schools into smaller parts, joining them with local authority pupils if necessary, rather than finding accommodation suitable for one single school. There was, therefore, a distinct possibility that Watson's might have become one of the first casualties of any future war.

On behalf of its schools the Merchant Company objected to the scheme and requested the right to evacuate its schools as complete units. The Department of Health had to make a decision. Three months later it declined to authorise evacuation by units. The Merchant Company exploded into activity to alter that decision, including a letter to old Watsonian John Anderson who was the Minister responsible for Civil Defence. At a subsequent meeting in London even he refused to oppose the Government scheme.

Big private schools such as Watson's now faced possible decline in the event of a crisis. Parents would be extremely reluctant to pay fees for an education which was exactly the same as that of the local authority to which their children had been evacuated. Also, who would then pay the salaries of the Watson's staff? The Merchant Company had to come up fast with its own emergency scheme.

It took the view that as Watson's and Stewart's were out of the city centre then they were unlikely to be bombed. As both girls' schools were in the centre, then it made sense to amalgamate using a shift system. The Ladies' College would leave George Square and use the facilities at Colinton Road.

TERM	SHIFT 1	SHIFT 2
Spring & Autumn	8.30–12.30	1–5pm

There would be Saturday morning school to help compensate for the loss of teaching time. Also, each month the shift would be alternated and during winter the afternoon shift would be shortened. School dinners were thus unnecessary, saving both time and trouble. However, if the schools were not to be evacuated then air-raid shelters would have to be provided at a huge cost and built extremely quickly. By the time Watson's broke up for the summer holidays in July 1939 an emergency plan had been agreed upon should the Polish Crisis be unresolved by peaceful means. But would the air-raid shelters be ready for the new term on 16 September?

Bye Bye Colinton Road

Britain declared war on Nazi Germany on 3 September 1939. Parents, understandably, took fright. The Merchant Company decision not to evacuate did not go down at all well with many, especially as it was commonly believed at the time that *"the bomber will always get through"*. Cities would be pulverised. Those who could – usually those with contacts and money – made private arrangements to evacuate their own children to areas and people of which they approved. The wealthier sections of society were already sending their children abroad and by June 1940 the parents of 275 Watsonians had indicated they wished their children to be evacuated to the white dominions (ie Canada, Australia, etc). By September 1939, parents had informed Watson's that just 621 pupils would be returning out of a pre-war total of 1,263.

Could the school survive with such reduced numbers and revenue? Economy measures were introduced which included the ruthless sacking of teachers – some within two years of retirement – but those retained were eventually rewarded with a 5% increase for all the massive extra work and trouble caused by the situation.

In March 1940, the Department of Health changed its mind and allowed schools to evacuate as single units with their own teachers. The difficulty was still finding accommodation sufficient for a large school. In June 1940, the Headmaster, George Robertson, visited several possible sites.

DECISIONS		
Watson's Senior Boys to go to KEITH	**Watson's Junior** Boys to go DRUMMUIR CASTLE	**The Ladies' College** to go to ELGIN

Thus, if the Government ordered immediate evacuation the schools would reopen in line with the local holiday dates in the Moray area. Parents were obviously not happy. Only 300 pupils were enrolled for such a scheme. In 1940, the threat of evacuation was 'imminent'. Could Watson's have survived? Happily, no such evacuation was ordered.

NB The Castle was the home of the Gordon-Duff family from 1621. It was rebuilt in 1847 in the then modern Gothic style and is now an International Corporate Hospitality Centre owned by the Guinness Group whose products include 'Johnnie Walker'.

Fire-Watching Memories

Fire-watching was begun in Watson's at the end of January 1941. This required a huge commitment as it involved a continuous vigilance both night and day by senior pupils and staff. Indeed, teachers had done all the night duties up to 10 February 1941.

Camp beds and blankets were provided as were sandbags, sandbins, ladders, hatchets and blackout necessary for the sitting and sleeping rooms. The green sandbags with their distinctive smell are in Mr Howie's room as is the field radio. The east tower at the front of the school was used as the lookout point. Pupils began their rota on 10 February 1941. Girls would relieve the boys at the weekends during daylight hours which seems to have been *"a task cheerfully undertaken."*

As usual, problems soon arose. Boys were not allowed on the roof and a paid fire-watcher had to be hired. Holidays were a nuisance, so staff were asked to volunteer. Only two were exempt: Major WR Cooper (Head of History) who was 2nd in Command of the Perimeter Reinforcing Battalion and Alex McKenzie (Adjutant of the Edinburgh Wing, ATC and in charge of 1,600 Cadets). Refreshments also posed a problem which was solved from September 1941 by giving an allowance of 1s 6d (7.5p) per night except for Sunday when a breakfast of unrationed food was supplied. Box mattresses also had to be supplied at £1 13s 6d each.

In October 1941, the blackout needed to be extended to cover the Secretary's and the Cashier's Rooms, plus an additional lavatory. This cost £12. The blinds for the kitchen and staircase cost even more – £34. Imagine what blackout for the entire school would have cost!

Helmets were supplied in November 1941 by Maurice Heggie, the Divisional Warden.

Since March 1941, four teachers, one janitor and ten boys (ie five parties of three) had provided 'the watch' overnight, but on the night of 1 February 1942 they should have been watching the Assembly Hall. The new stage curtains, the new pelmet, the stage, seating and the harmonium were totally destroyed by fire. A few nasty people blamed the fire-watchers, but the local CID could prove nothing. The police suggested locking the school at night, but the problem was the ARP post which had to be kept open night and day. The solution was to lock all doors and fit locks to the swing doors at Reception with the ARP Warden holding the key. The total damage amounted to £653 12s 10d.

By 1942 it was becoming increasingly difficult to get pupils to volunteer as most preferred outdoor summer work, but fire-watching nevertheless continued until June 1945 mainly due to an increasing proportion of teachers to pupils on duty. After that any equipment which was of no use to the school was sold, but the blankets, sheets and mattresses were gifted to the Scottish Youth Hostels Association.

Edinburgh experienced only 14 Luftwaffe raids in WW2. In all, 18 people were killed and 212 injured.

From left to right— Archibald H. Ferguson, John H. Glover, John W. Lapraik, Rev. John Maclagan, Lord Provost Biggar, Mr Jack Paterson, Mrs Maclagan; Members of the Fire Services.

Monday, 5 December 1941. Glasgow and West of Scotland Watsonian Club presents a mobile kichen to the National Fire Service.

Who can have watched our Airmen, or have read of their exploits, without deep pride in their mastery of the air? These are the men who, when on leave, pursue a golf ball with as much determination as they pursue their quarry. And when that ball is a NORTH BRITISH 'S.S.' screaming from the club-head with *supercharged* force, how it must remind them of their own swift and purposeful flight!

NORTH BRITISH
GOLF BALLS
Not only British—but 'NORTH BRITISH'

SUPERCHARGED S.S.	PIN-HI *high performance*
the choice of champions.	*at low cost.*

MADE IN EDINBURGH BY THE NORTH BRITISH RUBBER COMPANY LTD.

December 1940.

Some memories are given here by John Walter, using memory and his trusty diary.

"*Saturday 25 January 1941. Went to school. Today there was a meeting for the new Fire-Watching scheme. All boys from 16 upwards will take turns and will begin next week. Some of the Staff are on over the week-end. It was my job as CQMS to provide camp beds and some greatcoats for blankets for them tonight.*

As far as I can remember we slept in the Green Room at the back of the stage at least that's where our beds were! Because we spent most of the night exploring parts of the school building which were closed to us and carrying on generally. Three adventures I remember were walking about in the roof space of the Assembly Hall, walking on the bottom of the (empty) swimming bath, and riding our bikes at high speed along the long corridor applying the brakes on passing the Headmaster's Office (now the Staff Room) so that you skidded well into the Maths Department."

"*13 March 1941. At about 9.10pm there was an air-alert. From then on there was a continuous procession of Nazi raiders going across from East to West. There was a heavy barrage from AA Guns. I do not think our fighters did very much although it was a full moon.*

We heard next day that the raid, the longest of the war so far, had been on Glasgow Clydebank."

"*14 March 1941. A parachute flare landed in the school grounds during last night, but was unignited and taken away by police.*"

"*15 March 1941. A rugby match I was watching between our 1st XV and Lismore was abandoned when an Air Raid alert sounded. However, Watsonians v Heriots nearby continued and during this match we saw marvellous trails in the sky caused by a dog-fight. The All-Clear sounded at 5pm. All this during the Highers!*

It was our duty as fire-watchers to look for the fall of relatively small incendiary bombs on our buildings and those of our neighbours, to alert ARP or AFS who would deal with them. In the meantime we were to tackle them and any fire they started using special equipment. We used the stirrup pump with its bucket, a long-handled half enclosed scoop, a rake and a bin with handle to be half-filled with sand."

The drill was that you approached the incendiary on your belly spraying it with water from the pump operated by another member of the team. Then when the fire was out you used the scoop to lift the remains of the bomb-casing and deposited it in the bin which you then carried back down the ladder. Sandbags were also used. The team for fire-watching consisted of 12 operating in pairs and each did two hours duty in the night. On 16 March 1941 70 incendiaries were dropped at Abbeyhill, but none caused any serious damage.

Spring 1941.

A rugby match I was watching between our 1st XV and Lismore was abandoned when an Air Raid alert sounded. However, Watsonians v Heriots nearby continued and during this match we saw marvellous trails in the sky caused by a dog-fight.

War Work

John Walter.

A great deal of war work was carried out by Watson's youngsters. This included stretcher bearing, aerodrome preparation, fire-fighting, crop cultivation and work at the Agricultural Experimental Farm at Craigs Road, Corstorphine. Farm work during the summer holidays was extremely popular. Private arrangements were made with local farmers and in 1943, for example, 200 boys were employed in harvest work. However, the most enthusiastically supported scheme of all was undoubtedly cutting timber.

Lumber Camps

In May 1940, the Forestry Commission asked the Headmaster if any pupils over the age of fourteen might like to volunteer for summer work. Only expenses would be paid. The response was astonishing: 90 volunteers by June. The first camp was held at Selkirk and proved an enormous success so much so that numbers were limited for the following year. In 1941, two camps were established at Cromdale and Grantown-on-Spey, each with 25 boys.

Harvest Camps

From 1943 to 1945 farming camps were held at Eccles (1943–5), Leitholm (1943) and Swinton (1944). 100 boys and teachers were taking part in 1944. The 1945 camp lasted six weeks.

Memories of the First Lumber Camp at Selkirk, 1940

The following is an account of that first camp written by one who was actually there – John Walter – using a diary he kept at the time.

"Clarilawmoor was the site of the camp in Forestry Commission woods to the South of the A699 Selkirk-St Boswells road at the junction with the B6453 to Middlem. Although I joined the 'Advance Party' on 21st July a 'Skeleton Camp' had been established for some three weeks.

Four of us from the Craiglockhart/Colinton Road area set off by bicycle and our route was Newington-Eskbank-Heriot-Galashiels-Selkirk. We cycled everywhere in those days.

We were in tents although when the main body arrived on 29 July they were accommodated in the Selkirk High School building. We had five or six tents and a marquee. Nic Gray and I had a tent to ourselves which was very nice."

CHOP CHOP

"Reveille was at 0700 and breakfast at 0715. We went up to the wood at 0800. "There are acres of felled trees around here and our job is to make brush-wood paths through the woods so that the tractors may get round and pick up the trees." The felling had been carried out by Newfoundland lumberjacks who had a camp near Broadmeadows. The Forestry Commission foreman was very critical of the way the work had been carried out as the whole site was left with stumps of 6–18 inches. Our job was de-stumping."

CHIP CHIP

"Those on duty as cooks brought us OXO and sandwiches at 1000 hours and I can remember how welcome that was! We had a five minute break every hour and came back to camp for lunch at 1200 and then back to work at 1300. Coffee was at 1500 and then back to camp for high tea at 1700.

Evenings were very often spent in Selkirk, sometimes at 'The Pictures' and invariably with a call on the way out of town at the fish and chip shop before trying to cycle up a hill full of fizzy drinks."

"Here with a Loaf of Bread beneath the Bough, A Flask of Wine, a Book of verse and —" DS Bennet, H McTaggart and Mr Shanks.

GANGS OF SELKIRK

We made 'Corded Roads', each of which was given a name, usually after a teacher involved, eg Albert Parade, Watson Walk and Collie Crescent.

I was a Ganger and as such was paid £2 19s 6d per week, from which was deducted 2/8d for insurance and then we paid £1 per week for food, so there was £1 16s 10d (£1.84) left. This must have gone a long way judging from the number of times we went to the cinema!

My first gang consisted of Nic Gray, Allan Jamieson, Allan Sharp, Jim Burns, Bobbie Calder? Stokoe, Ian Candlish, Andrew Young and our FP was Tommy Elgin.

One of the most popular tasks was loading lorries with varying lengths of timber usually to be used as pit props in the coal mines, and then travelling to St Boswells goods yard perched high on the top of the loads and unloading there. Every Saturday I cycled to Gala with one of my friends to get a steaming hot bath at the house of one of my father's business colleagues.

By damming a local stream we made quite a good pool in which we plunged 'starkers'!

Nic Gray was selected to go one day to Melrose to pre-record an item to be broadcast on the 'Wireless' about the camp; we also had photographs in The Scotsman and in The Bulletin.

We played Volleyball and Tenniquoits at the camp. A school cricket team played St Boswells on 8 August, but St B won. Evening Sing-Songs were arranged by those living in the High School. When Selkirk High went back after their holiday on 26 August more tents were erected at Clarilaw to take the 90 who had been living in the school building.

The war was never far from our thoughts, "After breakfast today (27 August) there was a great talk of bombs. I did not hear them, but three or four bombs fell pretty near here last night."

Returning from one of the concerts in the High School: "On the way home we were stopped by the local Home Guard who, on seeing about twenty bicycles appear out of the night were heard to say, 'It's the invasion this time!'

OUR GERMAN BOYS

"Wolfgang Ziegel, one of our German boys, was at the camp and caused me to confide in my diary, "I wish all Germans were as nice as him."

Scouts and Cubs

Scouts

War caused the first ever cancellation of a summer camp which was planned for Gullane, but Scouts did their bit for the war effort by acting as harvest helpers (eg Ford, 1939 and Romannobridge, 1941), ARP messengers, stretcher bearers, evacuation helpers, lumberjacks and messengers with the Citizens' Advice Bureau.

School was not available at night for Troop meetings because of the lack of blackout, so patrols met in the house of each Scout in turn and outdoor activities were organised to help bring the Troop together. By 1940 the lighter summer evenings were used by the whole Troop which met in the School Gymnasia, but for the darker months the Troop was divided into three sections meeting at the Scout Hut in Springvalley, Spylaw House and South Morningside Church Hall. In 1941, the Spylaw House section moved to Chalmers Memorial Hall, Slateford. In 1944, the Troop was reorganised into two sections meeting in Bruntsfield School during the winter. By 1946, the pre-war meetings were restored, ie Friday evenings in Watson's.

Night-scouting games, treks and barn camps were all organised despite the difficulties. *"Bitter is the memory of the Scout who forgot his sugar ration."* In September 1940, a big camp lasting two weeks was held at Bellanridge Farm Manor, but, *"owing to Adolf the ranks were slightly depleted."* In 1941, Youth Hostels and hikes took over from treks (ie rucksacks, not barrows) for the first time since WW1. But Scouting survived!

Cubs

The 1939 Summer Camp went ahead in July at Nether Fala, but war totally disrupted activities as many parents privately evacuated their children out of the city. Cubs were urged to join a local Pack wherever they were. Only two Watson's meetings were held, one at Akela's house and the other at Hillend Park. Severe weather in early 1940 further disrupted any plans and, of course, the lack of expensive blackout prevented after school meetings in school.

An alternative was sought in North Morningside Church Hall, but worried parents had to be assured that the Hall was *"protected as a shelter"*. Meetings were held there on Friday evenings until it became too dark. Saturday afternoon meetings started on 16 November 1940 and lasted until the lighter March evenings whence the Pack returned to Watson's with a 5.10pm start.

There were now no summer camps, but the fields near the school were used for open-air games. District activities also suffered, but on 21 November 1943 the entire District went en masse to the Dominion Cinema to see *The Jungle Book*.

By September 1944 there were 45 on the roll and Akela was looking for helpers. Instead of the usual eight, there was only one.

By July 1946 there had been a gradual return to normality. The Bun Feed Night in the Bun Room had been revived (despite continued rationing) along with songs, plays and a film in the Lecture Theatre. Camps were planned and things were looking up once again!

The Craigmillar Boys' Club

It may come as a surprise to our present pupils, but Watson's used to run a successful club in the Craigmillar area for many, many years. The impetus came from the Watsonian Pioneer Club, inspired, of course, by the energetic and irrepressible co-founder of Watson's Scouts, Sandie Somerville. By 1926, Watson's was running three Troops and one Cub Pack in the Old Town. In February 1926, the Scouts rented a big flat at 10 Nicolson Street and turned its six rooms into a Boys' Club. From that base the Scouts led camps, football teams and even acted as Probation Officers! As the slums were demolished and new affordable local authority housing was built on the outskirts of the city it seemed that such a Club was no longer necessary in the Old Town. However, no social or recreational activities had been provided in the new estates built far from the city centre. There were few affordable transport links. The Boys' Club leaders were in no doubt that something had to be done:

"If we fail, then there is nothing for it but leaving the area to be a breeding ground for all the anti-social "-isms" that are the curse of the modern world."

As most of its members had gone to Craigmillar, then so must the Club. The resources required would be far beyond that of the Scouts, so the Watson's community was asked to respond. The result was astonishing and reflects the growing concern about social divisions and its dangers that began to dominate post-WW1 Britain. Over £3,000 was raised by Garden Fetes alone in 1935 and 1938. Watsonians the world over sent donations, enough to finance the Club for five years.

Sandie was chosen as the first Club leader ably supported by J Blair, W Crawford, G Horne, J Allan and N Campbell, plus the ever-enthusiastic Norman Bruce who later did so much to revive the Pipe Band and even designed the Watsonian Tartan.

The Club opened during October 1935 in a disused church hall in Peffermill Road and soon had 90 members involved in PE, games, drama, crafts, billiards, bagatelle, ping-pong and football. Thirty Watsonian helpers were involved. In 1937 funds were raised for a permanent, separate building which was opened in May 1939 at Craigmillar Castle Avenue. So, just when the Club really got going, the war began and the military commandeered the building!

Nine months later the military left. In the meantime the Club still kept three football teams going and took some boys to camp along with others connected to the Edinburgh Union of Boys' Clubs. Back in its building the Club flourished despite lack of adult helpers due to the war. Workshop activities revived as did music, gym and drama. New American basketball became 'a special feature' 20 years before it was 'pioneered' in local authority schools. Membership exploded to an amazing 200 aged between 12–19. The guiding force was still Sandie, a committed Christian, whose aim was "*the formation of character.*" Sandie only resigned in 1947.

Sandie Somerville – A Watson's Hero.

Scouts on trek, 1934.

Club Camp at Bowland, Galashiels, 1936.

Boys' Club New Building, Craigmillar, 1938.

Did You Know?

1940: GWC to be used as an emergency hospital for air raid casualties.

1940: As a last resort three gymnasia to be used to house people dispossessed by air raids. Thick wooden poles erected at Myreside to stop gliders landing if there was an invasion.

1940: College adopted the *'Milk in Schools'* scheme whereby one-third of a pint was supplied to each pupil per day at a cost of ½d. Extremely popular.

1940: Quads used by F Coy No 6 Battalion Home Guard to drill on Sundays.

1940: 3rd Battalion Home Guard started to use the Rifle Range.

1941: Women's Auxiliary Police and Perimeter Reinforcement Unit both use the quads to drill.

1940: Women's Voluntary Services began to store emergency clothing in College rooms in case of the school being used as a hospital. In George Square, the Ladies' College was being used by the Red Cross. Bandages were rolled and wound dressings were made using Sphagnum Moss gathered on the Pentlands!

1943: Outdoor gym used by Women's Home Defence.

1940: SE Area Hospital Service offered to train senior pupils as stretcher bearers at hospitals.

"It was reported that the Headmaster had introduced a system of imposing a fine of 2d on boys leaving articles of clothing etc. lying around the school, the proceeds to go to the Red Cross."
(*Education Board Minutes*, Dec 1940)

1941: PE block was to be used as a *'Gas Decontamination Centre'* in any emergency.

1941: Rationing meant that school uniform was not insisted upon. A scheme for second-hand uniforms was started in March 1942 which perhaps was the origin of our Thrift Shop.

Photo by]   [J. R. Coltart & Son, Edinburgh

Prefects George Watson's Boys' College 1939/40
BACK ROW: FP Henderson, LD Laidlaw, H Clark.
MIDDLE ROW: WG Keddie, GAM Sharman, IJM Lumsden, EAM Wood, AWM Smith, PM Hamilton, D Whamond, WN Crooke.
FRONT ROW: J Elliot, JH Burns, NPG Smith, WC Jamieson (School Captain), Mr G Robertson (Headmaster), G Hislop (School Vice-Captain), RCW Lowe, IM McLean, RO Calder.
INSET: R Finlay, EH McEwan.

During one alert the youngsters were making their way across to the shelters when a Heinkel bomber flew extremely low over Tipperlinn. The pilot could easily have opened fire, but didn't. A few moments later he was killed by the fighter pursuing him. Another time, during school hours, a stick of five bombs was dropped on Merchiston.

1939: The cycle shed was strengthened and became an air raid shelter. Without this the school could not have opened on 16 October 1939 as there had to be sufficient shelters for all pupils. That day saw the first air raid in our area – on Rosyth/Forth Bridge. At least one aerial dog fight close to the school.

1939: Valuables from the other Merchant Company schools were placed in the basement underneath the Assembly Hall.

1944: Dickie Patterson and Hans Schneider resurrected *Phoenix*. Printing costs? £8.

Assembly Hall Usage
June 1940: Merchiston Ward First Aid.
Oct 1940: Air Raid Precautions meeting.
May 1943: Wings for Victory concert.
May 1943: Women's Rural Institute entertain Women's Land Army.

The bricked-up windows of the Janitors' Room (now Reception).

1939: The Janitors' Room (now Reception) was turned into an Air Raid Precautions Post, a major position for the Colinton area manned day and night. It had to be strengthened to be *"splinter and blast proof"*. The rebuilding was completed in October 1941.

1939: The Boys' College got its first organ (a Hammond) on loan from the Ladies' College. Later in the war the parents of Stuart Watt (School Captain 1938/9) gifted a similar one in memory of their son who was killed attempting to put out a fire in a minefield. Recently the brass plaque which was on that organ has been attached to the modern one.

Rugby became a war victim with a 30% player shortage, two main coaches gone, difficulties of practices in a shift system, changing difficulties (girls), unfit pupils, lack of fixtures due to evacuations or enforced idleness of other schools, bad weather in 1940/1, poor crowds, shortage of referees, insufficient clothing coupons for kit and a general lack of interest which went well beyond 1945. Nevertheless, rugby survived.

"The silver badge is evidently not deemed sufficient adornment for this session's prefects, so the addition of a tie with special crest is now to be made to their insignia of office. We wonder which of their number has been reading Scott's definition of true love:–

> *It is the secret sympathy,*
> *The silver link, the silken tie,*
> *Which heart to heart,*
>   *and mind to mind,*
> *In body and soul can bind."*

(The Watsonian, April 1940)

"'Summer Revels' proved a great success on Saturday 28 June. Trumpeter J Loraine and his Boys provided music for the young ladies of Watson's Ladies College and our own revellers. May we suggest that some of the latter would do well to take some dancing lessons before their next appearance on the dance floor?"
(The Watsonian, July 1941)

The appeal issued by the controller of Salvage to salve bones from the kitchen limbo has met with a ready response from the boys.

"Mighty, might, mite" has been suggested as a title for our picture (opposite page 23) of Gordon Hislop, "Bobbie" Brice and the diminutive Brian D Gibb, the smallest boy in the School, and son of the worthy Secretary of The Watsonian Club. Our photographer may have had in mind a study of Robert de Bruce and Brian Boru when 6ft 5ins of Hislop stepped into the picture!"
(The Watsonian, December 1940)

(Gordon Hislop was wounded in 1943 and had a leg amputated.)

"The appeal issued by the controller of Salvage to salve bones from the kitchen limbo has met with a ready response from the boys. The parcel which little Tommy carries all neatly parcelled up to avoid a "choppy finger", contains not "an apple for the teacher" but the less lyrical, yet more patriotic, relic of the week-end joint! We suggest that the receptacles provided in the playground for the collection of bones should bear the inscription not simply "Bones" but "Cui bono? Pro bono publico."
(The Watsonian, April 1940)

The scheme began on 7 February 1940. Bones were used to make glue, or 'dope' for use in aircraft production.

■ *Tommy Elgin, Sandie Somerville, Gordon Hislop, Sandy Montgomery, John Walter.*

The Schoolboys' Club was founded by Stanley Nairn who lived in Lockharton Avenue. At Easter 1940, 23 boys and 5 officers (led by Sandie Somerville) camped at Fingleton Mill (near Newton Mearns). Tommy Elgin was a Watsonian cricketer and Club helper. Sandy Montgomery was a young, popular and brilliant Cambridge graduate who had recently joined the Watsonian English staff. He became Headmaster of Marr College, Troon. Favoured candidate for Head of GWC in 1958, but pipped at the post by Roger Young.

Ex Corde Carrots

Digging For Victory

In late 1940, the Scottish Education Department asked Watson's if any ground could be cultivated. At first, an area of 730 square yards from the Head Janitor's House to the War Memorial was targeted. It was ploughed as 'trenching' (double digging) *"might be beyond the strength of the boys"*.

By March 1941 it had been decided to extend this to, *"an area west of the hockey pitch in front of the school"*, plus a plot, *"west of the Prep. School"*. Seeds and equipment amounting to £22 4s 5d were purchased. Also, the users of the Merchiston Pleasure Garden (between the Junior School and Colinton Road) agreed to have their garden cultivated too! Leeks, cabbages, savoys, turnips and parsley were all grown. By late 1941 it was clear that a tractor was needed, but unlikely to be supplied. By early summer there were four plots amounting to an amazing 4,000 square yards all ploughed, harrowed and planted.

Old Myreside

The scheme was extended to include two undersized pitches at Myreside, *"running parallel with Colinton Road and between the shelters and Myreside Road."* This gave an extra three acres. By October 1944 there was, understandably, a complete loss of interest in the drudgery of agricultural work. One year later it was decided to restore the fields to their pre-war uses. Potatoes were planted to clear the ground and, by 1946, everything was back to normal.

The Retirement of Miss Black

'Since Eve ate apples much depends on dinner,' said Byron and during the past 15 years schoolboy appetites have depended for satisfaction largley on the skill and consideration of Miss Black, who retired at the end of last term. No one understood more readlily than Miss Black the dictum that schoolboys are always 'as hungry as the sea and can digest as much.' May she enjoy a long and happy retirement form her culinary labour."

(*The Watsonian*, July 1941)

Photo by]   SCHOOL GARDENERS   [*D. L. Macdonald, Esq.*

Food Production

Owing to the necessity for increased food production, the boys, both Senior and Junior, have been asked this term to contribute their share of effort to grow more food. Four plots of land in the College grounds were ploughed and harrowed at the end of April. The plots are worked by the boys under the direction of Messrs Budge and McLean and already have quite an attractive appearance, the potato patch at the College entrance being particularly good. It is hoped to supply the kitchen with green and root crops during next session. Our photograph shows some of our young enthusiasts busy planting cauliflowers at the back of the School.

"In my wee gas mask ..."
Calvin Hider, Alistair Milliken, Raymond Forbes. c 1940.

The Air-Raid Shelters

Work started in July 1939 at a cost of £6,000 and each pupil was charged 5s over two terms. Work was due to be finished in time for the new term on 19 September, but *"other prior claims on reinforced concrete"* forced a postponement until Monday 16 October. Parents were assured that these shelters were bomb proof, *"approved of by the Home Office"* and supplied with Air Raid Precaution equipment.

Twenty 'Girling' shelters were built by Aerocrete Ltd, fewer than expected because of the drop in pupil numbers. The Scottish Education Department paid 50% of the cost which was an enormous relief as income had fallen. Swimming had been banned because if the pool were bombed then the boilers would be flooded and the entire school closed down. An unhappy Swimming Instructor, Mr Lemmon, lost his job and only reluctantly accepted a post as joint Shelter Warden for GWC and Stewart's at £175 per year. In October 1940, four stretchers and 12 blankets were provided, but, because of the cost, no gas blankets.

Dampness became a major problem and duckboards had to be put into shelters 8 and 20. In May 1941, heavy rain flooded the shelters because the builders had cut the old drainage system. Earlier that year, four surface-type public shelters were planned for the areas beside the entrance gates to be paid for by a 100% Government grant, but these were never built.

At the time the big fear was that gas would be dropped and, in January 1941, the issue of the missing gas blankets was raised with the Merchant Company. It argued that solid gas doors were necessary, not just blankets, but that would mean new lighting too. The total cost would be £800. As the Home Office, however, did not require gas-proof shelters no action was taken.

Music School Site

Hospital Wall

Shelter Entrances

The Price of Privilege

In July 1940, a privilege was granted to Dr RM Fraser of 28 Morningside Place to use the shelters. He paid £5 and was given a key to Tipperlinn Road gates so long as it was *"used only at night"*, ie should he be 'caught short' during an air raid. Just over a year later he was demanding his money back because he claimed other members of the public were using the shelters free of charge. The *'other members of the public'* turned out to be the local Air Raid Warden!

At the time the big fear was that gas would be dropped.

"The occupants of a certain air-raid shelter, who lingered there the other day for twenty minutes after the 'All Clear' siren had been sounded, evidently preferred their subterranean sojourn to what Burke called 'the siren Song of Ambition'. Or, perhaps, like 'Old Bill', they thought the shelter had 'a better 'ole' than the classroom! Not so the studious, who hastened back to read in Pope's Dunciad:–

> *Others the siren sisters warble round,*
> *And empty heads console with empty sound,*
> *No more, alas, the voice of Fame they hear,*
> *The balm of dulness tricking in their ear.*

(December 1939)

Fighting Fascism

John Dunlop, 1923.

John Dunlop was born in 1915 to wealthy parents, lived at 9 East Fettes Avenue, entered Watson's in 1922 and left 10 years later to become an apprentice accountant in Glasgow. Uninterested in politics until he was 21 in 1936, John considered his options. Disenchanted with the major parties, he considered the new fascists and communists. The fascists sent him *"… scurrilous literature about the Jews which outraged me. I shoved it in the bin."*

"That left the communists. I lived in a house with three storeys and we had two maids …, but I went to the home of one of the boys I played football with and found it was just one room. You had to see the conditions in the slum areas of Edinburgh and Glasgow, where 5 or 6 households had one lavatory between them. My eyes were further opened to social inequalities when my firm of accountants carried out an audit on a mining company. … I got to see the wage sheets and disparity between the workers' pay and directors' salaries.

Reading the Communist Manifesto, I also found the internationalism of communism very attractive. In my Sunday School there had been a picture of Jesus sitting with a black child on his knee, an Indian girl, a Chinese, all the races about him. I was totally taken in by this idea. I had an internationalist outlook, though I was proud to be a Scot."

In 1936, the elected Popular Front Spanish Government was attacked by conservative forces supported by Spanish fascists. Soon the Italian fascists and German Nazis were aiding the rebels whilst the only country ostensibly aiding the democrats was Communist Russia. To John, and thousands of others in Britain, the Spanish Civil War was what Vietnam would be to Americans in the 1960s.

"I joined the Communist Party a few months before I went to Spain in 1937. The war against Franco's fascists was in all the papers … I went to an Aid Spain meeting addressed by a young man who had been wounded there. … After the meeting I said:' I'm going to Spain.' I thought it was a wonderful adventure. It wasn't until I got there and things started falling down around me that I got scared."

John served with an an Anti-Tank Battery and was wounded in the Battle of Brunete, got to a convalescent home in Denia and met there a red-haired Herioter called John Tunnah who used to get the same tram as he did from Comely Bank to Lauriston Place. *"What the Hell are you doing here?"* was the greeting of each to the other!

The two Johns were lucky to be alive and were repatriated in December 1938. *"When we returned there was a reception for us in Edinburgh. My parents were there and my father said to me: 'John, looking around these are not the kind of people my son should be associating with'. I never forgave him for that. It sickened me."*

During WW2 John volunteered (he had been born in Canada and was therefore not conscripted) to join the Scots Guards.

Mock Election, 1933

A NAZI TRIUMPH

(At the Watson's College by-election, held on Friday, 17th November, the Nazi candidate—Herr Adolph Bowman—was returned by a substantial majority.—*Fleet Street*.)

THE return of the Nazi candidate by what is considered to be one of the sanest and most serious bodies of electors in the country has precipitated a grave national crisis in the country.

Herr Adolph Hitler, who was reviewing his storm-troops, is reported to have shouted "Bowman über alles," amidst cries of " Heil" from his followers.

Swastikas have gripped our College in a manner unsurpassed by any other political symbol, despite some dubiety as to whether a Nazi swastika is clockwise or anti-clockwise; and when the swastika is completed, there still remains considerable doubt not only as to whether it should be clockwise or anti-clockwise, but whether it is clockwise or anti-clockwise. A puzzling business !

The Watsonian, *December 1933.*

The Watsonian, *December 1934.*

"I Was Born in Edinburgh at the Age of 12"

Both Hans' parents (Hugo and Bella) were dentists in Vienna. When he was 11 years old the German army occupied Austria, Hitler's birthplace. For three months Hans lived under Nazi rule with little change to his life. For the story in his own words go to: www.math.wisc.edu/~hans/pers_hist.txt

In June 1938, Hans' father decided to get the family out. Escape from Austria was difficult enough, but entry to another country was even more so. In Austria he had to deal with a state department run by the notorious bureaucrat of the Holocaust, Adolf Eichmann, but only by bribing a Czech border guard did the family manage to enter Czechoslovakia by train as illegal immigrants.

"Thus ended what had been a secure, middle-class existence up to the annexation of Austria by Germany, and we became refugees without resources, status or prospects; three lives in limbo."

The Schneiders went to live in Karvina where Hugo had been born and stayed with Hugo's brother. In October 1938 the Munich Agreement gave the town to Poland, so the family were now illegal immigrants in a country where anti-Semitism was rife.

Hans was then sent by his parents to a Quaker school in Holland which had been established for German and Austrian refugee children. He had to travel to Warsaw to obtain a visa from the Dutch consul there and then, to get to Holland without entering Germany. He missed the first plane and had to wait in Warsaw for 10 days with his father to get the next one. Amazingly he stayed with a member of the German Embassy!

Hans' parents were denounced to the authorities who, astonishingly, allowed them 24 hours to flee to the Polish interior where they stayed with distant relatives whilst waiting for US or British visas.

Luckily, in April 1939, Hugo was one of the 40 dentists allowed to enter Britain. He and his wife sailed by boat from Poland. They lived in London for a while, but there was pressure to move elsewhere as so many asylum seekers were living there.

Hans Schneider.

"My parents chose to move to Edinburgh where I rejoined them in August 1939 … I do not know if I realised during our separation that I might never see them again …."

Hugo's brother, wife and son in Karvina died later in the Holocaust.

The fear of German spies resulted in Hugo's internment while Bella was exiled to Glasgow away from the East Coast invasion area. His parents had sent him to Watson's *("one of the best schools")*, but now Hans was left alone. He was taken in by a rich lady and member of the Usher brewing family, Helen Johnstone (3 Great Stuart Street), who was a sincere Christian and pacifist.

Hugo was released in August 1940 through the efforts of the Church and politicians. *"During the next five years we shared the experience of the British people at war, a remarkable people whom the world owes gratitude for their decision to fight Hitler. … Particularly for me as a teenager there was a tremendous need for assimilation and adaptation. Attachment to a dead past is a burden … I used to remark "I was born in Edinburgh at the age of 12", a joke with serious content."*

Hans loved and appreciated Watson's. *"Attitudes? I don't recall one hostile remark … I flourished under academic competition."* He became Professor of Mathematics at Wisconsin University, USA.

There were pupils with German names and relatives. Some like Doreen, Pamela and Jill Gruber plus Elaine, Elizabeth and Janetta Bauermeister at the Ladies' College and George Theurer at the Boys came from families resident in Edinburgh long before the First World War. *"I started in Watson's when I was nearly ten in 1942 in 6MJ and I cannot remember ever encountering any adverse feelings or comments from my classmates as a result of my parentage or name"* (George Theurer)

However, there were German and Austrian individuals who had arrived more recently in Edinburgh as refugees fleeing racial persecution by the Nazis. The vast majority were Jewish. When WW2 began the British Government interned all 'aliens' over the age of 16 in camps on the Isle of Man. The scheme, incidentally, was administered by Sir John Anderson. A plan to deport them all to the colonies ended with the sinking of the *Arandora Star* in 1940. Vigorous protests against internment meant that most were released by 1942.

WERNER WOLFF
Born 10 October 1923.
Joined Watson's on 10 February 1939. Interned on 23 July 1940. His Guardian was Rabbi the Rev Dr Salis Daiches (father of David).

KLAUS SCHIRMER
Born 26 August 1924.
Fled from Berlin. Joined Watson's on 15 May 1939. Interned on 23 July 1940. Guardian was James Gardiner, Convenor of St. George's West Church Refugee Committee.

PETER ZIEGEL
Born 27 May 1924.
Joined Watson's on 8 May 1939. Interned on 10 June 1940.

WOLFGANG ZIEGEL
Born 21 May 1926.
Attended the Goethe Realschule, Berlin. Joined Watson's 13 June 1939. Too young to be interned. Left for Edinburgh University on 21 July 1943 to do a B Com.

GEORGE AND JULIAN GROSS
From Austria. Joined 1942.

LISELOTTE ADLER
From Austria. Joined 1943.

The Watsonian Club

The 41st Annual Dinner was held on 20 January 1939 in the school Dining Hall. The cartoons (right) were drawn by the famous Edinburgh publisher, BB Captain, politician and cartoonist, Tom Curr. A record gathering of 320, presided over by Mr D Foulis, enjoyed good food, humour, speeches and toasts. In his speech the Headmaster – doing his propaganda bit – said he estimated that Watson's had turned out some 1,500 doctors in its history as a day school. Unfortunately it would be the last 'big do' for quite some time. Ominously, as George Byres was reading cables and telegrams from Watsonian Clubs throughout the world, the newly installed ARP sirens wailed their warning notes over the city.

THE WATSONIAN CLUB—   FORTY-FIRST ANNUAL DINNER

Once begun the war began to have an effect on this thriving, prosperous international organisation. Plans to improve schoolboy accommodation at Myreside as well as the Grandstand had to be shelved. The SRU cancelled all fixtures, but Myreside was kept open for training. Nothing daunted, scratch games were arranged and a temporary fixture list formed. By December 1939, Watsonians still managed to put out three teams each Saturday.

The following year the Annual Dinner and Ball were cancelled and there was *"a steady decrease"* in sports membership. The Council, meeting in the Liberal Club in Princes Street, adopted a new strategy. As there was a gap between leaving school and joining the armed forces there was a clear need to keep fit and that was the message to sell S6. Cricket, Golf and Athletics should all be 'pushed'. Also, improvements *would* be made wherever possible, eg renewal of the upstairs rooms at Myreside Pavilion and the introduction of gas lighting gifted by Stanley Bennet and RF Kelly.

By 1941 the sports section had begun to recover whilst both membership and finances remained in good shape. Rugby games were back and one 'East-West' fixture raised a magnificent £230 for Red Cross funds. Only the Club's Junior Section had been abandoned as most potential members were either in the Forces, or on some other form of National Service.

Communication with its overseas clubs remained a problem throughout the war, but the main organisation survived intact and in good heart. A Victory Ball was held in the Assembly Hall on Friday 18 January 1946, but the main event for the Club was its first Post-War Dinner held on 'Watsonian Day', 17 January 1947. A record 400 sat down in the Hall for a meal which included items rare in the days of rationing: rice pudding and Drambuie.

This was even superseded by the 600 who turned up for the Ball. A great start for a new era!

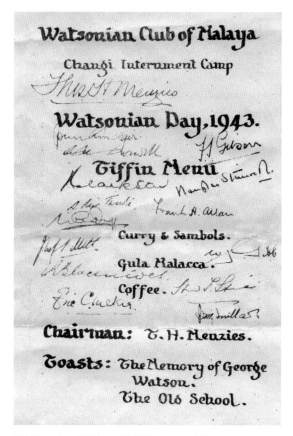

There were 29 Watsonian POWs and 22 Watsonian civilians in the notorious Changi Prison Complex in Singapore. Amazingly, in 1943, they celebrated Watsonian Day!

Hands Across the Sea

As during WW1 The Watsonian Club of North America generously sent money and goods not only to Watsonians at home, but also to those taken prisoner. The driving force was, as in WW1, Dr Arthur Hunter of Montclair in New Jersey, aided by J Loutit of New York.

James Hogarth.

> MADISON SQUARE,
> NEW YORK, N.Y.
> *April* 30, 1941.
>
> DEAR MR GIBB,—In the last *Watsonian* I noticed that there were three prisoners of war in Germany. I have taken pleasure in sending to them, through the International Red Cross at Geneva, two packages of food each, consisting of the following :—
>
> | | | |
> |---|---|---|
> | Milk, evaporated, unsweetened . | . . | 2 14½ oz. cans. |
> | Cocoa, instant . | . . | 8 1 oz. envelopes. |
> | Biscuits, hard . | . . | 1 8 oz. package. |
> | Sardines . | . . | 2 3¼ oz. cans. |
> | Beef, corned . | . . | 1 12 oz. can. |
> | Oleomargarine with Vitamin A . | . . | 1 1 lb. can. |
> | Prunes . | . . | 1 1 lb. package. |
> | Orange juice, concentrated . | . . | 2 3½ oz. jars. |
> | Cigarettes . | . . | 2 " 20's " |
> | " VioBin " (defatted, dehydrated wheat germ product) . | . . . | 1 15 oz. package. |
>
> I have brought the foregoing to the attention of several other Watsonians, who will undoubtedly assist in this line. If you will let me have the names of other Watsonians who are prisoners of war in Germany, with full information, I shall endeavour to interest other Watsonians in this country. We must have the full name and nationality of the prisoner, his rank, his prisoner of war number, the designation of prison camp and the country in which it is located.   ARTHUR HUNTER.

Ex-Head John Alison gave some heavy hints as to what he would like from the USA. His letter is dated 8 March 1942.

```
        Paper is so scarce that you may be put in jail if
you burn any or put your waste paper among the ashes.  A small
amount to kindle the morning fire is allowed.

        I must apologise for the faintness of my writing.
But it reminds me that no fountain pens can be bought in
Edinburgh or elsewhere so far as I can discover; and none
are expected in the shops till May.  I suppose that the pen
works must for the most part be now on munitions.

        There is very little that we eat or drink or wear
that is not rationed.  That is as it should be for it allows
all to share equally.  Nobody is starving or anything like it.

        With best wishes for yourself and for my Watsonian
friends with you.

                        Yours faithfully,
                        John Alison
```

James Hogarth lived at 7 Carlton Terrace, Edinburgh and left Watson's in 1935. He was a very keen Territorial soldier and went to France in January 1940 with the Lothian and Border Yeomanry. He spent his 21st birthday in the Maginot Line.

When the German forces attacked in June 1940 James was severely wounded in both legs, taken prisoner and spent eight months in hospital, undergoing ten operations. The Germans then decided to repatriate him back to Britain. His photograph was taken at Rouen awaiting repatriation, but things went wrong and James spent the next four years as a POW in Germany. The Germans sent him to the camp where his regimental comrades were imprisoned.

There is absolutely no doubt that Watsonian parcels made a huge difference. His mother wrote to Arthur Hunter, *"whoopee! … a Godsend."* Many others would echo that joyous response.

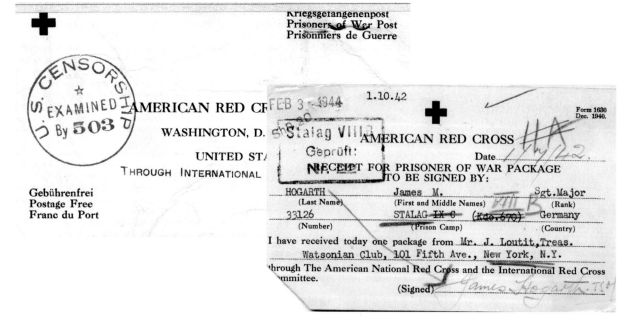

Girls and a Shifty Timetable

The Ladies' and Boys' Colleges were united in October 1939. The girls moved from George Square to Colinton Road whilst the Red Cross moved into their building. There were two shifts, 8.30am–11.45am (including Saturday morning) and 12.15pm–3.30pm. Boys were on the first shift and girls on the second. The changeover began at mid-term, but, later, alternated monthly. The times were altered during the summer months (8.30am–12.30pm and 1.00pm–5.00pm, with no Saturday school).

The shifts were to be used for *tuition* only and all written work was to be done at home. To cut costs and periods, RE was discontinued (although morning prayers remained) as was music tuition, Russian, shorthand and swimming. All except Elementary pupils were to attend Saturday school. Despite the care taken, all this amounted to was half-time schooling and was seen as such by those parents who had removed their children from the roll.

The Junior School was least affected because the large number of privately evacuated pupils meant that there was free space. The girls used the upper floor and the boys remained on the lower one.

From November 1940 it was agreed that if an air-raid disturbed pupils after 2am (from December between 10pm and 6am) then they could come in late, ie the beginning of period two.

By January 1941 the main invasion crisis was clearly over. Full-time schooling for national examinations was demanded by both parents and teachers, but the problem was getting the girls back into George Square. The Red Cross would go if asked, but the real problem was sufficient air-raid shelters. Only once this had been settled with the local council did the Merchant Company ask, in March 1941, the Red Cross to vacate the building. Thus by October 1941 the double shift system ended and the boys remained by themselves until the girls came along once again in 1974, but, this time, didn't leave!

Incidentally, the new Headmaster, Ian Andrew (who was installed on 30 September 1943), decided in May 1944 to put five minutes on the end of each school day, except for Wednesday. This meant that the school day was divisible into seven periods of 40 minutes each. Each Wednesday the school closed at 2.45 to allow matches to be played against other schools. This was the real beginning of our modern timetable.

> Naturally, there was some concern for the proprieties during the occasions when the boys and girls were both in the school at the same time, which happened under a later arrangement for Tuesday and Thursday afternoons and Saturday mornings when all Leaving Certificate candidates were taught. Screens were put up in common corridors to keep the sexes apart; seats in the examination hall were placed so that the boys and the girls sat with their backs to each other; and the girls were not allowed to take off their gym tunics during physical education periods lest they create a scandal by having to run to the air-raid shelters in their knickers.

▌ *Hector Waugh:* George Watson's College: History and Record, 1724–1970 *(Clark, Edinburgh 1970), p147.*

The story is best told by John Walter using memory and his diary.

As is well known the authorities at the two schools behaved in what we would now call an extraordinary manner in their attempts to segregate the boys and girls. An example from my own experience leaving school late at lunchtime I met, by co-incidence, my then girlfriend at what we called the Senior Gate on to Colinton Road and she insisted that we must not speak together as she would be in trouble if seen. We were both Prefects!

The real trouble began when, with the approach of Highers, it was felt us candidates needed more tuition and would have to share certain corridors, particularly the upper one (now Classics, etc), when sharing the building. I remember vividly a division erected in the above corridor using screens of the type in drawing rooms to keep out draughts. You certainly could not see over or through them!

Obviously the timetable for Swimming was carefully constructed in order that lascivious schoolboys should not see the girls be-sporting themselves, albeit in one-piece costumes!

In addition to the main air-raid shelters there was a shelter for sixth-formers in what had been a bicycle shed beneath two floors of the main building. Now for some reason the lighting had failed in there when an air-raid warning sounded. We nipped down from History and ensconced ourselves in the farthest reaches. When the girls arrived there was absolute pandemonium and I suspect some of the Mistresses were on the verge of 'The Vapours' – "*Horrid boys … and in the dark!!!*"

A Better Future

But what was the war for? Would people stomach a return to pre-war unemployment, poor housing, bullying management, private medicine, class divisions, poverty and international insecurity? Such thoughts sparked off a huge interest in modern domestic and world affairs, especially among the young. Unfortunately, the school systems in the United Kingdom totally neglected both modern history and modern studies.

All this found expression in July 1943 with the foundation of ESCA (Edinburgh Schools Citizenship Association) which was the first of its kind in Scotland and open to S4–S6 in all Edinburgh schools. It was run from the League of Nations Union (3 Rutland Square). Its first lectures were Nazi Youth (by Frau Litten) and Education in the USSR (by Mrs Dahlin), plus discussion groups on anti-Semitism, the Beveridge Report and Education.

By September 1944 ESCA was thriving. Watson's pupils used to a sparkling 'Lit Club' – dominated in

The League of Nations
What a shame,
Has done its best,
But ain't that tame?
Results are always
Just the same—
NOTHING.

the '30s by Scottish Nationalists and Socialists – took full advantage of this new organisation with heavyweight speakers such as Sir George Morton (British Democracy) and William H Marwick (Local Government). Watson's Russian expert, Madame Semeonoff, lectured on the USSR while Lieutenant US Navy, Gerald Fox, did the same for the USA. Debates then followed : "The influence of the USA in post-war Europe", "British Imperialism" and "Town Planning". All were hugely important issues in 1944 as Hitler's empire crumbled.

The organisation continued to go from strength to strength. By December 1946 18 Edinburgh secondary schools were attached with a

total membership of 500. The lifting of the ice cream ban in late 1945 certainly helped make the Christmas social a great success. Lectures that year had varied from China to Scottish Hydro-Electricity. The Easter Conference had dealt with Social Security, Europe's Frontiers and Health.

"At the last meeting, 'Outlook for Tomorrow', Sir William Beveridge outlined his plan and congratulated the Association on the successful reports which were read at the beginning of this meeting."

ESCA lasted well beyond 1945 and was mostly serious, but one of the best debates of that year was: "Whether Edinburgh should put up with the Members of George Heriot's School."

Watsonians in Government

The Second World War, unlike the First, did not throw giants like the Geddes brothers onto the political stage. However, there were Watsonians in and around Government from 1939 to 1945 – WS Morrison, Harvie Watt, TM Cooper – but, undoubtedly, the two most famous were John Anderson and David P Maxwell Fyfe.

John Anderson
Born on 8 July 1882 at Eskbank. Educated at GWC (Dux 1899). Also at Edinburgh and Leipzig Universities. Home Secretary (1939–40) and Chancellor of the Exchequer (1943–5). When Labour won the 1945 election he left Government. He lost his seat in 1950. Knighted in 1919 he was created Viscount Waverley of Westdean in 1952.

Probably most famous for creating the Anderson Shelter (which he tested by jumping on one with both feet) and the PAYE system for income tax

payment. He died in London on 4 January 1958.

The following extract is taken from Angus Calder's *The People's War* (Granada, 1971), pp 119–20.

"Sir John Anderson, on the other hand, represented no section of the human race whatsoever, unless he can be seen as the epitome of the Civil Service where he had made his career. Before the computer was perfected, Anderson was a tolerable substitute. Early in 1940, Mass Observation had noted that 'Probably no cabinet minister has a lower public appeal... His rather formal and uncompromising manner has never infused into the machinery for which he is responsible any warmth, humour or general sympathy likely to appeal to the many'. Even among civil servants where he was most at home, he was nicknamed 'Pompous John' or 'Jehovah'. He was alleged, by one or two admirers, to have a streak of dour humour in him; if so his wit was as dry as a fine, invisible dust. The Bishop of

John Anderson, Founder's Day 1947.

Winchester was present on one occasion when Anderson was talking to King George on the subject of air raid shelters. At one point, Anderson absent mindedly responded to the King's remarks with 'But my dear Man!!'. The King roared with laughter. Anderson remained impassive.

The son of a petty Edinburgh fancy stationer, he had entered the Civil Service with the second highest mark ever recorded in its examination; had his paper on political science not been poor, he would have been second to no one. He had then followed a distinguished course of repression. He had controlled the Black and Tans in Ireland; he had invented the regional machinery now used in Civil Defence for the purpose of repressing the General Strike; he had left the Home Office to go to India, as Governor of Bengal, to repress the natives, then restless. Returning in 1938 and entering parliament, his unique talent for repression had been recognised by Chamberlain, who had made him Lord Privy Seal to perfect the mechanisms whereby a panicking population might be repressed in the event of air raids; in three letters ARP. 'Don't talk to us as though we were a lot of niggers', an exasperated Labour MP once shouted across the Commons during one of Anderson's uniquely tedious speeches.

Yet, after Bevin, Anderson was probably the most essential of Churchill's ministers. Who else, with centralised planning in a rudimentary state, could so easily have confronted the enormous statistics of the war economy and coped with them? When in October 1940, Anderson was removed from the delicate position of Home Secretary to succeed Chamberlain as Lord President, the press, hooting after him, thought he had been 'kicked upstairs'. In fact, the Lord President's Committee became, in Churchill's words 'almost a parallel cabinet concerned with home affairs'. Had the mocking Gods chosen, they might easily have made Anderson, whom Churchill once referred to as his 'automatic pilot', the Prime Minister of Britain. When both Churchill and Eden flew to Yalta near the end of the war, Churchill advised the King that Anderson should succeed him if both died in a crash."

Mr John Anderson.

MR JOHN ANDERSON, whose portrait we reproduce above, was one of our most brilliant pupils. In his last year at school he gained the Jenkins' Prize, the Lizars, Mathematical (resigned), and Dux Medals, and one of the College Bursaries.

His career at the University was no less distinguished. During his course he gained ten medals in addition to many other prizes and certificates, the Hope Prize and the Vans Dunlop Scholarship in chemistry. Finally he graduated with first-class honours in mathematics and natural philosophy.

His greatest success, however, was achieved during the past autumn. In the open competition for appointments to the Home and Indian Civil Service he gained the first place, an honour which has once before been carried off by a former pupil.

The Watsonian, *December 1905.*

Had the mocking Gods chosen, they might easily have made Anderson, whom Churchill once referred to as his 'automatic pilot', the Prime Minister of Britain.

David P Maxwell Fyfe

Born in 1900 in Aberdeen. Educated at GWC, Edinburgh and Oxford Universities. Became Britain's youngest KC for 250 years. Elected in 1934 as a Conservative. In 1942, Churchill appointed him Solicitor General, but he became an internationally renowned figure as Deputy Chief Prosecutor at the Nuremberg Trials. Maxwell Fyfe lost office in 1945, but returned as Home Secretary (1951–4) and Lord Chancellor (1954–62). Created Lord Kilmuir, Earl Fyfe of Dornoch. He died in 1967. The two articles here come from *The Watsonian* for 1939 and then 1946.

Sir David meets the School, 1949.

"Nevertheless, it may be some consolation to MR Cooper (GWC history teacher) to know that his... pupil is the only British advocate who has ever been complimented by an ex-Chancellor of Germany, in the middle of cross-examination, on his great knowledge of German history. Whether it was a true appraisment of my knowledge, or an attempt to lighten cross-examination I leave those who knew Franz von Papen to decide."
(Sir David's Founder's Day speech, 8 July 1949)

D. P. Maxwell Fyfe, K.C., M.P.

The February 1939 number of *The Liverpolitan* contains an interesting sketch of the career of the young Watsonian Parliamentarian, D. P. Maxwell Fyfe, K.C., who is M.P. for the West Derby Division of Liverpool. From it we quote one paragraph which we are sure will be of interest to our readers.

" To look for the first time at his stocky, yet massive, figure, with its short-cropped, Mussolini-like head, is to give one an impression of the masterful, the domineering. The impression is false. He does not dazzle by the showy gifts of the cheap-jack party hack. He is not clever in the sense of employing little tricks of demagogic oratory. Cleverness is volatile and can cloak an inferior personality. But it is character that makes the man. And it is because Maxwell Fyfe has character plus brains above the average that he is now an honoured and outstanding figure in his profession and one of our leading Parliamentarians. In both spheres he has won universal regard. No judge has ever admonished him; no political opponent has ever uttered an unkind word about him."

SIR D. MAXWELL FYFE: A PEN-PICTURE FROM NUREMBERG

(Reprinted by kind permission of " The Sunday Times ")

THE British delegation dominates, and the genius of the place is Sir David Maxwell Fyfe, who so far excels the other prosecutors that he has almost played them off the stage. Indeed, his skill in cross-examination has alone prevented the Germans from turning the court into a theatre for the display of patriotic histrionics.

Those who have followed Sir David's career from its early days will not be surprised by his Nuremberg successes. Educated at George Watson's College—an Edinburgh school which during this century has produced a cricket eleven, if not, indeed, a " rugger " fifteen, of Ministers, including Sir John Anderson, the Geddes brothers, and the late Lord Horne—this Liverpool Scot combines a first-class brain with a greater capacity for hard work than any barrister I have ever known.

He has, too, that important quality of greatness—a complete mastery of his time. This asset enhances a most attractive personality and leaves him sufficient leisure to keep in touch with a wide circle of friends. He was comparatively unknown when he entered Parliament in 1935. But his fearlessness, his qualities of leadership, and his capacity for shouldering even the most irksome responsibility soon brought him to the front, and given office in 1942, he established himself as one of the best Solicitor-Generals of modern times.

ATTICUS

They were so heavy we could hardly lift them let alone wield them in battle!

One final tale from John Walter:

"Something I have always wanted to record happened in September or October 1939 when we were not in school. Donald Maitland (now Sir Donald) and I were asked to come in to the school armoury to load our beautiful Short Magazine Lee-Enfield rifles onto an Army lorry and off they went to war.

Sometime later, and because we were a Home Guard unit as well as OTC, we helped unload their replacements ... PIKES!! These consisted of a length of tubular steel scaffolding with the long bayonet welded on to the top. They were so heavy we could hardly lift them let alone wield them in battle!"

Victory

It seems impossible to go anywhere without coming across a Watsonian and so it was for the German Army. On 3 May 1945, representatives of the German Government after Hitler's suicide came to Field Marshal Sir Bernard Montgomery's headquarters on the Luneburg Heath, near Hamburg, to ask for surrender terms for all the German forces in Holland, NW Germany and Denmark. In charge of this historic meeting was a Watsonian, James Oliver (Jo) Ewart.

Ewart was living at 2 Craiglockhart Crescent when, in 1929, he came to Watson's from the Royal High School. He was a brilliant all-rounder at school who then went on to take a First Class Honours Degree in Classics at Edinburgh University. As a student he had travelled widely in Europe and spoke French, German, Dutch, modern Greek, Spanish and Italian.

In 1939, he joined the 9th Royal Scots. At the age of 25 he was a Lieutenant-Colonel; at 28 he had been awarded the OBE and CBE and had attained the rank of Colonel. Ewart was killed in a mysterious road accident near Ostenwalde Castle, Germany, on 1 July 1945.

James Oliver Ewart. 2nd XI, 1935.

Prefect, 1935.

Ewart, Montgomery, Friedeburg.

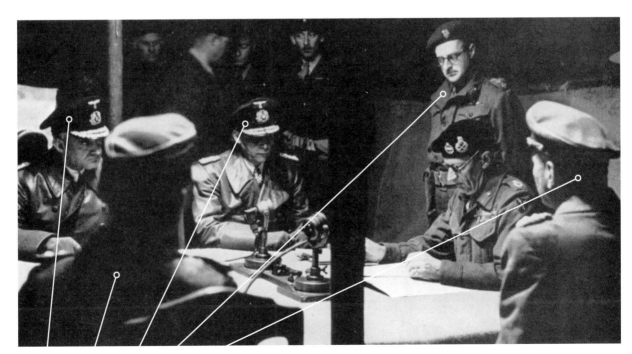
Wagner, Polleck, Friedeburg, Ewart, Kinzel.
The German delegates were Admiral von Friedeburg, C-in C. German Navy, Gen. Kinzel, Chief of Staff to Field Marshal Busch, Rear-Admiral Wagner and a SS staff officer. Friedeburg committed suicide on 23 May.

Remembrance

The Watsonian War Relief Fund

This was established in 1941 to relieve those Watsonians who were suffering as a result of war, *"...wrecked lives, wrecked homes, wrecked businesses."* Watsonians in North America – led by Dr A T Hunter of New York who had organised a similar fund in the First World War – kick-started this scheme with a generous donation of £300. Within three months £4,900 had been donated, but even by 1945 the aim of reaching £10,000 had not been achieved. After all, the war had not caused, in Britain, the massive devastation expected. An appeal during the summer pushed the amount upwards so that by 1946 the final total was only about £600 short of the target. There is no question that many Watsonians did benefit from the fund.

During the war huge amounts of goods came into Watson's from the United States. The following was recorded in April 1942:

> 1 case anæsthetics,
> 4 cases medical supplies,
> 2 cases toys (donated by Miss Gertrude Lawrence),
> 5 cases camp beds and bedding,
> 11 cases fur coats and odd fur pieces,
> 66 cases of men's, women's and children's clothing,

of which the greater part is new.

Arrangements have already been made to have the first three items distributed at once to appropriate recipients, such as hospitals, day nursery schools, etc. The remaining items, valued at approximately £3000, await distribution through our War Relief Fund Committee.

THE WATSONIAN
WAR RECORD
1939-1945

In 1948 a permanent record of Watsonian war service was decided upon, but, compared to that for the First World War, it *"will be of necessity less copious in its information."* The reason for this? A national paper shortage. Each day a new page is still turned by the Librarian.

> We are told, and have reason to believe it true, that the war has increased national unity and improved neighbourly relations. Politicians have turned from reviling each other to working together ; class distinctions seem less important than they were ; neighbours who were almost complete strangers are sharing common duties and dangers, and acquiring a broader humanity ; self-centred lives are spreading out in new directions under the impulse of working for others ; even in international relations we are acquiring a deeper understanding from association with the representatives of the Allied peoples in our midst. This is the better side of war, and much of it just means being mutually helpful.

The War Relief Fund, July 1941.

The War Memorial

The Council of The Watsonian Club decided in 1946 to extend the existing War Memorial to include the Roll of Honour for those who had died in the Second World War. The original architect, Mr J A Carfrae, was approached for ideas.

The following year two photographs of a model showing the proposed changes was published in *The Watsonian*. The model had been made by members of the Art Department: R Scott Irvine, Euan Walker and James Coull. The proposed extension was not carried out.

Headmasters

Ian Graham Andrew, 1943–53.

Ian Graham Andrew

Ian Andrew was installed as Head on Thursday, 30 September 1943 following the retiral of George Robertson after 17 years at Watson's.

Andrew was a native of Barrhill, Ayrshire, who had attended Glasgow High School. By the time he came to Watson's Andrew had already been a Head for 20 years, 10 at Elgin Academy and 10 at Robert Gordon's. He was a safe bet. Quiet, highly efficient and unassuming, Andrew was the perfect bureaucratic Head who would rock no boat and keep the good ship Watson's on an even keel. He took occasional classes in English and French, but regularly taught RE and American History to Sixth Year. He was charming and friendly, played golf, followed rugby, loved gardening, read profusely and once arrived in school with a gorgeous black eye achieved in the pursuit of cricket.

New Departments

Andrew did not arrive at the best of times – war, casualties, teacher shortages, overcrowding and restrictions – but he did have some successes.

In 1945, he revived the Commercial Subjects Department which had faded over the years. Arthur Brown was appointed as Head of Department, as well as doubling as Careers' Master. It eventually expanded so that by 1974 it included Economics, Economic History, Principles of Accounts and Modern Studies.

In the same year Andrew also established a separate Department of Technical Subjects. Previously, wood- and metal-work had declined so much since 1914 that they had become after-school activities sponsored by the Art Department. A new Leaving Certificate in Technical subjects was the spur to change. Two new members of staff, James Milligan and Ben Dunbar, transformed the subject, creating a successful new Department.

For boys, however, his greatest achievement was getting rid of the ridiculous short trousers in which his predecessor had imprisoned all from S1 to S6.

Andrew is credited with bringing the Blair Library to a successful conclusion, pursuing the Preparatory School extension and introducing a formidable annual Founder's Day celebration. More controversially he appointed a School Chaplain given "… *the irreligious spirit of our time."* Russian language teaching was pioneered, as was a full-time teacher of Biology. Also a games period was introduced into the timetable which made possible compulsory rugby and cricket for S1 to S3. This was not entirely popular and was soon reduced to one year. Although his idea for a boarding house came to nothing, it was put into operation 10 years later.

For boys, however, his greatest achievement was getting rid of the ridiculous short trousers in which his predecessor had imprisoned all from S1 to S6 and bringing back 'longs' for seniors.

A New Ethos?

He also emphasised different values than other Heads, describing what Ogilvie and others had created as, "… *this conveyor-belt delivery of successful scholars."* He had no desire to attack academic standards (or exam-passing techniques as expressed by some), but instead emphasised "… *the tradition of service: to the School first, then to the community, and particularly to those less fortunate than ourselves."* Others had sought to emphasise 'Sport' and/or 'School Loyalty', but Andrew's approach would stand the test of time.

In July 1953, following Robertson's example, Andrew retired at 60 after 10 years at Watson's.

Ian Donald McIntosh, 1953–8.

Ian Donald McIntosh

The new Head was a "Moray Loon" hailing from the same area as Dr Ogilvie. Born in Forres he received most of his schooling at Inverness Royal Academy and then proceeded to Aberdeen University where he graduated First Class Honours in French and German, picking up a Gold Medal for Modern Languages and a Cricket Blue. McIntosh then studied at Trinity College, Cambridge where he took a BA with First Class Honours and a Soccer Blue. He taught in Berkshire for a while and then was appointed in 1937 as Head of Modern Languages to Winchester College where he also commanded the Air Training Corps for both town and College. Unusually he was also a member of Hampshire Education Committee and Chairman of Governors of the Secondary Modern Schools at Winchester.

With this background much was expected. Unfortunately, little was delivered. Within five years McIntosh had packed his bags and retreated to gentler pastures as Head of Fettes. He may have been a talented linguist and sportsman, but as an intellectual, educationalist and manager he left a lot to be desired.

"My policy is to regard as major sports those which are essentially team games and not individual recreations, especially Cricket and Rugby, the one a game of high skill and the other of violent effort, both containing healthy possibilities of discomfort and even danger."

"It is hoped gradually to raise musical standards in the school, both of performance and appreciation, no easy matter in these days of jazz music which has a peculiarly strong appeal to young people."

McIntosh was perfectly affable and genial, solid and competent, but his most notable innovation amounted to an unannounced arrival in a classroom followed by sitting quietly and listening to the teacher. He resigned on 20 March 1958 admitting to the Governors that he had been too cautious, but quickly blamed Watson's stating that it was part of a Scottish system which resisted change through "the weight of inertia". In reality the job was far too big, inducing mental paralysis. Firm decisions were quite beyond him. Few regretted his passing.

Roger William Young, 1958–85.

Sir Roger

The next Head would become one of the best known in the country. Controversial, both hated and loved, but also unforgettable and sadly missed on his retiral, Roger Young was the finest Head since the days of Dr Ogilvie.

Roger was born in Delhi. His father was Vice Principal of St Stephen's College. His mother was a surgeon and Principal of Lady Hardinge Medical College. Roger was educated at Westminster and Oxford, taught Classics and English mostly at Manchester Grammar and had seen active service in the North Atlantic and D-Day with the RNVR. He was a keen walker and climber, and had organised trips to both the Alps and Dolomites. While he was still teaching Roger studied for the Lambeth Diploma in Theology and wrote 'Philosophical Exercises for Sixth Formers'. Here was a Head with a real distinction of mind, genuinely interested in a wider concept of education than merely passing exams and, above all, with the energy and bravery to attempt to put his ideas into action within a school rooted in the past and content with its own comfortable existence. His first Report in 1959 contained his deeply held convictions about what a school should be:

"... So intense is the feeling for the Leaving Certificate and so determined is the struggle to obtain passes that there is

a real danger that the educational ends we are striving for may be lost and the examinations themselves become the final end instead of merely a means. This is bad in itself and some of its consequences are also very bad – for example, the pressure exerted by some parents to get their sons into unsuitable courses merely to get some kind of certificate; or the accusation of 'doing a boy an injustice' when members of staff attempt to help parents think realistically about their son's schooling. More serious in practice is the fact that, on the assumption that teaching for passes in the Leaving Certificate is the most important function of the school, a boy will stay on until he has got as many passes as he can."

Sir Roger was determined that Watson's should stop being 'a crammer' – the sausage machine as some locals called it – and start educating. He would be taking on some very entrenched conservative attitudes right across the board from parents, teachers and, indeed, pupils.

In 1960, the Merchant Company Education Board asked Heads to formulate their aims for the next 20 years. Sir Roger lost no time in preparing a 17-page memorandum. His first aim was to create what he called a school community. What he meant by that was not just a school with clubs, societies, sports and an FP organisation, but also where teachers would take responsibility for *"the boy and his education"* rather than specialist subjects alone. *"There are*

[Roger] was a Head with a real distinction of mind, genuinely interested in a wider concept of education than merely passing exams.

however signs that day schools should more and more concern themselves with the education of the whole person." Of crucial importance to this concept was the creation of a Form Teacher, "… and all that this implies in pastoral and personal concern for each boy in the form." Secondly, a boy's education should be suited to his needs and aptitudes and, thirdly, the need to develop "private study and independent work."

"If effect is given to these three aims Scottish schools will be humanised and liberalised and made personal in ways which are badly needed. It is here that Watson's can, I believe, set the pace in the next twenty years."

He was also convinced that the ablest pupils were not being stretched. "The present Scottish system has of course the great virtue of allowing the more or less average boy (academically speaking) to obtain University and professional qualifications in combination with a reasonably good general education. There is no need to abandon this advantage, geared as it rightly is to the requirements of the majority of senior school pupils. Indeed, I should be very sorry to see it disappear." How precisely this raising of standards was to be achieved was left a little vague except that each department was exhorted to

do so. "The really important changes must occur in the minds and attitudes of teachers. This is a slow process which organisational changes may assist but cannot of themselves bring about."

The new Ordinary Grade courses were welcomed as suiting boys who until then had nothing to aim for, but the ablest were allowed to by-pass and make their main target the Higher Grade. At one end S6 would be encouraged to take 'Advanced' examinations and be allocated a 'Tutor', preferably a Head of Department, "… who is teaching him regularly in one of his main subjects. … to guide and advise him in work and other matters … and provide the information I need for Testimonials, Confidential Reports, etc.." At the other, a special class called '1S' would be established for the immature and academically weak in P7, " … a 'sandwich' Form between the top form in the Junior School and Form 1 in the Senior School." Class sizes were to be reduced from 35 to 30 in the Junior School and in the Senior School (S1–S3) from 36–38 down to 30 as well. Certificate classes were huge: 30–34 and were lowered to a maximum of 25 for Higher and 30 for Ordinary Grade.

Staff had to be attracted, but at that time salaries were not paid above the national scale. Other inducements had to be good teaching, accommodation and amenities, smaller classes than elsewhere, prestige and a stimulating community life. He did, however, foresee the danger of people not moving once appointed. "Indeed, it is only this immense fund of loyalty to the school and willingness to take on out-of-school activities that enables us to organise the astonishing variety of activities which are presently open to boys in the school." Sir Roger made an oblique plea for extra payments and some thought to further inducements.

All this amounted to a revolution. The winds of change would indeed howl through hallowed Watson's corridors.

> *The winds of change would indeed howl through hallowed Watson's corridors.*

Staff Football XI, 1964. Back: C Binns, D Fergusson, J Smith, J MacLagan, D Scott, J Craig
Front: J Hunter, R Young, R Hendry (Captain), J Cowan, P Edington.

The Building

Victory may have been won in 1945, but there was no immediate return to normality, so a period of austerity continued into the 1950s. Watson's desperately needed to expand with 1,500 boys crammed into a building designed for only 1,200, but a Government Licence was required for any building work and not granted easily.

Minor conversion work took place in 1950 with two art rooms being created out of one and the male Staff Room moved into the Reception Area.

In the following year the Prefects' Room was revamped. Of greater importance was the opening on 15 September 1953 of two new classrooms built above the east wing of the Preparatory School. In addition, the Hall was redecorated in *"delicate tones"* designed by Watsonian architect Basil Spence. The pelmet above the stage had attached, *"... a beautifully embroidered Coat of Arms."* None of this, however, solved the overcrowding problem.

In March 1948, The Head, Ian Graham Andrew, publicly expressed a desire to have a school boarding house

perhaps sponsored by The Watsonian Club, but nothing came of it. An important internal rearrangement was finished in January 1953 when the Head's Room was moved adjacent to the Main Entrance in what had been the Male Staff Room. The Secretary and Assistant Secretary moved next to the Head in what had been the Cashier's Room. The Cashier then moved into what had been an unsightly storeroom to the left just inside the Main Entrance. The Male Staff Room was moved into the room formerly used by the Head. All at the considerable cost of £522.

The Soul of the School

With little else to acclaim much was made of the intent to create a new Library. It is astonishing that as late as 1945 a school claiming to be a major educational institution had such dismal Library provision. Even in 1949, it had only 2,384 volumes and lent a pathetic 560. There was no professional Librarian, the work being left to the part-time activity of a volunteer teacher. The Editor of *The Watsonian*, Alex Mackenzie, lamented in July 1947 that *"... our Library is lacking in the dignity, beauty and comfort which are so desirable if the Library is to be as it should he, the spiritual centre of the school."*

John S Blair

All that was to change. An FP and Master of the Merchant Company, John S Blair, had gifted £3,500 to build a new facility. Unfortunately, no Government building licence was granted until 1949. Eventually, on 13 November 1950, it was opened by John Blair in person. At the ceremony the Head expressed a genuine personal sentiment: *"I have always felt that a school may possess splendid buildings and spacious playing fields, and yet, if it does not have a good library as the centre of all school activities, it is a body without a soul."* He suggested that every S6 leaver should donate a book like adding a pebble to a cairn.

The Library was superbly constructed given the constraints of the time with the entire panelling and shelves made from waxed walnut. All the careful hand-carving was done

John S Blair.

by Edinburgh sculptor Thomas Good who took a quotation from Proverbs plus designs based on the College and Merchant Company arms. Indirect lighting was introduced and the floor made sound-proof. Two cases for the War Records were designed by the Library architect W Hardie Kininmonth, a Watsonian. The Head hoped it would be called 'The Blair Library'.

The school now had a Library, but hardly any books. A plea brought a deluge. The ever-faithful Arthur Hunter in New Jersey donated 70 volumes dealing with the USA, South African Wasonians gave 30 concerning their adopted homeland, even the Head generously offered 100 on assorted topics while individuals gave gifts ranging from single books to the entire works of *Punch*. By 1953, the number of volumes rose to 6,797. That these were popular works was indicated by a rise in lending of 900%!

Unfortunately, not everything changed. Once initial enthusiasm had waned the College again reverted to penny-pinching. Professional help from the Central and National Libraries had been used to establish a modern system, but no professional Librarian/ Archivist was appointed. George More, amateur Teacher-Librarian since 1949, obviously felt the job was now beyond him and resigned in favour of another teacher, Donald Doull.

McIntosh stated in 1954 that although the Education Board's grant was generous, it was only so in comparison to local authority schools where the position was 'deplorable'. Nevertheless, in 1954, 600 volumes had been added and borrowing was up by 1,000. The Junior Section had been expanded 300% with S1–S3 boys gifting 200 books. The Junior School now ran its section while 30 Library helpers supervised by five Library

Prefects helped run the senior one. Above all, the Head was interested and gave full support. In 1958, the Head, McIntosh, took a different tack: *"gradually to reduce the stock of popular books hitherto used as ground bait and to raise the standard of the stock held – now over 10,000 volumes."*

Roger Young strongly believed that pupil use of the Library was a major factor in preparing youngsters to be students and deplored the fact that the amount granted by the Education Board was well below the level advised by the School Library Association and the National Book League. Above all pupils needed to learn the importance of self-disciplined work. To that end, he organised, as an experiment, unsupervised library periods in 1959–60 for S5 and S6. Needless to say it failed, yet he continued hoping that a separation of those two year groups might help the situation as would the extra space in the new Library room which would soon be available.

Next year Sir Roger was still complaining about overcrowding and a second Library room was desperately needed now as S4 had timetabled Library periods in order to help train them in the joys of private study. Book losses were serious, but Mr Doull and Mr Bell (Library Adviser) were on the case only to discover that about 800 books were missing.

In 1961, the cost of altering R64 into a Library rose from £500 to £1,570. By June 1962, the new Morrison Library had been *"... transformed out of a very dingy classroom"*. Despite this there was still overcrowding. The Blair Library's chairs had their arm rests removed and were strengthened. By 1964 Messrs Doull and Bell had finally got a grip on 'shrinkage' which had been reduced to a paltry 70 and Sir Roger was still bleating that the grant was too small, *"... in comparison with any similar sized Grammar School."*

In 1965, the Junior Library was moved to the old 'Stage Room' behind the stage which had been used as a Music Room and the books for use in the Sixth Form Library had been sorted and were awaiting its completion in January 1967. In 1968, the new Library was dubbed, 'The Blair and Morrison Libraries'.

The Great Fire of Watson's, 1951

31ST OCTOBER 1951

THE douce inhabitants of Morningside were, as usual, watching the daily procession of boys towards Tipperlinn when, suddenly, another procession began to stream in the opposite direction, with morning faces shining considerably more brightly than usual. In the words of the *Dispatch*, the dream of every schoolboy had come true—the School was on fire !

Within the building, as we surveyed the damage done to our beautiful School, satisfaction at the enforced holiday was less evident ; but the realisation soon came that, grim as it was, the devastation might so easily have been much greater. The Library, close to the scene of the fire, was undamaged ; the Hall with its great expanse of roof, the Ship, symbol of our traditions, were unscathed ; the kitchens, though blackened with soot and deprived of power, had suffered no more serious hurt.

Our photographs show the state of Mr Dickson's chemistry laboratory and the roof above it. In addition, the adjoining laboratory and the lecture room are affected by fire or water ; the rest of the north-west wing on the upper floor is cut off owing to the danger from falling plaster ; and in the rooms below—the Staff-room, the adjoining offices and the main music room—water still drips from ceilings and walls, and plaster hangs disconsolately. The walls of the two north staircases are smoke-blackened and an acrid smell lingers ; but nothing irreplaceable has been lost or seriously affected. It says much for the soundness of the building that the damage was so confined.

By the efforts of many, and to the disappointment of those who had hoped for an extended mid-term weekend, we were able the next day to carry through the normal programme with a minimum of discomfort, even to the serving of school lunches. But it will be many a day before the whole extent of the damage can be made good.

An inquiry could find no cause for the fire, but the Fire Brigade complained that it had difficulty getting in the east front gate and advocated the demolition of bollards and safety rails plus a widening of the entrance width to 10' 6".

Myreside Makeover

By the 1950s, the Grandstand at Myreside was Watson's Disgrace: *"... a continual reproach to Watsonians .... no credit to the School or the Club."* Not only had it lain unfinished since 1932, but it was also inadequate as regards accommodation and facilities. Eighty players were obliged to share one bath, 7 by 5ft. There were no separate changing rooms for referees, or even teachers. As a result the Pavilion was under severe pressure.

In 1956, the Merchant Company offered to pay one-half of the estimated £4,000 improvement costs. However, this would only improve the situation by providing two more changing rooms, a referees' room and modern showers. It did not include completing the main eyesore, the back of the Grandstand. Here it was hoped that two further changing rooms could be created and, in the remaining space, an indoor practice wicket. An anonymous Watsonian had already offered £500 towards the latter. It later transpired that this generous benefactor was Dr J G Martin. It would not be the last time that this fine gentleman would help improve the lot of present and future Watsonians. The total cost was estimated at £10,500, thus leaving the school to find £8,000.

The generosity of the Watson's 'family' can only be marvelled at. Before Christmas 1956, £4000 had been received and £2,500 promised, thus leaving only £2000 to be found. Given this amazing response it was decided to make an early start to the works. Plans were drawn up by Messrs J & F Johnston. Costs went up as well, but so too did the imaginative powers of donors. One elderly chap who had attended Watson's between 1884 and 1894 decided to give 1d for each hour spent at school. He calculated 21,000 days at 6 hours per day. The final total? £52.50.

The work was being completed in 1957 at an increased cost of £11,500. There was still enough room in the north end of the stand for another two rooms, plus bath and shower facilities. The work would cost another £2,500 and would go ahead

when the money became available. By 1958, Myreside was ready and only required *"... a cream-coloured coat of Snowcem."*

Cricket Wicket

Few people appreciate how much thought and detail went into this project which was finally completed in 1960. To ensure the best possible surface various bodies were consulted including the MCC and the National Playing Fields Association. Finally the best of its kind was agreed to be the Warwickshire indoor wicket at Edgbaston which had only been in use for three years. Three surfaces were in use there: slow, medium and fast. For learners it was considered that the slow surface would be the best and that was what was reproduced at Myreside. The base was made of concrete with mastic asphalt on top with a 3/16th inch rubber playing surface. The bowler's run-up and follow-through was made of cork. The entire surface was in a shade of grass green. It took 2½ months to make.

A New Pavilion

Following improvements to the Grandstand it was the old Pavilion which now was in sore need of attention. Unfortunately, it would prove very expensive indeed to adapt and renovate the old place, so, in 1965, a new building was planned in front of the Squash Courts facing the Cricket Square. This would act as an attractive new social centre with a mixed lounge and bar, plus office accommodation. The old Pavilion would be renovated with the old Tea Room being divided into smaller changing areas.

Four years later the reconstructed Pavilion was opened, *"...the first pint was drawn in the new bar at 4pm on Saturday, 8 March."* The new buildings transformed Myreside and included a new groundsman's house built to the left of the entrance drive. The old veranda was glazed its entire length, while upstairs the long room was extended and deepened to make the now familiar lounge and bar. Off it was a ladies' room and a mixed lounge. Myreside could now boast some of the best and most comfortable facilities in Edinburgh.

Myreside, 1956.

Indoor cricket, 1960.

New Entrance Hall and Veranda at Pavilion, 1969.

Costs went up, but so too did the imaginative powers of donors. One elderly chap who had attended Watson's between 1884 and 1894 decided to give 1d for each hour spent at school.

New and Better

Science Rules

In 1957, helped by grants from the Industrial Fund for the Advancement of Scientific Education in Schools, three new laboratories for Physics and Chemistry were opened, the School Museum was turned into a biology department and a lot of new apparatus purchased. Subsequently the number of science teachers increased, the time spent by S6 in laboratory work increased by 50% and a second Biology class was established for S4–S5. Despite all this the Head still bemoaned the fact that there was still a woeful lack of experimental science, but at least it was better than the position of technical which McIntosh described as *"barely adequate."*

Demolishing the Head's Toilet

As early as March 1959 Roger Young had identified the needs of his new school: an Interview Room for the Careers' Master, an addition to the Library, a Technician's workshop and, above all, a suitable Male Staff Room which could cope with a staff of 55. Even the latter was all a part of Roger's grand plan for *"... a pleasant and lively Common Room not only breeds contentment, but can create a stimulating intellectual life which is carried over into the teaching and is so communicated to the boys."* To achieve this Roger Young suggested demolishing the wall between the old Head's Room and the former Secretary's Room. The Education Board agreed and suggested demolishing the Head's Toilet, thus giving more space and building a new toilet on the north side of the corridor in a *"small closed courtyard"*. The Library problem was solved by the addition of Room 64. The Technician got a room on first-floor corridor and the Careers' Master got a partitioned-off classroom. Not bad for a start and nearly all this has stood the test of time.

Coal to Oil

The School changed from coal to oil ready for the winter of 1960. The possibility then arose of pulling

Sketch by the architects of the new Science sections.

Common Room and Study Block, 1966.

Library.

down the dominant and ugly brick chimney which *The Watsonian* commented *"... would cause no regrets."* One casualty was the furnace man, Ronnie Ansell, who decided to retire after 29 years with Watson's. A veteran of the Battle of the Falkland Islands and Gallipoli, Ronnie had also been Stage Manager of Pringle's Theatre (The Gateway) in Leith Walk before joining the new school in 1932. He retired, as many others ex-employees, to one of the cottages in Colinton Dell.

Building Fund

In 1961 a serious effort was made to improve and expand facilities with help from the Watson's 'family'. The appeal target, in December 1961, was £200,000. This was a school appeal, not a Merchant Company or Watsonian one and organised by a professional firm, John F Rich & Co. In June 1962, Arthur Hunter had expressed an interest in helping, so Sir Roger visited him and then went to meet Watsonians in Toronto and Montreal. A brochure was prepared and launched in 1962.

By the end of January 1963, the campaign was doing far better than expected and had raised £67,249. Plans were now prepared for the new S6 Block and Science Laboratories. By December, £150,000 had been raised with only a few *"hypercritical or hostile comments."* £246,000 had been raised by July 1964. The target was now revised upwards to £270,000.

This was undoubtedly the most important innovation of the period. Even the name evolved from *"The Building Fund"* to the existing *"Development Fund."* The aim was to build a new block of experimental laboratories, class and tutorial rooms plus a common room, all with the intention of encouraging reading and private study by Sixth Year. The justification was that numbers were increasing in S6 far more than ever before, that the nature of S6 students was more sophisticated and that far more was expected from them by further education and employers. In an increasingly competitive world the deciding factor would not be purely examination success as before, but include powers of self-expression,

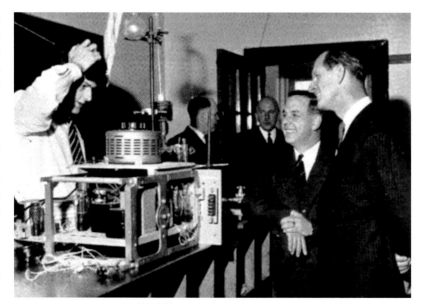

| *The Master of the Merchant Company, The Duke of Edinburgh, visited the School in 1966.*

the ability to think for oneself and tackle work in a resourceful, self-reliant manner. There is no question that Roger Young's clarity of thought and purpose would stamp itself on Watson's just as Doc Ogilvie's had done post 1870.

By 1965, £250,000 had been raised. Estimated costs had risen, thus a further £20,000 was required which all were confident of achieving. Construction was begun and the site visited by the Duke of Edinburgh on 6 May 1966. One year later, in March 1967, the S6 building was opened. It had a large Common Room with chairs and low tables, a Library of 3,000 books,

four study rooms and seven small tutorial rooms with chairs fitted with note-taking boards. It was stressed at the opening that the first year university failure rate was enormous and that Watson's must prepare pupils for more independent work. Also, pupils must be encouraged to be more responsible. To that end the S6 Library and Common Room were to run by an elected committee which would meet once a week instead of attending morning Assembly. Cynics, however, commented that the new facilities would aid only soporific activity and be open to gross abuse by the *"uncouth and ungodly."*

Musical Watson's

One of the truly great success stories of the 1950s was undoubtedly the Music Department more than ably led by Norman 'Pongo' Hyde with considerable help from Richard (Dick) Telfer. Hyde came from England via the Army and Robert Gordon's and replaced Mr Holmes who retired in 1951. He more than anyone else raised the profile of music within the school and helped destroy old-fashioned Scottish prejudice against the subject. The real beginning of music in Watson's started with the foundation by 'Pa' Lennie of the school orchestra as an 'experiment' in 1918 and its first performance on 9 July, 1919. It was boosted in 1926 when the SED required that music be taught throughout the school. Watson's then started a scheme to teach instrumental music after school hours. The orchestra flourished as did a jazz group in the 1930s led by David Veitch. Nevertheless, it was still regarded in the main as a fringe interest and not a subject for a 'real' boy.

Hyde and Telfer helped change all that. Above all, their enthusiasm was absolutely infectious. It was they, in 1953, who began the now famous Christmas Service. They also invited talented musicians to play in special concerts. In 1954 it was the Eric Roberts String Orchestra with Lady Barbirolli as oboe soloist. Also in 1954, they revived the Music Festival (an internal competition) after a lapse of three years. The standard was not high. The new Head only wanted it repeated in 1956 and definitely not the next year. This competition lasted a full day in June, plus two evenings, and ended with a concert.

A spreading of musical wings began during the 1955 Easter Holiday when 23 members of the orchestra and 26 choristers invaded the south of England, "... *where boy musicians are less a rarity than in Scotland.*" Most of the time was spent in Yeovil School where Hyde had been a teacher. This was Watson's first 'musical tour'.

Nearer home the choir took part in singing at Holyroodhouse for the 1954 and 1956 Royal visits.

The newly formed Junior School Orchestra played for the first time in 1954 at the Junior School closing concert. Hyde and Telfer even encouraged a Campanology Group which he hoped would succeed unless its members were "*.. hanged by the bell ropes.*" In June 1956, they revived the School Concert independent of Prize Giving. Another important and early breakthrough was the support for vernacular Scottish music ignored and ridiculed elsewhere by so-called classically trained and anglicised teachers. In 1957, they invited the Saltire Group to give a performance which included Scots and Gaelic items plus Jean Campbell on the clarsach, an instrument then only played by a very tiny minority. Not content with that, the far-sighted pair founded a Recorder Group in the same year which they hoped would interest the youngest pupils in music. At the second School Concert in 1957, the Head noted, *"There is some genuine musical talent in Watson's which may lead to the level which ought to be appropriate to a great school."* Hyde and Telfer deserve a memorial!

All this musical improvement, however, didn't rub off on singing at Assembly which McIntosh described politely in 1957 as *"uninspiring and so far has not been amenable to improvement. Indeed, non-singing or mumbling appears to have become just another of our many traditions, but anything can change ..."*

The second Music Tour was to Denmark at Easter 1961 organised by Norman Hyde and the Danish Institute. A choir and orchestra of 56 boys played three concerts and enjoyed the sights, including the pipe-smoking pupil of the venerable Soro Academy. In 1964 they were off to Paris during March and April. The Lycée Henri IV was visited, the ancient school with which Watson's had an exchange and a performance was given on French television. In 1966, the South of England was re-visited with 90 boys. This was a rehearsal for the proposed trip to the USA in 1968 and shows the careful and dedicated preparation typical of Norman Hyde. Both secular and church music were played.

Norman Hyde, 1972.

The Music School under construction.

The kind, talented and popular Dick Telfer (GWC 1952–74) who did as much as Norman Hyde to create a vibrant and healthy atmosphere in which Music was to thrive at Watson's. Also, along with Alexander Gibson, he set up Scottish Opera.

The Music School

Carol Concert, 1956.

This was the first to benefit from the Development Fund and the amazing generosity of one former pupil. What must be remembered is the totally unsuitable accommodation the Music Department had been working from since 1932. There were two, widely separated Music Rooms, Richard Telfer's being a cramped and narrow one behind the stage not designed as a classroom at all. Both rooms were subject to outside noise and their own. There were no individual teaching or practice rooms at all. *"Instrumental teachers are harried from room to room to find space or peace or a piano, to their own and other people's inconvenience; for the only rooms available are ordinary classrooms which happen to contain a piano."* (Roger Young, May 1960)

A Music School was highly desirable and had to be separate from the rest of the school. The first idea was a block to be built between the Janitor's Lodge and the War Memorial for which 'Pongo' Hyde had drawn a sketch at the suggestion of Sir Roger. Hyde even proposed raising part of the money through playing music for cash and using some of the boys to build it, an extension of 'Projects'. If built, it would free 'Pongo' Hyde's room to become a Sixth Form Common Room.

A huge opportunity presented itself when £35,000 was presented anonymously by an FP to build a Music School. Little did people know that Dr Jack Martin (23 Hatton Place), who had openly gifted £200 for the purchase of recorders, a xylophone and glockenspiel, was also the anonymous donor. Basil Spence was unable to accept the commission to design it because of other commitments. Michael Laird accepted the challenge, *"... with the approval of the donor."* By 1962, the estimated cost rose to £48,630 5s 6d plus some additional expenditure getting rid of five air-raid shelters and landscaping.

The foundations were laid in 1962. The design was ultra-modern, including a Concert Room with a hyperbolic paraboloid roof. It was opened following the Founder's Day Service on 10 March 1964 by Lord Harewood. A short concert followed the highlight of which was a poem by Hilaire Belloc (*He does not die*) specially set to music by the composer Alan Rawsthorne who was there to conduct it. The other works performed were Gustav Holst's *Turn Back o Man*, Peter Warlock's *The Capriol Suite*, Nos 1,5 and 6 and George Dyson's *Reveille'* from his *Three Songs of Courage*. Thereafter, light concerts took place on 10–14 and 16–18 March. This was followed by a concert tour of London and Paris at Easter, a half-hour programme on French TV, an open-air Concert in July at Penicuik House and, to finish a magnificent year, a special Christmas Carol Service. Five hundred boys were now involved in music which, for a Scottish school, was an amazing success.

A special abstract sculpture was erected at the entrance to the Music School, the work of Anne Henderson. It was described as a mystery with its own secret language. Hector Waugh, the Editor of *The Watsonian*, described it perfectly as both *"eloquent yet enigmatic."* In 1966, the Music School was chosen for the presentation of the awards by the Council for Industrial Design.

US Tour by Choir & Orchestra

At the end of August 1968 the choir and orchestra left on a three-week tour of the USA. The party was composed of 95 boys, two girls from the Ladies' College (clarsach & soloist), and teams of Country and Highland Dancers. Nine concerts were played as were two church services and two school assemblies. All agreed that the most memorable had been the performance in Washington Cathedral although the climax of the tour had been the massively warm welcome given to the party at Hamilton College.

The two men responsible for creating a centre of musical excellence at Watson's, retired in the 1970s, Hyde in 1972 and Telfer in 1974. As *The Watsonian* commented: *"Norman Hyde's attitude to modern values in life and music was clear: unremitting negation of the rubbish and active encouragement of talent, hard-work and good manners."* His farewell concert on 28 June was the largest ever seen in Watson's: 200 choristers, an orchestra of 70 with the biggest audience ever witnessed crammed into the Assembly Hall. A recording was made and 250 copies issued.

A huge opportunity presented itself when £35,000 was presented anonymously by an FP to build a Music School.

Boarding Boys

The first 'official' boarding house was opened in September 1956 and named in memory of the first playing field, 'Bainfield'. As about 110–120 boys boarded annually scattered around various private families, it was decided that a school boarding house, or houses, be set up which might even attract more parents to send their children to Watson's. When one old-established boarding house run by Mrs Cooper was about to close, it was suggested that the school take it over in co-operation with The Watsonian Club.

While plans were being formulated, however, a bigger and better house at a good price became available at 4 Gillsland Road.

A non-profit making organisation was formed to run it: George Watson's Boarding Houses (note the use of the plural). It was run by seven Directors: the Headmaster, three Merchant Company representatives and three from the Council of The Watsonian Club. £10,000 was required and the Education Board granted £4,000. The rest would be raised by issuing debentures in multiples of £100 paying 6% interest.

Mr W Clark of the Maths Department and his wife became the first to run Bainfield with a staff of three. It was a large three-storey house with an acre of garden plus stable and coach-house. Five dormitories were created varying in size from ten to five beds each. A Common Room and Dining Room were provided along with oil central heating. The plan was to create a warm, intimate, snug, safe and home-like atmosphere. There would be plenty warm water and no chance of "... *small boys setting themselves ablaze.*" On the top storey the eight smallest boys would have their own dormitory with dreamy views across the city.

In 1966, a fire engulfed the stable block destroying the Games and Store Rooms. It was decided to rebuild, but include rooms for a resident Tutor. In 1967, Alex Weston left as Housemaster and was replaced by Mr and Mrs

Bainfield House.

Meadows House, 1958.

Donald Scott with David Christie as Resident Tutor.

Meadows House

The second boarding house was opened in 1958 at 7 Spylaw Road. Formerly it had been 'Athole Lodge' run as a Watson's boarding establishment by Miss Ritchie who had retired. Its first Housemaster was Oliver L McLauchlan and catered for 32 boys. It was named Meadows House "... *to recall the site of the old School and George Watson's Hospital.*"

Third Boarding House

Opened on 18 September 1961 at 10 Ettrick Road and named Myreside House. Catering for 34 pupils, S6 had its own dormitory on the ground floor while S3–S5 shared rooms at the top of the house. It was run by Dr and Mrs Walter Baston.

There would be plenty warm water and no chance of "... small boys setting themselves ablaze."

Towards the Merger, 1974

In November 1967, the plan was publicly announced to join the two Watson's Colleges together to form one co-educational establishment in Colinton Road. George Square was zoned for an extension of the University while Colinton Road had been largely modernised and had room to expand. In 1961, the Education Board had asked the City to rezone the University Playing Fields at Craiglockhart as the new site of GWLC and that had been agreed. The idea now was to 'link' the schools. Once the site had been acquired it would take five years to build thus being ready by 1974–5. The St Alban's Road building used for P1–P5 would be sold and the amount raised used to build at Craiglockhart plus a Dining Hall and Kitchen. The Prep Block at Watson's would be used for P6 and P7 although one new classroom would have to be built. P6 and P7 would move from the Main Building (where Maths now is) and this would allow the Senior girls to move in provided that a new Art/Craft/Domestic Science building was completed along with classrooms and a Social Subjects wing.

In 1973, plans were finalised. This was the most ambitious scheme since 1932:

• Yet more science laboratories.
• More kitchen space.
• A new block for P1–P3 on Tipperlinn playing fields to the west of the line of trees between rugby pitches T2 and T3. The loss of the playing fields would be offset by the acquisition of the present University Sports Ground at Craiglockhart.
• A covered Games Hall.
• A Design Centre which would accommodate Art, Technical and Home Economics.
• A Social Studies block to incorporate History, Geography, Economics, Modern Studies and RE. This would be built across the east side of the then Junior Playground (now the East Quad), in front of the Rifle Range. It would house its own library, projection facilities and tutorial rooms.

There was no mention of a purpose-built theatre which many at the time felt was a glaring omission, especially given the popularity of drama in both schools. Unfortunately, not all of this plan was executed.

Assembly Hall Makeover
By the late '60s, the Assembly Hall had become more than a bit shoddy. It was also underutilised. In November 1972, it had been revamped and redecorated: a new stage curtain was installed; the lighting improved; the floor stripped, sanded and varnished; walls and ceiling repainted in a pale French mustard colour plus two shades of grey and the area under the gallery was curtained off for use by small discussion groups. Although used for Morning Assembly the Hall was mostly empty for the rest of the day. In an effort to get clubs, sports, gym and drama to use it a volley-ball pitch was laid out as was a badminton court. Eventually it became such a popular venue that a booking system had to be introduced.

Myreside House.

Meadows House.

Myreside House.

Tipperlinn: From the Gaelic 'to ber' or 'toper' meaning a well and 'linn' meaning a pool or river. The site of the old well is in the grounds of Viewfield House on the corner of Tipperlinn Road and Albert Terrace. The river was the Jordan, or Pow Burn which has disappeared underground.

Coronation Trees, 1953

On 6 February 1952, George VI died. To celebrate the forthcoming Coronation on 2 June 1953 of his daughter, Elizabeth, 23 cherry and crab apple trees were planted at the front of the school on 1 April by old and some very young members of the Watsonian 'family'.

EccE (see page 159) announced that one of the Coronation Trees, planted by the Lit Club, had died a dastardly death on 11 July 1955. The Lit Club Secretary, *"... accused the Dramatic Club of poisoning the tree by administering an over-dose of weed killer."* The truth was that a Chemistry class had been experimenting with arsenic and a solution of the said liquid had been left on a windowsill. Another class came in and one boy, who thought it was water, threw the beaker's contents out.

The Preparatory School trees were planted by Brian Thom, son of Jim Thom of rugby fame, and by one of the smallest of all the boys, Colin Young. The boys were later asked to describe the event:

> " A Boy is planting a tree he has ai spesd and erth and he is shuvling it on a Big Boy is hodling the tree."
> " On wedensday we planted a coronation tree at wotsons and Colon yong with his spad poot the erth in the hol on that day it was very windy the boys wer making a noys."

> " I am planting the tree at wosnsns I am colin yung I hoiv got good musls."

> " The trees are planted now at least we hop thea are groing now."

> " I so a luvly tree for the Coronation I wos very very hapy We plantid trees for the Coronation the trees wil tern into blosim of ol culers."

> " It was windy we wer cold dont let the wind make you cold."
> " A tree was planted at the coronation at wastsins boys. I hope it grow the wind was being a nyoosens I was cold I had to stand."

The Preparatory School. Brian Thom, Colin Young.

The Master.

> In presence of the whole School, trees were planted by the following :—
> The Master of The Merchant Company and Mrs Dick Wood ; the Headmaster and Mrs Andrew ; the Treasurer of The Merchant Company and Mrs Bennet ; Mr J. Ainslie Thin, President of The Watsonian Club ; Mr Norman McK. Manclark, Vice-Convener for the School ; Dr George Robertson, former Headmaster of the School, and Mrs Robertson ; Mr Williams, on behalf of the Staff ; and representatives of the four Houses, the Prefects, the First Fifteen and First Eleven, the Literary Club, the Field Club, the C.C.F., the Scouts, the Choir and Orchestra, the Young Farmers' Club and the Junior and Preparatory Schools and Cubs. At the close of the ceremony the Vice-Captain of the School presented a pepper-mill to the Master as a memento of the occasion.

Dr George Robertson.

The President.

The Blair Morrison Library

The 'Morrison' part of the Library (ex-Room 64) was named after William Shepherd Morrison, born 8 October 1893 in Torinturk (Argyll & Bute) of North Uist parents. Educated at Watson's and Edinburgh University Morrison joined the Royal Artillery in WW1 during which he was thrice wounded, mentioned in despatches twice and won the Military Cross. He became a lawyer in England and was elected as Conservative MP for Cirencester and Tewkesbury in 1929. In Parliament he acquired the nickname 'Shakes' because of his habit of quoting Shakespeare. Morrison had a long career under four Prime Ministers: MacDonald, Baldwin, Chamberlain and Churchill. He became Parliamentary Secretary to the Attorney-General (1931–5), Financial Secretary to the Treasury (1935–6), Minister of Agriculture and Fisheries (1936–9), Minister of Food (1939–40), Postmaster General

Lord Dunrossil being sworn in as Governor-General of Australia.

(1940–3) and Minister for Town and Country Planning (1943–5). In 1951, Morrison was elected as Speaker of the House of Commons in the first contested election in the twentieth century. Morrison was the first Gaelic-speaker to hold the position. He resigned from Parliament in 1959, taking the title of Viscount Dunrossil of Vallaquie which is on N Uist, the land of his forebears. His resignation meant that for the first time since 1911 there were no Watsonian Members of Parliament, the first of whom had been Lord Strathcarron. Robert Menzies, Prime Minister of Australia, then invited Morrison to become Governor-General which he held for exactly one year until his death on 3 February 1961. He is buried in St John's Churchyard in Canberra.

This part of the Library should, however, be a memorial not only to William Morrison, but also his five Gaelic-speaking, bagpipe-playing brothers (Donald, Donald John, Sandy, Cecil and Neil) who all came to Watson's in 1899. John became Chief of Clan Morrison, but the most famous of all was Sandy, Watsonian extraordinaire, killed-in-action at Loos on 25 September 1915.

The Cadets

Junior Training Corps
The JTC was still going strong in 1945 with 200 boys on parade per week. The usual activities continued, plus several visits to the Usher Hall in order to witness 'Freedom of the City' ceremonies for wartime dignitaries such as General Montgomery.

By 1947, army surplus equipment was showered on the College which soon found itself with an abundance of weapons once again. Greatcoats were issued for the first time which the boys thought were very 'cool', "… *particularly the type without brass buttons.*" Even army boots were issued without the need for coupons.

'Back to normal' for Watson's Cadets meant getting out of battle dress and back into kilts. Unfortunately, boys had 'borrowed' so many kilts during the war that there were hardly any left. A plea was made for a return of the said items.

Another attraction of the Cadets, of course, was being invited by Mary Erskine's GTC to its dance in Queen Street. Seventy Cadets trouped along with the exciting prospect of a return event.

Cadets, 1958. Down Ben MacDhui into the Larig Ghru.

Air-Training Corps
As early as 1943 there was a falling-off of numbers and enthusiasm in this one-time most glamorous wing of the Cadet Force. Numbers hovered about the 60–70 mark and measures were taken to attract youngsters by introducing radio and practical navigation. The radio idea proved to be popular with modern radio equipment being used … and protected by the Physics Department. Another attraction was a certificate course in gliding.

The Combined Cadet Force
In October 1948 the two organisations above were united into one, although separate identities continued.

Bell-Bottoms
A Naval Section was first introduced into Watson's in the winter of 1949 under the command of Sub-L D MacInnes. Sixteen boys joined in its first year.

Corps Camp, 1951
For the first time the Annual Camp

included a climbing expedition which 'did' The Saddle in Argyll. This sparked a lot of interest. By October 1952 there was a record number of boys in the Corps: 264. By 1954, that number had increased to 296.

Watson's Big Gun

In 1951, an artillery section was formed by the Head *"on his own responsibility"* and trained using a 25-pounder field gun lent by 278th Regiment TA. A garage was made ready underneath the Open Air Gym at a cost of over £100 which would be paid for out of the 'School Canteen Fund.' By October 1956, the school, however, was proposing to return the artillery piece because of continuing maintenance difficulties. The Education Board demanded to know what the freed accommodation would be used for. It was suggested that the staff joiner be given it as he had no workshop. The Head replied that he was hoping to get an army truck which would be garaged in the gun shelter. As for the joiner, it was suggested that the air raid shelter near the Junior Cycle Shed would do as, *"it was a solid structure and it is a pity having it lying there derelict."* The Merchant Company Superintendent of Works, B Wilson, was having none of it as the gun shelter was not ventilated, alternative ventilation would have to be provided for the pool's Purification Plant Room, fire insurance premiums might be raised as a garage was a risk and the depth of the shelter was only 11ft 3in, sufficient only *".... for a very small car."* He suggested that the derelict

Cadets, 1961.

Cadets, 1963. Artillery Section, winners of the Scottish CCF Gun-Drill Competition.

> *The joiner's old store [became the] Cadet Clothing area which was duly fitted out as such by 1958 and promptly broken into twice.*

shelter would make a better garage at a cost of about £70 excluding a road across the grass. Watson's joiner obviously had influential friends.

By April 1957, the field gun had been returned and the garage was empty. The Head wrote pointedly to Harvey Jamieson, the Secretary of the Merchant Company: *"I understand you would like to have it for the school joiner."* As the Armoury was crowded the Head requested the joiner's old store as a Cadet Clothing area which was duly fitted out as such by 1958 and promptly broken into twice during one weekend in September. The only item taken was an empty box of. 22 ammunition, but the police were not amused and an extra-strong padlock was furnished. Gunner training continued at the

Drill Hall of 278 Field Regt (TA) in Grindlay Street.

National Service

In 1957, as National Service was wound down, the fear was that boys would resign en masse from the Cadets once they had gained Part 1 of Certificate A. To attract youngsters they needed to concentrate on leadership and initiative skills. As McIntosh put it: *"that rather more emphasis be placed on activities developing those qualities and rather less on formal military training."*

The fall away never happened. In 1958, there were still 269 Cadets. The new initiative training techniques borrowed from The Duke of Edinburgh's Award scheme and the Scouts were proving very popular.

| *Music Radio Club, 1956.*

Glider Glee

In September 1955, the RAF Section suggested that it might be a good idea to obtain a primary glider, but were advised that the necessary shed provided by the RAF might just delay matters. If the school could offer accommodation it might speed things up. The Head, Mr McIntosh, suggested using one of the air raid shelters on Tipperlinn as the dimensions were correct. If the interior could be cleared and a door made then *"… it would be pleasant to put it to some use."* In November 1955, the RAF said it would definitely supply a glider, but not financially aid the alteration of the shelter because it was private property. Also, the supply of glider sheds had dried up. Estimates were sought as regards the necessary work and one for £45 recommended for acceptance.

GM3 BCD

Attracting new recruits in a brave new technological world was continued by the creation of a Radio Club in 1955 which was attached to the Signals Section, supported by the Technical Department. In 1956, it got a licence to set up a short-wave radio station the call sign of which was GM3 BCD. It was run by Mr Simpson from a small room under the Hall, *"… giving easy access to the roof for the aerial feeders."* Soon Watson's was in daily contact with Alaska, Greenland and Malaya which was astonishingly exciting in the days before computers and the Internet. Younger members built receivers and all learnt Morse. Even a public address system at the Annual Games was installed by Club members.

Camps

Two very different camps were attended in 1956 and 1958. The former was the English Public Schools Camp at Aldershot at which Watson's was the sole Scottish representative. Indeed, it was the first time a Scottish school had been invited by Southern Command and was regarded as a considerable honour. In 1958, another first was achieved when Watson's Cadets attended the very first Leadership Course sponsored by the War Office. It took the form of an outward-bound course in the Cairngorms with sleeping bags and anoraks. It was very popular as were similar initiative tests held in the Lammermuirs.

Trouble Ahead

It was McIntosh who first observed in October 1957 that the Cadets might have a limited future.

"It will be interesting to note the effects of declining National Service on recruitment of Cadets. My guess is that a more serious and vital problem will be the recruitment of officers. Difficulty is already being experienced in finding staff a) qualified and b) keen enough to undertake the work."

The same applied to sport. There was a *"scarcity in the teaching profession"*, so the academic side was considered above all else.

In October 1959, the difficulty of appointing officers was raised by Roger Young after Fl/Lt Sherriff of the Air Section resigned. In the following year the Corps lost four officers and only one was replaced. Roger Young now recommended that NCOs be trained to take command of various activities rather than depend upon officers.

Radio Club, 1959.

The Glorious Sixties

1960 was the Centenary of the Cadet Forces, so Watson's helped with Beating Retreat at the Castle, took part in the service at St Giles' and three Cadets went to take part in the London parade.

In 1960, a glider operated from the school as part of the Air Section's activities. The maximum number of launches in one day was 40. In 1961, the Cadets continued outward-bound training in Wester Ross which "... *was not intended to be a military exercise."* The Corps Commander, Oliver McLauchlan, resigned in 1961 and Robin Morgan took over after only being in the school for six months. Next year he was in charge of the biggest Army Section in years and hoped to form a section of the Royal Electrical and Mechanical Engineers which involved popular skills such as vehicle maintenance. In April 1962, they were involved in 'leadership and organisation' training in Killilan Forest, Wester Ross, which involved a treasure hunt and an adventure journey. A camp was also held in Norway.

"... Campsites are more and more difficult to get from the Army, and schools are forced to cast a fairly wide net in order to ensure that the CCF Summer Camp will be able to hold the interest of boys and extend them. Taking a leaf out of Eton's book, the idea of sending a party to Norway was conceived some 12 months ago ... the party will consist of 85 boys, Major Morgan in charge, Major Doull, Captain N Clark, Lieutenant R Hendry, Captain Gee (a Watsonian TA officer) and a Watsonian Cadet from Sandhurst, J Robertson... The Camp will be held at Sauda, north of Stavanger."
(Roger Young to Harvey-Jamieson, 7 June 1962)

The following year the Annual Camp was held in in Belgium. In 1966, they were in Ullapool engaging in an imaginative 'escape and evasion' game modelled on Eric Linklater's popular book *The Prince in the Heather* but mostly it was mountaineering with the climax being an ascent of Stac Polly. Officer recruitment was being described as acute. In 1968, they went to Belgium for a second time, this time by air, and also visited WW1 battlefields including Verdun. In 1969, a party went to Skye while the Annual Camp was held at Killilan.

This was a vibrant and forward-looking school organisation involved in naval aviation, navigation, gunnery, catering, signals, Duke of Edinburgh's Awards, electrical and mechanical engineering, railway and port operating, flying and gliding. Even Highland Dancing appeared in 1967 as an activity with a team, *"most ably coached by Miss Dilbey and Mr Hunter"* which came second in the Team and Individual dancing events at the Scottish Pipe Band Competition. In 1968, Watson's Cadets became the first Army Section in Scotland to drop battle-dress in favour of *"a more comfortable khaki jersey."* There was, however, a severe staffing crisis again in 1968 and 1969.

Nevertheless, it came as a stunning shock when the school disbanded the entire organisation in 1970, including its independently financed Pipe Band. A Corps Reunion was held in November 1970 in the spirit of *"sorrow and nostalgia"*:

"... the pipers ... made a very brave show and struck the right note of defiance. The Corps marched out with its head held high."
(*The Watsonian*, 1970)

The last camp was held at Ardtrostan with the now usual outdoor activities ranging from sailing to rock-climbing. There was no school Pipe Band at the 1970 Annual Games. The Cadet Corps was finished.

The Demise of the Corps, 1970

The sudden disbandment of the Cadet Corps after its Annual Camp in 1970 was met by anger, shock and disbelief. Over the years that anger has not been assuaged, so it is right that some time be spent examining the issue. The Corps was disbanded, according to Sir Roger, because there was no no-one willing to take over the Corps from inside the school while the appointment of an outsider would cause problems. Sir Roger did, however, sum up perfectly how people felt:

"The Corps is an old and honourable institution, it has a fine record of achievement, it has meant a great deal to large numbers of boys, and their parents, it has absorbed much of the leisure time of a small band of dedicated officers, it is a part of the school and its history, and to consider disbanding it is a hateful business. And yet after considering every means of overcoming the officer deficiency I am forced to conclude there is no alternative."
(Roger Young to the Education Board, 20 January 1970)

There is no question that the Corps was a vibrant and go-ahead organisation when Roger Young arrived in 1958. Certainly it was not as strong as it had been under Bill 'Cappie Dick' Dickson, CO from 1936 to 1949, but, given the growing anti-military mood amongst post-war youngsters, the Watson's Corps was not only merely holding its own, but thriving. Indeed, the Corps was actively involved in promoting outdoor pursuits in order to encourage both personal independence and self-reliance. It was not an archaic organisation stuck in some pre-war time-warp. This is the Inspector's Report given on 22 June 1956 by Col WI Moberley, two years before Roger Young was appointed Head:

"The strength of the Contingent is obviously conditioned by the counter-attractions of leisure of day boys as compared to boarders. In the conditions the strength of the Contingent is satisfactory, and is sustained by obvious enthusiasm on the part of officers and by good support from the Headmaster.
The main ingredients of the
individual and collective performances seen were dash and vigour, but the standard of instruction and supervision was creditable in view of the comparative lack of time for practising the details in a CCF contingent.
The local shortage of practical training areas is liable to have accumulative effect on the enthusiasm of the Contingent officers and the more senior cadets through becoming too well acquainted with the details of the ground. ...
I consider that, generally, the activity and standards demonstrated by the Contingents did the School credit."

The problem lay not in a lack of interest by youngsters, but with adult leadership. Those involved in 1958 were Norman Clark (Classics), Roy Mackay, Roger Sherriff (Modern Languages) and Oliver MacLaughlin (Classics) who was CO, 1957–61. The problem was that Norman was getting near retirement and promotion might account for the younger ones. Sir Roger regularly asked candidates for teaching posts whether or not they would be interested in helping with the Corps and was met by an equally negative response. Younger candidates no longer had the experience of National Service, or even CCF experience at school, while older ones felt they were beyond giving help of that kind. Oliver MacLaughlin was succeeded by Robin Morgan (CO from 1961). The situation stabilised, but the underlying problem did not disappear. The matter was made worse as there was a shortage of teachers and Sir Roger could not make *"... a particular kind of extra-curricular service to the school a condition of appointment ..."*

The Crisis

The crisis arose when Robin Morgan was promoted to be Headmaster of Campbell College, Belfast. Norman Clark, who ran the Army Section, had the experience to take over, but, being close to retirement, he wanted to give up. Roy Mackay, who ran the Air Force Section, said much the same thing, though he was not close to retirement. Roy had become quite keen on S3 Projects and felt he could not do both. Donald Doull who ran the Signals Section also stated that
he intended to retire. There is no question that Sir Roger did canvass staff members such as Pat Edington (Biology), but met with no success. Pat felt, for example, that his main interest was sport. The Education Board was notified by Sir Roger on 13 November 1969 that he intended to disband the Corps the following summer.

Advice was offered and taken from many sources. The Admiral Commanding Reserves stated that no realistic help could be expected from the Navy and it was better to *"hang up its colours"* with dignity. Group Captain Hunter of the RAF could not see any officers being available to help and the best solution was for boys to join the ATC. The Army proved to be the most helpful and as early as 20 November Major Hamill was suggesting possible sources of help such as the universities, officer cadets, the TA and Reserve Officers. Indeed, they were prepared to offer the services of Officer Cadet McCall-Smith of Edinburgh University OTC. However, this would be for a limited period only and he was not an experienced officer. Brigadier Balharrie could see no long-term solution, namely, *"... the continuous direction and control of training in the school."*

Neither the Merchant Company, nor Watsonians were at all pleased to see the Corps disband and a number of meetings were held to find a solution. Even as late as mid-March 1970 no decision had been taken by the Education Board. One possible solution was a joint Corps with Daniel Stewart's. This, Sir Roger felt, was *"...administratively of doubtful viability and at best a stop-gap."* The only serious suggestion was that a commissioned officer, or officers, be brought in from outside Watson's. Sir Roger was not convinced, however, that this was a really feasible or wise solution. His main objection was that the value of the Cadets, apart from the usual educational and character-building aspects, lay in creating valuable bonds between staff and pupils. That vital staff-pupil link would be lost by introducing an outsider. As Sir Roger put it: *"The loyalty of boys in the CCF is a loyalty to the school expressed through the*

Contingent, not basically a loyalty to the Army, Navy or Air Force as such."

If pupils felt they really wanted to join a military organisation, and not a Watson's one, then there were many other Cadet units in and around Edinburgh. Sir Roger's other objection was the issue of 'responsibility' if problems arose because the CO would not be an employee of the school, or Merchant Company. A solution was not reached. The suddenness of the disbandment was explained by Sir Roger:

"We agreed that despite the disappointment and dismay of many Watsonians and others, disbanding the CCF was the only proper solution. Moreover, we all agreed that it was important to go out with a bang and not a whimper: a slow decline in support and interest would be far worse than immediate closure with due recognition of the value the CCF had been to the School."

Sir Roger also felt that the Duke of Edinburgh's Award scheme and S3 Projects were engaged in similar activities as the CCF. Projects involved all pupils and large numbers of staff which the CCF did not.

Critics, however, state that the will was not there to succeed: that members of staff could have been found who were interested in supporting the Corps and a solution to 'responsibility' could have been discovered. Sir Roger did not try hard enough. The concept of a vital staff-pupil link necessary in any extracurricular activity was not consistently followed. The dynamic Rowing Club, for example, was led by George Hunter who was not a member of staff. Critics argue that Sir Roger wanted the military influence out of the school and used the lack of staff involvement as an excuse to do it. All of this Sir Roger strenuously denies and the surviving evidence does tend to support his case.

The issue did not disappear and for many years attempts were made to reinstate the Cadets as a school activity. Brigadier Frank Coutts, Colonel, The King's Own Scottish Borderers, wrote on 25 January 1974 to the Master of the Merchant Company, Hugh Rose, complaining that the lack of a CCF unit was *"... a very serious handicap for a boy going forward to*

For many years attempts were made to reinstate the Cadets as a school activity.

Regular Commissions Board." Coutts was hoping that the Education Board might do something as it was packed with Territorial Officers. As regards the lack of leaders:

"I simply cannot believe this. There must be about 90 masters at Watson's, and there must be several who would be prepared to have a bash. I have recently met two young schoolmasters at another Merchant Company school and they told me how much they had enjoyed the new Sandhurst course for CCF officers with no previous experience."

He was sure the Army would help, but in the meantime the school should start and attach a Watson's unit to a Cadet Contingent in town. Indeed, Frank Coutts offered to help as he had moved close to the school. It was as successful as all other well-meaning attempts. In this instance because of arrangements for the coming merger a Cadet resurrection was put on the back burner, but Coutts did not give up:

"I am delighted to learn that your Board might be prepared to take my proposal into account when considering plans for the new co-educational George Watson's College. This would appear to open up a wonderful opportunity, not only to re-activate the boys CCF, but to start one for the girls as well. You may know that Dollar Academy are now running the Pilot Scheme for a girls' contingent of the CCF, and I am told by my sister-in-law who is a teacher in the school that it is a great success." (To Hugh Rose, 4 February 1974)

On 19 October 1976 Hugh Rose was holding Roger Young to a promise made in 1974 that *"... once the two schools were integrated he would look at the matter. I think the time is ripe for consideration of reforming the Watson's CCF."* Nothing, however, came of it.

After only two years in the job Sir Roger began a campaign which all new Heads attempt: the Campaign for Smartness and Standards. Sir Roger, in 1961, declared war on unpunctuality, irresponsibility, untidy dress and poor attendance. The staff were to blame, of course, with some members failing, "... to maintain vigilance and real supervision."

For the first time since the late '40s a dress code was emphasised:

- *Highland Dress: kilt, tweed jacket (NOT a Blazer) and suitable stockings or Cadet/Scout Uniform or Blazer*
- *Trousers: (Dark blue flannel shorts at least until the end of S2) S3 boys could wear longs, 'with turn-ups'. The height of 5ft 6in restriction was abandoned.*
- *Stockings: maroon*
- *Socks: grey*
- *Shoes: black (rounded toe and three lacings). Brown sandels permitted in summer.*
- *Shirt: grey or white (white for special occasions).*
- *Pullover: V-necked, plain white or grey*
- *Raincoat: Navy Blue — S6 Fawn*
- *Scarf: maroon and white.*

He was still fighting that campaign in 1964 when Watson's was hit by a spate of vandalism with switches, radiators, windows and library tables all receiving particular attention. Not only that, but some members of S3 devised their own special Project: shoplifting. A run-ragged Sir Roger explained: "There is no doubt that there is a group of undesirable boys at the centre of much of this .... only 2 or 3 strong, but influencing other boys out of all proportion to their number." By 1966, Sir Roger was still not winning: "The casual attitude and vandalistic tendencies of a minority element are disturbing and give us some cause for concern." Who were to blame? Yes, of course, certain members of staff!

The Pipes and Drums

Just as the British Army did not maintain its pipe bands, so the Army Cadet Force did not finance Watson's band. Instead, it was supported out of annual subscriptions paid by Corps members. After 1945, however, attitudes had changed. As in other matters the mood was 'fair shares for all': a subscription might debar some children. Thus, by November 1952, the Pipe Band was left high and dry with no means of support. It desperately needed to replace its old dark green uniforms which were faded, patched and darned. Khaki jackets were not regarded as an attractive option. The Band also needed modern drums and more sets of pipes. A support fund was opened and fund-raising began in earnest.

A New Beginning

"Glamorous new uniforms" were on parade for the first time in 1956, made possible at the last minute by a gift of £180 from an old Watsonian who had left in 1914, but preferred to remain anonymous. The uniform remained much as it had been pre-1939, but striking maroon doublets with white piping had been substituted for the old ones of bottle green. Under the able leadership of Pipe Major Murdo Montgomery, Watson's achieved its first victory at the novel East of Scotland Schools Band Competition held at Glenalmond. Enthusiasm for the band was at a high and, for the first time, the idea of a Watsonian Band was mooted, if only *"... for New Year's Day at least!"*

Fifty-three members ranging from 7HJ to VIA were boasted of in 1958. The Band was 5th out of 11 in the annual Cadets' Band Competition held that year in Crieff and took part with other East of Scotland units in Beating Retreat at Edinburgh Castle. Black steel rod-tension drums with plastic heads now replaced the old brass and rope-tensioned ones with skins which burst easily in heavy rain. A modern and smart band had been revived. As the Head said:

"The Pipes and Drums are growing and keen and should by 1959/60 be one of the best School CCF bands in Scotland."

The Pipe Band, 1955.

The Cadet Band, 1963.

Next year, the annual competition was held for the first time at Myreside. Again, the Band was placed 5th although I Turnbull won the individual drumming for the second year running.

A smart Pipe Banner was presented by Mrs Darling and Mrs Sinclair while the Highland Watsonian Club presented a quaich as a trophy for the internal open piping competition. The Band also got a Band Room. Piping was taught by Mr Logie, Drumming by Mr Fergusson and Bugling by Ted the Janitor. Those were the days when army drummers were all required to play the bugle in case, of course, modern radios failed and the British Army had to resort to drum and bugle calls against the armed might of the Soviet Union. The Band was flourishing.

In 1960, the band was composed of young players with the oldest being in S4, a sure sign of neglect at some time in the recent past. Nevertheless, it was asked to play for the passing-out parade of the Royal Highland Fusiliers and also beat retreat at the USAF base at Prestwick. In 1961, Sir Roger said its *"morale and standard of play are high"*. It came 3rd in the Band Contest.

All that disguised a real problem: lack of strength in depth. In 1965, the Band was *"... on the brink of extinction."* A recruiting drive resulted in an influx of S2, but the Band did not enter the Band Contest.

By 1968, a small group of Watsonians were resuscitating the Band: Robert Sawers, John Manson and Robert Simpson. They were too late. The Corps was scrapped in 1970. Had the Band been in a healthier state it might have survived as an independent unit.

Parental Bliss

Children may be a blessing, but some parents are most definitely not, especially when defending an obnoxious fledgling or brood. In the Cadets an inordinate amount of time was spent by Officers trying to retrieve bits of equipment and uniform from wayward boys. In October 1961, Major Robin Morgan's patience snapped after attempting to get uniforms returned.

"Doubtless your reasons are the human ones of sloth, indolence or forgetfulness, but I do not propose to let your failings result in losses to the unit, and, as I consider that you have had a sufficiently long time to muster the energy to visit the Armoury, I propose to place this matter in the hands of the Police, unless these items are returned forthwith."

(Major Robin Morgan, Commanding Officer)

The boy's father replied …

"In your letter dated 25 October 1961 received by my son today (11 November) you accuse him of 'sloth, indolence or forgetfulness' and it is obvious that the accusation is born of personal experience in such failings. …I consider your letter such an impertinence that I am communicating direct with the Merchant Company and Headmaster. …"

In his letter to the Merchant Company the father maintained that:

"According to my son this is the only intimation he has received requesting return of the equipment."

Teacher readers may have come across that one before. As usual, however, the issue was partly a misunderstanding and could have been avoided. A tactful reply by Roger Young apologised for Robin Morgan's strong letter, but pointed out that the initial letter requesting a return of equipment and uniform had not been sent by Captain Lymn although Robin had thought it had been. The father was thanked for getting his son to return equipment, but five items were still missing: cap badge, tie, oil bottle, pull through and denim buckle. There is a moral or two somewhere in this story.

A Wappenschaw

A Wappenschaw (a Scots military display, from the German Wappenschau) was held in the Summer of 1954 at Myreside in order to raise money for the Pipe Band. It included drill without commands with a final fusillade, a fly past by two members of the air section, a model aircraft with a 5½ ft wingspan which refused to become airborne, the inevitable PE display, spirited, but dodgy Highland dancing, a ragged signalling demonstration plus a 25-pounder gun which *"… fired off a dozen imaginary rounds of high explosive in the general direction of Heriot's."* All that and a big shaggy dog which threatened to disrupt each new act.

[a 25-pounder gun] … fired off a dozen imaginary rounds of high explosive in the general direction of Heriot's.

Of Heriot's or Watson's ghaist
or yours, I wonder whilk is maist
dumbfounert, dozent and bumbazed
  wi indignation
to see our modern Embro taste
  in education.

We may jalouse George Watson's banes
will gowl the maist wi grieslie maens
nou that his schule for puirtith's weans,
  foundit sae weill,
chairges sic fees and taks sic pains
  to be genteel.

Extracted from Robert Garioch's poem addressed to Robert Fergusson. Garioch (1909–81) was an FP of the Royal High School.

Up in Smoke

The final Cadet Camp at Ardtrostan on Loch Earn ended with a feeble singsong around a bonfire, 1970.

A School Chaplain was appointed for the first time in 1955. He would be responsible for Morning Service four times a week, RE for Protestant youngsters and hospital visits.

The Armoury

The Cadet Armoury used to be below the entrance to the PE Block. It is now used by the school joiner. In 1956, there was a real concern that terrorists might break in, especially the IRA. Although the door was steel-lined, the windows barred and the 300 rifles chained, the fact that it was in a semi-basement not overlooked by houses and far away from the road led the police to conclude *"... that determined men could cut their way in with little difficulty and no possibility of interruption."* The solution was a burglar alarm which would automatically phone the police. That was, however, not so easy, especially when dealing with the Army and War Office.

The saga began in 1955 when the Corps Commander asked the Scottish Command Conference for an alarm. No reply was received except a circular letter requesting requirements and costs. The Armoury was then inspected by the police and representatives of two burglar alarm firms. The details were sent to the Army on 13 January 1956. Again, no immediate reply was received, but a reminder was sent in March which advised that authorisation was being awaited from the War Office. By 22 June, the day of the Annual Inspection, nothing had been done. The Inspecting Officer, therefore, incorporated the matter in his report. The Army then demanded to know when the proposals had been initially submitted, but no further reply was received. In November 1956, however, the Scottish Command Conference stated that *"work is now in hand and will be completed as soon as possible."* The fact was, however, that even by December no work whatsoever had been done and it took several more months for it to be completed.

Six years later the Army was intent on improving the alarm to the Armoury door. Despite the Head's disapproval of a wire being strung out along from the PE Block to the Main Building's roof and thence to the Janitor's Lodge (now Reception) where a big gong would sound if the door was tampered with, soldiers from the TA Field Artillery completed the work during the summer while the Head was on holiday! No authorisation for

Gordon Mowat (Head Janitor, 2005).

the work had been received from either the school or the Merchant Company, and, worse, the troops had pierced the asphalt-covered roofs and stone pointing with clips for the wire. All were bemused and no adequate explanation was ever received. Artillery chaps subsequently repaired the damage. Later in the year the Army wanted the rifle racks transferred from the outer to the inner Armoury, proper storage facilities erected in the outer Armoury and a partitioned office made there too. As the Army had taken over maintenance of CCF accommodation there was no problem. Roger Young was even hoping to get them to finance part of the Rifle Range considering that at Fettes they built virtually a complete

Range. Plans for the Armoury were submitted in December 1963. In 1969, the door frame was covered in metal and a wall safe built. All to no purpose, of course, as in 1970 the Corps was disbanded.

A big gong would sound if the door was tampered with.

School Clubs & Societies, 1945-1974

Old-established societies continued as if nothing had happened. The old Lit Club was doing its stuff by showing lantern slides of 'Pre-War Berlin' and debating motions such as 'Psychology is the Curse of our Time' against Heriot's, Mary Erskine's and Gillespie's.

The Radio Club erected a frame aerial on the roof of the Geography Department while the Cubs and Scouts continued to be prepared as ever. However, the popularity of the Scottish Schoolboys' Club had fallen since 1939. One hundred had gone to camp in 1939, but only four 10 years later. The Edinburgh Schools' Citizenship Association – catering for an interest in modern studies before its inclusion in the curriculum – continued with a wide variety of activities including films, debates, discussions and conferences on such subjects as 'Racial Discrimination' and 'Self-Government for the Colonies'.

A new Society was founded in 1949: The Edinburgh Schools' Scientific Society. It soon claimed an astonishing 300 members within the school. Its first lecture was on 'Colour Vision' by Dr Eggleton of Edinburgh University followed by one on genetics by Dr Auerbach.

Another new activity was one combined with The Watsonian Club: sailing. In 1949, a small group of eighteen were co-operating with the Royal Forth Yacht Club in its activities such as building dinghies and cruising on the Clyde.

Thus, by about 1949, both school and Watsonian Club activities were up and running.

The Fabulous Fifties

Thirty youngsters banded together in 1956 to form the Photographic Society with DL Macdonald as President. Their aim was not to record school events, but learn the principles of photography. As part of their fund-raising a Calendar was produced for 1957 which proved a lucrative money-spinning venture.

What would become one of Watson's biggest and most famous Clubs was founded in October 1957

by the enthusiasm of George Hunter, Secretary of the Scottish Amateur Rowing Association. The Club was formed as a member of the St Andrew Boat Club which gave it the use of boats and oars on the Union Canal. First of many gifts was a set of oars and the first of its many wins was in June 1958 at the Dumfries Regatta.

The Art Society was formed in April 1958 under the Head of Art, Scott Irvine. Unusually for a school society it restricted its number to 20 with a Committee approving membership. Obviously it had not heard of democracy, or even Robespierre. Its first meeting was held on 1 May 1958.

The usual school societies continued, some flourishing more than others. Lit Club debates continued, for example, *"That National Service is harming, not helping, this country."* One of its most enjoyable occasions was the Balloon Night. In 1954, *"Leonardo da Vinci stoutly claimed he should be the one to stay in the balloon, as he had invented it. The Adjudicating Gods agreed with him."* The 75th Anniversary Burns's Supper was celebrated by 75 members. The Lit Club also produced *Phoenix.* McIntosh's comment in October 1957 was:

"Their magazine Phoenix *was disappointing, as the Editor's anxiety to make it pay was permitted to lower the purely literary standards – not uncommon in modern journalism."*

The following year McIntosh was even more scathing. Watson's, he said, *" … should be able to support a production that depends on literary merit and not a parish pump journalism more suitably catered for, if at all necessary, by the weekly summer news-sheet* EccE.*"*

Despite the absence of girls the Scottish Country Dance Society, founded in 1946, continued to birl and twirl with the aid of any lady to hand, teacher or wife. Another organisation interested in a bit of flesh was the Young Farmers' Club. This had existed in Watson's seemingly since time immemorial, but was finding the mid-50s as tough as old steak with a distinct lack of customers. Nevertheless, in 1954, it hoped to gain new blood with a visit to the Corporation Slaughterhouse.

The Swinging Sixties – 1974
The Duke of Edinburgh's Award Scheme

This began in Session 1962/3 as part of the Cadet Corps activities with 30 boys three of whom were tackling Silver and 27 Bronze. The physical fitness part was being ably organised by that star of the PE Department, Donald Scott. By 1965, Watson's had gained 2 Gold, 26 Silver and 17 Bronze. The scheme had *"… been run almost single-handed by Sgt I B Stewart."* Sir Roger hoped it would spread beyond the Cadets, but also emphasised that many boys were achieving its aims but without being involved in the Scheme. Away ahead of the merger, in 1967, one group was organised as a joint venture with the Ladies' College. The following year a strong and definite effort was made to organise D of E far more widely in the school and attract those not in the Cadet Corps.

It was that 1968 campaign which really made The Duke of Edinburgh's Award scheme take off in Watson's. It began with a film and talk by the ever enthusiastic Charles Corsar (Col 8/9th Royal Scots and Secretary of D of E in Scotland) who charmed 71 pupils to take part. The Scheme has never looked back since.

Archaeological Society

Founded in 1963 and run in a highly professional manner which included learning the Egyptian language and, in June 1964, the beginning of a long-running excavation seeking Dere Street near Soutra Hill. In 1963, the leading light was Ian Cassells who was soon to leave for Cambridge. Sir Roger wondered whether this society would merely become *"a nine days' wonder."* He need not have worried for its members were made of sterner stuff. Three years later the society was still going strong. At a dig at Douglas Burn a medieval wooden-handled dagger was found and this enthusiastic group even persuaded the great Sir Mortimer Wheeler to speak to them. In 1968, a dig was held at Braidwood Fort, Silverburn, under the supervision of one of the finest archaeologists of the age, Professor Stuart Piggott of Edinburgh University. If only all school societies were organised thus!

Exploration Club

Founded in February 1963 with 68 boys from S5 and S6. The first exploration was on 23 March of Upper Tweeddale, a 15 mile hike over the hills around Stobo. One party surveyed a cottage on Minch Moor with the idea of using it as a weekend house. 1964 saw three expeditions: Crianlarich, Garth Youth Hostel and Dollar Law, Tweedsmuir. Session 1964/5 saw the first canoe expedition along the Union Canal. It proved so popular that a separate section of 35 boys was formed who went on excursions to Linlithgow Loch, Loch Tay and the Firth of Forth. In 1966, the Merchant Company acquired Ardtrostan House on the south shore of Loch Earn, Perthshire, to act as a centre for field studies and outdoor pursuits. This old farmhouse had been transformed, could cater for 24–30 pupils and had a resident couple who acted as caretakers (Mr and Mrs Fraser). This Centre was for all four of the Merchant Company schools. In addition, two mini-buses were available for the 2 ½ hour trip. In 1967, Old Howpasley, a shepherd's cottage in the Border hills, was leased to Watson's on a trial basis. Staff and parents furnished it. Users were charged 1s a night.

The George Washington Society

Founded in December 1962 to encourage the study of American history.

Kipling-Kitchener Society

Begun in early 1962 to study British History during the latter half of the nineteenth century. The first talks included the Temperance Movement and the Ashanti Wars.

Poetry Reading Society

This small informal group began in 1959 to read poetry of all kinds from Chaucer to Ginsberg.

Motor Sport Club

Begun by Mr Morgan in January 1960 with a membership of 30 with films, lectures and visits such as to Ingliston motor racing circuit. The owner of Ecurie Ecosse, David Murray, also showed pupils his latest racing car. In 1967, some members went to Silverstone in uniform and, said Sir Roger proudly, "... *must surely have helped to spur Jim Clark to victory.*"

Record Club/Music Society

Begun in October 1969 to foster all kinds of music. A large membership of 90 which held lunchtime meetings with its own version of *Desert Island Discs* as well as monthly ones in order to listen to music informally. Sir Roger loved this Society hailing it as *"a significant development... It underlines the 'grass-roots' interest in music and will create yet another use for the new Music School."* Two societies here? 1965 – joint programme with large mixed choir from Simcoe Composite School, Canada.

Cinematographic Society

Founded on 14 September 1970 to help amateurs make better films. Mr Cowan commissioned a sound film of the Centenary Exhibition held during Charities Week.

Bus and Rail Club, 1969: Model Railway Club, 1970: Philatelic Society, April 1970: Geographical Society, 1970: Wargames Club, 1972

Economics Society

Founded September 1968. Its 30 members made the first trip on 1 October. The venue? Usher's Brewery.

Community Service Group

Begun in December 1968, with "... *the object of making service to the community a permanent activity throughout the school year.*" The Group immediately began work with Shelter and hoped to expand into work with the Simon Square Centre and the Cheshire Homes. By 1972, this ambitious and imaginative group was involved in work with the Royal Edinburgh Hospital and Craighouse, had designed an Adventure Playground 'kit' which could be marketed, repaired footbridges in Glen Tilt and Kintail, got S2 boys to help the elderly at Pitsligo House, involved pupils to help in Children's Homes in Colinton Road and Corstorphine as well as signposting footpaths across the Pentlands. Its most ambitious project, however, was sending eight boys to India to live with Indian families in a scheme run by the English Speaking Union and the Indian Government. This Group was strongly supported within the school.

Hair

For the first time in living memory long hair came back not only as a fashion, but also as a statement of teenage rebellion and individual freedom. Watson's, of course, devised a rule in 1968 that hair could not be longer than the cheekbones in front of the ear, but some boys wondered whether this also applied to the three girls from George Square who were attending Colinton Road in preparation for their Oxbridge exams! This select little band was the advance guard of things to come.

A member of staff was appointed to take charge of each of the four senior year groups. In other schools these people were known as 'Principal Teachers of Guidance', but that might send the wrong message to those choosing a safe haven for their offspring. Watson's thus created 'Year Heads' whose main job was said to create a sense of identity beyond House and Form, but who would also give extra help and guidance to a very small number of occasionally wayward or troubled pupils. Cynics, however, said they were 'jobs for the boys'.

An S5 Common Room was created in 1968 from the cloakroom nearest the Maths corridor. The boys furnished it themselves, even raising £80 for a new carpet.

Better Late than Never
A plaque was affixed to the wall just inside the main door commemorating the opening of the school on 22 September 1932.
The year? 1956.

You Sixthy Thing

In 1961, S6 were being encouraged to make far more of the last term by doing their own version of 'S3 Projects' which involved excursions, lab work, model building (working mini-hovercraft and car) and listening to various talks by university-based Watsonians. Nevertheless, in 1963, Sir Roger was still faced with a 'couldn't care less attitude' by many and this led to a highly structured venture known as the S6 Project Programme, but fitting in with Sir Roger's idea of training boys for life. The entire scheme lasted for two weeks, was unsupervised and all suggestions came from the boys alone, except for the computer part and help for the Cheshire Home at Granton. Groups went to Torridon (to help the National Trust), Kinlochewe (Nature Conservancy), Iona and the Cairngorms. The following year, projects had to fit into one of three categories: service, a practical school-based idea or a survey furth of Edinburgh. One in particular shone: *"Christopher Smith's record of his survey of the Pennine Way is a fascinating illustrated guide and 'companion' running to some 80 pages!"* (Sir Roger Young, 1969) Much of the success of this scheme was due to Donald MacDonald who had a real flair for bringing out the best in people.

The Education Board, in 1961, accepted Sir Roger's idea of Tutorial Groups, but suggested groups of six instead of four to make for better discussion and that the topics should be given in advance. By 1962, the only complaint was that suitable books were difficult to find. In 1964, pupils were given four periods of preparation for two periods in Tutorial Groups. By 1967, the syllabus has been formalised as nine periods of RE, art and music, philosophy of science, literature, economics and politics.

Another important development by Sir Roger was the high profile given to careers advice with the appointment in 1967 of a dedicated member of staff, Donald MacDonald, who became responsible for arranging careers talks, interview training and liaison with universities. As a result Donald nurtured one of the best Departments of its kind in Scotland.

As Prefects' Badges were retained by the boys stocks had become exhausted by 1947. The girls in George Square had the same problem, so, in austerity Britain, a joint badge in silver was designed, the boys as a buttonhole and the girls as a brooch. Unfortunately, purchase tax was raised to 125% soon after this decision was made forcing an oxidised silver-plated version to be authorised in January 1948. One hundred of each kind were produced at a total cost of £25 as against £100 for the silver ones. The badges were made by Kirkwood's. The Watsonian Club came up with an alternative shield-shaped design in March 1952, but nothing came of it. In 1961, the die stamp from which lapel badges for the School Captain would be produced was presented by Andrew Burnie who had left school in 1960.

SVI Tutorial Classes, modelled on the University pattern, began in 1962 to help the transition between school and university. The substance of these Tutorials would be, *" ... to study some of the great questions of our day and civilisation."* Some teachers felt quite happy with this, but others felt adrift and wanted guidance. "Who am I?" was a 136 page type-written booklet prepared in 1971 by Roger Young to give some uniformity and depth to SVI Tutorials. The latter were completely revised aiming to achieve a maximum of eight boys and three members of staff, preferably a mix of humanities, arts and science. In addition, each boy was allocated a Tutor who would help with his UCCA forms and write the necessary reference. Again, it was hoped that this too would open up new, closer and friendlier lines of communication between staff and senior pupils.

Before the War the School Captain had received from The Watsonian Club a silver-framed picture of the school. This now proved to be too expensive because of wartime restrictions and an alternative was devised: a replica of the school torch designed by Messrs Charles Henshaw & Son. In 1951, all Captains from 1941 would be presented with this memento.

To replace the former silver medal for Scholarship and Games, a plaque was designed showing the Founder's coat of arms. These were also presented to all winners retrospectively.

"Presented by The Watsonian Club for Scholarship & Athletics".

1971/2 saw a new Prefectorial system adopted which involved all of S6 and not just a select few. The number of Prefects was reduced from 30 to 17:

- School Captain
- 7 Form Captains
- 2 Vice Captains
- 2 S6 Returners
- 4 House Captains
- 1 Library Prefect

Form Captains were chosen from a list of pupils elected by those in S5 who intended to return in S6. The major change here was that all of S6 would now have duties to perform by rotating the Form Group responsible for them every two weeks. During that time those pupils would be permitted to use the Prefects' Room. This system would help prepare S6 for university, but also go some way to appease the more democratic spirit of the times. The Prefectorial System was giving way to one of 'Office Bearers'. In 1972, S6 planned a Charities Week which would include a 'Sixth Form Revue'. Both were encouraged by Mr JG Scott who became the guru for all things Sixthy.

The School Council, 1974

This began in October 1969 to help develop House activities. The four House Masters would be helped by two boys elected by each House. Weekly meetings were held under the genial, good-natured Chairmanship of Jim Cowan.

Post-School Projects

John Sanson, a Bristol surgeon who had left GWC in 1900, left money for pupils to engage in a "worthwhile activity". The first seven pupils to benefit were:

- Peter Craig and Stewart Crawford who spent three weeks in South Acquintaine studying the Albigensians and the Crusade launched against them by the Catholic Church.
- Ian Hetherington and Fraser Grigor travelled to Yugoslavia to collect Montenegrin folk-tales.
- Richard Beaton and John Fleming who became involved in the restoration of the Kennet and Avon Canal.
- Craig Mair who spent nine months in Anatolia searching for sealed Byzantine Churches. A satisfying career followed writing books and teaching History.

Dr Arthur Hunter

Arthur Hunter, 1964.

Dr Arthur Hunter, a loyal and generous supporter of his old school, announced in 1955 that he would provide a scholarship for a Watson's boy to study for a year in a United States residential college, namely Hamilton College in Clinton, New York. That College had a strong Presbyterian tradition with an emphasis on the liberal arts. The first 'Dr Hunter Scholar' was C Leslie Murison (6a) who was joint Leader of the Orchestra, Secretary of the Lit Club, an NCO in the Air Cadets, a member of the Highland Dancing team and an accomplished scholar. The scholarship would pay college fees, board and lodging, but, as it was felt that parents should contribute something, Murison would pay his own passage. Hunter probably got the idea from an earlier successful scholarship programme in 1947 when the British and American Schools Scholarship Selection Committee

chose George L Walker to study in the US during 1947/8.

Dr Hunter hoped his exchange would become an annual scholarship, but it was too costly for him and other members of the North American Club to fund indefinitely. Hamilton College valued the connection and was prepared to fund it liberally, but not entirely. The English Speaking Union administered and fostered the plan, but could not support it financially. Dr Hunter visited Watson's in 1958 and gave a substantial gift in order for it to continue. It is not known how much Dr Hunter gave, but the trustees, the English Speaking Union, was now administering a fund of £9,000. The scholarship, incidentally, was in memory of 'Ethel Parsons Hunter'. Dr Hunter died in Montclair, New Jersey, in 1964.

> *Dr Arthur Hunter announced in 1955 that he would provide a scholarship for a Watson's boy to study for a year in a United States residential college.*

Hamilton College, 1959.

Founder's Day

Graham Andrew rightly gains the credit for introducing a highly structured series of events which included pupils as well as Former Pupils. He did claim that it was *"The first Founder's Day in the history of the school"* which is technically correct, but he had little knowledge of Hospital history.

"It has long been felt that a day should be set apart when pupils, past and present, of George Watson's College should join in an act of homage to their generous and far-seeing Founder." (Graham Andrew, April 1947)

Andrew chose Friday 11 July as Founder's Day for the good reason that it was the day before the Annual Games (called by 1947 'School Sports Day'). He hoped it would become 'an occasion' visited by all the Watson's community.

The boys, like their Hospital forebears, probably would have been happy with a 'play day', or holiday, but that was far from Andrew's mind.

- First, there would be a morning Service in the Hall where an oration would be given by 'a distinguished Watsonian'. The first choice was who many regarded as the then greatest living Watsonian, Sir John Anderson. Wreaths would be laid at the foot of the Memorial Tablet in the Entrance Hall by the President of The Watsonian Club and the School Captain.
- Second, a Luncheon would be provided for invited guests in the School Dining Hall once, of course, rationing had been relaxed, or even ended. (At the first lunch in 1947, three survivors were present of the first day in 1870: DM Forrester, G Boyd and R Gibson.)
- Thirdly, an afternoon cricket match would be played between a College and a Watsonian XI.
- In the evening the School Dramatic Society would provide the *"… climax to a great day of remembrance and reunion."* The first play was *Saint Joan* by Bernard Shaw, produced by Scott Allan who had founded the Dramatic Society in the 1920s and done so much to popularise drama in Watson's.

The following year all this was being called 'tradition' and the cricket fixture became 'the usual match'. Thus are Watson's traditions made!

Given the rather refined nature of the new Founder's Day, Andrew then looked for a more dignified school song. In a thinly veiled attack on the raw and often raucous 'Hail to the Old School' sung to the tune of 'Hail to the Chief' he suggested a new approach:

"Is it too much to hope, though, that some Watsonians with the necessary dramatic flair may one day produce a great School chronicle play to prove a fitting climax to our Founder's Day? … There is an opportunity also for a poet or a musician to combine in composing a worthy School song for the occasion so that we may no longer have to deal with ours in borrowed plumes – or rather tunes!" (Graham Andrew, April 1947)

No-one took the bait.

Founder's Day Moves, 1962

One casualty of the new exam system was Founder's Day. It is often forgotten that under the old Leaving Certificate the exams were taken around Easter thus leaving a marvellous 12-week period of freedom, especially for S6 which allowed them to become involved with many other school activities. The new Certificate exams were now timetabled for May. The result was that the date of Founder's Day in 1962 was altered from the day before the Annual Games to Friday 16 March. That date was chosen simply because a Calcutta Cup match would be played at Murrayfield and it was hoped that wandering Watsonians would visit both events. The afternoon cricket match, however, was ditched in favour of House Rugby.

FRONT: Turner Ewing, Esq, master of the Merchant Company; Lord Provost Sir John I Falconer; The Headmaster; The Rt Hon Sir John Anderson.

1870 meets 1949: Messrs George Boyd, Robert Gibson, Charles Ainslie and Rev Dr DM Forrester, (1870), with Dr Arthur and the School Captain.

The Jubilee, 1970:
100 Years as a Day School

GWC: History and Record, 1724–1970 compiled and edited by Hector Waugh with Jimmie Allan collating the statistics. Hector was Head of History, Editor of *The Watsonian* and a Director of the family building company. Jimmie inherited the famous family firm of J & R Allan on the Bridges, but decided on a massive career change later in life, training as a teacher and then doing yeoman service in Bellevue Junior Secondary School (now Drummond). Jimmie's pal was Jack Martin who did something very similar: inherited the family bakery business, switched to studying medicine in his thirties and then began financially supporting good causes. Both Jimmie and Jack were committed Christians.

At the end of the 1970 Summer Term a joint concert with the choirs and orchestras of the four Merchant Company schools was held in the Usher Hall when a special work by Dr William Mathias was performed.

A Founder's Day service and lunch was held on Friday, 25 September 1970 to celebrate the opening of the Day School on 26 September 1870.

During the entire 1970/1 Session the school was open to visitors.

Other activities included a Fancy Dress Dance, a S6 Revue and a Centenary Rugby Match.

On 24 February 1955 it was agreed to have a copy of Watson's portrait painted by Mr Haswall Miller for £150 plus expenses of £40–£50, all paid from the Lamb Bequest. The copy would be hung in the Entrance Hall along with Dr Ogilvie's portrait.

Record Russian

On 22 February 1947 a BBC recording van parked itself outside the main entrance to record a Russian lesson by Mme Anna Semeonoff, the foremost teacher of Russian in Scotland. It was broadcast on the European Service and proved to be so popular that the BBC asked permission to record Watson's boys singing Russian songs.

1947 was also the first year that Russian was offered as part of the Higher Leaving Certificate, an exam pioneered by Anna. Three Watson's pupils achieved passes.

Dux Discovery, 1951

Deep in the bowels underneath the Hall a board was discovered with all the names of the School Duxes from 1828 to 1870. This had come originally from the Hospital, but then had been placed above the great door of the Hall in Archibald Place. As the Board had seen better days it was decided to record the names, "… in the alcove off the front entrance hall" above the Founder's Memorial Tablet. The Vice Convener of the Education Board, Mr Reid, offered to pay the entire cost himself.

The arms on the old board was "renovated and erected in the prefects' room." Does anyone know what happened to it and the board?

Last Tram for Shrubhill

Friday 16 November 1956 saw the last eight trams leave the Braids for Shrubhill Depot in Leith Walk. A Watson's pupil, J Inglis of 6a, was in Reserved Car No 2 which was third in the procession. Huge crowds lined the route, many risking life and limb to lay a penny on a rail. Inglis, "… thought it very strange that I would never be in an Edinburgh tram again." The end of an era.

The Watsonian Boy

This film was made in 1946 by Will Fyffe, Junior when he was an S6 pupil at the school. It lasted an hour and showed wonderful scenes of everyday school life and activities. It was originally a silent film with titles by Charles Dawson although a commentary was dubbed on later. The school has one copy which is disintegrating fast, but at least six copies were made. Do you have one?

Will Fyffe was the son of the late actor and comedian of the same name. In 1944, he had gone to North Africa to play piano for his father who was entertaining the troops. Eventually Will joined the Rank Organisation.

AM Paton, AK Black & J Stewart fishing on the Tweed, 1959.

The Progress of Music

Alastair Cameron McGill Duncan died of septicaemia in 1941 shortly after leaving school. Six years later his grieving father presented a bronze relief, *The Progress of Music* by Pittendrigh Macgillivray which was described as *"... a fine example of the work of the distinguished Scottish sculptor."*

Music was, indeed, progressing. At one time the choir and orchestra only performed once a year. Mr Holmes began to improve that. The first major innovation was a Music Festival begun in 1947 which was really an internal competition to help raise standards. Inspired by Mr Holmes a gramophone recording of choir and orchestra was made in 1950 and was on sale. It included the Lord's Prayer, the 23rd Psalm, The School Song and an orchestral piece, Mozart's *Eine kleine Nachtmusik*.

In 1951, Mr Hyde was appointed as Head of Department and quickly set about creating a vast programme compared to previous years which involved choral works for both the Carol Service and Founder's Day. A new conductor of the orchestra, Mr Telfer, began improving standards by establishing a Pupils' Concert in March 1953, a small junior choir and a junior orchestra with 24 members.

The Music Department was on its way to creating the deservedly high status that it currently enjoys.

A Fishy Business

In 1951, one of the strangest gifts ever offered was one of Fishing Rights on the Tweed presented by Mr JHW Lownie. At first it was refused because of the dangers of the Tweed. As an experiment Lownie offered the Field Club 50 tickets which boys could use provided a parental letter of consent was received. It was so successful that pupils – and teachers – have been fishing there ever since.

The stretch is a two-mile one at Thornielee midway between Walkerburn and Clovenfords. Part of the agreement was the creation of a School Angling Club, which, if ever disbanded, would result in the fishing rights being withdrawn.

Due to local complaints about the 'waste' of good fishing rights to a bunch of 'townies', boys who went to fish were instructed to wear their blazers so that the local Borderers could see that it was being properly used, and often.

EccE

This wonderful, satirical–cum–news magazine was founded in 1952 by G Orr and WR Oatley as a Summer Term enterprise. Twelve issues had been produced in two years and, by 1954, *EccE* was selling a healthy 490 copies per week. Each issue contained 45 inches of column space and was sold on Thursday mornings. Profits were split between a donation to the Craigmillar Boys' Club and the Blair Library, provided that books were bought which, in the spirit of *EccE*, could only be read, *"... for the fun of it."*

EccE admitted that many critics thought there was too much sport while the anti-Cadet Corps faction considered there was too much easy pro-Corps advertising.

"A strongly worded and vigorous article was easily written, but as often as not invited the blue pencil. The temperate article, which one hoped would hold the buyer's interest, but not invite him to burn down the school, came more slowly from the pen. Censorship is too strong a word, but something of this kind was necessary if the demise of The Wallpaper *in the 1920s was not to be repeated. The editors were also saved the worry of wondering whether this issue could be their last."* (*The Watsonian*, 1954)

In 1956, the Head stated that *EccE* was doing fine, *"... with a master as censor. This is a necessary precaution as I have been at pains to indicate to the boys that, since I regard the school less a people's democracy than as an enlightened despotism, the Press cannot wholly be free."* (McIntosh)

EccE continued walking the tightrope for many delightful, entertaining years. In 1962 it was bringing out a twice-termly Lit Supplement called *EHEU*. Five years later it was claiming to be *" ... the longest running, if not the only, weekly school newspaper in the country."*

The term 'Bug Hut' to describe the Boarding House may have begun with an 'underground' rival to *EccE* begun by Ian Macmurrich in Meadows House about 1956/7 entitled *The Bug Hut News*.

The Kirking of the Master
This venerable and ancient ceremony first took place on 20 January 1956 in St Giles' Cathedral. By the following year, of course, it had become 'a school tradition'.

Cycling Proficiency Tests

Police cars zoomed into Watson's in November 1954, but only for 10 officers to put 103 First Year through Cycling Proficiency Tests. Inspector McLaren, an FP, supervised the proceedings. Boys had to show a knowledge of the Highway Code, the dangers of being in traffic and how to maintain a bike.

Ninety-five passed. The eight who did not must be the ancestors of those today who ride straight through red lights. And getting away with it may be down to a paucity of Watsonian Inspectors!

Get the Point?
The Royal Company of Archers was given permission in 1950 to shoot in the College grounds during evenings when the Lord High Commissioner was in residence at Holyrood. This was granted in perpetuity, "subject to school requirements." Perhaps we should remind these elderly gentlemen ....

A Little B
The Editor of The Watsonian, Hector Waugh, was stung by a bee at Assembly (This sounds like a poem. – Ed). The Field Club, it transpired, had taken delivery of two new hives donated by Dr D Hutchison of Musselburgh.

The Chipmunk

In 1955, a Chipmunk training aircraft flew over the Prep School and landed in the middle of the playing fields. This member of Edinburgh University Air Squadron had to make a forced landing on the cricket square at Myreside, narrowly missing the school chimney. The pilot (an Academical) was unhurt and flew off the next day.

New Reports

Old Report Cards were a statistician's joy filled with % marks, places in class and median marks. In his first Report in 1959 Sir Roger was clear and forthright: " ... our present Reports are wholly inadequate as a means of keeping Parents informed about their son's progress, conduct and welfare. ... I hope we may gradually improve our school reports so that they may be fully informative about the whole boy rather than a list of the marks he has obtained in examinations," In 1961, these were scrapped in favour of more personal comments not only from class teachers, but also the Form Teacher and Headmaster. The Watsonian commented that this would give the teacher " ... a real challenge to his confidence and command of the language." Teachers rose to that easily enough ("Works at his own pace, very gently."), but, unfortunately, absolutely no extra time was given to write such reports.

The Six-Day Cycle

Although the Education Board gave its approval in 1959 to the new 7-period day and the lengthening of each period by 5 minutes to 40 minutes, it was not so sure about the 6-Day Cycle which was thought to have *"practical difficulties."* Nevertheless, it was agreed to give it a trial.

The rationale for change was as follows: the old school day had 8 periods of 40 minutes each in a day which started at 9.15am (after Morning Assembly) and ended at 3.25pm. Thus 15 minutes was available for a mid-morning break and 35 minutes for lunch. The Junior School (aged 9–12) ended at 3.05pm. Sir Roger felt that these were only nominal 40 minutes as boys moved across a widespread campus. The resulting 35 minutes in practice was *"… not an economic teaching span."* In addition, such short breaks combined with a rush to class at the beginning of each period turned the school into *"a helter-skelter"* without time for intellectual reflection or refreshment.

Sir Roger proposed a 7-period day from September 1959. The loss of one period would result in the lunch interval being extended from 35 to 55 minutes and a five-minute 'change-over' time between periods. Thus a full 40-minute period would be achieved while the quality of afternoon classwork should rise after an *"adequate lunch and recreation interval."*

One major consequence of all this, however, was that a 7-period day would only give 35 periods to be apportioned between the same number of classes as the previous 40. Sir Roger then proposed the revolutionary step that the timetable be no longer tied to the days of the week. Instead, he proposed the 6-Day Cycle. The advantages, he claimed, would be that 42 periods would be available for allocation and holidays would not hit the same subjects each time. Staffing would not be affected except in PE where there was a clear case for one redundancy.

Renaming Classes

The Leaving Certificate examinations introduced in 1888 emphasised academic excellence. This Certificate was divided between Highers and Lowers taken in Fifth and Sixth Year respectively and, up until 1950, a candidate had to pass a group of subjects (like the current German Abitur) in order to pass the Certificate. In Watson's, pupils were academically streamed within each year group (U down through A, W, X, Y), class U (University) being expected to pass the Higher Certificate without much difficulty.

From 1950 onwards the condition of a group pass was eased and an award could now be made for each individual subject. In 1961, the Leaving Certificate was renamed the Scottish Certificate for Education and the Lower Grade was replaced by a less demanding Ordinary Grade taken in Fourth instead of Fifth Year. The intention was, of course, that able pupils would bypass Ordinary Grades and aim straight for Higher in Fifth. As no subject was made compulsory in order to gain a subject this led to a blossoming of courses such as biology, modern studies, applied maths, navigation and horticulture. The last major change was in 1968 when Sixth Year Studies emerged despite criticisms that it was the beginning of despised and unwanted English specialisation.

In 1959, Watson's renamed its classes in accordance with changing attitudes and conditions. From S4 classes were set not streamed and renamed according to the main subject, or group, chosen eg Science, French, Spanish, Classics, etc.. Thus '4 Fre 1' indicated a pupil in Fourth Year who had chosen French/ languages and was in the first class or group. Pupils now chose their subjects in S2 and all boys were to take five examinable subjects. A relatively free choice was meant to counter *"indifference and apathy".* Sir Roger argued that the old system encouraged a 'Register Teacher' when he wanted a 'Form Teacher', ie someone who would see the youngsters more regularly, probably teach some or most of them, get to know strengths and weaknesses and carry out pastoral duties. He wanted *"a close-knit, fairly intimate community within the larger community of the school in which each boy knows his personal place and value."* A similar approach would be applied to S6: Cl (assical), M (odern) and Sc (ience).

Parental Involvement

In 1957, two serious attempts were made by McIntosh to involve parents in the education of their children. The first was a Parents' Afternoon where all the work and tests produced by a child were place, on his desk for inspection by his parents. Secondly, for the very first time, a Parents' Evening was held for S1, S2 and S3 in the Senior School. After a civilised cup of tea in the Dining Hall parents could interview a teacher in his own room. All this was regarded as useful, but it was only once a year and no written reports were being produced.

It was Sir Roger who radically changed the situation. Once the new reporting system was in place and a frank exchange of views was now being invited then the inevitable followed: parents' meetings which eventually gave rise to hour upon hour of exhausting evenings with no compensation whatsoever for the teachers involved. The first instigated by Sir Roger were for P7 and S3. But that was only the tip of the iceberg to come: *"I hope it will be possible to arrange, through the year, several meetings for parents along these lines so that each parent will have the opportunity by the time their sons leave of consulting the school at the most important points in his career: eg at 9, 12, 15 and 17 years of age."*

The '60s saw the beginning of teacher exploitation on a grand scale. If Sir Roger had an Achilles' Heel then it was his lack of sympathy with the financial plight of young teachers expected to give their all in return for a disgracefully low salary amounting, in the early 1970s, to about £90 per month!

By 1969, Sir Roger was launching another campaign with a fresh target: "What I want to see happen in the school is an awakening of the visual Arts within the curriculum. We are not doing all we should in the time allocated to Art in the timetable."

Getting Away

The first post-war school trip abroad took place between 17 August and 3 September 1946. Forty boys aged between 14 and 18 spent two weeks in Haarlem in Holland living with local families. This was an exchange visit organised by the World Friendship Association and, despite shortages of meat and eggs, the group managed to survive on vegetables and fruit. Among the many visits was one to the West Wall fortifications vacated in 1945 by the Wehrmacht.

The 'trip' bug soon caught on. In March 1947, 72 pupils journeyed to Paris by boat and train although John Stewart in 3U spent more time in London than the others by having his appendix removed in Charing Cross Hospital.

In July 1948, 24 pupils spent a week in Normandy as guests of the Lycée Malherbe. This connection had been established as early as 1945 when all sorts of items were sent as a goodwill gesture to a town destroyed by the Allies from 6 June to 7 July 1945. Watson's pupils visited the D-Day beaches, Pegasus Bridge and some cemeteries.

In 1948, the Scottish Education Department sponsored a scheme to link Scottish and French schools. Watson's was linked with the Lycée Henri IV in Paris and six boys travelled unescorted in the summer to spend six weeks there while six French boys came to Edinburgh. The Head described this as " ... *an interesting experiment.*" It was so successful that it was repeated in 1949 with 21 pupils and continued throughout the 1950s.

Other trips in 1949 included Easter visits to the Riviera, Switzerland and Spain. In 1950, a Winter Sports trip went to Champery in Switzerland and an Easter trip to Paris. This formula was repeated in 1951.

The 'South African Aid to Britain' organised a schoolboys' tour of East Africa, the Rhodesias and South Africa for the summer of 1950. One of the three boys chosen from Scotland to take part was Donald P Braid (6A). This was a first for Watson's, but it wouldn't be the last time that Watson's boys would travel to play rugby in that part of the world.

Holland bound, 1946.

To Paris, 30 March 1947.

Henri IV at Watson's, 1949.

Harvest Moon

The idea of a 'Harvest Camp' must be strange to modern youngsters, but after the War shortages of labour and food led to the creation of special summer camps where youngsters could help take in the harvest, get paid for it and have fun too. In 1945, the first camp was at Eccles, but Watson's special place was on the Earl of Home's estate at The Hirsel, near Coldstream. At the first camp in 1948, 1,098 days of work were done on surrounding farms amounting to a colossal 10,000 work hours. This went on until 1951, but by that time the holiday 'fun' element had risen considerably. Indeed, that camp was the last one.

Outward Bound

In May 1950 an article appeared in *The Watsonian* written by a boy in 5U called HH Webster. He described at length his experience of a month's course at the Outward Bound Sea School at Aberdovey in Merioneth which was *"… a novel and strenuous holiday"* involving seamanship, cruising, athletics and expedition work such as a 30-mile hike over the Welsh hills. On a successful conclusion to the course a special buttonhole badge was issued, being *" blue, circular …with the letters OBSS on it."* Webster had seen the shape of things to come.

Watson's Wanderlust continued unabated throughout the 1950s. Two Easter trips in 1954 to Switzerland and Norway were aided by The Scottish Secondary Schools' Travel Trust. The Commandant of the ship to Norway was none other than ex-Head, Graham Andrew. The following year saw two trips to Switzerland, the Christmas one being a skiing holiday in the Alps. An ambitious Edinburgh-Rome Exchange was organised for 1956 when 18 boys led by Mr Penman entrained at Easter for two weeks in the Eternal City. Another trip to Austria was led by Mr More. In May the Lycée Henri IV Exchange took place. The first exchange with a German school since WW2 was organised in 1957 with the Schickhardt Gymnasium in Stuttgart. All this was part of a wider horizon enjoyed by mostly middle-class youngsters in the 1950s. The

days of an annual canvas camp, or week in Dunbar, were well and truly numbered.

The 1960s and 1970s saw an ever-increasing number of trips, even a joint skiing one in 1964 to Switzerland with Melville College. There was no Lycée Henri IV exchange in 1968 because of student-worker protest in Paris and the prospect of violent revolutionary activity. Instead, 22 peaceful German boys came over.

World Refugee Year, 1960

Aid for this Charity began in Watson's – as it began in almost every Edinburgh school – during the Winter Term of 1959. It struck a cord with youngsters everywhere and Watson's raised £1,561, ie one pound for every boy in the school. That money would go to finance five orphaned refugee youngsters for the next three years at the Spittal Training Centre in Austria to help them gain skills to support themselves. This Centre had been built by the World Council of Churches.

This charity campaign was skilfully done and a model of its kind. Every class was first shown a film on conditions in refugee camps. Then each boy received a photograph of a camp and a sheet of 6d 'stamps'. Every time a stamp was sold it would be stuck on the photograph. When all stamps had been sold, the camp picture had been obliterated and 10s raised for the cause. Other fund-raising ventures included the annual Carol Concert where half of the proceeds was donated.

"Boys need to be encouraged to spend part of their time and energies on behalf of other people's needs and to experience the deep satisfaction that such service brings. Not for nothing is our motto Ex Corde Caritas." (The Watsonian, 1960)

Ex Corde Caritas

Charities supported 1945– 74 included:

Craigmillar Boys' Club	Caen Fund
United Aid to China	Watsonian Benevolent Society
Scottish Veterans' Gardens	British Red Cross
Help Holland Fund	Poppy and Rose Day
Spastic Children	Trefoil School for Handicapped
Lifeboats	National Playing Fields
UNICEF	Hungarian Relief Fund
Famine Relief	Freedom from Hunger

The boys of the Lycée Henri IV Exchange raised money to purchase a light oak cross for use in the Sanctuary of the Scots Kirk in Paris.

The Craigmillar Boys' Club

In 1954, James Allan, a power behind the Club for 19 years, appointed Alan Cowieson as Club Leader. The Club's main attraction was undoubtedly boxing – in line with similar institutions throughout the country – but basketball was played to a high standard as was football. Table tennis was another popular feature as was the annual pantomime, now into its sixth year. A canteen was a novel addition, but necessary for café-addicted teenagers of the '50s desirous of nothing stronger, of course, than coke, hot orange and Bovril (but not together).

Cowieson attempted to widen the Club's support by introducing workshop crafts such as modelling and woodwork. This worked well with younger boys, but did little to halt the drift of older ones away from the Club. Cowieson found it hard going to persuade the 15+ age group to take part in activities, but he didn't give up. In 1955, he even tried athletics during the summer months.

Local Authorities were required to make provision for youth services in the late 1950s. Although the School and The Watsonian Club provided £700, the biggest grant (£375) was coming from Edinburgh Corporation. A full-time trained and experienced Leader was now required who would be supported by a Youth Service Officer appointed by the Education Committee. In the summer of 1957 Cowieson was replaced by GM Lightheart. Despite increasing professionalism the Club still desperately needed volunteer support and that was in short supply. By 1958, the writing was on the wall. The Head, McIntosh, noted that contributions to the Club were markedly down: *"This may reflect a changing public attitude to Boys' Clubs … Flogging a dead horse is less than useless if it is half-hearted into the bargain."*

By 1960, the Club was surviving, but constrained. It was living within its means, but had a chronic shortage of leaders. In 1962, Lightheart left. Mr John Clunie from Fife took over in June. The Club needed

maintenance so he asked the local authority (the Corporation) for a grant and the Carnegie Trust for support. A third of the costs was now being met by the Corporation, one-third by voluntary subscriptions and one-third by friends. The leaders were specialists or from the local community and the Club was open every weekday from 6 to 10pm. In 1963, piping lessons were started, but the big innovation was a Club Camp which included canoeing and mountain climbing. Help was given by S3 Projects, but the link with the school was beginning to be lost.

In 1966, Clunie resigned and Mr P Haggett took over. He wanted to give the Club a makeover and widen the activities into sailing, diving, visits, gliding and parachuting, but he didn't last long. Hector McGregor took over in December 1966. A big character who always wore the kilt he wanted to take a new direction.

McGregor had trained in Outward Bound activities in the North of Scotland and Pakistan and wanted more adventurous activities. He took a small party to the Cairngorms with the help of the army and even introduced the boys to skiing. He and the boys even repainted the front of the building. Very sadly Hector resigned in September 1967 and went to a new post in Pakistan. His decision was most certainly related to Club Camp at Killin when one boy was tragically drowned.

Tom Pitcairn was appointed Leader. He introduced an Adventure Playground for younger boys. Tarzan ropes proved popular, but Tom left to undergo training on a Youth Leadership Course. The Club was suffering too many changes of leadership. In 1968, it got a full-time experienced Leader from Oban, Mr Headridge. The Corporation was accepting direct responsibility for Youth Service Work and had built four Centres so far. Only financial restrictions had halted expansion. So, there was still a role for the Club.

But, by 1972, 80% of the Club's finance came from the Corporation and no Watsonians were involved in running the Club. The Watsonian-Craigmillar connection was effectively at an end.

Sandie Somerville Died, 1 December 1961

Sandie was Watson's first Scoutmaster and remained so for half a century. He had been a divinity student and then caught up in the Great War where he was thrice wounded and nearly blinded at the Somme while serving with the Seaforth Highlanders. Sandie had a Christian concern with the under-privileged and helped Rev Harry Millar in his ministry in the Old Town slums. It was Sandie who encouraged older Rover Scouts from Watson's to establish the Watsonian Scout Centre during the 1920s which set up Scouting organisations in the High Street, St Mary's, the West Port and the Pleasance. It was this which led to the formation of the Craigmillar Boys' Club, manned initially by many Watsonian Scouts. With his friend Stanley Nairne, Sandie also created the Scottish Schoolboys Club in 1912 with Sandie as Chairman of the Edinburgh Branch. In 1953, he was honoured with the highest award in Scouting: the Silver Wolf. In 1956, the state awarded him a thoroughly well-deserved MBE. Sandie died of a stroke at 33 Merchiston Crescent. In 1964, the Scouts created their own memorials: a photo in the Scout Room, a trophy to the best patrol and a fund to buy equipment for the winner of the Inter-Patrol Trophy.

"Among all the gifted diversity of Watsonians there has been no other like him. He was unique."
(The Watsonian)

Making canoes for the Scouts, 1962.

S3 Projects

The first mention of S3 Projects in *The Watsonian* was during a report of the 1962 Watsonian Club Annual Dinner. Sixty-four S3 had gone to Glenmore Lodge for a two-week course in hill and field craft. The others had gone on Edinburgh projects to benefit themselves and the community, eg working on the Niddrie Adventure Playground, local surveys, three days' woodworking in a workshop and industrial visits. The second year of Projects (1963) saw 64 go to Glenmore again. Eleven went with Messrs McLauchlan and Robson to *"… the first National Trust Adventure Camp at Kintail"*. There they helped the local community of foresters and crofters and indulged in hill-walking, canoeing, natural and local history. Others did work for the Craigmillar Boys' Club. One highly imaginative Craft Project made three garden huts and set up a mass-production pottery factory which made 300 items in nine days. It was hoped to expand this in future.

In 1964, a delighted Sir Roger declared that *"… the whole scheme has caught on and is proving of incalculable value out of proportion to the time spent on it."* Sixty-eight boys were involved in Edinburgh Projects: the pottery factory was repeated, wicket covers were made for Myreside, a sandpit was built for a local Children's Home, Craigmillar Boys' Club was helped out, OAPs' gardens were dug and boys learned some cooking. By 1966 more groups were going 'furth' of Edinburgh, including a special one to St Kilda to help the National Trust. Thanks to severe gales, this group arrived back five days late. Sixth Year helped with the Edinburgh Groups and this experiment worked well.

The rest is history. Projects became one of the best-loved of all activities.

The Watsonian Club

After '45 the Club pushed its 'War Relief and Benevolent Fund' begun in 1943 to alleviate hardship caused by war. The aim was to get £10,000 and use the income of £350 per year, which even then was not regarded as much. The capital sum had still not been achieved by 1945. Nevertheless, it did sterling work distributing Christmas parcels, helping widows with no, or inadequate, pensions, aiding orphans and long-stay hospital patients.

The War Memorial had now to be extended to include those from the most recent war. The original architect, JA Carfrae, was consulted and the original idea was to extend the Memorial outwards. A model was made by the Art Department (R Scott Irvine, Euan Walker and James Coull), but a much cheaper variant was opted for consisting of two bronze panels. This was unveiled after the Founder's Day Service on 7 July 1950.

A War Record was decided upon in March 1948 which would be similar to that of the Great War, but in condensed form. It was published in 1951.

During the 1945 Armistice Service the Head read out to the School the name of each of the Watsonian dead. In 1946, he stated *" … it would have been easy to let the occasion slip and allow our School Service to pass into the limbo of forgotten and outworn ceremonies."* That would not be allowed to happen because the price paid by the school in both wars had been so heavy.

Causing much concern in 1945 was the state of the Craigmillar Boys' Club. Membership and support in the area was not a problem, but the fact was that very few Watsonians were actively helping and the Club was in financial trouble. Indeed, by 1950 only 11 were prepared to give up one evening per week and the Club had a financial deficit. Sandie Somerville resigned as Leader in 1947 urging a full-time appointment which, unfortunately, could not be fulfilled without adequate funding. It was a great pity that very few younger Watsonians were not prepared to support what was a thriving venture with three championship football teams, a string of successes in boxing and, in 1948, one of the first basketball teams in Scotland.

The Watsonian Clubs at home and abroad survived and flourished. The first post-war Ball was held in 1947 with the 600 tickets being snapped up almost immediately. It was described as *"gaiety and beauty"* all to the music of Tim Wright and his Broadcasting Band. The good days seemed to be back. But an ominous note was struck in 1952:

"The old members are getting older and new members are not coming forward. The School has always drawn boys from overseas and has always sent boys overseas, but in recent years the numbers have shrunk."
(*The Watsonian*, 1952)

The Empire was declining rapidly, the winds of change were blowing and overseas prospects subsequently diminished. How long would these overseas Clubs last?

Proposed new War Memorial.

Watsonian Club of India, 1955.

Sporty Chaps

Boys

School sports gradually got back to normal, some a little quicker than others.

Cricket and Swimming soldiered on bravely, but Rugby was hard hit. In 1946, the PE Department was complaining about the *"... small number of boys who turn out to play Rugby."* Only 17 XVs were playing regularly, but there should have been a lot more. The real problem was not one of changing attitudes, but a real practical one of the *"... present-day difficulty of obtaining boots, jerseys and shorts."* An improvement was hoped for when rationing was ended. In the meantime a plea was made for jerseys, shorts and boots.

Hockey was also hard hit, but in a different way: its pitch at the front of the school had disappeared under crops. Also, there was a problem finding teams to play as school hockey was not widespread, so girls'

and adult teams were challenged. Indeed, 80% of their post-war games were against adults and some could become a bit rough: *"male opposition has been dealt some violent blows."* In late 1947, a new pitch at Myreside was used, but the main pitch was not regained until the Winter of 1949. The Head encouraged hockey by allowing, from 1949 onwards, boys from S2 upwards to join, but there was always a problem that the rugby people felt their position was being undermined. In 1951, for example, membership was restricted to S4 boys and upwards which cut numbers drastically. After complaints, this was reduced to S3. Despite everything this highly enthusiastic organisation was clamouring for full Colours by 1948.

Squash was also being enthusiastically espoused by a hard-core of about 25 players and given a huge boost in 1947 when JW Everett won the new Scottish Boys' Squash Championships.

Old Boys

Rugby and Cricket quickly returned to normal, but other Clubs were not so lucky.

The Curling Club had been suspended in 1939 when Haymarket Ice Rink was requisitioned by the Admiralty and not 'de-requisitioned' until 1947. Curling's fresh start began in October of that year.

The Hockey Club had lost its main front pitch (*"O wad some Pow'r the pitchie gie us."*), so the 1st XI had an all-away programme. Despite everything the Club flourished. The Rifle Club had an even worse problem: no rifles. After Dunkirk these had been loaned to the Home Guard and it was not until 1948 that reconditioned rifles were returned.

The Athletic Club went into abeyance during the war years, but it got going once more in the Spring of '45. However, there was no competition as soldiers had yet to return from their units. The Swimming Club also resumed under the redoubtable Fred Lemmon.

GEORGE WATSON'S COLLEGE SWIMMING TEAM 1973·74

E. R. YERBURY & SON
EDINBURGH

D. Cook   D. Johnstone   D. Hall   R. Iggo   J. Rashbash   S. Biagi

Mr R.A. Mack   N. Henderson   G. Jardine   S. Livingstone   G. Finlayson   I. Kerr-Hunter   M. Turner
D.P.E.

H. Turnbull   C.F. Morgan   M.W. Laidlaw   M.R. Wagner
Secretary   Vice-Captain

Absent I.W.M. Burton

Squash had kept going throughout the emergency years, but whereas it had 90 members in 1939, it was down to 40 in '45. Golf managed to continue and a *"lively interest"* was recorded by 1948. These activities survived largely due to the fact that older individuals could keep them going, but the problem now became one of attracting younger people, especially when National Service had first priority.

D Reid wins the 440 Handicap, 1965.

Badminton
The Badminton Club was formed in 1954 with 25 members.

Rugby
1960. The first time that Watsonians failed to produce a championship, winning side since the 1930s. The Stand at Myreside was empty on Saturdays.

Rowing
In 1960, the Club won the greatest honour to be won in Scotland: Scottish Schoolboy Senior Championships, but 1963 would prove its most successful year ever. In that year it bought its first boat for £200 in co-operation with Heriot's. In 1964, it had its most successful year with 21 wins between five crews. In 1966, the Education Board lent £800 to the Club to erect a Boat House on the site of the Old University Boat Club on the Union Canal at Slateford. The site was leased from British Rail at a nominal rent. In 1968, it dominated schoolboy rowing.

Tiddlywinks
4Sc1 formed the first Tiddlywinks Club in 1960.

Fencing Club
Begun in July 1967 by Mr Wells.

Sailing Club
1967/8 saw *"… the real start of sailing at Watson's"* Got off the ground by a group of 20 boys on S3 Projects based at Balquhidder Youth Hostel and helped by the Loch Earn Sailing School.

Basketball Club
Started in 1966 and used the Senior Quadrangle (West Quad). The Club was supervised by the new PE teacher, Peter Gallagher, who had taken over from Fred Lemmon.

Curling Club
A school Club, as distinct from the Watsonian version, was begun during the Winter of 1961. Curling Colours were presented for the first time in 1968. The recipients were Ian Brown, James Hunter, Arthur Hendry and Colin Baxter.

GEORGE WATSON'S COLLEGE   ATHLETIC CLUB 1970

E. R. YERBURY & SON   EDINBURGH.

C. S. A. Wayte   G. McKinlay   C. E. Bruce   A. G. Strasser   B. Robertson   N. A. Craig   C. G. Baird   M. J. Andrews

Mr R. M. Hunter   G. R. Walker   D. I. Smith   G. A. Cooper   C. M. Beggs   J. R. Miller   I. Anderson   A. E. Dick   P. J. Wililamson   D. Y. Veitch   R. Hall   I. H. Finnie   L. D. McLachlan
Recorder

D. M. Smith   K. R. Ridley   C. J. M. Sandilands   I. C. R. Butt   D. D. Robertson   N. M. Sandilands   T. M. Barr   J. L. McWhinnie
Captain   Vice-Captain

D. M. Walker   G. E. F. Laing   H. K. Watson   C. W. Lemmon

Entrance Doorway to George Watson's Ladies' College painted by Ken Lochhead in 1976.

Its Physical Presence and the Spirit That Dwelt Within

When Charlotte Ainslie, Headmistress of George Watson's Ladies' College between 1902 and 1926, sat down at her desk in December 1910 to write the first article for a new magazine for the pupils and former pupils of her school she could hardly have known what history she was about to make.

She admits to a major headache in deciding what to call the new magazine, and having made the choice *The George Square Chronicle*, she felt it necessary to apologise for assuming a name that could so easily imply the report of a much wider set of institutions than that which was housed within numbers 3,4,5,6 and 7 George Square.

Yet 'George Square' remains the accepted and preferred description of the school attended by generations of former pupils of George Watson's Ladies' College. Even now, in some quarters of Edinburgh, you might still find you are judged by whether you attended 'Queen Street' (The Mary Erskine School) or 'George Square'.

George Square itself dates back to 1766, being built as the first residential development beyond the City of Edinburgh's Flodden Wall. At this time there was a growing demand amongst some of the more wealthy Edinburgh families to move away from the *Lands* and *Closes* of the High Street into open ground with more space, more light and more air. The new square immediately attracted some of the city's most fashionable citizens.

At first it was called the Great Square, then George's Square after the Christian name of the brother (George Brown) of the architect (James Brown), but in 1815, at the time when the centre of the Square was redeveloped from an area for grazing cattle into attractive gardens, it became known simply as George Square.

Many famous people went to live in George Square. Amongst the early residents were the Countess of Sutherland (No 14), Lord Braxfield

No 5 George Square.

(No 13), known as the 'Hanging Judge' for the harsh sentences he handed down and as the character who inspired RL Stevenson's *Weir of Hermiston*, and the Earl of Kintore (No 55), but there were also many professionals; ministers, schoolmasters, physicians, professors, lawyers and soldiers and writers.

Arthur Conan Doyle, creator of Sherlock Holmes, wrote his first short story whilst resident in George Square (No 23) and the young Walter Scott lived in George Square (No 25) between 1772 and 1797. Despite his frequent suffering with a debilitating fever, the young Scott would

sometimes get involved in street fights or *"bickers"* as he refers to them in the introduction to his *Waverley Novels*. These 'bickers', which could turn quite nasty, took place between boys of different localities and backgrounds and, as is described on page 13, were often confrontations between the boys of George Heriot's Hospital and the boys of George Watson's Hospital.

In later years, well-known residents included the legendary Olympian Eric Liddell (No 56) and Professor Peter Guthrie Tait (No 38) who worked alongside Lord Kelvin on mathematical and physical studies and who was believed to have one of Edinburgh's

Nos 23–25 George Square, homes to Arthur Conan Doyle and Walter Scott.

finest private collections of books and old manuscripts, including some which related to his pioneering studies of the flight of golf balls. However, it was Walter Scott of Harden in his adult years who built what eventually became known as Melville House (No 5) on the north side of the Square and which would eventually become the first setting for the School. It was a particularly grand house built with its entrance at right angles to the roadway and it was the only house in the Square to have its own garden, both features which were later to become immensely important in the development of George Watson's Ladies' College.

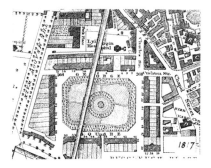

Architect's plan of George Square, 1817.

Room 4.

Sir Walter Scott (1771–1832) by Sir Henry Raeburn, Scottish National Portrait Gallery.

…or the wild callants bicker wi'snawballs as they whiles do

Built in 1770, it faced the gable of No 4 and its entrance was from the garden which connected George Square to Charles Street. In the basement it housed the splendid 'Admiral's Kitchen' *(see photo page 235)* just like the galley of the grandest sailing ship, and upstairs there were some handsome architectural features in the public rooms, including the classical frieze above the mantelpiece

and Adam fireplace in what was to become Room 4 of George Watson's Ladies' College.

Without ever having lived in it, Walter Scott of Harden sold the house in 1773 to the Lord Advocate, Henry Dundas, later Viscount Melville, or 'Harry the Ninth' as he was known. In those days it was the Lord Advocate who effectively controlled the government of Scotland and Dundas resided there from 1775 until his impeachment in 1805, an often torrid period of office in Scottish politics.

In 1792 various eyewitnesses of the time recall scenes, reminiscent of the French Revolution three years previous, when Dundas's effigy, made of rags and straw, was burned in the Square by an unruly mob which was protesting against his repressive measures as the equivalent of a modern-day Home Secretary. The windows of the house were shattered, but on instruction one servant escaped by the back lane and sped up to the

castle garrison for aid. The soldiers rushed down, the Riot Act was read and when the mob still refused to disperse, the military opened fire leaving several corpses on the street in front of Melville House.

A niece of Lord Melville, as Dundas became known after his elevation to the peerage, married Captain Duncan of Lundie who, in 1786, acquired Melville House. Captain Duncan became Admiral of the Fleet and later, in honour of his victory against the Dutch at the Battle of Camperdown in 1797, Viscount Duncan of Camperdown.

To celebrate this occasion a very large procession of infantry, cavalry and artillery marched in his honour through the Square. They were accompanied by naval officers and a naval car on which a mast was stepped. From the top of it flew the Union Jack and beneath it drooped the flag of the Dutch Admiral de Winter which had been taken in battle. Viscount

Melville House, 1871.

Adam Duncan, 1st Viscount Duncan of Camperdown (1731–1804) by Henri-Pierre Danloux, Scottish National Portrait Gallery.

Duncan of Camperdown stood outside his house to take the salute before attending a public banquet in his honour.

After Admiral Lord Duncan's widow died in 1832 the house had several different private occupants but it was first used as a school, known as Miss Shiells' Boarding School, for a brief period between 1834–7 and then as the Edinburgh Southern Academy between 1837–53. Mr George Lorimer, Master of the Merchant Company between 1910–11, was a pupil at the Academy around 1850 and he recalled travelling to school across the Meadows, just to the south of George Square, where there were high palings and lands let to those interested in the cattle trade. There were also mounds concealing the water pipe that took water from Glencorse to the reservoir on Castle Hill and he remembers it bursting during the winter when the whole area froze up.

He also recalled, at the age of nine, being asked to write an essay on *The difference between the Jewish and Christian dispensation*, being told that his source was the *Epistle to the Hebrews* and to go away and not return until the work was complete! He found this a very tedious exercise and much preferred the day in 1911 when, as Master of the Merchant Company, he sat in on a domestic science lesson in the new east wing of George Watson's

Ladies' College when it was opened by the Marchioness of Tullibardine. The tea and scones were apparently a much better experience than the essay!

For a brief period of six years Melville House returned to private occupancy but in 1859 it once more became a school which offered boarding facilities for young ladies. The Headmaster was Alexander Thomson who submitted the following advertisement to *The Edinburgh Directory* in 1868–9:

Mr Thomson's School, Melville House, George Square

This establishment consists of classes for Young Ladies and a Preparatory School for Boys. Pupils are received at five years of age. The course of Instruction for Young Ladies extends to all the various branches of a polite education, and Young Gentlemen are fully prepared for entering any of the higher class schools. Mr Thomson receives a limited number of Young Gentlemen as Boarders.

In the Minutes of a meeting of the Edinburgh Merchant Company in February 1871, it was suggested that Melville House and the adjoining building of which Mr Thomson was a tenant, would be suitable for a new day school for girls – a development planned by the Company in response to the growing demand for a good secondary education for girls. This move followed an amendment to the Merchant Company's *Provisional Order of George Watson's College* which, in accordance with the terms of George Watson's will, had not previously made provision for a girls' school.

At this time, the perceived wisdom was that the old hospital system of education benefited only a few, and at great cost, so major reform was called for. In 1868 Simon S Laurie, then the Secretary of the Education Committee of the Church of Scotland, was asked to present a report on the Merchant Company's four hospital schools; the Merchant Maiden, George Watson's, Daniel Stewart's and James Gillespie's. The governors of the time were confident of an *"unpartial and candid report"* from *"a gentleman of such experience and independence of character and position."*

At the same time, a Royal Commission on Education had been investigating the use, in Scotland, of educational endowments, and in the case of Edinburgh, had suggested that *"there are great educational mortifications in the city which do comparatively little educational good"* and that the system in general was *"not a wholesome one either morally or intellectually"*. This prompted the Merchant Company Education Committee in July 1868 to ask Parliament for powers to carry out major alterations to the organisation of their schools and to the use of their endowments so that education was more widely available.

And so in February 1871, the Merchant Company took over the lease of Melville House and the adjoining property. At the same time they approached Alexander Thomson, who had been running his own school in Melville House since 1865, to take over the running of the new George Watson's College Schools for Young Ladies (the name was changed to George Watson's College for Ladies in 1877 and to George Watson's Ladies' College in 1890). His salary was £400 per annum and 5s per annum for every day scholar on the roll and £15 for *"the extra trouble in engaging teachers"*. Nonetheless, this £15 was immediately taken back from him in order to pay the rent on his accommodation! A Lady Superintendent, Miss Alice C Wilson, was also appointed at a salary of £100 per annum.

In the first session there were well over 500 pupils on the roll and 45 men and women on the staff and it was soon obvious that the buildings were inadequate. Plans were shortly underway to build in the garden of Melville House and a new wing at right angles to the old house backing on to Charles Street Lane.

There were various legal difficulties that got in the way but by 1876 building was in progress and the decision was taken to heat the whole building with hot water pipes. It is interesting to note that in Mr Thomson's Headmaster's report of 1877, he said that some of his staff and pupils were *"doing their best with not any fire at all"* but others were *"blaming hot water pipes for giving them headaches."* There was also a delicate issue about a staff proposal for Venetian

"George Watson's Ladies' College; Mr Alexander Thomson, the Headmaster, and Miss Alice C Wilson, the Lady Superintendent, having, after long service resigned their respective offices, to take effect at the end of September next, the Governors at their meeting yesterday, resolved to advertise for a Headmistress", The Scotsman (6 June 1902.)

blinds *"to keep out the insufferable heat of the sun"* but, much to their annoyance, this was turned down by the Merchant Company officials who said that Venetian blinds were *"not in the least bit suitable for a girls' school"*. Instead, it was decreed that the school would be provided with ordinary cloth blinds on rollers. Obviously, the headmaster couldn't win the battle of comfort!

Yet more internal troubles occurred in 1883 and this time the issue was staff salaries. Having faced a delegation of male staff who let it be known that they thought they should be paid more, Mr Thomson was eventually persuaded to approach the Merchant Company. Company Minutes from that year indicate there were some tense meetings on the subject in Merchants' Hall but it was finally agreed to award what amounted to an average 10% increase per annum to the senior staff with the junior staff receiving more limited increases. For a staff of 60 men and women, one janitor and one matron, the increases in salaries not only imposed quite a bit of extra cost on the Merchant Company but they also increased the pay differentials for men and women. Indeed, it was striking that the Lady Superintendent, the equivalent of the modern Deputy Head, was paid £95 less than a Maths master. So much for sexual equality in those days!

Per annum salaries after the 1883 increases:

Lady Superintendent	£185
French Mistress	£ 80
English Mistress	£ 50
Music Mistress	£ 60
Classics Master	£140
English Master	£250
Maths Master	£280

By this stage other developments were also taking place: the Elementary pupils had been moved into a room on the north side of the building (what became Room 27) to allow a new Lecture Room (Room 22) and a new Writing Room (Room 19) to be built. The old garden was transformed into an attractive courtyard and a flight of steps was built to connect this with a new entrance at the north-east corner of Melville House, the doorway which, in later years, was to lead from the Tiled Hall to the Gallery.

Charlotte Ainslie (Headmistress 1902-26 and pupil when Mr Thomson's school first opened its doors) described the early school buildings as very compact and without much space for a school that was clearly in demand; *"There was no east wing and no west wing, no gymnasium, no sports ground, and no dinner (to which she obviously took some exception as a hungry young lady!). There was no gallery and no central hall."*

The most important room she recalls was Room 25 with its *"inconvenient pillar in the middle"*. She remembers most functions being held here, where prizes were given out and where lectures and dancing and singing classes took place. She also mentions the purposeful atmosphere of the arithmetic classes that took place in the Tiled Hall and watching the Janitor walking through into the small passage leading from it where the gongs were struck for the end of each lesson (no bells in those days).

But if Charlotte Ainslie as a pupil recalls the Tiled Hall with fond memories, the same could not be said for many of her own pupils a generation later when it assumed a much more sinister character as the chamber which awaited those who had been sent down to the headmistress (*see page 237*).

Yet further pressure on accommodation occurred in 1886 and Mr Thomson had to declare that he could take no more pupils – understandable with a roll of 896. Quite simply, it was a question of adding more space or reducing the number of pupils so it was decided to make further purchases of adjoining properties at 4 George Square and 3 Charles Street Lane. No 4 George Square had, for a brief period between 1855–60, been used as the Misses Menzies' Ladies Boarding School so the Merchant Company officials believed they were taking on a relatively straight-forward proposition.

The courtyard between this new wing and the original Melville House would be excavated and roofed over to form a hall below street level. There would be a gallery round the hall and a new entrance onto the Square above which, on the pediment, Mr Thomson insisted that the Coat of Arms of the Merchant Company should be placed.

Room 22 in the early days.

Furthermore, there would be improvements to the existing school buildings with the total cost reckoned to be £9,200. These changes would allow one classroom for every 50 pupils and a music-room for every 30. State-of-the-art gas stoves were installed for cookery lessons and 'Otto's Gas Engine' was fitted to control a new system of ventilation. Even electric bells were installed (at a cost of £94 6s) but so too was an elaborate system of speaking tubes which connected the Headmaster's study with other rooms (the last of these speaking tubes remained in place until the 1960s much to the amusement of the pupils who thought it came straight out of the stage-set from St Trinian's). It was a matter of regret that the new hall was to take away some outdoor space but the compensation was a new gymnasium, also used as a play area, and a more spacious luncheon room which became known as the Court and which was adjacent to the Admiral's Kitchen.

In 1893 the new school buildings designed by Mr Washington Browne, were finally opened by Lord Elgin, Viceroy of India. But it was not long before the school roll rose yet again – to over a thousand pupils this time and, with curriculum changes looming, yet more purchase of property was required, this time at No 3 George Square.

Remarkably, just after the second new extension encompassing No 3 had been opened in 1903 by Lord Balfour of Burleigh, the Merchant Company was tipped off that No 6 would be on the market the following year. This proved to be the case and in 1909 No 7 also became available.

The seemingly endless building works were finally complete by 1911 and at last the school had time to settle into its more permanent accommodation. The extension which now occupied Nos 6 and 7 George Square was four stories high; the Elementary Department was housed in five rooms on the ground floor, senior classes in five rooms on the 2nd and 3rd floors and the Domestic Science Department on the top floor.

With all the moves it was little wonder that the internal numbering of rooms bore little resemblance to arithmetical sequence or to most people's perception of common sense and it often became a real headache for new staff and pupils. The building changes had been brought about by the expansion of the curriculum, and most especially the recognition that the curriculum of a girls' school need not mirror that of the boys' school, by new examination syllabuses and the need to reduce class sizes.

Never again did the school undertake such extensive new building and structural changes although there were to be several changes to the interior design and use of rooms. By the mid 1930s there had been improvements to the Art Room and the Library, followed in 1949 by new developments to the Waiting Room, school cloakrooms, the Dining Room and the stage facilities in Room 22. Apart from a short period during the Evacuation years of the Second World War, when the school was transformed into a Red Cross Depot, George Square had taken on its most established form and the one which is so easily remembered by the George Square family today.

Of course, as with many famous old buildings, there is the unique folklore to consider just as much part of the place as the rooms. As time progressed the corridors of George Square were often said to be haunted by ghosts, two in particular.

Firstly, there was the ghost of Admiral Duncan himself, described in the December 1940 issue of *The George Square Chronicle* by Sarah Wintcombe who worked with the Red Cross when they occupied George Square and

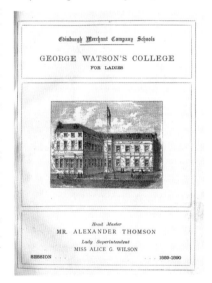

The Coat of Arms of the Merchant Company.

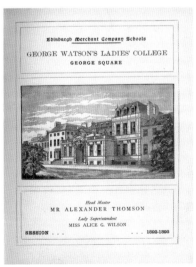

The changing frontage of the School buildings in the late 19th century.

who, through her membership of the Society for Psychical Research, clearly had an interest in the study of poltergeists and hauntings.

Miss Wintcombe claims that on 27 January 1940 she had been about to leave the building when she heard the door being shut and locked and steps of the person ascending. She rushed to shout and detain them. To no avail and so she had to try to find another door in the dark interior. Near the Central Hall she tripped over something and lost consciousness for a very short period of time. When she awoke she described the scene:

> *"Over me there was a bended man, in fancy dress I judged, who laved my forehead with a sweet-smelling liquid.*
>
> *I looked round and to my amazement saw a large fire blazing in the fireplace in the corner and several shining pots and pans…*
>
> *…suddenly I heard footsteps, faint at first, but coming nearer. I looked at the man, but he did not seem to notice anything and continued to wipe my face.*
>
> *The door opened, and the scene faded as the old caretaker entered. Puzzled, I went with him upstairs to his room where he was just going to bed after his final look round the premises.*
>
> *"Weel," he said, "it's no' often I gang into the kitchen afore I turn in, but it's lucky for you I did. What are ye staring at?" he added. Above him was a large painting, the image of the man I had just seen.*
>
> *"That's just the auld Admiral, him wha focht at Camperdown, ye ken."*
>
> *"Did he ever live here?" I stammered out.*
>
> *"Why, yes, bless your soul; did ye no' ken it was his kitchen you was in?"*
>
> *I have since made enquiries and examined all the authenticated portraits of Admiral Duncan I could find – and the resemblance to the figure I saw is convincing in the highest degree. Although since, I have, accompanied by friends, spent nights in the Admiral's kitchen and no more strange phenomena were observed."*

Secondly, and perhaps more mysteriously, there was the ghost of the Grey Lady – a relic of stories told by pupils during the First World War. Initially, the tales of the Grey Lady described her as a youthful and elegant Georgian figure who at one time had been the mistress of an inhabitant of Melville House. The story ran that she fell out of love and in her misery locked herself away in one of the top attic rooms of the school.

But thereafter, the story seemed to take on a more sinister tone. As the Grey Lady aged and became increasingly bitter she was said to keep her vigil in the 'Dark Passage' and all the sombre depths below street level. By all accounts she seemed to be a very dark and forbidding character whose ghostly presence was a constant source of fear. Some said she was the ghost of a headmistress, dressed in a black gown, and with the daily ritual of sweeping up her prey at the unsuspecting

moment. Junior girls in the 1950s and 1960s used to shout to each other at the end of the school day when they were collecting their coats to make haste before the Grey Lady appeared.

Junior class, 1958.

Two Images of The Grey Lady

As midnight strikes, a groan heard,
And yet another after,
Then echoing through the passage comes
The sound of ghostly laughter.

A grey form glides down the dark stairs,
And leans against the railing,
Now from the haunted classrooms comes
The sound of mournful wailing.

For hours, till dawn, she glides around,
Her groans are never ending
Until, at last, her vigil o'er,
To the haunted room ascending.

L G IK , *The Chronicle,* Winter 1960

'Tis said there is a lady fair,
On topmost floor of our George Square;
No mistress she nor sprightly lass,
The corridor by night she'll pass.

She is in truth the Grey Lady,
Her background is a little shady;
What does she hear by night or day?
What does she whisper, what does she say?

Is she still haunting the cooking class?
Or does our ghost mutter "amo, amas…?"
How long she's been here none can remember,
But our ghost is quite a mystery member.

F R IL, *The Chronicle,* Winter 1963

Pupil's image of the Grey Lady, 1966.

Junior class in Mr Thomson's School, 1896.

No-one seems to know exactly from whence she came or where she went and maybe there are some who will not tell!

History class, 1953.

The Attic Room where the Grey Lady was supposed to live.

The Central Hall.

St Alban's Road.

Beyond the Buildings in George Square

Of course latterly, 'George Square' wasn't just confined to its address in the centre of Edinburgh. In September 1943, the new Preparatory Department was opened at 58 St Alban's Road, in a house which had been built in 1883 as a private home for a William Barron and his family (whose initials could be seen etched in the stained glass window in the stairway). In 1892 the house was sold and used as a small private girls' school known as Bellwood, but this lasted for only nine years after which the building was returned to private ownership and lived in by the Alston family.

Situated in the leafy Edinburgh suburb of The Grange, 58 St Alban's Road was a graceful Georgian house in which the rooms were spacious, beautifully proportioned and very light. The property also afforded attractive gardens into which the Merchant Company planted its symbolic Stock of Broom as well as fruit trees, vegetables, shrubs and roses, and there was also a delightful summerhouse and old-fashioned greenhouse close to where small air-raid shelters had been built by the previous owners.

By September 1954 the whole Junior School apart from Forms 4 and 5 Junior (who remained with the Senior School at George Square), plus all the Preparatory classes, were housed at St Alban's Road thanks to the Merchant Company's purchases of the two private residences at Nos 60 and 62 St Alban's Road, known as Craigmichen House and Monkton Lodge respectively. It was during this year that the School crest was placed above the entrance to the main building. The crest which was a stone carving of the leaves of the oak tree surrounded by acorns, and with the letters GWLC and date 1954 engraved upon it, was later found in 1981 *"lying near the joiner's workshop in Daniel*

Stewart's and Melville College." No-one is quite sure how it got there but even more mysteriously it was later built into a wall in the old DSMC headmaster's house and remains there today, at least for the time being!

It is not hard to find Women Watsonians who speak very fondly about their early schooldays spent at St Alban's Road and many former members of staff describe it as a very special place in which to teach even if the approach was firmly traditional and modern ideas were sometimes rejected as *"unsuitable for young ladies"*. Set in one of the most pleasant residential parts of Edinburgh with easy access for the vast majority of pupils, it commanded an air of quiet dignity and purposeful learning. The classrooms, most of which had originally been the public rooms of private residences, were ideal for primary classes and each of the two parts of the school, the Preparatory Department and the Lower Junior School, boasted a hall area which could easily accommodate the classes for morning assembly and special occasions although it was a bit more of a squeeze on days when parents were invited along to watch a nativity play or a harvest festival.

There was also the magnificent Rose Cairney Library in the Lower Junior School which was opened in 1964 in memory of Miss Rose Cairney who had been Head of the Lower Junior School from 1955 to 1963.

The staff were, on the whole, extremely caring and very able and conscientious champions of their profession. It was striking, too, that all staff, whether teaching or non-teaching, were considered part of the St Alban's Road family, and therefore pupils found it just as easy to relate to their janitor and their matron (Mr and Mr Officer) as they did to their own class teachers.

At morning break and lunchtimes, there was extensive room in the playground for the whole school despite the school authorities' decision to declare the beautifully mown lawns and weedless vegetable garden out of bounds to the hordes who might have got their shoes dirty. As it was compulsory to have indoor and outdoor shoes it was always a source of some mystery as to why it should

The Stock of Broom

The Emblem of the Merchant Company

Stone crest above the entrance to the Lower Junior School presented by the Women Watsonians' Club in 1954.

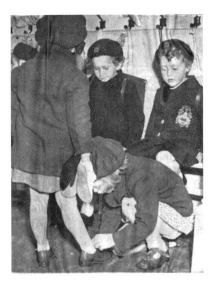

Preparatory Schoolgirls, 1951.

matter but then these were school rules – obviously taken very seriously!

Opposite the school buildings in St Alban's Road there was an open field that was used by the pupils for recreation and gymnastics periods in the summer term and for the annual sports day, but for real games in terms of hockey and tennis practices and competitive matches against other schools you had to wait until you were in the Upper Junior and Senior Schools.

When George Square closed in 1974, the properties at St Alban's Road were sold to the Bank of Scotland which used the old school as its training facilities right up until 2003. As part of the deal, the newly merged George Watson's College acquired the old Bank of Scotland training facilities in Tipperlinn House, Tipperlinn Road, and this was used as the boarding house for Watson's girls and was run by Housemistress, Mrs Joan Thomson.

If St Alban's Road is synonymous with preparatory education at George Watson's Ladies' College then the names Falconhall and Liberton mean games. The first school records of games activities date back to 1886 when one of the music governesses, Miss Lizzie Knott, decided to start a tennis club for the staff making use of some private courts on the south side of Edinburgh (sometimes at 7am!). Not long after this, she lobbied the Merchant Company about the possibility of purchasing land in the Strathearn area for the girls to play

tennis but it was thought to be too expensive, and so the girls had to make do with sharing some of the boys' tennis facilities at George Watson's College for which four racquets and 12 tennis balls were duly purchased!

It was only in 1893 that the use of playing fields at Falconhall became available, largely the area which now covers the territory between Falcon Gardens and Morningside Road east to west and which stretches from Newbattle Terrace in the north to Canaan Lane in the south. In 1780, Lord Provost William Coulter built Morningside Lodge just at the end of what is today Steel's Place and in the early years of the 19th century he purchased more of the surrounding land. In 1814 he sold both the house and the estate to Alexander Falconer, who had retired as Chief Secretary to the Governor of Madras, and who renamed the private residence Falcon Hall – hence the stone falcons which adorned the frontage and gate pillars of the house and which became the badge for girls in Falconhall House.

Falcon Hall and a copy of the label of the Falconhall blend of Scotch Whisky as pictured in Charles A Smith's book, Historic South Edinburgh, Vol 1.

The estate at Falconhall was purchased for £30,000 by the Merchant Company in 1889 and until 1923 the grounds were shared by the girls of Mary Erskine and George Square (as well as some less frequent users). Thereafter, there was a period of 14 years, once the Mary Erskine pupils had moved to new facilities at Inverleith, when George Square pupils had Falconhall to themselves.

For the early sportswomen of the school, trips to games at Falconhall via one of the stately Morningside trams were obviously a much-loved part of the week. Initially, there were four tennis courts of which George Watson's Ladies' College had the use of two, but two more were built in 1909 and another two in 1920. By 1894 the girls were allowed to make use of a short-hole golf course which had been constructed in the north-east corner of the grounds and two grass hockey pitches which had been specially sewn for the use of both Mary Erskine and George Watson's Ladies' College (the grass for a cricket field to be used by the boys of James Gillespie's School was also sown at this time.)

While the location of the playing fields and small pavilion had much charm, just like the delightful groundsman, Mr Preston, mentioned in several issues of *The George Square Chronicle*, there was obviously some concern about the state of some of the playing surface. In particular, it was noted that the very small hand mower used for grass-cutting *"did nothing for the coarse grass that found its way all too easily onto the tennis courts and hockey pitches"* and which was blamed, more than once, for a bad bounce that swung the result of a match the wrong way!

If St Alban's Road is synonymous with preparatory education… …then Falconhall and Liberton mean games.

Staff and parents at the strawberry tea party, 1934.

Sports Day, Falconhall 1935, BACK ROW, left to right: Doreen Melvin, Kathleen Redpath, Jean Young, Isobel McDowall, FRONT ROW, left to right: Irene Scott, Janet Darling, Agnes McLaren, Dorothy Goote.

Dr Ainslie at Falconhall.

Mr Sutherland (top hat), School Janitor at Falconhall with Mr Preston, Groundsman.

In Dr Ainslie's time it was recognised that not all girls either wanted to or could enjoy games and therefore she encouraged those of less physical persuasion to simply enjoy the surroundings and participate in other recreations such as the special reading groups that took place on summer days under the shade of the many large oak trees and in the small garden which she had planted in 1920.

But as Headmistress, she also took great pride in the tradition of sports days and strawberry tea parties to which parents and visitors were invited each summer term. These occasions lasted virtually all day with special tennis matches being played as well as the first attempts at staff/pupil competitions.

In 1937, by which time there had been some discussion about whether the school at George Square would move to a new and more modern campus, more extensive playing fields at Liberton were purchased and officially opened in December of that year by Sir Robert Gordon Gilmour, Bt, of Liberton and Craigmillar who also generously donated 10 trees to be planted in the grounds. Shortly after this, the Master of the Merchant Company, Mr W Kinloch Anderson, was reported as saying:

"There is no immediate prospect of a new school being built on this site, but, recognising the desirability of having a school and playgrounds contiguous, and looking to future requirements, we have acquired sufficient land to build a school when that time comes. (25 acres)."

Liberton was some way from George Square and for games afternoons in the later period of the school's history buses were hired from the private company Hunter's rather than depend on public transport in the form of a no 7 or no 8 bus from the Bridges. The time that had to be allowed for travel as well as for changing did much to curtail the pupils' time on the games field (perhaps a blessing for some!) and while Liberton was greatly enjoyed by all those hockey and tennis enthusiasts, it was a great relief when the merger eventually arrived and all you had to do was walk out the door of the school onto the playing fields.

Liberton itself was quite different from Falconhall; much less sheltered and, because it stood high, it was much more open to the elements, especially the howling winter gales for which Edinburgh is renowned. Looking back at the records of tennis and hockey teams over the course of school history, a higher percentage of matches were cancelled per season at Liberton than they were at Falconhall but this must be set against the fact that the greater number of pitches and courts at Liberton allowed for more fixtures and more school teams. The change most certainly did not appear to have any detrimental effect on the quality of play and certainly not on the numbers participating.

Perhaps, Liberton was at its best on the Annual Senior School Sports Day which took place on a Saturday towards the end of session. It was as much a social as an athletic occasion

and was one of the few sporting events in the school calendar which could guarantee a very substantial turn-out of parents and family relations. Large numbers of chairs lined the track and each family, heavily laden with picnic hampers and warm rugs, was asked to take up its position in time for the first starting pistol to be fired. The races lasted most of the afternoon and were followed by the House Relays which aroused more passion than any other event. But it was the arrival of the ice-cream van which was always seen as the real highlight and a much-needed consolation prize for all those whose short-lived athletics careers had ended in disappointment.

Like Falconhall earlier, Liberton was a very important part of the life of the school and for many hundreds of George Square girls they both provided much needed recreational facilities outwith the school buildings. They may have taken up many hours in a tram or a bus, they may evoke some painful memories for those who were not persuaded of the merits of outdoor pursuits but they laid the foundation on which was built a distinguished record of sporting achievement not just for the school but for Scotland at a national level.

In her preface for the first *George Square Chronicle* Charlotte Ainslie writes:

"History speaks to us not only in the text-books of the classrooms, but in the sober and dignified houses which we see from our windows, and which will be famous to all time because they have sheltered such honoured heads. Imagination might perhaps conjure up an old world figure, resolute and alert, listening with interest to history lessons dealing with naval victories and silently approving the growth of pious and patriotic sentiment among the present occupants of his former home… and those who claim as their motto the words, Ex Corde Caritas."

George Square means many things to the vast armies of women who have passed through her doors as staff and pupils. …they each have their own stories and they all know they have been privileged to have the lasting acquaintance of the spirit that dwelt within.

Portrait of Dr Ainslie wearing the scarlet and blue robes of the LL D degree. The artist was Stanley Cursiter OBE, ARSA, Keeper of the National Gallery of Scotland.

The Alexander Thomson Memorial Tablet presented to the School in 1918 by the Former Pupils' Club.

The Watsonian Chair gifted to the School by Miss Charlotte E Ainslie on her retirement as Headmistress. The chair is 6ft tall, made of Scottish oak and has the School coat of arms carved on the back panel.

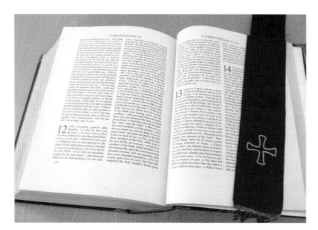

The George Square School Bible, presented in memory of Headmistress Dorothy Nicolson, 1958.

The Gallery Clock designed by Mr Cooper, Art Master, 1921–7, and presented by the Women Watsonians' Club to mark the 25th Jubilee of the Club.

The First World War

As soon as the shock of the invasion by Germany and the outbreak of war had been absorbed, staff, girls and former pupils turned energetically to a rapidly widening range of activities designed to support Britain's war effort and above all to help the wounded, the sick and the refugees.

On the morning of Wednesday 7 October 1914, Miss Ainslie assembled the school. She provided the staff and pupils with an overview of the war situation and then urged them to consider the importance of the issues at stake:

"Our statesmen have striven to maintain peace, but when peace with honour could not be had, the nation has preferred war to an unworthy peace. Britain is fighting for freedom and in self-defence. If she does not fight now she will lose her freedom which is dearer than life itself. The fight is for a good and a great cause; there never was a more righteous war. I now urge each and every one of you to engage in activities that will help to relieve distress."

Her appeals for comforts for the troops did not fall on deaf ears. Pillows, shirts, flannel vests, knitted helmets, waistcoats, scarves, gloves, cuffs and socks, as well as books, currant loaves, jam and shortbread were sent in parcels to the front line, to the many hospitals caring for the wounded and to the Grand Fleet. In December 1915 each member of the 80-strong crew of the battleship 'Orion' received a Christmas pudding (each weighing exactly 9lb!) sent specially by the girls from George Square. There were also special requests made by Lady Tullibardine (who opened the new wing of the school in 1911) to send hose-tops to the Scottish Horse Regiment and by the Deaconess Hospital for food parcels of jam and shortbread.

George Square also sent funds to support hospital beds, most notably the George Square Bed at Royaumont Hospital which was established by Elsie Inglis in the houses of the ancient L'Abbaye de Royaumont in 1914 and which was staffed entirely by women doctors and nurses. In January 1916 a young soldier of 22 years, Jean Semur, a patient who had spent several weeks in the George Square Bed wrote;

"On 24 October 1914 we left for Belgium. It was there that I made my first trenches and saw my companions killed for the first time. It was there too, that I saw the most terrible sights of the campaign. On 10 November I was wounded in the head by a bullet and in hospital I contracted typhoid fever which meant I had to remain in hospital for four months. When I was fit again in May 1915, I returned to the Front at Neuville St Vaast where I spent the most terrible hours of my life. The trenches were choked and crumbled to pieces; there were many dead and wounded. I was sent to Arras in September and here I was wounded in my left arm by a shell. The comrade standing at my side fell dead, his chest torn apart by a shell. I am now in this charming hospital of Royaumont where I am very well looked after. Thank you to the pupils and staff at George Watson's Ladies' College."

Past and present members of staff undertook a variety of tasks. Staff volunteered their services to teach French to soldiers and nurses going to the Front; male staff enrolled for the Home Defence while female staff joined the Red Cross and did all kinds of voluntary work such as berry-picking and catering in munitions factories. School archives record former Headmaster, Mr Thomson (by then aged 83!) drilling with the High Constables, Mrs Boa, a former matron, coming out of retirement to take up duty as a chief stoker and the School Janitor, Robert Guthrie, enrolling in the Army.

Former pupils served with distinction at home and abroad. In hospitals in France, Belgium and Serbia they served as doctors, matrons and nurses, as cooks and canteen-workers, as members of the newly formed Women's Services, and they proved, as if any proof was necessary, the worth of a sound education for women. Miss Alice Hutchison, who at

Members of the crew of the *Orion*, 1915.

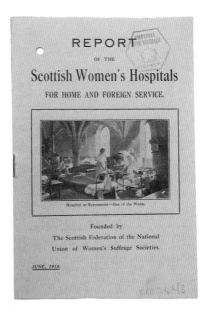

The George Square Bed.

Nurse Whitson.

one time had been the School Doctor, was appointed head of the Belgian Base Hospital in Boulogne and Dr Barbara Cunningham, also a School Doctor at George Square, was appointed as a Senior Nurse at Limoges Hospital. In Dr Cunningham's case, medical expertise was combined with a knowledge of Hindustani which proved to be a huge advantage with the presence of several Indian troops stationed in the town. She became a full-time translator as well as a nurse.

Nurse Maud Fletcher worked as a medical officer in Ghent and stuck to that post throughout the German invasion, sometimes having to serve in large private houses which had been turned into hospitals for wounded senior officers. These were closely guarded by the Germans but occasionally, she managed to get letters smuggled out (through friends in Holland) to her sister in George Square. On 30 November 1914 she wrote:

"Our English officer has died. We could not bury him with any military honours, but very quietly in an ordinary hearse, followed by the two English nurses and myself. At his grave we read the Burial Service and with this he was laid to rest. We made a cross of various flowers from the garden and my special offering to him was my little bit of Scotch heather which had been enclosed in a letter to me. This I tied with a big bow of red, white and blue ribbon and laid it at the head of his grave."

On the home front things were no different. The George Square 'army' assisted the war effort in many ways, working in factories, shops, munitions depots, and of course continuing with all the work of supplying parcels for soldiers and their families. Some who were based in Edinburgh even found themselves working as conductresses on the new tram service and expressing their gratitude to the school for the elocution lessons which enabled them to call out the tram stops *"with a clarity that aroused very favourable comment from our passengers!"*

A 'War Intelligence Corner' was set up on the Gallery by an English master, Mr Young, which provided the girls with newspaper cuttings, pamphlets, books and pictures to help keep them in touch with what was going on in the War. There was a large map on which was charted the weekly movement of troops and on which was marked the names of battles. They were dark days but as one pupil describes, the gloom was pierced by *"moments of unholy joy such as when we stuck the Russian Cross into the waxy surface of East Prussia, in imagination prodding the body of the Kaiser himself. If there is any truth in mediaeval necromancy he must have felt many a twinge of body if not of conscience!"*

At a school event in 1916 Mr Young staged an exhibition of war souvenirs, including a British steel helmet, bombs and hand-grenades, a French shell and part of the German bomb which fell on the Boys' College during an air-raid on Edinburgh.

During these years there were few spheres, industrial, social or commercial, in which women from George Square did not play a part, demonstrating beyond doubt their ability to perform with competence work hitherto considered unsuitable or beyond their powers.

There can be no more difficult a task for a headmistress than to guide her staff and pupils through the personal tragedy of war. But Miss Ainslie's calm authority, compassion, consideration for others and her determination not to yield to the forces of evil were exactly what was called for in a period of unprecedented military engagement. Her speeches resonated with hope, often inspired by passages from the Scriptures, but also with a sense of reality and an understanding that the world would never quite return to its old order. She met that challenge head on, unafraid of the dangers that still lay ahead and unbowed by the personal sacrifices that she herself had to make.

On 3 July 1919, Miss Ainslie ordered a celebration of peace. The gallery was decorated with Union Jacks and banners from various regiments but while the overriding mood was one of relief and joy, there was also humility. Passages from her moving speech to the school and the music and readings performed on that occasion fostered many of the traditions that are central to the annual Armistice Service still held every year on 11 November.

"We fought for Truth and Right, and

the protection of the weak against brutal aggression. But let us spare a little pity too, for our vanquished enemies; it is a bitter thing to be beaten, and not all of them we think, are guilty of the worst crimes that have stained their country's shield." (Charlotte Ainslie, 3 July 1919)

Arthur Nalborough, Singing Master at GWLC, who died of pneumonia in 1915 following severe war wounds. He probably has the distinction of being the only member of staff to be photographed whilst smoking.

There can be no more difficult a task for a headmistress than to guide her staff and pupils through the personal tragedy of war.

Home From the Front by Vida Paterson, aged seven.

"We had a soldier-friend home from the front, and he let us see the box he got from Princess Mary. It had cigarettes a pipe, tobacco, a Christmas card and a photograph of Princess Mary.

He also let us see his emergency ration-kit. It contained five biscuits (which looked like dog-biscuits), tea and sugar, three Oxo cubes, and a tin or corned beef.

At the same time we saw French, German and British bullets, and some pieces of cordite.

His spurs were covered with Belgian and French mud, and he would not allow anyone to brush it off.

He had his case with needles, thread, buttons and safety-pins.

He had been in thirteen engagements."

Somewhere in France by Helen Farquharson and printed in the December 1916 number of *The George Square Chronicle*.

Somewhere in France there's a
lonely grave,
Where a lonely man lies buried deep;
After the turmoil and strife of War,
Sleeping the last long sleep.

Somewhere at home there's a
lonely house,
Where a lonely woman mourns
her dead;
Mourns for the joys that are lost
to her,
Mourns for the beauty in life that
has fled.

Somewhere in heaven there's a
recompense
For those who have given their life
and love;
And the loneliness felt on the earth
below
Will all be forgot in the joys above.

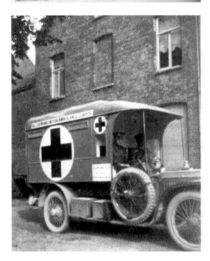

Somewhere in Flanders.

Extract from *Reminiscences* – pupil known as JIC and printed in centenary number of *The George Square Chronicle*.

"It was wartime, we were living through the First World War, and we were all involved, both staff and pupils. There were cookery classes in the downstairs kitchen where we learned to bake with maize. We served teas for parents and friends in the central hall for war funds, we bought war savings stamps and we knitted socks and scarves that were put in parcels for soldiers in the trenches. Even the small children enclosed something they had made and when a letter came back to us it came from 'Somewhere in France' it meant a great deal to us.

Scores of pairs of socks knitted by George Square pupils arrived in boxes for soldiers based near Ypres in 1916. This pair was given to a soldier who turned out to be the uncle of a girl in class IIIb at the time and they still exist today despite being a bit worse for wear!

Sometimes a class produced a magazine for Red Cross Funds and often its first page was devoted to the Roll of Honour. The names of fathers and brothers were written there and read with pride, and alas, often with sadness.

At length the war came to and end and then came our first Armistice Service. No-one who was there could forget it – the school gathered together in the central hall, the hymns we sang, the silence, the loud boom of the gun from the Castle, the signal that the two minutes' silence was over, and then the quiet hush as we walked back to the classrooms. The war was still very close to us."

In 1919 a memorial service was held in St Giles' Cathedral for all those from Merchant Company schools who had lost their lives in the Great War. At this, moving tributes were accompanied by a plea to all those who were lucky enough to survive to continue their efforts to support the national programme for reconstruction and charitable services. The delightful booklet *Our Square* which was written by a Former Pupil, Miss Macdonald in 1925, was just one of the examples of George Square's frequent contributions to support the National Funds which continued for several years after the end of the Great War.

The Second World War

In the July 1939 number of *The George Square Chronicle* the Editor writes that the reader will *"find little in our pages to indicate the existence of anything abnormal"*, such was the determination not to let the international crisis interfere any more than was necessary with the lives of the young ladies of George Square. There were even some light-hearted references to the entire staff undertaking gas-drill lessons and to *"reverend signors swathed in bandages"* taking part in the demonstrations in the first aid classes.

The staff also undertook air-raid training on successive Wednesday evenings – delivered by a Sergeant Pearson and a Sergeant Rodger. *"In spite of the grim necessity which occasioned the instruction, the audience felt sorry when the talks came to an end."*

But the 'business as usual' slogan became increasingly difficult to uphold not least because the decision was taken early to transfer the girls to the boys' school at Colinton Road. The school working day was lengthened to accommodate 'shifts' of teaching the different sexes, there was considerable curtailment to games and House activities, and there was the loss of many valued members of staff as they volunteered for the Forces.

A Former Pupil, Dr Seonaid Cameron, describes 'the move':

"January 1940 was a totally new experience as we found ourselves at school in the relatively new buildings at Colinton Road. We were strictly segregated; in the first half of term the

girls attended in the morning and the boys attended in the afternoon but it was the other way round after half term. Morning school began an hour earlier each day and afternoon school finished an hour later and horror of horrors we had school on Saturdays too, but it was surprising how quickly we adapted to this regime.

Girls came from other Edinburgh schools like Cranley and Queen Street and they were allowed to wear their own uniforms so we were a motley crew although the George Square girls still had to wear gloves and hats even in the hot weather!

We had to carry gas masks everywhere and attend air raid shelter practice but these didn't occur too often. I was given a small bar of plain chocolate to put down the side of my gas mask case and this was only to be eaten if we were in the air raid shelter for over an hour. We never were and I have a horrible feeling that the chocolate was still there when I handed in my gas mask several years later in Southampton.

On one occasion we were allowed to attend a school charity dance with the boys although both myself and another girl did not want to go. However it turned out to be quite a pleasant evening as we sat and talked with my cousin Ian and some of his friends and we managed to avoid dancing all evening!

When I got the telephone call from my father's office in London to say that our family would be returning to Rhodesia, I can remember telling Miss Robertson, the Headmistress, that my elder sister and I would be leaving school immediately. We had not consulted my mother at all but 'CC' accepted us at our word. She was wonderful and I'm sure she understood that the War had made each of us grow up very quickly."

By April 1940, there was talk of evacuation to other parts of Scotland and it was at this time that the dark days of war began to take their heavy toll. News of casualties was all too often a feature of weekly school bulletins and reports within the school magazines.

News of the first member of staff to be injured at the Front, Monsieur Guy La Bastide, came through to the Headmistress shortly before Christmas 1939. Gifts, which were largely the work of two pupils, Joyce Smuts and

EVACUATION TASKS

Parents' Support of Merchant Company Plan

Dispatch ————— 17. v. 39.

NO FAVOURITISM

Two days ago we published a leading article on this subject in which we mentioned that the proposals of the Merchant Company Education Board for the evacuation of its schools in the event of an emergency had been turned down by the Government authorities.

Lest there be any doubt in the minds of our readers as to what the proposals of the Merchant Company are, we publish the following statement, which has been supplied to us by those who speak with authority for the Merchant Company Education Board.

The Merchant Company Education Board considers that it has two duties towards the pupils who attend its schools, first, their safety, and, secondly, the continuance of their education. So far as safety is concerned, the Board desire that all pupils whose parents wish them to be evacuated shall be evacuated to the receiving area for the City of Edinburgh.

The Department of Health for Scotland has made a survey of the accommodation available in the receiving area and should be in a position to say that accommodation for, say, one of the Merchant Company Schools is available in one town, and for another school in another town. It might, depending on the accommodation available, be necessary in some cases to evacuate the elementary portion of the school to one town and the secondary portion to another.

AS A UNIT

Such a scheme ensures that as each school would be evacuated as a unit under its own teachers, there would be less chance of confusion with resulting danger during the actual evacuation and better facilities for continuance of education after evacuation.

It must be kept in view that under this scheme the pupils of the Merchant Company schools would be no safer than the children of the city schools. Lest there should be, to quote the leading article in the *Evening Dispatch*, "anything savouring of favouritism or privilege," the Education Board offered that the whole of the city schools should be evacuated before a start was made on the schools of the Company.

Again, to quote the leading article referred to, the Merchant Company's proposals mean a "departure from the policy of the Government that children of the same family be kept together." That may be the policy of the Department of Health, but the circular issued by the Ministry of Health in charge of evacuation in England reads:— "In other words, the Government are giving priority to school children treated as school units." Accordingly, the Merchant Company are merely asking that the Department of Health allow them to do what is being done in England, where evacuation is on a much larger scale than here.

AN OVERWHELMING MAJORITY

That request has been turned down, and the Merchant Company is told that its pupils will be allowed to go to the nearest city school from which, in charge of teachers whom they do not know, they will be taken to places unknown, their education on arrival being in the hands of the Education Committee for the receiving area.

Again to quote the article mentioned, "Such a decision is likely to win the confidence of the public." It has not won the confidence of the parents of Merchant Company pupils, who by an overwhelming majority have shown their support of the Education Board's proposals.

The answers to the questionnaire issued by the Education Board are (to date) as follows:—Consider evacuation is not necessary, 193; have made private arrangements, 804; in favour of the Company's proposals, 1946; in favour of evacuation with the city schools, 16.

"Evacuation Tasks", Evening Dispatch, *17 May 1939.*

GWLC evacuees in Canada, Margaret McRitchie, Anne Robertson and her brother, 1941.

Her Majesty Queen Elizabeth visits the Red Cross Depot in George Square on 24 February 1940.

Isobel Shade, and a member of staff, Miss Reid were dispatched to his hospital in France. The following letter was sent back:

"Sur le point de repartir pour le front je reçois le magnifique cadeau qu'ont tricoté pour moi les mains très experts de vos élèves. Je suis très touché de ces attentions si délicates. Ce passe-montagne et ces gants me seront un très chaud et précieux témoignage de notre bonne amitié a laquelle je suis et demeurerai très attaché.

Je vous charge, chère Miss Robertson, de transmettre à Miss Reid, Miss Joyce Smuts et Miss Isobel Shade mes bien vifs remerciements."

Following evacuation to Colinton Road 'George Square' became a main Depot for Red Cross activities. A large Red Cross insignia hung over the main entrance and inside the Waiting Room officials would take names and addresses of those wanting to sign up for voluntary service.

The Gallery and classrooms were turned into a miniature factory where parcels of hospital comforts were made up for soldiers, sailors and airmen who had been wounded in the front line.

Former Pupil and a Commandant of the British Red Cross Society, Mrs Sinclair (1940) describes the scene:

"Volunteers would bring all sorts of items of sewn and knitted clothes, take away new materials and patterns, carry in bundles of dried sphagnum moss and old boots and shoes which were to be repaired and made good for further use.

In the basement gym area volunteers laid out the large quantities of sphagnum moss and the cloakrooms were turned into the store rooms for materials such as wincey, flannelette and calico for making uniform shirts and underclothes.

There was also a large army of catering volunteers serving up meals from the Admiral's Kitchen at a shilling a head for those who had signed into the Lunch Book."

Mrs Sinclair also describes the visit of Her Majesty Queen Elizabeth to the Red Cross Depot in George Square on Saturday 24 February 1940.

"The School on this particular morning presented a sight of great activity and there hung around about it an air of great expectancy. Why? Her Majesty the Queen was honouring the old School with a visit.

The Hall was laid out with tables holding all kinds of hospital equipment, sewed garments, knitted garments, sphagnum moss, surgical appliances and dressings which had been made at the various depots and collected here.

As the hour approached for Her Majesty's arrival, the Hall became a hive of industry and animation. All the people connected with the various departments of the Depot took up their places round the tables.

To come down to my own little bit of work – namely, the Canteen – I will now try to describe the scene there. The old Dining-room looked at its very best and we all stood ready for our great moment. Her Majesty approached. I and another Woman Watsonian had the honour of being presented to Her Majesty and serving her with tea, which she graciously consented to take. On Her Majesty's entrance to the Dining-room, she remarked on the lovely flowers, and on leaving she accepted one of the baskets of flowers. In course of conversation, Her Majesty enquired where the pupils of the School had gone, thereby showing her great sympathy and interest in the children.

It was indeed a great thrill to me and my assistants, numbering among them three Women Watsonians, that we were privileged to keep the old flag flying in the old School."

Editors of *The George Square Chronicle* received floods of letters from Former Pupils recounting their wartime efforts ranging from the standard service of knitting and sewing, to keeping ducks and goats, looking after evacuee children, collecting books for the Forces and delivering Government ear-plugs and spades.

In the 1940 number of *The George Square Chronicle* it was reported that Mrs Barker (Edith Henderson at school) ran the Ypyres League Comforts Depot at Purley, Mrs Churcher (Dorothy Morris) ran the Services Club at North Farnborough, Miss Cator and Miss Fletcher took on the work of organising the street collections of the National Savings Scheme throughout Horsham, Mrs Goodfellow (Bertha Gunn) was doing the same in Wembley, Elizabeth Gray worked with the Canning Town Women's Settlement, Helen Gillespie was driving ambulances, K McLeish and Mrs Turner (Nora Loudon) worked as Air Raid Wardens and Jessie and Margaret Carter ran the Ministry of Food 'Save the Fruit' scheme for a district of Surrey; just one paragraph in just one war-time number of the School magazine which highlighted the efforts of Women Watsonians at home and abroad.

The war-time school magazines were also full of the pupils' literary contributions:

For Freedom

When my thoughts wander from the perfect beauty of nature to present day events a great gloom comes upon me. I can see no longer the shining splendour of the earth. I can see only a world stark mad.

Yet even out of the inky blackness of war, signs of man's immortality shine out. I see the constant bravery of the fighting forces and I remember the epic of Dunkirk, when rich and poor alike went down to the sea in ships, to face death itself, in a valiant effort to save their fellow men.

I believe that out of this war, with its total disregard for human life, will emerge a new realisation of life's endless possibilities. There will be a reawakening to the sheer wonder of the universe, a new understanding of the immense value of each and every human life.

Thousands of young lives are at this minute being sacrificed for freedom. Freedom for what? If we feel justified in waging war on the battlefield of France, we must, at the same time, wage war with tenfold vigour on the battlefield of our own souls. We must, each one of us, seek to evolve a personality which draws every action, word and thought into line with the "straight and narrow way", which is the way of true freedom – freedom from sin.

When we affirm that we are seeking to preserve the cause of freedom in the world, we must bear in mind that there is but one freedom worthwhile. It is the freedom to put every atom of our being behind an enormous creative effort to build a better and finer country. It is the freedom to make ourselves fit for the leading place in building a better and finer world.

(C C F, Vb, July 1940, *The George Square Chronicle*)

The Jerry's Patrol

One moonlight night, a Jerry came
To Edinburgh town of ancient fame,
But the fighter squadrons had all been warned,
And the Spits and Hurricanes had upwards swarmed.
So when Jerry saw they were now within range,
He thought he'd better be off for a change,
So he jettisoned his bombs in a very great hurry,
(They fell, by the way, in the village of Currie),
And with wild endeavour, began a race
To try to rejoin his friends and his base.
But alas! And Alack! For that Jerry 'plane,
It was soon a great mass of bright orange flame,
And fell spinning to earth all out of control,
So that was the end of Jerry's patrol.

(Doreen Ireland, IVa, July 1940, *The George Square Chronicle*)

MISS RUBY GRIERSON
City of Benares Victim
WAS FILMING VOYAGE

AMONG the passengers who lost their lives when the City of Benares, the evacuee vessel bound for Canada, was torpedoed last week was Miss Ruby I. Grierson, youngest sister of Mr John Grierson, the Scottish film producer. Miss Grierson, who had directed a number of documentary films, had joined the vessel as a passenger in order to make a film of the voyage, commissioned by the Canadian Government.

Youngest daughter of the late Mr Robert M. Grierson, headmaster, Cambusbarron, Stirlingshire, Miss Grierson was educated at Glasgow University. She taught for several years at George Watson's Ladies' College, Edinburgh, and during this period lived at Balerno. She shared her brother's enthusiasm for films, however, and, in 1936, after several vacations spent working with film units in London, she severed her connection with the College and began her career in films.

The first production with which she was associated was "Housing Problems," a stirring plea for improvement in social conditions. A later film with a similar purpose was "Eastern Valley." For Strand Films she made "Zoo and You," which amusingly gave the animals' view of zoo visitors. Her most important film was "Cargo from Ardrossan," filmed largely in Mull. Before leaving for Canada she had been working on a series of cooking films for the Ministry of Food.

A friend writes:

"She was the type of woman this country needs now and even more when the war is over. She had courage, faith, a fighting spirit and a lifetime of rebuilding ahead – and yet she died in the gale of terror and darkness created by Nazi savagery."

SCOTSMAN 25:9:40

News of the death of Miss Ruby Grierson, The Scotsman, *25 September 1940.*

Miss Ruby Grierson who was a member of the English Department between 1928 and 1936 was one of the first recognised female film directors. She was a sister of the more famous John Grierson who was responsible for producing several films in the 1930s which focused on the economic deprivation of industrial Britain and who, as a result, is largely credited with being the founder of documentary film-making. Ruby made her own films for early cinema, the most notable of which were those recording life inside the city slums.

On 17 September 1940 Ruby Grierson was on board 'The City of Benares', an original Ellerman City Line passenger ship which was carrying British evacuees, many of them children, from Liverpool to Montreal. Miss Grierson had been commissioned by the Canadian Government to film the voyage but disaster struck when the ship was sunk by a torpedo from a German U48 submarine; 250 people, including Miss Grierson were drowned. Also on the same ship and lost at sea were the two sons of the then Treasurer of the London Women Watsonians' Club, Mrs Goodfellow.

Thoughts in the Black-Out

At the present time the outside world seems to hold little or no attraction for us. At a too early hour we seem suddenly to be enveloped in a great cloak of darkness which hems us in on every side and from which the night walker has no means of escape. We stumble blindly, confused by the eternal darkness, in which we ca find no guiding star and vague thoughts of possible demons and unearthly beings fill our minds. Dazed, we are suddenly awakened from our stupor by a glare of headlights, to be immediately followed by an even thicker and denser darkness.

Having groped his way for what seems an immeasurable length of time, the walker eventually arrives in a quieter and more open part of town, and is soon able to discern the outlines of phantom houses, trees and possibly masses of clouds making their way across the somewhat stormy sky. The houses look gloomy and sinister and we wonder to think of the masses of brilliancy and light bottled up behind those dark, silent shutters. Peering into the gardens we are at once confronted by weird shapes, and imagine stealthy figures lurking behind trees, – figures likely at any moment to spring out upon us.

Steeped in distressing thoughts and hardly noticing where we are going, we are relieved to find ourselves again on our own doorstep. At the sight of a ruddy fire and the sound of cheery voices, our phantom visions and nightmares flee to their own places – and we are left in peace.

(D E I, IVa, *The George Square Chronicle*, December 1939)

Excerpt from a letter sent to *The Scotsman* by Cicily Isabel Fairfield (later known as Rebecca West) in 1907 at the age of 14 *(see also page 254).*

"….I was very much interested in the letter signed 'Mater' in this morning's issue as it seems to reflect no inconsiderable part of feminine opinion. The writer is not very clear as to her opening point. She denounces the National Women's Social and Political Union as unpatriotic on the declaration of war on the Liberal Government, independent of their divers political

creeds. And why? Because it is the duty of women to support our constitution against all revolutionary efforts; to, in short, defend the nation from Socialism. I for one cannot follow "Mater" here as I do not think she realises the profound national effects of the subjugation of women on the nation".

One wonders if Cicily Fairfield got into trouble with any George Square staff for writing her letter or whether they secretly agreed with her!

It goes without saying that the Second World War left a deep psychological scar on the lives of all those who attended George Square just as it had on the nation, but within the ashes of devastation, both physical and mental, new strengths had been found as had a new sense of purpose for the future of the School.

No-one knows how many George Square FPs were lost in the two World Wars, possibly no-one ever will, but they will never be forgotten by successive generations.

In Memoriam

Daisy Kathleen Mary Coles, daughter of Mr and Mrs Walter G Coles of 18 St Ninian's Terrace, Edinburgh, and Priorsford House, Peebles, was killed at the age of 24 in an enemy air raid on 30 September 1917 whilst working for the 58th General Hospital Unit of the Voluntary Aid Detachment (Red Cross) near the town of St Omer in France. She is buried in the Longuenesse Cemetery, three kilometres from St Omer.

Daisy Coles' grave, Longuenesse Cemetery, St Omer, France.

At the going down of the sun and in the morning, we will remember them.

Edinburgh
Merchant Company
Schools.

GEORGE WATSON'S
LADIES'
COLLEGE.

HEAD MISTRESS—CHARLOTTE E. AINSLIE, B.A. (Lond.).

Session 1905-1906.

The College will be re-opened on Tuesday, 3rd October 1905.
All information may be obtained on application to the Secretary of the Merchant Company,
The Merchants' Hall, Edinburgh.

ORGANISATION.

ELEMENTARY DEPARTMENT.

PUPILS are received from five years of age, and continue for two years in the Elementary Department. The course includes:—Reading, Spelling, Recitation, Writing, Arithmetic, Stories from Scripture, History and Literature, Language Lessons, Geography, Nature Study, Kindergarten Subjects, including Modelling and Brushwork, Needlework, Singing, Musical Drill, Dancing and Calisthenics.

	PER TERM.	PER SESSION.
FEE	17s. 6d.	£2, 12, 6.

AND

Matriculation Fee—Two Shillings per Session.*

JUNIOR DEPARTMENT.

In the Junior Department the study of Pianoforte Music is begun, and the other subjects include Scripture Knowledge, Arithmetic, English, Grammar, Geography, History, Needlework, Singing, Dancing and Calisthenics.

In the Upper Junior Classes these subjects, suitably advanced, are continued, and the pupils are able profitably to begin French and Drawing.

		PER TERM.	PER SESSION.
Fees {	LOWER DIVISION ...	£1, 17, 6.	£5, 12, 6.
	HIGHER DIVISION ...	£2, 15, 0.	£8, 5, 0.

AND

Matriculation Fee—Four Shillings per Session.*

SENIOR DEPARTMENT.

In the Senior Department the studies begun in the Junior are continued, and pupils, as they are able, take Latin, Mathematics and German.

In the Senior Advanced Classes the studies include English Classics with the History of English Literature, French and German Languages, Literature and Conversation, Latin with Prose Composition, Science including Hygiene, Arithmetic generally with Mathematics, including Euclid, Algebra and Trigonometry.

In the Sewing Classes instruction is given in Pattern Drawing, Shaping and Cutting.

		PER TERM.	PER SESSION.
Fees {	LOWER DIVISION—Lower Grade	£3, 7, 6.	£10, 2, 6.
	LOWER DIVISION—Upper Grade	£3, 15, 0.	£11, 5, 0.
	HIGHER DIVISION ...	£4, 0, 0.	£12, 0, 0.

AND

Matriculation Fee—Four Shillings per Session.*

MEDICAL EXAMINATION OF PUPILS.

The Governors inaugurated last session a system of Medical Examination of pupils. The object of the examination is to ascertain how far each girl is physically fit for the ordinary school course, and in what respects the course should be modified to meet the needs of individual pupils. If the Lady Medical Examiner of the School finds any weakness which can be corrected by remedial exercises given in school, the Physical Mistress will be instructed as to the exercises necessary. If special attention should otherwise be needed in any case, the parent or guardian will be asked to consult the family medical adviser, but in no case will the school doctor prescribe. The examination is entirely optional on the part of parents and guardians, but in view of the importance of the subject, the Governors hope to receive their hearty co-operation. The charge for the examination is included in the Matriculation Fee.

The Medical Examiner is Miss B. M. CUNNINGHAM, M.B., Ch. B. (Edin.).

* Includes cost of Stationery detailed on page 6.

5

STATIONERY.

All articles of Stationery required for use in School, as undernoted, will be supplied to the pupils:—

ELEMENTARY DEPARTMENT.—Copy-books, Drawing-books, Exercise-books, Pencils and India-rubber for Drawing.

JUNIOR DEPARTMENT.—Copy-books, Drawing-books, Exercise-books, Examination Paper, Pencils and India-rubber for Drawing.

SENIOR DEPARTMENT.—Scroll-books for Arithmetic and Mathematics, Copy-books, Drawing-books, Science Note-books, Examination Paper, Pencils and India-rubber for Drawing.

SCHOOL REGULATIONS.

1. Pupils must be punctual and regular in their attendance, orderly in their habits, and polite in their conduct both in and out of School.

2. When a pupil is absent, intimation of the reason should be sent at once to the Head Mistress. No excuse, except illness, is regarded as satisfactory for absence or neglect of lessons.

3. No pupil is allowed to leave during school hours without a written request, signed by the parent or guardian, and addressed to the Head Mistress.

4. School Books, &c., should be marked with the Name and Class of the pupil, so that any article found may be at once returned to the owner.

5. Parents or Guardians must give intimation to the Head Mistress if infectious disease occurs in the house. Pupils who have suffered from any infectious disease, or who have been living in a house where such a disease has occurred, are not allowed to attend School until a medical certificate has been produced to the Head Mistress stating that there is no longer any risk of infection, and that suitable disinfection has been practised. This certificate should be sent by post, and should reach the Head Mistress at least twenty-four hours before the pupil proposes to resume attendance.

6. The Head Mistress will be glad to see the parents or guardians of pupils on Wednesday in each week, from 10 to 3 o'clock, and at other times by appointment.

7. As General Prayers are held each morning at 9 o'clock, pupils are required to assemble five minutes before that hour. Requests for exemption from attendance at Prayers should be addressed to the Head Mistress in writing.

SCHOOL HOURS.

ELEMENTARY DEPARTMENT.—In the Junior Division the hours are from 9 a.m. to 1 p.m. ; in the Senior Division from 9 a.m. to 1.30 p.m.

JUNIOR AND SENIOR DEPARTMENTS.—The hours are as follows:—

| Morning School (for all girls) | . | . | . | 9 a.m. to 1.30 p.m. |
| Afternoon School (for some girls) | . | . | . | 2.30 p.m. to 4 p.m. |

During the morning, there is a short interval between classes, and an interval of about twenty minutes for lunch and recreation.

The afternoon hours are devoted to extra classes for advanced or exceptional pupils, including subjects such as Languages, Cookery, Shorthand, Music, Physical Training, &c., and to the preparation of lessons for next day by those girls whose parents may desire them to return to School for the purpose.

Those pupils who may require occasionally to attend afternoon classes, and are not within easy reach of home, may partake in the School buildings of food brought with them, or of a dinner provided by the School authorities at a moderate charge.

6

SCHOOL SESSION.

The session extends from 3rd October to about the end of July, and is divided into three Terms. The *first* Term extends to the Christmas holidays ; the *second*, to the Spring holidays ; and the *third*, to the end of the session. The Fees are payable each Term in advance.

When pupils are withdrawn during the course of the session, written notice should be sent to the Head Mistress not less than fourteen days before the end of a Term ; otherwise liability is incurred for the Fee for the next Term.

HOLIDAYS.

The Governors, subject to a power reserved to them to make such alterations as they may consider proper, have fixed the School Holidays during session 1905-1906 to be as follows, viz.:—

1. Christmas Holidays—From the afternoon of Thursday, 21st December 1905, to the morning of Tuesday, 9th January 1906.

2. Good Friday.

3. Spring Holidays—A Fortnight in April.

4. Victoria Day.

5. Summer Holidays—Two Months.

RECREATION HALL.

7

A selection of pages from the George Watson's Ladies' College Prospectus, Session 1905/6.

From Merchant Company records written in 1870 there is evidence that its members considered the opening of a girls' school to be a relatively straight-forward matter. They didn't think there was any need for elaborate science equipment or laboratories, art studios or gymnasia; you just had to find a building, some benches, desks, blackboards and pianos, find a suitable headmaster and open the doors. The rest would take care of itself!

Certainly, when it came to finding a suitable headmaster, the Merchant Company made one of the wisest choices in its long, distinguished history. Alexander Thomson, about whom more is written later in this book, was the perfect man for the job, and on 2 October 1871 he opened the new school with 500 pupils, offering *"instruction in English, French, German and Latin Languages, Lectures on Literature, Science, Writing, Arithmetic, Book-keeping, Algebra, Mathematics, Drawing, Vocal Music, Instruction on the Pianoforte, Drill, Calisthenics, Dancing, Needlework and Cookery".*

In its range of academic subjects the curriculum was very like that of the boys' school except that there was less Science and no Greek. And, like the boys' school, there were meticulous records kept of the admissions procedure.

The School's Register of Admission provided a record of each pupil's personal and academic profile within the three departments of the School; Elementary (class E), Junior (classes 1 to 6 with 1 being the equivalent of Primary 7) and Senior (classes I to VI with I being the equivalent of the Sixth Form). The Registers show the very high percentage of pupils who came to George Square from the Grange, Marchmont and Newington areas of the city, a tradition that was to continue throughout the School's history, but it is also interesting to note that several pupils travelled quite a long way to school from places like Winchburgh, Denny, Musselburgh, and Dalkeith, some of whom used the passenger rail service between

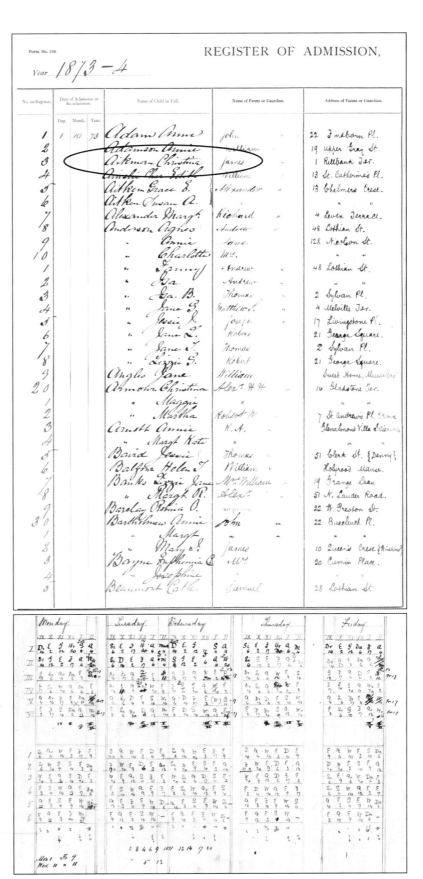

1873 School Register on which the name of Charlotte E Ainslie appears and copy of the 1871/2 session timetable.

Eskbank Station from which many George Square girls alighted the train to Waverley.

Class Governess with Elementary pupils.

Hardengreen and Waverley that had been opened in 1855. But these pupils were in the minority with the vast majority enjoying a relatively short travel time between home and school.

In the 1870s, fees ranged from 12s 6d per quarter for the Elementary Department to £3 for the Senior Department. Foundations and school bursaries were available, and to these were soon added *"Bursaries for the Educational Advancement of Girls"* to enable girls of *"merit and promise"* to continue their education after leaving school, and there were also bursaries available for the Edinburgh School of Cookery and Domestic Science (ten of them at £5 per annum).

Up until this point, the tradition for staffing most educational establishments for girls had been the employment of governesses; highly respectable and well-intentioned women but they did not usually have professional training. And so, while there was always the guarantee of governesses teaching basic reading, writing and arithmetic skills to the more junior classes, other teachers and schoolmasters, recognisable by their distinctive black frock-coats, were hired in to take charge of the more senior classes and provide the opportunity for some of the more able girls to sit local university examinations. Looking after the best interests of the most able was a priority within the curriculum and for this reason the Merchant Company frequently invited inspection of their schools by University professors. Such inspections were usually short and to the point and rarely gave rise to any adverse comment although there is some evidence of a few problems with a teacher of German in the 1880s who seemed a bit too ready to discuss his extra-marital affairs with his pupils!

However, while careful inspection of certificate classes was rigorously pursued, this was not the case for

1875
May 7 I have gone over the whole of the establishment to day and am extremely pleased with all that I have seen. The classes were all busily at work and the pupils evidently interested in the various branches of instruction they are receiving. The classrooms were all well ventilated and cleanly
Sd Marshall.

School Inspector's comment 1875.

lower classes. The wider curriculum often reflected the special interests of staff and so there was nothing unusual about different classes being exposed to slightly different material within each subject area. There was virtually no pressure from any outside bodies to influence exactly what was taught or how – heads were trusted to do things their own way and by and large nobody interfered unless there was a major scandal of some sort.

How much everything was to change; beginning with the advent of the Endowed Institutions Acts of 1878 and 1882 (allowing former hospital foundations to be turned

into secondary schools) and followed by legislation in 1892 which promoted free grant-aided secondary education throughout Scotland and provided additional funding for schools which were wishing to specialise in art or science.

There were two main results of these changes: Firstly, the new 'free' schools were very attractive to parents who were worried about the financial constraints of paying fees and so they quickly attracted pupils. This made the fee-paying institutions have to fight much harder to retain high numbers on their school rolls. Secondly, as a direct result of the increased market

Science Room, built in 1906/7.

Cuisenaire rods.

and competition, boards of governors started to take a much greater interest in the running of their schools and the teaching abilities of staff within them. They also knew that they would have to spend money on improving facilities to ensure that they kept the competitive edge over their rivals.

And so it was not coincidence that the Merchant Company took action in all its schools, George Square included, to provide better accommodation and more extensive opportunities within the curriculum. Indeed, it is the combination of the foresight of the Merchant Company and two excellent heads in the persons of Mr Thomson and Miss Ainslie that brought such success to the early years of the school – so much success that in 1879 it inspired an examiner in Mathematics and Arithmetic to comment that *"the institution of the Merchant Company's Schools for Girls has to a great extent created the Secondary education of girls."*

By 1888 the Scottish Leaving Certificate had been introduced and there was quite clearly a move to make the curriculum much more appealing to pupils and parents, particularly in the extra-curricular dimension. Gradually, there was the recognition that education should no longer be limited to sound instruction in the three Rs but instead laying more stress on the development of individuality and the skills necessary to enjoy a rich and fulfilling life as a good citizen.

By the time Charlotte Ainslie became headmistress in 1902, there was a desire to staff the school with full-time qualified teachers and with as many women as possible although not to the exclusion of men. The Scottish Education Department was, by this stage, advising the governors of girls' schools to appoint headmistresses rather than headmasters and to *"take on women of culture and character from wherever you can find them."* Charlotte Ainslie set out to do just that and when it came to the teaching of languages she was determined to find those who had studied abroad as well as having been educated at a British school. Visiting masters and governesses became a redundant concept although a few of them were absorbed into the school teaching staff. Heads of department were recommended *"to relieve the Headmistress of some clerical work"* and a Senior Assistant Mistress was appointed to take over the duties of the Lady Superintendent.

However, it was to be more substantial developments in the curriculum which were to bring about the most noticeable changes to school life. Before the extension of 1903 there was only one small room adapted for science work with few girls taking up its individual disciplines with any degree of enthusiasm. However, with the advent of a new approach by the Scottish Education Department and new developments in the fields of scientific research and technology, the Merchant Company invested in brand new laboratories; one laboratory for Physics, one for Chemistry and one for Domestic Science. Instead of one science master there were six and the number of pupils sitting certificate courses in science rose from 40 to 100.

There followed a complete reorganisation of the timetable and, a little later, a complete overhaul of internal organisation. Previously the school hours operated from 9am till 3pm with lesson times of an hour with an hour's break for lunch. After 1903 the lesson time was shortened 9.00am–1.30pm, an hour for lunch then lessons resumed 1.30pm–4.00pm including time for preparation. New subjects appeared on the curriculum such as Greek and Secretarial Studies and Elementary education was also completely reorganised along kindergarten lines with the phonetic method of reading introduced (later known as the *"look and say"* method whose model children were the famous Dick and Dora), the use of *"Speer's arithmetic"* and *"Froebel's bricks"* which eventually gave way to *"Cuisenaire rods"* at a much later date.

The institution of the Merchant Company's Schools for Girls has to a great extent created the Secondary education of girls.

It is interesting to note that reports from the Elementary Department, which were given considerable prominence in early issues of *The George Square Chronicle*, relate a striking breadth of activity in the infant classes, ranging from *"doing sums and words all day"*, to nature rambles on Blackford Hill, visits to the Castle *"to see real soldiers"*, acting historical pageants, entertaining Timothy the Tortoise and drawing pictures of George Watson and his family.

Young pupils' drawings of George Watson and his family. 1. George Watson, his aunt and his brother James by Beatrice Wilson – age 7 years. 2. George Watson at work by Eleanor Cowlin - age 7 years. 3. George Watson with two Dutch friends by Celia Fowler – age 7 years.

"George Wotsen left his mony to bild sckools and he has a wig on his hair and I lice him very mutch and so do other peepl he is very nise and good to you he has a luvly wig" – comment from Isobel Meikle, class Eb, 1930.

The style of writing in the reports is also worthy of note; a very caring Infant Mistress who understands the ways of her charges very well, knows their interests, what they enjoy best and what will stimulate their creative skills. But she is also firm and it is clear she is preparing them for the more rigorous discipline they will meet further up the school.

An 'honours' system operated in the Elementary School which consisted of red stars and blue stars being respectively handed out for 'excellent' and 'very good' work in class, but there

was also a system of order marks for those who fell below expectations and there was the possibility of removal from class for very bad conduct. By all accounts, this was a very rare occurrence and it involved more disgrace falling on the parents, who were summoned into school, than it did on the pupil. Nor did the misdemeanours of the few have any lasting detrimental effect on the high standards of the many and on the high expectations of those who were teaching them. *The George Square Chronicles* of the early years are bursting with news about the activities of the youngest members of the school community and there is no doubt that they played a very full part in the life of the School. Even in wartime this contribution was vitally important as their vast collection of silver paper and paint tubes for the Prisoners of War Fund in 1916 demonstrates.

By the first decade of the twentieth century, new developments were taking shape in extra-curricular activities and there was a very clear move to promote a curriculum, both inside and outside the schoolroom that went well beyond the teaching of just basic academic knowledge. Charlotte Ainslie said in her end-of-session report in 1914 that the school had a responsibility, particularly in a world fraught with international tension, to inculcate a sense of duty in all its girls, to be for ever cheerful, helpful and to understand that good manners and good conduct are the essence of good character. Personal service in the cause of others, she said, was just as important as success in the examination hall. School was much more than just your books.

George Square during the First World War is covered elsewhere in this volume but there was remarkably little disruption to lessons and the routine of the school day. However, there is no doubt that the war had a profound effect on the school community and the approach to education thereafter. In 1920, Miss Ainslie commented upon the unrest found in many quarters of society and the need to meet its challenge by demanding the maintenance of high standards of work and insisting that service to the community must come before selfish interests. She recommended

concentration on duty rather than the pursuit of pleasure as a motive for action in life.

The first 50 years of the school's life were summed up in the words of the Editor of *The George Square Chronicle* in 1926 (when Miss Ainslie retired): *"The old order which passed with Mr Thomson has left us treasured memories; the new order established by Miss Ainslie marks an achievement so great that we may not yet compute it. The two combined leave us a tradition which is the heritage of the future generations."*

In the 1920s and 1930s George Square moved forward, still very much in the vanguard of Scottish education. Following a Games Club initiative in 1920 to stimulate more competitive games, the school was divided into Houses *"to aid discipline and organisation"* and in 1927, during Miss CC Robertson's first year as Headmistress, a new class structure was introduced with an interesting reference to it in the very first line of the editorial for the December 1927 issue of the school magazine;

"The rearrangement of the designation of the classes has brought us into line with the generally accepted system of nomenclature, and the new arrangements generally are conducive to a certain liveliness, leaving little time for reposeful meditation between classes. The sixth form seems to have gained in weight and responsibility, and in influence plays well its leading part in the school."

Reflecting the changes to the curriculum the form classes in the Senior School were named VI, Va, Vb, V Secretarial, V Domestic, IVa, IVb, IV Secretarial, IV Domestic, IIIa, IIIb, IIIc, IIa, IIc, Ia, Ib, I Alpha. In 1929 IIx form was an interesting and, for some girls and staff, a controversial, addition. The brightest pupils in the pre-qualifying class sat their main exam a year early and were often taught alongside some of the pupils a year older than them. It was the present-day equivalent of missing out O-Grades or latterly Standard Grades to progress straight into Higher work. One Former Pupil of the time, Christina Berry, says that *"the move caused quite a bit of ill-feeling as some of the superior pupils got a bit uppity and caused problems."* In the class round-ups of the day it is easy to see that feelings ran high!

IIx
Poor IIx!
See how they work;
They work long after it's twelve
at night,
And think, and learn, and read
and write,
If they do it much longer
they'll ruin their sight.
Poor IIx.

In IIX.
There are ten M's.
They're mostly moral, and mild,
and mute,
But some are magpies and
methods dispute,
They are mingled and mixed,
I'm sure you'll impute,
In IIx.

Comments about Form IIx.

Laboratory work, 1950s.

In the Junior School, classes were named 5a, 5b, 4a and 4b, 3a and 3b, 2a and 2b and 1a and 1b with the kindergarten below that (elementary classes A,B,C, and D). These changes reflected a reduction in size of class from 35 to 30 although the curriculum remained largely the same: English, Grammar, Nature Study, French, Arithmetic, Geography, History, Latin, Gymnastics and Dancing and Sewing. Towards the Upper Junior School, academic grading became very important and there were quite separate timetables operating for those with top academic potential and those who were less able. Sets were decided upon linguistic ability and for those in the bottom sets there was a more vocational programme available with extra English classes regarded as compulsory.

In the early 1930s the school fees ranged between £3 and £6 a term dependent upon the age of the pupil and there were special reductions offered for girls from Church of Scotland families, a privilege that was later to be awarded to those who were daughters of members of staff at a Merchant Company School and a girl who was the last in line as the third sibling attending a Merchant Company School.

Wartime had certainly changed attitudes; there was a much stronger belief in the important role of women in economic and political life and there was a much more practical application of the curriculum which involved a greater use of teaching aids and a further broadening of the subjects offered both in the junior and senior schools. In the Headmistress's Report of 1949, Miss Nicolson proudly reported that the School had now invested in all modern facilities: electric light, gramophones, wirelesses and typewriters and, as such, would compare favourably with any girls' school in the land.

Other innovations of this time were current affairs classes and parents' evenings. In Session 1947, a series of five evening lectures by visiting speakers was arranged for interested parents in which the topics for debate were diverse: *"Religious Instruction in the Home and School"*, *"Health Care for Young Ladies"*, *"Art and Science – Is there a conflict?"*, *"Wartime Experiences"*, *"Moral Issues for Young People"*.

What was interesting here was that parents were encouraged to participate in the discussion rather than simply be lectured to showing that there was a desire to make them feel as much a part of the school community as their daughters – always one of the strongest assets of both George Watson's. The meetings soon became opportunities for the parents to discuss their daughters' progress and to hear about their endeavours beyond the classroom.

But it was perhaps within the mainstream curriculum that most change took place. In the postwar years, there was a much more utilitarian approach to education at national level, not least because of the growth of the school population especially in the upper years of the senior school. There was a reaction against study simply for the sake of training the mind rather than for its practical application to the modern world and there was also a reaction against such formal discipline, although possibly not many George Square girls of the time would claim to have noticed!

Science became much more important, the traditional dependence on the Classics was broken and there were new opportunities in the field of Social Science. Part of this development was a reaction to economic and social trends, part an acceptance that these changes had worked well in the boys' schools, and part a reflection of an increasingly secular society which put a much higher value on practical skills than ever before. That is not to say that George Square suddenly transformed itself into a bastion of the modern enlightenment and abandoned its traditional curriculum. Certainly, there were changes and both

Dorothy Nicolson and Hilda Fleming were unafraid to move into uncharted waters – in the former instance in the development of new methods in primary education and in the latter case developing a much greater insight into the benefits of science teaching and the development of a formal programme of extra-curricular activity.

It was also noticeable in the 1950s and 1960s that there was a desire to extend the horizons of the girls to encompass more breadth in the curriculum and an opportunity to participate in more activities that had previously been the preserve of their male counterparts. In particular this developed in the extra-curricular field but there was no doubt that changing social and cultural attitudes were also reflected in the curriculum. While some subjects were still considered less appropriate for a girls' school (eg Politics), there was a growth in technical subjects and a much more enlightened attitude to business-related careers or industry. With women's access to university improving all the time good schools knew they could not be left behind and therefore they were anxious to undertake changes that suited new curricular opportunities in further and higher education.

But there is no doubt that the catalyst for more substantial change occurred towards the end of the 1960s. On the surface, many pupils would not notice much difference at school. In its prospectus, George Square remained firmly wedded to the traditional principles that underpinned girls' private schooling and most especially an emphasis on the core curriculum in terms of the three 'Rs'. As well as basic arithmetic, spelling, grammar and writing skills, pupils would be expected to read aloud in class, to learn endless lists of vocabulary and mathematical formulae; History was still taught chronologically if open to a wider variety of teaching methods, Geography was still physical, and non-academic education was still all about cooking and sewing and various handcrafts that were thought essential to the management of a good home and the acquisition of a good husband.

Discipline remained rigorous with no question of informality between staff and pupils, except perhaps when the pupil had reached the dizzy heights of the Sixth Form; rules were rules and

---

GEORGE WATSON'S LADIES' COLLEGE

Form III 1970 – 71

Girls entering Form III in September 1970 must select their subjects for O grade in 1972 and possibly H grade in 1973 or 4. ALL girls take

1. English
2. French
3. Mathematics – except those now in $\int$ who take arithmetic only. They must also choose one subject from each of three groups and reject one group.
4. Physics or history.
5. Chemistry, German, Greek, Art, Commerce.
6. Biology
7. Geography or Latin.

There are two chemistry divisions, one for the scientists taking physics as well, and a slower stream taking O grade in 1973 for domestic science, etc. There is a beginners' course in German for good linguists but not a beginners' course in Latin. Art and commerce courses do not lead to O grade in IV but can be expanded to specialisation in V and VI when home management, dress and design, music are also available.

Biology is an alternative to mathematics for university qualification.

HILDA FLEMING
Headmistress.

Subject choice sheet, 1970.

Staff photo 1955 by which time gentlemen staff numbered only four.

---

the Headmistress's word was law, with staff as well as pupils.

But, little by little, perceptible innovations appeared. Although success in national examinations (which, after 1961, were sat in May and not March) remained paramount, they were forced to give some quarter to more assignments and projects which were designed to encourage greater creativity and more self-discipline in the classroom. French had appeared in the Junior School curriculum, as had formal sex education for the early years of senior school, and there was a much stronger emphasis on debating skills and the expressive arts. On the staff, after a long tradition of relying on male heads in the major academic departments (Dr Langdon, Mr Millar, Mr Trail, Mr Bogie and Mr Henderson) more women were appointed to these posts and there was clear evidence that yet more change to the departmental structure of school was on the way.

Class nomenclature changed again with the advent of the new Higher Examination system which was introduced in 1964 under the management of a new national board. The Preparatory nomenclature remained as it always had as classes A,B,C,and D, but classes in the Lower Junior School were renamed 3a, 3b, 4a, 4b, 5a and 5b. Thereafter, to accommodate a new intake of girls who had not previously been at Watson's, the Upper Junior School was divided into three classes in each year: 6a, 6b, 6c, 7a, 7b and 7c. The Senior School operated on the basis of Forms I to VI but with strict academic grading (in Greek nomenclature, α, β, γ, δ) for English, Mathematics and French. *The George Square Chronicles* of the early 1960s were scathing about the changes, and most especially about those which had been imposed from 'on high'. *"It is a matter of regret that the Scottish Certificate Examinations continue to be held in May... when girls in Forms 1V and V have no real holiday from one summer till the next and when they suffer a curtailment of outdoor activities. Schools may as well be swotting institutions these days."*

Other changes took place on the political front. In 1965 the Scottish Education Department issued a statement that Scottish secondary schools were to become fully comprehensive on a six-year non-selective basis. George Watson's Ladies' College was one of the country's Grant-Aided Schools whereby parents were charged fees but at a lower rate than the schools in the fully independent sector thanks to the Scottish Education Department providing a grant that matched approximately 40% of the expenditure on the Grant-Aided Sector. Given that many state sector teachers and administrators had an in-built dislike of the Grant-Aided Schools who they believed were creaming off their best pupils, there was a fear that the new edict would be divisive. More importantly, there was a fear that a Labour Government of the future might decide to freeze the Grant Aid meaning that these schools would either have to become fully independent with the resulting hike in fees, or they would have to join the comprehensive sector, just as some previously local authority run fee-paying schools had done.

But the major change was in society. The unquestioning adherence to discipline and authority was about to be challenged. 'Traditional values' were about to be confronted by laissez-faire liberalism, the core curriculum was to be re-examined as the pace of technology put the advantage in the hands of the scientists rather than the linguists or the historians, a new politics threatened the Establishment and youth became synonymous with protest and 'flower power'. Skirts were even being hitched up to reveal a daring stretch of leg and in Paris in 1968 students were throwing cobblestones – an act which led the Merchant Company and George Square authorities of the time to cancel the French Exchange to Lycée Camille Sée. The future was definitely not what it used to be!

The wind of change was also blowing through the Merchant Company. In 1966 the Chairman of the Education Board reminded his colleagues of the fact that the Merchant Company had led educational thinking back in 1870 and that it was time to do so again and he urged his colleagues to give serious thought to the future of all the Merchant Company schools.

By the late 1960s, following much discussion within the Merchant Company and between the heads of all four Merchant Company schools, it was recognised that radical change would be necessary. On 30 June 1967 a letter was prepared for all parents and staff of the two George Watson's Colleges immediately prior to the publication of a banner headline in *The Scotsman*:

Merchant Company plan to combine two colleges: "A unique opportunity".

Reaction was either delight or despair.

For some, including Headmistress, Hilda Fleming, it meant an exciting new beginning, but for others, especially to be found in some ranks of the Former Pupil Club, it sounded the death knell of a famous school and something with which it was going to be very hard to come to terms. Some felt inspired, some felt badly let down, but whatever they felt they were united in the belief that George Square was something very special.

Miss Fleming wrote in June 1974:

"We send our school to Colinton Road confident that they take with them, and will maintain, our traditions and that they have much to contribute to the future happiness and success of George Watson's College."

She asked the girls to contemplate what makes a great school; it wasn't the building, or the work within the classrooms, the staff or the pupils, but the compound of humour, warmth and genuine humanity which was its essence. Every effort had been made to take to Colinton Road not only everything which could be physically transported but the values which made George Square such a good school. Had George Watson been around at the time of "the move" he would most surely have approved. George Square had not only been a priceless enrichment of his legacy, but it was also about to be a crucial part in the remarkable success of the most ambitious mergers in Scottish education.

Art

The original Drawing Master in the early days of Mr Thomson's headship was Mr Robert Frier, an artist of repute who was assisted by his son and later by his daughter. Classes undertook freehand and chalk drawing copied from the flat and also model drawing using geometrical shapes. In 1893 Mr John Dun succeeded Mr Frier and he was instrumental in preparing the way for a new Art Department in 1905. Subject matter was expanded to include still life from nature in light and shade, water colour painting, design for earthenware and jewellery, embroidery especially for collars and cuffs and there were also lectures given on house decoration and furnishings.

From *George Square Chronicle* reports of Session 1910/11 it is clear that at least six pupils from the previous year had taken up places at the Edinburgh College of Art and that each of them was busily engaged in a diploma course of drawing and painting including a piece of work on the college skeleton (*"not so much still life as stiff life"* one student remarked) and studies in the history of art and sculpture. George Square art was gaining a strong reputation in the city and this was clearly a matter of great pride to staff and governors alike.

In 1920 the major project of the Art Department was the production of a school banner *"to be of the natural colour of linen, upon which will be applied about forty embroidered silk panels designed by present and former pupils. The principal panels will consist of the coat-of-arms of George Watson, the arms of the Merchant Company and of the City of Edinburgh, and the ornament will be of Christian Celtic character, consisting of interlacing bands intertwined with animal forms."* The banner was to be an important symbol of the foundation of the school and was hung for the first time of the wall of the Gallery on Commemoration Day in 1925.

By the late inter-war period George Square had amassed one of the best sculpture collections to be found in any Scottish school. This included casts of the Elgin Marbles, and a statuette of mother and

Art Room session 1896/7.

Early pupils' art and embroidery work.

School banner, 1925.

Art Medal Competition 1912 Winner Mary Lamonby.

Statuette of Mother and Child.

FROM THE ART ROOM WINDOW

School Christmas card competition
1951 – winner Isabel Reid.

child sculpted by the distinguished sculptor Alexander Carrick RSA and which had been exhibited in Paris, Berlin, Vienna and Prague. The Art Collection also included 54 colour reproductions of Old Masters plus some papers that related to the history of Italian art between the fifteenth and eighteenth centuries. These were presented by Mr Stewart Morton who was Vice Convenor of the School in Session 1930/1 and who had spent much of his time travelling abroad in Europe and North America.

During this period one of George Square's art masters, T Elder Dickson, became a well-known University figure following his award of Doctor of Philosophy for his work in psychological studies of art and his translation of many art works from French, German and Italian into English. In 1940 he was elected a Fellow of the Royal Society of Edinburgh, only the second artist besides Mr Stanley Cursiter *(painter of Miss Ainslie's official portrait – see page 180)*, to receive this distinction. The following year, both Mr Cursiter and Dr Dickson were instrumental in arranging for the work of George Square girls to be shown in the National Gallery of Scotland, a remarkable tribute to Dr Dickson's work as Head of Department and it was no surprise when he was invited to become Vice Principal of the Edinburgh College of Art in 1949.

Dr Dickson's successor for 21 years was the much-loved and respected James Henderson whose wife, Nan, was also a member of the Art Department. A distinguished schoolmaster as well as artist (he was a regular exhibitor at the RSA and well known to many Scottish artists including William Gillies), Mr Henderson built on the fine legacy of his predecessor. The standard of art work continued to impress well beyond the doors of George Square and many of his pupils went on to earn distinctions in art colleges across the land. As well as instilling a love of art in his pupils and sharing with them his personal artistic gifts, Mr Henderson recognised the importance of an integrated approach in the expressive arts and so he was always keen to develop new links with other disciplines such as music, photography and film-making. The first George Watson's Colleges' Arts Festival in 1968 included displays of paintings, sculptures and photographic material and it also featured a new experimental film some musical compositions and poetry reading.

Mr Henderson took his pupils on archaeological outings, he helped them to learn to sail, he ran competitions for the design of the school Christmas card and he produced the George Square script which was used in handwriting competitions. Almost everyone who has recorded their schooldays of the 1950s and 1960s speaks highly of Mr Henderson and the many happy hours in the art rooms.

The quality of the expressive arts tells you much about the quality of a school and there is no doubt that George Square was able to offer pupils a rich diversity of artistic opportunities that were not available in many other schools. That so much talent was fostered inside the art rooms and directed by some of the finest schoolmasters of their generation was the reason why the new Head of Department, Rosemary Schofield, and the George Square artists could hold their heads up high when they moved to Colinton Road.

The standard of art work continued to impress well beyond the doors of George Square and many of his pupils went on to earn distinctions in art colleges across the land.

Domestic Science and Craft

There is no question that the teaching of Domestic Science, particularly in terms of needlework and cookery, was a very important aspect of the curriculum at George Square right from the start. Every girl, whether academic or not, was expected to learn practical skills for the home and thus Domestic Science lessons were compulsory and seen as complementary to rather than a substitute for other lessons. A measure of this importance was firstly, the fact that in 1875 100 girls (out of 564) attended cookery classes in the Edinburgh School of Arts and secondly, that one of the building priorities at the turn of the century was a new wing for well-equipped school kitchens which was opened on 8 November 1911 by the Marchioness of Tullibardine. This was an event which attracted considerable interest in the press as well as the attendance of many important guests including the Earl of Rosebery, Sir William Turner, Secretary of the Scottish Education Department, and Lord Dunedin, the Lord Justice-Clerk. The entire extension projects cost £43,000, £38,000 of which was raised through Merchant Company endowments and £5,000 was a direct gift from Andrew Carnegie who was an Honorary Member of the Merchant Company.

In her speech at the opening ceremony, the Marchioness of Tullibardine echoed the Merchant Company philosophy of the time

The new kitchens, 1911.

which stated that it should be the aim of all great schools to turn out *"good and useful women"* just as much as it should be their aim to ensure that girls could pass examinations. It should not be the aim to carry away from school a mass of useless facts but rather a mass of helpful skills that would assist them in their daily lives and particularly in the home. In a carefully crafted and at times humorous address, the Marchioness claimed that everyone had to eat, everyone had to have their clothes clean and everyone had to have their homes neatly swept even if this was sometimes a dull and painful experience. With reference to herself she made it clear that even if someone didn't have to do these tasks themselves then it made it much easier to superintend the task if you knew something about them. In other words she had never really had to undertake much housework but as far as she could see the new kitchens had everything a modern woman could want!

Every so often during the school year, George Square pupils would be expected to run a school bazaar at which the culinary, baking, needlework and handcraft skills would not only be on display but also be on sale for charitable causes. The Central Hall, Court and Admiral's Kitchen areas would all be turned into stalls and mini cafés and restaurants and the presentation of the pupils, all dressed in immaculate uniforms and aprons, would be just as much on show as the products of Domestic Science classes.

These bazaars as well as the occasional exhibitions and open days were a very important part of school life and standards were high, a fact remarked upon by the school inspectors on several occasions and most especially during the 1922 Exhibition. Items ranged from hand-knitted garments, to embroidery, to handmade toys, basket work and weaving, baking and cooked food and all sorts of plants and flower arrangements. The pupils' exhibits were closely inspected by the mistress in charge and it was not unusual for the object to be returned several times until an acceptable standard had been reached. Many former pupils recall being held back after school hours until a garment or a piece of embroidery was properly presented.

There is no question that George Square came into its own when it came to assisting the war effort. A series of six demonstrations of war time cookery took place in 1914 and gradually every girl in the school was involved in helping to make garments or provide parcels to send out to the front line *(see chapter 3.2, "George Square in Wartime")*. Miss Ainslie left them in no doubt that taking part in such activities was an important part of their duty as well as an important part of their curriculum.

Lessons in personal and family hygiene were also given not least because of the higher incidence of disease at this time. Typhus, gastric fevers, measles, smallpox, chickenpox, diphtheria, scarlet fever, whooping

The Marchioness of Tullibardine.

cough, mumps and ringworm were all still forces to be reckoned with and it caused no end of consternation in the ranks when the medical officer closed the school between 4–25 November 1918 on account of 340 cases of influenza amongst the pupils (2 deaths) and 42 cases (out of 72) amongst the staff.

In the later years at George Square, pupils became a bit more ambivalent about Domestic Science lessons. While there undoubtedly remained for many an appreciation of receiving a solid foundation in cooking and needlework, the changing curriculum meant that these subjects were no longer the priorities they had once been and therefore the powers that be did not always promote them in the same manner nor did some of the pupils attach much importance to them.

The rooms which had been state of the art in 1911 had now become antiquated and they were not well equipped. Schoolgirls are notorious for exaggerating their stories of the classroom but there did appear to be some ruffling of feathers when the parents of two girls from a 1960s class complained that the equipment wasn't up to scratch. Their moans about *"the non-electric irons which took an eternity to heat, gas cookers which seemed to blow up at regular intervals, and old-fashioned wooden stools that frequently fell apart"* resulted in the Headmistress hurriedly dispatching the janitorial staff to check all the fittings and furnishings just in case there were issues of health and safety. No doubt the two girls had not endeared themselves to the Domestic Science staff of the time (who probably had to suffer the same frustrations) and matters were not helped by their further complaint that they were never allowed to eat the products of their efforts in class. *"Our teacher had just taught us how to make a delicious dish of bacon and eggs when she told us we had to put it in a Tupperware box and take it home to show our parents. What a mess!"* But for all the girls who might question the wisdom of compulsory Domestic Science there were many more who were eternally grateful for the time they had spent in the school kitchens and sewing rooms learning their homecraft, even if it

MARJORIE OLIVER, GRETA CAIRNS, JENNY BLACK, DORA BRUCE, HILDA AN DER HALDEN, PEGGY LAWSON, ELSIE GILROY, Miss CRICK, Miss JOHNSTON, FRANCES GUNN, MARJORY PARK, NORAH HAY.

Class Ib (Domestic), 1912.

meant there was the endless problem of persuading their mothers to trail to Jenners, Patrick Thompsons and J & R Allan's seeking the recommended Dorcas Dressmakers steel pins or reels of Coates thread.

Craft, which was largely undertaken by the top Junior School forms, had by this time branched out into cane-work, raffia-work and painted papier-mâché modelling. Receiving instructions from a member of staff to visit the extraordinary cane cupboard near the Library (which some pupils initially mistook for more sinister purposes) were not to be taken lightly. Yards and yards of very thin cane used for basket-work sprang out as soon as the door was opened and it often ended up in a jumbled mess on the floor but not before it had left its mark on any available bit of flesh. Worse still, this cupboard included the dreaded wooden looms which were used for woven garments (loose description only) and which occasionally had to be transported home inside a pillow case. At one time, in the very early 1970s the timetable for Primary 7 meant that the hapless pupil had to carry with her a normal school satchel, a loom, a hockey stick and a bag containing gym kit. It was certainly not an easy journey to school on a double-decker bus during the rush hour and perhaps one of the reasons why Domestic Science didn't always receive the credit it was surely due.

Physical Education; Gymnastics and Dance

In an age where women have climbed Mount Everest, sailed solo around the world, been on space missions and run the length of Britain it is hard to imagine what would have been thought of such physical activities by the girls, and more importantly the staff, who were at George Square in the late nineteenth century.

Late Victorian Britain was a forbidding place for any woman who wished to participate in physical games – something which led Florence Nightingale in her essay *Cassandra* written in 1859 to condemn the constraints, both intellectual and physical, that were placed on women. The ladies from Hambleton may have made cricketing history because the shape of their crinoline dresses inspired overarm rather than underarm bowling, but women's physical activities were almost always restricted to nothing more than genteel and dignified exercise.

Yet, we should not underestimate the recognition that physical exercise was both physiologically essential and enjoyable for the first generation of George Square girls. Early physical education consisted of drill, callisthenics and dancing although there were no proper facilities available in terms of a gymnasium or playing-fields. When the Drill Sergeant,

Mr Donnelly retired in 1893, an opportunity arose to restructure the physical education curriculum and employ a fully qualified gymnast. The Headmaster, however, was not well disposed to any really radical changes, believing that musical drill would easily substitute for gymnastics: *"I should be content with two hours a week"*, he proclaimed, *"and dumb-bells for one class."* Nonetheless, it was not long before the Merchant Company applied pressure and insisted that he shared the services of a professional gymnast, Miss Tisdall, with Queen Street although there seemed to be a minor to-do about how much she should be paid.

Much of the physical activity in school related to dance lessons; a decision that no doubt had social intent as well as the development of the girls' agility in mind. There was no formal PE curriculum in the way we know today and certainly girls were not expected to engage in anything that could loosely be seen as competitive physical activity. That would come later once school games appeared.

By the turn of the century dancing lessons took place on a regular twice a week basis and in 1903 the school appointed its first full-time PE mistress. Every girl was required to wear expanders, a pair of black sandals or dancing pumps and white gloves: just a little different from the lycra shorts and loose-fitting T-shirts that are the uniform of today's sporting exponents. Forgetting any of these items was considered a major sin by the Dancing Mistress, and in the case of Miss Graham's class, it would often result in physical punishment for *"the naughty darlings"*.

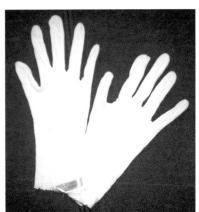

White gloves for dancing lessons.

Physical Education class, 1906/07.

Dancing exhibitions were quite clearly a major event of the school year and one where the school was definitely on show. A former pupil recalls a dancing exhibition consisting of *"a long line of girls marching into the hall from the little playroom, led by the dancing mistress with the smallest child by one hand, the other holding a bouquet given her by the dancers."* – a ceremony that bears at least some resemblance to the final stage of the present-day Junior Prizegiving when the smallest girl and boy in the School accompany the Infant Mistress of the Preparatory Department across the stage to present a bouquet of flowers to the wife of the Chairman of Governors and red rose button-holes to the Headmaster of the Junior School and the Chairman of Governors. It has a poignancy all of its own which, I am sure, was just as true in 1914 as it is today.

Attitudes changed during the War when women were expected to play their part, not only in helping to fight an enemy abroad, but in coping with the hard labour of looking after the domestic scene. Stamina was no longer just about being able to last out an Eightsome Reel or a Dashing White Sergeant but about enduring long hard hours and the pressures of running a home on their own.

Major changes occurred within physical education in the inter-war period which also coincided with the introduction of the House System in 1923. Within the timetable pupils were taught one lesson of gymnastics per week and one lesson of dance mainly taught by Miss Jenkins and Miss Graham and some other part-time assistants but there was also the option of games afternoons once a week. School finished at 1.15pm on a Thursday and girls could go off to Falconhall if they so chose (see section on school games).

In 1932 Miss Janet Armstrong became head of department and this marked a watershed in the organisation of the PE curriculum, giving it more profile within the timetable. While much greater emphasis was put on games both through the House and inter-school structures, there was also more emphasis on a formal structure of gymnastics and a recognition that PE classes should be an integral part of the working week. They had a discipline of their own and they were part of the expressive arts just as much as they were about keeping fit.

There is an amusing article in the December 1951 number of *The George Square Chronicle* in which a pupil tries to imagine what George Watson would be thinking of the 'modern' trends in George Square education, most especially the classes in physical education. She thought he would get a shock as he watched a gymnastics class with girls leaping fearlessly from wooden horses and turning somersaults with confidence. Even the boys of his day, the pupil surmises, would have been loath, not to say unable, to do the exercises they could manage. George Watson would be forced to *"hide his face in shame"* as, looking down from the Gallery, he spies a dancing class *"showing unheard of quantities of leg"* engaging in activities that *"more resemble the sacred rites of a heathen tribe"*. This was modern dance, for which the school was well renowned as a leading player in new curricular developments, maybe not appreciated by all pupils!

Miss Armstrong's successor, Miss Doreen Smith, both expanded and enhanced this thinking and in the 1960s George Square was one of the first schools to introduce new 'modern dance' facilities taught by a series of specialist dance teachers. PE classes went from strength to strength and were relatively well provided for in terms of equipment. The PE Department Staff inevitably appeared much younger than the rest of the teaching staff and they were often the staff who had the best knowledge of the pupils as they progressed from the Elementary stage to the Sixth Form. But gymnastics and dance were only half the story.

Games

No subject in the annals of George Square history has produced more diametrically opposed opinions than school games. You were either a passionate believer in their ability to mould women of the world or you were not. You either enjoyed running up and down muddy fields in icy cold rain and wind, bedecked in inappropriate outfits and wielding dangerous sticks, or you did not. Ne'er the twain would meet, but what most Women Watsonians do agree is that many of the most vivid memories of their schooldays relate to the activities on the games field, whether at Falconhall or Liberton.

As was mentioned previously, it took time for games to appear on the formal curriculum and extra-curriculum but there is no doubt that the school was very lucky to have use of extensive facilities at Falconhall from 1893 even if these had to be shared in the first years with their schoolgirl counterparts from the north side.

It is not entirely clear from the school records when the first competitive matches were played against other schools but by 1895 there was a George Square tennis team, by 1899 a George Square hockey team and in 1903 £5 was spent on the equipment required for *"the new game of netball"*. By the first decade of the 1900s, hockey and tennis matches were regular features of Thursday afternoons and Saturday mornings, each activity being overseen by a committee which operated under the careful guidance of a member of staff. The first numbers of *The George Square Chronicle* suggest that such activities were taken very seriously.

'Criticism meetings' were held every Monday when members of the committees met to discuss the Saturday fixture. A written record was kept of these meetings and, as can be seen, from some of the entries, no punches were pulled!

Games cartoons by pupil Edith Stewart, 1924 & 1925.

Goalkeeper *"sometimes clears well but at times is far too slow"*

Right Half *" will never hit well until she learns to hold her stick properly"*

Left Half *" is plucky, at times showing considerable dash but, like the rest of the team, her hitting is feeble"*

1st couple Tennis VI *"plays a lazy game steadily, but is rather slow"*

3rd couple Tennis VI *" really rather useless at the moment"*

In 1909/10 special hockey colours were awarded to three girls, T Thomson (captain and right wing), M Foy (left wing) and MB Smith (centre-half) for outstanding achievement including their selection for an Edinburgh City Schools XI which played against the Glasgow City schools that year, and in 1912–13 special mention is made of Helen Logan (left back) who was the first girl to receive colours three years in a row.

By 1909/10, two and sometimes three teams were participating in each of these sports with fixtures, both home and away, against Edinburgh Ladies' College, St George's School, St Margaret's School (hockey and tennis), Edinburgh University, Dollar Academy and a team which consisted of ministers' daughters (hockey only). By and large the results were usually wins for GWLC and it is noticeable how many hockey goals were scored in those days.

But Falconhall was also home to Games Club Garden Parties which featured the School Tennis Championship Finals, Sports Days

and the famous Strawberry Feast which, for many pupils, was the highlight of the school year. Just after lunchtime large groups of spectators would arrive through the little wooden door that was set high in the wall that surrounded Falconhall (an entrance that was on Morningside Road half way between Falcon Road West and Steel's Place), carrying rugs and bags and spare clothes in case it turned wet. The grounds boasted magnificent old trees under which the spectators would sit and enjoy a long afternoon of entertainment, sometimes with musical accompaniment, and refreshments.

The races at sports day included the more traditional flat, sack and obstacle races but there were also competitions for blindfold driving, dressing the potato (an elaborate affair by all accounts much enjoyed by the more junior girls) and a race for teachers *"not that too many were really capable"* according to one youngster in 1914!

Hockey and tennis went from strength to strength over the next few years with more and more girls wanting to play despite concerns from some member of the Merchant Company who bemoaned the fact that *"about two thirds of pupils never go near the games field"*. An Edinburgh schools' hockey league was established in 1920, a seven, a-side tournament was played by nine Edinburgh schools in 1924, and, as a result of concerns that Falconhall was becoming overcrowded, a third hockey pitch was built in the same year.

As was the case with boys' rugby and cricket reports in *The Watsonian*, *The George Square Chronicles* devoted a lot of column space to sports reports indicating just how important games had become in the life of the School.

The introduction of the House System did everything to increase enthusiasm for games and was greeted with great excitement. One FP recalls *"the great joy of wearing the badge firmly stitched on one's tunic and the satisfaction of belonging to a House. But the joy didn't stop there; Now, we worked and played for one's House and games and sports at the playing field took on a new meaning."* House matches over the years were fought over just as keenly as inter-school matches and there is no doubt that many more girls took part as a result.

If hockey and tennis were the dominant games, George Square offered plenty other opportunities. Participation in badminton matches, rounders, horse-riding lessons, swimming galas and rowing regattas was part of school life in the 1920s and there were even reports of some 'informal' cricket matches at Falconhall, opposition unstated but probably with the boys of James Gillespie's School.

With the appointment of Miss Armstrong as Head of Department in 1932, there began a long and unbroken period of sporting achievement. In 1930, Miss Armstrong had gone to South Africa as a member of the first Scottish Women's hockey touring side and there is no doubt that her enthusiasm for the game was part of the reason why so many George Square girls went on to win district and national honours in hockey. The transfer of the school games fields from Falconhall to Liberton in 1937 marked further growth in the number of girls participating in the main school games. Fixture lists expanded and with them the distances travelled beyond the confines of Edinburgh. Instead of Dollar being the only real 'excursion', hockey team visits are recorded to North Berwick, Dunfermline, and Glasgow only for the Second World War to intervene and curtail extra-curricular activities.

Activities soon picked up after the War and so too did the organisation of fixtures or pupils further down the

Helen Logan (circled), the first girl to receive hockey colours three years in a row.

Hockey 1st XI, 1930.
BACK ROW: Amy Mathers, Peggy Craig, Joyce Mathers, Marjory Penman.
MIDDLE ROW: Jessie Adam, Isobel McNeill, Rachael Ross (Capt), Jean Kay,
Winnie Westwater.
FRONT ROW: Dorothy Middleton, Jean Wilson.

Hockey 1st XI, 1956/7.
BACK ROW: Lois Beevers, Shona Spence, Pat Thomson, Stella Lyle, Katherine Kerr,
Jill Dawson.
FRONT ROW: Jean Burnett, Moira Scott, Susan Barnes (Capt), Elisabeth Inglis (Vice
Capt), Alison Allan.

Joan Hay, Senior School Hurdles winner, 1950.

school. In Session 1949/50, 60 pupils were regularly playing Saturday morning hockey fixtures, 44 had entered for the East of Scotland Junior Tennis Championship, 128 girls were members of the Badminton club and the Swimming club boasted 40 members but only because the baths at George Watson's College and Drumsheugh couldn't cope with any more.

In 1964 Miss Doreen Smith took over the reins in the PE Department and along with her colleague Miss Dorothy Brown, the appointments meant that there would continue to be top-quality sportswomen on the games staff, and a most important asset when it came to inspiring their pupils.

Miss Smith had taught as an assistant at George Square in the ten years previous and had been instrumental in the development of athletics and skiing as school sports. Moves were afoot to offer more games further down the school and in the top junior years and to make use of the sporting talents of other staff including those in the junior school. Miss Smith and Miss Brown both believed that as many girls as possible should be encouraged to take part in physical activities and the more variety that was offered the easier this would be. Golf, sailing, volleyball, hillwalking, orienteering all joined the games curriculum as did a number of new sporting competitions for which there were school prizes. By the 1970s good numbers of girls were also regularly participating in canoeing, rowing and fencing.

But if the variety increased there were no sacrifices in excellence. Standards rose in almost every area and there was also a higher emphasis put on the development of match fitness to complement those of team spirit and sportsmanship. George Square girls flourished in games everywhere and while there were inevitably good seasons and bad seasons, the records of George Square teams, most especially in hockey, are outstanding. It was certainly not surprising that many national sporting bodies such as the Scottish Women's Hockey Association viewed Watson's as one of the important institutions through which to build their representative teams.

| *Early piano lessons in the attic rooms 1896/7.*

Music

When Mr Thomson's School opened its doors, music featured very prominently. Both singing and learning to play the pianoforte were considered to be essential aspects of a good education for young ladies. All pupils, after they entered the Junior Department, took piano lessons in groups of six – a system which involved great expense in the purchase of sufficient pianos and a minor fracas amongst the staff who, in the summer of 1882, sent a deputation of their members to complain to the Headmaster about the *"insufferable noise from the abundance of pianofortes in the attic-rooms"* and promptly followed this by a petition for sound-proofing! This seemed to be borne out by the pupils who bemoaned the appalling noise from piano lessons and the ghastly ordeal of the Annual Recital in the Music Hall, George Street, when eight pianos were placed in a row on the platform and three 'pianists' sat at each hammering out an operatic overture. It was said that the great applause with which the audience greeted them at the end was given out of *"sheer relief"* rather than delight.

This was not the only aspect of music that aroused strong feelings at the time; an official complaint was made to Mr Thomson via the Merchant Company that the cantata performed at the 1881 concert was *"of popish character"* and should have been proscribed on the basis of its unsuitable content. The Vice Convenor added to the Headmaster's discomfort by

complaining that *"no matter how excellent the music provided, no concert should be longer than an hour. It upsets the audience if it lasts longer."*

Things obviously settled down a bit, more music staff were appointed and one of these, Mr Tom Craig, was often singled out for special mention as a devoted tutor and accomplished instrumentalist. By the turn of the century, George Square girls were not only performing regular concerts for their parents and friends, but also taking part in a variety of musical entertainments for the public. Some like Mary Grierson *(see page 254)* were about to embark on distinguished musical careers.

The second number of *The George Square Chronicle* reports that a *"red-letter night"* took place in the Lawnmarket's Orwell Halls on the evening of 3 February 1911 when the girls of George Square combined with the Guards Brigade (musically only we presume) to provide what became an established annual concert for both parents and members of the public. As well as the girls providing a varied programme of both song and dance, the Guards Brigade during the interval apparently provided a demonstration of how to get someone into an ambulance. *The George Square Chronicle* notes, however, that when the ambulance appeared *"the stretchers were more needed for the audience than for the victims."*

In 1915, a special concert was held in aid of war funds (raising £46 17s 6d) and helping to ensure the provision of another year's maintenance for the

| Tom Craig, the accomplished instrumentalist, decided in 1892 that a Gold Medal for Music should be awarded on the basis that pupils were "to play separately and screened by a curtain from the judges."

George Square bed in Rouen Hospital. By all accounts, the concert, which was held in the School Hall in Archibald Place, was a patriotic affair as well as one rich in musical talent.

There is no doubt that George Square music was establishing a name for itself in the city and this was to continue. As well as educating young ladies, the school arranged seminars in musical topics of the day, ranging from the romanticism of French composers through to the celebration of Beethoven in 1927 and it extended an invitation to a choir from the Berlin College of Music in 1937.

Much of the success was due to the exceptional talents of one man, Dr W B Ross. After 30 years (1907–37) he had become a legendary figure in the

Dr W B Ross.

Cartoons depicting Mr Dudley Langdon.

school (*The George Square Chronicle* described him as "an institution"). He was widely acclaimed well beyond Edinburgh as both a talented organist and as an expert on the construction of the king of instruments. He gave regular recitals in the Usher Hall and St Mary's Cathedral and he was often sought after in the early years of BBC music broadcasting. Indeed it was the invitation from the congregational board of the Church of the Holy Rude in Stirling for Dr Ross to become their organist that was the reason for his departure from George Square.

His memory is enshrined for ever in the music of the School Hymn (*see page 217*) – music which he composed at the secret request of Dr Ainslie who had earlier composed the six verses of the School Hymn – and for the descant of 'Crimond' which was specially requested by Princess Elizabeth at her wedding and which became the traditional hymn for the School's Annual Closing Concert. Dr Ross's outstanding contribution to music was recognised by Oxford University which conferred upon him the degree of Doctor of Music (also later awarded to another Music Master at George Square, Mr Lee Ashton) – an accolade that was unusual for Scottish musicians but even more coveted as a result.

After some difficult years during the Second World War when there was inevitable disruption to music teaching and public performances, a new approach was pioneered under Head of Music, Mr Dudley Langdon (1942–62). He refused to believe that any girl was incapable of singing and of leaving school without the permanent possession of an appreciation of music. George Square became a singing school under Mr Langdon and he was instrumental in introducing the Leaving Certificate in Music. He paid great attention to the music for special occasions: Commemoration Day, Armistice Day, the Christmas Service, the formal functions of the Merchant Company, most especially the Kirking of the Master, the Easter Service, the school plays and the Closing Concert, a legacy he left to his successor Margery Traves who not only built on this tradition but expanded the extra-curricular dimension of music.

At the time of the George Square Centenary in 1971 there were three choirs with at least 50 voices in each, an orchestra, folk groups, madrigals, recorder groups and a music club, many of them enjoying joint activities with the boys' school. Distinguished school musicians were regularly taking part in, and winning medals in 'schools' festivals and in a few cases, performing on the national and international stage.

In the Junior School, under the inspired direction of Cecilia Cavaye (who was also a highly accomplished pianist), singing and instrumental music grew from strength to strength and was clearly a source of great enjoyment as well as learning for a large number of junior girls. Miss Cavaye also worked with PE classes playing the piano for dance classes and various performances of the expressive arts and must have been one of the fittest members of staff having to rush back and forwards between George Square and St Alban's Road all the time on a number 42 bus!

The Traves/Cavaye years not only provided George Square with many musical successes but a celebration of music as entertainment as well as an academic discipline and there is no doubt that this legacy did much to enrich the lives of musicians at Watson's after the merger.

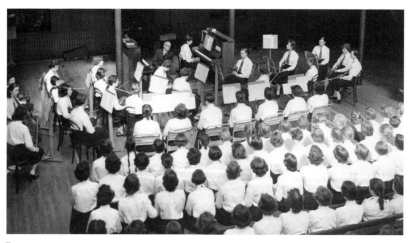

School Orchestra and Choirs, 1958.

Distinguished George Square Musicians

Miss Muriel Dickson – soprano of the D'Oyly Carte Opera.

Libby Ritchie (opera singer).

Fiona McPherson (violinist).

Miss A Milne playing with Max Piram, Freemasons' Hall.

Alison Kinnaird (clarsach).

Susan Tomes (piano and harpsichord).

"Our classroom for the whole two weeks was the stunning beauty of the Cairngorm. No cathedral could lead us to anything more uplifting."
S3 Projects pupil 1972

Like their male counterparts at George Watson's Boys' College, the girls of George Square were in a privileged position when it came to extra-curricular activities. If the variety and extent of adventure in these activities did not fully develop till the mid 1960s (much earlier than in many other similar schools) there is no question about their importance even as far back as the 1880s.

Light years away from the age of 'political correctness', extra-curricular activities were allowed to flourish in whichever direction reflected the interests of staff and pupils alike and in ways that would contribute to the education of responsible, active and imaginative adults. As such, they did much to enrich the life of the school throughout its hundred and three year history and the lives of all those who worked within it. Above all, they provided fun and a much needed relief from the daily grind of the classroom!

Debating at The Square

The Literary and Debating Society was the leading light in extra-curricular activities for many years, always producing a full and varied programme of events for girls in the Senior and Middle Schools. From the early days at the turn of the century, debates were held at least once a month and visiting speakers were invited at least once a term. The standard was exceptionally high and George Square had a proud run of success in several Edinburgh Schools' competitions and within the activities of the English Speaking Union.

There were some amusing moments, however, starting with a minor hiccup at the time of the 1911 General Election. Shortly after the visit of Major Jameson, MP for West Edinburgh, who spoke about life in the House of Commons and the issues confronting the parties, the girls asked the English Department if they could hold a Mock Election. The staff agreed, but since women were not allowed to stand for Parliament they told the girls that those who were selected as candidates would have to dress up as men. This was eventually agreed and names were chosen, costumes sought and election campaigns planned.

The first Election rallies took place in Room 22 and there was no scarcity of speakers; A group of 'Republicans' was caught smuggling the Red Flag into the room, 'Tory Twisters' were accused of *"talking tariff twaddle"* and there was some severe heckling and even jeers and boos when the Liberal candidate spoke. All this resulted in some stiff reprimands from a senior member of staff who said the whole thing would have to be called off unless dignity was restored with immediate effect.

But just as events were threatening to get very dull, a Prefect burst into the room to say that she had been tipped off that the Liberals were planning to kidnap the Tory candidate and that some members of staff might be next! By all accounts, proceedings were quickly brought to a close and the pupils were asked to fill in their ballot papers as they left the room. The result?

Samuel Chapman Brown (Con) 76

William Gladstone Fraser (Lib) 50

William Graham Savage (Lab) 18

And there were no spoilt papers.

Things clearly calmed down a little after this but the Literary and Debating Society did not lose its taste for controversy. In 1923 a few of the senior girls made a representation to Miss Ainslie that they might be allowed to run some debating events without the presence of staff so that

SYLLABUS

FIRST TERM.	SECOND TERM.

FIRST TERM.

Wed., 29th September.
Inaugural Meeting.

Fri., 8th October.
Inter-debate with George Heriot's School Debating Society.

Wed., 13th October.
Talk by **Miss Ramsay** of the Scott Club.

Wed., 27th October.
Short Debates.

Fri., 5th November.
Inter-debate with George Watson's Boys' College Debating Society.

Wed., 10th November.
Ministry of Information Films.

Wed., 24th November.
Literary Night.

Wed., 8th December.
Brains Trust.

Fri., 10th December.
Quadrangular Debate between the Merchant Company Schools.

SECOND TERM.

Wed., 12th January.
Mock Trial.

Wed., 26th January.
Talk by **Miss Carnon.**

Fri., 4th February.
Inter-debate with Daniel Stewart's Debating Society.

Wed., 9th February.
Debate.

Wed., 23rd February.
Talk.

Wed., 9th March.
III's. and IV's. Meeting.

Wed., 23rd March.
?

Fri., 25th March.
Inter-debate with the Royal High School Debating Society.

THIRD TERM.
Annual General Meeting.

Debating Society syllabus 1948/9.

the younger pupils wouldn't feel so inhibited about speaking from the floor. To their great surprise the Headmistress agreed to allow a limited number of debates to take place without supervision but sadly, the ploy didn't work. At the first debate without staff (*"This House believes that ignorance with contentment is preferable to wisdom with discontentment"*) no-one spoke from the floor at all and the event had to finish early!

This was not the only cause of disquiet in the 1920s. The senior pupils were soon back at Miss Ainslie's door bemoaning the fact the more important debating events, such as the Merchant Company Schools Debate, were taking place far too early in the session and well before *"the more juvenile and frivolous members of the Society had gained experience in speaking in open debate."* They told her they were not going to organise debates unless the Middle School pupils behaved as young ladies should.

In April 1936 much amusement was had in a double-header end-of-term debate where the topics were *"Elder brothers are preferable to elder sisters"* and *"The present Form Three are degenerate"*. It was noted that there was a larger than usual turn-out of staff at this event and that there was a unanimous vote within their number in favour of the second motion! The next day several members of Form Three were seen awaiting the attention of the Headmistress in the Tiled Hall following what one member of staff described as *"unfortunate pranks and protestations"* as the pupils sought their revenge. Jars of tadpoles seem to have been involved somewhere along the line.

In 1949 Sir John Falconer gave a wonderful address to the Debating Society on *"The Beginnings of the Edinburgh Festival"*. Immediately after this it was decided that if the pupils were going to have the privilege of listening to this quality of speaker they should be charged the princely sum of 2d as a subscription!

By the late 1950s and throughout the 1960s and early 1970s the Literary and Debating Society was excelling itself in national competitions particularly those run by *The Scotsman* and *The Daily Express* newspapers and the English Speaking Union although it is interesting to note that the attention given to it within the reports in *The George Square Chronicle* diminished. Maybe success was taken for granted for there is no question that the performances of several pupils continued to bring great credit to the school.

> "Elder brothers are preferable to elder sisters" *and* "The present Form Three are degenerate".

Drama at The Square

The Tercentenary Celebration of William Shakespeare's death – Poet's Corner, Friday 26 May 1916:

"The recitations were all finely rendered, the tragic recital of his grisly dream by the doomed Clarence, Henry V's stirring speech to his army before the gates of Harfleur, and, in lighter vein, a scene from As You Like It where the love-torn Orlando was teased and hood-winked by a Rosalind coy and coquettish beyond her tender years.

Each piece was prefaced by Mr Budge with a brief but lucid explanation, which fortunately made clear its setting and connection with the plot."

The first House Drama Competition, 5 April 1921

Each House had to act out three scenes depicting what George Watson's Ladies' College would have looked like 50 years ago. A young Junior School pupil writes about what she saw:

Lauriston:

"A game of clock golf was in progress, although a conversation about weddings and Bismarck's occupation of Paris engrossed the actors attention more than the ball. The next scene shifted to Falconhall where girls were playing hockey and then for the last scene we were all asked to imagine girls fifty years from now playing rugby! The team did not look unattractive!"

Melville:

"The first scene was a dressing room of fifty years ago but everyone was decorously dressed. Scene two was about the difficulties of taking a class photograph and Scene Three brought us into contact with the supernatural agencies which was hard to understand."

Falconhall:

"This began in a drawing room with the well known sound of the gong. Everyone departs except for one discontented mortal who is taken away by a monster into a sewing class of 1871, and then after a period of boredom is transported into a sewing class of 1971."

Greyfriars:

"This play took place in room 42 with girls all swotting for exams and through the window were gazing all sorts of onlookers who got very interested in what they were doing. To return to less thrilling matters... ...Falconhall won the prize."

Beatrice Denies Her Salutation, *School Play, 1921.*

The Admirable Crichton *by JM Barrie, GWLC pupils, 1935.*

Statuette sculpted by Miss Mabel Locke in 1930 presented for individual excellence in Dramatic Art.

Ex Corde Caritas

Given the school motto, it is perhaps unsurprising that support for charitable causes was always regarded as a very important responsibility of any George Square pupil. This feeling was summed up by the little girl who when she heard that one of the workmen working on the new east wing in 1903 had a sick daughter, brought in her only teddy bear the next day and told him to take it home to her in the hope that she might get better soon. It was an unsolicited and natural act of charity which hopefully exemplified the strength of the pupils' compassionate spirit down the ages.

Naturally, much of the early charity work focused on the Great War and this is described in pages 181–4. But the pupils and former pupils were asked to make more permanent contributions too. In July 1913 a letter was sent from Margaret Alexander, one of the Honorary Members of the Women Watsonians' Club, to all Former Pupils in which she urged far more than just a contribution to the war effort.

"Will you all come to our next meeting determined to adopt some scheme which instead of bringing pleasure to ourselves shall carry with it the opportunity, if not the obligation, to do some good to others? Mere almsgiving will not do. There is already too much of that! Surely our Club can be a rich recruiting ground."

Four schools – George Watson's Ladies' College, Edinburgh Ladies' College, St Bride's and St George's – combined in the winter of 1921 to help French village children in Falaise, Seraincourt and Margny in the Ardennes. Eighteen parcels of clothes and food were sent away from George Square and a week later were received in the village of Falaise in which, on the bell of the town hall, there is still the inscription: *"Aux Généreux citoyens d'Édimbourg, Écosse. La commune de Falaise reconnaissance."*

A joint work party at 19 Greenhill Place met every Tuesday afternoon during the period 1940–2 when pupils and former pupils could be found busy cleaning sphagnum moss for dressings and knitting and sewing at great pace

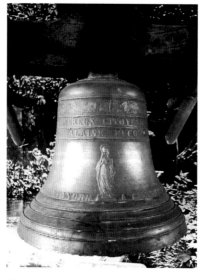

Pour Falaise, Seraincourt et Margny.

19 Greenhill Place.

CHARITIES' REPORT
June 1964-June 1965

I. DONATIONS

Scottish Council for the Care of Spastics	-	-	-	£33 7 8
*Queensberry House	-	-	-	10 0 0
*Queen's Institute of District Nursing	-	-	-	15 0 0
Earl Haig Poppy Fund	-	-	-	23 7 6
Oxfam	-	-	-	34 5 0
Abdulovic family Christmas gift	-	-	-	10 0 0
Churchill Memorial Trust	-	-	-	50 0 0
Dr Kate Young's Mission to Lepers	-	-	-	19 7 6
Royal National Lifeboat Institution	-	-	-	2 0 6
Pestalozzi Children's Village Trust	-	-	-	6 10 0
People's Dispensary for Sick Animals	-	-	-	5 15 0
Royal Scottish Zoological Society (" Joey ")	-	-	-	24 0 0
Quarrier's Homes	-	-	-	1 1 0
Edinburgh Cripple Aid Society	-	-	-	1 1 0
" Save the Children " Fund Sponsorship Scheme	-	-	-	15 0 0
				£251 5 2

* July, 1964 collection.

Charities Account 1964/5.

to meet the demand for the parcels the Red Cross Headquarters in the school at George Square.

Long-standing Charity Commitments for the Houses

Greyfriars – *Niddrie Nursery School*
Falconhall – *Cowgate Nursery School*
Lauriston – *Widowers' Children's Home, Corstorphine*
Melville – *Grassmarket Nursery School*

Sixth Form Community Service Projects 1972 (for those girls not involved with examinations for Oxford and Cambridge or on outdoor education or foreign exchanges)

8 girls working with Nature Conservancy
20 girls working in hospitals with handicapped children and geriatric patients
3 girls working with the Family Planning Association
2 girls helping to teach English to Immigrants at the Women's International Centre
1 girl assisting the National Bible Society with missionary work

Excursion to the zoo, 1915.

A school journey in Germany, 1936.

Excursions from The Square

George Square girls were to be found in every corner of the world

The *First George Square Chronicle* in 1910 includes four articles recounting adventures around the world:

"*Eine Schottin in Deutschland*"

"*Life as I found it in an école normale*"

"*Calcutta School for Girls*"

"*Shanghai: an impression*"

Extract from a young pupil's (A C Davie) diary on a trip to the Battlefields, September 1922:

"*At different intervals along the road on the Menin Road we saw a single grave with either a 'Tommy's' tin hat, or a German helmet on top of it. This I think was even sadder than all the miles of graves. It tells us that some poor soldier had been shot by his enemies and his comrades had buried him just where they found him.*"

Former President of the Women Watsonians' Club, Ida Anderson (Ida Watt) was on 1936 the trip to Germany as a 16-year-old:

"*I remember the excitement when we gathered at Waverley Station wearing our maroon blazers and panama hats. Having spent a night in London, we crossed the Channel by boat and, after a long journey, we arrived in Cologne. The accompanying staff, Miss Thomson (German mistress) and Miss Mitchell (English), told us we would have to walk to the Youth Hostel and that we should proceed quickly. But just as Miss Thomson was pointing out the magnificent cathedral of Cologne, it was*

illuminated by a great flash of lightning. There followed a thunderstorm and torrential rain, but undaunted we kept walking and eventually reached the youth hostel, only to find that the other occupants were staring out the windows laughing at the fact that the brims of our hats were all full of water; 'Die schöne hütte!' was the cry and we were more than a little embarrassed.

Believe it or not, the staff allowed the guide in Heidelberg to take us to the Hitler Youth Camp from where the boys, immaculate in their storm-trooper uniforms, took us to some of the historic parts of the city. We were oblivious to the reality of the situation.*"

George Square Girls and Drugs

The Headmistress and the science staff took a group of pupils to the laboratories of Duncan & Flockhart's Factory in Holyrood Road, 1936:

"*We were led into a small laboratory where were laid out the ingredients of various well-known medicines, including the notorious Gregory's Mixture. Then drugs! In a laboratory whose door is always locked we were permitted to see a great many of the very dangerous drugs used in medicines, soporific opium, murderous strychnine, pain deadening morphia. With great interest, mixed with not a few qualms as to the effect of the smell, we were taken to see a huge vat where chloroform was being washed and then we were taken to see huge barrels of absolute alcohol for the preparation of ether..... Odd little questions were asked by various people and it was with infinite regret that we went home.*"

Visit of 71 Danish Schoolgirls, 1947

Their arrival at Waverley Station caused not a little excitement amongst our girls and speculation ran high. The School sponsored a tour of the castle, a visit to the GPO, a memorable day by bus to Loch Lomond and Glencoe where the Danes saw mountains and waterfalls for the first time and a visit to see the Royal Family in Princes Street.

The School Exchange to France, 1952

"*Unfortunately we arrived in Paris at rush hour and proceeded through crowds of gesticulating French pedestrians who were using words we couldn't find in our dictionaries.

The school is colossal. Multiply Watson's boys by two and you will have a rough idea of the size. The corridors are all tiled and very slippery. Between periods they are filled with screaming French girls, all in blue overalls, who behave as if they were on a skating rink. Incidentally, no one except the lazy Scots ever falls.

Our misfortune was at Dieppe when one suitcase fell into the sea. It was quickly retrieved but the other passengers were regaled with the sight of the owner's clothes being dried in the corridor. The porters were very helpful and we suspect they are used to this sort of thing. The French customs officer however, did not examine our cases but pinched the cheek of one of our number and left it at that. This, we presume, is another old French custom.*"

Societies and Clubs at the Square

As well as the highly popular music, drama and literary and debating clubs, George Square girls had many other opportunities to expand their interests and hobbies:

Nature Club

This was an immensely popular club founded in 1910 and numbering well over 100 pupils in the Middle School. Pupils were expected to play a very active role in preparing short papers, conducting short experiments, making collections and taking part in various excursions, mainly to the Royal Botanic Garden and the Zoo.

George Watson's Ladies' College Games Club

Founded in 1907, to be responsible for the management of the athletic activities of the School, namely, hockey, tennis and badminton. It was open to all staff and all girls in the Upper School. By 1920 it had over 400 members not all of whom could be accommodated at Falconhall. This continued until the advent of the House system.

Current Events Club

For members of 1A and 1B (equivalent of the Sixth Form) 1922 set up by Mr Budge:

"The girls who have no time or no opportunity out of school for acquiring a general idea of the state of the country will find that whenever they have any spare time they may spend it, if not very pleasantly, at least to their advantage. They will have available the Daily Mail, The Observer, Sunday Times, L'Echo de Paris, Punch, The Children's Newspaper, Chamber's Journal.*"*

"Regrettably Clubs and Societies have been suspended in order to accommodate black-out instructions" Notice in the Central Hall, Summer 1939.

Gramophone Club

The first meeting of the Gramophone Club was held on Friday 1 May 1942 – the programme: the overture from Wagner's *Die Meistersinger von Nürnberg*, arias by Puccini and Verdi and the Intermezzo from *Cavalleria Rusticana* by Mascagni.

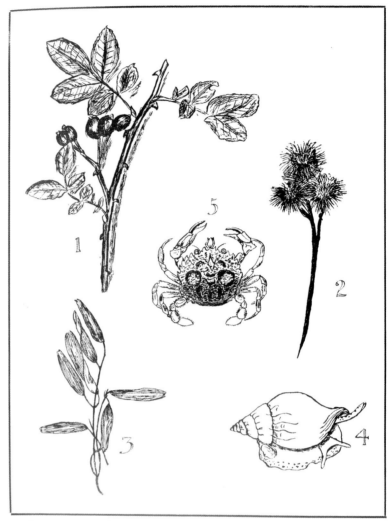

Some of the Treasures found on our Nature Excursions.

1. Dog-rose spray with hips.
   LENA GUMLEY.
2. Fruit of the Burdock.
   MOLLIE GRIERSON.
3. Fruit of the Ash Tree.
   BESSIE BENNETT.
5. Swimming Crab.
   BESSIE BENNETT.
4. Whelk.
   JENNIE BRUCE LOW.

Nature Club drawings.

Winning entry from a competition organised by the Photographic Club which was started in 1966. Christ and the Apostles *by Jennifer Bowman.*

George Square pupils took part in the Edinburgh Schools' Citizenship Association, the Edinburgh Schools' Film Society and the Edinburgh Schools' Scientific Society

History Society extract from *Foco* (the Pupils' School magazine), 1973:

Classical and Archaeological Society, visit to Hadrian's Wall, 1971.

1st year pupils at Redheughs Farm, 1969.

THE HISTORY SOCIETY

In answer to a summons from Colinton Road for some GIRLS to enhance their pursuance of culture in the form of our heritage, a sister-society has been formed. Two seperate committees have been elected as some activities will be separate and some with the boys. If the support from IIIrd year continues the society should blossom in future years – in fact no-one had realised just how keen they were on history – or could it be something else?

Since our joint committee meeting on Monday 17th December, a programme for next term has been discussed. On Tuesday, January 15th, we launch the society properly with a quiz in the Music School at 7.30pm. It should be in the form of a "Top of the Form" quiz and we hope for lots of support. In the middle of January a party is going to see "The Lion in Winter" – a historical play in the Churchhill Theatre.

Lists will be up on the notice-board on the gallery for nominations for the quiz, and for numbers for "Lion in Winter". We optimistically look for plenty of support.

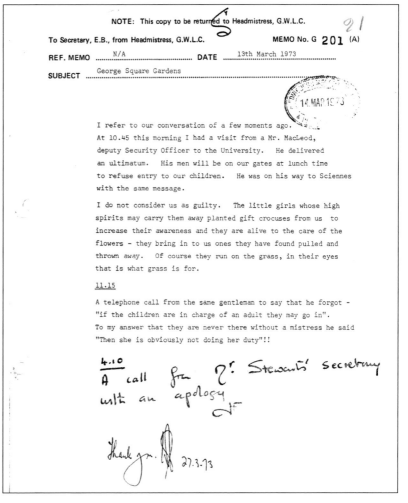

Extra-curricular activity of a different sort!

Projects at The Square

In session 1962/3, members of the PE staff discussed the possibility of offering a week away at Glenmore Lodge so that pupils would have greater opportunity to explore the wilds, gain some basic skills in hill-walking and water sports and encounter an environment far removed from that of a classroom in Edinburgh. Places were filled on a voluntary, first come, first served basis, but it was immediately clear that this new extra-curricular activity was popular and in heavy demand. Visits to Glenmore Lodge continued for the next three years and in 1967 the group went to the Edinburgh Outdoor Centre in Benmore, Argyll. Professional staff were employed to assist with the basic training, although George Watson's Ladies' College staff organised all the activities.

In 1968, it seemed appropriate that the George Watson's Ladies' College staff should organise and staff their own outdoor programme similar to that operating at Colinton Road, and in essence this was the beginning of Projects at the girls' school. The first Project, on a voluntary basis for the Fifth Form, was located at Balquhidder Youth Hostel, where the girls learnt about hill-walking and orienteering and made use of the Loch Earn Sailing Club for canoeing and sailing. The next year saw the opening of the Merchant Company Outdoor Centre at Ardtrostan on the south side of Loch Earn, and this was then used annually until sadly the building was burnt down in 1981. The School developed its own sailing club in 1972 under the direction of Margaret Lee.

In the early 1970s, Hilda Fleming took the decision to extend Projects to include everyone in the Third Form. It was compulsory for every pupil to undertake two weeks of outdoor activities, although provision was made for an Edinburgh group for those who were unable to go away for some reason. For the summers of 1973, 1974 and 1975 the entire Third Form went away for two weeks in early May. There were four groups each year and the venues used were Ardtrostan, Garth Youth Hostel in Glen Lyon, Abernethy Field Centre, Dalguise House, Melrose Youth Hostel and various locations along Hadrian's Wall.

The Projects Staff at George Square: PE staff: Doreen Smith, Dot Brown, Margaret Lee, Anna Sherriff; other members of the academic staff – Eileen Sharples, Margery Traves, Margaret Elder, Sara Watt, Trudi Bolland, Elma Coghill, Margaret Hutchison, Margaret Mackenzie, Caroline Fortescue, Cecilia Cavaye, Maggie Smith, Marion Froude, Sheila Sargeant and Eleanor Wallis.

Ardtrostan: The Adventure Centre, 1973.

Glen Lyon: The Garth Youth Hostel, 1970.

Speyside: The Nethy Bridge Outdoor Centre, 1975.

Staff at Ardtrostan, 1969.

Her traditions were many and varied, some even bordering on the eccentric, but more than anything else they remain the basis of the cherished schooldays memories which define George Watson's Ladies' College.

Being Part of the Watsonian Family

"Blood is thicker than water and the blood in this family, including yours, is maroon!" That's how one former pupil described how she learnt from her father that she was to be sent to George Square.

"Even at the age of five I greatly resented the fact that there was to be no argument about where I should be sent to school and so I made up my mind that I would not enjoy myself. However, my childish antics didn't last more than five minutes. No sooner was I in the door at St Alban's Road, than I was led by the hand by the Infant Mistress and introduced to my new classmates. I knew then I had just joined a big family and that these people would always be my friends."

With regard to her 'family' George Square was incredibly lucky. For a start, a very high percentage of parents and grand-parents, uncles and aunts were Watsonians and therefore they too had a strong commitment to the school. A high percentage of brothers went to Watson's and with an increasing number of joint activities taking place over the years there was bound to be a common bond and mutual support. It was also true that a large number of staff, two headmistresses included, chose to return to teach in their old school; not everyone approved of this trend, but the critics found it difficult to find fault with the desire of many former pupils to give something back to the community from which they had derived so much in their own schooldays. And so it was not uncommon, throughout all the years of her history, to find families in which every member had some connection with the school.

Mr and Mrs William Mackay Budge, Mr Budge was English and History master at GWLC, 1895–1931, Mrs Mackay Budge was President of the George Square Former Pupils' Club, 1913/14, and their daughter, Joan M Budge was Dux 1927/8.

The Carmichael Family, Mr JH Carmichael was Vice Convenor of GWLC, 1950/1, Mrs Carmichael was President of the Women Watsonians' Club 1953/4, their daughter Brenda, their two sons, Dennis and Jasper, and Mrs Carmichael's brother, Aubrey Wood Hawks, were all distinguished Watsonians in their own right.

There was also the added advantage of strong connections with the Merchant Company. The post of Vice Convenor was hugely significant in helping to strengthen the links between school and governors and ensuring that George Square girls would always have a sense of belonging to the wider Edinburgh community.

In his diary which records two years in office, the Vice Convenor of 1965–67, Mr J Melrose Smibert, acknowledges the crucial role which anyone in his position had when it came to ensuring that neither the Merchant Company nor the school ever lost sight of the importance of their family ties.

The Merchant Company link went much deeper too; if siblings of George Square girls were not at George Watson's College they were very likely to be at Mary Erskine or Daniel Stewart's and so the bond between the 'north side' and the 'south side' was also very strong and much to the benefit of all four schools.

The School Badge and Motto

In the December 1910 number of *The George Square Chronicle* there was much discussion about the possibility of giving silver badges to the Prefects as a souvenir of their time in office. This stirred up some correspondence from former pupils who wondered why a badge should not be given to all girls. A letter to the Editor in April 1911 (signed only '*Esprit de Corps*') states:

"George Square girls when they go out into the world have no outward symbol to show that they belong to our glorious community. After a certain age they get beyond sailor hats with school colours and maroon and white ties are not suitable for every toilette.........not only would the world in general be benefited by knowing George Square girls at once – for, of course, a George Square badge would be a passport anywhere – but, how many an old girl, labouring in far off Africa, or in the scorching Indian sun, would be cheered every time she looked at her badge and thought of her School. The badge would console her in her loneliness and act as a talisman to her."

If there was some degree of imperial bombast accompanying the

O T H E R   D U T I E S

The Vice-Convener should visit the School weekly, at a time suitable to him and the Headmistress.

He will act as liaison between the School and the Merchant Hall, and to assist him the Headmistress provides copies of all the correspondence sent from the School to the Merchant Hall.

The Vice-Convener when invited, will sit in on all discussions when the Headmistress is interviewing and selecting Staff.

He may be called upon by the Headmistress to attend any interviews she is having with a difficult Parent or with a Member of the Staff.

Extract from the diary of Mr J Melrose Smibert, Vice Convenor 1965/7.

Suggestions for the first School Badge.

The Badge of George Watson's Ladies' College.

The School Hymn

One Merchant Company visitor to a School Commemoration Day shortly after the Second World War asked whereabouts in the church hymnary she could find the words to the hymn that began "God of our Youth". Expressing slight shame that she had failed to notice *"this great hymn"* before, she asked whether it had been written by Wesley or Blake or Watts.

On being told that it was none of them, but by Charlotte Ainslie, a former Headmistress, the visitor remarked; *"Then she must have been a great lady"*.

The School Hymn was first sung on 24 October 1918 although at that stage the identity of the author was unknown except that it was the work of a Former Pupil. In its original version the hymn contained six verses and the musical settings were composed by Former Pupils Miss Winnie Fry and Miss Molly Grierson. A special calligraphic edition of the words was produced on parchment by Miss Norah Paterson and the reproduction of the music score was undertaken by Miss Harper and Miss Winnie Harvey. The fact that the collective work was produced by Former Pupils was received with great delight and it was quite clearly a reason for the hymn's immediate popularity.

On her retirement in 1926, Miss Ainslie admitted her authorship and the fact that she had asked Dr WB Ross to undertake an arrangement of the music which included a descant and special introduction to the final verse. Theirs was a successful partnership, the fruits of which gave both George Square and the modern George Watson's College something unique.

There were however, other attempts to produce a school song.

In April 1913 Margaret JH Marwick of Form IIc wrote an *Ode to the School* (which was awarded a prize by the Women Watsonians' Club) and in the autumn of 1918 Helen W Thomson used the themes from the brand new School Hymn to write a School Song. In neither case did their efforts survive on the same basis as the existing School Hymn but it was perhaps an indication of the strength of feeling at the time as to how music could inspire both loyalty and lasting affection.

Music could inspire both loyalty and lasting affection.

request, it worked! An Art Master, Mr Wyse, was soon beavering away with suggested designs and in the next issue of *The George Square Chronicle* he asked for opinions which he received in copious number. Deliberations continued, and following a successful school sale in May 1913, sufficient funds were made available to allow the Art Department to commission a competition and the net result was a badge featuring the George Watson coat of arms (dating from 1736), the familiar oak tree and three besants upon a shield over which is the flaming heart. The School Motto appeared on a scroll along with the date of the Founder's death.

At Commemoration Day in 1917 Miss Ainslie spoke of the significance of the Badge and Motto. The tree was typical of growth and progress, and of achievement which is its fruit; the flaming heart symbolises the fervour, sensitivity, kindness and love which is represented by the School Motto; and the besants are symbols of the commercial trade through which George Watson had been able to make his money and create his benefaction.

The exact design of School Badge, which was slightly different from the Badge of the Boys' School underwent some minor changes in its early days but there is no mistaking the lasting emblem of George Square which was granted by the Lord Lyon King of Arms in the autumn of 1917.

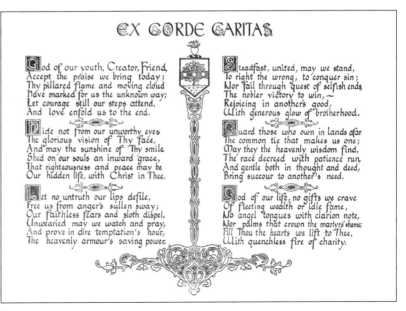

The School Hymn.

Uniform Through the Ages

As well as keeping their old school ties, physically as well as metaphorically, many former pupils have kept their blazers, their colours, their House Badges and other badges of office. This pictorial section gives some idea of the changes over the period 1871–1974.

Senior School, 1910/11.

Senior School, 1945/6.

Senior School, 1948/9.

Junior School, 1937/8.

Junior School, 1965.

Elementary Class, 1922/3.

Prefects

Prefect's stripe, 1935.

Prefect's Tie Pin, 1970.

Games Wear

Hockey Uniform, 1909/10.

Hockey Uniform, 1945/6.

Hockey Uniform, 1973/4.

St Alban's Road School Sports, 1961.

Blazer Badge and colours flashes.

1st XI Tunic Badge.

1st XI Skirt Badge.

Hats

School Beret.

School beret with Prefect's stripes and 2nd XI colours tassle.

School beret with Prefect's stripes and 1st XI colours tassle.

School Ties

Gymn & Dance Wear

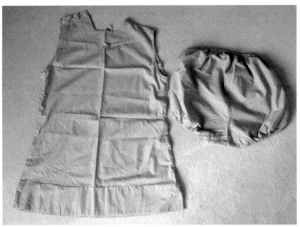

Dancing tunic.

There is a great deal to be said for school hats, one way and another. If some people's definition of poetry is correct, then school hats are poetry; they certainly have the power to awaken many and varied emotions in the school-girl's soul.
ME Va, 1949

The Houses

The House System, both Junior and Senior, was based on the long-standing traditions of the House System in boys' public schools which was designed to foster respect for authority, a spirit of pride and loyalty and act as an agent of discipline.

Started at the Senior level in 1920 and the Junior level in 1923 as a result of moves within the Games Club to promote greater competition and better team spirit, there is no question the House System was immediately popular. Judging by the many reports of the girls' excitement at the time of House Competitions and how many old George Square girls have hung onto their House Badges, belonging to Melville or Lauriston, Falconhall or Greyfriars was a very important part of school life, just as important in some cases as belonging to George Square itself.

Girls were entered for a House primarily as a result of any connections that her family might have. Families were kept together and there was always an attempt to find an appropriate link however tenuous this might be (one girl was told she was to be in Melville because a cousin was called Duncan!).

Each House had its own House Mistress, House Captain and House Games Captain (in the latter two cases elected by the pupils themselves) and they were expected to provide the necessary teams to compete in numerous House Competitions. The Alexander Thomson Memorial Cup was presented to the Senior House Games Champions following competitions in hockey, tennis, badminton and athletics, and the Young Trophy for Scholarship and Conduct was presented to the House, both Junior and Senior sections, which had gained the most points for academic success and deportment. In the early days there were also House competitions for spelling, mental arithmetic, literary composition and debating.

As time continued, House Competitions expanded into every area of games, into Shakespearean drama productions, singing and art. Added to this was the later attachment of Houses to various charitable projects around Edinburgh, mainly helping the needy and sick.

House Officials for Session 1923/4

SENIOR	FALCONHALL	GREYFRIARS	LAURISTON	MELVILLE
HOUSE MISTRESS	Miss Longson	Miss Rivington	Miss Carrie	Miss Harper
HOUSE CAPTAIN	M Smith	O Linton	A Savage	E McCracken
GAMES CAPTAIN	M Stewart	N Glover	B Johnston	C Hogg
JUNIOR				
HOUSE MISTRESS	Miss Russell	Miss Carruthers	Miss Simpson	Miss Wylie
HOUSE CAPTAIN	J Dalgleish	D Hunter	B Meason	N Miller
GAMES CAPTAIN	N Fallas	B Arnold	W Marshall	E Miller

Falconhall (House Colour: Yellow)

A description of the origins of Falconhall appears on page 177 and there is no doubt that the name was synonymous with the wonderful grounds that had once surrounded Falcon Hall, the mansion belonging to Alexander Falconar. Like his father before him, Alexander Falconar made his fortune in India, and in 1811 at the age of 44 he decided to retire with his wife and family to Scotland. The family were highly respected members of the Morningside community for almost eighty years during which time they were generous benefactors of Morningside Parish Church and also Christ's Episcopal Church at Holy Corner. Alexander Falconar died in 1867 and is buried in the Falconar family tomb in Greyfriars' Churchyard where both William Coulter, the first owner of Falcon Hall, and George Watson are buried.

Following the death of Alexander Falconar, Falcon Hall belonged to Henry Craigie, husband of Jessie Pigou one of the Falconar daughters, and four other daughters continued

LEFT: One of the stone falcons which is now above the entrance to Edinburgh Zoo. RIGHT: The Palladian portico from Falcon Hall, now part of the Edinburgh Geographical Institute.

to reside in the house until the last of them died in 1887. The house was then sold and became a boys' boarding school for a short time. Two parts of Falcon Hall survive. The best known is the pair of falcons which guard the entrance to Edinburgh Zoo. Less well known is the entire Palladian portico (1824) which was removed from the John George Bartholomew residence at Falcon Hall to adorn the new building in Duncan Street, Newington. It is now known as Bartholomew House, the home of the Edinburgh Geographical Institute.

Falconhall Head of House Badge.

Greyfriars (House Colour: Grey)

Not far to the north of George Square is Greyfriars' Churchyard which, for the best part of three hundred years after the Restoration, was the principal graveyard for the city. Upon the west wall of the Churchyard is a small tablet on which are inscribed the words *"near this spot lie the remains of George Watson"*. Our Founder is buried there alongside many other famous citizens of Edinburgh and his grave has been the focus for various pilgrimages of George Square girls over the years as well as a sneaking desire to see the statue of Greyfriars' Bobby, the Skye Terrier, who followed the body of his poor, friendless master to the grave, refusing to leave the spot despite repeated attempts to drive him away. Eventually the proprietor of a near-by restaurant took pity and agreed to supply the little dog with one meal a day. One cannot help but feel George Watson would have approved.

Greyfriars Head of House Badge.

Lauriston (House Colour: Green)

In the year 1600 much of the land lying to the West Port of Edinburgh was owned by a family called Turris who appointed a resident factor by the name of Thomas Lowrie to look after their interests. Thomas Lowrie did so well that he was followed by two other members of his family, John and Francis, and when they too were highly successful, the Lowrie family became a recognised part of Edinburgh's gentry. In 1681 they changed their name to Laurie. 'Lauriston Yairds' became a much-sought-after piece of land part of which the Merchant Company feued in 1738 to build George Watson's Hospital. Thus began the long Merchant Company association with the lands at Lauriston and the romance which surrounded the first years of George Watson's foundation. The fact that the Founder was buried a few hundred yards away was part of the family trust. That both brothers and sisters could belong to Lauriston was an additional bond between George Square and George Watson's College.

Lauriston Head of House Badge.

Melville (House Colour: Blue)

Those who are fond of reading about the public schools will know that there is always one House that considers itself to be "School House". If any of George Square's four Houses can lay claim to this distinction it is Melville because of the fact that the George Square buildings include the original Melville House caption. Owned by Henry Dundas of Melville as described on page 170, it seems likely that the dominating personality inside Melville House was his mother, an old lady with a decided will of her own, who spoke broad Scots and who tried to induce her young grandsons and their friends to skip lessons in order to run errands for her. When they expressed concern about the thrashings they would receive she apparently replied with scorn that they would be nothing compared with the thrashings she had received as a young girl. It must have been quite a sight in 1792 when the old dame took on the Edinburgh mob who were protesting about Lord Melville's proposals to increase the price of a sack of oatmeal. Rumour has it she took them on bare fisted just like Tom Brown had taken on Flashman in School House in Rugby!

Melville Head of House Badge.

Greyfriars' Bobby.

Edinburgh's Flodden Wall close to Lauriston Yairds.

Henry Dundas of Melville.

Greyfriars for Brains Lauriston for Games Falconhall and Melville are just silly names.

– A House Ditty from the 1960s

The first Prefects, 1910/11.

The Prefects

Prefects were first introduced on a formal basis to George Square in 1902 although prior to that, senior pupils carried out various duties within the school. In Mr Thomson's time these older pupils were asked to help look after some of the younger classes from time to time in order to assist a governess and there were certainly instances where older girls were given specific responsibilities and duties, usually in terms of organising school events.

Miss Ainslie believed strongly in the prefect system and allowing those who held office (around a dozen each year) to be responsible in part for the daily routine of the school. To this end, some Prefects were elected by the girls themselves and some were appointed by the Headmistress. High standards were expected by Miss Ainslie and demotions would occur if they were not met. It was the ultimate disgrace to have one's office removed but records from Miss Ainslie's time suggest that it did happen at least once.

There is no doubt that the Prefects were held in awe, and not just in the early days. 'Idolatory' was the term used to describe the 'disease' said to be rank amongst the 12–14 year olds in the 1920s as they worshipped a chosen Prefect, preferably one who belonged to the 1st XI. One pupil in 1923 was even heard to beg her parents to move house to Braid Road

The last Prefects, 1974/5.

in Morningside so that she would be close to a Prefect's house and might therefore get the chance to walk to school with her! Another pupil in 1968 recalls the honour bestowed in being the recipient of a hockey stick that had belonged to a Head of House and member of the 1st XI!

Prefects, of course, meant discipline. In Miss Ainslie's time Prefects wore a distinctive maroon and white rosette and were able to issue the dreaded order marks which counted against your House as well as issue lines, essays and punishment exercises. Worst of all, in these days, they had the authority to send a pupil to the Tiled Hall to await the attention of the Headmistress. Given that notification of these order marks and punishments were attached to school reports and

kept in a book for the frequent perusal of the Headmistress, it is not surprising that Prefects commanded respect. A summons by a Prefect was, in many instances, to be feared more than a summons by one of the staff.

Over the years, the duties of Prefects changed from those undertaken in Miss Ainslie's time but successive heads of George Square continued to consider their presence vital to the discipline of the school. During Miss Fleming's time, all Prefects, including the Senior and Deputy Senior Prefects, were elected by the body of their own year group, although the staff kept a close watching brief, and the remainder of the VIth Form and some of the Vth Form were appointed Deputy Prefects. The Prefects also had their own room just off the Court.

Prefects could enjoy a day in the summer term when the they were allowed to take classes and be in full charge of the discipline of the school!

Order marks disappeared in the 1960s but Prefects were still able to issue other punishments and they would have to take their turn on duty to ensure various standards were upheld; most especially that silence was observed on the stairs on the way down to Prayers, that there were orderly queues for break and lunch, and that pupils were inside in good time from the Gardens.

In the 1950s and 1960s the Prefects also took it in turn to invite three members of staff to coffee each week so that better links could be established between the staff and the girls and so that was a regular opportunity to discuss any concerns. Not everyone felt at ease however; one former Prefect describing the event as a *"more than a little awkward and embarrassing although matters improved because my mother had been persuaded to bake a cake which the most difficult of the teachers seemed to enjoy!"*

Even in the 1970s, by which time numbers had swelled to two dozen, Prefects still had a great deal of authority even to the extent of enjoying a day in the summer term when the they were allowed to take classes and be in full charge of the discipline of the school! And on the last day of session they could be found in full regalia, distinctive berets and all, armed with vast bouquets of flowers to be given to their favourite and maybe not so favourite teachers. Prefects had a life of their own, not easily understood by the rest of the School.

The Senior Prefect and Deputy Senior Prefect Badges and Prizes

Between 1903 and 1974 one girl in the Sixth Form had the honour to be elected Senior Prefect although during Miss Ainslie's Headship Senior Prefects were appointed and only when there was an outstanding candidate. For most of the same period there was also a Deputy Senior Prefect. These girls worked closely with the Headmistress of the day and were responsible for the organisation of the Prefects' duties. They were also the public face of the School and were expected to play a full part in special occasions, most especially Commemoration Day, but also on Armistice Day, Empire Day, the Closing Concert and the Kirking of the Master of the Merchant Company.

Badge presented by Anna Scarlet, President of the Women Watsonians' Club 1946/7 and worn by the Senior Prefect.

Badge presented by JM Smibert, Vice Convenor 1965/7 and worn by the Deputy Senior Prefect.

In 1934 the Women Watsonians' Club decided to use the memorial funds for Miss Mona Brebner, School Secretary, who died in a road accident in 1933, to fund a holiday for a pupil whose family had fallen on hard times and also the Mona Brebner Prize for Service and Merit which was initially awarded to the Senior Prefect. In 1958, following the death of the Headmistress, Miss Nicolson, a further memorial fund was set up, part of which was used to fund the Dorothy Nicolson Prize for Service and Merit. Since then, and throughout the years since the merger the Senior Prefect has received the Dorothy Nicolson Prize and the Deputy Senior Prefect has received the Mona Brebner Prize.

The style of the badges of office worn by the Senior Prefects changed slightly three times between 1916 and 1974 but in each case it consisted of a ribbon decoration worn on the left hand side of the school blouse from which was hung either a plain silver or a silver and enamel badge of the school crest. The most splendid are undoubtedly those still worn today and pictured left.

The Badge Ceremony took place at the end of the Closing Concert, a tradition which continues today as part of the Torch and Badge Ceremony at the Annual Prizegiving. The Senior Prefect would remove the Badge from her own person and pin it to the person of her successor in a ceremony which was always conducted in silence in front of the whole School and which used to arouse considerable emotion, especially for the Sixth Form leavers.

The Senior Prefect would remove the Badge from her own person and pin it to the person of her successor.

Mr Thomson took delight in highlighting the major academic successes of his girls.

George Square Prize List

Early prospectuses of the Merchant Company Schools demonstrate a very firm commitment to academic excellence and for George Square, it was no different. As well as a list of available bursaries, the prospectuses included a list of the principal prizewinners and reference to any awards received at regional or national and sometimes even international level. In Mr Thomson's annual reports to Merchant Company governors he clearly took delight in highlighting the major academic successes of his girls and made the case strongly for both bursary funding and medal awards for duxes and other distinguished pupils.

By the time of publication of the first *George Square Chronicle* in 1910, the full prize list numbered 13 special prizes, 46 bursary awards and a roll of honour of all graduation results for Former Pupils around the various universities and colleges. The magazine also devoted a special page to the School Dux sparing no end of glowing tribute to the incumbent's achievements in the academic field.

With the advent of the House competitions in the 1920s the prize list was extended to include many more House awards and sporting trophies, some of which were presented to the school by the Women Watsonians' Club.

By the 1930s and 1940s the prize list increased again thanks to new gifts to the School from former staff, retiring Vice-Convenors, Merchant Company office-bearers and various other friends of George Square. These provided more opportunities for the younger pupils to win awards both on an individual and House basis making the publication of the Prize List in early June an eagerly awaited ritual. After the Closing Concert of June 1974 a total of 72 prizes were awarded.

From top to bottom: The Alexander Thomson Memorial Cup, The Morrison Inches Rose Bowl for House Hockey, The Mary Beattie Baton for the House choir Competition, The Vice Convenor's Targe for Work and conduct, The Winkler Trophy for Posture.

Duxes of the School

THE RHINEGOLD
& THE VALKYRIE
BY RICHARD WAGNER
WITH ILLUSTRATIONS
BY ARTHUR RACKHAM

TRANSLATED BY MARGARET ARMOUR
LONDON: WILLIAM HEINEMANN LTD.

Margaret Armour, Dux, 1878
Poet, Prose Author and Translator most famous for her translations of commentaries on the works of Richard Wagner, notably *The Fall of the Niebelungs*. She also wrote *Songs of Love and Death* and *Agnes of Edinburgh*.

Eleanor Pairman, Dux, 1914
Top Prize Winner in the John Welsh Mathematical Bursary, the first occasion in the history of Edinburgh University when such a prize was awarded to a woman. She was also the joint winner of the Newton Bursary in Mathematics, the Winner of the Kelland Memorial Prize in Mathematics and a Medallist in Natural Philosophy. On leaving University which she completed in only three years she won the Vans Dunlop Scholarship in Mathematics worth £300, before taking up a senior post in the Department of Applied Statistics at University College London.

The School Dux Medal and Gold Watch, early twentieth century, and the Modern Languages Gold Medal, 1894.

The Michie Sisters, Violet and Doreen, Duxes in 1937 and 1938
The Michies have the unique distinction of being the only two sisters to be Duxes in the history of the school. They were remarkable for their outstanding achievements across a broad range of the curriculum.

Joan Smith, Dux, 1940
In 1979, Dr Smith was appointed Secretary of the Bank of Scotland, the first woman to hold such a post in a major Scottish Bank. This appointment followed a highly successful academic career in which Dr Smith achieved distinction in the University of Edinburgh's Bursary Competitions and acquired the degrees MA, LLB and PhD. Prior to her appointment as Secretary to the Bank of Scotland, she worked in the law department of the Bank after which, in 1973, she was appointed Secretary of the Bank of Scotland Finance Company (renamed the British Linen Bank Ltd in 1977).

Elizabeth Young, Dux, 1971

After leaving George Watson's Ladies' College, Elizabeth went to the Boys' College to sit her Oxford Entrance examination before spending six months studying Italian at the Universita Stranieri in Perugia. Elizabeth won an Exhibition to St Anne's College where she read Honours Mods and Greats and from where she graduated in 1976. She trained as a nurse and midwife, following which she married and then she and her family moved to Japan for four years. Between 1985 to 1996 the family lived and worked in Spain where she learned Spanish and trained as a shiatsu specialist; two years in Dunoon as a midwife were followed by a move to Brussels where she has been teaching English to Japanese 8–14 year-olds since 1999.

Julia Sanderson, Dux, 1972

Following her distinguished school career Julia Sanderson read physics at Manchester University and then chose a career in IT. She joined ICL as a programmer and worked in systems development and implementation for 12 years, with Shell and Mercantile Credit, before joining a firm of management consultants. She is now a director with leading professional services firm Deloitte. In her current role she helps organisations to bring about business transformation through the implementation of enterprise-wide systems. Julia is married, with two grown-up stepchildren and lives in Warwickshire.

The gymnastics competition took place each year in the summer term. A Sixth Form pupil, Brenda Carmichael, describes the event:

"Preparation for this historic event starts months beforehand. Prospective candidates start deep breathing exercises at a wide open window, go to bed half an hour earlier than usual and try to loosen themselves up with back bends, front bends, side bends and other contortions. During the Easter holidays after the competition exercises have been disclosed to the participants, the occupants of certain select hotel bedrooms are subjected to an entertainment of groans, bumps, sighs and thuds.

At home, parents turning up in their daughter's bedroom at the wrong time, or the right time, depending on how you view matters, may find her in an unexpected and not exactly ladylike position.

Parents need to sign a note to say that their offspring is sufficiently capable of being left in the school gymnasium early morning, sine custode, in order to practise. Exhausting practice results in pulled muscles, sprained wrists and ankles and bruised ribs. Some go the length of looking in a full mirror to see that knees do not bend, that toes are pointed, that the head is up, the back straight and the tongue kept well in.

The preliminary contest approaches and a dozen quivering girls will be asked to perform their routine. Four will be disappointed. The other eight will be so nervous that they will wish they hadn't got into the final.

The day of the final dawns bright and clear, actually it's dull and wet, and we all have to go through the routines again in complete silence. After we have all been in we are ushered out into the Court and we have then to go back in individually to perform an unrehearsed routine presented to us by the judges. In the final ordeal, before we hear who's won, we all have to go into the gym and run round until we are told to stop. We each vow we will never take part again, but we do because the lure of the prize is too great."

The preliminary contest approaches and a dozen quivering girls will be asked to perform their routine. Four will be disappointed. The other eight will be so nervous that they will wish they hadn't got into the final.

The Annual Closing Concert and Prizegiving in the Usher Hall

There is no question that one of the best loved events at George Square was the end of session Concert and Prizegiving the tradition of which dates from 1874. It was a hugely impressive occasion, the first and last of which took place in the Music Hall of the Assembly Rooms, George Street, and in the intervening period, in the Usher Hall, although there were occasions when the Central Hall in Tollcross was used.

At all stages in the school's history this was a showcase event and one at which the input from the Music Department was substantial. In the Usher Hall in the 1920s, the massed ranks of the senior choirs in pristine dresses and white gloves marched in to the organ gallery after which there would be choral, orchestral and Highland dance performances on stage prior to the Annual Prizegiving. This tradition continued for many years making it a very formal and dignified occasion planned with military-style precision and providing the Head of the day with the opportunity not only to report on the activities of the school but also to make pronouncements about the issues confronting the world of education.

There was only the odd hiccup over the years. In 1943 the father of the recipient of the first prize (a junior pupil receiving the T Douglas Dobson Prize for handwriting) allowed his French Mauritian roots to get the better of him; as he proudly watched his daughter cross the stage to receive her prize he exclaimed with great gusto and wild gesticulation, *"Bravo, Bravo!"* only to find that the rest of the Edinburgh middle class audience was a little less enthusiastic. The incident, which caused a minor stir at the time, was used years later by the daughter when she became an actress and script writer. It appeared as the opening theme for a radio play entitled *Ask No Questions* and was broadcast on the Home Service on 26 September 1989.

After 1907, it was also the occasion after which it was traditional for the Vice Convenor to hold an official

The Annual Closing Concert in the Usher Hall.

dinner party for the Headmistress and her Deputy, the retiring members of staff, the President of the Women Watsonians' Club and various Merchant Company officials. On one such occasion in the 1950s the Vice Convenor of the day had clearly done his bit with the invitations but had forgotten to tell his wife that she was hosting 12 people to dinner!

In the later years of Usher Hall concerts, by which time the pupils wore navy skirts and white blouses with school ties, the School would march in to the tune of *Marche Triomphale* by the Schoolmaster, Lee Ashton. Thereafter, the Senior Music Mistress would lead the assembled company in The School Hymn and the 'Crimond' version of the 23rd Psalm before proceeding to a dozen or so other items of orchestral and choral work for both senior and junior pupils. On occasion there were also solo performances. The standard of music was high and the occasion was often attended by members of Edinburgh's musical societies as well as parents and family friends.

At the conclusion of the Concert the School Orchestra left the stage and long trestle tables were carried in on which there would be two very substantial trays of prizes trophies ordered from the most junior awards to those for the Senior Prefects and Duxes. At the command of silence the platform party, led by the Master

of the Merchant Company in his distinctive robes, emerged from the Green Room entrance beneath the organ gallery to take its place on stage where they stood awaiting the Headmistress to emerge in full academic regalia. The Headmistress would present her Annual Report detailing the activities of the School during the session just ending and then invite the wife of the Master of the Merchant Company to present the prizes. The *National Anthem* was sung after the Senior Prefect Badge Ceremony had been completed.

> *The standard of music was high and the occasion was often attended by members of Edinburgh's musical societies as well as parents and family friends.*

The Central Hall.

In the early days, the school day opened with a prayer in each form class although there were certain occasions on which Mr Thomson assembled the whole school together. This was not easy given the absence of a hall at that time but he effectively called for silence with the use of a whistle (interesting that silence for today's assemblies at Colinton Road is also called for by use of the whistle at the command of either the Head Boy or Head Girl).

Mr Thomson's whistle.

The Central Hall and Gallery

Being at one time the garden of Melville House, the Central Hall with its Gallery was officially opened in 1893 and from that date provided the focus for whole school events including special occasions, morning prayers, recreation, former pupil events and exhibitions. Visitors to the school entered by the door on the south side of the Gallery from where there was a wonderful view of the Central Hall.

Leading off from the west side of the Gallery there was a waiting room which was just behind the Head's study, and two other small rooms which had initially been junior classrooms but which were latterly used for staff administration. At the north-west corner of the Gallery was the entrance to the Tiled Hall which was the main door to the school when the first building developments took place in 1876 and on the north and east sides of the Gallery it was easy to see the stone façade of No 4 George Square. The Gallery added a distinctive architectural feature to the School which visibly preserved much of its early history.

On special occasions such as Commemoration Day, Empire Day and Armistice Day the whole school would be assembled to hear the Head and often a visiting speaker.

But the Central Hall was in constant daily use as well. Pupils who were at school in the first two decades of the twentieth century remember dancing classes and drill classes being held in the Central Hall and also remember the notice-boards on which was posted much of the information about the school week. Booking sheets were posted for use of the tennis courts at Falconhall, as were various notices about school discipline.

In wartime these notice-boards were used to keep pupils and staff up to date on what was happening at the Front and the various activities in the war effort at home. Later, the Central Hall was used for some music classes, gym and dance and a wide range of clubs and societies activities including badminton, basketball, charities work and debating. It was never out of use both for daily use and special occasions which is why so many former pupils have such vivid memories of their time spent there.

When Miss Ainslie became Headmistress in 1902 full morning assemblies took place each day in the Central Hall and there is no doubt that it was an impressive place to be, especially when the whole school was assembled. A gong, or latterly a bell, would ring to call the School from form classes and Prefects would be expected to stand on the stairs and in the corridors to ensure the School assembled in silence. The lower forms would stand in the Central Hall itself, the youngest classes to the front and the middle school classes to the back and then the senior forms would be placed in the Gallery also in rank order of year group.

Into the north side of the Gallery railing was built a wooden lectern from which the duty member of staff would call for silence before the appearance of the Head. In later years a small electric bell was used to call for the silence, although in the case of a few staff there might have to be more than one attempt! It was the gravest sin to be caught talking at this point. In front of the entire school the miscreant would be asked to leave her place and attend the Tiled Hall to await the Head after Prayers.

Once silence reigned the Head, followed by a dignified procession of the male members of staff, would appear from the Tiled Hall entrance to the Gallery. It was not a sight for the faint-hearted especially those junior members of the school community who were looking up at their headmaster or headmistress from the lower decks. *"She was like a goddess"*, said Vera Carmichael (neé Wood Hawks) of her headmistress, Charlotte Ainslie, *"her dignity, her lovely white hair and her graceful dress left no-one in any doubt that she was the Head. There was a sudden hush, compounded of awe and admiration.......we knew she was a strict disciplinarian and rightly so."*

For some pupils, their Heads, all of whom had a striking physical presence, were sometimes seen as rather remote and unapproachable figures to whom you would not dare to speak. They commanded respect simply by being there and it was only in the heights of the Sixth Form that pupils might appreciate the more human side.

Each morning, the service consisted of an opening hymn, prayers, a reading and often a second hymn or piece by the orchestra. Once a week, in Miss Fleming's time, a form class would take responsibility for the reading and the choosing of the hymn. There was a period at the end of the service for the reading of notices, sometimes by the Headmistress and sometimes by the Prefects or pupils responsible for clubs and societies or school teams. Even the reading out of a two-line notice used to put fear into the heart of the girl concerned!

For pupils who had just returned from absence, there was the added discomfort of presenting themselves after prayers to the Headmistress with a note from their parents explaining the nature of their ailment and hoping no awkward questions would be asked.

Even the reading out of a two line notice used to put fear into the heart of the girl concerned!

The Coronation Service, 21 June 1911.

Special Occasions

(i) A Celebration of Mr Thomson

One of the first recorded special occasions in George Square was the celebration of the Jubilee of Headmaster Alexander Thomson in 1897. Fifty years as a schoolmaster had prompted him to host what he described as 'a social event' to thank all those with whom he had worked during his career. The evening which was hosted in room 23 (later room 25), was divided into two parts: in the first part guests listened to a programme of vocal and instrumental music and then there was a presentation of a silver tea service and silver ink stand to Mr Thomson from former pupils of the school, and a writing-table and book-stand from the staff. The second part of the evening was a dance accompanied by refreshments.

This occasion proved to be a lot more than a celebration of the professional career of one of Edinburgh's outstanding headmasters; it is also witnessed the birth of the Former Pupils' Club *(see page 247)* and established the tradition that George Square was far more than the sum of her present pupils and staff. It was more of a family than a school with a unique bond of loyalty and affection that was to sustain the institution throughout its history and which is one of the hallmarks of the modern Watson's.

(ii) Royal Events

A notable Royal occasion was the Coronation Service on 21 June 1911: *"A Christian ceremony at which the Empire renews its vows and receives consecration in the person of its Sovereign."* The Central Hall was bedecked in red, white and blue with a centrepiece Union Jack flanked by the feathers of the Prince Wales and a large banner on which was inscribed 'God Save the King'. A solemn religious service followed during which Miss Ainslie described the spiritual meaning of the Coronation Service in Westminster Abbey and reminded her school of their duty to serve King and Country. After this, 'the Elementaries' (preparatory school pupils) trooped in, each carrying a miniature Union Jack and a shield showing the emblems of the three kingdoms. Once they had assembled on the Gallery behind Miss Ainslie the National Anthem was sung after which there was *"much cheering and rejoicing."* As a souvenir each pupil was presented with a copy of Lord Rosebery's address on the Union Jack.

The celebration of Royal occasions continued: on 24 May 1923 the first Empire Day event took place at which a tape-recorded message from the King was played to the assembled company in the Central Hall. Honour, love of country and duty were the themes of the subsequent speech from Miss Ainslie.

King George V's Silver Jubilee in 1935 was marked by a special service of thanksgiving and in the *"deliberate absence of too much external pomp and circumstance"* the School was asked to consider what it could do to help those who were still in need around the world and what it could do to assist those in need in its home city. Various collections were made for charities working abroad and £30 was raised to help the Princess Margaret Rose Hospital in Fairmilehead.

On Tuesday 21 January 1936 the School assembled to hear Miss Robertson announce the death of King George V. She recalled the events of the last 25 years and the fact that she had been present at the Mercat Cross at the time of his Proclamation. She referred to his unfailing loyalty, his strenuous devotion to duty before the School sang the 23rd Psalm and filed out of the Central Hall in silence. A few days later some senior pupils were taken by Miss Robertson to the Mercat Cross to hear the Lord Provost and Sir Francis Grant make the Proclamation of King Edward VIII. Other pupils were taken in groups to the Singing Room to hear excerpts of the radio coverage and then in May 1937, a group of staff and senior pupils attended a special ceremony to mark the Coronation of George VI.

Events repeated themselves on 6 February 1952 when Miss Nicolson called the School together in the Central Hall to announce the death of King George VI.

The Duke and Duchess of Edinburgh became Honorary Members of the Merchant Company, 3 March 1949.

(iii) Commemoration Day
In a memo to her staff, Charlotte Ainslie intimated that Friday 16 January 1914 would be observed by Watsonians all over the world as Founder's Commemoration Day, and so began the long tradition of a Founder's Day service and oration dedicated to the memory of George Watson. The first visiting Speaker was Mr W K Allan, Vice Convenor of the School in Session 1917/18 who chose as his theme the life of George Watson. At this service there was a

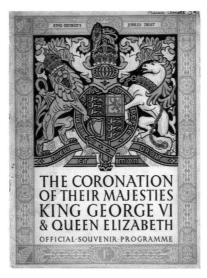

Souvenir programme signed by all those from George Square who attended the special ceremony in the City of Edinburgh to mark the Coronation, 12 May 1937.

George Watson's Ladies' College planting rhododendrons in George Square Garden to commemorate the Coronation.

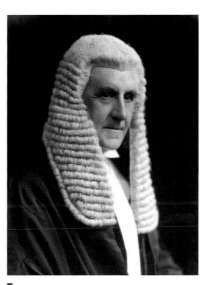

Sheriff Robert L Orr.

reading of the well-known passage from Ecclesiasticus 44 *"Let us now praise famous men"* and the singing of the *Te Deum.* On Commemoration Days after 1918 the School Hymn was sung and the Senior Prefect read the 13th Chapter of 1st Corinthians. The Headmistress also read special Commemoration prayers (still read today).

Amongst the Commemoration Day/Founder's Day Speakers have been distinguished men and women such as Sheriff Orr, Lady Rhondda and Mrs Vera Carmichael :

1. Sheriff Orr, Commemoration Day, 1933
Robert L Orr, 1853–1944, was the first Dux of George Watson's College and in 1895/6 was President of The Watsonian Club. He was Sheriff Substitute for Lothian and Peebles 1908-38. *"The purest joy is being able to recall what you have done to help others".*

2. Lady Rhondda, Commemoration Day, 1939
Margaret Haig Thomas, Viscountess Rhondda, 'The Welsh Boadicea' (1883–1958), joined Emmeline Pankhurst's Suffragette movement and organised their first meeting at Newport, despite the fact that this was against the wishes of her husband, Humphrey Mackworth. She was arrested and imprisoned for five days in 1908 for attempting to blow up a letterbox. In 1917 she was appointed Director of the Women's Department

Lady Rhondda.

at the Department for National Service and she was also instrumental in reforming the Women's squadrons in the Royal Air Force. She founded the magazine *Time and Tide* which concentrated on women's issues but which also provided outlets for the writing talents of authors such as Virginia Woolf, George Orwell and DH Lawrence. "I know that you will never shirk the responsibilities you recognise in your society – your type does not do that."

3. Vera Carmichael, Commemoration Day, 1954

Vera Wood Hawks was born in 1900 attending George Square between 1905–18. She trained initially as a secretary before marrying Jimmy Carmichael, a Scottish rugby internationalist, and before embarking on a distinguished career in public life. Her wide-ranging interests in politics, in the Church, in sport and in charity work gave her a breadth of vision and experience which made her a valued member of numerous committees. This, together with her capacity for hard work and unfailing loyalty to those whom she served, was the reason why she was awarded the OBE in 1956 for political services in Scotland. *"Never forget Red Letter Days. They define our traditions and they open new doors for each and every one of us."*

Vera Carmichael OBE.

From 1943 onwards, Commemoration Day began with a short ceremony at St Alban's Road at 9am, after which the Merchant Company officials, Vice Convenor and Headmistress would go to George Square for the main service at 11.30am. Thereafter, a Commemoration Day Lunch was held.

(iv) Armistice Day 1919

Armistice Day 1919 was the first service of Remembrance to be held in George Square. By all accounts, it was an extremely moving occasion at which Miss Ainslie read out a letter from King George in which he expressed his unfailing sympathy for all his subjects who had lost loved ones and his deep gratitude for the sacrifice that had been made in order that Right could triumph over Wrong. Armistice Day, Miss Ainslie said, was an important occasion on which we should remember all those who gave their lives so that we might live in peace. A religious service followed in which there were hymns and readings and a dedication of remembrance. It was an occasion which marked the beginning of a long and important tradition in the school.

GEORGE WATSON'S
- LADIES' COLLEGE -

FOUNDER'S DAY
LUNCHEON
1935

Menu
❖
Crème d'Asperges
❖
Tournedos de Bœuf
Champignons
Choux-fleurs
Croquettes de Pommes
de Terre
❖
Pouding d'Oranges
Bavaroise au Chocolat
❖
Prunes Farcies
❖
Café

Design by HILARY BRADSHAW, VI.

Commemoration Day menu.

Greyfriars' Church.

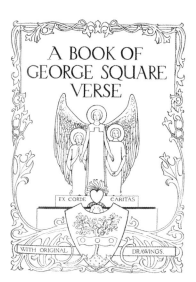

A Book of George Square Verse.

(v) The Carol Service

Annual carol services took place within every part of the school right from the early days of Mr Thomson although some were very much less formal than others especially some of those in the Elementary Department which involved a nativity presentation by the youngest pupils. Apparently, these did not always go to plan; on one occasion, a young poodle dog was dressed up in blankets to be used as a lamb but unfortunately got loose and hid under the piano in the Central Hall much to the consternation of the shepherds and kings. On another occasion at St Alban's Road, Mary lost her dress when Joseph unwittingly stepped on the cord that was keeping it together and the baby Jesus who was supposedly asleep in the crib piped up *"Don't worry, I haven't got my clothes on either."*

From the ridiculous to the sublime, and to Greyfriars' Church where each Christmas in the 1960s and early 1970s, at the instigation of Hilda Fleming, the School assembled on the last Sunday before the end of term for a service of Nine Lessons and Carols. This was a wonderful occasion, known for its solo of the first verse of *Once in Royal David's City* and the powerful readings of the Christmas story which were undertaken by a pupil from each year group Primary 6 to Form V, the Senior Prefect, and the Headmistress.

(vi) Other Events in the George Square Diary

1907 Visit of the Japanese Education Minister – Baron Kikuchi:1920 Jubilee of Merchant Company Schools

Signature of Baron Kikuchi, Japanese Education Minister, 1907, in the School visitors' book.

1932 Opening of Colinton Road

1932 *A Book of George Square Verse* published

1935 Form 3a Junior was chosen to take part in a cinema film of historic Scotland *Key to Scotland.*

1953 Pupils taken to see film of Everest ascent

1969 School choir takes part in the recording of the Soundtrack for the film *The Prime of Miss Jean Brodie* starring Maggie Smith

1975 "Goodby to George Square" Dinner

Everest
Above the hymalayas, the mountains of Tibet,
Two flags are bravely flying, 'mid ice and cold and wet,
The rich reward of thirty years of bravery and toil,
By bulldog Britains, sturdy Swiss, the aim of one and all
Is onward, ever onward, to the top.

From fever-ridden jungle, from mountain pasture sweet,
To the cold, cold wintry weather high above the dust and heat,
The loyal band of mountaineers with wandering spirits strong,
Within the heart of everyone there throbs the ancient song;
'Tis onward, ever onward, to the top.

Their minds are filled with wonder as the sun sets overhead,
And clothes the sappire mountain in a robe of ruby red.
The pale moon's light bathes all around in gold and silver strewn,
They climb with acheing limbs the icy steps that they have hewn –
Still onward, ever onward, to the top.

But now, through perseverence we have reached the mighty brow;
With joy and tears our minds reflect that after this we now
Have scaled the highest mountian, no higher can we go;
Our minds are warmed and lightened like the melting of the snow;
It's downward, ever downward, from the top.

Winning Everest poem, Betty Murray, 5b.

The Cookie-Shine

The Cookie-Shine was, for many pupils, the highlight of the school year. Held in December it was the equivalent of the School Dance we know today but with lots of differences! There was no male company other than the handful of gentlemen on the staff who suddenly found themselves the most popular people in the school; dance cards were issued at the start of the evening and these had to be religiously kept to lest anyone was left out, and there was an early end to the evening to allow parents to collect their daughters and escort them home.

The dancing was what one pupil in 1926 described as 'sedate but amateur' and it was all too short given the huge amount of time that had gone into choosing and, in many cases making, the right dress to wear. There were also some musical interludes and short performances which took place just before and after the supper and refreshments stage of the evening.

In 1932 there was much concern because the Cookie-Shine was moved from its usual Christmas time slot to the beginning of the second term in order to allow a special celebration of the 250th anniversary of the Merchant Company. For this, the girls of George Square had to play their part in *The Masque*: a small theatrical production based on the lives of the famous residents of George Square in the eighteenth century. This decision didn't go down very well with the girls especially when, *"in the interests of national economy, various items in* The Masque *had to be shorn away"*. There was no doubt about where the girls would rather have been!

The Cookie-Shine, however, remained the pride and joy of the Upper School and it was not until 1955 that the Senior Prefect of the time, Margaret Somerville, was despatched by her peers to approach the Headmistress, Miss Nicolson, to ask if partners might be permitted. To the huge surprise of everyone (and by all accounts, the horror of some staff!) Miss Nicolson agreed although not without first enforcing some strict rules. The girls' parents had to write to the Headmistress informing her of the name of both the boy and his

school; if the boy was a University student he must be in his first year of undergraduate study and he could not be a medical student (one can only speculate as to what was the reasoning behind this decision!), and on the night itself the poor boy had to be introduced to what was described as a *"triumvirate of Miss Nicolson, Miss Lindsay and Miss Carruthers"*. The couple had to stay in the Central Hall unless either had to use the 'bathrooms' (substantial queues at the tiny male staff 'bathroom') and they would be under strict escort (by a female member of staff) as they collected their coats from the cloakrooms in the Dark Passage.

Despite the excitement of a mixed dance, finding partners was no easy matter for many girls as few had boyfriends, or if they did they kept quiet about them! The School Captain of George Watson's College was commandeered to act as an intermediary, brothers were press-ganged and in a few cases, mothers had to work quickly to find the male offspring of some long-lost cousin.

Sadly, the name Cookie-Shine was disbanded in 1962, but was replaced with a more familiar school dance.

Cookie-Shine Rhyme
(with apologies to Gilbert and Sullivan)

Three little maids from school are we
All dressed up for a dance you see.
One little maid says – "We'll be late,
Taxis go at a snail's slow rate!"
Three little maids arrive at last,
Early because the clock was fast.
All of the maids look very swell –
Who's a teacher we cannot tell.
Three little maids and many more,
Dance about on the shiny floor.
One little maid says "I'm so hot,
Next's a play by our friend Miss Scott."
One little maid steps on her dress
Frills are torn – oh my, what a mess!
Three little maids have tired sore feet;
Supper comes and we eat and eat.
After the rest we neatly do
Lancers, polkas and foxtrots too.
Enters the band while we all cool –
Sailors who sing Britannia Rule
Three little maids on ices dine,
Then we end with For Auld Lang Syne.

But;
Next month three little maids feel ill
Why? Well, look at the taxi bill!

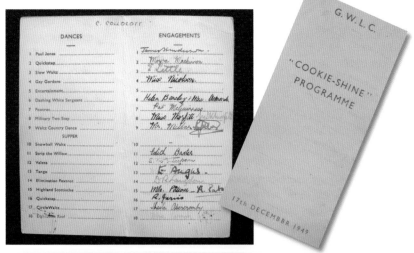

Cookie-Shine dance card and Cookie-Shine entertainment.

22: A Room with a View

For those pupils who attended George Square in the second half of its history, Room 22 became the focus of many events in school life. Built as a Lecture Room, Room 22 was spacious and light as the result of the fact that it had large windows on both its north and south sides. By the late 1940s it was equipped for theatrical productions complete with a wooden stage and large trap-door (the hinges of which were saved by one drama enthusiast as an important piece of George Square memorabilia) And all the necessary space for stage lights and scenery screens. It was also used as a meeting room, an examination hall and, latterly, as a Music Room and as such it contained a grand piano and old-fashioned gramophone on which the girls used to listen to opera.

However, the greater attraction of Room 22 was the fact that its north windows faced the refectory in the students' union in Teviot Row which, at lunchtimes, was crammed full of University students. The fact that many of these students were of the opposite sex, handsome or otherwise, was a source of great delight to many George Square girls (and the odd younger member of staff) who sometimes felt being cooped up inside George Square all day was a bit like being in a nunnery. Room 22 was undoubtedly the room with a view and very popular as a result.

Music Classes in Room 22, 1950.

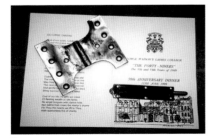

The hinges of the trap-door on the stage in Room 22.

The Admiral's Kitchen.

The Admiral's Kitchen and Court

One can only imagine what it must have been like in the galley of *The Venerable* when Admiral Duncan set out on his journeys on the high seas but the image is one of frenetic activity with cooks rushing about between large wooden tables and steaming stoves in order to serve up solid nourishment to the hungry company. It was the hub of the ship and the Admiral's Kitchen was the hub of George Square from its earliest days.

Next to the Admiral's Kitchen was the Court which, in Mr Thomson's time, was used as the dining room. Here, lunch would be put out on two groups of large trays, one for 'ha'penny things' and one for 'penny things'. Coffee and cocoa cost a ha'penny and soup cost a penny. Apparently the 'currant bricks' weren't worth either!

The Admiral's Kitchen tended to be a much warmer part of the building, close to the school boilers and enjoying the additional heat of the large ovens. It had been the kitchen for Melville House and was distinctive because of its arched ceiling and heavy pillars. Later generations of girls and staff received their hot drinks and milk (and by all accounts a very special brand of cocoa) from the Admiral's Kitchen, plus their scones and buns brought in on long wooden trays by local bakers' boys just before break-time. Sometimes they would be late and chaos would ensue. Not that all was lost, as there was always the possibility of a quick trip out to the sweetie shop in Charles Street although this had to be undertaken with precision timing and preferably with an atlas to hand as the best size of book in which to hide the largest bar of chocolate. The owner could generally be relied upon to keep her counsel but there were also the odd occasions where she reported girls for being out of class.

Back in the Admiral's Kitchen once the girls had been served by the kitchen staff they sat round the Court area on wooden benches. Several notice boards were pinned to the wall including those on which the all-important games teams were posted and which were the subject of much discussion on Thursdays and Fridays just before the Saturday matches.

The Court, however, also had another meaning rather than just the physical aspect of what had been the original dining room of the school. In the 1960s, Hilda Fleming instituted a weekly meeting of Prefects and Form Captains, known as 'Court' at which the daily business of the school was discussed. It was an opportunity for the pupils to make their representations to their Headmistress but few dared to say much in case they were accused of renegade activity!

The Dark Passage

Nowhere inside George Square was shrouded in more mystery than the Dark Passage. Running the length of the Central Hall between the Court and Lower Dining Room (connecting nos. 4 and 5 George Square) it was a rabbit warren of small cloakrooms and cupboards boxed in by pillars, a series of low ceilings and casings which carried the pipes that were the mainstay of the school heating system (not always on top form).

It never saw the light of day as it was tucked away at the back of the school, under street level and without much ventilation. Dark it most certainly was and for some pupils this also bordered on the spectral. The so-called 'sightings' of the Grey Lady often occurred in the Dark Passage and it was certainly a likely environment in which to meet a member of staff on the prowl to find recalcitrant pupils. According to one old master of the School, *"Ninety percent of misdemeanours took place in the Dark Passage because it was so difficult to patrol."*

The cloakrooms were like wooden box rooms with wire netting standing atop each partition and they were far too small to house a whole class of girls all struggling to put on or take off outdoor clothes and shoes. When it came to changing for gym lessons it was nothing short of a nightmare. More energy was expended in the 'pre and après gym' than was expended on the ropes and wall-bars or on learning the Foxtrot or the Dashing White Sergeant.

Changing for gym over the years had a dynamic all of its own because of the most extraordinary range of garments that were deemed suitable for exercise, ranging from long flowing dresses and white gloves, to box tunics, to the garish colours of House dancing tunics and finally leotards minus the customary stretch. Girls today can think themselves very lucky not only to enjoy ample space in which to change with warm, private showers but also sensible sports wear. This was never the case at George Square.

It was advisable to arrive at the cloakroom either very early or very late so as to avoid the worst of the

The back door to the Dark Passage.

undignified crush. In theory everyone had a peg but reaching it was virtually out the window, especially for the more petite citizens who did not have the physical ability to jostle with their more substantial peers. Bits of bare limbs went in all directions as they struggled to fit into the appropriate arm and leg-holes in garments that were certainly not designed by athletes. Voices became more staccato as inevitably some poor souls would find that their juice had leaked over their shoe bag and a rather irritable gym mistress would arrive wondering what on earth was causing all the delay.

When it got to the era of dancing tunics, the mayhem was ten times worse. These bizarre uniforms came in two sizes only; large and extra-large and they consisted of two parts; tunic and pantaloons which were a mixture of styles common to Roman soldiers and circus acrobats. They came in four colours ostensibly matching the blue, green, yellow and grey of Melville, Lauriston, Falconhall and Greyfriars respectively, but more in tune with the lurid paint mixes of *The Magic Roundabout*.

It was a sight to behold and pity the class that was once forced to attend George Square Theatre clad in its multi-colours as a result of a bomb scare evacuation. The ensuing sing-song whilst the emergency services checked the building rivalled anything of the regalia worn on the Last Night of the Proms. It was a great relief to see on the uniform list of 1973 the words *"leotards will replace dancing tunics"*.

The Dark Passage had a life all of its own. If there was any subterfuge it would be found here as would huddles of girls discussing any major gossip or scandal. Likewise, those who were not well inclined to take their recreation in the gardens tried their best to hide in the Dark Passage only to be stopped by a covert rearguard action of the staff on duty and woe betide anyone who could not produce a valid excuse.

The Tiled Hall as drawn by Catriona Stewart, V, 1974.

The Tiled Hall

When the building developments of 1876 took place, the original entrance to Melville House disappeared and a new entrance was built at the north east corner of the old house. Having come into the garden from street level pupils and staff would climb a few steps and enter the school by a Tiled Hall. In relation to décor this room was very Victorian, both in terms of the ornate tiling round the walls and the rather garish colour scheme. It had hints of the interior of an Orthodox church and the entrance to one of the older London Underground stations. It was a dark chamber because of the absence of strong daylight and, despite its large fireplace, often rather cold.

In Mr Thomson's time the Tiled Hall was sometimes used as an area for Elementary classes and some junior arithmetic classes and it was also from here that the school gong would be sounded for the end of lessons.

But by Miss Ainslie's time, and for the succeeding headships, the Tiled Hall assumed a much more sinister character as it was to here that any girl who had committed an act of wrongdoing would be sent to await the Headmistress whose study was close by. If awaiting the wrath of the Headmistress in the austere setting of the Tiled Hall was bad enough there was the added shame of the rest of the school being able to watch. The main staircase in No 5 George Square ascended from the Tiled Hall and, following the 1909 building developments, it was the meeting place of two of the busiest corridors in the school. Everyone saw what happened in the Tiled Hall and so there was no doubt about the disgrace of the miscreant's predicament.

By Miss Robertson's time a wooden bench had been placed in the Tiled Hall in a position where it could be seen from the door of the Headmistress's study. This did nothing to relieve the discomfort of the situation especially as it meant that the Headmistress simply had to emerge from behind her door and call out the pupil's name. It was a long walk down the corridor to meet one's fate.

In July 1938, however, a rumour spread like wildfire that a notice had been posted in room 9: *"Delinquents will no longer be sent to the Tiled Hall"*. Rejoicing, however, was short lived when it was revealed that some minor vandalism had taken place and there was in fact another bit of the paper which continued: *"they will instead first be sent to room 6"*, but only so that a senior mistress could make the judgement as to whether or not the Headmistress's time was going to be wasted if the girl was sent down! In most cases the judgement was very firmly that it was not, so there was the double purgatory of waiting outside room 6 as well as being sent to the Tiled Hall. The staff obviously decided this bureaucracy wasn't worth the effort so they abandoned the 'room 6 rule' a few months later. The Tiled Hall retained its *"air of foreboding"* throughout both Miss Nicolson's and Miss Fleming's headships and by all accounts the fear of being sent there had not diminished when George Square closed her doors in 1975.

The Tiled Hall decor.

Classroom Discipline

In the very early days, there were few recorded incidents of indiscipline requiring the attention of the Headmaster although there are some notes within the reports sent to the Merchant Company by Mr Thomson that he had *"found it profitable to engage the help of two sets of parents of girls showing a disinclination towards their studies"*. There are also reports of girls being summoned to the Lady Superintendent, Miss Wilson, *"to explain lapses of concentration", "lengthy periods of daydreaming"* and, in one case in 1881 *"unladylike behaviour"* although the notes do not divulge the details!

Bad behaviour was neither acceptable nor expected in Mr Thomson's school and it seems unlikely that he had to waste much of his time dealing with unruly pupils. *"His reproofs were so often touched with humour, yet his discipline was perfect,"* was how one pupil summed him up. He was always around the school and made it abundantly clear that he would tolerate no nonsense. Disappointment rather than anger was his wont.

Classroom discipline was tight – not surprising in Victorian times – but it was not draconian in the way that was the case at many boys' schools. Governesses and masters had few problems when it came to keeping order and if problems did occur they were very quickly dealt with.

By Miss Ainslie's time, with a larger school to consider, the disciplinary procedures became more formal, partly because of the Prefects' system, but also because of the greater responsibilities invested in Form Staff and House Staff. There was still a noticeable absence of serious misdemeanour and very few of the school records of the time mention any trouble.

In the early years of the twentieth century girls were expected to stand to answer in class and at the end of each lesson they were expected to present their work. If, for any reason it was deemed unsatisfactory, the pupil would, in front of the rest of the class, be asked to provide the reason for the failure to satisfy and may well be required to wait behind or *"adorn the vacant spot beside the blackboard"*.

Order marks (or 'black marks' as they were known by the more junior pupils) were regarded a serious discipline, made much more so by the fact that they were posted, in full view of every pupil and every member of staff, on House notice-boards displayed in the Central Hall. Incur an order mark and you were guaranteed to be up before your Head of House and asked to provide an explanation. Failure to do so would result in double punishment, and it seemed much worse if it was from another pupil.

Attitudes to discipline underwent some changes in the mid 1960s following the national debate which questioned the wisdom of leaving senior pupils to take charge of so many matters of discipline. As the curriculum changed so too did the structure of the school and the focus for discipline shifted away from Houses to Year Groups.

George Square Gardens

One of the great physical assets of George Square is its spacious gardens, first laid out in 1815. The magnificent trees and shrubberies, some of which were imported from countries far away, and the sunken garden (which sadly was removed in 1972) provided a tranquil setting for the graceful elegance of the buildings around the Square and several of the later generations of George Square staff and girls were very privileged to be able to enjoy their lunchtime recreation in such surroundings. Looking out from any window on the south side of the school building afforded wonderful views especially in the early morning sun, and girls (and staff) could not be blamed for the odd bit of day-dreaming.

Not every pupil appreciated the splendour of the gardens. Such was the lunchtime rigmarole one had to go through to get there that it put the less hardy individual off. The compulsory change of shoes was an inconvenience to say the least as was the donning of gabardine raincoats, their unworkable material belts and maroon berets. After this it was necessary to line up so that the duty mistress could check numbers before she escorted the procession from the nether regions

of the Court up the steps to street level and to the appropriate kerbside. There, under the watchful eye of the Headmistress whose study window was right beside this crossing point, she acted as a lollipop lady (a very dignified one, of course) and ensured that no girl escaped from any one of the three gates on the east, south and west sides (too dangerous in case you encountered a university student).

By the time all this routine was complete it was time to come back and therefore there were some who decided to cut their losses and make up all sorts of excuses to remain inside. They didn't usually work but it was always worth a try.

The Gardens also boasted beautiful lawns on which it was a joy to play all sorts of games. Sadly, there came a day when ball games were forbidden by the school authorities on the ground that they were not being played in a lady-like manner!

In the summertime there were occasions where an adventurous member of staff would conduct a class outside but this was frowned upon in some quarters and the practice was soon discontinued much to the annoyance of the girls who saw outdoor classes as a real treat.

George Square Gardens.

GEORGE WATSON'S LADIES' COLLEGE.   Age 9.

Standard of Work to be reached for Entrance to Form 3 Junior.

1. Arithmetic   Multiplication tables 2 to 12.
                  Money table.
                  Addition, subtraction, multiplication by 2 figures
                      and long division.
                  Addition, subtraction, multiplication by 1 figure
                      and short division of money.

2. English   Ability to read fluently and give a lucid account
                      of passage read.
                  Ability to write clear simple sentences.
                  Memorising of poetry.
                  Spelling.
                              During 3 Junior.
              Analysis of Simple sentences
              Recognition of Parts of Speech.

Aged 9 standards of work requirements.

St Alban's Road in the Later Years

Work

The Nursery Department at St Alban's Road catered for around 20 girls in the pre-school age group and was situated in rooms to the west side of the building at No 58. It was a large and bright room and was well equipped, providing the children not just with the basics of learning in small groups, but with plenty opportunity for constructive playtime. Favourite activities of the day were often at break time when the children might be allowed to play in the small sandpit or ride the old-fashioned rocking horse or don their overalls for some painting. The Nursery was a much-loved part of St Alban's Road and was often the first point of contact because of its proximity to the front entrance and the fact that many future Primary pupils sat their entrance test in this room.

At the end of the session, the 20 or so Nursery pupils would be joined by another 30–35 pupils to form two Elementary classes and these classes would remain roughly the same until the end of the fifth year of Primary School when a further intake would occur and which allowed for a third class in the year group.

Life at St Alban's Road was both purposeful and disciplined. The weekly timetable was spelt out in precise detail, the lessons were subject based and the set books

Class D, 1965, which includes two GWC staff, Liz Smith and Sally Marshall – 1st and 2nd from the right respectively.

(which always had to be covered in brown paper!) were strictly adhered to with substantial punishments for girls who forgot any of them. Daily lesson diaries had to be kept by staff and they had to hand in their lesson notes from time to time; nor was there much latitude for staff or pupils who wanted to branch out into other activities that might be considered a bit non-conformist such as drawing interconnecting chalk circles on the floor to represent Venn diagrams!

Nonetheless, the teaching was extremely sound and there were plenty opportunities for practical activities too. Each class grew bulbs and kept tadpoles, performed little plays that would be presented to other class groups and, from time to time, there would be trips out to the castle or Holyrood or visits from guests who came to speak about a special hobby or outside interest. The Lower Junior School was very fortunate to have the services of other specialist staff from the PE, Music, Art and Domestic Science Departments and there was always the annual visit of the Junior Choir to the Assembly Rooms to compete in the Edinburgh Schools' Festival Competition.

Playtime

All sorts of games were played at school intervals at St Alban's Road. During mid morning there was a short playground interval of 20 minutes, although this could not be enjoyed until the compulsory daily intake of school milk, often revoltingly tepid in temperature because it had been sitting next to a radiator, was complete. Then, at lunchtime, there was the extended interval of an hour which contained time for both school lunch and the playground. School lunches were an institution and again playground activities could not begin in earnest until they were over, made much more of a problem because pupils were not permitted to leave one scrap of food on their plates unless their were extenuating circumstances (which there never were!). Such was the concern about getting value for money from the termly dinner cheques which, in the last session at George Square, were the princely sum of £6.12.

In the Elementary Department there was a wonderful array of swings and climbing frames and plenty space in which to play. In the Lower Junior School there were numerous skipping games (mothers must have wondered where their washing lines went), British bulldog competitions (no hint of political correctness), superball matches (small marble-like bouncy balls that had a habit of clearing every garden wall in sight) and 'elastics' – a game that consisted of knotting together lots of elastic bands that would then be placed around one team's ankles. The rules were somewhat vague but it didn't matter too much as the interval seemed to be over before one team was *"strung up"*.

Ball games could only take place if a gym mistress was present. This was because the girls, if left to their own devices, could not be trusted to keep the ball out of the famous cabbage patch (which seemed to produce nothing other than a wonderful array of caterpillars) or the gardens of the surrounding residents. The plethora of mini footballs that were given away at petrol stations after England's World Cup victory in 1966 had no place in St Alban's Road as they did in all the other playgrounds around the country but perhaps there were good reasons. With the existence of Miss Clark Wilson's camel whip it wasn't worth finding out!

Sports Days at St Alban's Road field were regarded by the Preparatory and Lower Junior girls as mini Olympic Games. There were endless rehearsals for the races although they weren't really necessary since the same girls won every time. These races included a flat race, an obstacle race, a sack race, a three-legged race (these nearly always ended in tears whichever way you choose to pronounce the word) and an egg and spoon race for which tennis balls were wisely substituted for real eggs.

The 80 yards running track was carefully marked out for weeks in advance and so every available free moment of lunchtime was taken up with practising the various skills. Many a tie and summer dress belt came to grief as they were used for makeshift three-legged bindings and many a parent must have cursed the grass stains and skin burns which went hand in hand with sack racing.

When the big day came, it was usually wet, and so there were frantic discussions with the janitor and the groundsman about the likely forecast and whether or not there should be the dreaded postponement. Eventually the races would take place with much screaming and shouting from the sidelines and with parents running up and down trying to operate cine-cameras to capture the golden moments on film. Pride of place went to all those who managed to secure a chestful of red badges by being first in as many races as possible. Blues and yellows counted too but it was the red ones that mattered most and which would later find their way onto blazer lapels for the rest of term.

Little People's Reflections on Life at St Alban's Road:
On work: "I went to eluclooshin klasis yesterday and I had breefing ecsirsis." *S Rae, Class D, 1968/9*

On play: "On Christmas when my Mummy and Daddy opend the presints that I had made at school thia wer dlitd". *C Reid, Primary 2, 1968/9*

On visits: "I sow the Douk of Ednbarar and he was in a blak and whuyt soot." *J Stewart, Class D, 1965/6*

On the way to school: "Our car brock down and Daddy came out and his pjamas wer shoing." *L Stewart, Class A, 1967/8*

Jane Gault and Jane Inch cross the winning line in the Lower Junior School Sports, 4 July 1959.

Pamella Beveridge in the obstacle race at St Alban's Road Sports Day, 1960.

Alexander Thomson FEIS
Headmaster 1871–1902

Alexander Thomson was born on 15 October 1831 in Cupar in Fife but he spent most of his own schooldays near Duns before moving to Edinburgh to train as a teacher at Moray House. Between 1853 and 1864 he held a Tutorship, an appointment at Dr Guthrie's Ragged School and thereafter he occupied various posts in some of Edinburgh's small private schools.

In 1864 he decided to set up his own private school in Melville House, George Square, which he ran very successfully before being approached by the Edinburgh Merchant Company to run their new school for young ladies. Thus Alexander Thomson was introduced to the school over which for so long a period he was to preside and which became so much part of his life.

Apart from studying a wide range in the curriculum, he was keen that his girls *"learnt to be useful, that the spirit of independence should be imparted and the habit of preserving effort should be acquired."* He strove to educate by principle, by virtue and by moral worth and he was determined to lead by example, never failing to consult his staff or seek the measures that would unify the school community.

Alexander Thomson's own teaching within his school and at his assemblies was embodied within the Scriptures and especially within the passages of the Old Testament which extol the virtues of the joys of living a Christian life. In this, he was compared by some of his fellow heads to Dr Arnold of Rugby, whose preaching at the great English public school was to lay the foundations of a new educational philosophy that spread across the land in the second half of the nineteenth century.

A tall, dignified figure with white beard and moustache, Alexander Thomson was a frequent visitor to the classrooms of his colleagues, not only to keep a watchful eye on their teaching abilities but also to seek a better acquaintance with all his pupils. Former pupils report that he knew them all by name and that he would often spend time chatting to them during breaks and lunchtimes. He was always interested in them as human beings rather than just as pupils at his school.

There is no doubt that he was held in the highest regard by his pupils and his colleagues and there is no doubt that his qualities were much to do with the increasing demand for places at the school. He oversaw several extensions to the buildings mainly on the east side of Melville House and he was instrumental in developing new interests within the classroom and in extra-curricular activities. Education was in a period of robust change in the last decade of the nineteenth Century and Thomson was not going to let George Watson's Ladies' College stand still.

Perhaps his greatest legacy was the George Square Former Pupils' Club which was instituted at his jubilee celebrations in 1897 *(see chapter 3.7)* and there is no doubt that he continued to take enormous pleasure in visiting the school after he retired in 1902 particularly during his frequent visits to the Elementary Department.

When war came Alexander Thomson continued his drills with the High Constables of Edinburgh which he had been doing for the preceding 41 years and he unselfishly offered his assistance to Charlotte Ainslie and her pupils as they prepared their parcels to be sent to the war effort.

Alexander Thomson died in the spring of 1916 as the result of a road accident and on 9 November 1918 his memorial tablet, made out of oak and bearing the arms of both the school and Mr Thomson himself, was unveiled on the west wall of the Gallery, not far from where Mr Thomson's study had been. It read *"As an educationist he rendered great service to this city: as a man he won the affection and gratitude of many generations of pupils."* It was a happy coincidence that this occasion took place on the 21st birthday of the Former Pupils' Club, the institution for which all George Square pupils would be eternally grateful to Alexander Thomson.

Alexander Thomson.

He strove to educate by principle, by virtue and by moral worth and he was determined to lead by example.

Charlotte E Ainslie OBE, BA, LLD
Headmistress, 1902–26

In her valediction Charlotte Ainslie said *"In one respect the School will know no change. It will call forth in those who work within its walls loyalty and affection which time and distance will be powerless to touch."*

If Charlotte Ainslie was the creator of 'George Square' she was also the Head (for she was always called that and not Headmistress) whose life and work epitomised these words and who did more than anyone to foster the common tie that bound her pupils and former pupils together both in Edinburgh and in lands afar. She was not only a celebrated Head but a distinguished academic and a highly respected member of the Edinburgh establishment.

Born in Edinburgh in 1863, Charlotte Ainslie entered Mr Thomson's George Watson's College Schools for Young Ladies in Session 1873/4 and left as Dux in 1880. Having left school already an accomplished linguist, she graduated from St Andrews University before embarking on studies abroad in France, Germany and Switzerland, before being appointed Head of Modern Languages at Dunheved College, Launceston, Cornwall.

Before returning to George Square, she was awarded a scholarship by the Reid Trustees following her outstanding success in the Matriculation Examination of the University of London and she won the Gilchrist Scholarship bestowed on the best candidate in the year, something that precipitated an invitation to lecture at the Cambridge Training College in Education and Psychology.

If the Merchant Company already knew the wisdom of their choice of Head to succeed Alexander Thomson there was both suspense and apprehension amongst the pupils and staff as to what the new Head might be like, especially as they were apprehensive about losing the much-loved Mr Thomson. They were not to be disappointed. Described as a goddess by a pupil who attended Miss Ainslie's very first assembly, the school stood in awe of this graceful and dignified lady whose very presence was sufficient to command respect and

Charlotte E Ainslie.

self-discipline. She was a passionate believer in womanhood and all that it could accomplish through a sense of purpose in life even in the difficult times of the First World War (recounted in Chapter 2).

Her first thought was for the welfare and promotion of her pupils no matter whether they were brilliant, average or weak, and there would be only words of encouragement for those who could not or chose not to go to university. Her sensitivity and her generosity of spirit as well as her pawky sense of humour were greatly admired traits and much appreciated by those pupils who found themselves in genuine difficulty. She could also teach any class on any subject and frequently entered a class to find out what subject was being discussed. As a linguist she was fluent in French and German, she was well read in History and Music, and she had a deep love of literature which was evident in a series of lectures she delivered in 1920 on Dante's 'Purgatorio'.

But for those who offended the good name of George Square there was a firm hand of discipline. Woe betide any girl who was sent to the Tiled Hall should Miss Ainslie happen to find her there. A cold terrifying reprimand would be issued, sometimes along with more severe punishment, and the girl would be left in no doubt that she was the source of considerable disappointment as well as displeasure.

It was some time before Charlotte Ainslie admitted to being the author of the School Hymn *(see chapter 3.5)* which continues to this day to inspire generations of Watson's pupils, both boys and girls, and which speaks volumes about the values through which Miss Ainslie sought to educate her pupils.

Over the course of 24 years, Miss Ainslie oversaw fundamental change within the curriculum and within the buildings at George Square. Never afraid to confront difficult choices and respond to new educational practices, Miss Ainslie's calm dignity reflected her courage and inward strength and provided her with an unfailing ability to respond to every crisis. In George Square Miss Ainslie believed in the power of absolute value. Its ethos was sacred to her and so with all sincerity she could point to the school as an inspiration to work and service, as a source of pride and as the focus for Christian values.

The University of Edinburgh conferred a Doctorate of Laws on Charlotte Ainslie in 1926, the year she retired and in 1929 she received an OBE for services to education. They were richly deserved and no-one could doubt the pleasure she received from both. Yet they meant little when compared to the legacy of George Square and all that it meant to its pupils and staff. Charlotte Ainslie was the outstanding head of her generation but she was also a remarkable woman on whose heart is for ever etched the words *"Ex Corde Caritas"*.

Charlotte Ainslie… did more than anyone to foster the common tie that bound her pupils and former pupils together.

Catherine C Robertson MA
Headmistress, 1926–45

Miss Robertson, or 'CC' as she was known to many people, was born in Perth in 1886 and it was at Perth Academy where she was heavily influenced by the great English scholar DB Nicholson. To him, she claimed, she owed a considerable debt not only for inspiring her in his subject and the arts, but also in learning the skills required for successful classroom teaching. It was also at home in Perthshire where she first developed a love of hill-walking.

From Perth, Miss Robertson went to the Universities of Edinburgh and Oxford and thereafter to spend time in Grenoble from where she made several excursions into the Savoy Alps and the medieval villages of southern France. She also had a short period in the USA following an award she won with the English Speaking Union.

Before becoming Headmistress at George Square, Miss Robertson taught at Madras College, Rothesay Academy, Fraserburgh Academy, Daniel Stewart's College and Edinburgh Ladies' College.

If the image of headmistresses in 1926 was remote and austere, Miss Robertson was anything but. Her relatively youthful elegance and assured manner were combined with unflagging energy, a delightful wit and compassionate understanding of human nature. She had a wide circle of friends which reflected her entertaining conversation and her shrewd observance of the contemporary scene. In her pupils she inspired an automatic loyalty and sense of responsibility because she led by example.

She refused to become rigid and doctrinaire. Her penetrating intuitive insight into workings of the minds of young children meant she could easily dispense with the 'isms' and 'ologies' and this allowed her to remain fully wedded to what was good practice rather than fashionable theory.

It was not easy to take on a headship at a time when so much had to change. Nationally, there was great uncertainty. The economic crisis of the early 1930s was followed by the uneasy years which led to war in 1939 and in education she was faced

Catherine C Robertson.

with new demands on the curriculum which necessitated changes to the teaching structure of the school, the creation of a more formal Sixth Form and the development of new facilities including many in the extra-curricular field. Miss Robertson was instrumental in planning the move from Falconhall to Liberton, perhaps additionally inspired by her own interest in hockey, she set up the first school camp at Cupar, the first Girls' Training Corps and she used to take the Sixth Form on hill-walking trips across the Pentland Hills before treating them all to supper afterwards. She was also responsible for much of the thinking that went into St Alban's Road, the development which probably brought her the greatest degree of personal satisfaction in all her time at George Square.

Miss Robertson was always keen to see the school as a whole and it was for this reason that she was an enthusiastic and regular supporter of the Women Watsonians' Club, making trips to the various branches as often as she could even at times when war-time restrictions made it difficult. She recognised the immense importance of the former pupil community and she was always anxious that they should be able to return to school whenever they wished.

One former pupil, Evelyn Haselgrove, said that to talk with Miss Robertson was an education in itself. Her love of life was obvious; she

could hold court on a wide range of different topics and be well informed about them all. She had connections in every corner of the world and she could talk with great eloquence about her childhood spent in Perthshire, her family connections in Edinburgh, her experiences abroad and meeting many veterans of the Great War. She had many hobbies, she enjoyed good food and good wine (tastes she had developed from her Professor at Edinburgh University who held one of the best cellars in the city), she was a member of various academic societies and she continued to enjoy her hill-walking. But above all she remained a devoted servant of her school and all that it stood for.

Her retirement in 1945 was hastened as a result of damaged eyesight caused by an accident when she was taking part in a war-time fire-fighting exercise. Characteristically, she seldom referred to this incident but it clearly brought her much pain as did her increasing ill-health in the later years of retirement, many of which compelled her to have long periods in hospital.

George Square was immensely fortunate, in the years which bridged the old world and the new, to have a headmistress with the understanding and the empathy to enter into both. She was a remarkable lady whose death at the age of 99 was mourned by Former Pupils all over the world because of the enormous debt of gratitude they owed to 'CC'.

Her love of life was obvious; she could hold court on a wide range of different topics and be well informed about them all.

M Dorothy Nicolson MA
Headmistress, 1945–57

When Miss Muriel Jennings was appointed Headmistress of the Mary Erskine School in 1946 a letter arrived on her desk from an MD Nicolson welcoming her into the fold of Edinburgh headmistresses and issuing an invitation to meet as soon as possible. What Miss Jennings took to be a courteous gesture soon became the foundation for a very firm friendship and was typical of the warm-hearted woman who became Headmistress of George Square at the end of the Second World War.

When Dorothy Nicolson was appointed Headmistress from a talented field of applicants there was great delight in Watsonian circles that the important post had been awarded to one of its former pupils. Her early connection with the school was a result of the fact that her father was pastor of the old Bristo Place Baptist Church just round the corner from George Square. She attended the 'local school' for a period of 12 years making her mark academically but never wanting too much of the limelight.

Following school, she went to Edinburgh University where she graduated MA with Honours in French and Latin and it was during this time that she spent several months in the French city of Nîmes where she claimed to have acquired her deep love of its classical culture. After graduating Miss Nicolson received her professional training at St George's Training College in Edinburgh and thereafter gained a wide experience of teaching in Carlisle, Aberdeen and Bath before becoming Headmistress of Wigan High School for Girls.

Undoubtedly a woman of great integrity and sincerity, Dorothy Nicolson was an academic whose capacity for clear thinking and hard work made her a highly successful administrator as well as teacher. Her sense of values, founded on tolerance and on her strong faith, made her a sympathetic ear as well as a trusted friend and she was always keen to put the interests of others before those of herself.

M Dorothy Nicolson.

If some might describe her as rather remote, she always knew the importance of human relationships within her school and the need to take her colleagues with her when it came to the implementation of major changes. Respect for tradition had to be tempered by an appreciation of the need for new ideas and she was unafraid to enter uncharted waters in seeking greater freedoms for her senior pupils. It was Miss Nicolson who introduced the new Library at George Square which permitted the Fifth and Sixth Forms to have more time and more space in which to study on their own and it was Miss Nicolson who developed the Lower Primary School at St Alban's Road.

As well as her activities inside George Square Miss Nicolson was a guiding light in the Scottish Headmistresses' Association, being elected President for the period 1953–5. In this role she gained a reputation for sound judgement and wise counsel and for someone who could carry off her duties with dignity, intellectual drive and good humour in equal measure.

It gave Miss Nicolson the greatest pleasure to be elected President of the Women Watsonians' Club in their Jubilee year in 1947 and most especially because of the presence at the Annual General Meeting of both her predecessors Charlotte Ainslie and CC Robertson, both of whom, in her judgement, were the reason for the strength of the former pupil network. In her address she acknowledged the unique family ties that had become the essence of George Square and paid tribute to the warmth of spirit she had encountered throughout her schooldays and from the Watsonian communities she visited across the land.

Her untimely death in 1957, whilst still in office, was a sharp reminder of the fragility of human life and it deeply shocked the school as well as the Edinburgh community. Those present in the Central Hall when the announcement of her death came through still describe the disbelief and emptiness with which the room was filled. Consequently, it was not surprising that a substantial sum of money was raised for the Dorothy Nicolson Memorial Fund from which was purchased a lectern Bible, a bronze statue for the Library, a stone statue for St Alban's Road and the Dorothy Nicolson Memorial Prize.

Each year, the Head Girl of Watson's receives this Prize with pride; a symbol of Miss Nicolson's enormous contribution to the school and its lasting traditions. As pupil, Headmistress and President of The Watsonian Club she gave everything to the service of George Watson's Ladies' College. She did not ask for anything more.

Her sense of values, founded on tolerance and on her strong faith, made her a sympathetic ear as well as a trusted friend.

Hilda Fleming BSc
Headmistress, 1958–74

Hilda Fleming, arrived at George Square in 1958 at a time when the relationship between the Arts and the Sciences was a matter of great educational debate. She was fortunate that her upbringing and intellect provided her with an interest in both and the knowledge of how the two disciplines were interwoven.

She was born on a small rocky promontory, whipped by the winds of the North Sea, under the lee of the grey Abbey Church of St Hilda near Hartlepool, with its ancient pillars and buttresses, which provided a certain beauty against the stark cranes and gantries of the shipyards across the bay and the bleak outline of the Cleveland Hills. Cradled thus, midway between two worlds, Hilda Fleming developed both a deep love of history and literature and a precocious interest in science – and most especially in Physics. She never forgot her roots and the fact that she came from a part of the world where many people did not enjoy privilege or wealth; and it was partly because of this that she wanted to enter the teaching profession.

Having left the Old Hartlepool Grammar School, she went to St Mary's College in the University of Durham from where she graduated with an Honours degree in Physics. Her year of professional training was in London and immediately after this she spent her first few years in Edinburgh teaching at Craigmount School. At the end of the Second World War, during which she returned to Durham, she was appointed Senior Mistress (and later Acting Headmistress) at Howell's School, Denbigh, a girls' boarding school run by the Drapers' Company, but she was not there long before being appointed Headmistress of Bately Girls' Grammar School in Yorkshire.

In deciding to accept the headship at George Square, Hilda Fleming made a very conscious decision to return to a city with which she had fallen in love several years earlier and one in which she rightly believed she would find scope to follow her varied interests and lead others to discover theirs too.

Hilda Fleming.

Resolutely determined, with the occasional touch of what she describes as "*a dose of Yorkshire stubbornness*", Hilda Fleming was sometimes seen by her pupils as a rather daunting figure, not least because of her tall, commanding appearance in black gown and mortar board. Yet underneath, there was a very human personality which was deeply interested in people and the communities in which they found themselves.

Her vision for George Square was one of academic excellence, for science teaching in particular, and the provision of a multi-faceted education that went well beyond the classroom. Like her predecessors she believed that women should be educated citizens as well as scholars but she was also persuaded that there was need for practical training as well as intellectual rigour. Along with her senior colleagues, she had soon embarked on a programme of developing new opportunities for clubs and societies and outdoor education, many of which became available as a result of the Merchant Company's purchase of property at Ardtrostan for an outdoor centre. During this period she was also Chairman of the Scottish Council of the Duke of Edinburgh's Award scheme.

Under her leadership the school resisted the assault of the meretricious. She was always alive to the need for change but never if it meant

compromise or a sacrifice of the values, especially those taught in the Scriptures and in successful academic institutions around the country.

As a member of the Scottish Certificate of Education Examination Board, Hilda Fleming was never afraid to speak her mind even if it provoked some uncomfortable reaction. Forthright she undoubtedly was, but only because she believed she was right and that it was her duty to take difficult decisions when other people might prevaricate. Her devotion to the 'The Square', as she would prefer to call it, was unquestioned, as has been her warm and continuing interest in her former pupils and former colleagues.

Given the changing political, economic and social climate of the 1960s and yet more pressures from the external examination bodies, Hilda Fleming had the wisdom and foresight to see the need for change if the fruits of George Watson's benefaction were to continue to flourish in the years ahead. The vision that had led her in her first few months in the job to make some important changes to the timetable now led her in 1964 to the most enlightened suggestion of her professional career.

When pressure had been applied by the University of Edinburgh regarding the future of George Square, the response from several officials within the Merchant Company was to consider a new site for the girls' school, including the possibility of building on the Craiglockhart site which adjoined Myreside. But for Hilda Fleming there was a much better and more radical solution which entailed the proposal for a fully co-educational merger of the two George Watson schools on the existing site at Colinton Road.

There were many who did not approve. Indeed there were some who thought that this was a betrayal of the good name of George Square. But if they had any doubts they need only look at what has happened since to understand that Hilda Fleming was right. For this and much else, she deserves the gratitude of Watsonians everywhere.

The Women Watsonians' Club Badge.

The George Square Former Pupils' Club 1897–1924; The Women Watsonians' Club, 1924–79

In the 18 December 1897 issue of *The Edinburgh Evening Dispatch* there appeared an article about the Jubilee of a distinguished Edinburgh Headmaster who was approaching the celebration of 50 years as a schoolmaster. In a small insignificant sentence in minute text at the bottom of the page it states:

"It was afterwards resolved to form a former pupils' club in connection with the College, which it is proposed should have an annual reunion."

And so, with a celebration of the service given by the only Headmaster of GWLC (1871–1902), Alexander Thomson's proposals to host a party and a dance to thank all those with whom he had worked throughout his career provided the foundation for the George Square Former Pupils' Club.

Throughout the first part of the evening, which was hosted in Room 23 (later altered to Room 25), there was a programme of vocal and instrumental music and the presentation of a silver tea service and silver ink stand from the former pupils, and a writing-table and book stand as a memento from the staff. Following a speech by the Chairman of Governors, Mr Thomson was asked what he would most like to be his legacy: *"the reunion of former pupils,"* he said without a moment's hesitation.

The 213 'Old Girls' who enrolled in Mr Thomson's Club intended meeting at least once every year inside their old school and it was not long before the discussion of a more formal former pupil structure was under way. It included two Honorary Presidents (Mr Thomson and Miss Wilson), 15 Honorary Members, a President (Miss Janet Haig), an Honorary Secretary (Dr Frances Melville), and an Honorary Treasurer (Miss Rhua Thomson who was Mr Thomson's daughter). A constitution was drawn up, the committee met five times a year and an annual written report was presented to each member. The first constitution stated that there should be at least two meetings a year for ordinary members. The first subscription was set at 2s 6d (country members 1s).

By 1910, when Charlotte Ainslie sought the annual report from the former pupil body for the first number of *The George Square Chronicle* there were over 500 members enrolled and new committees had formed. The main events of the year were always the reunions at School at which the President welcomed members before both she and Miss Ainslie reported on school and club events. However, the most eagerly awaited part of the evening was the entertainment, usually a mixture of songs and recitals and some dance routines. After this there were refreshments and a chance to catch up with old friends. The evenings ended with more dancing and singing and general merriment.

The Club never looked back. In March 1913 some members formed a music club with the intention of organising several recitals and lectures during the year (one of which, on the subject of early musical training, was given by Miss Ainslie's sister). At this time, too, discussion took place about the formation of the first English branch and about how Former Pupils could become involved in social and charitable work in their home city, building on the ethos of the Provident Fund that had been set up in 1901. At the beginning of the Great War, a number of Edinburgh based Former Pupils responded to this call and were regularly helping disadvantaged families either in the home or providing financial assistance. The scheme was organised by Miss M Alexander who ran operations from her house at 5 McLaren Road.

At this stage, the annual subscription for Edinburgh dwellers was 3s, for country dwellers 1s, and the annual fee for Life Members was £1. While the annual reports from the respective Presidents of the time, (who in 1914 included Mr Thomson's daughter Rhua), tended to concentrate

OFFICE-BEARERS, 1897–98.

Hon. Presidents.
ALEXANDER THOMSON, ESQ.
MISS ALICE GRANT WILSON.

President.
MISS JANET HAIG, L.L.A.

Hon. Secretary.
MISS FRANCES H. MELVILLE, M.A., 10 Fettes Row.

Hon. Treasurer.
MISS RHUA THOMSON, 40B George Square.

Committee.
Mrs CUNNINGHAM (Jean Craigie).
Miss DRUMMOND, M.A.
Miss KATE LOCKHART.
Miss CHARLOTTE LOWNIE.
Mrs MACKINTOSH [Jessie D. Dobie].
Miss BESSIE MILLER.
Miss JESSIE MUIR, M.A.
Miss AGNES NAPIER.
Miss MARION RIDPATH.
Miss MABEL ROSS.
Miss ROSA STOLTZ, M.A.
Miss ROBINA M. SMITH [elected by Staff].

Office Bearers, 1897/8.

Name.
The Club shall be known as the "George Square former Pupils' Club".

Object
The Object of the George Square Former Pupils' Club shall be to unite in a common bond all former pupils of George Watson's Ladies' College.

Membership
All former pupils of George Watson's Ladies' College over sixteen years of age shall be eligible for membership of the club. Members of the College Staff, present or past, although not former pupils of the College, shall be eligible for membership.

The first constitution for the George Square Former Pupils' Club.

on providing very detailed accounts of the Club's events, right down to what had been consumed for afternoon tea, there were some encouraging words for those in the far-flung corners of the world who wanted to assist the Former Pupil cause. Small branches appeared in the USA, Canada, India and China although in the latter two cases they lasted only a few years because of the exigencies of war. There was quite clearly the desire to spread *Ex Corde Caritas* to all continents and the recognition, perhaps inspired by Mr Thomson himself, that George Watson's Ladies' College was more than just a school.

If there were good intentions to continue the various branches and sections as normal, there is no doubt that the Great War played a major part in shaping the activities of the Club from 1914 throughout the 1920s. The usual events had to be curtailed and many of the reports from the Former Pupil Club concentrated instead on information about the war effort and how former pupils could help.

As a result of Lord Derby's Recruiting Scheme, a plea was made to Former Pupils in 1915 that *"well-educated women may be needed in banks, offices and warehouses"*, and that they should alert Miss Ainslie if they were willing to assist. A Shilling Fund was also established as a form of war relief assistance, partly to ensure that the George Square Bed in Royaumont Hospital could be maintained (this cost £50 per year) but also to provide much-needed help for the sick and wounded at the front line. A large number of Former Pupils contributed and many also took part in efforts to send food and clothes parcels through to the front line troops.

But by far the biggest event was the fête held on 28 June 1919. This occasion was the Former Pupils' Club's opportunity to donate substantial funds to the Watsonian Memorial Fund which had been set up to assist families of Watsonians who had lost their lives (one in six of all those from GWC who had responded to the call to serve their country). The event was opened by Watson's youngest winner of the Victoria Cross, Lieutenant DL MacIntyre, at 2.30pm which was the time coinciding with the time of the

signing of the Treaty of Versailles. After this, there were moving speeches from the Headmaster of the boys' school, Mr Alison, and from the Vice Convenor Mr Malcolm Smith. There were all sorts of stalls and games, plenty entertainment and refreshments and the day ended with £310 raised for the Fund.

By the time of the Silver Jubilee in 1922 the Club was well established. The London Branch was also formed during this year following discussion at a small gathering of former pupils which had been organised by Mrs Chetwode Crawley (Nessa Luke). The idea appeared to have immediate appeal; no fewer than 70 members, including Dame Rebecca West turned up to the 2nd AGM of the London Club held in Kensington Gardens Kiosk. The Club held its first dinner in 1931 shortly after which discussions began with regard to the design and purchase of the London President's Badge.

While meetings continued during the war years thanks to the dedicated work of the Secretary, Miss Margaret Carter, it was after 1946 when the Club enjoyed its heyday. Apart from the formal annual dinner, often held in the Grosvenor Hotel and attended by a Guest Speaker, there were at least three other social events each year. Many members also took part in organised outings to places of interest such as the Houses of Parliament, Hatfield House and Harrow School and the events organised by the Former Pupils of the other Merchant Company schools.

The London Women Watsonians celebrated their Golden Jubilee in October 1972 with a luncheon at the Russell Hotel which was attended by virtually the entire Club, the Headmistress, the Vice Convenor and the Master of the Merchant Company. It was agreed that the highlight of the occasion was the special presentation of a cake confection in the form of the Club's badge, particularly as it had been prepared by a Former Pupil of the Royal High School!

The Glasgow branch first met in December 1925 and boasted 66 members by 1927, and in 1928 a dozen former pupils living in Vancouver (two of whom attended Mr Thomson's school on its first day)

The London Women Watsonians' Club President's Badge was damaged in a fire which started in a factory as a result of an air raid in 1940. This was the factory where the then London President, Miss Hay, was working in the war effort and where, luckily for the Club, there were strong safes. The Badge "made history but lost its beauty a bit. The silver was a bit tarnished, the enamel slightly cracked and the maroon ribbon, though neither burnt nor charred and as strong as ever, turned black, something said to be the result of the heat and some adjacent copper coins in the safe." The Badge was successfully restored a year later.

met to start the first overseas branch. This was as a result of the friendship between Agnes Maitland and Dorothy Jack, who had met in Vancouver General Hospital in 1916 whilst on a nurses' training course.

In 1924 a major change took place in the Edinburgh-based Club. After much discussion at the AGM and a subsequent vote, the name was changed to the Women Watsonians' Club and the President, Mrs Ritchie, also reported that she had received various suggestions from members about how the Club could extend its activities. In particular there had been discussions about provision for sporting pursuits via a Women Watsonians' Athletic Club, greater support for charitable causes and the possibility of Club colours being designed by school outfitters Aitken & Niven.

It is also interesting to note at this stage that the annual reports of the Club no longer concentrated on the mundane reports of minutes and events but began to include many more personal contributions from Former Pupils, such as Mary Stewart's article about her experiences watching the chaotic ending to the famous and controversial tennis match between Suzanne Lenglen and Helen Wills in the French Open in Cannes in 1926 when the umpire made the wrong decision on match point! There was also considerable effort made to report on the diversity of achievement within the Former Pupil community and to encourage greater links between Former Pupils and pupils at the School.

Perhaps the most important social event of this decade was the dinner held in Merchants' Hall on 10 May 1929 in honour of Charlotte Ainslie on the occasion of her investiture as Officer of Order of the British Empire. Glowing tributes were paid by several speakers to the woman who had been the first head of a large Scottish School, a leading academic and a very loyal servant to both the George Square Former Pupils' Club and the Women Watsonians' Club. In her time as Headmistress she had clearly meant a huge amount to the Club, not least because she was a Woman Watsonian herself, but also because of the high regard in which she was held by the educational establishment.

By 1931 Club membership had risen to 1262. No fewer than 81 new members joined that year and therefore perhaps it is no surprise that the first Women Watsonians' Club Dance was such a huge success. Indeed, the Club prospered greatly in the 1930s and 1940s with a pleasing growth in the number of younger Former Pupils joining straight from school. A Junior London Branch was formed in 1936 and was only open to anyone who had been a Former Pupil of 15 years or less.

The first Women Watsonians' Dinner was held on 3 November 1934 at Merchants' Hall. Dr Ainslie proposed the Toast to the School and it is interesting to note that her themes included what she described as *"the growing bonds of trust between teachers and pupils"*, and the unwelcome diversions which confronted the teaching profession such as *"the complexities talked about by "psycho-*

The OBE decoration awarded to Charlotte Ainslie.

The Women Watsonians' Club Dance, 1935.

Jubilee Dinner, 1947.

analysts and doctors who try to relate diet and discipline".

Women Watsonian Dinners became important events in the Edinburgh social calendar. Held in either Merchants' Hall or one of the larger Edinburgh hotels, often the Roxburghe or North British, they numbered anywhere between 150 and 300 guests and were attended by officials from the Merchant Company as well as staff at the School. They were very formal occasions (white tie and tails for the gentlemen and long evening dresses for the ladies) and were seen as an important focus for the Club's activities both at home and abroad. In 1936 two places were even reserved for journalists of the day, free of charge!

In 1947 the Club held its Jubilee celebrations which consisted of various events in school, a reunion reception and the annual dinner. The day began with an exhibition of archive material and related school artefacts, one of which was the diary of the legendary Headmistress of the North London Collegiate School, Miss Frances Mary Buss, which had been lent to the School for the special occasion. Thereafter there were entertainments and speeches by several dignitaries including Dr Frances Melville, first Secretary of the Women Watsonians' Club. Special silver editions of the Club Badge were presented to 15 Past Presidents and the occasion ended with the singing of the School Hymn.

In a report of the Jubilee, a founder member recounts the success of the Club over the 50 years: *"The Club has sung the fame of distinguished pupils, welcomed home adventurers and wanderers from all parts of the earth, kept close and bright the link with the beneficent Merchant Company and all its schools, whose representatives have been our guests a so many functions and above all, whose members have glorified in calling themselves George Square girls."*

However, she also sounded a note of caution warning that there was a feeling amongst some members that the Club had never taken itself seriously enough. In particular, there was criticism that the Club had missed opportunities to be a glowing beacon in the field of organised social service and that it had also missed out on some opportunities to raise more money. She warned about what she described as *"the magic inner circle"* which tended to dominate the Club and how, in her opinion, the Club should try to reach out to more people.

Perhaps her concerns were heeded. In the 1950s more events appeared on the calendar. In 1950 a former pupil choir was formed with 26 members and under the conductorship of Dr Langdon, the school's music master. It met every Wednesday in school at 7.15pm and it cost 5s to join. It was also optional to stay on afterwards to attend country dancing classes at 15s for a session's tuition. In 1954 a very successful junior dance was held and once again many of the former pupils became involved with work in local charity organisations and with the Earl Haig Fund.

The Aberdeen branch was formed in 1953 with 17 members and this quickly rose to 33 and, like the sister Clubs in London and Glasgow/West of Scotland, it arranged several outings during the course of the year. It also benefited greatly from the strength of ties within the Aberdeen area with the other Merchant Company schools and the opportunity to take part in several joint events.

The normal calendar of events continued throughout the 1960s and the early 1970s and when George Square closed her doors in 1975 the membership of the Women Watsonians' Club had risen to 1,366. The annual subscription was only 50p and Life Membership cost no more than £3.15 a small price to pay for lasting human friendship and an eager interest in all matters Watsonian. However, while the Merger of the Schools took place in 1974, the Merger of the Clubs did not take place until five years later and only after fairly difficult negotiations within the respective committees of both former pupil clubs. During this five-year period, the Women Watsonians' Club and its branches continued with their traditional programme of events and indeed a new 'branch' was formed in Perth in 1976 following a chance meeting by two Former Pupils, Mrs Heather Anderson and Mrs Jenny Campbell. The Perth Ladies currently have 45 members and they continue to meet on an informal basis three times a year.

There were many in the Women Watsonians' Club who felt aggrieved at the prospect of the merger and sharing their Former Pupils' Club with the men. They were not to be persuaded by the member who pointed out at a meeting in 1974 that the George Square Former Pupils' Club had been started by the first male head of the school and had included several male honorary members who had given 15 years or more of unbroken service to George Square.

Some of their male counterparts felt aggrieved, too, a few suggesting that The Women Watsonians' Club could be tolerated if it became a section of The Watsonian Club! However, after lengthy negotiations it was clear that the diehards on both sides were in the minority. A motion was put to The Women Watsonians' Club and The Watsonian Club at the same time on the same day and the vote in both cases was in favour of amalgamation, even if The Watsonian Club vote took an hour longer! The two Clubs amalgamated on equal terms in October 1979.

Times had moved on, and the success of the present Watsonian Club owes just as much to the values of George Square as it does to those of Lauriston Place, Archibald Place and Colinton Road. Women Watsonians found a common bond everywhere, whether they were present at Mr Thomson's Jubilee celebrations in 1897 or at the final Women Watsonians' Club Dinner in 1979. There are many George Square girls of yesterday who give considerable support to the Watson's pupils of today and who continue in the future to be very active and loyal members of The Watsonian Club.

Dr Margaret Brotherston MB, ChB, DPH, MBE (Miss Merry Smith), Club President 1921/2 and present at almost every AGM from 1901 to 1970! She died aged 94 in 1971.

The Women Watsonians' Club President's Badge presented by Mrs Fallas, President between 1932/3.

Women Watsonians' Club gift of brush, mirror and comb set.

Times had moved on, and the success of the present Watsonian Club owes just as much to the values of George Square as it does to those of Lauriston Place, Archibald Place and Colinton Road.

The Gilbert Archer Competition, Kilspindie Golf Club, 1930s.

The Women Watsonians' Golf Club outing to Gifford 2002.
BACK ROW: Gill McNeillage, Joan Henderson, Mabel Montgomery, Pat Morrison
FRONT ROW: Moira Thom, Anne Buchan, Marjory Curtis, Maggie Pringle,
Moira Murray.

The 75th anniversary dinner of the Women Watsonians' Golf Cub, 2005.

Women Watsonians' Golf Club

The Women Watsonians' Golf Club was established in 1930 when Miss Alice C Wilson was in the Chair as President of the Women Watsonians' Athletic Club. Thirty-seven members had expressed an interest and so it was decided to form a golf section for which the subscription would be 2s 6d and which would make use of various Edinburgh golf clubs for a programme of outings. The first of these outings was held at Carnwath on 26 April 1930 and three months later the Club played the first of its annual matches against the Merchant Maidens' Golf Club which Women Watsonians' won by three matches to none. A little later that summer saw the first match between Watsonian Club and Women Watsonian Club pairings and Daniel Stewart's Club and Merchant Maiden pairings which the former pairings won 5 in 3. After 1931 this annual match, which is still played today, became known as the Gilbert Archer Cup.

During wartime, activities were suspended but the Club resumed its fixture card in 1946 with four annual outings and two matches. There was also a hole in hole competition for which the Kay Maxwell Trophy was awarded. The Mary Robinson Spoon was awarded to the person with the best two cards over the season.

The Women Watsonians' Golf Club still exists today and has just celebrated its 75th Anniversary at which a large number of members, past and present, were in attendance.

Each year there are four outings in May, July, August and September and the Club continues to field teams for the annual fixtures against Mary Erskine and the combined Mary Erskine/David Stewart's and Mary Erskine team in the Gilbert Archer Cup. Venues normally include Lundin Links, Auchterarder, Kilspindie, Broomieknowe and Gifford.

The Women Watsonians' Golf Club still exists today.

Women Watsonians' Hockey Club

The Women Watsonians' Hockey Club, established in 1933, was destined to become one of the strongest links in the Former Pupil community. By 1935 it was fielding three XIs (the 3rd XI included some Mary Erskine former pupils) and it could boast some of the finest players in the country including Dr Nora Campbell who was Captain of the Scottish Women's XI in 1936 and the first Woman Watsonian to represent her country (*see page 255*). Dorothy Middleton won 7 caps between 1936 and 1938 and Molly Anderson won 22 caps between 1937 and 1949 whilst playing for Ayr Ladies' Hockey Club.

Originally allowed the use of a pitch at Colinton Road, the hockey club moved to Liberton in 1939, a move greatly appreciated by the players because the changing facilities within the new clubhouse were much preferable to Room 7 in the boys' school and because the Club could now provide its own teas after each match.

The Club went from strength to strength even fending off the controversy of being the first club to introduce divided skirts and dispense with the old-fashioned tunics. At a special meeting Club members initially deemed the new uniform too expensive on the grounds that it would cost 27s 3d to purchase but they were soon swayed by the fact that one member spoke out strongly about the old tunics *"which inhibited general comfort and ease of movement"*.

The Club's heyday was perhaps the late 1950s when it provided four members of the Scottish Women's XI, Jean Calder, Joan Hay, Wendy Pink and Doreen Smith (Dorothy Brown was in the Scottish Reserves), and when the team won several domestic competitions. In 1960, following the Scottish Women's Hockey Association Diamond Jubilee Tournament, the Women Watsonians' 1st XI was considered the best side in Scotland on account of the fact that it was the only undefeated home side out of 16 playing against other British and European club sides. The team toured to Orkney, Holland, the Isle of Man and Spain and in 1962 Isobel Jarvis

Date.	1st XI.	2nd XI.
1933		
Oct. 7.	*Edinburgh Western.	Boroughmuir F.P.
„ 14.	*Gillespie's F.P.	
„ 21.	*Dunfermline.	Dunfermline.
„ 28.	East Seven-a-sides.	East Seven-a-sides.
Nov. 4.	*Trinity.	Edinburgh Western.
„ 11.	*Edin. College Dom. Science.	
„ 18.		Edinburgh.
„ 25.	*Liberton.	G.W.L.C. (a.m.).
Dec. 2.	*Park School (a.m.).	*Liberton.
„ 9.	*G.W.L.C. (a.m.).	Edinburgh Women's A.C.
„ 16.	*Broughty Ferry G.C.	Gillespie's F.P.
„ 23.	*Merchant Maiden.	
„ 26.	Perth Academy F.P.	
1934		
Jan. 6.	Edinburgh.	*Dunfermline.
„ 13.	*Boroughmuir F.P.	Glasgow University 3rd.
„ 20.	Edinburgh Western.	*Edinburgh Western.
„ 27.	*Merchant Maiden.	East Lothian 1st.
Feb. 3.		St Andrews University (a.m.).
„ 10.	*Perth Academy F.P.	*Boroughmuir F.P.
„ 17.	Dunfermline.	*Edinburgh.
„ 24.	*Edinburgh Gymnasts (a.m.).	Liberton.
Mar. 3.	*G.W.L.C. (a.m.).	*G.W.L.C. (a.m.).
„ 10.	Liberton.	*East Lothian 1st.
„ 17.	Edin. College Dom. Science.	*Edinburgh University.
„ 24.	Aberdeen (a.m.).	
„ 31.	Edinburgh Gymnasts.	*Edinburgh Women's A.C.
Apr. 7.		*Merchant Maiden.

* Denotes matches played away from home ground.

First Hockey Club fixture list.

A Scottish Touring Team, 1956. Left to Right: 3rd Dorothy Brown, 4th Doreen Smith, 10th Jean Calder.

was also awarded with international honours.

Until the late 1960s the hockey club boasted at least one international player in its ranks and over its history eight members played for their country, another three played for Scottish Reserves, 45 played for the East District and one played for the South District. It also played a major part in providing match officials and office bearers for the SWHA, most notably Miss Jean Calder who gained 25 caps between 1957 and 1965 and who was President of SWHA between 1974 and 1977.

Rather paradoxically, it was this success that led, in part, to decline.

Younger players found it very difficult to get a place in a long-established and successful team and drifted off to clubs elsewhere. It was also the time when far more youngsters went away to university and college and so there were fewer members for the Club to draw on for lower teams. It became increasingly difficult for the Club to field a 2nd XI and as it was a similar story at Mary Erskine the decision was taken in 1972 to merge the Women Watsonians' Hockey Club with the Merchant Maiden Hockey Club and form the new Merchant Ladies' Hockey Club. The merger, which was born out of realpolitik, was never really popular with either group of former pupils and there was much rejoicing in 1994 when the Clubs split once again and the Watsonian section was renamed Watsonian Ladies' Hockey Club.

There were variously named sports sections throughout the history of the club and while hockey and golf may have stolen much of the limelight, former George Square girls flourished in other sports too. Brenda Carmichael (at one time the most capped female player in the world) and Irene Rowe won international honours in squash as did Christine Heatly in badminton and Susan Bowie and Kathy Stewart in swimming.

Susan Bowie.

Scottish Women's Squash Team 1976, Stirling University, Home Internationals.
Left to Right: Pat Green, Dorothy McNeil, Brenda Carmichael (Captain), Liz Elgood, Jean Reynolds & Irene Rowe.

Kathy Stewart.

Well-Known Women Watsonians

Frances Melville OBE, MA, BD, LLD (1873–1962)

Dr Frances Melville was one of the first women undergraduates at Edinburgh University from where she graduated with first class honours in Philosophy. She became a member of staff at Cheltenham Ladies' College for a brief period before being appointed Warden of Women Students at St Andrews University. During this time she completed her studies for a degree in Divinity and as such became the first woman to graduate with a BD from a Scottish University. She was appointed Mistress of Queen Margaret College, Glasgow, in 1909, a position unique in Scottish universities, and which she occupied until she retired in 1935, the year she also received the OBE. Glasgow University marked her outstanding achievements in education by conferring on her the honorary degree of LLB, again, the first time a woman had been honoured in this way. Frances Melville was a Founder Member of the George Square Former Pupils' Club and became an Honorary Member of the Women Watsonians' Club.

Mary Grierson OBE, Mus Doc

Mary Grierson was one of the first Former Pupils to gain distinction in the world of music. Known as Mollie Grierson at school she graduated from Edinburgh University as a Bachelor of Music and as an LRAM and then became the understudy to Professor Tovey in his work as conductor

Frances Melville.

Mary Grierson.

Christine Black née Heatly.

Rebecca West (photograph: National Portrait Gallery, London).

with the Reid Orchestra during the period 1902–13, a most unusual appointment for a woman. A highly accomplished pianist, Miss Grierson was an established music tutor in Edinburgh for many years and during this time gained the degree of Doctor of Music. She was the composer of the music for the School Hymn before Dr Ross provided the present setting and was a regular examiner for the Junior School Music Prize. She was Conductor of the Edinburgh Bach Choir, 1928–61, and was responsible for the annual performance of the St Matthew Passion. She was President of the Women Watsonians' Club 1926/7 and in 1953 she gave the Commemoration Day address.

Rebecca West (1892–1983)

Cicely Isabel Fairfield was born on 21 December 1892 and attended George Square between 1904 and 1907 before embarking on a dramatic career at the Academy of Dramatic Art in London. Although she did not complete her studies there she left with the stage name Rebecca West, the name she had taken from the heroine of Ibsen's *Rosmersholm*. Committed to both the Suffragette movement and the Fabian Society, Rebecca West became a journalist and author and became noted for her incisive reviews of the works of HG Wells (with whom she had a son in 1914), TS Eliot, DH Lawrence and Virginia Woolf. Her own works included *The Return of the Soldier* (made into a film in 1982 and produced on the London stage in 1996) and *The Judge*. In the 1930s, Rebecca West focused her writing on the rise of Fascism (*Black Lamb and Grey Falcon*, 2 vols, 1942) and she undertook extensive travel in Europe. In her post-war writings she became famous for her political commentaries, most especially those which dealt with espionage and anti-communist propaganda. Rebecca West was President of the London Women Watsonians' Club 1937/8.

Nora Campbell (1909–96)

Arguably, Nora Campbell was the School's and the Club's most celebrated sportswoman. After an outstanding academic and sporting career at school where she was both Head Girl

Nora Cambell, 1948 (front left).

Martha Kearney, Founder's Day, 2003.

Alison Kinnaird.

and Captain of the 1st XI, as well as winner of a special science prize, Nora Campbell, spent time at university in Germany before returning to pursue a distinguished academic career in Scotland. Following her selection for the Scottish Women's Hockey team in 1931 and her successes in the international fixtures between 1931 and 1935, she became the first Women Watsonian to captain the international team (season 1935–6). She was a talented golfer as well as hockey player and a very loyal and dedicated member of The Women Watsonians' Club. She received 33 caps between 1931 and 1950.

Martha Kearney (1956–)

Martha Kearney has presented *Woman's Hour* on Mondays and Tuesdays since 1998. After School and a Classics degree at Oxford Martha started her media career at LBC/IRN Radio. She worked as a phone operator and a news information researcher, a reporter, a

presenter and a lobby correspondent before a spending a year on *A Week in Politics* for Channel 4. On joining the BBC she worked as a reporter for BBC1's *On the Record* between 1988 and 1994 before going to *Newsnight*. She is now political editor of *Newsnight* and still presents the programme from time to time. Martha was nominated for a BAFTA award for her coverage of the Northern Ireland Peace Process in 1998, and was nominated with Jenni Murray for a Sony Award as News and Talk Broadcaster of the Year in 2000.

Alison Kinnaird MBE (1949–)

Alison Kinnaird is an internationally recognised glass artist as well as clarsach musician. In 2002 she received a Creative Scotland Award which enabled her to create 'Psalmsong', a 3.1 metre long glass installation which was initially on display at the entrance to the Victoria and Albert Museum and which is now on permanent display in the

Scottish Parliament building. The quality of this piece has also led to her winning the Glass Sellers' Award 2004. Using lissajous patterns and light mixed with the inspiration of Gaelic psalms she has combined her passion for music with her skills as a glass artist to create a unique and innovative artwork for which she was awarded the MBE in 1997.

Distinguished Visitors to the Women Watsonians' Club Dinners

Gertrude Herzfeld MB, FRCSEd (portrait by Sir William Hutchison).

Saturday 28 October 1939
Gertrude Herzfeld MB, FRCSEd
(1890–1981)

Gertrude Herzfeld was born and educated in London her parents having emigrated from Austria. After qualifying MBChB in Edinburgh in 1914, she became the first woman House Surgeon to Sir Harold Stiles at the Royal Hospital for Sick Children and the Chalmers Hospital. In 1917 she became a surgeon at the RAMC Cambridge Hospital, Aldershot, and from 1917 to 1919 was senior House Surgeon at Bolton Infirmary. In 1920, she was the first woman to be appointed honorary Assistant Surgeon to the Royal Hospital for Sick Children in Edinburgh and became a Fellow of the Royal College of Surgeons, only the second woman to be admitted. In 1925, following the resignation of Sir John Fraser, she and Norman Dott were together appointed as Surgeons to the Royal Hospital for Sick Children.

She was the first practising woman surgeon in Scotland. In those days, paediatric surgery embraced the whole

range of plastic, orthopaedic, abdominal and neonatal work and included the treatment of burns and trauma. At the same time she undertook a wide range of general and gynaecological surgery at Bruntsfield Hospital.

She helped to found the Edinburgh School of Chiropody and the Edinburgh Orthopaedic Clinic and was medical adviser to the Edinburgh Cripple Aid Society and the Trefoil School for Physically Handicapped Children. She joined the British Medical Association in 1915 and was Chairman of the Edinburgh Division from 1960 to 1962.

Baron Boothby (photograph: National Portrait Gallery, London).

Friday 21 October 1966
Baron Boothby of Buchan and Rattray Head KBE, LLD
(1900–86)

Robert Boothby was born in Edinburgh and was educated at Eton and Oxford. He was the Conservative Member of Parliament for Aberdeenshire and Kincardine East between 1924 and 1950 and then for Aberdeenshire East, 1950–8, when the constituency boundaries were changed. He was Private Parliamentary Secretary to Winston Churchill between 1926 and 1929 and Private Secretary to the Ministry of Food between 1940–1. He was appointed to the Council of United Europe in 1948, was knighted in 1953 and raised to the peerage in 1958. Robert Boothby was a well-known and skilled public affairs commentator on radio and television although his personal life was often troubled with controversy.

PRESENTS OF THE GEORGE SQUARE FORMER PUPILS' CLUB

1897/8	Miss Janet Haig
1898/9	Mrs Cunningham
1899/1900	Miss Kate Lockhart
1900/1	Mrs JS Anderson
1901/2	Miss M Drummond
1902/3	Mrs John Alison
1903/4	Mrs James Buchanan
1904/6	Miss Clara A Fairgrieve
1906/7	Mrs EA Roberts
1907/8	Miss Andrine Burnet
1908/9	Miss Rosa GC Stoltz (Mrs Waugh)
1909/10	Miss Jean K Borland
1910/11	Miss Bessie Robson
1911/12	Mrs Tait
1912/13	Miss Charlotte S Young (Mrs Sinclair)
1913/14	Mrs Mackay Budge
1914/15	Miss Rhua Thomson
1915/16	Mrs H Thomson
1916/17	Miss Joan Drummond (Mrs Thomson)
1917/18	Mrs Gibb
1918/19	Miss Ranolina Stewart
1919/20	Mrs Adams
192021	Mrs Taylor
1921/2	Dr Margaret Brotherston
1922/3	Mrs Ritchie
1923/4	Miss JE MacDonald

PRESIDENTS OF THE WOMEN WATSONIANS' CLUB

1924/5	Miss A Henderson
1925/6	Miss JC Thorburn
1926/7	Miss Mary Grierson
1927/8	Mrs Hagan
1928/9	Mrs Allan
1929/30	Miss M Carrie
1930/1	Mrs Tullo
1931/2	Miss Agnes Shaw
1932/3	Mrs Fallas
1933/4	Miss Margaret Fleming
1934/5	Mrs Martin Hobkirk
1935/6	Mrs Cowper
1936/7	Mrs AB Hyslop
1937/8	Mrs Gill
1938–40	Mrs Jardine
1940–2	Mrs Douglas
1942/3	Mrs Stewart
1943/4	Miss Proudfoot
1944/5	Mrs McCall
1945/6	Mrs Ferguson
1946/7	Miss Anna Scarlett
1947/8	Miss M Dorothy Nicolson
1948/9	Mrs C Curr
1949/50	Mrs B Hall
1950/1	Mrs L Fentiman
1951/2	Miss ASP Gilmour
1952/3	Mrs M Gardner
1953/4	Mrs Vera Carmichael
1954/5	Mrs Margaret E S Matheson
1955/6	Miss Vida Paterson
1956/7	Mrs J Gilchrist
1957–9	Miss Nancy Gordon
1959–1	Dr MSB Langton
1961–3	Mrs E C Malcolm
1963/4	Mrs WS Campbell
1964–6	Mrs AY Hamilton
1966–8	Miss E G Chalmers
1968–71	Mrs Betty Ross
1971–3	Mrs Betty Ewing
1973–5	Mrs Yvonne Foubister
1975–7	Mrs Ida Anderson
1977–9	Mrs Patricia Morrison

Appendix 1

GEORGE WATSON'S LADIES' COLLEGE STAFF 1871–1974

For several decades in the school's history the Merchant Company's records of staff employment dates are incomplete. The following lists provide what information is available; List 1 contains the names of those staff (including visiting staff) whose first date of employment appears on the Merchant Company register, 'Register of Teachers' between sessions 1873 and 1913 (only some retirement dates are available) and List 2 is the most complete list of staff who taught at George Watson's Ladies' College between 1914 and 1974 (a few retirement dates are missing).

NB: the School changed its name to George Watson's College for Ladies in 1877 and to George Watson's Ladies' College in 1890.

LIST 1 (from the Merchant Company's Register of Schoolmasters and Schoolmistresses): staff in alphabetical order of register entry with date of first appointment between 1873 and 1914. Subject(s) taught and leaving dates are given where known.

Miss Elizabeth Adam, Governess, 1878
Miss Alice Aigne, Music, 1879
Miss Alison Aikman, Music, 1878
Miss Charlotte Ainslie, Headmistress, 1902–26
Miss Lizzie Aitken, Swedish Drill and Gymnastics, 1903–14
Miss Lizzie Alexander, Music, 1878
Miss Margaret Alexander, Secretarial, 1903
Mrs Margaret Alexander, Elementary, 1890–1915
Mrs Alexander, Needlework, left 1914
Miss Catherine Allan, Elementary, 1899–1935
Miss Eleanor Anderson, Music, 1904–38
Miss Ella Anderson, Music, 1891–1928
Miss Jane Anderson, Music, left 1931
Mr John Anderson, Music, 1873–1910
Miss Lizzie Anderson, Elementary, 1873
Mr David Annandale, English, 1873
Miss Agnes Armstrong, Music, 1879
Miss Annie Arnot, Art, 1873–1922
Miss Kate Arnott, English, 1873
Miss Mary Arnott, Junior, 1889–1915
Miss Doris Arthur, 1913–21
Dr Lee Ashton, Music, 1910–38
Miss Maggie Baxter, Science, 1907
Mrs Bell, Matron, 1913
Mr Edward Blades, Mathematics, 1905–20
Monsieur René de Blanchard, French, 1893
Mrs Boa, Matron, 1902–34
Miss Elizabeth Bower, Music, 1904–30
Miss Mona Brebner, Secretary, 1911–34
Miss Catherine Brown, Elementary, 1891–1917
Miss Elizabeth Brown, Music, 1873
Miss Nelly Brown, Music and Drawing, 1873
Mr William Brown, English, 1886–1913
Miss Bella Bryden, Governess, 1889
Mr James Buchanan, English, 1878–90
Mr William Budge, History, English and Elocution, 1895–1931
Miss Rose Burnett, Music, 1907–39
Miss Margaret Burns, Governess, 1878

Miss Campbell, Music, 1910–14
Miss Hannah Caton, Mathematics, 1908
Mr John Clark, English and Latin, 1880
Miss Florence Coates, Dancing, 1899
Miss Agnes Cochrane, Sewing, 1891
Miss Elizabeth Combe, Pianist, 1899
Miss Margaret Cowpar, Sewing, 1878
Mr John Craig, Singing, 1891
Mr Miller Craig, Singing, 1897–1910
Mr Tom Craig, Music, 1888–1909
Miss Harriet Crawford, Writing, 1873
Miss Mary Crawford, Elementary and Music, 1901–39
Miss Dorothy Crick, Domestic Science, 1911
Mr George Croall, Piano, 1889
Miss Crockart, Neddlework, left 1911
Miss Catherine Cunningham, Governess, 1893
Miss Annie Davidson, Music, 1901–30
Mr Walter D'Egville, Dancing, 1873
Monsieur de Palmas, 1873
Miss Sybella Dick, English, 1873
Miss Margaret Dickson, Governess, 1873
Miss Donald, Music, 1911–13
Miss Ella Donaldson, Music, 1898
Sergeant William Donnelly, Drill, 1873
Miss Agnes Dowie, Music, 1913–23
Miss Rachel Drummond, Sewing, 1900
Miss Helen Dudgeon, Gymnastics, 1903
Mr John Dun, Drawing, 1893
Miss Maragret Elliot, Music, 1899
Miss Katherine Erskine, Governess, 1890
Miss Mabel Erskine, Music, 1873
Miss Mary Evans, Gymnastics, 1913
Miss Clara Fairgrieve, French, 1889–1923
Miss Anna Falconer, Governess and French, 1895–1932
Mr Donald Ferguson, English, 1878
Miss Jane Finch, French, 1878
Miss Morag Fletcher, Needlework, 1911–18
Miss Bessie Flint, Music, 1899
Miss Annie Forbes, Music, 1879
Miss Fordham, Head of French, left 1916
Miss Mary Forsyth, Music, 1873
Miss Margaret Frier, Drawing, 1893
Miss Mary Frier, Drawing, 1879
Mr Robert Frier, Drawing, 1873
Miss Elizabeth Gibb, Science, 1913–16
Miss Isabella Goldie, Governess, 1878
Miss Elizabeth Gowanlock, Elementary, 1889
Miss Annie Graham, Governess, 1891–1916
Miss Jessie Graham, Dancing, 1899–1932
Mrs Margaret Graham, Music, 1883–1937
Miss Mary Grease, Music, 1889
Miss Ida Green, Piano, 1904
Mr Robert Guthrie, Janitor, 1912–24
Miss Janet Haig, Music, 1879
Miss Emily Hall, Governess, 1896
Miss Mary Hamilton, Music, 1878
Miss Etheloynne Harvey, Art, 1908–39
Miss Kate Hay, Elementary, 1878
Miss Agnes Henderson, Junior, 1888–1923
Miss Margaret Hennan, Music, 1873
Miss Lizzie Hogg, Governess, 1878
Mrs Horsburgh, Matron and Kitchen Staff, 1904–43
Miss Louisa Hory, Mathematics, 1904
Miss Jane Hunter, Latin, 1911–18
Miss Margaret Hunter, Drill, 1907
Mr William Hunter, English, 1878

Miss Maida Irons, Governess, 1873–1917
Miss Helen Irving, Governess, 1873
Mr Augustus Jamieson, Music, 1878–1916
Miss Jenny Johnson, French, 1904
Miss Johnston, Domestic Science, 1910
Mr JG Keller, French, 1878
Miss Kinloch, Sewing
Miss Elizabeth Knott, Music, 1873
Miss Mary Laing, Music, 1898–1910
Miss Letham, Sewing
Miss Eva Lingard, Music, 1896
Miss Logan, Gymnastics, 1910
Miss Jeanie Lowe, Music, 1892
Miss Lizzie Lyle, Governess, 1873
Miss Edith Macartney, Governess and Junior, 1892–1935
Miss Margaret McBean, Head of German, 1912–16
Miss Jessie McDonald, Latin, 1880–1923
Mr John Macdonald, Science and Mathematics, 1900
Miss Margaret Macdonald, Governess, 1893
Miss Effie McFarlane, Governess, 1879
Miss Kate McKattie, Elementary, 1878
Miss Elizabeth Mackay, Governess, 1891–1910
Miss Margaret McLagan, Governess, 1889
Mrs Ann McLeod, Matron, 1889
Mr John McLeod, Janitor, 1873–1908
Miss Minnie Macmath, Governess, 1892
Miss C McNair, Governess, 1878
Miss Annie McWalter, Governess, 1879
Miss Agnes McWilliam, German, 1908–12
Miss Mason, Science, 1916
Miss Masterton, 1923
Miss Isabella Matthew, Governess, 1889–1910
Miss Grace Meiklejohn, Elementary, 1904–17
Mr Alexander Meyerowicz, German, 1873
Miss Elizabeth Mickel, Elementary, 1904–34
Miss Jessie Mickel, Elementary, 1896
Miss Amy Middlemiss, Music, 1880
Miss Mary Middlemiss, Governess, 1873
Miss Elizabeth Millar, Modern Languages, left 1911
Miss Kate Miller, Music, 1878
Mr James Miller, Writing, 1878
Rev Robert Miller, Mathematics, 1871–1904
Mr Robert Mitchell, Janitor, 1908–11
Mr Andrew Moffat, Arithmetic, 1873
Miss Jessie Morham, Music, 1873
Mr James Morrison, Arithmetic, 1878
Miss Charlotte Muckle, Head of Elementary, 1903–27
Monsieur Edmond Muriset, French, 1873
Miss Alice Murray, Governess, 1878
Mr Arthur Nalborough, Music, died in action 1915
Miss Isobel Nisbet, Governess, 1897
Miss Margaret Nisbet, Catering, 1891–1922
Mr Whaley Bouchier Nutt, Elocution, 1873
Mr John Paterson, Arithmetic, 1878
Mr John Patterson, Arithmetic, 1878
Miss Christian Peddie, Drawing, 1897
Miss Mary Perkins, Swedish Drill, 1899
Miss Jessie Peterson, Governess, 1873
Miss Adelaide Pockney, Head of Sewing, 1909–30
Monsieur Henri Pompe, French, 1873
Miss Rae, Domestic Science, left 1910
Miss Reith, left 1910
Miss Margaret Riddell Watt, Governess, 1892

Miss Marion Ridpath, Elementary, 1904

Miss Elizabeth Robertson, Drill, 1908–10

Miss Helena Robertson, Elementary, 1912–14

Miss Minnie Robertson Lyle, Governess, 1889–1914

Miss Margaret Robinson, Music and Drill, 1873

Miss Marion Robinson, Music, 1873–8

Miss Elizabeth Robson, French and German 1900–14

Mr John Ross, Head of English 1889–1922

Miss Lilian Ross, Latin and Mathematics, 1906

Dr William Ross, Head of Music 1908–37

Miss Aline Rothera, Swedish Drill, 1899

Miss Florence Roy, Sewing, 1873

Miss Mary Russell, Singing, 1897–1931

Mr Charles Scott, Geography, 1895–1926

Miss Jane Shannon, Music, 1878

Miss Jeanie Simpson, Governess, 1899

Miss Ida Smith, Elementary, 1902

Miss Margaret Smith, Governess, 1873

Miss Robina Smith, German, 1880–1919, and Senior Mistress, 1902–19

Mrs Jane Smythe, Elementary, 1889

Miss Somerville, Mathematics, 1901

Miss Amy Steele, Classics, 1906–10

Miss Stevenson, Gymnastics, left 1913

Miss Annie Stewart, Junior, 1885–1928

Miss Edith Stokes, 1908–18

Miss Story, left 1910

Mr Walter Strang, Singing, 1873

Miss Isa Sutherland, Elementary, 1878

Miss Jean Sutherland, Elementary, 1878

Miss Helen Taylor, Music, 1891

Miss Jane Tennant, Elementary, 1878

Mr Alexander Thomson, Headmaster, 1871–1902

Mr Alexander Thomson, Science, 1906–26

Miss Barbara Thomson, Elementary, 1873

Miss Jessie Thomson, Governess, 1891

Miss Rhua Thomson, Clerk, 1889

Miss Janie Thorburn, Governess,Junior, Languages, 1897–1938

Mr Frederick Todd, Shorthand, 1873

Miss Mary Turner, Music, 1898–1922

Mr David Vallance, Art, 1873

Mr William Walker, Arithmetic, 1896

Mr Samuel Warren, Music, 1909–31

Miss Margaret Wells, French and Singing, 1873

Miss Mary Wells, Governess, 1878

Miss Alice Wilson, Lady Superintendent, 1871–1902

Miss Mary Wood, Sewing, 1873

Mr Henry Wyse, Head of Art, 1904–22

Miss Charlotte Young, Governess, 1898–1912

Miss Young, Science, left 1913

Miss Robina Young, Music, 1873

Mr Thomas Young, English and History, 1896–1920

Miss Helen Younger, Governess, 1891

LIST 2: GWLC staff appointed between 1914 and 1974
(some of the later appointments continued their teaching careers at GWC after the merger of the two schools)*

Mrs Acaster, Physical Education, 1956

Miss Eliza Adam Junior, 12 years

Miss Jean Adam (Mrs Smith), Art 1952–6

Mrs Dorothy Adams*, Domestic Science, 1974

Miss Elizabeth Aitken, Junior, 1922–44

Miss Elizabeth Aitken, Junior and Drama, 1948–51

Miss Mary Aitken, Head of Music, 1914–33

Mrs Mary Aitkenhead, History, 1966–9

Mrs Janet Allan 1951–9

Miss Sheila Allan, 1954–5

Miss Edwina Angus, Dancing, 1945–50

Miss Eliza Angus, Latin, 1923–7

Miss Janet Armstrong, Head of Physical Education, 1928–64

Miss Grace Auchterlonie, Head of Biology, 1964–74

Miss Austra Augenbergs, Russian, 1963–71

Miss Marjorie Baird (Mrs Archer), Piano, 1932–6

Mrs Anne Baird*, Junior, 1974

Mrs Ball, Junior, 1974

Miss Caroline Ballantine, 1925

Miss Mary Bannerman*, Junior, 1962–74

Dr Marie Barber, German, 1915–23

Miss Elsa Barker, Music, 1919–25

Miss Elizabeth Barnetson, Secretarial, 1930–2

Miss Anita Bartleman, Dancing, 1921–8

Miss Molly Baul (Mrs Whittenburn) 1955

Mr Baxter, Janitor, 1947

Miss Helen Beaton, Secretarial, 1937–42

Miss Jean Beattie, Junior, 1960–1

Miss Beaumont, English, 1918

Miss Margaret Belcher 1933

Mr John Bennett 1946–7

Miss Jean Bertram, Mathematics, 1945–5 Deputy Headmistress, 1955–67

Miss Elizabeth Blair, Head of Domestic Science 1932–47

Miss Boa, Catering, 1935

Miss Boag, Preparatory, 1973–4

Miss Jane Boath, Physical Education, 1924–6

Mr Reginald Bogie, Head of Physics, 1949–69

Miss Gertrude Bolland*, Head of Classics, 1968–74

Miss Elspeth Boog Watson, Head of History, 1931–60

Miss Kathleen Bonnington, Nursery, 1962–4

Miss Margaret Borthwick, Junior, 1936

Miss Marie Bowman, Head of Preparatory, 1928–49

Mrs Jean Bowman, Primary, 1973–4

Rev Norman Bowman*, Religious Studies, 1967–74

Miss Jean Boyd, Junior and French, 1917–38

Miss Kathleen Brebner, Secretary, 1937–48

Miss Eileen Brian, English, 1968–71

Miss Kathleen Brockway (Mrs Winter), Sewing, 1954–60, Head of Sewing, 1960–9

Miss Catherine Brown, Head of Commerce, 1950–66

Miss Dorothy Brown*, Physical Education, 1964–74

Miss Mary Brown, Religious Education, 1950–4

Miss Kathleen Brown, Junior, 1952–64

Miss L Brown, Music, 1920–2

Miss Nan Brydon*, Primary, 1945–74

Miss Burgess, left 1965

Mrs Mary Burke*, Junior, 1968–74

Miss Eileen Burrell

Miss Margaret Burrows, Junior, 1947–50

Miss Rose Cairney, Junior, 1928–63, Head of Lower Junior School, 1955–63

Miss Cecilia Calder, English, 1923–33

Miss Elizabeth Caldwell 1939

Mrs Elaine Campbell, Secretarial 1971–4

Miss Sylvia Campbell, Sewing, 1969–71

Miss Eleanor Carnon, English, 1945–74, Head of English 1968–74

Miss Edith Carrie, Head of French and German 1917–44

Miss Jessie Carter, 1931

Miss Winifred Carter, 1935

Miss Isobel Carruthers, Junior, 1916–42, 1942–55, Head of the Junior School

Miss Sheila Cater, Dancing, 1938–46

Miss Cecilia Cavaye*, Music, 1972–4

Miss Elizabeth Chalmers*, Senior School Secretary, 1963–74

Mr Chambers, Groundsman, 1944–66

Miss Clark, left 1922

Miss Mary Clark, Domestic Science, 1918–32

Miss Clark Wilson, Junior 1930–71, Head of the Lower Junior School, 1963–71

Miss Isabella Cochrane*, Chemistry, 1962–74

Miss Elma Coghill, Primary, 1958–74

Mrs Isobel Collee, Primary, 1970/1

Miss Patricia Colley 1965–9

Miss Frances Collinson, 1955/6

Miss Alexandra Cooper, 1960/1

Mr Francis Cooper, Art, 1921–7

Miss Elizabeth Corrigall, Physical Education, 1938/9

Miss Joy Courtney, Catering Officer, 1949–74

Miss Mary Cowan*, Junior and French, 1945–74

Miss Dorothy Cownie (Mrs Carnon), Music, 1946–56

Miss Charlotte Craig, Needlework, 1914–39

Miss Effie Craig, 1927

Miss Elizabeth Craw, 1941–4

Miss Mary Crawford, 1943/4

Miss Margaret Crichton*, Mathematics, 1958–74

Miss Muriel Croll, Physical Education, 1946–51

Miss Eleanor Cromb, Junior, 1926–30

Miss Agnes Crowe, Chemistry, 1919–31

Mr Dalton, Janitor, left 1971

Mrs Davie, Art, 1974

Mrs Davidson, left 1945

Miss Margaret Derome*, Geography, 1974

Mrs Elizabeth Dick, Junior, 1963–72, Head of Lower Junior School, 1972–4

Mrs Janet Dickie, Preparatory, 1973–74

Dr Thomas Dickson, Head of Art, 1927–49

Miss Dodds, German and Russian, 1972–4

Miss Christine Donald, Preparatory, 1953–4

Miss Donald, Gymnastics, 1917–23

Miss Ella Donaldson, 1922

Miss Margaret Doull, French, 1945–69

Miss Jane Dow, 1929

Miss Agnes Dowie, 1926

Miss Grace Downie, Domestic Science, 1921

Mrs Mary Drysdale, Physical Education, 1973/4

Miss Morag Duckering, 1964–5

Mrs Mildred Duncan, Secretary, 1943–45

Miss Janette Dunlop, left 1922

Miss May Dunn, 1931

Mrs Isabel Dunnett, Junior, 1968–74

Mrs Kathleen Easton, German, 1949–72, Head of German, 1972–4

Mrs Dana Edgar, History, left 1962

Miss Violet Edwards, 1938

Miss Margaret Elder*, Biology, 1966–74

Miss Ellis, 1916

Miss Ethel Ewan, English,History and Religious Studies 1919–50

Miss Nellie Fairbairn, Science and Mathematics, 1920–59

Mrs Mary Fairley*, Matron, 1972–74

Mrs Julia Falconer, 1950

Miss M Falconer, Music, 1920

Dr William Falconer, English, 1922–47

Mrs Janette Fancey, Physics, 1969–74

Miss Jean Farquharson (Mrs Davidson) 1937–46

Miss Elizabeth Ferguson, 1930

Miss Alice Fleming, Music, 1967–72

Miss Hilda Fleming, Headmistress, 1958–74

Miss Forbes, Gymnastics and Dancing, 1921

Miss Edith Ford, Secretary, 1948–52

Miss Ford (Mrs Sloan), Domestic Science, 1960–2

Miss Ford (Mrs Brady), Art, 1972–4

Miss Margaret Forsyth, Preparatory, 1950–8, Infant Mistress, 1958–70

Miss Caroline Fortescue*, English, 1955–74

Miss Isobel Fraser*, Primary, 1945–74

Mrs Muriel Fraser*, Primary, 1966–74

Miss Susan Fraser, 1941–9

Miss Nora Frater, Dancing, 1932–4

Miss Alice Frost (Mrs Arthur), Preparatory, 1951–4

Miss Marion Froude, Head of Geography, 1946–74

Miss Winnie Fry, Music, 1916/17

Miss Susan Gardham, French, 1921–45

Miss Valerie Garrow, Needlework, 1956–9

Miss Marion Gauld, Music, 1936–8

Miss Margaret George, Biology, 1962–63

Miss Margaret Gibson, Physical Education, 1952–5

Miss Marjory Gilbert, 1944–74, French, Deputy Headmistress, 1967–74

Mrs Janet Gilbraith, Mathematics, 1971–4

Miss Gladys Gilfillan, Secretary, 1947–53

Miss Georgina Gillespie, 1924–9

Miss Anna Gilmour, Head of Chemistry, 1931–62

Miss Margaret Gilmour, Junior, 1944–65

Mrs Glennie, Mathematics, 1965

Miss Frances Gourlay, 1938

Miss Margaret Grant *, Junior, 1960–74

Miss Margaret Gray 1933–44

Miss Janet Gray, 1945

Miss Hilda Green, Head of Needlework, 1954–6

Miss Ann Greig ,1926

Miss Ruby Grierson, English, 1927–36

Miss Margaret Grieve, English, 1933–7

Mrs Hamilton, Matron, left 1972

Miss Hancock, 1964–68

Miss Christian Harper, Senior School Secretary, 1915–43

Miss Pamela Hart, Biology, 1974

Miss Hassall, Junior, 1972–4

Miss Isobel Hawes, Elementary, 1957–62

Mrs Janet Hayes, Biology, 1962–4

Mrs Agnes Henderson, Art, 1962–74

Mr James Henderson, Head of Art, 1949–70

Miss E. Henderson, Secretarial, 1922–30

Miss Henderson, Junior, 1974

Miss Frances Heney, 1930

Miss Margaret Herd, Preparatory, 1964–6

Miss Phyllis Hodges, Art, 1922–52

Miss Brenda Hudson (Mrs McCann), Dancing, 1957–64

Miss Agnes Hughes, 1934–8

Mrs Margaret Hutchison, French, 1959–74

Mrs Dorothy Inglis*, Chemistry, 1974

Miss Mary Innes, Music, 1930

Miss Margaret Jaboor 1941

Miss Helen James 1933

Mr Arthur Jamieson, Geography, 1926–46

Miss Rhoda Jarvis, Latin, 1921–55

Miss Jelly, Spanish, 1916/17

Mr John Jenkins, Head of Science, 1926–49

Miss Margaret Jenkins, Gymnastics, 1921–31

Miss Josephine Johnston, 1928

Miss Mary Johnston, Dancing, 1960/1

Miss Rene Johnston, 1955–8

Mrs Johnstone, 1955

Miss Joyner, Latin, 1918–1922

Miss Kempson, Science, 1916/17

Miss Davina Kerr,1956

Miss Margaret Kerr, 1932

Miss Mary Kerr, Mathematics, 1924–30

Miss Mary Kerr, Domestic Science and Catering 1927

Miss Margaret Kilpatrick, Preparatory, 1965–8

Miss King, Science, 1917/18

Miss Edith Kinloch, Needlework, 1946–60, Head of Needlework, 1956–60

Miss Mysie Kyle, History, 1962–6

Monsieur Guy La Bastide, French, left 1939

Miss Jean Laird (Mrs Muir), Junior, 1962–6

Miss Jean Lamb, Gymnastics, 1931–5

Miss Catherine Lambert, Physical Education, 1951/2

Dr Dudley Langdon, Head of Music, 1942–62

Miss Margaret Lawrence, 1931

Miss Janet Lawrie, Secretary, 1952–4

Miss Beatrice Leatham (Mrs Lowe), Needlework, 1949–54

Miss Eleanor Lee, Secretary, 1945–7

Miss Margaret Lee, Dancing, 1969–74

Miss Jean Lindsay, Head of Classics, 1927–38, Deputy Headmistress, 1938–55

Miss Mary Linton

Miss Edith Little, Head of German, 1949–71

Miss Margaret Littlewood (Mrs Pogue), English, 1947–74

Miss Caroline Lochead, 1931

Miss Charlotte Longson, History, 1919–29, Senior Mistress 1929–38

Miss Christine Lothian, English, 1971–4

Miss Mary Lothian, Dancing, 1920–8

Mrs Jean Lupton*, French 1971–4

Mr McAdam, 1922

Miss McCaig, Head of French, 1916–23

Miss Agnes McCallum, French and German, 1923–7

Miss Fiona MacCormick (Mrs Reid), Art, 1956–62

Mr Tom McCourt, Head of Music, 1938–42

Miss Eva Macdonald, Junior, 1917

Mrs Margaret Macdonald, Junior, 1966–72

Miss MacDonald, Latin, left 1932

Miss Mary McDougall, Needlework 1921–30, Junior, 1930–58

Miss MacDuff, Mathematics, 1920

Miss McElderry, left 1916

Miss McHardy, Junior, 1930–40

Miss McIntosh, Music, 1922–5

Mrs McIntosh, Matron, 1965–9

Miss Jean McIntyre, History, 1955–60

Miss Myra McKeachie, Secretary, 1953–5

Dr MacKenzie, English

Miss Henrietta Mackenzie, Science, 1925

Mrs Margaret Mackenzie, 1958–68, Head of Classics, 1968–72

Miss Maimie Mackenzie, Classics, 1955–7

Miss Mackinnon, Secretary, 1954–63

Miss Evelyn MacLachlan, 1946–47

Miss Gaynor McLachlan, Physical Education, 1967–9

Miss Margaret MacLeod, 1963–5

Mrs Alexandra MacLeod, Secretary, 1961–74

Miss Diana McMichael, Mathematics, 1973/4

Mrs Genevieve McMillan 1951

Miss Annie MacPherson, Junior, 1944/5

Miss Elizabeth McPherson, 1956

Miss Margaret Macpherson, 1925

Mrs Macpherson, left 1963

Mrs McPherson, Music, 1954–67

Miss Catherine Marshall, Head of Domestic Science, 1947–53

Miss Marais, Elementary, 1914–17

Miss Martin, 1945

Miss Masterton, 1918–23

Miss Katherine Matthew (Mrs Gunn) 1956–62

Miss Mary Mathewson, Gymnastics, 1926–8

Mr Alexander Merrilees, Head of Mathematics, 1919–45

Miss N Metcalfe, Elementary, 1950–3

Miss Miller, Cook, 1922

Miss Kathleen Millar, 1938

Mr Robert Millar, Head of English, 1947–68

Miss Elizabeth Miller, Domestic Science, 1952–54

Miss Jean Mitchell, 1934–8

Miss Miller, 1963

Miss Moir, Mathematics, 1918–24

Miss Moir, Music, 1921/2

Miss Daphne Moody, Elementary, 1945–8

Miss Margaret Morfitt, Mathematics, 1945–67

Mr Alexander Morris*, Physics, 1974

Miss Dorothy Morris*, French, 1946–72, Head of French, 1972–4

Miss Catherine Moyes, Domestic Science, 1960–3

Miss Mudie, Sewing, 1918

Miss Muirhead, Sewing, left 1918

Miss Valerie Munro, Junior, 1960–5

Miss Lorna Murray, Preparatory, 1970–2

Miss Margaret Naughton*, History 1943–74, Head of Upper Junior School, 1955–74

Miss Nelson, left 1962

Miss Helen Ness, Science, 1963–6

Miss Isabella Newton, Biology,1921–62

Miss May Nicol*, Head of History, 1960–74, Deputy Headmistress, 1974/5

Miss Dorothy Nicolson, Headmistress, 1945–57

Miss Dorothy Nisbet (Mrs Anderson), Junior, 1969–72

Miss Grace Normand, Commerce, 1942–50

Miss Vaila Norrish (Mrs Croudace), Junior, 1954–6

Mrs Officer, Matron

Mr Officer, Janitor

Miss Dorothea Ogilvie, Gymnastics, 1935–

Miss Mary Ogilvie, Head of Domestic Science, 1953–74

Mrs Annie Ogg, Head of Mathematics, 1967–74

Miss Catherine Omon, Elementary, 1926

Miss Alice Parnell, Music, 1925–30

Miss Elizabeth Paterson, 1956–57

Mrs Elizabeth Paterson, 1943–46

Miss Katharine Paterson, 1946–48

Miss Elizabeth Patterson, French, 1969–72

Miss Alice Paxton, Art, 1928

Miss Margaret Pearson, Head of Commerce, 1966–71

Miss Betty Pennycook, Commerce, 1949–50

Miss Pettigrew, Sewing, 1918

Mrs Maxine Pettigrew, Junior, 1971–4

Miss Marjorie Pollitt, Preparatory, 1954–6

Miss Irene Purves, Preparatory, 1956–64

Mrs A Rae, Junior, left 1940

Mrs Margaret Ramsay, Junior, 1954–57

Miss Marion Reid, Head of Sewing, 1930–49

Miss Johmina Reilly, Mathematics and Science, 1931

Miss Margaret Renton, Junior, 1961–5

Miss Jean Richardson, Junior, 1964–70

Miss Marguerite Riddel, Elementary, 1917–50

Miss Marian Riddell, Elementary, 1938/9

Miss Dorothea Rivington, English, 1920–38

Miss Jean Robb (Mrs Nelson), Science,1959–62

Mrs Anne Roberts*, Domestic Science, 1970–4

Miss CC Robertson, Headmistress, 1926–1945

Miss Dorothy Robertson (Mrs Anderson), Needlework, 1962–9

Miss Elspeth Robertson, Music, 1919–39

Miss Isabel Robertson, French and German, Head of German, 1924–49

Miss Catherine Rodger, Primary, 1939–44

Miss Elizabeth Rose, Commerce, 1950–2

Miss Annie Rosie, Music, 1938

Miss Doris Ross, Domestic Science, 1946/7

Miss Dorothy Ross, School Secretary, 1934–7

Mrs Anne Runnalls*, History, 1970–4

Miss Annie Russell, Junior, Mathematics and Science, 1922–58

Miss Marianne Russell, Junior, 1941–4

Miss Sheila Sargeant, Head of French, 1960–71

Madame Andreé Schmidt, French, 1945

Miss Kathleen Schofield*, Art, 1962–74, Head of Art 1970–4

Miss Bertha Scott, 1946/7

Miss Anna Semeonoff, Russian, 1946

Miss Shanks, Secretarial, 1929–30

Mrs Margaret Sharp*, Junior, 1968–74

Mrs Eileen Sharples, Chemistry, 1963–73

Miss Nellie Shepley, Mathematics, 1936–8

Miss Anna Sherriff (Mrs Sutherland), Physical Education, 1970–4

Miss Eleanor Simpson, Head of French, 1920–60

Miss Nancy Simpson*, Sewing, 1972–4

Miss Sinclair, English and Geography, 1921/2

Miss Mary Sinclair, Secretarial, 1931

Miss Sheila Sinclair, PE, 1965

Mrs Sloan, Junior, left 1962

Miss Doreen Smith*, PE, 1954–74, Head of PE 1964–74

Mrs Joan Smith, Biology, 1969–74

Miss Margaret Smith, Mathematics, 1967–71

Miss Marjorie Smith, Art, 1943–61

Miss Jean Snow, Infant Department, 1954–6

Miss Rachel Somerville, Mathematics, 1921–4

Miss Sommerville, German, 1923/4

Miss Spafford, Physical Education, 1915–22

Miss Rona Speirs, Physical Education, 1954–6

Miss Squire, left 1917

Miss Lena Stein, French, 1937–44

Miss Eva Stephen, English, 1917–1933

Miss Mary Stevenson, Elementary, 1944/5

Miss Elsie Stewart, Elementary, 1948–51

Miss Marion Stewart*, Junior, 1965–74

Mrs Stewart, 1965

Miss Valerie Stone, Domestic Science, 1963–7

Miss Stoops, 1916

Miss Rosemary Summers, Dancing, left 1954

Mr Sutherland, Janitor, 1924

Miss Elizabeth Swinton, Mathematics and Science, 1930–63

Mr Bill Symon,* Janitor, 1972–74

Miss Taggart, Secretarial, 1917

Miss Anne Taylor, Junior, 1934

Miss Elizabeth Taylor, Junior, 1958–68

Miss Merricks Taylor, Elementary, 1935

Mrs Thin, 1956

Miss Grace Thomson, English, 1939–44

Miss Mary Thomson, Mathematics, 1915–55

Miss Mary Thomson, French and German, 1936–40

Miss Tocher, French, 1916–22

Mr William Trail, Head of Classics, 1955–68

Miss Margery Traves*, Head of Music, 1962–74

Miss Mary Turnbull, 1925

Miss Helen Turner (Mrs Mackenzie), English, 1936–47

Mrs Rosalind Ungar*, Classics, 1973/4

Mrs Wales, Latin, 1973/4

Miss Walker, Gymnastics, 1922

Mrs Elizabeth Watson, German and Russian, 1971–4

Miss Frances Watson, Domestic Science, 1949–52

Miss Sara Watt*, Geography, 1966–74

Miss Mary Waugh, PE, 1956/7

Miss Josephine Whetson, PE, 1936

Miss Margaret White*, Mathematics, 1958–74

Miss Dorothy Wilson, Elementary, 1930–71, Head of Elementary 1957–71

Miss Jeanie Wilson, Head of Elementary, 1925–57

Miss Wilson, left 1917

Mr Hugh Wilson, Janitor, left 1972

Miss Hilda Winchester, French, 1932–7

Mrs Evelyn Wolstencroft, Junior, 1945–60

Mrs Wood, French, 1973/4

Miss Margaret Wright, Needlework, 1935

Miss Danis Wright, Junior, 1958–60

Miss Jean Wylie, Junior, 1922–44

Mrs Gillian Young, Geography, 1974

Appendix 2

SENIOR PREFECTS OF GEORGE WATSON'S LADIES' COLLEGE 1903–74

1903/4	M E S Moodie
1906/7	Mary Wright
1907/8	Annette Hunter
1908/9	Ella Ritchie
1909/10	Dorothy Paton
1910/11	Margaret White
1916/17	Grace Dover
1917/18	Clementina Findlay
1918/19	Sidney Croskery
1919/20	Winifred Flett
1920/1	Madeleine Mackay
1921/2	Doris Fenton
1922/3	Nockold Bisset Smith
1923/4	May Smith
1924/5	Dorothy McGill
1925/6	Isobel Yeoman
1926/7	Marian Linton
1927/8	Nora Campbell
1928/9	Betty Forsyth
1929/0	Helen Linton
1930/1	Emily Fisher
1931/2	Margaret Duncan
1932/3	Agnes Sanderson
1933/4	Alison Ewan
1934/5	Joan McWilliam
1935/6	Margaret Berneaud
1936/7	Margaret Macdonald
1937/8	Margaret Macdonald
1938/9	Margaret Ewan
1939/40	Elizabeth Davidson
1940/1	Maud Wood
1941/2	Anne Calder
1942/3	Joan Jarvis
1943/4	Gertrude Whyte
1944/5	Jean Hardie
1945/6	Sheana Kennedy
1946/7	Agnes Ewan
1947/8	Dorothy Grieve
1948/9	Winifred Galloway
1949/50	Sheila Henderson
1950/1	Kathleen Ritchie
1951/2	Mona Ryrie
1952/3	Christine Dandie
1953/4	Lorna Craig
1954/5	Margaret Allan
1955/6	Shelagh Barnard
1956/7	Lois Beevers
1957/8	Patricia Barnard
1958/9	Barbara Bridges

1959/60	Janet Whitteridge
1960/1	Jenifer Malcolm
1961/2	Ingrid Smith
1962/3	Jennifer Black
1963/4	Jenny Easton
1964/5	Fiona Mackay
1965/6	Rosemary Colquhoun
1966/7	Jane Langlands
1967/8	Kathryn Taylor
1968/9	Lorna Macdonald
1969/70	Sally Chalmers
1970/1	Margaret Macdonald
1971/2	Julia Hamilton
1972/3	Frances Morton
1973/4	Louise Stewart
1974/5	Christine Baird

DUXES OF THE SCHOOL 1872–1974

1872	Margaret H Brown
1873	Walterina M Gouinlock
1874	Janet S Haig
1875	Isabella Craig
1876	Jessie J McKean
1877	Janie S Craigie
1878	Margaret Armour
1879	Helen M Irving
1880	Charlotte E Ainslie
1881	Grace M Cameron
1882	Jessie A Young
1883	Agnes Sutherland
1884	Margaret J Bryden
1885	Helen L Robson
1886	Agnes K Rudd
1887	Janet A Scott
1888	Helen Taylor
1889	Catherine H Fleming
1890	Margaret Drummond
1891	Sarah W Davison
1892	Jeanie W Robertson
1893	Helen Cameron
1894	Bessie H Robson
1895	Jessie A Linton
1896	Bessie K Hogg
1897	Margaret A Alexander
1898	Nellie N Gow
1899	Davidina J Davidson
1900	Margaret C Aitken
1901	Helen A Hunter
1902	Audrey C Edgar
1903	Euphemia M Bain
1904	Isa A Allan
1905	Dora M Neill
1905	Janie C Stewart
1906	Mabel D Curtis
1907	Annette A Hunter
1908	Ella L Ritchie
1909	Janette G Dunlop
1909	Dorothy Paton
1910	Thelma Thomson
1911	Margaret P White
1912	Hannah Lister
1913	Maysie Dees
1914	Eleanor Pairman
1915	A Sheila Macleod
1916	Isobel M Finlayson
1917	Mary A Kerr
1918	Netta R Seath
1919	Sidney E Croskery
1920	M Evelyn McLaren
1921	Helen L Wood
1922	Doris J A Fenton
1923	Mary O Linton
1924	I Marjorie McKechnie
1925	Muriel E Bentham
1925	Mary L Gilbert

1926	Margaret J P Laurence
1927	Lois M D Patrick
1928	Joan I M Budge
1929	A Marjorie Robertson
1930	E Muriel Welsh
1931	Marion A M Wilson
1932	Evelyn H Johnston
1933	Agnes L Sanderson
1934	Alison L Ewan
1935	Hilary J Bradshaw
1936	J Margaret Berneaud
1937	Violet F Michie
1938	Doreen W Michie
1939	Beryl GM Young
1940	Helen M Joan Smith
1941	Beryl Daiches
1942	Elizabeth Elkin
1943	C Joan D Jarvis
1944	Gertrude WN Whyte
1945	Winifred M Temple
1946	Sheana M Kennedy
1947	HM Joyce Richey
1948	Frances M Crombie
1949	Anne A Johnston
1950	Edith M Baxter
1951	Kathleen J Ritchie
1952	Mona B Ryrie
1953	Heather D A Wood
1954	Janet M Norbury
1955	Maragret J C Somerville
1956	Katherine A Reid
1957	Wilma M Trail
1958	Kathleen M Gardner
1959	Pamela M Bisset
1960	Katharine M Schlapp
1961	H Mhairi J Macnicol
1962	Muriel M Cassie
1963	Jennifer R Black
1964	Gillean E Somerville
1965	Alison Gould
1965	Gillian Dingwall–Smith
1966	Heather E S Robertson
1967	Jane R Langlands
1967	Fiona S Clayton
1968	Sally V Millar
1968	Kathryn A Taylor
1969	Sheila J McWilliam
1969	Jean E Innes
1969	Janet E Morton
1970	Gillian E MacLean
1970	M Anne Naughton
1971	Nicola J Graham
1971	Sarah C A Robertson
1971	Elizabeth M Young
1972	Julia L Sanderson
1973	Deirdre A Cunningham
1973	Janet A Wilson
1974	Gillian S Peart
1974	Linda M McAndrew
1974	Lesley H Brown

17 girls were both Senior Prefect and Dux of the School although not always in the same session.

VICE CONVENORS OF GEORGE WATSON'S LADIES' COLLEGE 1909–74

1909–11	John R Findlay
1911/12	W Fraser Dobbie
1912/14	James H Thin
1914/16	George Murray
1916/18	William K Allan
1918/19	Malcolm Smith
1919–21	J W Shennan
1921–3	Archibald Young CBE
1923–5	WS Morton
1925–7	Robert Grant
1927–9	J MacDonald Smith
1929/30	William R Macmillan
1930/1	John Reid
1931–3	Charles J Cousland
1933–5	David M Boyd
1935–7	Thomas Hay
1937–9	George Veitch
1939–40	J Chalmers Brown
1940/1	Thomas Band
1941–3	WOB Winkler
1943–5	J Morrison Inches
1945–7	Alexander Ross
1947–9	Andrew G F Adams
1949–51	James H Carmichael
1951–3	James B Allan OBE
1953–5	William Fergus Harris
1955–7	Thomas W Harper
1957–9	Alastair M Stewart
1959–61	Hugh P McMaster TD
1961–3	Alexander R Mathewson CBE
1963–5	Ian WS Wilson
1965–7	James M Smibert
1967–9	Kenneth Ryden MC
1969–71	RCH Boothman DFC
1971/2	W Colin Brown JP
1972/3	R M Morrison MBE

CAPTAINS OF THE WOMEN WATSONIANS' GOLF CLUB 1930–2005

1930–1	Miss Alice Wilson
1932–3	Miss Nora Campbell
1934–5	Miss Kirsten Allan
1936–7	Miss Margaret Hay
1938–9	Miss Greta Hall
1945–7	Miss Chris
1948–51	Miss Brodie Hall
1952–3	Miss Margaret Hay
1954–6	Miss Nellie MacHugh
1957–9	Mrs Ruby Hay
1960–1	Miss Sheila Renton
1962–3	Miss Marjorie MacGregor
1964–5	Mrs Betty Ross
1966–7	Mrs Barbara Cooper
1968–9	Mrs Dorothy Anderson
1970–1	Mrs Dorothy Wilson
1972–3	Miss Muriel Burrows
1974–5	Mrs Marjory Curtis
1976–7	Mrs Joyce Forbes
1978–9	Miss Peggy Hunter
1980–1	Mrs Mabel Montgomery
1982–3	Mrs Joan Henderson
1984–5	Miss Doreen Smith
1986–7	Miss Susan Bell
1988–9	Mrs Netta Brooks
1990–1	Mrs Anne Scott
1992–3	Mrs Pat Morrison
1994–5	Mrs Rhoda Cowie
1996–7	Miss Jean Calder
1998–9	Mrs Moira Thom
2000–1	Mrs Gill McNeillage
2002–3	Mrs Maggie Pringle
2004–5	Miss Liz Childs

CAPTAINS OF THE WOMEN WATSONIANS' HOCKEY CLUB 1933–72

1933/4	Miss Kate Weatherhead
1934/5	Miss Jenny Grossart
1935/6	Miss Marjorie Stewart
1936/7	Miss Marjorie Stewart
1937/8	Miss Dorothy Middleton
1938/9	Dr Nora Campbell
1939/40	Miss MM Carmichael
1940/1	Miss MM Carmichael
1941/2	wartime
1942/3	wartime
1943/4	wartime
1944/5	wartime
1945/6	Dr Isobel Jarvis
1946/7	Miss Ellen Heron
1947/8	Miss Joy Brebner
1948/9	Miss Joy Brebner
1949/0	Miss Alison Mathers
1950/1	Miss Alison Mathers
1951/2	Dr Isobel Jarvis
1952/3	Dr Isobel Jarvis
1953/4	Dr Isobel Jarvis
1954/5	Miss Margaret Moncrieff
1955/6	Miss Joan Hay
1956/7	Miss Doreen Smith
1957/8	Miss Doreen Smith
1958/9	Miss Maureen MacKenzie
1959/60	Mrs Wendy Gould
1960/1	Miss Dorothy Brown
1961/2	Miss Dorothy Brown
1962/3	Miss Brenda Carmichael
1963/4	Miss Jill Dawson
1964/5	Mrs Jill Scotland
1965/6	Miss Irene Andrew
1966/7	Miss Dorothy Brown
1967/8	Miss Dorothy Brown
1968/9	Miss Lorna Melville
1969/70	Miss Anne Mackay
1970/1	Miss Anne Mackay
1971/2	Miss Rosemary Henderson

Distinguished Service as Recorded by Their Pupils and Their Colleagues

**Mr William Budge
1895–1932**

"His very presence in a school corridor seemed to give a guarantee, even to the casual visitor, that all must be well with the School."

**Miss Robina Smith
1880–1919**

"She thought much of her duty, and had loftier and clearer notions of it than most people, and held fast to them with more success. To rise from Governess to Deputy Headmistress in those days was a remarkable achievement."

**Miss Janet Carruthers
1916–55**

"With Miss Carruthers the unruly became gentle and the lazy enthusiastic. She had an amazing gift."

**Mr Alexander
Merrilees 1919–45**

"The wisest of counsellors and a brilliant scholar, by whom it was a privilege to be taught."

**Miss Boog Watson
1931–60**

"She had a splendid gift for transmuting drudgery by imaginative and ingenious means. She was a truly remarkable teacher."

**Miss Jean Lindsay
1938–55**

"A model of toleration born of wisdom and experience."

**Miss Peggy Naughton
1943–74**

"No–one understood George Square and all that it meant better than Peggy Naughton. She was the complete Watsonian."

**Nora Carnon
1945–74**

"A distinguished scholar and an inspirational schoolmistress."

**Miss Jean Bertram
1945–67**

"Her integrity, her level–headed and perceptive judgment and her sheer practical common sense have been of inestimable value to the school."

**Mr Robert Millar
1947–68**

"A man of great intellect and a very special human being."

**Mr James Henderson
1949–70**

"James Henderson as a teacher and man was made for George Square and George Square was made for James Henderson."

**Miss May Nicol
1960–74**

"Quite simply the best teacher I ever had."

The merger of George Watson's Boys' College in 1974 to form a co-educational school at Colinton Road was one of the most important decisions the Merchant Company Education Board has ever taken in its history. It was as momentous, in some ways, as the decision in 1870 to change the status of George Watson's Hospital to a day school and to found a separate day school for girls in George Square.

There were a number of reasons for the Merchant Company's radical proposals, some educational, others reacting to the political and economic pressures arising from the education policies of the Labour Government of the mid 1960s.

In a policy statement on 30 June 1967 the Merchant Company Education Board indicated it was intending *"within the foreseeable future to make provision for co-education"* at the two George Watson's schools. The Board had requested an update of the Quinquennial Review of the City Development Plan which had previously earmarked the George Square building for incorporation in the University's plans. At the same time the University playing fields at Craiglockhart had been earmarked for the site of a new George Watson's Ladies' College. It seemed a small, but important step for the Board to proceed with a single co-educational college at Colinton Road, believing it made more economic and educational sense. The Board also emphasised that the new co-ed George Watson's College was a major plank in its policy of providing choice for Merchant Company parents between co-education on the South side and single sex education on the North side where Mary Erskine and Daniel Stewart's Melville Schools were being modernised to keep them abreast of developments in education.

The Merchant Company Education Board was also aware of the possible implications for their schools of two educational initiatives that the Labour Government was undertaking. In 1965 the Secretary of State for Scotland, Willie Ross, issued a circular

The last Boys' School March Hare.

to all Local Education Authorities to introduce comprehensive education for all secondary schools based on a non-selective intake of pupils at the end of primary schooling. At about the same time the UK Government set up the Public Schools' Commission to look into the future operation of the Direct Grant Schools (equivalent to Grant-Aided schools in Scotland).

While there must have been some misgivings in the two Watson's school communities with regard to the proposed merger, the overall view seems to have been one of cautious welcome. The editorial of *The Scotsman* of 4 July 1967 was generally in favour of the decision saying:

"...departure from tradition is welcome recognition that fee-paying schools should adapt themselves to changing social conditions, even if it means becoming more like local authority schools... Merchant Company schools have never been isolated from the community like the so-called "public" schools... Merchant Company schools would like to charge fees according to the ability to pay if the Government would permit this... (that they) stress the claim of the non-academic pupils offers reassuring evidence that Merchant Company schools are enterprising in methods and liberal in outlook as well as efficient in teaching..."

At the Watsonian Annual Dinner in January 1968, the Master of the Merchant Company, Ian Forbes, stated that the proposed merger of the *"two maroon-clad"* schools was no political

gimmick to appease the authorities, but was based on the assessment of educational benefits. He denied any question of changing the schools' names and emphasised that the recent cuts in the level of Government Grant need not affect the Merchant Company schools too adversely. A month previously (December 1967) the Merchant Company had launched a Development Fund Campaign to enable Watson's boys to continue to benefit from new buildings, indicating that from the mid-seventies such benefits would be available to the girls after the merger.

On a more light-hearted note, Wilfred Taylor in his inimitable 'A Scotsman's Log', passed some amusing comments on the effects the thought of a co-educational Watson's might have on the traditional male Watsonian:

"...the disclosure that the old school is to go co-ed has deeply shaken a number of Watsonians..... some are still pretty dazed... [the news] has sent shock waves... a sonic boom round the world."
And yet Taylor was optimistic about the long-term outcome:

"... instinct for realistic compromise is a hallmark of successful Watson's legislation and has come into play... [there is] no doubt that the famous boys' college which survived the extension of the franchise will in time assimilate the newcomers [girls]... the co-efficient of grace at Watson's will notch imperceptibly upwards!"

In a letter of 3 July 1973 to both sets of parents, the Merchant

The first joint Founder's Day, June 1974.

Company Education Board indicated that the proposals for the merger had been approved in principle by the Scottish Education Department. The planned merger would take place in Session 1974/5, with 1 October 1974 as the date for the administrative and staff merger. Roger Young was to be the first Principal of the new college, with Hilda Fleming appointed as Associate Principal at George Watson's Ladies' College for Session 1974/5. It was envisaged that there would be 450 pupils in the Lower Primary, 600 in the Upper Primary and 1,400 in the Senior School.

One of the key constituents in a successful merger would be a substantial building programme on the Colinton Road site. Accordingly it was envisaged that in addition to extending existing buildings to provide more science laboratories, kitchen facilities and other necessities, a new block for primaries 1 to 3 on the Tipperlinn playing fields would have to be built. (The loss of this playing field would be compensated by the acquisition of the University Sports ground at Craiglockhart.) On the same site a covered games hall and a Design Centre were to be built. The latter would embrace all the functions of the existing Art, Technical and Home Economics departments of the two schools. In addition, a Social Studies Block, with up-to-date facilities, was to house History, Geography, Economics and Modern Studies, and Religious Education, to be constructed across the existing Junior playground in front of the Rifle Range.

However, a few years previously, in March 1970, the long-awaited Report of the Public Schools' Commission on Direct Grant Schools was published. Its main recommendation was the phasing out of the Government grant to the schools concerned, with the anticipated result of Direct Grant schools facing the choice of opting for independence or merging with the Local Authority education system within a two to three year timescale. The unexpected Conservative General Election victory of June 1970 seemed to be a boost for maintaining the status quo with regard to the Direct Grant schools. Indeed at the Annual Dinner of The Watsonian Club in January 1972, the principal guest, Gordon Campbell, Secretary of State for Scotland, emphasised his determination to support grant-aided schools and the principle of parental choice. Such pronouncements, however, did generate a feeling of uncertainty about the future of the Merchant Company schools. Roger Young, Watson's Headmaster, had earlier stated that the worst thing for the schools was the continuing uncertainty. He urged the Merchant Company schools to lose no time in determining their own future status.

On a practical note Roger Young, in a letter to Watson's parents in September 1972, indicated that the new structure of promoted posts in Secondary Schools introduced by the Scottish Education Department in August 1972 would be implemented in Watson's. This involved creating a Guidance system of Year Staff to look after the pastoral and administrative responsibilities more effectively, with the Secondary Department being divided into two – a Middle School comprising years 1 to 3 and an Upper School consisting of Years 4 to 6, each with its own Head. At the

same time a Head of School Careers Advisory Service was appointed. It is interesting to note that within two years of the introduction of the new Guidance system, the Editor of *The Watsonian* in May 1974, was convinced that special benefits had been identified. With the increasing complexities of life it was felt that the pupils needed more help in adjusting to society as a whole. There were fewer unhappy boys in school, the relationship between staff and boys was becoming less formal and discipline was more discriminating. Tribute was paid to past generations of Form teachers who under the new system remained the first point of contact for the individual pupil.

As the deadline for the merger, Session 1974/5 approached, one can only imagine the 'behind the scenes' detailed forward planning involved, the frenetic activity on both Watson's sites, the countless negotiations with the builders to ensure completion on time of the new building to accommodate the transfer of the girls to Colinton Road. One member of staff (a Head of Department) recalls the period of the merger as *"stimulating and busy"* with much preparation to amalgamate stores and libraries, and meetings to agree staff and timetables. He concedes that it must have been particularly stressful for the Girls' School staff, with strange new buildings and new colleagues. On a more positive note the process of integration of the two school communities had already begun. The first joint Founder's Day was held in June 1974, the first integrated drama production – *The Importance of Being Earnest* – took place in June 1973, as well as the *June Revue*. In the autumn of 1974/5 a joint Historical Society was set up with an audience of 150 for a history quiz. Subsequent numbers never fell below 80 for the rest of the session. Most significantly, the first joint school assembly took place on 1 October 1974 (the actual date of the merger) with the presence of a number of senior girls in the Colinton Road Assembly Hall. The new joint school hymn *Ex Corde Caritas* was sung.

Earlier, at The Watsonian Club Dinner in January 1974, Roger Young was introduced as 'the Principal' for the first time, giving rise to speculation amongst members that he could be very well headhunted by a university! At the same dinner, the principal speaker was Sir Frederick Graham (late of the Argyll and Sutherland Highlanders) who made a clarion call to save Watson's from the *"sinister political forces"* wanting to compel integration of Grant-Aided Schools into the state sector, reminding his audience of the recently successful campaign to 'Save the Argylls'!

December 1974 saw the last issue of the old style *Watsonian*, after a history of 70 years. It was to be replaced by a new *Watsonian* incorporating the strengths of the boys' *Watsonian* and the girls' *George Square Chronicle*. Henceforth, there would be wide coverage of school and Watsonian affairs but much greater space would be given for pupils'

creative writing, a prominent feature of the *George Square Chronicle*. In that issue the joint editors of the *Chronicle*, pointed out that they were sad to see the disappearance of a long-standing tradition, but were eagerly looking forward to the merger and creating a new tradition. Furthermore their participation in joint assemblies and activities had made them more aware of the customs of the other place.

In her final Christmas address to the school, Hilda Fleming said:

"In August when you go to Colinton Road, remember that it will be just as strange for the boys there as it will be for you... It will be a new beginning for you, a new school."

Previously she had given all pupils and staff a card on which was printed the school song, and to all staff she distributed a carnation buttonhole.

Rugby 1st XV.

Girls' Hockey 1st XI.

Aftermath of the Merger

The various challenges of trying to achieve as smooth a transition from the two schools to a new merged school were further complicated by the last-minute need to accommodate over a hundred staff and pupils from John Watson's School in Belford Road. The governors of John Watson's had taken the sad but seemingly inevitable decision to close the school at the end of the summer term against a background of a seriously deteriorating financial position. Both staff and pupils from John Watson's soon settled down and were to make an invaluable contribution to the future of the merged Watson's.

The return of a Labour Government in 1974 intensified the debate about the future of the Merchant Company schools. The Government soon indicated its intention to phase out the grant from August 1976, over a period of six years and requested local education authorities to proceed with the re-organisation of secondary education on comprehensive lines. The Merchant Company eventually agreed to offer the Mary Erskine School to Lothian Region Education Authority, but ironically the Secretary of State for Scotland, Willie Ross, refused to sanction this proposal on the grounds that Lothian already had too many schools in the north-west area of Edinburgh. (Rumour had it at the time that Lothian Education Authority had their eyes on the new co-educational Watson's!) This now left the Merchant Company free to choose independent status for their schools. To this end, in 1976, the Merchant Company launched an appeal to set up an endowment fund of £1 million:

"To enable the Merchant Company Education Board to reinforce their traditional policy of assisting those in need and of creating wider opportunities of a Merchant Company Education."

In addition the new fund would help to overcome problems caused by the phasing out of the grant and to plan for the future.

A little earlier in June 1974, Roger Young in his Principal's Report had engaged in the debate over the future of Watson's. He argued that Watson's capacity to provide the right education for pupils of different abilities could be hampered if it was forced to become a

Last session for the St Alban's Road girls.

neighbourhood school. He rejected the idea that schools should do no more than reflect society which he called a form of sociological determinism. In particular he emphasised that the needs of pupils with learning difficulties at Watson's would be effectively tackled by the new Learning Support Department of Catriona Collins (the Cabin) which was to gain a deserved reputation over the next few years as a centre of excellence in helping pupils with specific learning difficulties such as dyslexia.

The editor of *The Watsonian* in June 1975 felt the need to reassure the Watsonian community that:

"The current changes in George Watson's College are being carried out in a most responsible fashion… with the correct objective in mind, namely the most efficient use of resources to maintain and improve the traditional high quality education offered by Merchant Company schools."

What of the new Watson's? Numerically it entered the *Guinness Book of Records* as Scotland's largest co-educational school, with over 2,400 pupils. In October 1975 the *Edinburgh Evening News* reflecting on the new Watson's stated that the resultant changes meant different things to different people. For example, the boys were *"quieter, more polite – the girls less giggly and silly"*.

Again the boys in cookery lessons wanted to eat the food straight out of the ovens, while the girls' progress in technical subjects revealed *"a fine eye for detail and intricate work"*. Another boy/male teacher is quoted as saying, *"it is nice to see a decent pair of legs around"*.

More seriously the new buildings and refurbishment at Colinton Road were completed in time for August 1975. A notable exception was the Social Science block which had to be abandoned because of financial considerations. Instead, the Social Science subjects were temporarily housed in transportable units (huts to those staff who taught in them). In the new Design Centre, Mike Gill, the new co-ordinator, laid down that all first and second year boys and girls would do cooking, work with fabrics and experience metalwork and woodwork.

Although inevitably there were numerous irritations and frustrations in the first full session of the new Watson's (1975/6), *The Watsonian* struck a very optimistic note:

"The first full year of amalgamation has now passed with a smoothness and efficiency that has astonished many. The prophets of doom have been confounded, although of course not silenced."

The article goes on to state that the administrative changes affected the staff more than the pupils. Although class numbers changed little, there was a problem of the school size which was apparent in recreation areas and corridors. Timetabling must have been a major headache. A tribute is paid to the new guidance staff who more than earned their salaries in tackling pupil problems in the new school. Finally, most staff were delighted to hear the Principal state that changes would in future be kept to a minimum, giving way to a period of consolidation.

It is interesting to comment on a few random reactions to the merger. Perhaps with tongue in cheek, *The Watsonian* commented on the choice of Baroness Tweedsmuir (daughter of John Buchan, novelist) as the first female Founder's Day Speaker in June 1975:

"Diehard chauvinist Watsonians possibly inured to the idea of a mixed school Founder's Day… were shocked to discover that the speaker was a lady… and no doubt mildly surprised that the roof of the school hall remained intact at the end."

In 1976, the editor of *The Watsonian* explained to readers that the new S1 and S2 class nomenclature 'GWH' stood for George Watson's Hospital and not *"good, worse, horrible"*. In the same article, he regrets that new names for the school Houses had not been agreed and that the use of hyphenated names might prove cumbersome. However, perhaps a judgement of the first few years of the merger is best expressed

in the words of Peggy Naughton, Assistant Principal at the time:

The first day at GWC: everyone, staff and pupils, boys and girls, in unfamiliar territory, among unfamiliar faces and following an unfamiliar timetable – a camaraderie of shared ignorance!

Second/third term of amalgamation: teething troubles of co-education disappearing. Some apparent 'diehards' on the staff – of both sexes – even admitting to a certain pleasure in some facets of their work.

At last: 'The Amalgamation' stamped as a success – in terms of disbelief a boy actually says, *"Do you really mean the boys and girls of Watson's were once kept in separate schools?"*

It had been agreed to phase out corporal punishment at Colinton Road before the merger. However, in the first year of the merger, a celebrated example of corporal punishment involved the Deputy Principal, Alex Weston, administering six of the best to a foolhardy VIth former who had ridden his motorcycle across the grass in front of the main school at lunchtime.

In June 1976, an Open Week was held at Watson's to celebrate the first completed session of the new co-educational school, during which the school buildings, old and new, on the campus, departmental activities, school clubs and societies were on show.

A few days later, in his annual report, the Principal paid fulsome tribute to the team of people involved in the nine years of the amalgamation exercise. All contributed to the process of creating a school with special qualities to offer, not only to education in Edinburgh, but also to the wider community of Scotland and Europe:

"Qualities which will be distinctly constructive, distinctly caring, distinctly excellent and distinctly Watson's."

Sir Roger Young, 1958–85.

The final few years of Roger Young's stewardship witnessed not only a successful consolidation of the new George Watson's, but also a series of events celebrating important landmarks in the school's history, viz the Merchant Company tercentenary (1981), HM Queen's visit in June 1982, marking the fiftieth anniversary of Watson's move to Colinton Road and the celebrations of the Arts (FEAST) in Watson's to mark the retirement of Roger Young in June 1985.

However, on a more practical level challenges to the progress and special nature of Watson's had to be met. On a number of occasions the Principal defended the school's traditional policy of presenting its senior pupils for certification by the Scottish Examinations Board, rather than giving in to the demands of a minority of parents wishing to follow the GCE A and O level exam programme. In his Principal's report of Session 1980/1, he attempted to reassure such anxious parents that the chances of Watson's pupils going to non-Scottish universities were in no way diminished by Watson's being firmly based in the Scottish examination system. His assertion was supported by the following statistics:

"In 1979, no less than 42 out of 128 university-bound pupils from Watson's went to non-Scottish universities and 24 out of 129 in 1980; thus over a third took up places outside Scotland in 1979 and a fifth in 1980."

With the return of a Conservative government in 1979, Watson's hopes of maintaining its long-standing tradition of providing school places for children from low-income families were raised by the setting up of the Assisted Places Scheme.

The first of the high-profile events of the 1980s were the celebrations marking the Merchant Company Tercentenary in 1981. A Schools Festival Week (20–27 June) was organised, consisting of cultural, historical and sporting activities in the three Merchant Company Schools. One of the highlights was the Opening Gala Concert held in Watson's Assembly Hall. Appropriately the new pipe organ painstakingly assembled by a volunteer

Back Row (left to right): W. Symon, B. Alexander, R. Mallinson, J. Anderson, I. Coutts, G. Skirving, M. Gill, J. Braithwaite, R. Vandersteen, I. Murray, M. Matheson, M. Hunter, A. Murray, D. Carter, Dr P. Edington.

Row 8: E. Stewart, E. Rogers, M. Burke, C. Young, M. Vandersteen, C. Thomson, H. Ogilvie, P. Benton, M. Grant, R. Renton, E. Dunnett, K. De Luca, M. Gillies, E. Smith, A. Brobbel, J. Campbell, C. McNab, C. Robinson.

Row 7: G. Mowat, D. Edwardson, P. Taylor, A. Keith, K. Strachan, A. Robertson, T. Fairley, I. Gilray, I. Callender, P. Gaudin, R. Mackay, I. Brown, C. Binns, A. MacLaren, P. Skingley, E. Thomson.

Row 6: R. Mack, R. Tavener, J. Quinn, F. McCallum, A. Boyer, A. Runnalls, J. Thomson, P. Boyd, A. Roberts, L. Tait, P. Gibson, M. C. Stewart, B. Mann, S. Arnott, E. Hepburn, C. Fortescue, M. Wilson, A. Evans, I. McAinsh, P. Boyer.

Row 5: I. Bannerman, D. Fyfe, E. Edington, O. Watters, A. Mitchell, P. Curran, L. Strong, F. Denyer, V. Hogg, K. Christie, E. Strachan, P. Paterson, S. Campbell, A. Singleton, G. Durham, R. Ungar, F. Osborne, M. Shaw, P. Dickson, M. Muir, J. Smart, D. Hamilton, W. Nisbet.

Row 4: Dr C. Collins, J. McColl, R. Small, R. Looker, P. Marshall, G. McVitie, D. Hughes, D. Cowan, D. Croudace, P. Stark, J. Barrow, I. McHaffie, D. McLaggan, L. Lyall, W. Rees, L. Smith.

Row 3: G. Strang, P. Stewart, M. Allan, M. Derome, D. Inglis, P. MacGregor, J. Dickie, C. Collins, J. Burgess, M. Stewart, N. Bell, E. K. Smith, A. Aitken, J. Green, S. Thornton, J. Hanley, M. Stevenson, D. MacLeod, M. Baxter, C. Cavaye.

Row 2: M. Quinn, D. Paton, S. Carbarns, E. Easton, A. Hoffie, A. Collins, W. Anderson, F. Dorward, C. Fleming, N. Brydon, M. Elder, D. Brown, B. Wise, P. McNaught, P. Bogie, K. Smith, J. Kinglsey, A. Oremus, H. Rifkind.

Front Row: D. Smith, P. Edington, R. Cutforth, E. Brown, M. Sharp, A. Peden, J. Cowan, D. MacDonald, M. Nicol, Sir Roger Young, A. Macdonald, G. Scott, D. McGougan, M. Dilbey, I. Wells, R. Slater, D. Scott, S. Castle-Smith, T. Burton.

Absent: C. Rush, C. Sharpe, H. Quinn, P. Criswell, J. Lightbody, C. Mears, I. Peebles, M. Strange, S. Jackman.

George Watson's College staff photo, 1985.

group of staff and pupils was given its first official public performance. The concert programme was a mixture of the traditional and new with a work for chorus and orchestra by William Sweeney (a leading contemporary Scottish composer) commissioned for the occasion by Watson's and the Scottish Arts Council and based on two poems by Christopher Rush of Watson's English department. Moray Welsh (former pupil) played Elgar's *Cello Concerto*. Schubert's *Incidental Music to Rosamunde*, with a ballet, orchestra and chorus of Watson's conducted by Roderick Brydon (Artistic Director of the Scottish Chamber Orchestra and a former pupil of Daniel Stewart's), completed the programme. In addition, Watson's organised an Open Week which integrated with the Tercentenary Celebrations and consisted of the whole spectrum of school activities ranging from science displays to quizzes and debates.

On the very same day as the Tercentenary Concert the New Myreside Boarding House with accommodation for 80 boys and girls was opened by Malcolm Rifkind, MP, a Scottish Office Minister and himself a Watsonian.

On 29 June 1982 took place one of the most memorable events in the long history of George Watson's – the visit of Her Majesty Queen Elizabeth. It was to be undoubtedly the climax of the celebrations marking the Golden Jubilee of the move in 1932 from Archibald Place to Colinton Road. It was especially fitting that the Queen herself should make the visit as her uncle, Prince George of Kent, had officially opened the new school building at Colinton Road.

The programme of the Royal visit lasted for two hours during which the Queen made a 'Royal Progress' taking in as many of the different sections of the Watson's campus as time would allow. One of the highlights was a short concert in the Assembly Hall which featured Walton's *Fanfare*, the *National Anthem* arranged by Sir David Willcocks, Bizet's *Carmen Overture* and Handel's *Zadok the Priest*. The ceremony concluded with the Queen presenting the principal prizes to senior pupils and the unveiling of a plaque to commemorate the Royal visit.

Her Majesty signs the Visitors' Book and autographs a portrait.

Tea in the staff room. Her Majesty meets senior pupils.

The farewell from the School.

The unveiling of the Commemorative Plaque.

Sir Roger and his five deputies. Left to Right: Alex Weston, May Nicol, Sir Roger, John Sinclair, Angus Macdonald, Keith Pearson.

Two days later the Principal indicated to the school at Prize-giving on 1 July, that he had received from the Queen's Private Secretary a letter of thanks and appreciation on behalf of the Queen on the following lines:

"My Dear Headmaster,

The Queen has instructed me to write at once to say how much she enjoyed her visit to Watson's. Her Majesty was enormously impressed by everything she saw and she was particularly delighted to have the opportunity of talking to so many of the staff and pupils. There was a splendid atmosphere in the school throughout the Queen's visit and she was very touched by the warmth of the reception given to her in the Assembly Hall......... It is the boys and girls who determine the quality of a school and what struck Her Majesty most this afternoon was the intelligence, enthusiasm and good manners of the boys and girls of George Watson's College. They were delightful."

In a special Golden Jubilee issue of the *Watson's Bulletin*, Roger Young wrote an article (taking the place of the traditional Principal's Report) in which his theme was the importance of the philosophical concept of the 'Golden Mean' at Watson's. He argued that:

"We at Watson's seek the Golden Mean in encouraging a balanced view of the world and in reconciling contrasting loyalties: self-centredness must be restrained by a sense of service: excessive demands of society countered by individual initiative and self-fulfilment...The character and size of Watson's enable it to unite loyalty to the community with personal integrity, and to enhance a sense of our common humanity across the world no less than here in Edinburgh without destroying our delightful diversity."

As part of the Golden Jubilee celebrations an exhibition was mounted in the school of the remarkable collection of Chinese scrolls, fan painting and objets d'art gathered by James Haldane Stewart-Lockhart (dux of the school and rugby captain in 1874) during his years in Hong Kong and Wei Hai Wei.

June 1985 witnessed the retiral of Roger Young as Principal. It is difficult to exaggerate the enormous impact and contribution he made to Watson's.

Recognition had been made of Roger Young's contribution to the wider world of education by Hamilton College, a Liberal Arts College in Clinton, New York State, awarding

June 1985 witnessed the retiral of Roger Young as Principal. It is difficult to exaggerate the enormous impact and contribution he made to Watson's.

Roger and Mary, relaxing in the garden.

him an Honorary Doctorate in Humane Letters in 1978. Watson's /Hamilton links go back to 1954 with the appointment of Charles Murison as the first Hamilton Scholar and in 1978 Tom Wertimer becoming the first Hamilton Fellow. In October 1983, the Principal was knighted *"for educational and public services, particularly in Scotland and Edinburgh"*.

To mark the end of the Young era, a Festival of the Arts in the Summer Term (FEAST) took place from 17 to 22 June. It comprised 70 performances in drama, music and fine arts, involving Watson's pupils past and present and parents and friends of the school. It was emphasised that the *"educational dimension of FEAST is quite as important as the actual performance or products"*. The director of FEAST was Dr John Barrow of the Physics Department. Highlights included the orchestral concert conducted by James Lockhart (left Watson's 1947), conductor of the Koblenz Opera, Rock and Firework concerts, art exhibitions of pupils' work, a programme of modern and country-dance and a mini-retrospective of the famous Watsonian actor Finlay Currie in the film classics *Great Expectations* and *Whisky Galore*.

The Watson's of 1985 was in some ways substantially different from that of 1958. In a special number of the *Watson's Bulletin*, editor Anne Brobbel catalogued the *"landmarks of change"*

in the 27 years. Pre-merger, were mentioned the six-day and seven-day teaching cycles, opening of the Music School (1964), Third Year Projects (1962), the re-organisation of the Sixth Year with tutors, tutorial groups, a sixth form common room, and a library with tutorial rooms. Post-merger, the need for physical change was exemplified by the new Remedial Department, the Design Centre, Nursery Unit and Primary Libraries. Pupils were encouraged to take some responsibility in the running of the school, for example, sixth form duties, form monitors, Morning Assembly Committee, School Council, and library administration. The concept of Watson's as a family was strengthened with the introduction of year groups, parental liaison groups, the *Bulletin* and the Watson's Broadcasting Service.

What were the personal qualities that made Sir Roger Young one of the outstanding headmasters of his generation? Again quoting Anne Brobbel:

"Roger Young generated and responded positively to change in the quest for progress and improvement... He possessed the steadfast constancy of a philosopher who had a clear set of educational and humanitarian principles which were desirable and attainable... with a philosophy of pursuit of individual excellence within a caring family community."

The following tributes were paid by William McDonald and Judith Sischy (Secretary and Deputy Secretary of

the Merchant Company Education Board):

"Behind the charts, plans and structures lies a sensitive, imaginative, wise and decisive mind... who also made it look so easy... his effortless leadership is indicative of his huge capacity and skill."

May Nicol (Deputy Principal from 1974 to 1991) summed up Sir Roger's achievements as follows:

"...a man of immense ability and energy with almost workaholic tendencies... inspiration and driving force behind all that Watson's has achieved in the last 27 years... belief in the pursuit of excellence has encouraged both pupils and staff to achieve more that they would have believed possible whether it be in academic work, in sport, or in the arts."

Sir Roger Young himself believed that the Merchant Company Education Board's decision to create a co-educational school was *"the happiest and wisest decision since founding its schools"*. In addition to the list of changes noted above, he identified innovations such as the careers advisory service and work experience under Donald Macdonald, parents' evenings, a sizeable extension to extra-curricular activities and a greater variety of travel and projects awards. These, he thought, were significant in his years at the helm. In his valedictory address at the Senior Prize-Giving on 27 June 1985 he defined what he thought were the abiding values for Watson's, namely, that a good school needed to be a happy school, one which was an open society welcoming new ideas and tolerant of different viewpoints, and one in which the pursuit of excellence in one's self and others was paramount. As Sir Roger pointed out:

A man's reach should exceed his grasp or what's a heaven for? (Robert Browning)

The Master of the Merchant Company, Mr Charles Paterson, welcomes Mr Gerstenberg as the new Principal at the installation ceremony before the whole Senior School on Tuesday 27 August 1985. At side (left to right) are Rev Peter Marshall, Kirsty Zealley, Fraser Tolmie and Mrs Gerstenberg.

Frank Gerstenberg.

The new Principal was Mr Frank E Gerstenberg MA (Cantab) who was installed on the first day of the new session, 27 August 1985, by the Master of the Merchant Company, Mr Charles Paterson, before the whole Senior School in the Assembly Hall. The Master welcomed Mr and Mrs Gerstenberg and their family to Edinburgh and Watson's. In his reply Mr Gerstenberg intimated an old family link with the school through his grandfather who had started at Watson's in 1882. He exhorted pupils to set themselves standards and especially, *"...to aim high. Be your own man and woman and consider other people."*

What kind of man was the new Principal? In the April 1985 number of the *Watson's Bulletin*, Frank Gerstenberg and his wife Val gave a detailed and informative interview about themselves and their family. Frank was born in the village of Balfron about 20 miles north of Glasgow, educated at Glasgow Academy during his early primary years, then Croftinloan School in Perthshire, completing his secondary education at Trinity College, Glenalmond. He graduated from Cambridge with a degree in History and completed his postgraduate certificate in Education at the University of London. He began his teaching career in 1963 in Devon

before becoming Head of History and Modern Studies at Millfield School in Somerset. He was appointed as Senior Boarding House Master at Millfield, with Val acting as House Matron. In 1974 he became Headmaster of Oswestry School (founded in 1407) which then had a co-educational population of about 620 pupils.

The Gerstenbergs had three children, the oldest Neil and identical twin daughters, Wendy and Anna. At the time of his appointment the grapevine indicated that the Oswestry School community were very sad to lose their headmaster after eleven years – a good omen. The new Principal affirmed that his great interests were his family, books, sport, music and travel. He also emphasised that while he had enjoyed his years teaching in the classroom, he had derived great pleasure from being a Headmaster, which gave him scope for organisation, and seeing his ideas eventually being implemented. He was also greatly interested in witnessing individual pupils and pupil groups developing in their time at school.

In his Principal's Report in June 1986, Frank Gerstenberg gave his impressions of Watson's after a year. It truly was a family with a warm welcome for himself and *his* family.

He was, however, acutely aware of the huge challenge of *"the colossal legacy"* of his predecessor who had left Watson's in good heart and excellent condition. Nevertheless he identified the challenge of change at *"a time when one has to run fast to keep still... when changes in the educational world are almost frightening in their intensity."*

He cited the problems associated with the introduction of the Standard Grade exams (with the philosophy of certification for all). He stressed the need for Watson's to embrace the new technology with facilities for the study of technology and related subjects.

However, in associating Watson's with 1986 as the Year of Industry the Principal was identifying a theme which was to feature prominently in his time at Watson's. Initiatives that session included staff attending short courses at national companies, seminars involving senior pupils, a symposium on British Industry Past, Present and Future run by the Economics Department and involving six other schools. There was also a new management-shadowing scheme for sixth formers which prompted one amusing but untypical reaction:

"It was tremendous. I spent the whole day driving around in a Mercedes and had smoked salmon and champagne for lunch!"

It should be pointed out the new Principal enjoyed one piece of good fortune, namely the end of unrest in Scottish schools arising from dissatisfaction among teachers over pay and conditions which had affected Watson's in the previous few years.

The challenge of preparing Watson's pupils for the world of business and industry was taken up with a number of initiatives over the next few years. An Industrial Liaison Advisor was appointed to assist the Careers Advisory Service, the 1987 Founder's Day speaker was a leading Scottish industrialist, Sir Monty Finniston, technology was introduced to the curriculum in S1 and for some S5 and S6 pupils Young Enterprise companies were formed to introduce them to the practicalities of running a business.

Also at this time two unrelated developments took place. The class nomenclature of 'G' and 'W' for S1 and S2 was abolished on the grounds that it was both educationally and socially divisive. With the continuation of the Conservative Government after the 1987 General Election, the Assisted Places Scheme, which enabled Watson's to broaden their pupil intake, was safeguarded for the foreseeable future.

In his Principal's Report in June 1988 Frank Gerstenberg, noting the centenary of the Scottish Higher exam, observed that Watson's presented most candidates. However, as then the authorities were concerned that exams *"might develop a tyrannical control over our educational system"*, a fear that was to grow stronger with future changes in the exam system over the next 20 years, the Principal sought to assure parents that Watson's pupils were offered, *"a breadth of activity, all of which adds up to the education of the rounded Watsonian."*

One of the most important challenges facing Watson's at this time was the need to modernise buildings and facilities. Accordingly the Merchant Company Education Board embarked on an ambitious building programme for Session 1988/9, consisting of relocating the Fiction Library upstairs next to the Sixth Form Library, allowing an expanding Computer Studies Department to be integrated with the Secretarial Studies

The new Convie Wing. Mr Les Howie teaching in one of the new classrooms.

One of the most important challenges facing Watson's at this time was the need to modernise buildings and facilities.

Department on the ground floor. However, one of the most significant building developments at this time was the completion of the Convie Wing on the south side of the East Quad, consisting of seven classrooms and a resource centre. This was to house the Economics and History Departments which had occupied huts in the East Quad for 14 years since the merger of 1975 and made good the intention, pre-merger, of building a Social Science Block, abandoned then because of lack of finance.

Incidentally, both staff and pupils using the new facilities immediately appreciated being piped into the main school's heating system instead of venturing out to the huts in all weathers!

One of the most far-reaching and radical decisions in the way Merchant Company schools were run was taken in Session 1989/90 when the Merchant Company Education Board agreed

to devolve a great deal of power and financial administration to individual school Governing Councils. For some time it had been felt by some members of the Merchant Company, including the Master, Michael Walker, that the decision-making system and the time-scale of implementation of agreed decisions affecting the schools had been bogged down by excessive bureaucracy. Accordingly the Master and the majority of the Merchant Company members proposed a Governing Council for each school with powers to run their own financial affairs on a daily basis. These changes were very much in line with Frank Gerstenberg's thoughts as he had experienced a degree of frustration at the limited scope for individual decision-making compared to that which he had enjoyed at Oswestry. Not surprisingly there was a serious division of opinion among Merchant Company members and the Secretariat over the proposed changes. The opponents argued that they would seriously weaken both the Merchant Company and its schools. After much discussion and argument the reformist view prevailed in the Master's Court just in time to avoid any need for a new Act of Parliament.

The new Governing Council had as its first Chairman Geoffrey Ball, last Vice Convenor and a Watson's parent who knew fairly well how the school worked. A Bursar was appointed in charge of the school's devolved finances. To tackle the new challenge of running the school it was stipulated that the Governing Council should have at least one lawyer, accountant, educationalist and architect. Within a short time the benefits of devolution were manifest with the Watson's management able, after wide consultations, to make their own decisions on the spot and implement them more quickly. For the most part staff, pupils and parents probably saw little difference at first but soon the Governing Council was able to make decisions affecting the whole Watson's community such as setting fees, holiday dates and staff salaries independent of the other Merchant Company schools.

For three weeks in January and February 1990, Watson's underwent a General Inspection by Her Majesty's School Inspectorate (HMI), unbelievably the first since 1965. The anticipation of this dreaded experience turned out on the whole to be worse than the actual event. What it undoubtedly produced was a mountain of paperwork, policy statements, lesson plan revision and a dusting down of visual aids, symptomatic of the dead hand of bureaucracy on contemporary education. Two amusing reactions from senior members of staff captured the spirit of the inspection. May Nicol, Deputy Principal, in frustration, asked the Principal, "*Where is my policy for writing policy statements?*"

Ivan Wells, Head of the Maths Department, having taught a Higher Maths lesson to very able pupils which had impressed the inspector, suggested to him, "*Now if you want to see how that lesson is usually taught come back tomorrow, same time same place.*"

On a more serious note the inspection was a very good and positive experience for the whole school. The Report produced a very satisfactory outcome although there were a few areas for improvement – more resources for computer access across the curriculum, more balance in the curriculum and the wisdom or otherwise of bypassing Standard Grade exams for the more able pupils in some subjects in S4. The extent and variety of extra-curricular activities surprised the HMI, especially Watson's insisting on traditional team sports such as rugby, cricket and hockey as well as a myriad of activities affording individual experiences.

Perhaps the last word should be that of the HMI themselves:

"*Pupils were articulate and well motivated. Relationships between staff*

The Douglas Robertson Memorial Photograph.

Anniversary Thanksgiving Service, 1991.

Some of the congregation.

and pupils were good... the school was particularly strong in the many opportunities it offered its pupils to participate in activities outside the formal curriculum and to develop qualities and leadership... it had gone a long way towards meeting its aim of equipping pupils with the academic, practical and social skills needed for the last decade of the twentieth century in a happy and caring environment."

One of the positive steps taken by the Merchant Company and the new Governing Council was to reward the teaching staff with an allowance above the national salary scales, as a mark of appreciation of the collective teaching body, for their efforts in the classroom, the burden of Standard Grade course development and their widespread extra-curricular contribution.

1991 was to be another significant landmark in the history of Watson's marking the 250th Anniversary of the opening of George Watson's Hospital and the 120th Anniversary of the opening of the Ladies' College. To begin with in a practical way in September 1990, the Governing Council decided to launch the Watson's 250 Appeal which exceeded its £1 million target by the time the appeal closed at the end of March 1991. Until 1985 under grant-aided regulations the use of fee income for capital projects was prohibited. Despite this the new Information Technology Unit and the Convie Wing were made possible through private bequests, sale of land and careful management of school resources. Accordingly the Watson's 250 Appeal was to finance a number of school development projects. Two new physics laboratories and a new biology laboratory were created to help meet increased demand for science subjects; six new all-weather artificial tennis courts under floodlights were laid which could double as hockey and PE facilities and an upgrading of drama facilities in the Assembly Hall, with raked seating and a permanent lighting and sound system were carried out.

The 250/120 anniversaries were of course celebrated in a variety of ways. In March one of the outstanding events was the Founder's Day Concert in the Usher Hall at which a pupil, Paul Burt, played Shostakovich's *Piano Concerto No 2* (one of the most challenging in the concert repertoire). On 27 March a special Thanksgiving Service was held in the old Royal Infirmary Chapel (formerly the chapel of the original George Watson's Hospital). On 11 October a Service of Celebration for the life of George Watson was held in Greyfriars' Kirk at which the Moderator of the General Assembly of the Church of Scotland, the Very Reverend Dr William Macmillan, preached the sermon. After the service a memorial plaque was dedicated to George Watson and can be seen in the Flodden Wall in Greyfriars' churchyard. Other events included a pipe band competition, some celebrity lectures, and an end-of-year Carol Concert in St Giles' Cathedral.

The *Watsonian* for Session 1991/2 pinpointed a growing sense of unease at the problem of excessive

Founder's Day Concert, Usher Hall.

Murray Fergusson, Leader of the Orchestra.

Paul Burt, Piano Soloist.

bureaucracy in education. In his editorial, Christopher Rush made an impassioned plea to *"protect the ancient values of George Watson's College against the meretricious ideologies from the false gods of statistics, bureaucracy, finance, change, position, and power."*

This sentiment was partially echoed in the same issue by the Principal when he expressed his abhorrence that *"...creeping bureaucracy was in danger of strangling education."*

One undoubted cause of increasing paperwork was the continuous change in the national exam curriculum during this period involving the introduction of Standard Grades, Revised Higher and Advanced Higher, SCOTVEC modules and the 5 to 14 Programme, all involving increased

pupil assessment and more regular progress reporting.

On a more positive note Watson's continued to expand its international links. For decades parties of pupils had benefited from foreign travel exchanges. In the early 1990s a number of initiatives were taken to emphasise that the school was part of the wider international community. A European committee was set up to encourage pupils 'to think European'. The European flag was flown from the top of the school to mark Britain's presidency of the European Community in the second half of 1993 and in December during the Edinburgh European Summit, Sir Edward Heath (former Prime Minister who took Britain into Europe in 1973) was invited to give an address. The Founder's Day speaker in March 1994 was Monsieur Pierre Joxe, former French Minister of Defence who had spent three months as a Watson's pupil in 1950. Other foreign initiatives included the school orchestra's concert tour in Assisi, in Italy, during Session 1991/2 and the extension of work experience for S5 pupils to include placements in France and Denmark. In response to a request that British schools with boarding facilities should accept pupils from Eastern Europe four Ukrainian pupils joined Watson's. A Bosnian girl, Aida Dedic (who had acted for many months as an interpreter for British UN forces in Bosnia) joined Watson's for a few months to try to catch up with her 'lost years' of education during the Bosnian tragedy of the early 1990s.

One of the most exciting building projects under Frank Gerstenberg was the opening of Watson's new Technology Centre in late 1993. It was launched at a hi-tech ceremony incorporating a multi-screen conference link-up between Helen Sharman (Britain's first and only astronaut) who officially opened the building, and Professor Heinz Wolff in London. At a cost of nearly £1million, the new facility, amongst the most modern in Britain, was dedicated to technology studies and graphic communication, and geared very much to education in the twenty-first century. Coincidentally, a major refurbishment of the Design Centre was now undertaken, both projects being financed by the Watson's 250 Appeal.

Watson's links with industry and commerce were further strengthened by

the introduction of an 'Understanding Industry' course for the vast majority of S5 pupils. In 1995, to celebrate its tercentenary, the Bank of Scotland endowed a study and travel scholarship worth £500 per annum to enable the recipient to travel in Europe and undertake an academic investigation on a commercial topic. This initiative seemed especially fitting with George Watson being the first Accountant of the Bank of Scotland in the late seventeenth century.

A heightened awareness of management and business ethos and practices seemed to percolate down into school life during the 1990s encapsulated by the concept of development. Traditionally Watson's had as its main goal the all-round development of the pupil. To this was added a few innovations to develop further the different parts of the Watson's community. Five-year management-type development plans for the whole school and individual departments were initiated, the professional status of the staff was to be enhanced by a staff appraisal and development scheme which was supplemented by Watson's being accredited as 'Investors in People'. However, with the appointment of a School Development Officer in a later expanding Development Office, the development reached its height.

The basic function of the new Development Office was fundraising to supplement fee income and publicity. One of its main roles was to administer the Watson's Family Foundation set up in 1997. The new Labour Government of 1997 very quickly indicated its desire

The Principal welcoming the Rt Hon Sir Edward Heath on 10 December, when he spoke in the Music School to staff and senior pupils.

to scrap the Assisted Places Scheme which had allowed 250 pupils to attend Watson's on reduced or nil fees. As the Labour Party had indicated as early as 1992 their intention to abolish the scheme when in government, the Governing Council had deliberated *"over ways of minimising the financial blow of abolition"* and yet still satisfy George Watson's original aim in his will to provide for Foundationers. Accordingly, by 1997 the Governing Council had agreed to set up a Watson's Family Foundation which would be permanent with the twin aims of raising funds to replace the Assisted Places Scheme and to finance future building projects. Such was the success of the Foundation that within six years of its launch 125 pupils annually received financial assistance, which would certainly have gladdened the heart of George Watson.

The last few years of the twentieth century saw Watson's, under Frank Gerstenberg, continuing to focus on the wider community. During Session 1997/8, the Castlebrae High School/Watson's Joint Drug Project culminated in a study visit to New York, an excellent example of co-operation between state and independent schools. In October 1997, Watson's hosted a Student Commonwealth Heads of Government Meeting involving 31 state and independent schools. In April 1998, 10 S5 and S6 pupils were chosen to represent the United Kingdom in the European Youth Parliament in Granada in Spain.

At the same time the Principal voiced concern about the effect of

Service of Celebration at Greyfriars' Kirk.

possible litigation acting as a deterrent to staff responsible for pupil groups embarking on outdoor education projects such as Third Year Projects. He also sought to reassure the Watson's community that despite the problems associated with the introduction of the new Higher Still exam programme in August 1999, the school would resist any clamour to adopt the A Level exam system or even contemplate a fanciful notion of Watson's setting up its own private exam system. On a positive note, Certificates of Graduation were awarded for the first time to all S6 leavers in June 1997.

The biggest challenge facing Watson's (and all other Scottish secondary schools) in the last years of Frank Gerstenberg's principalship was the need to rebuild the credibility of the new Higher Still exams after the fiasco of the 2000 SQA exam results when thousands of inaccurate results were sent out to candidates. In his farewell address on 29 June 2001, the Principal noted the irony of his retiral coinciding with Scottish education in crisis with teaching unions threatening to boycott the internal assessment element of Higher Still. (When he came to Watson's in 1985, the teaching unions had boycotted the development of the new Standard Grade exam by instituting a work-to-rule leading to the demise of much extra-curricular activity in state schools.) Yet Frank Gerstenberg was optimistic about the future and in particular the growing oral competence of pupils during his 16 years at Watson's, believing that the emphasis on more pupil discussion demanded by Standard Grade was the catalyst. He also praised the younger generation for displaying a greater awareness of the environment. However, inadequate salaries for teachers and higher than inflation fee increases were sources of disappointment for him.

Frank Gerstenberg's time at the helm at Watson's was a period of breathtaking change in society and education. Perhaps the most appropriate tribute was a member of the Governing Council's description of him as a *"quiet revolutionary"*. The physical appearance of Watson's in 2001 was in many ways different from that of 1985 with the new

Technology Building, a refurbished Art School, the Convie Wing in the East Quad, updated drama facilities in the Assembly Hall, a floodlit astro-turf pitch adaptable for a number of sports, an expanded IT Department and not least the Myreside Bridge linking the school with the playing fields. In addition he managed very successfully the devolution of powers to the Governing Council, the HMI school inspection, the Watson's 250/120 celebrations and appeal, and the launching of the Development Office and the Family Foundation.

Developments which must have given particular pleasure were tangible benefits for the teaching staff with the Watson's Allowance, the IIP accreditation revealing concern for both teaching and supporting staff, and the innovation of a sabbatical term for staff. The enhanced status of the visual and performing arts was also a great source of pleasure to the Principal,

especially the emergence of art and drama as activities to be considered on a par with music. The introduction of the St Giles' Carol Service in 1991 was a *"glorious celebration of worship and musical talent"* and a most happy legacy of the Gerstenberg years.

Frank Gerstenberg was an unassuming leader who worked tirelessly for the benefit of the whole community. He consistently showed his genuine interest in the pupils and the staff, never more so than at times of illness and bereavement. Anne Brobbel (Deputy Principal 1991–2000) paid a glowing tribute to the Principal in the 2001 *Watsonian*. She said: *"…as change in education relentlessly gathered pace Frank steered Watson's along its own route, taking on board the best of the new ideas, amending and adapting others to suit our ethos and standards and rejecting those which were fads and claptrap… he was inspired by change and not inhibited by it."*

The original Steering Committee of George Watson's Family Foundation.(Left to Right) Mr Robert Bellis, Mrs Anne Hamilton, Mr Roy Mack (Director of Projects), Mr Frank Gerstenberg (Principal), Mrs Lesley McKean, Mr Andrew Cubie (Chairman of the Governing Council), Mrs Anne Brobbel, Mr James Cowan, Mr Donald McGougan.

Frank Gerstenberg, 2001.

European Youth Parliament.

George Watson's College welcomes the new Principal, August 2001.

The Governors appointed Mr Gareth Edwards MA, Rector and Principal of Morrison's Academy, Crieff since 1996, to be the new Principal from August 2001. Aged 42 and married to Jane, with a 16-year-old daughter, Gareth Edwards was educated at Tudor Grange Grammar School, then at the Sixth Form College, both in Solihull and studied for an MA Degree in Classics at Exeter College, Oxford. His first teaching appointment was as Assistant Classics Master at King Edward School, Birmingham, followed by Head of Classics and Year Head at Bolton School, and becoming Vice Principal of Newcastle-under-Lyme School before he took up his appointment at Morrison's Academy. His interests included rugby, cricket, hill walking, operatic singing, travel and church work, and he was an elder in the Church of Scotland.

HRH The Princess Royal, Master of the Merchant Company, officially opens the Lower Primary, January 2001.

The new Music School, opened 2003.

In his first Prizegiving Address, in June 2002, Gareth Edwards outlined his educational objectives: "*My philosophy is simple… schools must try to achieve what each of us as individuals must strive to achieve….. amidst exciting new educational ideas we must still retain a focus upon the role schools play in providing an exemplar of society for the young to absorb and to improve on in their adult lives.*"

About this time in an interview in the *Watsonian*, with the Deputy Head Boy, Ryan Bowie, the new Principal outlined his impressions at the end of his first year at Watson's. He was surprised at the "*small school feel*" despite its size and was grateful for the family-like welcome he had received. He indicated his priority for Watson's was to maintain a close-knit, yet open and enthusiastic community which was not afraid to challenge itself, ie "*a school of and for all sorts*". He believed the School was successful in living up to its motto "*Ex Corde Caritas*". The range of extra-curricular activities had particularly impressed him, and he singled out Third Year Projects as a 'hallmark' of the School.

In return the consensus around the School was that after just one session, Gareth Edwards had been a pleasure to work with, being open, thoughtful and caring with a very strong sense of fairness – a promising beginning to his time at Watson's.

In 2003 evidence was forthcoming that Watson's was continuing to make very satisfactory progress in areas where it had been traditionally prominent. The autumn of 2003 saw Watson's undergoing a successful, full HMIe Inspection (the first since 1990). The Report noted: "*The strength of the quality of relationships that exists across the whole school community which encapsulates not only pupils and staff but also parents and governors.*" A new school prospectus emphasised that Watson's measured its success as much by what pupils were as by what they did.

The tradition of educational innovation was maintained by the introduction of an eight-day teaching cycle, partly to accommodate the increase to eight subjects that each S3 and S4 pupil had to take on his or her timetable.

A highlight of Session 2003/4 was the concert, on 15 October 2003, to celebrate the opening of the refurbished Music School, at which two celebrated Watsonians in the music world, the pianist Malcolm Martineau and the bass, Brian Bannatyne-Scott, performed. The latest modernisation featured an extension with a modern keyboard studio, an ensemble and practice room and disabled facilities. The opportunity was also taken to unveil a plaque in memory of Dr Jack Martin, the original anonymous donor of £60,000 who financed the New Music School opened in 1964. The Music School had been refurbished in 1975 to accommodate the new merged Watson's.

It should also be pointed out that the Family Foundation provided £600,000 to finance this latest modernisation, a good example of the important work of the School Development Office and the Foundation. Perhaps its importance will be seen against a background of the devolved Scottish Parliament's intention to examine the charitable status of schools like Watson's in the near future with a view to weakening or abolishing it altogether. Perish the thought!

The strength of the quality of relationships that exists across the whole school community which encapsulates not only pupils and staff but also parents and governors.

The Watson's Bulletin, *December 1988.*

The front cover of the *Watson's Bulletin* of December 1988 encapsulates for many the infinite variety of extra-curricular activities at the school. During both the 1990 and 2003 full Inspections the HMI expressed surprise at the scope and variety of the 'hidden curriculum' at Watson's. Indeed it would need a separate history to describe them all. Accordingly in the following section a selection only is made to give a flavour of this very important dimension of school life.

The main team sports such as rugby, cricket, girls' and boys' hockey, as well as badminton, curling, tennis, rowing have been recorded in detail over the years in the *Watsonian*.

Watsonian, *2005*

Foreign Travel

There has been a dramatic expansion of foreign travel opportunities for Watson's pupils in the last 30 years which can be divided into three broad categories. The following lists give only an indication of foreign trips available during this period.

- S4 Lycee Henri IV (for boys began 1950)
- S4 Camille See (for girls began 1952)
- S2 Thonon-les-Bains
- S2 Ile de Ré (began 1988/9) – all France
- German-Scottish Exchange, Munich (Senior pupils began 1980)
- Italian-Scottish Exchange, Sondrio, North Italy (for S5/6 began 1988)
- Spanish-Scottish Exchange, Fuengirola (for S4/5)
- American-Scottish Exchange, Harley High School, Rochester, New York State (began 1980 for S6)
- Russian-Scottish Exchange, Moscow High School 1209 (began 1990 for S4/5)
- Second American-Scottish Exchange, Edinburgh, Richmond, Virginia (involving 8 pupils from St Christopher's and St Katherine's Schools, began 1998/9)

French exchange to Thonon-Les-Bains.

Russian exchange, 1991.

Tours and Trips (examples)

- Vancouver, 1980 and 1984, Rugby and Curling teams in return for two visits to Edinburgh during 1977–9 by St George's School
- Skiing Abroad – 11 trips alone between 1975–81
- Educational Cruise on board SS *Uganda* for 85 pupils (July 1981)
- History Department First World War Battlefield Field Trips (began 1991)
- in 2002, Symphony Orchestra – Holland
  Pipe Band – Japan
  S3 Rugby – France
  First XV Rugby – New Zealand
  Girls' and Boys' First X1 Hockey – Holland
  Modern Studies (16 Sixth Formers) – New York

Expeditions

- Iceland, 1990
- Himalayas (Ladakh), 2001
- Ecuador, 2004

Charities

Watson's has endeavoured to put into practice the school motto, *"Ex Corde Caritas"*, in a variety of ways. The following is a brief list of the main charitable activities, co-ordinated by a Charities Committee.

- **Charities Day** – non uniform day (various fund-raising events usually in the Tipperlinn area) - raised nearly £5000 in 2003
- **Cockburn Sevens**
- **Aid to Bosnia** in 1990s
- **Sixth Year Charity** – Rachel House for Terminally Ill Children
- **Senior Pupil** involvement with the Ark (for Edinburgh homeless)

In addition nearly every week some individual pupil group, a Form or Year, raises money for a charity of their choice.

History Department field trip to First World War Battlefield, 1991.

Ecuador 2004, Ice Training on Cotopaxi.

Slave market, Charities Day, 1979.

Third Year Projects

No history of Watson's would be complete without some mention of Third Year Projects (for a detailed History of Projects see *The Story of Projects at George Watson's College* edited by Liz Smith and Roger Young, and published in October 2003). In turn Third Year Projects originating in Session 1961/2, has been described as:

"*The best thing we ever did.*" (RogerYoung)

"*One of the jewels in Watson's crown.*" (Frank Gerstenberg)

"*Part of the fabric of Watson's.*" (Gareth Edwards)

The educational philosophy of Projects was to give pupils experience of the 'great outdoors', engaging in a myriad of physical activities such as walking, climbing, exploring, canoeing, sailing and cycling. Complementary to the above was the desire to expose pupils to new experiences, and to encourage them to visit the rich inheritance of Scotland's outdoor life. In 1967 the Merchant Company purchased Ardtrostan, on the south side of Loch Earn, as an adventure centre for all four schools. This was sadly burned down in 1981 and was eventually replaced by Middleton Cottages Centre in Glen Isla, Perthshire, in 1983. However, over the last four decades projecteers have gone much further afield to nearly every corner of Scotland and regularly to parts of England and Wales.

It is difficult to overestimate the importance of Third Year Projects. For most Watsonians in later life, the experience of their first taste of communal living, away from home and tackling the physical challenges involved, was a watershed in their time at school and a turning point in their lives. For a minority of pupils the experience was a never-ending nightmare, separated as they were from the luxuries of modern living. As one very experienced Staff Leader (Ian Murray) noted: "*Too much luxury prevents you from appreciating what real outdoor life is all about.*"

However, over the last decade or so doubts over the future of Projects in their traditional form have become more prominent. What is important is to try to maintain the right balance between adventurous physical challenges and reassuring pupils and parents that everything possible is being done to maximise health and the safety of pupils and to minimise risk. As Frank Gerstenberg put it, "*There is an ever present danger that Third Year Projects will become watered down and come to resemble activity holidays rather than a voyage of self-discovery.*"

Happily, he was hugely successful in preserving the original ethos.

It is difficult to overestimate the importance of Third Year Projects. For most Watsonians, [it] was a watershed in their time at school and a turning point in their lives.

Music and Drama

Over the years there has been a tremendous range of successful and enjoyable productions – both musical and dramatic – performed by pupils throughout the school. Here are some notable examples of these:

Immediately After the Merger:
- *Oliver!* – musical, 1974
- *The Adventurer* by Terence Rattigan – the story of Alexander of Macedon, in 1975
- *Hassan*, music by Delius, in 1976
- *Orpheus in the Underworld* by J Offenbach, in 1977
- *The Crucible* by Arthur Miller, in 1978
- *West Side Story*, in 1979

In More Recent Times:
- *Cabaret*, in 2000
- *The Cheviot, Stag and the Black, Black Oil* (John McGrath) in 2000
- *My Fair Lady*, in 2001
- *Sweet Charity*, in 2002
- *Oklahoma!*, in 2004
- *Grease*, in 2005

And by Shakespeare
- *Macbeth*, in 2002
- *Much Ado About Nothing* and A *Midsummer Night's Dream*, in 2003
- *Hamlet*, in 2004

One of the most popular Drama events is the annual Inter-House Drama Competition.

My Fair Lady, *2001.*

The Music Department

In the 30 years since the merger, no department has had a higher profile at Watson's than the Music Department. It has enjoyed a well-deserved reputation for consistent excellence. This was in no small part due to the leadership and musicality of the three heads of department. Margery Traves, with an association at George Square going back to 1945, became joint Head of Music at the merger in 1974. By her enthusiasm, energy and devotion to the cause of music she inspired generations of pupils to reveal a musical talent previously hidden. She shared the running of the Department with Patrick Criswell until her retirement in 1979. Patrick, who joined Watson's in 1972, ran the department until 1988. During these years the Orchestra and Chorus performed regularly at Founder's Day and Spring Concerts, at the Annual Carol Service, at the Kirking of the Master in St Giles' and on numerous other occasions.

The Music Department was heavily involved in the Merchant Company Tercentenary in 1981 and in FEAST in 1985. Watson's musicians also regularly participated in operas and concerts in Haddo House in Aberdeenshire. From 1988 to 2004, Norman Mitchell was Director of Music. During this period the active pupil participation increased dramatically with about 1,000 pupils learning to play instruments in 2004. Again the various musical groups gave countless public performances including the First Orchestra and College Chorus, the Ex Corde Choir and Strings and the Chamber and Baroque Orchestra. Highlights in this period included the orchestral concert in the Usher Hall to celebrate the 250/ 120 anniversaries, the innovation of Nine Lessons and Carols in St Giles' in 1991, more recently the College Chorus' performance of Fauré's *Requiem* in 2001 and the special concert in October 2003 to mark the completion of the refurbishment of the Jack Martin Music School.

The New Organ

In 1978, a volunteer group of staff under Sandy Keith and Ron Looker began the process of replacing the Hammond electric organ in the Assembly Hall, which had been donated in memory of Stuart Cameron Watt, a former School Captain who was killed early in WW2. Chambers for a pipe organ had featured in the original plan for Colinton Road in 1932. The painstaking task of dismantling the organ from the Chaplaincy Centre in Forrest Road (formerly the New North Church) and rebuilding it in the Assembly Hall was carried out under the expert supervision of Ron Smith, an organ builder. Appropriately the new piped organ was given a public performance in the Opening Gala Concert during the Merchant Company Tercentenary Celebrations in June 1981. Then in June 1985, during FEAST, John Kitchen (St Andrews University), a leading Scottish organist, *"put the Keith/Looker through its paces"* in a recital of Bach and romantic organ music.

| *The Orchestra and Choir, 2001.*

British Lions, Gavin and Scott Hastings, 1993.

Louise Burton (left) and Janet Jack (née Nimmo), 1989.

After school Watson's pupils have made their mark in all walks of life. However, in the world of sport the following quintet have taken sporting excellence to a new level.

In rugby, the brothers Gavin and Scott Hastings (outstanding members of Watson's rugby XVs) won well over one hundred Scottish caps between them. Both were selected to play for the British Lions in New Zealand in 1993, Gavin also being chosen as Captain of the tourists.

In women's hockey, Janet Jack (née Nimmo) won over 140 Scottish caps and represented Britain. In 1998 she represented Scotland in both the World Cup Hockey Finals in Holland and in the Commonwealth Games in Kuala Lumpur, Malaysia, as did Louise Burton (left 1989) who also gained over 50 Scottish caps.

Perhaps the pinnacle of sporting glory was achieved on 20 August 2004 when Chris Hoy won the Olympic Gold Medal in Athens for the Cycling One Kilometre Time Trial. Chris had already won the World Championship and was the existing Commonwealth Champion.

Chris Hoy, Athens 1994.

Sir Basil Spence

Basil Urwin Spence was born in 1907 in Bombay, India, but was sent back to Scotland to study at George Watson's. He then attended Edinburgh College of Art (1927–32) and completed his architectural studies at the Bartlett School of Architecture in London.

His first post was as an assistant to Sir Edwin Lutyens who had a profound influence on his style. He worked on the designs for the Viceroy's House in New Delhi. After a spell at Rowland Anderson Paul he returned to Edinburgh in 1930.

In 1950, a British Commonwealth competition for a design for a new Anglican Cathedral in Coventry attracted 200 entries. Spence's radical design won. Work began in 1956 and was completed in 1962. Spence was knighted for his efforts and also served as President of the Royal Institute of British Architects (1958–60).

Unfortunately – due to a restrictive Council housing brief – he was also responsible for some of the worst and infamous high-rise monstrosities in Glasgow which replaced old slums with modern ones. Despite that low point in his career, he produced other more lasting and interesting designs, eg Mortonhall Crematorium (Edinburgh), St Aidan's College (Durham), Knightsbridge Barracks (London), the British Embassy (Rome), Glasgow Airport, the Erasmus Building (Cambridge), King's Buildings (Edinburgh), Edinburgh University Library and the Head's house at Watson's! He is regarded as one of Britain's finest architects.

Spence died in November 1976 and is buried at Thornham Parva, Suffolk.

[Sir Basil Spence] is regarded as one of Britain's finest architects.

Basil Spence with his model for the new Coventry Cathedral.

A Staff as diverse and talented as Watson's had many notables during this period. In this History it is impossible and not really necessary to record the achievements of and contributions to Watson's of all the staff. This has already been done most eloquently for individual staff annually in *The Watsonian*, on retirement, on moving to pastures new or, in a few cases, by marking their premature deaths in service.

The notables detailed below comprise merely a small selection of staff.

Alex Weston, seen here doing the dishes at the Pavilion after the tea break during the Staff v Boys' Cricket Match, 1973/4.

Alex Weston (Staff 1953–78)

Alex Weston joined Watson's at Colinton Road as Head of the Technical Department. He successfully oversaw the move to a more theoretical approach to technical subjects without losing sight of the importance of practical skills. He and his wife Connie also ran the boys' Bainfield Boarding House for eight years. In 1968 he was appointed Deputy Headmaster (later Deputy Principal), a position he held with great distinction until his retirement in December 1978. Although the bulk of his time at Watson's was pre-merger, Alex's qualities which

Donald Doull.

had stood him in good stead, shone throughout the difficult and at times stressful period of the transitional years from 1973 to 1978. He was a first-class organiser and administrator. That the first few years of the merger were successful was partly due to Alex's timetabling skills. Although a disciplinarian, he was a modest and unassuming person, very approachable to staff, pupils and parents. The Weston Years, particularly when he was Deputy Principal, acquired a legendary status.

> *Although a disciplinarian [Alex] was a modest and unassuming person, very approachable to staff, pupils and parents.*

Peggy Naughton (Staff 1943–80)

Peggy Naughton could best be described as a 'true Watsonian'. Educated at George Watson's Ladies' College, from 1923 to 1933, she joined the Primary Department of the Girls' School in 1943. She was appointed in turn House Mistress of Melville, Head of the Primary Department and finally became Assistant Principal of the Middle School after the merger, a position she held until her retirement in 1980. She also taught History and French at GWLC and became an invaluable member of the combined History Department at Colinton Road from 1975 to 1980. In Roger Young's tribute to Peggy, on her untimely death after only six years of retirement, he described her as *"a great teacher, a great administrator, a great Watsonian and a great person"*. She was unfailingly courteous to all, a quiet disciplinarian with a very keen sense of humour and fun, who related very well to pupils, colleagues and parents. Her diplomacy was considerable and the smoothness of the schools' merger and later of the Women Watsonians with The Watsonian Club, were in no small part due to Peggy. It was especially fitting that she was the last President of the Women Watsonians and the first 'woman' President of The Watsonian Club.

> *She was unfailingly courteous to all, [and] a quiet disciplinarian with a very keen sense of humour and fun.*

Donald Doull (Staff 1947–79)

Donald Doull was a member of the English Department from 1947 to 1979, the last seven as Head of Department. Hundreds of pupils were privileged to be introduced to the wonders of English language and literature by Donald in such a humane and gentle manner. Many also benefited from Donald's expert involvement in the Combined Cadet Force from 1948 to 1970, in Third Year Projects, in the Lit. and Debating Society, and in the School Library. However, it is above all else for his personal qualities for which Donald will be best remembered. Everyone who met this most gentle, kind and courteous of men felt the better for knowing him. Sadly he enjoyed only three years of retirement.

After many successful years Donald Scott finished as 1st XV Rugby coach. Roy Mack thought the occasion should be marked and invited all Donald's former rugby captains to attend a function and contribute to a gift. Roy commissioned a bronze statue of John Rutherford scoring a try. John was a former staff member and Scottish internationalist. Donald's first Captain presented him with the bronze.

Donald Scott
(Staff 1952–89)

Donald Scott joined the PE Department in 1952 and was to give Watson's 37 years of outstanding commitment and service. He had been an outstanding rugby player winning 10 Scottish international caps and he was to transfer his innate rugby skills on to the school playing field. For the next 33 years Donald coached the 1st XV with a record of success second to none among his Scottish contemporaries. In the process he provided a number of well-known Scottish rugby internationalists, culminating in the inclusion of the Hastings brothers in the successful British Lions Test side in South Africa in 1989. Under Donald school cricket also flourished with his teams playing attractive cricket and immaculately turned out in their whites. In 1972 he was appointed Head of the PE Department, a position he held until his retirement in 1989. During this time the PE Department was a team of committed professionals (and a few characters too) and successfully extended the range of sporting activities at the school. In addition, Donald and his wife Pat made an invaluable contribution to the development of a boarding house system at Watson's, particularly in Bainfield House, first as assistant to Alex Weston and then for a number of years in charge. Donald has deservedly been described as *"a great sportsman schoolmaster"*. Perhaps he will be best remembered for his unfailing courtesy and good humour and for inculcating in the pupils a strongly held belief that games should be played for enjoyment and in a sporting manner, win or lose. Watson's has had few better ambassadors.

Perhaps [Donald] will be best remembered for his unfailing courtesy and good humour.

May Nicol
(Staff 1960–91)

May Nicol joined the History Department of GWLC in 1960. In a short time she became a teaching legend both at the Square and later at Colinton Road. When both a Senior History Lecturer at Edinburgh University and a recent Founder's Day Speaker (herself a well-known BBC figure) described May as *"quite the best teacher I ever had"*, then it was obvious that here was a classroom teacher *sans pareil*. It came as no surprise that on

In a short time [May Nicol] became a teaching legend both at the Square and later at Colinton Road.

the retirement of Dr Boog-Watson in 1960, May was appointed Head of the History Department. After the merger May was appointed Deputy Principal of the new Watson's and she continued to teach History in the inspiring and committed way we had taken for granted, winning the respect of the HMI during the Inspection of 1990. It was, however, as a most efficient and formidable Deputy Principal for 16 years until 1991, that May made a lasting impact on the co-educational Watson's. Her contribution (along with that of Peggy Naughton) to

Jim Cowan.

helping the former staff and pupils of the girls' school settle down in the new and strange environment of Colinton Road was incalculable. Her razor-sharp intellect and mind allied to a very sound practical common sense enabled her to see through the fog of discussion and bureaucracy and to come to clear-cut decisions. The two Principals and the four co-deputies regarded May as a pillar of stability, whose advice was indispensable. Yet she was a caring and genuinely interested staff and pupil mentor, with a lovely sense of humour and fun, and an endearing line in self-parody. She was devoted to the Watson's community and staff could count on her loyalty whether on the hockey touch line or on Third Year Project visits. On one memorable occasion her calm authority defused a difficult situation involving an inebriated young lady on a History trip to WWI Battlefields! Both Principals she served under were in no doubt that May Nicol would have been an outstanding Headmistress.

Jim Cowan (Staff 1959–97)

Jim Cowan joined the Watson's Technical Department in 1959 and became a very effective teacher of Technical subjects and Mathematics. He was then appointed Myreside House Master, along with his wife, Ella, where his outstanding ability to relate to and help boarders and stand in loco parentis soon became evident. For six years Jim was Assistant Principal in charge of the Middle School (1980–6). His last 11 years were spent as Deputy Principal until his retirement in 1997. Throughout this period of almost four decades Jim indulged in his great passion of cricket by coaching generations of young schoolboys in the basic skills and laying the foundations of a lifelong love of the game. In addition he coached rugby teams and was an enthusiastic supporter of the Model Railway Club. However, it was Jim's personal qualities that made him an outstanding member of the Watson's staff. To him every pupil and member of staff was important. He won universal respect in the Watson's community for his integrity, fair-mindedness and his 'man

management' skills before the term became a cliché. He possessed sound practical common sense based on a deep-seated humanity and genuine concern for the welfare of pupils and staff. Jim also possessed a great sense of humour and fun whether in the role of Santa Claus at Christmas parties or by his regular participation in Melville-Ogilvie pantomimes. In addition he was able to soothe 'the savage breast' of some agitated Head of Department over a complicated timetabling matter and to give members of staff 'green slips' to cover classes of absent staff in such a way that one felt it was almost a privilege to receive one! In his editorial tribute in *The Watsonian*, Chris Rush summed up Jim's place in the long history of the school: *"the school motto, Ex Corde Caritas, never found a truer exponent than in the example of this extraordinary schoolmaster and great human being".*

Sylvia Castle-Smith (Principal's Secretary 1974–2003)

Sylvia Castle-Smith became Roger Young's secretary in 1974 and proceeded to become a vital cog in the Watson's machine until her retirement in 2003. During this time she became the embodiment of all that was good in a school secretary. She displayed unquestioning loyalty and a dedication and trust

so necessary in a job involving confidential material. Very often she was the first in school and the last to leave. The three principals she served unanimously agreed she was indispensable to the smooth running of the school and were always grateful for the many little additional tasks she carried out, unobtrusively, and which were perhaps at times beyond the call of duty. Almost always optimistic and cheerful, Sylvia's contact with the staff and pupils was helpful and positive. Her knowledge of the Watson's community was encyclopedic and she was a regular supporter of school plays, concerts and musicals.

The three principals [Miss Castle-Smith] served unanimously agreed she was indispensable to the smooth running of the school.

Mr Gerstenberg with the power behind his throne (his secretary Miss Sylvia Castle-Smith), 2001.

The Junior School in the 20th Century

Article by Jim Currall.

I have been asked to produce a 'history' of the twentieth-century Junior School as I knew and experienced it. My personal recollections are as a pupil, from 1927 age five, to 1939, prior to the outbreak of WW2 and then as a teacher from 1950 to 1983. My family connection started with my father's appointment in 1904 to the language department, of which he became Head, and later, a formidable Deputy Head of the whole school. To the boys he was no doubt looked upon with a degree of awe as a man not to be crossed, and I'm sure they would have been very astonished to see the two of us racing flat out along the pavement when I had been issued suddenly with the challenge, *"Race you to the third lamppost, boy!"*

One of the extraordinary facts that he told me of his early teaching days was that those who presented themselves for the Edinburgh University Bursary Competition forfeited 50 marks overall if they offered French or German rather than Latin!

It was, of course, the 'old school' which I first attended. This was over a mile from home in Falcon Road, and after a week or so, it was considered quite reasonable for me to head off on my own, via Greenhill Gardens, the Links and the Meadows. That such a solo walk was considered safe for a five-year-old is a rather sad comment on modern society.

The floors of the classrooms were timber, well worn; we had long continuous desks, tiered, more like a lecture room, and glowing coal fires in the winter. The playground was in the front of the building, the surface being small, shiny pebbles, not ideal for football nor falling on, and there were two WW1 German guns, like 18-pounders, for playing with or fighting over. In the summer term we were allowed on the Meadows.

My first teacher was a young, pretty, gentle lady, Miss Gillespie. We had slates for writing on, on which the chalk squeaked horribly! Then we went to class C, with 'Big' Miss Smith of a booming contralto voice. She had that invaluable talent, especially for the lower school, of being a talented musician. For very many years the school worked short of a classroom and the top third of the year of three classes skipped to what was the equivalent of P4, in my case, to Mrs Smith, a young widow who appeared to be one of those unfortunates picked on by fate, her only son, Roger, being knocked down and killed by a drunken motorist. Miss Lamont in 3 Lower Junior followed. Perhaps ready for a male teacher, I now moved to 6 Middle Junior, with Alec Budge. A man interested in Nature Study as it was called in those days, I enjoyed his class, was encouraged to start collecting stamps which I have done all my life and we became good friends when I returned as a teacher. I remember he was the first teacher to give me the belt and, believe me, I was quite pleased! I had become aware that, as the Deputy Head's son, the ladies were sometimes letting me off with minor misdemeanours that deserved retribution, and here I was pulled up short, just an ordinary member of the class, a salutary lesson!

My first year in Colinton Road was in 9 Higher Junior (P7) with 'Pa' Lennie, Head of the Junior School, a very large man in every way, with a deep booming voice and jowls that shook. He was sometimes overpowering for small boys, but basically kindly, with a great sense of humour. He sat us, all 39, in order of height, I being number 38. Take hope, any young midgets, I have ended at five foot ten! I vividly recall one of the smallest boys going to Pa's desk and accidentally knocking over the red ink bottle. There was a roar which put the fear of death into us. *"Boy! That is redinkulous! It is inkredulous!"* Dead silence! Then a slow smile spread over his chubby face and the class burst into nervous laughter. My father told me that 'Pa' had written beside a boy's essay talking of a stormy 'Petrol', *"Hail to thee blithe spirit, bird thou never wert!"*

HEADS OF THE JUNIOR SCHOOL, 1925–PRESENT

1925–39:	Robert 'Pa' Lennie
1939–66:	James Rattray
1966–79:	James Smith
Jan–June 1979:	James Currall (Acting Head)
1979–91:	Alex Peden
1991–Present:	Donald McGougan

"…'Pa' Lennie … a very large man …"

'Pa' joined Watson's in 1903. A lover of opera, Pa played leading comedy parts and sang in many a school activity. Pa loved writing sketches and lyrics. He also founded the school orchestra in 1919. One of his favourite songs was, 'Apple Dumpling.'

James Rattray (pictured in 1935) joined Watson's in 1925 and took over Junior Rugby and Cricket. Later, he assisted with the formation of the Air Training Corps. James gave 40 years' dedicated and efficient service to Watson's.

On the academic side we had started Latin with a senior classics master and had sat Watson's Qualifying Exam for entry to the appropriate senior class, bearing in mind that all our classes, Junior and Senior, were at this time streamed as 'U' (University), A, B, C, D. I ended in A, but being too young, repeated the year in U, a sensible move which made life much happier. We also now had swimming, the most popular subject of all.

The next six years were spent in the Senior School, not really the subject of this article. For me the 1940s were taken up by university, war service in India and Burma, 1942–5; in the Royal Artillery Band in London, 1946; business in Glasgow and then four years' teaching in David Kilpatrick Junior Secondary, now defunct, in dockland Leith, a tough but invaluable training ground. I was invited by Graham Andrew, then Headmaster of GWC, to join the Junior School, which I accepted when it was agreed that my outside musical activities could continue.

I joined a tight ship, run by James Rattray, an excellent, strict but scrupulously fair Head of the lower school. Everything ran on old-fashioned patterns on the principle of, *"If it ain't broke' don't fix it!"* Everyone, staff and pupils, knew where they were. I was happy. When James decided to go earlier than was necessary in 1966, it fell to Jim Smith to become Head. A very different character from James Rattray, he was a pleasant-natured, courteous man who gave the impression of less necessity for everything having to be done by yesterday, but nonetheless ran things with quiet efficiency, gave his staff their heads and as his Deputy we had a friendly, easy relationship.

About this time separate desks for each child were abandoned and small tables for four pupils were substituted. As this meant that it was much harder for some children to see the blackboard and easier to talk to your neighbour, I never fathomed the sense in this development.

A radical change, of course, took place in 1974/5 when GWLC joined the boys' school. A new Primary building was necessary and again it seemed to me that fashion rather than common sense prevailed when it was built in Open Plan. It is interesting to note that 30 years later, at considerable cost, it has been redesigned with separate classrooms once more.

When Jim Smith collapsed and sadly died on the first day of the January term, 1979, I found myself pitched into Headship of the Junior School. Knowing that I had no intention of staying much longer than finances dictated, I encouraged the appointment of a new Head to enable me to get back to working directly with a class for my last year or two, and Alex Peden was appointed.

Jim Smith died suddenly on 9 January 1979. He had been appointed Head in 1966 and Watson's was his life. Indeed, as teacher and pupil it spanned 45 years. He met his wife Thelma at GWC and his daughter Liz has continued in the mould set by her father. Jim was an admirable person: calm, reasonable, encouraging, cheerful and co-operative. He was a superb teacher, brilliant Head and an unforgettable human being.

In Alex's short tenure as Head of the Junior School he introduced two major additions. He introduced class visits to large industrial and big businesses in town for P6 and P7 to give the young pupils an insight into the way their world worked. Also, we took these same pupils to camp at Meigle for a week which taught them to cope without mum and dad always being there, to get on with others and to see their teachers in a different light. Both were excellent ideas. As Alex was good at delegation it meant a lot of work for me, but very interesting. I retired at this time,

Alex Peden came from Moray House College and, in 12 years, substantially developed the curriculum and built a dedicated staff team. Alex loved running and was frequently seen jogging around the campus. Alex was a dedicated teacher who thoroughly enjoyed his vocation.

Jim with Duncan Veitch whose grandfather David helped to found the Jazz Band with Jim during the 1930s. Jim's father Richard, usually known as 'Piggy', came to Watson's in 1904 and retired after forty years service. In 1914, he became Head of Languages and, twelve years later, Deputy Head.

One has to feel that it is not a very nice world we are living in, but the school has responded very well to the conditions.

1983, aged 61. I enjoyed my work, but with music (both hobby and earner), garden, philately, travel and photography I had more than enough to fill my days. I had left an excellent library in the large ex-gymnasium, built up carefully over 25 years and what happened to it over the next year left me sad and angry. However, it has now been partially restored.

Donald McGougan, ex-colleague and present Head of the Junior School, has helped greatly in bringing the story to date. Music now has two specialist teachers full-time for the Junior School, music instrument tuition being given to some four hundred pupils during and after school. As the first boy ever to take Higher Music in Watson's, in 1939, I have a special interest in this development. Fred Holmes, in the 1930s, first altered the then condescending attitude to the subject. Now perhaps several of these 400 youngsters will take up music as their career in future. Another major change in the curriculum is the inclusion of French from P2 and from native French speakers. This is a wonderful, if long overdue, acknowledgement that it was high time we shook off our arrogant, lazy attitude to foreign languages in this country. Also, of course, since my day, a technology that has passed me by, the computer, is available and important to all pupils from their earliest days.

Linked to all these fundamental changes in educational matters are the social ones as well, with mother

and father working, and the apparent greater risks of safety of young children in daily life – all rather sad – there is the development of the nursery end of schooling and care; of a Breakfast Club for age 4 to 11 from 7.30am and an Afternoon Club to 5.45pm. The staff for these activities are additional to and independent from the normal school staff. The school doors are locked from 9.10am during the working hours, the playground is supervised, much form filling is the order of the day if children are being taken out on cultural, historical, general interest visits, much expanded since my day to include London, York, Bannockburn, etc. In 1983 we had one office staff, now there are six. One has to feel that it is not a very nice world we are living in, but the school has responded very well to the conditions as have Donald and Staff. Long may it be so!

Donald's Junior School

Article by Donald McGougan, Head of the Junior School since September 1991.

I was appointed as Form Teacher in the Junior School in September 1970. The school today is very different to the one I joined some 34 years before.

In the Beginning ...
Watson's was my first teaching post and I started on 7 September. Summer holidays were different in those day as we always worked the first two weeks in July and returned to school in early September.

I was appointed by two hugely impressive gentlemen: Roger Young, Head of the Senior School, and Jim Smith, the greatly loved Junior School Head who tragically died at far too young an age. In those days Jim's office was roughly where the Bursar's

office is today while the Head's/Principal's room is the same. Between them was the office administration which consisted of the redoubtable and much admired School Secretary, Miss Kathleen Davidson, and her assistant. Other than a young lady manning the telephones at Reception, I cannot recall other admin staff being employed at that time.

Staff returned from holiday at 9am and the boys came in at 11am. There was no 'In-Service' and very few staff returned early. The staff meeting was held in the newly built Music School auditorium and lasted an hour and a quarter. I remember vividly frantically scribbling down notes on a huge variety of matters which were to have no relevance whatsoever. *(Nice to see some things don't change –Ed.)*

Only a short time before a vote had been taken to allow female members into the main staff room, but a ladies' only one still existed at the north end of the east corridor. As today papers were supplied, but unlike today smoking was allowed and pipe smoke billowed from various corners. Indeed, almost everyone smoked in those days .

By about 11am the boys were in their respective playgrounds, the Upper Primary pupils in the East Quad (recently renamed 'George Square'), but there were no huts. The Senior Pupils were in the West Quad, but there were no cars. At 11am Jim Smith took me along to my new room: now Room 3 in the current maths corridor. By now I was wearing my gown as all staff did at that time when in the building. Jim then left me in charge of 30 boys as all classes in the Junior School were at that time. This was wonderful as in the outside world classes could be as high as 42 or 43.

My First Class
My first Form Class was P5Y. There were three classes at each stage in the Junior School and they were named E (eldest), M (middle) and Y (youngest) on the basis of age. My fellow P5 teachers were Elizabeth Spence and Catriona Collins who later went on to found 'The Cabin' and learning support.

The Campus

The layout was very different in those days. The Art School, the Games Hall, the Technology Building, the Boarding House and the Lower Primary did not exist and from the Music School to the Grandstand was a wonderful expanse of grass on which were four rugby pitches. The furthermost one (T4) ran west to east outside the current Upper Primary building and was used as a playground by our Lower Primary pupils during the summer.

The Junior School in 1970 was in a totally different location. The Upper Primary was in the current senior building and occupied classrooms 1–9 which were found in today's Maths corridor, taking in part of the present-day staffroom and R35 which was immediately above at the east end. This accommodated three classes each from P5 to P7 and one class, surprisingly, from P4 because of lack of space in the Lower Primary. Parents did not seem to bother. All Junior School classes in the main building attended Senior School Assemblies which were held on an almost daily basis and only on the odd occasion was an Upper Primary only Assembly held. Assemblies usually consisted of the hymn, the reading (usually read by a prefect or sixth former) and the notices. Occasionally, there were guest speakers.

The Lower Primary

The Lower Primary was based in the present-day Upper Primary building. Here was gym staffed by the PE Department, but the present Upper Primary Hall didn't exist, nor did the four classrooms facing north which are currently situated above the Hall. Pupils and staff came over to the main Dining Hall for lunch, but other than that, contact between the two sections of the Junior School was not great. P1 pupils at that time only did half a day at school for the entire first session.

The School Day

For Upper Primary pupils it was not much different from that of today except that it was five minutes shorter (to 3.10pm) The pupils followed a six-day cycle while the older pupils benefited from specialist teaching in PE, Art, Music and Latin, but there was no Games period within the cycle.

The concept of 'preparation time' was a wonderful plus as this did not happen in the state sector. Particularly attractive was the day on which Art occurred during the last two periods allowing me to go home at 2.35pm if cover was not required elsewhere. After-school sports were very limited with only rugby in winter and cricket in summer. Games against other schools took place on Saturday mornings, but the number of possible opponents was much greater: Melville College, Daniel Stewart's, John Watson's, Scotus Academy, Royal High Primary, Leith Academy, James Gillespie's and Trinity plus those which still exist today. To travel to an away fixture was almost unknown.

A Slower Pace

Within the school things seemed to happen at a slightly slower pace. The bun room, run by the legendary Mrs Robertson and Mrs Ross, functioned at morning intervals for both boys and staff. Lunches were the envy of other schools with staff seated at their own dedicated tables, all covered with white linen each with its own menu and served by uniformed ladies. Home-made soup was always first followed by a choice of three main courses and two or three sweets. At the end of each day afternoon tea was available for staff in the bun room for a very small cost and almost everyone went along to enjoy it and the usually stimulating and interesting company from all over the school. Lasting friendships were made and kept.

A Simpler Time

There was a much smaller team than today. Jim Smith was the only one without a teaching commitment. Mr Sawyers was his Deputy and Mr Currall, a long-established member of staff, had set up the Junior School Library which was situated where Matron's suite now stands. It was acknowledged as ahead of its time. The Infants Mistress was the promoted staff member in the Lower Primary, but even she had a class commitment. There was no Junior School admin team whilst auxiliaries and class helpers were unheard of. School trips were rare, but volunteer parent helpers were easy to find as few mothers then worked. Residential visits just did not happen!

Similarities and Differences

Founder's Day was celebrated as a special event and prizegivings for Junior and Senior pupils took place at the end of each session. The school did not, however, have its own Board of Governors and was run instead by Merchants' Hall. A Vice-Convenor was appointed by the Merchant Company to have particular responsibility for the school. Some of the things we just take for granted did not exist: the Nursery Unit, Breakfast Club and After School Club. In-Service Days were also unknown.

It was a happy place to work and still is. The turnover of staff was no greater than it is today, but the school was smaller with 630 pupils. Competition for places was keen, possibly keener than it is today.

5L visit to Purves Puppet Theatre, Biggar, 1990.

Arise the Lower Primary

From information provided by Mary Dilbey, GWC, Jan 1966–Sep 1989. Infants Mistress & Head of Lower Primary from 1974.

Following the momentous decision to amalgamate the two Watson's it was announced in 1971 that a new building for the Lower Primary would be erected as part of the plan to increase the school roll after 1974. A Staff Briefing Panel was then established to prepare the architectural brief and decide on educational policy, administration and organisation.

The Building

This was revolutionary for Watson's: open plan, not only for the Lower Primary, but also for the entire new Senior School Design Centre. Construction would follow the CLASP system introduced by Nottingham County Council in the 1960s. Begun in 1973, the new building rose with astonishing speed on the rugby pitches to the south of the old Prep School. Tons of cement were used to form a bed on which the structure would 'float' while a fretwork of Meccano-type metal pillars was inserted into the cement so that prefabricated wall panels could be wrapped around it and topped with a flat roof – a disastrous flat roof, as it turned out, which constantly leaked.

The result? Two hollow squares each built around a courtyard. The first was to house six Primary One classes and the other a mixture of P2–P4. In the centre, where the two squares met, lay the dining-cum-gym-cum-assembly hall, the kitchen, library and audio-visual centre. On the west side of the second square, looking across Myreside, lay the medical room, the office and staffroom. Six entrances existed and visitors could come and go unmonitored.

The Staff

Two challenges awaited: one was amalgamating two quite different institutions: St Alban's Road and Colinton Road Prep and the other was learning to operate in an open-plan area. Careful work was carried out between 1971 and 1974 which included visiting numerous open-plan schools from Aberdeenshire to Nottingham. The visit to the latter involved the Daimler carrying four members of staff sustaining a puncture on a busy motorway which was bravely tackled by its lady occupants without outside assistance.

Despite thorough preparations staff were still nervous, so it was decided that for the 18 months before amalgamation all classrooms doors would remain open throughout the day!

The Opening

The target was 22 August 1974, but the internal building work had not yet been completed and furniture had not arrived. Thus the opening was postponed until 4 September and further delayed until Monday 23rd. Even then it was a close-run thing!

First Steps

The first experience for P1 – once parents had gone – was the 'Home Base', a small alcove in the corner of a class area with an armchair for teacher. This was quiet time when the register was checked, news exchanged and the day's programme begun. Thus began the whole new world of school.

Youngsters settled in quickly and moved around with confidence, sometimes even toddling mistakenly into a different, but seemingly more interesting class. They painted, worked with water, read and chose options for the first time. Assembly was an adventure, a massive hall crowded with hundreds of bigger people.

Open plan proved not to be the nightmare anticipated. Indeed, a quiet settled working atmosphere prevailed, but that was the result of a highly skilled and dedicated staff team who gave far, far more than was demanded from them.

Incidentally, one victim of open-plan was the school bell. There were no bells in LP!

Ethos

Like his predecessor Dr Ogilvie, Roger Young took a deep interest in the Lower Primary. These pupils were the future thus its ethos was of vital importance. Each child should feel important, valued, respected and it was the teacher's role to provide the opportunities and challenges to help each pupil discover his or her talents and gifts. Just 'playing'? The truth was that a tight framework of skilful, structured teaching underpinned the picture of apparently spontaneous activity. From the outset the new Lower Primary was an open building: open in design, open to new ways of working and open to visitors who became a part of everyday life.

In Search of Structure

Watson's also co-operated during 1975/6 with the Scottish Council

Building the new Lower Primary.

Marissa Hardie and James Lee greet Her Majesty.

Her Majesty was presented with flowers mostly grown in the class gardens plus a book of pictures and stories covered with paper marbled by P3 pupils.

for Research in Education into the relationship between theory and practice in open-plan schools. The project was led by Dr David Hamilton. The result was a fascinating and stimulating experience for all involved and one which did much to develop the Department. Indeed, it was liberating in that it destroyed the attitude that things had to be perfect before visitors were allowed!

New Parents' Evenings
Begun in Autumn 1976 with a slide presentation of pupil activities and a 'meet the teacher' spot. This proved so popular that it was repeated, expanded to include P2–P3 and worked in tandem with individual parent-teacher interviews.

The Queen's Visit, 1982
The highlight of the decade. The tour began in the Lower Primary and Her Majesty was presented with flowers mostly grown in the class gardens plus a book of pictures and stories covered with paper marbled by P3 pupils. In a P2 class she stopped to admire the tower of bricks a group of boys had just completed. *"Is it meant to lean over at the top?"* she asked. *"Well, yes … and no"* came the reply from Elliot Picken. *"Obviously heading for the Diplomatic Service,"* said the Queen.

Nursery Unit Opened, 1982
This unit was converted from the class areas on the west side of the building. It began with two classes, but the children came for morning sessions only.

'Arts Alive', 1985
This was the first major exhibition of artwork: painting, modelling, clay work and weaving. The latter included a tapestry of a coat of arms suitable for the newly knighted Roger Young which was then presented to him on his last day as Principal.

Annual Highlights
Pupils and staff will remember with affection Harvest Thanksgiving, the Carol Party (begun 1974) including the Nativity Play and Christmas Story and Founder's Day with its lively rendition of the School Hymn. Term ended with Sports Day and Prizegiving. Wonderful memories.

Arise the Refurbished Lower Primary

Article based on information provided by Pam Snell, Deputy Head Junior School (Lower Primary).

Planning the Refurbishment
In the mid-1990s, consultation began to plan the refurbishment of the Lower Primary building. As P4 had moved to the Upper Primary building a specially designed building could be created for pupils in Nursery, P1, P2 and P3. The plans included improved class and activity areas, space for specialist staff and enlarged nursery facilities. In addition, a large reception area, enclosed hall, redesigned library and new administrative facilities were incorporated into the design. Most of these changes were planned within the existing outer shell although additional space was created by the imaginative glazing over of the two internal courtyards.

Work Begins
Work was begun in March 2000 on the only 'new build': the two nursery rooms. In August, work began on the classrooms and the refurbishment continued until October 2002. The use of glazing throughout the Lower Primary preserved much of the original 'semi-open plan' whilst providing classrooms with doors and enclosed activity areas. The refurbished building provides an excellent environment for early education. The surrounding play areas were redesigned and resurfaced when the refurbishment was completed.

Nursery Provision
This has continued to expand and there is now a pre-school morning class, a pre-school day class and an afternoon class for three-year-old children. As well as new rooms, a challenging outdoor play area was constructed. In August 2005, a new facility opened to provide after-nursery care for pre-school children in an attractive ground floor area of New Myreside House.

Annual Highlights
With the appointment of a dedicated LP music specialist in 1987, the opportunity was created to develop and enhance musical and dramatic performances. Annually, the LP has

class and year group performances for parents which aim to provide all children with the opportunity to 'dress up' and take 'centre stage'.

Founder's Day is celebrated in an imaginative manner and other highlights include sports, the Nursery Teddy Bears' Picnic, the annual charity fund-raising activity and a wide range of visits.

The Staff
Since 1989, PE and music staff have been joined by a learning support teacher, a P1 enrichment and support teacher, a French teacher and an art specialist. The Lower Primary staff now numbers over forty teaching, auxiliary and reception staff. After School Club staff are based in the Lower Primary at the end of the day.

The Curriculum
Today's P1 children begin school with full days and quickly integrate into the new world of school and the many and varied experiences on offer. Every day our youngest pupils expand their horizons in all the traditional areas of education whilst at the same time embracing opportunities offered by new technology.

Parents are invited to meet the staff each session to hear about the curriculum in general, as well as focused talks on aspects of curricular change.

The Cabin

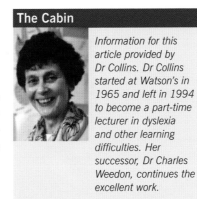

Information for this article provided by Dr Collins. Dr Collins started at Watson's in 1965 and left in 1994 to become a part-time lecturer in dyslexia and other learning difficulties. Her successor, Dr Charles Weedon, continues the excellent work.

Before coming to Watson's in 1965 Catriona Collins had worked in a London hospital for children with emotional and educational difficulties. Catriona didn't fully understand these difficulties, but did grasp that these children couldn't be educated in a mainstream classroom setting.

Catriona moved to join her family in Edinburgh and spent a year at Moray House to gain a Teaching Qualification. Her teaching practice was centred in Pilton in both Primary and Secondary schools where she continued her concern for pupils with learning difficulties.

From Little Acorns
Within two years of joining Watson's Catriona discovered a few boys who were having problems with reading and spelling. With permission from their parents – and themselves – Catriona proceeded to give assistance before and after school. Some progress was made, but she was puzzled and concerned about one boy whose progress was very slow and yet was verbally excellent. His ideas and vocabulary were extensive and he had leadership potential.

Word Blindness
At the end of term Catriona returned to London and attended a conference covering learning difficulties. There she discovered 'word blindness', later to be known as 'dyslexia', and became deeply interested in the condition. She also learned the importance of providing test materials as a means of diagnosis. This was the beginning of her mighty contribution to Watson's.

Catriona gained Roger Young's total support for a 'remedial class' provided she promised to see it through no matter the difficulties. His support was of the utmost importance for success would largely depend on staff co-operation. Each teacher would have to identify pupils with learning difficulties and accept their withdrawal from classes on a regular basis. Watson's staff proved to be helpful.

The Cabin
But where? A quiet and isolated space with few distractions was found beneath the stage, ideal for aiding concentration. It was also important that it looked unlike a classroom associated by such pupils with failure. A less formal space was desired. At first they had very little. A governor gave a carpet and pupils put up pictures. Catriona wanted it to be a space which they had helped to create and decorate, a place they felt comfortable and no longer intimidated by their difficulties. That was achieved. The first group of boys named it *The Cabin*. They felt they were on a ship – sailing forward.

A Right Royal Move
However, in 1982, when the Queen visited the school, her security officers demanded a separate entry and exit to The Cabin. It was therefore moved

The Visit of The Princess Royal, 29 January 2003
The official opening of the newly refurbished building was carried out by The Princess Royal, the Master of the Merchant Company. Pupils performed the story of the life of Robert Burns through music and drama in the new Hall. After unveiling the plaque, HRH toured the building to see classes 'in action.'

Special Sixth

From information provided by JG Scott and Ian Jordan. J Graham Scott arrived at GWC in 1959 as a German, French and Russian teacher. In 1971, he became Head of Modern Languages and then, in 1972, Head of the Upper School. 'JG' retired in August 1991. He was that rare thing in our schools: an intellectual, with the common touch plus a deep knowledge of Scottish history and culture.

to a large cloakroom at the end of the East Corridor where it links with the corridor that runs along the back of the main building. Three teaching areas were created: two small rooms and one open space. Areas were also created where pupils could be on their own to work, or enjoy conversation during interval breaks.

The new location was important as The Cabin staff and pupils now felt much more an integral part of the school, there was space for more children and, as its reputation spread, children began to arrive from other schools seeking expert help.

Compassion for All

The philosophy was simple: each pupil was seen as an individual who had the ability to reach his intellectual and educational potential. It was of paramount importance to discern pupils' strengths and build confidence sufficiently to tackle the English language. Pupils certainly responded and their gratitude can be measured by their determination to keep the name, The Cabin, despite attempts to change it.

There were 'ups and downs', but the latter were very few. The main criticisms were that Watson's high academic reputation was being lowered and that it was unfair that the services of a Reader/Scribe (and extra time for tests/examinations) should be given to some pupils. Catriona's reply was simple: *"Let Watson's be known as a school which also shows compassion towards all its pupils."*

Dyslexia became the focus of concern. Each year six pupils, fully

assessed as dyslexic by an educational psychologist, were admitted into first year in the senior school.

A Diploma

Catriona gave a series of six talks about dyslexia to the staff and explained how everyone could help. Many staff attended as did teachers from other schools. Catriona's work led to a huge interest within and without Watson's which culminated in the introduction of a one-year's course held in the school one evening per week which led to a Royal Society of Arts (RSA) Diploma Qualification in the Study of Dyslexia. This course was validated by an external verifier from London.

Changing Lives

The Cabin has been fortunate in its high quality of staff and by their concern for giving pupils appropriate schemes of work. When ex-pupils return they express their gratitude for the help they received in The Cabin and in most cases say it totally changed their lives. Many have gone on to become doctors, lawyers, geologists, nurses and teachers. One became a pharmacist, another a social worker based in prison and many others are involved in various businesses.

The Cabin gives Watson's a very special place in Scottish education, endorsed by teachers, pupils and parents. However, it must never be forgotten that The Cabin might never have existed without the invaluable support given by the Principal, Sir Roger Young, those many years ago.

Since the 1920s the Sixth Year, as it is called elsewhere in our country, has been referred to as 'The Sixth Form' although, happily, the use of this piece of Anglicisation has gradually weakened over the past few years.

Under Sir Roger Young the school broadened its horizons immeasurably. It became open to new ideas and to the world, and broke out from that self-congratulatory narrowness in which it has tended (or tends) to feel more comfortable. Under the policies of Sir Roger, the Sixth Form became open to all (in other words it was in the educational sense Comprehensive) and opened out to everywhere – universities, colleges, careers. Sir Roger's decision to work within the Scottish educational system, Highers and Sixth Year Studies examinations, was made for pragmatic reasons, and not nationalistic ones. The result was, however, that Watson's became the flagship of Scottish education and was seen as such by other schools which were straddling both Scottish and English (A-Level) examinations. The Scottish universities, the English universities, and Oxford and Cambridge, were all accessible. Perhaps this notion of a great flagship of the best that Scotland had to offer should have been used more widely in publicising the school, but then again, great schools don't have to boast.

The expansion of the Sixth Form during the 1960s and 1970s especially was due to several factors – pupils everywhere were tending to stay on longer in schools, the amalgamation of the two schools led to an immediate increase in numbers. But there was more to it than that – the Sixth Form became genuinely popular. It introduced a newish element into the school - a kind of intellectual liberation. Liberation is what education should be about in many respects, but it is not an idea that has been too willingly embraced in over-cautious systems. It was Whitehead who said that *"... the duty of the parent and the teacher is to withdraw, in both senses of the word, to bring out what is best, and to get out of the way."*

Those in charge of the (eventual) 10 Sixth Forms were chosen on a random basis, but there was one unspoken and perhaps even undefined principle: those chosen had to be open-minded, authoritative but not authoritarian, prepared to be tolerant and understanding – not fierce disciplinarians. The aim was to produce people who could think for themselves and who were at least 'semi' students by the end of the year.

Organisation

Numbers grew from about 60 in the 1960s to just over 200 in the 1980s. Pupils stayed on until the end of the session, even if this meant a great deal of checking up in the summer term. The year was pretty democratic, with as much choice and influence being given to the pupils themselves.

Tutors

Tutors were chosen by pupils at the end of Fifth Year. The Tutor acted as guide and mentor throughout the year, with the Form Teacher sometimes doubling up as a back-up.

Groups of pupils, generally with the same tutors, were then allocated to Forms. This could be a subtle process, as the strengths of the Form Teachers naturally varied, with different Form Teachers able in different ways to deal with different types of pupil.

Office bearers had also been chosen at the end of the Fifth Year.

The new Sixth Form then elected a Common Room Committee and a Library Committee, and these Committees were at least nominally in charge of the two main Sixth Form areas. Some were so excellent that they ran the areas and fulfilled their responsibilities well. Others needed much more support.

The Librarian was selected by the Staff School Librarian, and many were very efficient and highly skilled.

Tutorial Groups

These 'discussion' groups were intended to introduce pupils to a wide range of topics from the nature of the individual to all aspects of the world we live in. The devising of topics and courses depended on the willingness and co-operation of interested members of staff. The whole project was an exciting one, though much depended on the selection of staff for conducting these discussions.

Meetings Periods

These took place once a cycle. Once again, like Tutorial Groups, these were meant to be mind-broadening, and they certainly did succeed in raising awareness in many areas of concern which ranged from out-of-school projects in the summer term, gap years, university life, drug abuse, mental illness to international politics. Notables such as Hugh MacDiarmid, Sir Robert Grieve and Owen Dudley Edwards were also invited to speak.

Some talks offered follow-up opportunities, eg the talk by the Rev Murray Leishman (Royal Edinburgh Hospital) led to pupil visits which helped to break down prejudices, but some pupils then went voluntarily to entertain patients in small bands and orchestras.

A New Architecture

The change in structure and aims of the Sixth Form, away from class-room concepts towards social responsibility, large meetings, study periods and leisure periods, required a new architecture. The newly erected Library and Common Room were an essential part of this, but in a sense the living heart of the year was in the Music School auditorium. This was where the so-called 'Meetings'

periods were held, and where visiting speakers were introduced to the year group by the Head Boy or Girl, or other Sixth Form pupils. The Sixth, and the school, were fortunate indeed to have such surroundings of civilised elegance as existed in the Music School Auditorium.

The Summer Term

In this post-examination period various other elements were introduced. At one stage pupils selected and arranged an extra-school project and were allowed off school for a fortnight. Some of these were very successful, eg Nunraw Abbey, panning for gold at Kildonan or working with old people. The Sixth Form Revue and, eventually, a Sixth Form Year Book also became features of the summer term. 'JG' approved of the former, but disapproved of the latter with its shades of personality cults.

University and Careers Liaison

An essential requirement of a dynamic Sixth Form year is, of course, a superbly organised University and Careers liaison organisation. Watson's had a truly magnificent one managed by kind and civilised Donald MacDonald whose skills in handling the complexities involved became legendary.

The Fifth Year

Two attempts were made to introduce some of the ethos of the Sixth into the Fifth Year. One was a short-lived introduction of a Common Room. That failed. They should really have needed someone sitting there with them in some sort of a supervisory role.

The other was more interesting. It was an attempt to introduce discussions on the theme of moral dilemmas, eg *"What would you do if you were being bullied, if you were put under pressure to adopt group standards with which you disagreed?"* This gave rise to some interest, but perhaps the hearts of neither staff nor pupils were in the experiment, largely because of examination pressures, but mainly because the architecture was not there. 'JG' considers that it was the architecture which helped nurture the Sixth, leading, *"...to a geography of the mind with experiments which led at times to a re-mapping of both the external and the moral world."*

Post JG

The system inspired by Sir Roger and managed by JG remains largely in place although major changes have taken place, eg the library has been integrated with the School Library while the change in the dates of the major national examinations has undermined all post-examination activity, even threatening the much-loved Sixth Year musical.

The greatest experiment, however, began in Session 2005/6, when Ian Jordan (Head of Sixth Year) introduced the concept of 'Collegiate S6'. This intends to build upon the growing sense of independence and responsibility among S6 students by allowing them to come to school at their first lesson or school commitment. Registration is done by subject teachers, except on Tuesdays and Fridays when all S6 will have to be in school by 8.45am in order to attend full school assemblies.

The aim is to build a bridge between the highly structured world of school and the more fluid situation students will encounter when they move to college or university. Equally, any S6 pupils going immediately into the world of work will need to assume a great deal of responsibility for their time management. This is only for a trial period and remains to be evaluated.

The Cowan Room

The S6 Common Room was refurbished several years ago and was renamed the Cowan Room after Jim Cowan, a popular and much-liked Deputy Head. The finished result was a splendid space open to all S6 pupils before school, during non-teaching periods and after school; somewhere to escape the tumult of school. Table football is a great draw and the hi-fi plays an astonishingly wide range of music. Inevitably, however, a space as popular and widely used as this suffers considerable wear and tear.

Towards the end of the 2005 Autumn term Ian Jordan purchased some quality furniture from Ben Dawson, the Musselburgh-based furniture maker whose most well-known commission was to make all the furniture for the Scottish Parliament. He was having a clear-out sale and was offering chairs and tables at prices which were too good to resist. The Bursar agreed and the new furniture arrived just before Christmas 2005. Apart from its stunning aesthetic appeal, the bigger tables and more comfortable chairs seems to have encouraged a more collegiate, convivial atmosphere in the common room with pupils chatting round tables or working on various projects and homework essays. These new additions emphasise the fact that still more work needs done on the fabric of the common room and the plan for 2006 is to repaint. Like the Forth Bridge keeping the common room in good repair is a never-ending task.

Trousers & Haircuts

Article by Scott Geissler.

I recall in my third year at George Watson's, I was sent home by the Depute Rector (I can't remember his name, for the life of me, but he was a fearsome character!) on two occasions. Before an assembly, pupils were lined up outside the door and the DR would walk along the line and identify and withdraw any pupil whose hair was more than an inch below the neckline and send them to the local hairdressers to get a haircut! He would also select anyone whom he believed was unable to pull his trousers off over his shoes, ie they were too tight! Any victim was immediately sent home to change into a more appropriate pair of trousers. On both counts, pupils were told not to return to the school until the rules were complied with. I was caught on both counts! Actually, it wasn't all that embarrassing, as you were seen as a bit of a rebel!

I also recall that the school gained its first female pupils (two, I think) who were co-opted from the Ladies College in my Sixth Year (1967). All I remember is that one of them was the daughter of my Latin teacher. This was the beginning of the school moving towards being co-educational.

I remember we had a brilliant Sixth Form Common Room with its own library. A group of us used to avidly read the *Daily Telegraph*.

We even adopted an unfashionable English football team (Hereford, I think) and followed their fortunes every week. It had (and I guess still has) small side rooms that you could use for independent study. I confess that I regularly used them to skive off my English class, as we had a boring teacher who must have been about 70, and who never checked the register. I hasten to add that my time was spent reading Russian novels (some in Russian!), something I felt would broaden my education far better than falling asleep in English.

The Office

Article contributed by Sylvia Castle-Smith who was the Principal's Secretary at Watson's from 1974 to 2003. After her retiral Sylvia kept as busy as ever: Scouting, a guide at Hopetoun House and a Prison Visitor at Saughton.

When I first joined GWC the Head of the School was Mr Roger Young – Headmaster; the Merchant Company then decided that all Headmasters and Headmistresses should have the title of Principal – so the letter-headed paper was changed and we had to remember the change of title; Roger then received a Doctorate from Hamilton College in the USA – so he became Dr Roger Young – and the letterheaded paper was changed; then he was given a Knighthood and his title was then Sir Roger Young – yes, you have got it! – the letterheaded paper was again changed. Who says life in a school office is boring,

My earliest memories of life in Watson's were of a friendly and caring staff who wholeheartedly agreed that the teaching staff needed the non-teaching staff (as we were then called) and the non-teaching staff needed the teaching staff. My first social event took place within the first few weeks of my appointment and was the new Vice Convenor's introduction to the staff – a formal occasion when the Vice Convenor and his wife, together with the Headmaster and his wife, greeted the invited members of staff as they were introduced by the Company Officer. As I approached the door, a member of the Modern Languages staff, John

John Pearson
(GWC: 1972–9)
A wonderfully eccentric, kindly, ex-RAF Squadron Leader and History teacher who, in post-Cadet days, occasionally took his classes into the East Quad for squad drill much to the merriment and enjoyment of all.

Watson's version of Little and Large. Sylvia-Castle Smith with Barclay Phillips, 1979.

Pearson, was preparing to enter. He kindly waited for me to join him and then held open the door for me. As we approached the Company Officer he asked John for his name. 'John Pearson' was the reply. In a loud voice the Company Officer announced 'Mr & Mrs John Pearson'. Roger Young looked across in amazement and neither John nor myself knew what to say. Roger hurriedly came over to the Company Officer and informed him that the lady was not Mrs Pearson but in fact his new Secretary! Every morning for the first few weeks of my appointment Alex Weston stood on the front door step and when I arrived walked through to the office with me.

I will never forgot one sunny afternoon when the trees at the front of the school were full of blossom and Roger decided he wanted to pick some of the blossom. Out we went, Roger carrying the office stepladders, Liz Firoozi and myself, one of us carrying a long slim umbrella with a hooked handle. Having positioned the stepladders underneath the tree, which he considered, had the best looking blossom, up climbed Roger – with the hook of the umbrella over a branch he carefully pulled it down so that Liz and myself could pick the blossom. Once he thought he had sufficient blossom we returned to the office. Roger and I filled the large celadon bowl with water and carefully carried it up the corridor to the Conference Room. Having placed it in the middle of the table Roger then put in the centre of the bowl a ceramic frog and floated the blossom round the frog. It did look very attractive but I think Mike Gill had other ideas about the use of the celadon bowl.

The Admissions register was a very large tome covered with wooden boards which made it both extremely heavy and awkward to handle and

the pages were covered with line fibres. Alex Weston, the Deputy Headmaster at the time, was one of those rare people who could see when a member of staff was experiencing a difficulty and would, in his own quiet way, do something about it. He came into the office one day and found me standing at my desk bending over the admissions register entering in the details of the pupils who had joined the school that session. Next morning when I arrived at school there, beside my desk was the sloping desk, which Alex used when he was working on the timetable, together with a high stool for me to sit on. When Barclay Phillips, our Factorial Secretary (1974–80), strolled in later in the day he found me trying to pull the fibres out of the nib of my fountain pen. Like Gordon Mowat today, Barclay Phillips was wonderful at being able to find anything one wanted and he returned with a couple of pen shafts and a box of pen nibs. From that day onwards I quite happily perched on top of the stool to enter the details, much to the amusement of staff and pupils alike.

Computerisation came to the office of George Watson's College. Today's offices are full of sleek, sophisticated computers and photocopiers but 20 plus years ago it was a different story. We were the first school to have a computerized school office. And how proud we were of our IBM equipment. The disc drives were so large and heavy they had to have their own tables – the monitors were so large you could not see the member of staff sitting behind them and the printer – well that was something else – it was placed on a large table between our two desks and when the printer was in use it sounded like a machine gun! But we proudly showed off our equipment to all the visiting Heads who were most impressed, However I never did part with my typewriter!

Alex Weston, the Deputy Headmaster at the time, was one of those rare people who could see when a member of staff was experiencing a difficulty and would, in his own quiet way, do something about it.

The House System

Article contributed by Ron Looker, GWC 1971–2004 and Head of Classics, 1998–2004.

The school House system was the invention of Dr John Alison who was Headmaster from 1904 to 1926. In 1908, he decided to create four Houses modelled on the system prevalent in many English boarding schools. Dr Alison had been elected a member of the British Headmasters' Conference which effectively made Watson's one of the very few public schools in Scotland. Watson's, however, unlike the majority of English public schools, was not a boarding school, although there were a small number of boarding pupils. There is no record of how the names for the Houses were selected, whether Dr Alison chose them himself, or whether they were chosen by committee. The Headmaster's Report to the Governors for that year is not available.

House Names

Assuming that Dr Alison chose the names himself, how did he choose the names Cockburn, Lauriston, Ogilvie and Preston?

- Cockburn was the name of an estate near Balerno owned by the Merchant Company Education Board. The name still remains visible in the place and farm names south-west of Balerno. The estate was gradually sold off into separate farms and the Merchant Company no longer owns any of it.
- Lauriston commemorates the location of the original George Watson's Hospital.
- Ogilvie is named after another Headmaster, Dr George Ogilvie who was Headmaster from 1870 to 1898.
- Preston commemorates another Merchant Company estate close to Prestonpans. The estate was sold off for housing many years ago, but its boundary was the site of the Battle of Prestonpans (1745), marked by a thorn tree.

House Colours

The Houses were each given a colour, taken from the Union Flag representing the four home countries:

The House Championship Trophy
This carved oak panel was executed by a member of staff, Mr JR Parnell, and presented to the School in 1937.
It shows the School arms in the centre in inlay, surrounded by a laurel wreath with the four House Colours at the corners.

Scotland, England, Ireland and Wales, which ought to give the colours red, white and blue. However, the blue of Scotland was never used to avoid favouring one House over the others. Black was chosen because New Zealand had recently sent over their famous 'All Blacks' on a rugby tour. The allocation of a colour to a particular house was random.

The Merger

After the merger of George Watson's with George Watson's Ladies' College seven different Houses could have existed, but it was decided to limit the number to four. Neither school wished to lose its traditional House names and suggestions to abolish all of them and create four new ones were also rejected. Consequently it was decided to twin the names, but there was no logic other than euphony for the existing twinnings.

- Cockburn was twinned with Greyfriars.
- Lauriston was a House name the two schools had in common.
- Ogilvie was twinned with Melville.
- Preston was twinned with Falconhall

For the origin of the House names in the Ladies' College see Chapter 3.5.

House Badges CLOCKWISE FROM TOP LEFT: Cockburn Greyfriars, Lauriston, Melville Ogilvie & Preston Falconhall.

John Watson's School

Article contributed by Les Howie.

John Watson's Institution was opened in 1828 under the aegis of the Society of HM Writers to the Signet. Its original purpose was to house, maintain and educate destitute children. The Institution became John Watson's School in 1934 enrolling fee-paying pupils whilst maintaining its original purpose. By 1957, the school offered continuous education to all pupils from 5 to 18 years. In 1975, despite its growing reputation, it unexpectedly closed after the withdrawal of its grant. Many of its ex-pupils then attended GWC and its FPs still donate to the George Watson's Family Foundation thereby supporting pupils at the school. The building reopened in 1984 as the Scottish National Gallery of Modern Art. Less well known is the sad little school cemetery which still exists tucked away in a quiet, secluded corner.

John Watson's House Dress. By James Howie, c1890. Courtesy of Edinburgh City Archive.

Five Watsonian Generations – Can Any Other Family Beat This?

Lindsay Mackersy, *WS. 2 Rillbank Terrace. 1831–1902. Not at Watson's*

William R Mackersy
Entered Watson's in May 1873, aged 10 years.

William had three sons who attended Watson's:
1. **Lindsay S Mackersy** *MC. At Watson's from 1898 to 1906.*
   President of Imperial Bank of Commerce and Canadian Imperial Bank.
2. **William R Mackersy**. *Entered Watson's, April 1901.*
3. **Jack Mackersy.** *Entered Watson's, October 1904. See box below.*

Lindsay S Mackersy
Entered Watson's 4 October 1877, aged 6. Professional banker and fanatical amateur golfer.

Violet S Mackersy
Attended GWC 18 September 1918 to 5 April 1928. Dorothy's twin, seen here holding Graeme, married Bill White who had a carpet business in Lady Lawson Street.

Dorothy S Murray (née Mackersy)
Attended GWC from 18 September 1918 to 5 April 1928. Housewife and Champion of Craigmillar Park Golf Club.

Henry (Harry) S Mackersy
Born 24 December 1912 and attended GWC from 17 September 1919 to July 1929. A remarkably small chap and fine golfer. Champion of Duddingston and Longniddry Golf Clubs.

Jack Mackersy
Cousin of Violet, Dorothy and Harry.
Emigrated to Canada. Became Chairman of Royal Bank of Canada and President of the North American Watsonian Club. The American History Prize – donated by the Club – was won by Alan Murray!

Alan D Murray
Attended GWC 1941–53. Accountant, golfer, curler and Hibs fan.

Stuart D Murray
GWC 1944–55

Eileen P Goodall (née Murray)
GWC 1947–59.

Graeme D Murray
Attended GWC 1970–83. Accountant, golfer, squash player and Hibs supporter. Former Watsonian Squash Club Secretary.

Gillian E Neil (née Murray)
Attended GWC 1972–84. Housewife.

Cameron S Neil
GWC, 2001–Present

Lucy G Neil
GWC, 2003 –Present

Zack AW Neil
b. 2003. Future GWC.

The Convie Wing

Article contributed by Les Howie.

For those of you who remember the old wooden huts (sorry, mobile teaching units) in the East Quad, the opening of the Convie Wing was a mighty blessing and very much appreciated. So, who was Convie?

Henry Convie was born in Edinburgh, but emigrated to Canada, settling in Banff, Alberta. He worked as a handyman in a Convent there. The Sisters felt very sorry for him as he always seemed penniless. They paid him a wage, fed him for nothing and found him all his clothes. To save money Henry never took a bus, always preferring to walk. He also never went on holiday and worked every day of his 36 years with the Convent. A loyal staff member with a passion, however, for his old country, Scotland.

Henry's secret was that he was indeed penniless, but only because he invested every single available coin on the stock market. He seems to have been a shrewd, intelligent and lucky investor. By the late 1950s he had made a great deal of money.

But why give it to Watson's? In 1966, he wrote a letter to the Head, Roger Young with an explanation:

"I have always been interested in Edinburgh's 'Public Schools' and as a boy I used to admire those beautiful buildings, and the playing fields, and the uniforms of the boys with the distinctive school colours. I envied those boys because it was not my privilege to say in later years I was an 'old boy' of one of them. I feel proud to say, however, that I am one of the Scottish Capital's sons.

Of the several colleges within the City: Watson's, Daniel Stewart's, Fettes, Merchiston Castle, the Academy, the High and Heriot's, Watson's was my favourite. And although I liked the colours of Daniel Stewart's, I preferred the Maroon of Watson's. ...

I should like to see the 'Public Schools' remain, and carry on with their high standards of education and traditions for many, many years to come."

Thus Maroon did it! Henry visited the school in 1966 as an old man in his seventies and then returned to Canada. He was so quiet and retiring that he didn't even leave us a photograph, but, instead, enough money to erect a two-storey building. Henry's memorial will be with us forever.

> *Henry's secret was that he was indeed penniless, but only because he invested every single available coin on the stock market.*

The Duke of Edinburgh's Award

From information provided by Tim Young.

This Award has become one of the most popular, much loved and enduring of all pupil activities and most of that is due to the unceasing labours of its organiser, Tim Young. Tim came to Watson's in 1986 and took over the Expeditions from Ron Looker in that year. Ron, however, remained as the Award Officer (ie in charge) for a further two years when Tim took over the whole thing. Incidentally, Tim's interest began at school and he has stayed involved ever since.

During Session 1986/7 75 pupils participated in the Award (13 at Gold level, 14 at Silver and 48 at Bronze). The Bronze Expeditions took place on S3 Projects in Arran and Argyll. Silver and Gold Practice Expeditions took place in the Yorkshire Dales (with the Assessors camping in a field in Dentdale for the entire weekend) and the Qualifying Expeditions visited Wester Ross (with route planning taking place once we had arrived in Torridon).

Rapid Expansion

Numbers of participants increased rapidly and by 1993 about 300 pupils were involved. Since then numbers have remained consistently high, between 250 and 300 at any one time. Typically, about 100 Third Year pupils take part in the Bronze Award, 60–70 Fourth Year tackle the Silver Award and over 80 pupils, from among the Fifth and Sixth Years, attempt the Gold Award.

Emerging Patterns

After 1986 an established pattern of Expeditions settled down. Bronze Practice Expeditions take place in Glen Isla in September and Bronze Qualifying Expeditions in the Lowther Hills at Easter. The North of England is visited for the Silver and Gold Practice Expeditions, respectively in the Yorkshire Dales at Easter and the Northern Pennines in October. Silver and Gold Qualifying Expeditions take place over a fortnight in the North-West Highlands in June, alternating annually between

> *Bronze Qualifying Expedition, June 2004, near Tomintoul, Glenlivet.*

Sutherland and Wester Ross. As all this does not suit everyone 10 days of Expeditions are held at the start of July in the Southern Cairngorms.

Each year pupils are on Expeditions for at least 45 days and approximately 80 groups are attempting to complete Expeditions. There is a tradition of challenging hill-walking and camping Expeditions. Our pupils seem to enjoy a challenge, culminating for many of them with the arduous four-day, 50-mile Gold Qualifying venture, perhaps behind Ben More Assynt, through Fisherfield, or a circuit of the Cairngorms.

Community Service

The other Sections of the Award are also very important. The *Service Section* has enabled participants to contribute to the local community in a variety of ways, for example in conservation activities, with uniformed organisations, helping elderly people and in charity shops. Regular First Aid courses have been run in school and, recently, Lifesaving courses too.

Youngsters annually take part in a wide variety of *Skills and Physical Recreation activities*, many taking advantage of the wide variety of musical, artistic and sporting activities offered at Watson's. Specific courses have been offered for D of E participants, for example, cookery, pottery and batik.

Finally, Gold participants have undertaken diverse Residential Projects such as in environmental and restoration work, outdoor pursuits and a variety of camps.

Personal Development

The Award hopes to make a useful contribution to the personal development of those who take part by, for example, encouraging self-reliance through the Expedition work, in fostering initiative and independence and in making good use of some of an individual's free time.

No Man is an Island …

Large numbers of helpers and volunteers make all the above possible and Tim is very grateful indeed for their assistance, especially the many staff and Assessors. Watson's is fortunate to be an *Independent Operating Authority* within the Award and it is, therefore, important that high standards are maintained in future in all activities.

Massive Achievement

Between 1988 and 2005, Watson's pupils have gained over 500 Gold Awards, 700 Silver Awards and 1,100 Bronze Awards. About time Tim got an award too!

The D of E Award has become one of the most popular, much loved and enduring of all pupil activities.

> *Silver Qualifying Expedition, June 2004, near Nedd, Sutherland*
> *Left to Right: Jenny Chambers, Louise Anderson, Isla Robertson, Caroline Glauch.*

Magical Music

In 1972, Patrick Criswell came from Gordonstoun to be Watson's new Director of Music and develop further the notable work done by his predecessor. He was an ideal trainer of the school's orchestra and just as effective with voices. Indeed, his choral performances were a triumph. Everyone who entered the Music School became involved, even if just cataloguing the music library! The legendary Dick Telfer retired from Watson's just before the College became co-educational.

The 1974 merger involved necessary extensions to the Music School and Patrick had to make way for his George Square colleague, Margery Traves. This lasted two years during which time Margery brought her own particular skills, above all, excellent staged musical performances. Her colleague from George Square, Cecilia Cavaye, took responsibility for music in the Junior School – a task she undertook with relish until her retiral in 1995. Over the years a number of other staff have made a distinctive contribution. Tony Whatmough and the inspirational Jean Kingsley were noted for excellent teaching whilst John Anderson created the forerunner of a computer-based administration system, now refined, and in use today. In 1986, the Assembly Hall gained a Norman & Beard organ made possible by the generous gift of the Main family accompanied by the enthusiastic efforts of a band of teachers led by the late Sandy Keith. In 1988, after 16 years at Watson's, Patrick retired to Sherborne in Dorset.

Mighty Mitchell

Norman Mitchell was appointed in August 1988 with the main aim of generating an even greater interest in music. His background of quality performance as Cathedral Organist and co-founder/co-artistic director with Peter Maxwell Davies of the St Magnus Festival would serve the school well.

The time was ripe to advance the musical life of the College. Orchestras and choirs began to flourish as more pupils wanted to sing and learn to play an instrument. In 1988, the Music

In 1991 – the 250th Anniversary of the founding of the College – a celebratory concert was given in the Usher Hall to mark this important date with a programme which comprised Mozart's Symphony No 20 for Orchestra, Shostakovich's Second Piano Concerto and Handel's Ode for St Cecilia's Day for soloists, chorus and orchestra. Paul Burt is the soloist seen here.

School was coping with 500 individual lessons a week given by 23 visiting teachers. Very soon, however, space was at a premium. Three orchestras were formed, plus two new bands for brass, wind and percussionists not to mention a Jazz Band quickly followed by numerous chamber ensembles. The Music School looked tired and was suffering from 'elegant decay.'

Mighty Macdougall

In 1989, a new state-of-the-art Keyboards Studio was installed. This was a turning point in a new music curriculum from which only the best was chosen for Watson's. The arrival of the ever-enthusiastic Dr Ian Macdougall in 1989 added further to the dimension of music taught in class. The constant flux in the SEB examination syllabus sadly meant that much scholarly understanding of the subject was set aside in favour of a new style of musical learning.

Christmas Concert

The more secular Christmas Concert held at the College was discontinued and St Giles' became the focus for the Festival of Nine Lessons and Carols each December. Now firmly established, Christmas at Watson's would not be the same without it. The same applies to the annual springtime concerts which are the culmination of orchestral and choral work for each

session. In 1991 – as part of the 250th Anniversary celebrations – a concert was held in the Usher Hall.

In October 1991, the First Orchestra travelled to Assisi, Citta di Castello and Perugia – a hugely successful tour which was repeated in 1993.

Strings

Mention must be made of Viktor Pechar who brought his own distinctive style to teaching at Watson's. His contribution to orchestral work was memorable and his many pupils remember him fondly. In 1995, Hector Scott was appointed as Head of Strings and he brought string playing to even greater heights. The Baroque Orchestra, under his direction, gave concerts in Orkney (1998 & 2000) and Aberdeen and Inverness (2006).

Following Cecilia Cavaye's retiral in 1995, Rosemary McKerchar was appointed Head of Junior School Music and she continued to enthuse and train our younger pupils. She has been ably assisted by Katharine Jones in the Lower Primary.

Magical Musicals

The Summer term Senior School Musicals included such titles as *My Fair Lady, Anything Goes, Guys and Dolls, Fiddler on the Roof* and *Sweet Charity.* Everyone will remember the frantic two-week rehearsal schedule culminating in full-blooded performances which were a credit to the musicianship of the pupils and their dedicated teachers.

Success breeds ...

Chamber Music ensembles and soloists have given regular concerts in the Auditorium and our pupils are in demand 'in town' and further afield. In excess of 35 public music presentations are made each year. Mairi Leach has fostered an interest in Gaelic Music whilst Steven Griffin has brought new ideas – his particular interest being 'Rock' which had an immediate appeal for many pupils.

New Commissions

Two important new music commissions were undertaken whilst Norman was Head of Department. The Millennium was celebrated with a performance of *Birthday Sleep* written for Watson's by Sir John Tavener and sung by the Chamber Choir at St Giles'. In 2003, *The Angel Gabriel* was written for the Caritas Choir by Bob Chilcott. The latter celebrated the opening of the extended and refurbished Music School

New Music School

In 2000, it was recognised that the Music School needed to be enlarged. Upwards of 250 pupils were preparing for various certificates and almost 1,000 pupils were receiving individual lessons per week given by 39 instrumental teachers. In addition to all the orchestral instruments being taught, pupils also had access to lessons in piano, organ, clarsach, voice, bagpipes and pipe band drumming. The latter disciplines led to Watson's Pipe Band becoming World Champions.

By 2002, the Music School premises had doubled in size with important improvements to the Auditorium with better seating and an enlarged performance area. The formal re-opening in October 2003 was a concert given by Watsonians Brian Bannatyne Scott (Bass) and Malcolm Martineau (Piano). With this new Music School, and the extended appeal of the subject to pupils, Norman felt that he had completed the task given to him on his appointment in 1988.

Norman Mitchell before playing for his last Prizegiving Ceremony.

Norman was awarded an honorary doctorate by the University of Paisley to mark his distinguished career. He retired in 2004 after 16 years as Director of Music and has been succeeded by David Elliott from The William Latymer School in Edmonton, London.

Finlay Currie

Finlay Currie was born in Edinburgh on 20 January 1878, the only child of Finlay and Maude. A former church organist and choirmaster he began his 40 year career in entertainment as a singer in the music halls of the '20s, being first billed as 'Harry Calvo, the double-voiced vocalist' before starring in his first film in 1931. He had over 90 film roles among the best known of which are St Peter in Quo Vadis *(1951) and John Brown, Queen Victoria's personal attendant, in* The Mudlark *(1950). He was also the Narrator in* Whisky Galore *(1949). He died, one of Britain's best loved actors, on 9 May 1968 in Gerrards Cross.*

Malcolm Martineau

Malcolm Martineau was born in Edinburgh and began his musical training at Watson's before going on to read Music at St Catharine's College, Cambridge, and studying at the Royal College of Music. He accompanied at master classes at the Britten-Pears School in Aldeburgh for Joan Sutherland, Elisabeth Schwarzkopf, Suzanne Danco and Ileana Cotrubas. He presented his own series of the complete songs of Debussy and Poulenc as well as a Britten series which was broadcast by the BBC. Malcolm has accompanied many of the world's leading singers including Sir Thomas Allen, Dame Janet Baker and Barbara Bonney. He has appeared at prestigious festivals throughout the world. In 1998, Malcolm presented the complete Lieder of Hugo Wolf at the 1998 Edinburgh International Festival.

Chamber Music ensembles and soloists have given regular concerts in the Auditorium and our pupils are in demand 'in town' and further afield.

Robin Williamson

Born in Edinburgh in 1943, Robin Williamson left Watson's in the early sixties and very soon was a member of the Incredible String Band which had more album chart entries to 1974 than any group apart from The Beatles, The Stones, Cream and The Who. Robin plays over 40 instruments: plucked, blown, bowed and struck from all over the planet. Not content with that he is also a talented songwriter, a published poet, a novelist and storyteller. During the Summer of Love, Robin even played Woodstock and had a huge influence on the development of popular music. Robin has gone into Celtic music where the harp is the main instrument.
A multi-talented and creative mind, a model for all young aspiring Watsonian artistes.

Reforming the Pipe Band

The first attempt to restart the Pipe Band came about in 1978 – eight years after its demise along with the Cadet Corps – when three former pupils began to give instruction. Gordon Manson was the driving force amongst the pupils and, from 1979 to 1981, he was described as The Pipe Band President. Professional instruction began in 1979 with help from Duncan Smith and John McArley both pipers from Edinburgh City Police Pipe Band and joined later by drummer Jock Drysdale. Although the group described itself as a pipe band it never actually played as such.

The Angus Macdonald Era, 1982–6

Angus came to Watson's in 1982 as Head of Geography, but was soon promoted to Deputy Principal. He remarked to the Head, Roger Young, that he found it surprising that the school, unlike similar Scottish institutions, had no pipe band. Very bravely Angus decided to do something about it. A small group of learners did exist, the most prominent being Gavin Manson, younger brother of Gordon. Angus and Gavin, therefore, decided to hold a special S1–S2 Assembly to see if there was any interest in reforming the pipe band. The response was encouraging, so Angus contacted the Royal Scots for help with marching and playing as a group. Colour-Sergeant Keene and Captain Bannon came to the rescue and by July 1986 a band of twenty was playing together. Angus decided to learn the pipes and then began playing with the band, becoming the only bearded piper in its history.

Angus was operating a one-man band with no parental support whatsoever, but one FP, and former Vice President of The Watsonian Club, came to his assistance and began a long lasting association: Lt-Col Norman Bruce. Norman immediately began raising interest and money. Indeed, Norman raised £4,700 by 1986. In addition, a major scheme involved contacting clan chiefs and organisations with a view to providing extremely expensive pipe banners. Norman succeeded in persuading over a dozen clan societies to donate banners, plus others from the school, the Merchant Company, Dr Ronnie Seiler, The Royal Scots and the King's Own Scottish Borderers. The Master of the Merchant Company also presented the Drum Major's Mace. A most impressive presentation to the band was organised on the front lawn on Friday, 20 June 1986.

Unfortunately, Angus was appointed in 1986 as Head of Lomond School, Helensburgh. David Pyper (Geography) took over as teacher in charge, but David had no experience of running a band. Angus freely admits that the band always sounded *"a bit ropey"*, but after his exit it definitely became even ropier to the extent that it sadly became regarded as a bit of a joke by the rest of the school.

The Les Howie Era, 1987–93

The new Head, Frank Gerstenberg, was extremely keen to see a pipe band established within the school and regarded it as a major aim. At his instigation, on 7 January 1988, a parents' group – *Friends of the George Watson's College Pipe Band* – was formed to help the Band and to raise money. Its leading lights were Ronnie Seiler,

Charles Grant and George Wilson. In August 1987, Les Howie had become a member of the History Department and he did have experience of pipe bands having founded the highly successful Craigmount High School Band in 1974. David Pyper and Les Howie shared responsibility for the Band until Les took sole charge. At that time Chris Evans was the pupil Pipe Major and Alan Stobie was Leading Drummer.

The first task was to introduce first class instruction as from August 1988. Gordon Campbell had already been appointed as full-time piping instructor dependent upon fee income. Les invited Maggie Young to occupy a similar position for drumming. Maggie had been Leading Drummer with Craigmount, had recently taught at the Gaelic College in Nova Scotia, was a member of the Edinburgh City Police Pipe Band and had been placed 3rd in the World Solo Drumming Championships. Maggie's energy, enthusiasm, character and total commitment completely transformed the drumming section into a formidable corps. She was ably assisted by Findlay White of Edinburgh Police who taught bass and tenor.

The second task was to revive interest by making it clear that a quality competition band was being formed. By December 1988, pupils involved had risen from around a dozen to about fifty. Les Howie took over operations in the Senior School, while Anne Evans did yeoman service in raising the profile of the Band within the Junior School.

By Christmas 1988 a huge amount of work had been achieved. A graded GWC Certificate and Medal Scheme covering learners to advanced players had been introduced. The first certificates and medals were awarded to Mark Inchley (S2) and Alan Davidson (S3). Mark went on to become Leading Drummer and one of the finest drummers the school has ever produced. A new set of drums had been purchased at the then huge cost of £3,000. New uniforms were being considered, but instruments were the first priority. An in-band publication – *Band News* – was begun and produced by band members. By April 1989, £2,000 had been raised by the support

group – a huge effort pioneered by Messrs Wilson, Davidson and Rae – and one which had to continue if the band was to progress. A major Concert was held involving Alison Kinnaird. Even pupils organised their own fund-raising, eg Alastair Dinnis organised an S1 disco which raised £100. The main aim, however, was to get the band out competing in national competitions by the summer.

History was made at Dunbar on Saturday 13 May 1989 when the Band competed for the first time in a Royal Scottish Pipe Band Competition. It was also a first in the independent school sector as Cadet pipe bands tended to restrict themselves to internal closed contests from which GWC was excluded. All Band members showed up despite SCE examinations and S3 Projects (during which Heather Steel played her pipes on top of Ben Nevis). The Band was placed 4th in the Novice Juvenile Grade and won £60. It was a real 'eye opener' for our youngsters as regards the disciplined professionalism of other juvenile bands. Alastair Dinnis was Pipe Major.

By 1990, 77 pupils were involved. The first of the now famous 'Scottish Evenings' was held in the Assembly Hall on Friday 9 March 1990. The brilliant idea of self-catering was suggested by George and Carol Wilson. Meanwhile, at Carlops, the father of the Pipe Band, Norman Bruce, had devised *The Watsonian Tartan* on an old piece of cardboard. It, and a superb 'Ancient' version, were soon being produced by Dalgleish of Selkirk and turned into a variety of fund-raising products from ties to travelling rugs. Norman worked tirelessly on this project, but was helped enormously by Scott Hastings and Donald Scott. The first internal Annual Competition was held on Saturday 24 March 1990. (The first open Contest organised by GWC was held in 1991 to mark the 250th Anniversary. Many of the trophies continue to be used today.) Scott Rae devised a Constitution for the Parents' Association, the intention being to give it far more say in the future running of the Band. Gordon Campbell also left and was replaced by the multi-talented Robert

Pinkman. The Band was going from strength to strength. The first sign of things to come was being placed 1st in the open Novice Juvenile Contest run by the Glasgow and West of Scotland Branch of the RSPBA.

By 1992, Les had achieved his major aim culminating on Saturday 23 May at Stranraer when GWC became Novice Juvenile British Champions. From bottom to top in four years. Donald MacLeod was Pipe Major during two of those epoch-making years. The Band had been transformed, a second band was in the making taught by Neil Cameron and band members were winning solo competitions. The Band was also being run by a Parents' Committee elected by Association members. A first recording was made, *View From The Crag*. Drum Majors were now being taught: Rachel Hewitt, Alex Mitchell, Calum and Crawford Kidd.

John Davie Burgess
11 March 1934 – 30 June 2005

Without doubt one of the greatest exponents of the Highland bagpipe of all time with a huge knowledge of the subject put across in an unassuming manner and with great humour. John always claimed he had been educated at the Edinburgh Academy. It will come as a surprise to many that he was educated at Watson's from October 1941 to July 1944, played in its pipe band and left under a bit of a cloud. This is what his school record has to say.

"After trouble with parents, about boy swearing (was in Corps band), he left and went to Academy."

Nevertheless, we claim him as one of our great former band players.

Scottish & British Champions 1992/3
BACK ROW (Left to Right): Les Howie, Charlotte Kemp, David Wrench,
Sandy Henderson, Angus McGhie, Rob Lowe, Norman Bruce.
MIDDLE ROW: Pipe Major Robert Pinkman, Greg Chick, Robert Deans, Aylwin Chick,
Rachel Hewitt, Jean Adams, Alison Wilkie, Alastair Ross, Graham Glen.
FRONT ROW: David Ross, Simon Kemp, Colin Yule, Crawford Kidd, Colin Balfour,
Calumn Kidd, David Glen, GordonTait, Kate Hathway.
ABSENT: Pipe Major Donald MacLeod, Lee Forster, Kerry McGreechan, Maggie Young,
Colin Holton.

Ian Simpson.

Mick O'Neill.

1993, however, saw big changes. Norman Bruce, who had done so much, died the day before Prizegiving. The Band played 'For Norman'. Les resigned due to professional commitments and, unexpectedly, P/M Pinkman also left. Willie McBride took over as senior piping tutor and John Maloney (English Department) took over as teacher in charge.

The Jack Calder Era, 1993–2000

Jack was elected Chairman of the Parents' Committee in 1993. Seven years of solid consolidation and steady progress followed, culminating in a strategy which would not only save the Band, but also propel it on to a new and higher level. Jack's tireless efforts were remarkable, as was his determination to video every event.

Two bands were in existence by 1994 Both continued to play in competition and for engagements. When Maggie Young resigned in 1996 Mick O'Neill was appointed as drumming instructor. The band continued its steady progress in 1998 and was placed in all major competitions. When Willie McBride resigned in 2000 after a serious illness, Iain Simpson was appointed piping instructor. It was in that year that the band achieved its breakthrough: European and British Band and Drum Corps Champions. There was also strength in depth as over 100 pupils were now involved.

The Iain & Mick Era, 2000–Present

Frank Gerstenberg's legacy was to create a stable future for the Band by the adoption of a radical solution: the appointment of two full-time instructors on the same basis as other members of staff. These two would also manage the Band in place of the Parents' Association. Iain and Mick were perfect for the job. Frank was persuaded by Robert Bellis (Bursar), Roy Mack and Jack Calder that this was the way forward and they have been proven correct a thousand times over. Who could forget the Band's powerfully emotional, *Highland Cathedral*, played for Frank's retiral on 29 June 2001? It was well deserved.

2002 has to be the highest point in the Band's history when both the Band and the Drum Corps became World Champions for the first time, as well as Champion of Champions. That says it all.

Also in that year the Band began what has become its annual all-expenses paid trip to Japan. Since 2004 there have been three bands operating, the Novice Juvenile led by P/M George Wilson. Thus the organisation goes from strength to strength and most of that is due to the intense commitment and thorough professionalism of Iain and Mick combined with a marvellous group of youngsters, all supported by an enthusiastic parents' group.

2002 has to be the highest point in the Band's history when both the Band and the Drum Corps became World Champions for the first time, as well as Champion of Champions.

The Art Department

Article contributed by Mike Gill.

Mike Gill Arrives

The Art Department in 1971 was a small affair with a derisory budget. I had one assistant, Jimmy (Tam) Coull, a specialist in many crafts, one pupil doing Higher Art, two doing Lower Grade, and a treasure trove of the finest materials for working with watercolour such as handmade papers and the finest of sable brushes. I also inherited a plethora of postcards – the only means of teaching the highlights of the world's artistic achievements – painting, sculpture and architecture. I began to wonder as to what I had taken on.

Things did improve. I sold the papers and brushes, Roger Young helped me financially and, after a few years, the department was joined by Ian Coutts who turned out to be incredibly versatile. Somewhere at this stage I took on the teaching of the bulk of the Junior School pupils who had hitherto been ignored.

The New Design Centre

The imminent arrival of the ladies from George Square led to the creation of the Design Centre. This had considerable 'ups and downs' as the architects simply had no idea what was required for studio space. I requested lighting from the roof space and failed, even after months of negotiation. I requested large floor areas – and was immediately deprived of possible corridors. The modular building system of the Centre was then very popular because of its low costs and might have been suitable for conventional classrooms. It was simply too low to allow a lot of natural daylight in and we had to fall back on artificial lighting.

Three departments were moved in: Home Economics, Technical and Art. The idea was that since these subjects all made things they should be able to work together. It did not work. Pride in one's subject gives little leeway to any other. However, the arrival of the 'ladies' was a huge bonus as I had expected. They provided a degree of civilisation to the previous all-male society. Rosemary Schofield, Pat Benton and Christine Robinson were the start and, of course, I was

This 1985 photograph shows Mr MP Gill, head of the Design Centre, with his painting Watson's 1985 *to celebrate Sir Roger Young's 27 years as Headmaster/Principal. The painting compliments one done in 1914 of a Watson's schoolboy, and shows Catriona MacLean (S6), Christopher Small (S1) and Mr Gill's son Benjamin Gill (P1). In the background is shown a bamboo painting entitled* Bamboo *by Lan Fou Nong, part of the School's Chinese collection, which was given to the School during Sir Roger's time and in which he took a particular interest. Bamboo in Chinese symbolism represents 'inter alia' longevity, strength, resilience and tenderness. The painting now hangs in the Stewart Lockhart Suite.*

soon joined by Ian Coutts, Graham McVitie and later, Louise Black – a good team.

Expansion

The department began to grow ever bigger with more pupils and more taking examinations. After quite a few years, when Technology got its own building, we took over their part of the Design Centre (1994). This led to more arguments with architects, but eventually it was all to the good. I was helped and encouraged enormously at this stage by Graham McVitie who assisted me to draw up the penultimate design (more followed later). I had it named the Art School and since I retired the Home Economics Department has left (August 2001) and so my successor, Bill Robb, has seen the last of my dreams come true.

Success

Where once there were but three pupils taking exams, there are now hundreds, not only working very hard, but also enjoying themselves and the subject. Long before I retired I was becoming unhappy with the Scottish Examination system for art. It was too tight and, because of the finances in marking, the work produced was too small and unrelated to reality. I am truly glad that Bill moved to A Level.

A great number of pupils who went through the Design Centre experience, and later the Art School, have made their marks in a variety of careers. One is now a high-flying architect in Glasgow, recently awarded the job of refurbishing the Scottish National Museum. Earlier, two worked for Walt Disney in the production of *Bugs Bunny*, although one was in London and the other in Los Angeles. There are countless others who have succeeded in many ways: textile production, product design, photography, graphics and so on. Under Bill Robb the excellent work continues.

(Mike Gill retired in 1995. Mike was also involved in the conservation and restoration of many historical items such as the enormous armorial bearings above the Dining Hall door, the 'ship' windvane, the front doors and the difficult repair of the painting of the South Front of the Hospital building now to be seen outside the Headmaster's office. He was also responsible for the massive and extremely valuable Chinese Collection donated by James Stewart-Lockhart and now cared for by the National Museum. Mike also itemised and valued every work of art held by the school. All this amounted to a time-consuming and much underrated task for which Mike should be congratulated.)

Baldy Cooper's Boarding House

Article by Lindsay Watson & Colin Wood.

Both of us arrived at what was called 'Baldy Cooper's bug hut' at 'Castlegate', 2 Abbotsford Park, in September 1951. Nothing should be misinterpreted by the name which was applied to all the Boarding Houses at that time! They were privately owned, run by teachers at the School and it was to be many years before they were supplanted by the official School Boarding House at Myreside. By the time we arrived, Mr Cooper had retired as Head of History and most of the day-to-day running of the house was carried out by his wife. We soon realised that we had entered a regime run on fairly regimented lines, but considering the strict discipline at Watson's, and with National Service in full swing, it all related to the scene at the time.

The Regime

As you moved up the Senior School it was possible to become a boarding house prefect which gave a degree of authority. Punishment for various misdemeanours ranged from writing lines, copying out psalms or hymns, to a whacking from the LNER belt, the broad leather strap which raised or lowered a railway carriage window. Clean knee inspections were frequent (no long trousers were worn until

4th Year at school without special dispensation from the headmaster) and failure to wash properly at night was addressed by the LNER.

Many of the boys joined the CCF in 3rd Year and this created a lot of competition, certainly in the standard of kit-cleaning in the boarding house and a lot of rivalry between the Army, Navy and Air Sections. This all contributed to the discipline scene.

Working the System

After 'Baldy' Cooper's death the size of the boarding house was allowed to fall through natural wastage. Discipline was still applied, but there were many ways of working the system – the secret was not to get caught! Unauthorised activities which took place over the years included:

- Card gambling (small-scale).
- Summer sunbathing on the flat section of the house roof, with access through a dormer window in a 2nd floor room and by holding on tightly to a chimney stack.
- Larder raids to augment rations, producing very little (not even biscuits).
- Occasional visits at weekends to the semi-derelict Merchiston Castle across the road, now part of the Admin Department of the University. We can't remember how we got in, but rumour had it

that the timber floors were rotten – but we still managed to reach the battlements and return safely to the ground floor.

- To be caught smoking (and very few did smoke) was virtually a capital offence! Expulsion for smoking was the most severe of punishments. A favourite smokers' den was the toilets next to the Armoury.

Brylcreem Boys

Many activities were above board and approved by the Coopers. Saturday winter evenings offered the opportunity to visit the nearby Mardale Dancing School which encouraged us to scrub up, don sports jackets and apply liberal quantities of Brylcreem. Meeting girls from other private schools, particularly when they too were in mufti, was always a pleasant experience even if some of us realised we would never make ballroom dancers.

In the summer term, particularly after exams were finished, we were allowed out of the house after homework in addition to the normal weekend freedom. Various track and field sports were available at Myreside and Braids No 2 was used by the golfers amongst us. Others travelled to the open air pool at Portobello. Most of us kept a bicycle in the purpose-built shed and enjoyed some exciting races round the large rear garden on a gravel track. Alternatively, we went off on cycle runs. Occasionally a long run was carried out, eg to Glendevon, staying in a youth hostel and then returning. Looking back, life was much less complicated than it is nowadays.

Food

The food was quite good, but not plentiful in spite of the lifting of post-wartime rationing. Sunday evening meals were especially basic with beans or sardines on toast being the standby dish. The best arrangement was to have Sunday lunch and dinner invitations to family or friends within Edinburgh. Unlike Sundays, with little to do other than church, Saturdays could be busy. Many of the boys played rugby in the morning and watched Watsonians in the afternoon. The two international rugby matches at Murrayfield were highlights of the year, and we would

The Front Garden, Abbotsford Park, Summer 1956
BCK ROW: I Grant, A Stewart, D Stewart, R Sanderson, G Drever, unknown, L Watson, P Craig.
MIDDLE: C Wood, A Gray, Matron, Mrs J Cooper, Miss E Watson, R McClymont, I Scotland.
FRONT ROW: D McCreadie, ? Stewart, R Nettleton.

walk there, paying our entry at the gate if we didn't have the special schoolboy tickets. Princes Street was a joy, especially when playing Wales!

Home Comforts

We were not allowed access to the dormitories during the day when we used the two large rooms to the left coming in the front door. The first was used for dining and both were used for homework which was done after our evening meal. Storage heaters gave out a limited amount of heat, but the more senior boys used the large prep room which boasted a coke/log-burning stove. Those in Fifth or Sixth Year encircled the stove, so that juniors had to keep on their blazers for warmth. Homework was carried out in complete silence, the only exception being when an older pupil might help a younger one, and on completion Home Readers were the only books allowed until release for bed.

Bedtime

Bedtimes were staggered according to Year, with First Year and younger starting to get ready for bed at 8pm and in bed by 8.30pm Younger boys had to make a dressing gown appearance at the doorway of Mrs Cooper's sitting room. Washing facilities were basic – one large dormitory had a few basins, but the boys in the other dorms had to use the ground floor washroom. Apart from about four sinks, this had two baths (no showers). Each boy was timetabled to have a bath once a week. No such thing as privacy in these days, but neither was there at school, where if you forgot your swimming gear, you went without it (but Freddy Lemmon would at least throw you a swimming costume if a lady visitor came to the poolside). There was only *one* WC for the boys (at one stage there were 35 of us) although the Coopers and their staff had their own bathroom facilities in a part of the house which most of us never saw. Global warming was many years off and the winters were cold. Ice and snow would persist for weeks on end, and we were on occasion dragooned to chip it off the surrounding pavements. There was no heating in the dormitories and we used to gauge the night-time temperature by seeing how much of a glass of water froze overnight. There

were certainly some very cold spells which allowed us to skate after school on the canal at Craiglockhart and at Blackford duck pond.

Fagging

'Fagging' involved the more junior boys cleaning shoes for the seniors. The latter provided the shoe polish which enabled us to clean our own shoes at the same time! Pocket money was related to our Year (perhaps 3s 6d for the youngest), but we recall boys receiving the equivalent of Red Cross parcels from home to offset the occasional pangs of hunger. We all returned from holiday with additional supplies and the more generous parents sent Postal Orders to top-up tuck boxes. Part of pocket money was expected to be placed in the collection plate at the then Morningside Parish Church, on the corner of Newbattle Terrace. The Minister at the time completely ignored the 20–30 boys seated in one corner, so the 'takings' were not enormous. Some of the senior boys formed a breakaway group and, with Mrs Cooper's approval, walked all the way down to the West End to attend St George's Church.

The End

By 1956, the number of boys living at Abbotsford Park had diminished and Mrs Cooper retired that summer, moving into a small house in South Gillsland Road, adjoining the Watson's swimming pool. The rear garden abutted the Senior School playground and we sometimes wonder if she had a really strong affinity to the School and all it represented. She certainly could not have lived any closer! Her late husband taught the father of one of us (Lindsay) in the 1920s. We think Jean Cooper had at one time taught French, but can't remember at which school. The old boarding house was subsequently divided into two residential dwellings with detached garages.

When the boarding house closed, its occupants dispersed, some to university, some to the Services and the remainder with more years to serve at School to Mr Clark's boarding house in North Gillsland Road. One of us (Lindsay) was the exception and transferred to Peter Fleming's boarding house at 85 Colinton Road. In spite

of his reputation for strict discipline, we found him to be fair and had a lot of respect for him. Life in 'Butcher' Fleming's boarding house was very different from 'Baldy' Cooper's, but that is another tale!

(A vivid account of 'Butcher' Fleming's boarding house is given in Chapter 1 of High Endeavours. The Life and Legend of Robin Smith *by Jimmy Cruickshank (Canongate, 2005). It is the story of one iron will in collision with another! A superb book and one which every Watsonian should read.)*

In 1910, Major William R Cooper joined Watson's in the pioneer post of Head of History. Thus Watson's and Cooper led Scotland in treating History as a separate subject detached from English. He was a Founder Member of the Historical Association, Housemaster of Lauriston, Commanding Officer of the OTC and an enthusiastic exponent of rugby and cricket. He retired in September 1948 and died on 12 April 1954.

We used to gauge the night-time temperature by seeing how much of a glass of water froze overnight.

Our Janitors, 1939–2006

Ted Verdin

Ted was appointed Head Janitor in 1939. He came to Watson's after 25 years with The Royal Scots which he joined at the age of 15. Ted was always helpful and cheerful even when not in the best of health. His loyalty, kindliness, courteousness and consideration for others were renowned. Ted retired in 1959 and died in1964.

Bill Richardson

Bill Richardson, an ex-soldier, joined Watson's as an Under-Janitor in 1948 and was appointed Head Janitor in 1959. Even as early as 1948 he was being described as an 'institution' with a voice and character steeled by the parade ground. Bill never suffered delinquents gladly. A conscientious and trustworthy chap, Bill retired in 1967.

Bill Symon

In 1970, Bill Symon applied for the job as Janitor of the Ladies' College in George Square … as well as 420 others! The best man was appointed to keep order among 900 assorted girls, but Bill very soon had to cope with the massive organised chaos that was the merger. Catching lead thieves at night on the roof at Colinton Road was a particular speciality, as was dowsing smoky toasters in the Bug Hut. Bill enjoys pottery, woodwork, photography, DIY and classical music. Bill's daughter Linda attended Watson's and is now Junior School Director of Studies. Indeed, both grandchildren (Lorna and Euan) attended GWC, so perhaps there will be GWC great-grandchildren too!

Gordon Mowat

Ex-RAF Gordon Mowat flew into Watson's in 1976 and has, thankfully, been grounded here ever since. Appointed Head Janitor in 1988 – only the ninth since 1870 – Watson's gained a warm, friendly and totally efficient human being with a genuine interest in Watson's history.

Indeed, countless pieces of our heritage have been rescued by Gordon.

The Pipe Band also owes him a huge debt for without Gordon's massive input in the early days – from selling tartan to jumble sales – the Band could not have flourished.

The day Gordon retires will be a massive loss for the school.

Charles and Clare McDougall

Charles McDougall, an ex-Sergeant of The Black Watch, was a jovial giant of a jannie capable of stopping a child stampede with one roar plus a quietly uplifted hand. Charles was also much respected and loved, a genial friend to all, old and young. Nothing was ever too much trouble. He enjoyed a pint, a fag, a pretty leg, conviviality and the odd game of cards with S6 in the boiler room. His redoubtable and long-suffering wife (Clare or Mrs Mac) controlled the cleaners (and everyone else, including Charles) with a rod of iron. According to Mike Gill the school was, however, at its cleanest and never surpassed. Charles retired on 30 November 1975. Charles and Clare were an unforgettable double act. When will we see their like again?

School Sport

Sport in all its various forms has been very important to George Watson's. Indeed, it would take a book in itself to do justice to all the staff and pupils who have been involved over the years.

The evolution of sport at Watson's has reflected the changing nature of society. The coming of computers and hand-held game packs has brought a generation who are exposed to sport in a completely different way, where sports stars can be viewed from the comfort of a digital screen rather than trekking to watch a live game.

Sport at Watson's began through the interest of various subject teachers who understood the value of getting out of the classroom and taking healthy exercise. In the early days, those in authority did not really support sporting activities as academic work took priority. However, through the goodwill of these teachers our pupils learned to play games and, despite all the setbacks, sport flourished. Rugby, cricket and athletics became the most established games played and similar schools came together for competition.

New games came and went mainly on the availability of interested staff. The post of organising games in the school fell to Masters who, on their own initiative and in their own time, organised games. It was not until the mid-1930s that the Governors appointed the first member of staff responsible for the organising of games and the beginnings of curricular PT. The aptly named PEC Honeyman (Pech) took over 'Physical Training' (or 'Torture' to most). Specialists were mainly from a military background and lessons were very much aimed at fitness (a healthy mind in a healthy body).

Pre-WW2 pupils witnessed a tremendous growth in sport. Pupils were introduced to many aspects of the subject during the day and those with a particular interest could extend the experience after school.

WW2 had a detrimental effect on the progression of the subject as so many staff left to serve their country and were replaced by retired staff. These turbulent years saw a succession of men assume the role of Games Master: Montgomery, McLean and Thomson. It was only with the appointment of John Miller in 1947 that the first College-trained specialist was brought in.

Throughout the 1950s the PT Curriculum changed a great deal. Indeed, even the name changed to 'Physical Education.' A young Donald Scott began his career at Watson's followed by Malcolm Hunter and, into the 1960s, by Peter Gallagher. Each generated great enthusiasm for the subject and, with more subject teachers willing to give up their time to become involved in extra-curricular activities, sport thrived.

The merger of the two Watson's (girls and boys) would become a real focus in PE and the staff of both institutions began discussions as how best to deliver the curriculum and extra-curricular activities. Doreen Smith (Head of PE at George Square) along with Dot Brown and Anna Sheriff would meet their male counterparts to tackle the issues involved in bringing together two different cultures. The biggest issue would be accommodation. By 1975 a new games hall had been built alongside two squash courts. Changing facilities were upgraded whilst hockey pitches were created at Myreside. Meanwhile the Merchant Company had also completed discussions with Edinburgh University as regards taking over its playing fields at Craiglockhart. There was a need to increase the size of the PE Department to cater for the extra-curricular programme. The addition of Jane Campbell and John Rutherford gave increased provision. Donald Scott and Doreen Smith jointly headed the Department.

Percy Ewen Clunes Honeyman
Percy had attended a College of Agriculture, but joined the army in 1914 and remained there until 1935. He became an army PE instructor in 1923 and gained a further PE qualification in 1935 from the Scottish School of Physical Education in Glasgow. From 1935 to 1936 he was Organiser of PT to the Ministry of Labour. He was appointed to GWC in October 1936. Said to have much influence with the Head and responsible for persuading Robertson to put S6 into shorts!

Four Heads of the PE Department Sports Day Thursday 24 June 1999 Left to Right: Roy Mack, Donald Scott, John Miller, Iain Brown.

The Murray Family Pavilion at Myreside, January 2006.

As things settled down the condition of the rugby pitches on Tipperlinn was questioned and it was quickly decided that the next significant phase in the evolution of PE would begin with a complete redevelopment of that area. The tar tennis courts were flattened and flood lights were added beside the boarding house. The vast area of Tipperlinn became an all-weather, floodlit facility boasting a full-size astro hockey pitch which could be converted into extra tennis courts.

The size of the PE Department continued to grow and by the 1980s nine full-time PE teachers were looking after the physical welfare of some 2,200 children. George Skirving retired during that decade and Willie Morton, former Scottish Cricket internationalist, joined the staff as Head Groundsman.

All this set the scene for PE to develop into an examinable subject. For the first time PE was recognised as important enough to allow those with a talent in sport to be recognised with a qualification. Standard Grade was introduced at the end of the decade and was quickly followed by the Higher in the early 1990s.

The core curriculum for PE has grown over recent years to reflect the changing demands in sport, recreation and life styles. The next major innovation was to introduce a health and recreation provision, not only for pupils, but also for parents. In 2000, the Galleon Club was formed and initially managed by Kerry McNaughton and Murray Craig. In January 2006, Mark Gifford took over as Manager. The Club allowed for the extended opening of facilities with a wide range of activity classes for all ages plus the introduction of holiday courses. This highly successful venture is measured by a membership of just under 1,000. To accommodate this change staffing was increased to its present-day total of 15 plus two Heads of Junior School Sport (girls and boys).

The next stage of development will be the upgrading of the PE facilities, planning for which has been underway since 2004. New changing rooms (The Murray Family Pavilion) were opened at Myreside in November 2005 and the second phase (a second games hall) will commence in Summer 2006. The third and final phase will start in 2008 and will include renovation of the existing gyms and swimming pool, construction of a new three-storey gym and Fitness Centre, new lecture rooms, class rooms, viewing galleries and new staff offices. This exciting development will ensure that Watson's remains at the forefront of sport development and innovation in the twenty-first century.

Football

Closet Footballers

Or should it be Association Football, or soccer? In 1997, it was the sport that dared not speak its name. Nevertheless, soccer had been alive and well in the independent sector for many years. Indeed, former pupils from Charterhouse had founded a club in Barcelona. The English Independent Schools' Football Association had been in existence for 50 years and have a seat on the FA Council. In the 1880s, Alexander Watson Hutton, a teacher at Stewart's and Watson's, emigrated to Argentina, noticed they didn't play football and so started his own club. On his grave is enscribed *Father of Argentinian Football*.

But back in 1997 it simply wasn't school policy. Despite that Watson's produced footballers. One of them was Charlie Aitken who made the record number of appearances for Aston Villa from 1962 to 1976 and then went on to play with Pele, Beckenbauer and Cruyff as well as the New York Cosmos. David Johnson also played for Heart of Midlothian (and the British Lions).

The Challenge

There had been many attempts to get a team started, but had met with remarkable obstruction. At the first School Council meeting in September 1997, the Head Boy of the Boarding House, Gary Holton, asked the question, *"Why do we not have a football team?"* The Principal, Frank Gerstenberg, reiterated that it wasn't school policy, but passed the matter to the new Head of PE, Iain Brown. Iain stated again that it was not school policy, but pointed out that the astro turf was available at 4pm on a Friday. So, in Session 1997/8, there were 25–30 boys kicking a football about. It was enjoyable and so popular with some that in 1998/9 the time was changed to 6pm on Monday nights with no changing facilities.

Secret Conspirators?

At that point it was discovered that Stewart's Melville (under Jeff Marsh) had a team. Jeff informed Watson's that Strathallan also had a team who then provided the information that Queen Vic had a team! Thus in Season 1998/9 a few friendlies were played for the first time.

The Breakthrough

The next Season (1999/2000) saw some wonderful players emerge from the depths of Watson's: Johnny McWhirter, Sean Black and Andrew Turnbull. The lads were thrashing the independent schools and all were keen to play a state school. Thus Watson's entered the Lothian Schools' Cup. The first round match was against Musselburgh. The *Evening News* was asked to report the match, but was not interested in a novelty match where the victor was certain to be Musselburgh. The result, however, was that the four times holder of the Cup was resoundingly beaten 2–1 by Watson's!

S4, 1st XI Football, 2001/2
BACK ROW (Left to Right): Andrew Minto, Sean McDonald, Michael Tombs.
MIDDLE ROW: Andrew Roley, Dmitri Levitin, Calum Weir, Graham Urquhart,
Stephen Cooke, Murray Johnston, Matthew Pinnons.
FRONT ROW: Jamie Stevenson, Ross Mathison, Dario Crolla, Richard Lockerbie,
Scott Mayberry, Adam Smith, Andrew Watson.

Both the *News* and *The Scotsman* newspapers then started to run with the story. It was real Roy of the Rovers stuff as the next round was against Queensferry, the only unbeaten side in Lothian and Borders. Watson's beat them in a classic 6–3 victory. This was the breakthrough.

Although beaten in the quarter-finals, other schools, such as Heriot's, found they were under pupil pressure to form football teams on the Watson's model.

Players In-Depth
Firmer foundations were then dug by introducing football into S3. As a team needs time to develop, so this team would be the future golden generation.

National Organisation
By Season 2001/2 the Scottish Independent Schools' Football Association was established. Fourteen schools entered the inaugural cup played in pool stages. Watson's was knocked out in the semi-finals by a wonderfully entertaining Stewart's Melville team and Heriot's went on to win the final 3–2. That the final was held at Tynecastle Stadium gave the competition and organisation a certain kudos. The Cup was presented by Alex McLeish (whose son just happened to be playing for Stewart's Melville).

Lothian Leagues
Meanwhile, Watson's had been entered into the Lothian Leagues and was the only independent school playing at this level in Scotland. The school again reached the quarter finals of the Lothian Schools' Cup and was gaining vital experience.

The Big Year
Season 2002/3 was going to be the big year. Dario Crolla was on the Hearts' books, but also went on to represent Scottish Schools. Steven Cooke, Scott Mayberry, Richard Lockerbie, Ross Mathieson and Graham Urquhart were all superb players ably backed by S6 veterans Ian Carruthers and John Nisbet.

The team came third in the Lothian Leagues. It lost to the eventual winners in the Cup, but went on to win the Sisfa Cup at Tynecastle, 1–0. It eventually scored 101 goals that year, but the last was the worst one. It was scored by Steven Cooke!

The Staff
Mention must go to the pioneering members of staff who have helped over the years: Mike Casey, Roddy MacFarquhar, Matt Bergin and Ken Tait. Also, the many parents who have supported from the sidelines and sponsored the team.

**An Established
and Expanding Activity**
Since 2003, Watson's has reached the final of Sisfa (defeated by Hamilton College). The Sisfa organisation now has 28 schools in its organisation. There are also East-West and North-South District sides. In 2006, there should be a Scotland team.

Plus girls. In 2003, the first girls' cup was established. Watson's won.

The Rifle Club

Article by Bill Hamilton (Hon Match Secretary, 2004).

The Watsonian Rifle Club is unique in that it allows membership to school pupils, a provision instituted in 1935. As such it has been one of the most successful clubs of all time.

Origins
The Club sprang from the Cadet force which obviously had shooting as a major activity, but had no provision for FPs. The first attempt to rectify this was the 1919 Club, a mixture of Watsonians and pupils who wanted to restart activities after the Great War. Under its auspices the Watsonian Rifle Club was established March 1926, the first Chairman JL Cox with LB Patrick as Secretary. Shooting mostly took place in the indoor range at Archibald Place with outdoor shooting at Blackford Glen. The initial subscription was 3s 6d and membership varied between 20–40. The first trophy arrived in 1927 after winning Division IV in the Edinburgh & Midlothian League.

The Club benefited from the generosity of JK Munro Hall who was described in his obituary as *"the father of the Rifle Club."* He donated several rifles as prizes and was elected President in 1927. His son, JG Munro Hall, was Hon President from 1961 to 1968 after serving as Captain, Secretary and Treasurer between 1935–52. The first team captain was Archie Stevenson who was Honorary President from 1969 to 1991 after which the present incumbent, Stuart Guild, took over.

Colinton Road
Although the school moved in 1932, the rifle range was not completed until 1935. In the interim activities were carried on as guests of the Masonic Rifle

Club which had a range in the basement of the now demolished Poole's Synod Hall cinema in Castle Terrace.

The new school range lacked storage facilities for rifles and ammunition. The Cadets kept theirs in the armoury under the east gym. Eventually a purpose-built wooden locker was made by a Club member who happened to be a joiner.

Second World War and After

The Club's activities were suspended, but the range continued to be used by the Cadets and the five smallbore rifles were handed to the Home Guard. Post-war there were difficulties gaining members and equipment. Indeed, the Club has always been a small one, but today it has nine members who are current or past Scotland internationals and include a former Scottish Champion and two Commonwealth Games team members. Some have also represented Great Britain. Perhaps small, but elite.

Development

Prior to 1970, shooting was organised by the Cadets and being a member of the target shooting club was conditional on being in the CCF. Everything was free, but mostly of poor-quality MOD issue. The tradition of recording achievements on the brick walls came to an end when the range was painted. The Club shot at lunchtimes and one evening a week during the winter. Carrying guns through the school from the armoury was quite normal. Security was therefore a lot more lax than we would consider normal today. Indeed, the range had only wooden doors and windows which looked on to the playground and the houses next door. Also, the firing platform was open to the clubroom at the rear. Ear protection was seen as 'wimpish'. In 1961, a heavy curtain was installed which eliminated light and shadow interference, but not sound.

In the '50s and '60s shooting was supervised by John Sinclair (Maths) followed by 'Tex' Aitken (English) and after that by CCF CO Robin Morgan (History). There was no specialised clothing, just school or Cadet uniform. The rifle used was the basic Army No 8, but the Cadets had two specialist ones for the elite Shooting VIII: the BSA Martini International Mk II and the Anschutz Model 54. Competitions were regularly held with Cadet units

1996, the first P7 intake. Left to Right: Sarah Black, Gordon Cox, Ryan Bowie, Amy Irvine, Alex Brodie.

and other schools, notably for the magnificent Strathcona Shield.

During the Summer term the Club prepared for the Brock Shield (the Scottish Schools Championship) and the annual trip to Bisley in Surrey, all paid for by the CCF. The Brock Shield was won in 1910, 1914 and 1924, but the British Championship always eluded GWC.

The Watson's shooting jacket.

The Cadets Disband, 1970

Thus ended a supply of ready-made recruits and the Club was really struggling by 1974. The team was demoted to Division 2 of the local league. Selective recruiting secured promotion in 1975 and achievement of 'runners-up' in 1976.

In the late 1970s, coach Ian Thomson revolutionised the Club by 'targeting' S1 pupils. No-one objected to 12-year-olds being given a rifle. Such a scheme, however, would provide stability and growth. A monitorial system was introduced with older members being obliged to teach younger ones. A school grant was given and non-Cadet competitions entered. As the team became more successful, so the grant increased. Shooting jackets were also introduced as were spotting scopes previously forbidden by the Army.

Numbers soon rose to about 24 pupils and a second weekly session was begun on Saturday mornings. In the early '80s, a star joined the Club: Stephen Dunlop. Stephen soon progressed to the Scottish Junior Team and, as an FP, helped Ian to teach youngsters. Soon the junior section of the Club became a separate entity: GWC Rifle Club. Applications for membership still outnumbered capacity

The Neil Darker Trophy

The school Championship was formalised in 1920 when Neil Darker's parents presented a trophy in his memory. Neil had been a bugler in 1914 and killed-in-action in 1917 with the Royal Scots. In 1990, Stephen Dunlop organised the Open Meeting which has since been held annually and attracts competitors from all over the country. Above: David Champion won the trophy in 2004.

so a third session was introduced on Friday afternoons, followed by a session on Tuesday afternoons, run by Stephen, for Primary 7! The total membership was 48. Equipment was badly needed and parents began to raise huge amounts of money. The result was a multitude of trophies including the Scottish and British Junior Championships.

Tragically, in 1999, Stephen died. In 2000, Ian's job forced him to work abroad. Thus a successful partnership was broken. Fortunately Bill and Anne Hamilton came forward to fill the gap and, ably aided by Ronnie Sellar, Andrew Coates and David Nicoll, have succeeded magnificently in maintaining the high standard set. The Club was, and is, supported strongly by the school, even during the dark post-Dunblane period.

Meadowbank

The Club did move to Meadowbank Stadium in 1971, but it was back in 1972. The school facility was upgraded in 1979, 1983, 1989 and 1999. The result has been to create one of the best-appointed ranges and clubrooms in the area. An outdoor range depends upon land and money. Can anyone help?

Two heroes. Left: Ian Thomson, Right: The late Stephen Dunlop.

The Strathcona Shield won by GWCRC eight times between 1993 and 2004.

Bill Hamilton (Hon Match Secretary, 2004) seen here in 1989 behind the superb 50th Jubilee Trophy. A special Jubilee competition was held among other local clubs. Requests for designs were sent to the Art Departments of all Merchant Company Schools and a committee chose the winning design which was won by Fiona Miller of Mary Erskine. It was created out of stainless-steel by Alex Stewart and Dick Weir.

The Rowing Club

Article by Jim Ferguson. Jim started at GWC in 1995 and had coached rowing previously. He became a full-time Master in Charge of Rowing in 2002.

The Fifties

In 1955, George Hunter, OBE, invited pupils from Watson's to attend rowing sessions at St Andrew Rowing Club with a view to forming a Watson's College Boat Club. Out of a nucleus of a few rowers the Club was formed. In 1958, the Club attended several regattas, most of them in Glasgow, including the annual Scottish Schools' Championships, held on the Clyde, for which we entered three crews. At the Dumfries Regatta the first crew won their first Maiden Race and reached the semi-final.

In 1959, Watson's crews met with a fair cross-section of Scottish schools and remained undefeated. The first crew became Scottish Schoolboy Senior Champions by winning the Murchison Cup in the Scottish Championships at Glasgow. The Club's first new boat was

1963: The Most Successful Year
Left to Right: George Hunter, Graham Butler, Peter Ellis, Mike Masson, Alistair MacGregor, Bill Elwell-Sutton (behind), David Glass (Captain), Stuart Wilson, Ian MacFarlane, John Munn, Edward McIntosh, Hector Waugh.

ordered and would be ready for the next season. Boat Club Colours were introduced and awarded to DTBruce, EP Groves, HR Murray, PT Robertson and JGH Robertson. Half-Colours went to JD Morris who was cox.

The Sixties

In 1961, the first two crews combined to form a Watson's Eight for the Thames

Head of the River Race. The crew was indebted to Westminster School for hospitality, a tradition which still carries on. The new boat arrived and was christened *Caerketton*. The first crew, stroked by DT Bruce, were the winners of the Clyde Head plus five further events in Scottish regattas. Visits were made to Chester Regatta, Northwich and Tyne Regattas, and the City of

1996, Winners of London Schools Head and Scottish Schools Head Louise Potter, Izzy Walker, Laura Fitzgibbon, Faye McDowall.

Lancaster Regatta. The first crew won at the Tyne Regatta beating Durham School in the final by one foot.

At the 1962 Scottish Schools Championships Watson's won the championship fours and the School's Colts won the new Soutar Cup defeating Kingsridge School, Govan High School and Vale of Leven. At the Lancaster Regatta, the final saw the Watson's VIII win the trophy by beating Merchant Taylor's 2nd crew by half a length.

In 1963, the first crew won the Tyne Head of the River Race and at the Schools Championship it won the senior event, the Murchison Cup, beating Heriot's in the final. The Captain, DD Glass, was invited to row in the Scottish Eight at the Serpentine Regatta and won the international match against England, Ireland and Wales. A total of 127 crews competed for five trophies at the Scottish Schools Rowing Championships on the Clyde at Glasgow Green. Watson's won the Murchison, Boyd and George A Hunter cups.

The first Eight took part in Tideway Head in 1964 and at the end of the season was chosen to represent Scotland after gaining three wins at the Scottish Schools Championships. The 1st Crew showed that they were the best Scottish schools crew, the U16 crew won the Soutar Cup, while a very promising crew won the Hunter Cup for boys U15. Two more boats were bought from Club funds.

The Club went from strength to strength throughout the Sixties. In 1965, Watson's 1st and 2nd Fours represented Scotland against England in a Schools International. Meanwhile the new Boat House had become a reality. In 1967, Watson's were victors in the Schools Fours and Eights Championships, and enjoyed a five-day trip to N Ireland. In 1968, Watson's retained the Scottish Schools Head of the River Championship, heading the field of 34

crews by a clear fifteen seconds. Watson's again dominated schoolboy rowing in Scotland with the 1st VIII and 1st IV representing Scotland.

The Seventies
1970 saw the Club suffering from an acute lack of members, but the addition of crews from the Ladies' College was a welcome development. The Club acquired a Restricted Shell Four called *Bonaly*.

The 1971 1st Eight won the Scottish Schools Eights Championships. The following year the Club purchased its new "shell" Four, the *George Hunter*, the first of its type in Scotland. Towards the end of 1973, the Club acquired a second-hand clinker Four, which was renamed the *Titanic*.

In 1977, the Club attended 13 regattas recording 25 wins dominating women's rowing in Scotland, with the girls' first crew being defeated only twice and retaining its position as Scottish Schoolgirls' Fours Champions and becoming the Scottish Women's Junior Champions.

The Club then went into decline consistently failing to recruit enough members.

The Eighties
It was not until 1985 that rowing at the U14 level flourished again and in the following season the Senior Girls' IV won almost everything in sight with the younger crews performing very well indeed. The Club bought a new boat (a Janousek Racing IV) in outrageous pink, christened *Sir Roger Young* and a new set of racing blades.

In 1989, the Club was predominantly female with only 10 boys. The girls won the Women's Junior-18 coxed VIII and gained silver in the Women's Junior-18 IV at the National Schools' Championships at Nottingham. Watson's teams again successfully represented their country.

The Nineties
The girls continued to succeed. At the 1995 Munich Regatta and the World Championship, Isabel Walker, Katrina Hastings and Laura Fitzgibbon competed for Great Britain with Isabel and Katrina winning bronze as part of the GB Four.

It was not until 1998 that the boys showed real progress with Jonny Logan finishing 7th overall in the Scottish Scullers' Head winning the U18 single whilst still junior-15. He went on to represent his country.

The New Millennium
Watson's again won the overall trophy at the Scottish Schools Head in 2001, this time also having the fastest crew of the day. A younger boys crew was now beginning to gain success and by 2002 this crew was the fastest at the Tyne Head and won the Junior Quads at the Durham Head. Chris Logan was also overall winner at the Scottish Scullers Head and Kirsty Myles won the junior-18 girls event. Both went on to represent GB, Chris in the Worlds Squad and Kirsty in the Coupe double-scull where she won a Gold medal.

2004 saw the boys excelling with remarkable successes in both Scotland and England. Sean Dixon and Murray Wilkojc, despite being junior-15, reached the final in the U18 Single Sculls. They also gained a silver medal at the National Championships in the Double Sculls. Rishi Ramaesh and Jonathan Rankin gained medals in the same championships. The girls squad was also successful with Caroline McPherson, Jenny Chambers and Caroline Glauch representing Scotland at the Home Countries Regatta.

The Club has also attended the Ghent International Regatta for the past five years, producing some excellent results. In one year Watson's won 11 medals. There is also an annual trip to the Boston Marathon in Lincolnshire. The marathon is a very demanding 50K race and at present the Club holds eight record times.

In September, 2005 the Club held its 50th Anniversary Dinner with over 150 past and present members attending. Special guest of honour was George Hunter, the founder member. Many thanks must go to George for years of dedication.

Watson's Scouts & Cubs

From information provided by Jimmy Allan, Mike Steel and Richard Cavaye.

In the Beginning …

Scouting began in Watson's in 1908 as a Reconnaissance Section of the school Cadet Corps. It was founded by the legendary Sandy Morrison. Other independent patrols also began in Watson's around this time and Sandy was asked to unite these under his leadership. With other pressing commitments, however, Sandy felt he could not take on another, but his senior schoolboy, Lance-Sergeant Sandy Somerville, was undoubtedly the best man for the job. On the last Friday of the Spring Term 1908, in a crowded meeting in the Geography Room, it was decided to hold regular Scout meetings the following term.

The Ninth

Those first meetings were held on Thursday afternoons in the room at the foot of the Chapel steps opposite the old Burma Gong. In addition, many Field Days were held on Saturdays. During the Summer of 1908 the Midlothian Boy Scouts' Association was formed and a number allocated to each troop. It was impossible to know the correct order, so Sandy suggested he would be happy with 'nine'. Thus the first Watson's Troop of BP's. Boy Scouts became the 9th Edinburgh (Northern Division). Later it was in the Central District and subsequently in the Morningside District.

Scoutcraft

The first Summer Camp was held at Cademuir in July 1909 and a three-day cycling tour was organised for March 1910. Another such tour to Dumfriesshire in the same year involved another Watsonian, JL Lawrence, who was the first Organiser of the Boy Scouts in Scotland.

Badge work occupied a lot of time. Malcolm Wallace and Malcolm Macdonald were among the first Scouts in Scotland to gain all-round cords while Wallace was the first Scout in Scotland to gain a Silver Wolf (passing 24 proficiency badges).

The Trek

In 1911, the first Easter Trek was held, 75 miles being covered in four and a half days between Borthwick and Penicuik. In that year the Summer Camp found its home at Jovie's Neuk, Gullane. Scouts *walked* there with kit and tents on barrows until increased traffic made that dangerous during the Twenties.

The Great War

During the First World War the Scouts assisted with Red Cross work, the Recruiting Office, in forestry camps and on the depot ship HMS *Mars* at Invergordon. Many War Service Badges were gained. Sandy was badly wounded in 1916 and, invalided home, he returned to aid the Troop.

The Twenties

After the War, the Troop was divided into four Groups (later 'Sections'), each run largely as a separate unit.

About this time there were in the Troop more members of the Watsonian 1st XV and of the school 1st XV than ever before or since, and in four successive years the School Captain was a Scout.

Summer was the main time for outdoor work, thus Group or Section Camps have been held regularly then with, finally, a Camp at Jovie's Neuk, held since 1920 in the first fortnight of September.

To encourage progress in Scoutcraft many awards were made such as the Graham Burge Memorial Trophy for fieldcraft and services to the Troop and the Inter-Patrol Shield.

In July 1920, 22 Scouts attended the First World Jamboree at Olympia, London, and took part in displays of Highland Dancing. Many other gatherings and Jamborees followed.

The Second World War

During the Second World War, Camps were located away from the coast and the Troop couldn't meet in the school because of blackout difficulties. Houses and halls were used instead. Numbers inevitably dropped. Post-war saw a revival of interest with three Sections being created.

Wolf Cubs

A Wolf Cub Pack had been founded in 1922 by 'Bunny' Little who remained Cubmaster until 1937. The Pack has normally been limited to eight 'sixes'. The Pack meets for the hour before the Scouts and in the winter concentrates on games and star tests. In Summer,

Easter Trek, Aberfeldy, 28 April 1934.

a camp is held at the Victoria weekend and in July, first at Cockburnhill, then at Borthwick and latterly near Romanno Bridge.

The Watsonian Pioneer Club

In 1914, the Watsonian Pioneer Club was formed to help extend Scouting in poorer working-class areas and to establish a Boys' Club in one such area. The first Troop in the Old Town (16th Canongate) was staffed by members of the Pioneer Club. Other Troops and Packs followed, all using the Watsonian Scout Centre, a flat in Nicolson Street made into clubrooms and financed by older Watsonians. The Pioneer Club became the Watsonian Rover Crew and moved out to the new housing areas with the local population. It was then decided that one Boys' Club would be more useful than a number of little units, thus was born 'The Craigmillar Boys' Club'.

Sandy Honoured

Sandy was awarded the Medal of Merit in 1936 for services to the Scout Movement. In 1953, he was awarded the Silver Wolf and, in 1956, the MBE. He died in 1962. New leaders (Fraser Elgin, Ian Davidson and Tom Kelly) broke the continuity of a fixed summer camp and successfully encouraged lightweight hiking by both senior and junior boys.

Swingin' Sixties

The 1960s saw organisational change in the form of a Group Executive

Committee (parents plus leaders), the change from a green neckerchief to a maroon one with white edging, outdoor activities were expanded and, in 1967, a Venture Unit was born. A farm cottage at Eddlestone was used as an outdoor base from 1960 onwards, followed by Rachan Mill Hall in Broughton and then 'Knockenshang' in Dumfriesshire.

Fabulous Seventies

The 1970s saw The Ninth Magazine emerge followed by Ninth News which disseminated amusingly scurrilous news and comment. From 1970, the Cubs also flourished. Indeed, there are three Packs: Gilwell, Bonaly and Fordell.

Successful Eighties and Horrible Nineties

The 1980s was another successful decade with a third Troop (Beta) being formed. The Senior Hike was revived and trips to Denmark undertaken in 1982 and 1986. The 1990s, in line with other uniformed organisations, saw a reduction in numbers. By 1995, the Group was a fraction of the size it had been 10 years previously. Sterling work by Kenn Bryce-Stafford and Roddy Nelson saved the Troop and Pack respectively. A Beaver Colony was added in the late Nineties by Ronnie Sutherland. A shortage of adult leaders remained a problem.

Nevertheless, the Group did survive and continues to do so under the able leadership of Richard Cavaye.

Happy Memories!: Gullane, 1950s.

The Watsonian Club

Article from information provided by Donald Scott.

The first Watsonian Clubs came into existence soon after the Hospital transformed into a School: Rugby (1875), Cricket (1876), Golf Club (c 1887), soon followed by Cross Country and Curling. The Watson's College Athletic Club was established in 1882 to run the affairs of both past and present pupils.

The Edinburgh Watsonian Club was formed in 1894 and branch clubs sprang up: North America and South Africa (1898), London Club (1899), India Club (1905), Toronto, Montreal, Edmonton, British Columbia (1906), Bombay 1907, Winnipeg (1909), Burma (1910) Australia (1911). Over the next two decades these clubs increased in number to about forty.

In 1928, The Athletic Club and the other Watsonian Clubs amalgamated into The Watsonian Club. AW Angus was its first President and CM Byres its first Secretary. Both were much respected figures. In 1974, with the union of GWC with the Ladies' College the former pupils' clubs took stock and, in 1979, joined together, but retained the name, The Watsonan Club. Disappointingly, numbers of school leavers joining the Club continued to fall. With the co-operation of the College in 1992 leavers were offered free membership for a while, but, again, when that time elapsed few came forward to join. Further discussions ensued and, in the year 2000, all school leavers were automatically made life members of The Watsonian Club. In 2000, the administration of The Watsonian Club passed to Watson's College Development Office.

The Watsonian

In 1904, Henry John Findlay who had joined the English Department (GWC) in 1902, became the first editor of *The Watsonian*. Henry John did more than anyone else during his 31-year stint as Editor to bring Watsonians throughout

Donald Scott (Left) shown with two other fonts of Watson's knowledge, culture and heritage – Pat Edington and Malcolm Hunter.

the world into a close-knit family unit. The magazine was an instant success and was instrumental in bringing Watsonians world-wide in touch with their old school and with each other. Findlay was indefatigable in his duties and, by his vast correspondence with his readers, he was in effect the secretary of the world-wide Watsonian movement. Henry John should also be remembered for the massive work done to compile and edit *The Watsonian War Record, 1914–18*

The magazine continued to provide Watsonians everywhere with news from school and from all the branch clubs. There was a certain amount of competition between these clubs when it came to offering gifts and prizes, both academic and sporting, to their alma mater. During the 1940s, the magazine ceased to be published termly and came out in November and May each session. From 1976, due to increasing costs especially that of postage, it has been published annually.

The Watsonian Annual Dinner

In 1908, it was agreed that all branches of The Watsonian Club, no matter where they were, would all celebrate 'Watsonian Day' by sitting down to their annual dinner on the same day. The date chosen was the third Friday in January and the first occasion was held on 15 January 1909. This continued for many years with the

parent Club and the London Branch having large numbers while overseas Toronto continued to be a vibrant and successful Club. Gradually there was a movement away from a 'fixed' day, but while it still existed its highlight was the reading of the telegrams from all corners of the globe sending fraternal greetings. George Byres, Secretary of the Club, was entrusted with the task of reading these messages. His slight frame necessitated him standing upon his chair and his encyclopedic knowledge of Watsonians worldwide turned what might have been a mundane duty into a tour de force which over the years became an anticipated highlight of the annual dinner.

The cost of the new school in Colinton Road was estimated at £180,000 and The Watsonian Club, in consultation with the School and the Merchant Company, agreed to be responsible for the School boarding houses; a new rugby pitch and grandstand at Myreside and; the new school Assembly Hall. Unfortunately, the boarding facilities never materialised due to a lukewarm reaction by the Merchant Company and a shortfall in contributions by Watsonian members. The idea did not disappear completely, but it took until 1956 before a trust was set up with members equally divided between Watsonians and members of the Merchant Company Education Board.

The Benevolent Fund

The carnage and loss of life that took place during WW1 prompted Dr Arthur Hunter, a Watsonian living and working in New York, to suggest to John Alison, Headmaster of GWC, that a fund be established to help widows and orphans. This was the impetus that resulted in the Watsonian War Memorial Fund which came into being in November 1917.

The purpose of that fund was:
- The erection of a war memorial to commemorate those killed-in-action.
- The publication of a record of all those who served in the war.
- To provide education, and where necessary, giving other financial assistance to children or dependants of Watsonians killed or incapacitated in the war, and giving help to Watsonians who suffered by that war.

While victims of WW1 were being adequately catered for there was a growing conviction that some in civilian life were in need of help. Dr John Orr, President of The Watsonian Club, set in motion a fund to help these people. Never too well supported, this fund struggled on for some ten years before being incorporated, in 1943, into the new War Relief and Benevolent Fund. A considerable number of people had benefited from its efforts, while those administrating the Fund had become aware that there were a number of Watsonians who required financial help outwith the casualties of war.

Though prompted by WW2 there was a strong feeling that the new Fund should encompass not only those who suffered because of the war, but also include any deserving cases. Dr Arthur Hunter was again first in the field to offer support of £300 gathered from members of the North American Club and, in due course, the target of £10,000 was reached. The Benevolent Fund continues to this day and, although the number of recipients is not high, the Fund does alleviate hardship.

A brief tribute should be paid to the association of Wallace & Somerville, CA with the Fund. Mr Wallace was the first Secretary and then Secretary-Treasurer of the War Memorial Fund. He was succeeded in these offices by Sir John Somerville who carried on until the Fund was wound up. Miss Somerville, also a partner in the firm, acted as a voluntary visitor for both the earlier Fund and also the new Benevolent Fund.

The tradition of individuals giving long and committed voluntary service continued with David Anderson, another partner in the above firm, who served with distinction as Secretary and Treasurer for thirty years. The present incumbent is Dennis Carmichael who has now held the reins for 33 years and continues to ensure that the Fund is run sympathetically.

One of the most important voluntary efforts supported by The Watsonian Club was The Craigmillar Boys' Club, the story of which is covered elsewhere in this volume.

The Watsonian Club has had its 'ups and downs' over the years, but it has a proud record of service and commitment to the school. Long may that continue!

> **Some Gifts by Watsonians to the School**
> - The Music School, plus many instruments.
> - The Blair Library, plus many books.
> - The painting **The Harvest** in the Dining Room. A gift for the 'new' school.
> - The Chinese Collection.
> - The bronze statue **Summer** by George Lawson presented by RT Skinner, a former member of the mathematics staff.
> - The Progress of Music.
> - The Hammond Organ in the Assembly Hall gifted in memory of Stuart Watt, School Captain 1938/9, who was killed in WW2. This organ preceded the existing one.
> - The statuette **Youth** presented by the Edinburgh Ladies' College.
> - A stone taken from the Great Wall of China. Presented c1910 by George Houston.

In 1909, the first Annual Dinner of the Edinburgh Watsonian Club was held in the old School Hall in Lauriston Place. For the first time there was a toast to 'The Memory of George Watson' pledged in silence as it always has been since. The Dinner continued to be held there till 1928 (none between 1915–19). After amalgamation (see above), the new Club's first dinner was held in the Caledonian Hotel and for three years after that in the Freemasons' Hall. Then during 1933–9 the Dining Hall of the New School was the venue. A break of seven years was due to WW2, but the first post-war Dinner was attended by 400 Watsonians – a record number – the venue being the Assembly Hall. Thereafter the Dining

Room was large enough, except for 1953 when McVitie's Charlotte Rooms were preferred. In the mid-seventies, a formal Dinner ceased to exist, probably due to cost, and it was decided to dispense with 'Watsonian Day'. An experimental Dinner was held in October, but this proved no more popular and in 1976, 1980 and 1981 there was no Watsonian Dinner. Nevertheless, despite difficulties and it becoming a moveable feast, the tradition has remained intact to the present day.

The Watsonian Cricket Club

From information provided by Alan Borthwick.

The Watsonian Cricket Club was formed in 1875 playing first at Bainfield, near Dundee Street. In 1878, the site of today's Upper Junior School and Merchiston Gardens became available and was used until 1897 when the Club moved to its current venue. Two major cricket squares have been available at Myreside ever since, supplemented by a third from about 1978 at the Craiglockhart ground formerly used by Edinburgh University. For some years the Club also played some cricket at Tipperlinn, mostly on ground now occupied by the all-weather hockey pitch. War stopped play during 1914–18, but it continued right through WW2.

Membership

In the first 25 years some of the Club members were not former Watson's pupils. Then a former pupil (or teacher) became a requirement of Club membership until 1990 when, as a result of general pressure on former pupils' sports clubs to attract new members, the Club (and other Myreside sports sections) began to welcome outsiders as playing members. Now there are no restrictions on who may be a Club member. In recent years we have introduced a senior women's cricket team. Indeed, in 2003/4 the Club boasted a female, Australian Test wicket-keeper as the main permitted overseas player in the 2nd XI and coach for the women's team!

Teams

For many years only friendly matches were played as no cricket league existed, but the Club has fielded three teams for over a hundred years. The first East of Scotland League, in which the Firsts played, was formed in 1894, but it was short-lived. Watson's won it in 1895 and 1896. The present East of Scotland League dates from 1953 when the East of Scotland Cricket Association was formed. In 1996, the 1st XI became eligible to play in the putative Scottish national leagues, then being created. The national leagues are now apparently secure and we have played

in them from the start. Despite seldom winning leagues or cups the Club has held its own at the highest level at which our three teams can play. In the last decade, all our sides have either won a competition or come second, the most important being the winning of the National League's First Division in 2000, a feat repeated in 2005. At present, the Club is considered to be one of the top four in Edinburgh.

Greyhounds

Occasionally a friendly Sunday side has been fielded, called 'The Greyhounds'. The side always plays away with venues stretching from Dumfries to Aberfeldy. Begun in the 1960s to encourage 2nd and 3rd XI players it quickly became a successful means of introducing older schoolboys to adult cricket. In the 1990s, however, as a result of general social pressures, it fell into abeyance, but has recently been resurrected on a limited basis.

A Solid Record

The Club has produced 16 internationalists, including four who have been capped at both rugby and cricket: AW Angus (1907–35), ASB McNeil (1930s), Ian Lumsden (1940s) and David Bell (1967–80s). AW Angus was Club Captain for eight years, scored six centuries, had five caps for cricket and would have achieved more had WW1 not intervened. Another notable internationalist (at cricket only with 15 caps) was Douglas Watt (1908–38) who was Club Captain for four years. He succeeded Angus as Secretary of the Scottish Cricket Union in 1924, holding office until 1948. Remarkably, from 1919 to 1965, the three post-holders of the office of SCU Secretary were all Watsonians. After Watt came James Whitton.

Professional Guidance

A professional coach was appointed from the 1970s, but ten or so current members have coaching certificates. In the school spring term the Club runs popular, weekly indoor net sessions for age groups from about nine upwards, boys and girls. Our earliest professionals were Australians and have included Kim Hughes (1976), Terry Alderman (1980) and Robert Holland (1981). Hughes was the Club's most successful batting

The legendary John W Everett, pictured here in 1965.

At present, the Club is considered to be one of the top four in Edinburgh.

Watsonian Cricket Club 2nd XI Grade B Legue Champions 1991.
BACK ROW (Left to Right): D J Leonard, BD Henderson, MR Macari, WD Maguire,
I Torrens, JD Kidd, SB Lockhart, AR Borthwick, ND Cowan.
FRONT ROW: G Swan, MI Glynn, AGS Brian, JH Hood (Captain), B Adair (President),
KA Flannigan, TR Bunker, IAJ Paul.

professional, with 1,700 runs in a season, playing 70 Tests and Captained the famous 1981 Australian tour to England when Ian Botham seized the series almost single-handedly. Our most recent professional is the excellent South African, James Henderson, who has played for the Club for six years .

Heroes

Office bearers come and go, but the Club has two long-serving post-holders: Stewart Oliver (Secretary, 1974–95) and Duncan Graham (Treasurer, 1978–92). Apart from secretaries of the SCU, the Club has supplied four Presidents (James Martin, Tommy Elgin, Brian Adair and John Everett) and after internal reorganisation of the SCU, two Chairmen (Brian Adair and John Everett). John Everett's time as a player (from the 1950s) has allowed some to claim that they have played alongside father (John), son (Mark) and grandson (Andrew)!

Social Side

This has always been important, ranging from the legendary Myreside teas to a variety of functions such as the Crocks' Match, the Annual Dinner and various tours, the first being in 1926. Speakers at the Dinners have included the Earl of Home (the only Prime Minister to have played first-class cricket), Colin Cowdrey and Sir Garfield Sobers.

The Dublin tours (first in 1936) used to be biennial and many good friendships were made especially through games against Leinster and Pembroke. However, in recent years, the Club has not been so active on the touring front although it has hosted various sides from all over the world. More unusual tours, nevertheless, have included Holland and Corfu. Once the Myreside Pavilion was refurbished in 1968, it became easier to host other functions there.

Representative Cricket

In its centenary year the Club hosted a full week of games, including a match between England Ladies and Watson's, as well as the annual first-class match Scotland v MCC. The Club has also hosted one-day cup matches between Scotland and various English county sides. As a result some major English and foreign test stars have played at Myreside, including Derek Underwood and Graeme Hick. Since Scotland's matches now tend to be played elsewhere, the representative games are mostly now for junior age group sides.

A Pint in Hand

Myreside does, however, still present itself extremely well in the second half of the summer, once the ravages of the rugby season wear off, and the main square is highly rated by batsmen. The quality of the ground is almost certainly linked to the longevity of the head groundsmen: only six in the last 120 years. Few who have had the chance

to watch a match on a sunny Saturday from the pavilion balcony, pint in hand, forget the experience; and players know how lucky they are to play at Myreside, or indeed Craiglockhart with its rustic pavilion. Long may it continue!

Women's Cricket

From information provided by Liz Smith.

The role of women in cricket in days of old is amply illustrated by the picture (right) taken in 1959.

Girls in the Senior School at Watson's have been able to play cricket since 1986 when the first school fixture against Loretto took place, and since 2001 cricket has also been played by the girls in the Junior School. 1st XI matches have been played against 14 different schools in the UK and against three club sides. In recent seasons the girls have also participated in indoor tournaments organised by the Scottish Cricket Union and Cricket Scotland.

In addition to the school fixtures there is the annual Single Wicket Competition for the Adair Trophy and the competition for the most improved player who receives the Graham Trophy. Over the years, four girls have won Colours for cricket and the most notable achievements have been; Caroline Sweetman's 117 not out v Dollar Academy in 2001, Shona McIntyre's 102 not out v Loretto School in 1997 (the same match in which Watson's achieved its highest score of 233 for 2), Kelda Stevenson's 6 for 20 v Loretto in 1993 and Shona McIntyre's 5 for 4 v The Chase School in 2000.

The first team of Watsonian Ladies to play a competitive match took to the field under that name in July 2001 against a Scottish Women's Select XI, most members of which were about to depart for Bradfield College for a series of international matches against Holland, England and Ireland. Sadly, the match had to be abandoned because of bad weather after 12 overs when the Scottish Select were 60 for 1.

Four women Watsonians have played for Scotland: Shona Docherty (née McIntyre) 15 caps, Liz Smith 7 caps, Caroline Sweetman 4 caps and Gillian Graham 1 cap.

Women's Cricket: The Myreside Tea Ladies, 1959.
Left to Right: Mrs J Smith, Mrs HP Henderson, Mrs J Berrie, Mrs AS Adam, Mrs ER Yerbury, Mrs W McNab.

Women's Cricket: At Bradfield College v England, Ireland & Holland
The three Watsonians are: Back Row – 3rd from left, Caroline Sweetman 5th from left, Liz Smith.
Front Row – 2nd from right, Shona McIntyre.

Watsonian Curling Grand Match, 1979, Lake of Menteith
Back (Left to Right) Russel Young, O, John McLaren, Sandy Crerar, O, Napier Landale, Alastair Smith, Lauchlan MacLean, Robyn Slack.
Front: O, John Henderson, O
(O = Opponent)

The Watsonian Curling Club

From information provided by Lauchlan MacLean.

In the late 1950s, like most clubs, The Watsonian Club benefited from the increase in the popularity of curling. A number of young players joined and Robin Welsh, who had been Secretary for 26 years was appointed as Secretary of the Royal Caledonian Curling Club.

Games were played every night of the week instead of the Monday and Thursday format and more matches were arranged including games against Glasgow and Border Watsonians.

Bonspiel

The inception of the Bonspiel in 1967 saw Watsonians from London, Stranraer, Inverness, Fife and the Lothians coming to Edinburgh to play. One benefit was an influx of local players who had been invited to play with some of the Edinburgh and Leith teams.

School Curling

Curling was introduced to the school in 1961 and members of The Watsonian Club assisted with coaching and an annual match was arranged. Pat Edington was appointed teacher in charge. His enthusiasm and encouragement soon had the youngsters winning competitions.

Growth

In the '60s, membership rose to over 90 members and a Border team took part in our League, each Edinburgh team playing against them at the recently opened Kelso Rink and they, of course, played against the seven other teams at Haymarket.

More matches were arranged. The Edinburgh Academicals match is still one of the highlights of the season and the Club took part in local and national competitions with mixed success. A 'Pairs' competition became a regular feature and a 'Spring' league plus 'Knock Out' competition were introduced.

For a number of years a Fun Bonspiel has taken place and has been held at Kinross and Pitlochry as well as Murrayfield.

Notables

Throughout the years members have played a full part in the wider field of the game. Iain and Colin Baxter were in the team which won the Scottish Championships in 1971 and 1978 and were Silver medallists at the Canadian Silver Broom competition (curling equivalent of the World Cup) in 1971. Iain has also been the winner of the Scottish Pairs and was in the successful Scottish Seniors team. In 2002, a Watsonian team won the King George IV competition at Murrayfield. Pat Edington is the Secretary of Midlothian Province and has served on the Council of the Royal Club, as have JB 'Jimmy' Alexander, Ian Tulloch and Malcolm Patrick. Lauchlan MacLean, Jim Hunter, Ian Tulloch, Iain Baxter and Malcolm Patrick have been Presidents of Edinburgh Curling Club.

Watsonian Curling: Indoor Grand Match, 2005, Watsonians at Ayr Ice Rink. Left to Right: Dermont Dick, Dan Lean, John Stepney, Jim Hunter (Skip).

A number of members have toured in Canada, America and Switzerland. Paul Stevenson and Alistair Seftor became the Scottish Pairs Champions representing Murrayfield in 2005.

Grand Matches

The Club took part in Grand Matches played in 1962 and 1979 as well as the Indoor Grand Matches in 2000 and 2005.

Watsonian Hockey

From information provided by Richard Broadbent.

School hockey began in Spring 1921 at the request of boys to whom the strenuous pleasure of rugby did not appeal. Braving the taunts and gestures of rugby lovers the first team emerged playing two games against Edinburgh University. From these noble pioneers grew school and Watsonian Hockey.

Watsonian Hockey

This began in 1924 with a small group organised by Walter Murray to play against 2nd and 3rd XIs of local teams on a pitch at Damhead Farm, Gorgie. Changing accommodation was a barn and 'showers' consisted of a hose used to wash down the byre and its normal inhabitants.

A successful application to join the Watsonian Athletic Club was made. Thus the Watsonian Hockey Club officially began on 25 November 1924.

Season 1924/5 was the first Watsonian one, but also significant as the school team had for the first time a full fixture list. On 26 February 1926 the Club was officially admitted to the Scottish Hockey Association. In April 1928, the Club even organised its first open competition: a six-a-

Hockey enthusiasts, 1949. BACK ROW: J McD Wilson, J Heugh, EL Sharp, D Grant, G Allison, WT Scott, J McL Nicol, TG Salmon, CE Logan, IR Grant (Captain), DF Shearer, NE Sharp, IC Kirkwood, HCW Woolner, Al Patterson. FRONT ROW: FW Reynolds, JW Forbes, JD Carnegie (President) JGC Barr, GP Millar, D Allan, F Gruber, DD Campbell, D handford, IGR McKendrick.

side tournament organised by Jim McDowell Wilson who became an international umpire in 1930. The Club still had no pitch of its own, so this tournament was played on the 1st XV rugby pitch.

The New School, 1932

The pitch problem was solved when the Merchant Company Education Board decided to abandon the plan for a grand ceremonial driveway into the new school and opted instead for a more practical hockey pitch. On 14 March 1933, the first match was played starting a two month unbeaten home run which restored team confidence. Apart from the war years when potatoes and savoy cabbages graced the area it remained the first

team pitch until the advent of the artificial pitch on the other side of the school building.

Hockey Tours

A great feature of the Club has been its tours which started in Season 1936/7 with trips to the Borders playing Selkirk, Crichton Royal Hospital, Annandale, Nithsdale and Galashiels. Accommodation was provided by Youth Hostels and catering by a 2nd XI hotelier and chef. The first ever overseas tour took place in June 1981 with a visit to Canada. In 1983, a second tour went to the Caribbean. In 1988, the first school overseas tour took place when Colin Allison and Ron Looker organised a trip to Holland.

Honours

Watsonians were chosen to play at District level, but no-one represented Scotland until after WW2 when John Harley and Sandy Stephen were capped against England, Ireland (at Myreside) and Wales.

League Hockey

This began in 1952/3 with the introduction of the East of Scotland League with Watsonians finishing second bottom. However, this was compensated by Watsonian administrators: Jim McDowell Wilson (President), Jimmy Nicol (Vice-President), Ian Grant (Hon Sec), George Millar (Hon Treasurer) and Ian Carnegie (District Selector).

Tournaments

The Club re-introduced its own six-a-side tournament in 1959 when a Watsonian six went on to beat ICI in the final and retained the trophy in the following year. That tournament continued into the 1980s, but was only won once more by a Watsonian side. Watsonians featured regularly in other sixes tournaments in the early '60s winning the Midland Sixes, the Civil Service Sixes (1962 & 1963) and the Dunfermline sixes in 1964. Throughout this decade the Club recorded some other notable successes, culminating in that famous date of 12 October 1968 when Inverleith, fielding five full internationalists, were beaten by the incredible score of 6–0!

A brief setback came in 1970/1 when the 1st XV were relegated, but after a successful cup run the following season, reaching the semi-final, and a league reorganisation, the Club was back in the Premier Division of the East League where they stayed until the introduction of National Leagues.

Myreside Mirror

An astonishing innovation for a small Club was the foundation in January 1974, of the *Myreside Mirror* by Kerr Baillie. He was soon aided by John Murison. This broadsheet news publication is a major source for anyone interested in the history of the more recent Club.

National Leagues

Ignoring the wishes of the WHC, the SHA introduced these Leagues in 1975/6 with Watsonians entering in Pool B (the second of three pools which were then re-organised into six smaller ones in 1974/5. In 1976/7 the 1st XI finished 2nd in Division 3 and there it mostly stayed. The lowest point was in 1985/6 when out of 68 outdoor games played by the Club, only 10 were won. By February 1987, the 2nd XI could name their spectators – all two of them! At the same time the school teams, coached by Colin Allison, were highly successful : the 1st XI reaching the quarter finals of the Scottish Cup in 1988, six players in the East of Scotland U18 team and goalkeeper Craig Burton capped for Scotland at U16 level.

The resurrection of Watsonian Hockey began in the 1990s. By 1992 the 1st team was back in Division 2, but the lack of an artificial pitch was holding back progress. In 1993, the Club was using the new Astroturf at Fettes College. By 1994, the 1st team was in Division 1 and a 5th XI was formed intended to encourage and develop talent from the school. Things were on the move at last thanks to Mark Ferguson, Alan McKean, Morris Duncan and, above all, Colin Allison. Nevertheless, the 1st team was relegated in 1995, but the 5th team finished as Division 5 champions! The 1st team were back in Division 1 the following year. The teams went from strength to strength.

In 1995 it was announced that Watson's Astroturf was to be ready for season 1996/7 ... and it was!

Sponsorship

The first came from Duncan Young, CA, thanks to Morris Duncan and his partner. The Club now had financial security.

Girls!

With the arrival of dozens of hockey-playing females in 1974 the pitches began to wear out. Fortunately the Merchant Company had taken over the old Edinburgh University playing fields at Craiglockhart which were then used extensively.

Recognition

Scottish Schoolboy Caps were awarded to Chris Rielly and Neil Sharp in 1976. International representation was achieved in 1979 when Alan Sharp was selected for Scotland. Unfortunately, he never played a match and had to wait until 1981 for a game against Wales. Eventually he went on to gain two outdoor caps, 10 indoor and ten Scotland U21 caps.

In 1994/5, both Mike Leonard (U21) and Stuart McConachie (U18) were selected to play for Scotland while Jason Ng, Richard Broadbent and Robert Sinclair were chosen for East U18s. David Braithwaite (whilst playing for Gordonians) was capped in 1995/6 for Scotland and voted *Player of the Year*. Other U18 honours were gained by Colin Johnston, Scott Casey and Alasdair Swan, Jnr.

A Record?

Veteran player Nigel Sharp retired in 1998 having scored an amazing 1220 goals. His first goal was against RNATE Rosyth in September 1949.

An Open Club?

This had first been raised in 1976 when Watsonians and the University Clubs were the only closed ones in Scotland. In 1982, Kerr Baillie warned that the Club's future was in jeopardy. Three years later the first momentous step was taken by introducing House Membership which opened up the Club to relatives of any Watsonian member. The first non-Watsonians were Alasdair Swan and Dr Sandy Reid.

Watsonian Rugby

Article contributed by Alastair Nimmo.

Although football matches were played in Merchiston prior to 1875, it is generally accepted the Watsonian Football Club was founded in 1875 and records show its first recorded match took place on 30 January 1875 against St George, a team long since extinct. The match, which ended in a draw, was played at Bainfield, the first of the Club's four grounds. Watsonians played the match proudly sporting their orange and blue jerseys and it was a year later before maroon and white was introduced.

SFU/SRU

The Club became a member of the Scottish Football Union (SRU from 1924) in 1877 and won its first championship in season 1891/2. The

Watsonian Football Club 1st XV, 1969/70. Winners, Scottish (Unofficial) Club Championship: BACK ROW: DS Paterson, Dr Harvey, RJN Patrick, AM Hunter, RS Tolbert, JB Mitchell, PCA Baker, DED Neave, G Robertson, RH Blake. MIDDLE ROW: DD Mathieson, PC Forbes, I Robertson, AL McLaren (Vice-Captain); P Gallagher (Captain), AC McNish, WS Henderson, RG Young, DJ Hood. FRONT ROW: A Gregor, M Watters. (Photo by Yerbury).

Club was at its strongest in the six years from 1908 to 1914 during which period it won the club championship a further five times and lost only once in three seasons to Scottish opposition.

Myreside

The Club moved to its present ground at New Myreside in 1933 and celebrated by winning the championship again in seasons 1934/5 and 1936/7. The Club had to wait 33 years before winning its next championship in 1969/70 under the inspiring leadership of schoolmaster and coach, Peter Gallagher.

League Rugby

In 1973/4, league rugby was introduced and Watsonians were placed in Division 1, a position the Club has maintained for 27 of the 31 seasons played. The Club relaxed its rules after relegation in 1989, opening the Club to players outside of its previous GWC intake. After winning the 1997/8 Championship, Watsonians lost the majority of its victorious side to the professional ranks following the significant shift in attitude to professional rugby in Scotland. After a second spell of Division 2 rugby the Club returned to Division 1 in season 2003/4 and finished in fourth position.

A Proud Record

During its history the Club has had 63 players capped and has won the championship more often (16) than any other club apart from Hawick and Edinburgh Academicals. Seven British Lions have played for the Club,

27 Watsonians have appeared for the Barbarians and several have won rugby blues at Oxford or Cambridge. Watsonians have provided four international referees and nine SRU Presidents. Bill Hogg is the current SRU Secretary and Graham Young a recent SRU President. The Club has also triumphed at the abbreviated game winning 30 major sevens including nine at Melrose.

Most Capped

The Club's most capped members, Gavin and Scott Hastings, played major parts in three Rugby World Cups, two Lions tours and a Scotland Grand Slam with Gavin captaining the 1993 Lions in New Zealand. Gavin (61 caps) captained Scotland on 20 occasions before retiring from international rugby after the 1995 World Cup. Scott (65 caps) is Scotland's fourth highest capped player behind Gregor Townsend, Kenny Logan and Gordon Bulloch.

The Club Today

The recent pace of change in rugby is rapid and the Club has adapted to remain at the forefront of club rugby in Scotland. Significant Club sponsorship, the introduction of women's rugby and midi-rugby plus modern floodlighting at Myreside are evidence of this, a far cry from the mean field at Bainfield when an ill-judged kick would send the ball splashing into the Union Canal. The Club continues to make an outstanding contribution to Scottish rugby with expansive play combined with the aim of enjoying rugby football both on and off the field high on its list of priorities.

Watsonian Squash Rackets Club

Article contributed by Brenda Carmichael.

The Watsonian Squash Club, which was founded by Jimmie Allan and David Bogle in 1934, is still going strong. Jimmie Allan left Watson's in 1925 and spent three years at Cambridge University where he saw squash being played, and decided at once that it was a game he would like to take up when back in Edinburgh. Four years later he got his fellow Watsonian David Bogle enthusiastic, feued a site beside the Myreside pavilion from the Merchant Company and obtained permission to build on it. The next thing was to get the money (over £1,785), and this was raised though an Appeal in The Watsonian plus loans of £350 from The Watsonian Club together with smaller sums from the magazine's funds and from individuals. The courts were therefore physically owned by the Squash Club.

The two courts were built with glass roofs so no electricity was needed in daytime. (When the Second World War arrived the roof was required to be painted black to satisfy black-out regulations, and later a flat roof was added.) Unfortunately, there were the usual problems with the building, in that the roof leaked and the window frames were about to be put in when it was found there was no means of opening them! This was despite architects (WH Kininmonth and Basil Spence, both Watsonians and both of whom later received a knighthood for services to architecture, the latter being particularly famous for his building of Coventry Cathedral in 1951) having already encountered similar problems with the courts at Fettes and Edinburgh Academy with which they had also been involved. The facilities were basic, with the changing room being a corridor behind the courts, and the shower area hot water provided by a large copper boiler, the lighting of which was a highly dangerous operation involving holding a lit newspaper at arm's length and waiting for the gas to explode into action! The Club opened on 18 February 1935 with 90 members already signed up at an annual subscription £1 1s and an entry fee of the same amount, or as a

Watsonian Women's Team. Winners Lothian Leagues, 2003/4 & 2005/6.
BACK: Katy Buchanan,
Sarah McFadyen, Susie Laughland,
Alison Mackie.
FRONT: Christina Graham,
Margaret Clark, Christine Cochrane,
Alexis Manson.

life member for £10 10s. Rackets and lockers could be hired. This sub was soon increased to £2 2s as the club tried to pay back some of the loans. The first President was AG Cairns with the inevitable Jimmie Allan as first Secretary and David Bogle as Treasurer.

National Association
Very soon the intrepid pair decided to arrange the first Scottish Squash Championships at Myreside, and this was followed by a meeting in the Pavilion with a few other enthusiasts from which a Scottish Squash Rackets Association was formed. So, The Watsonian Club was in at the start of squash in Scotland and has played a part in its history ever since.

Early Days
At first there were no leagues, but regular matches were arranged against other early clubs such as the Edinburgh Sports Club, Edinburgh Academicals, Gala, and SSRC in Glasgow, sometimes for between 15 and 20 a side. In 1937, ladies were permitted to use the courts on three mornings a week for a reduced fee and separate membership; male members were banned from the courts and dressing room at these times. The squash building was freestanding, and with no on-court heating the temperature inside was the same as that outside, which proved to be a distinct advantage at most home matches against teams with heated courts. By the 1938/9 season there were 120 members and electric fires were supplied for the changing rooms, but

with the plea that they should be used no more than absolutely necessary, and that a similar economy should be applied to the on-court light.

Post-War Problems
The Second World War had a drastic effect on the fortunes of the club as membership tumbled, at one stage to five playing members, and the postwar years were very precarious with very low membership and financial deficits. Several of the loans were written off in 1951 including that from The Watsonian Club, and more £l0 loans were taken out to pay for repairs and dry rot, though these were all repaid in the following few years. All through the '50s and early '60s membership was low and the club swung between small surpluses and small deficits and, in 1959, the cost of repairs had become so onerous that the courts were gifted to the Merchant Company in exchange for the School taking over the maintenance costs, leaving the club with no fixed assets, but no debts other than loans from members. School pupils had use of the courts in mid-week afternoons and at weekends, and the school teams were looked after principally by Jimmie Allan until the mid-1960s, then notably by Jimmy Stevenson, Iain Murray and Robert Bellis. The club still tries to maintain good links with the school, and pupils have played for club teams in some seasons.

Development
The 1970s saw the start of the squash boom and things began to improve to the extent that in 1978 two new courts were planned as part of the refurbishment of the whole of Myreside at a cost of approximately £40,000. These courts opened in the autumn of 1980 and all courts were heated, thus relinquishing the home advantage mentioned earlier. As a result of the extra courts, membership reached a peak of just over 200 in 1980/1 with the admission of women to full membership thanks to the separate changing rooms. Financially things were still tight as repayment of the capital cost of the courts to the Merchant Company had to be undertaken through fundraising as well as subscription income. In addition, all sports clubs using Myreside had to

make a 'donation' to the parent club to help defray other costs of the Myreside refurbishment. When the new courts were opened the subscription doubled from £10 to £20 (having been only £3 up to 1997), but it was soon found that this was not enough and by 1993/4 the subscription had doubled again. This had the unfortunate result of reducing the number of members so the finances did not improve and the repayment terms to the parent club were amended to extend the period of payment and reduce the rate.

The club also widened its net, in 1986, to offer those who were House Members of the parent club (ie those who had some connection to the school though not having been a pupil) a season ticket to use the squash club. By 1990, however, there were still financial problems which were eased only when the capital contributions stopped about 1991 and since then the financial situation has been quite healthy, although more and more repairs can be anticipated. Membership was again widened in the 1990s with some 'invited' members as the parent club relaxed its rules further. House members are now classed as full members and more players are joining who have no specific link to the school, thus reducing further the restriction in membership requirements, in keeping with other sports sections.

Competition
On the competition front, the men's team joined the national leagues in the 1960s, winning the league in 1973/4, the inter-club cup in 1958/9, 1959/60 and the inaugural Scottish Quaich in 1973/4 and 1974/5. Having played some friendly matches in previous years, the 2nd team joined the East league in 1963, a 3rd team in 1972 and a 4th in 1976, and, despite regular struggles, there have been four teams ever since. In 1983 the 1st team abandoned the national leagues as the East leagues expanded into Lothian leagues, where the team were champions in 1995/6. In 1980, a women's team was formed and was joined by a second in 1983. The 2nds later dropped out to be restarted in 2002 when there was a resurgence of interest among women, which was rewarded in 2003/4 season by the

women's 1st team winning the league for the first time. An annual men's club championship has been held since 1935, apart from the War years. The first winner was Harry Roxburgh and the current holder for the past seven years is Richard McIntosh. His achievement is, however, dwarfed by the eight-year run and total of 11 won by the stylish Oliver Balfour, undeniably the best Watsonian player so far. The women's championship started in 1984 was won by Brenda Carmichael, with the current champion being Christina Graham, breaking a long run by Alexis Manson, although the event has not been completed in some seasons.

International

Former pupils of George Watson's have also performed at international level. Harry Roxburgh played before the War and since then the following were full internationalists: Jim Urmson, John and Peter Everett, Oliver Balfour, Bill Matheson, Jimmy Stevenson, Robin Chalmers, Iain McMurrich, Neil Martin, Brian Tait, Brenda Carmichael, Mrs Irene Rowe (Andrew), and, most recently, Harry and Lizzie Leitch and Pamela Nimmo, though never a squash club member, is a full-time player and in 2004 ranked in the world top 20. In 1968, Oliver Balfour was the most capped player in the world with 45 caps, and in 1978 Brenda Carmichael held the women's record with 53, still

having the longest Scottish span of 21 years and was awarded an MBE for services to squash in 1981. Other club members have represented Scotland at age group levels recently, including current members Jack Calder, Margaret Clark, Christina Graham, Alexis Manson, Peter Wilson.

National

To date there have been six Watsonian presidents of the Scottish Squash Rackets Association (now known as Scottish Squash): TJ Carlyle Gifford (pre-war), our founders Jimmie Allan and David Bogle, and Oliver Balfour, these all presidents of the men's association, and, since it became a joint association in 1972/3, Bruce Jamieson and George Mieras have officiated, with the latter still very active in the International Association. Both John and Peter Everett won the Scottish Boys' Junior Championship, as did Iain McMurrich and Neil Martin, while Oliver Balfour (twice, in 1959/60 and 1967/8) and Brenda Carmichael (in 1970/1) won the Scottish (Open) Amateur Championship. This event no longer exists, but Pamela Nimmo has won the National Championships three times to date.

Social

Social events and handicap tournaments, along with a ladder competition and/or mini leagues, have been tried regularly in order to

increase the social aspect of the club which had tended to be dominated by its many team matches. A celebratory Silver Jubilee Dinner was held in 1961 in the Epicure Restaurant, now long gone from Shandwick Place, at a time when founder Jimmie Allan was President. The Golden Jubilee Dinner was held in Myreside in December 1984 when Peter Lothian was President and speakers included Jimmie Allan again, plus Brian Adair and George Mieras (then the current SSRA President), as well as the then Principal Sir Roger Young. There were 106 members and guests present. It was agreed there that the two original, courts would be known as the 'Allan' and the 'Bogle' courts as a tribute to the two far-thinking initiators of the club. Recently the dinner has become a popular part of the annual social scene and is held on the same night as the finals of the club tournament.

Future

At present the membership is reasonably steady at just over 100 despite the general decline in the popularity of squash generally, so the club looks set to continue for the foreseeable future, as long as the courts can be maintained and volunteers found for the committee – a constant problem nowadays with most sports clubs and voluntary bodies – and is looking forward to celebrating its 75th anniversary in season 2009/10.

The Watsonian Swimming Club

Information contributed by
Roger G Smith, Captain 2003/4.

The Watsonian Swimming and Physical Training Club had its first meeting on 1 March 1933 with 144 members. Lessons were given by Freddy Lemmon to members. Tickets were sold (2s 6d for a single lesson and 10s for 5 lessons) and handed to Mr Lemmon. The initial subscription was fixed at 15s per annum. An honorarium was given to the Engineer, Furnaceman and Janitor for the required services.

Development

Membership increased in 1934 to 167 members which is the highest it

Watsonian Swimming & Physical Training Section – The Crocks' Cup, 1993:
BACK ROW (Left to Right): JM Inglis, WR Watt, CE Patton (Captain), GP Murray, KJ Lyon
MIDDLE ROW: GJ Bulmer, GFM Boddie
FRONT ROW: GW Russell, DF Stewart, IC Strachan, WA Milliken.

has ever been. It was agreed to have the Club swimming costumes (slips) and towels provided by the Club and washed after each evening's swimming. Physical Training was carried out in one of the gymnasia and over the years a number of staff members took the PT class for which they were given an honorarium. After the War basketball, badminton and quoits were also available. Now there is badminton and swimming only.

Ups and Downs

In 1938, the baths were closed for a term and a half over the Spring and Summer for 'improvements' and a refund of 5s was made to members. An outbreak of petty pilfering also occurred in the same year and, as a result, a box was provided in the janitor's office and two members were asked to go on the roof of the PT block to watch out for possible intruders!

By 1939, the Club finances were in a *"serious state of affairs"* due to falling membership and then, with the outbreak of War, the baths were closed until Easter 1941. They reopened for the Summer Term in 1941 with a subscription of 5s (1s for members of HM Forces). In 1943, The Watsonian Club asked the Swimming and PT Club to continue and agreed to meet any financial deficit. A Holding Committee was set up.

Members helped with the School Swimming Gala in 1944 as judges, timekeepers, doorkeepers and ushers. Normal nights resumed in October 1945 with an annual subscription of £1 5s, but membership numbers were low and by April 1946 the Club was in debt to the tune of £26 12s 6d. The Treasurer asked members to recruit more otherwise, *"... if the Merchant Company heard that attendance was so low they would close down the baths as it was such a waste of coal, wages, etc."* On one night there were there present Mr Lemmon, Mr Fleming (PT Instructor), the janitor, the engineer, the fireman, the Club Secretary and one member!

Later in 1946 the baths were closed in the winter term due to an outbreak of polio in the City. In January 1947 there was difficulty with the washing of towels and slips. One of the cleaners had done this work, but she had left and none of the others would agree

to do the work due to the difficulty of getting soap! Mr Lemmon came to the rescue and arranged for his assistant to do the job for £1.

The first mixed social evening was held in 1972 and this has become an annual event.

Personalities

One of the founder members was Dr Boyd Jamieson who was an office bearer for many years. He donated the Boyd Jamieson Crocks Cup for annual competition by members over the age of 45. He wished it to be free style over 50 yards, but *"... not to be a life and death matter, but more of an amusement."* The first winner was JGM McGregor in March 1939. The Cup is still competed for annually in March.

At the AGM in 1946, Freddy Lemmon raised under AOCB his concerns that the Captain (Dr Boyd Jamieson) was in the habit of celebrating his birthday by diving off the top board and his 80th birthday was imminent. The Doctor replied that his wife would second Mr Lemmon's motion to stop him!

Freddy Lemmon, who had been the Instructor since the Club's inception in 1933, retired in 1966. A presentation was made to Freddie at a social event held at the Iona Hotel on 13 July 1966 and at an Extraordinary General Meeting held that evening Freddie was made an Honorary Life Member of the Club. He was subsequently elected Captain for the year 1973/4.

1974–2004

In 1976, the Club's finances benefited from three wins in the Football Club's 100 Draw. In 1978, a cup was presented by the Club to the School for the Junior Girls Swimming Championship.

In the early 1980s the Club donated over £1,000 to the Myreside Development Fund and members took their share of Bar duties at Myreside Pavilion.

In 1984, there was 'lively' discussion about the amalgamation of the Club and the Watsonian Women's Sports Section (the ladies swimming club). No decision was made with *"... no urgency to pursue the matter."*

In 1985, the Club donated a Lifesaving Shield and annual voucher

to the School. Five years later, £750 was raised for the School Appeal. In the same year the first golf outing took place as well as the annual social.

In 1991, the annual subscription was raised from £1 to £6 with a 50% reduction for those over 65 years of age. In 1994, a trophy for P6 boys was presented to the School. Two years later, £200 was given to the Floodlight Fund at the Grandstand Pitch. That same year the ladies' section moved to Wednesday evenings. It was agreed to have four sessions of 45 minutes – one for ladies only, one for men only and two mixed. This has worked out very well and continues to this day.

In 2001, a proposal was made to amalgamate the two sections again, but the voting was six For and six Against. However, in 2003, common sense prevailed and the Watsonian Swimming Club with a new constitution approved by the Watsonian Council was born.

Freddy Lemmon, 1966.

Freddy Lemmon, despite his elf-like figure, was one of the greatest ever Watson's characters. Prior to 1914 he, along with his two brothers Douglas and Mark, used to do Trick Diving Exhibitions, a favourite with Scottish Galas. By 1920, Freddy was the East of Scotland Diving and 100 yards Champion. He was also the backbone of the Warrender Team who were the Scottish Team Race Champions for four years.

In 1923, Freddy accepted an appointment as a Teacher of Swimming with the Edinburgh Education Department and he came to Watson's in 1932 when the new school and pool were opened. His voice (and what a voice!) echoed around that pool for 34 years. He taught literally hundreds of boys to swim and save life. Fred won the Dobie Cup at Warrender Baths in 1908 and the Boyd Jamieson Cup in 1966.

Watsonian Lodge, Number 1375

Article by Lindsay Walls.

A Watsonian Lodge – Motto: *Ex Corde Caritas* – was the inspiration of William S Malloch. On 1 December 1930 he called a meeting of all interested to meet in 19 Hill Street to approve a Charter to be presented to Grand Lodge, to nominate the first Office Bearers and fix fees. Its Consecration took place in Freemasons' Hall, George Street, on 19 March 1931 by Grand Master Mason, Bro AA Hagart Spiers of Elderslie. The Lodge meetings were held in the ante-room of the Hall in Archibald Place. A scroll of Founder Members was made for posterity.

First Building Blocks

The first regular meeting was held on Thursday 9 April 1931 at 8pm. The first two applications for membership by affiliation were accepted from Ernest Godfrey (Roman Eagle No160) and William Jamie (St David No 36) while the first application came from none other than the then Editor of *The Watsonian*, Hendry James Findlay.

Colinton Road, 1932

The Merchant Company Education Board had granted the Lodge the use of a room within the new school and the first meeting was held there on 20 October 1932. In November it was announced that Bro Major Andrew, an Honorary Member, had been elected Master of the Merchant Company.

A sub-committee was soon formed to prepare designs for Lodge furnishings. Bro JM Johnston and Bro TW Marwich, both practising Architects, had their designs accepted. The new furniture – made by Scott's of George Street – was placed and used from November 1934 and insured for £300.

In 1935, Hon Membership was granted to Bro Robert W Miller, the Master Builder of the new school at Colinton Road.

Benevolence

In October 1936, Bro Leslie Grant proposed that the Lodge should help the school more. After discussions with the Head in July it was agreed that the Lodge would do valuable service in supporting boys who had just left school and wished to attend university or embark upon an apprenticeship, but whose parents then fell on hard times.

Standard Presented

On 9 December 1937, a Standard was presented to the Lodge by George Watson's Ladies' College. The Headmistress, Miss Robertson, not only sanctioned that the work be done by pupils of the Art Class, but gifted the silks and satins required for it. Miss Hodges, the Art Mistress, instructed and guided the girls to produce a masterpiece. Bro Jas Johnston and RWM Francis Inglis helped with the design and Bro Douglas Radford defrayed the cost of mounting, backing and binding the panel.

Old to New

On 17 November 1938, Mary's Chapel Lodge (the oldest Edinburgh Lodge) presented the youngest Lodge with three Tracing Boards which were to be returned to Lodge No 1 if the Watsonian Lodge became dormant.

WW2

The Merchant Company did not wish any of the school premises used when lighting was necessary, so the Lodge moved its meetings to Roman Eagle No 160, the first being held on 19 October 1939. Membership of the Lodge grew after the cessation of hostilities with many members continuing friendships made, not only at school, but in the armed forces.

To Morningside Drive

When the Blair Library expanded the Lodge moved to the 5th Year Common Room in the near to the Senior Quad. This did not prove a satisfactory venue and for some years from 1975 until the early 1980s, degrees were worked at the back of the Hall under the balcony. With the arrival of girls from George Square more and more pressure was put on available space, so the Lodge moved to the Upper Primary where a very good operational temple was created in the theatre/music room area with visitors sitting on the (then) raised area. Continuing pressure forced yet another move, in October 1994, to the Pavilion at Myreside. This was a popular venue

The Watsonian, *December 1934. The new furniture and special room, now part of the BM Library. Note the oaken wall fitting on the right made to take a copy of the War Record. Does anyone know where it is now?*

as Club members became aware of the existence of the Lodge and 1375 members were able to mix with them after meetings. Unfortunately, the franchising of the catering facilities meant that the Lodge could not always meet in a secure area and the decision was taken to rent premises more suited for Masonic purposes. Thus came about the move to the Dunedin Masonic Hall in Morningside Drive in October 1998, which heralded the discussions regarding a merger.

Membership Declines

During the period from 1946 until the mid-sixties, the Lodge continued to be well attended. It became customary for Depute Grand Masters to be given honorary membership and, in return, several Watsonians attained Grand Rank. Notable among these were Duncan Lowe, who became Grand Almoner, and AB (Sandy) Young, who became Grand Director of ceremonies.

From the mid-1960s, as was happening all too frequently, membership of Lodges throughout Scotland started to drop off. The Lodge attracted fewer and fewer members until, in 1980, the Brethren considered an application from a non-Watsonian. Consternation was expressed from several Past Masters and a special meeting was convened on 29 May 1980 to debate this turn of events. Bros Charles Wilson and Lindsay Walls proposed the cessation of restrictions which allowed membership exclusively for Watsonians and members of staff, especially in light of the fact that the Lodge was having extreme difficulty in attracting new members. After a debate lasting well over an hour, a vote was taken to open the membership or to retain the status quo. The status quo won by 22 votes to 2. Several Past Masters, who had not been seen in the Lodge for many years, packed their bags and were never seen again.

Rededication

On 5 February 1981 a Ceremony of Rededication, conducted by Bro Sir James W Mackay, Grand Master Mason, took place at Colinton Road. Among the Grand Lodge deputation were the following Watsonians: Bro Stuart Falconer (Grand Secretary), Bro Duncan M Lowe (Grand Almoner) and Bro Gabriel Jerdan and Dr WRC Andrew (Members of Grand Committee). It was with great regret that Bro Sandy Young had to tender his apologies for absence that night. Bro Sandy had recently been diagnosed as suffering from cancer and was too unwell to attend.

An Open Lodge?

It was not until 1991 when an application for membership was received from Lt Col RJS Smith, who was a former pupil of Stewarts-Melville, that the entire debate of opening up the Lodge re-opened. By that time The Watsonian Club had introduced Family Membership and it was felt that, to keep the Lodge viable, it too had to be opened. Several brethren,

either Watsonians, or with Merchant Company connections, affiliated and the Lodge enjoyed a new lease of life.

The Final Chapter

The move to Morningside Drive, however, enabled the final direct chapter of the Watsonian Lodge to be enacted. Lodge 1375 had several brethren moving through the offices and Lodge Dunedin No 1316 had a gap between recent members and those attaining the chair. Past Masters Lindsay Walls (1375) and Allan Jackson (1316) who had been firm friends for over twenty-five years looked at the broader picture and agreed that a merger would enable those gaps to be filled, would give an enhanced membership in a joint Lodge and would cement a relationship between the Lodges which had lasted for 70 years.

They approached Bro Robert Tait, then Provincial Grand Master of The Provincial Grand Lodge of Edinburgh, who endorsed the proposals and set in motion the chain of events which led to the merger of the two Lodges on 8 November 2002 as Lodge Dunedin Caritas No 1316.

It was fitting that the last initiate into Freemasonry in 1375 was Bro Andy Macrae, a teacher at Watson's. The final meeting was held in Morningside Drive on 25 October

2003 when Bro Andy was raised to the 3rd Degree. It was well attended by over eighty brethren from the Provinces of Edinburgh, Midlothian and further afield.

The Watsonian Furniture

The premises at Morningside Drive are owned by a consortium of six Lodges, all of whom have come together over a number of years. All of them brought furnishings with them, but it was not until the merger that the pièce de résistance took place. The beautiful Watsonian furniture, which had been stored in the school, was brought to Morningside Drive. There it was lovingly restored and it was agreed that all Lodges using the premises would use the furniture.

75 Years

The 75th Anniversary of the founding of The Watsonian Lodge. To mark the occasion, Past Master Bro Lindsay Walls has gone into the Chair. It is proposed to hold a special meeting in April, the 75th anniversary of the first Regular Meeting of 1375, when a degree was worked. It is hoped that Lodge Dunedin Caritas will carry on the true spirit of Freemasonry and that Watsonians wishing to join the ancient and honourable craft will consider it their natural point of entry.

Watsonian Club Branches

The first overseas Club to be formed was North America (February, 1898) with three members in Philadelphia: Peter Balfour, AP Ramage and Arthur Hunter. This was followed in the same year by South Africa. By 1905, branches had been established in Canada, India (1905), Cape Town (1905), the River Plate (1899) and London (1899). It was, however, the establishment of *The Watsonian* under the enthusiastic and vigorous editorship of Henry John Findlay which did more than anyone or anything else to promote branches of The Watsonian Club at home and overseas. He pumped blood into the system and and created something strong. Findlay retired in 1935.

By 1906, the American Branch was operating from five different centres: New York, Chicago, Milwaukee,

The American Club Badge.

We have much pleasure in reproducing a photo of the badge of the North American Club sent to the Headmaster recently. This little ornament, with its tasteful reproduction of the School arms, is worn as a watch-fob by our boys in "The States," and more than once the little trinket has drawn two men into friendly talk who would otherwise have remained strangers. The idea is a good one, and may recommend itself to the other branches of the Club.

The Watsonian, December 1905.

Springfield and Montreal. In April of that year an Australian Branch was proposed by WA Mackay of the Australian Steam Navigation Company. Unfortunately, it failed to come to anything and it was not until 21 January 1910 that the Western Australian Club

was born. Meanwhile, a small branch began operating in China by 1906 and the first Watsonian Dinner was held in Toronto on 12 December 1906. In the same year branches emerged in the Straits Settlement (4 September 2006), Alberta (30 November 2006) and Edmonton. In the following year a branch was formed in Bombay, but the River Plate Branch needed to be 'resuscitated.' Winnipeg began on 18 November 1909. In 1911, Leslie Grant founded a Branch in Eisenach, Germany, but celebrated Founder's Day by himself as he was the only member! On 11 July 1911 a branch was established in Sydney, but 1912 was a bumper year: Saskatoon, Lancashire, Calgary and New Zealand, although the latter didn't officially begin until its Dinner in Dunedin on 17 January 1913. In August 1914, Britain and its Empire went to war. The development of The Watsonian Club would have to wait.

A Watsonian Day?

This was proposed on 12 January 1907 by President J Gemmell of the Indian Watsonian Club meeting for its annual Dinner in Calcutta on 12 January 1907. He suggested that all branches across the world celebrate on the same day just like St Andrew's Night. He felt it would strengthen fellow-feeling, help people get to know each other and so give additional prestige to the old school. Henry John Findlay enthusiastically adopted the idea and the details were left with the parent Edinburgh Club. It decided on 18 June 1908 that Founder's Day should be the 3rd Friday of January. The first celebration was held in the College Hall on 15 January 1909 with '*Watsonian Pudding*', '*Chirnside Tart*', '*Myreside Patlids*' and '*Meadows Grouse on Toast*' all created by Mr Boettger of the Union Hotel. This Dinner became the model for all others, but the highlight of each evening was undoubtedly the reading of fraternal telegrams from branches all over the world.

Indeed, the annual Dinner was, for most members, the most important part of Club membership. Overseas, with members often scattered over wide areas, it was the only event that members could realistically attend. However, branches did try to create attractive programmes of other activities, mainly centring on golf and cricket, events which even those of advancing years could manage.

Younger Members

Attracting younger members was

The Canada Cup.
Gifted in 1909 and delivered in 1910.

a perennial problem. One solution came from the youngsters: a branch based on when you left school. Thus was born the 'Year Club'. In 1909, the 1905 Club emerged which catered for those who left between 1905 and 1909. It started a more energetic and high-spirited programme of golf matches, a cricket match against the school, target shooting as well as rides and walks across the Pentlands. On 17 July 1909 it played its first Annual Golf Competition at Brunstane.

It was followed in 1911 by the 1910 Club which attracted a huge membership mainly because of its lively leadership and attractive programme which included a smoking convert, gymnastics, rugby, golf, shooting and 'tramping'.

Helping the School

One aim of the Club was to help the school in any appropriate manner and its branches generously donated prizes. Among the earliest – even before an official Club had been created - was the massive Calcutta Cup presented in the 1880s by FPs in India. Members in China also presented a similar item. In 1909, the London Watsonian Club gave a fine shield for Inter-House Rugby and the Canadian Club presented a similar item for the ever-popular Inter-House Relay Race. In 1911, Mr MacLeod of the London Club donated a massive silver Challenge Bowl for the Quarter Mile Race at the Sports.

MacLeod had been the winner of the Quarter Mile and Hurdles at the very first School Sports. At the 1911 Prizegiving no fewer than 25 prizes had been awarded by the Club and its branches, including two gold watches and a Ross Rifle!

The Inter-War Years

The effect of WW1 on the overseas branches was devastating, but, by 1919, the following had recovered: Lancashire, North America, Montreal, Toronto, Winnipeg, Regina, Edmonton, Calgary, British Columbia, India (Ceylon and Burma), South Africa, Australia and New Zealand. A 1919 Club was also on the go.

This period saw the high point of branch development and the following Clubs were either reformed or founded: Glasgow (1921), Mesopotamia (1920), Fiji and Hawaii (by 1921), China (by 1922), Newcastle (1922), Border (1923), East Africa (1924), Malaya (1924), Dundee and District (1924), North West Frontier (1925), Yorkshire (1925), Central Scotland (1927), Oxford (1928), Junior 1919 Club, Washington (1928), Southern Rhodesia (1929), Transvaal (1930), Melbourne (1930), Sudan (1930), Victoria (1930), Midlands (1930), West of England and South Wales (1933), North California (1934), Brazil (1935), Highlands (1935), Aberdeen (1935) and one was proposed for Paris in 1936, but it appears only to have met once. Two Year Clubs were also begun: 1919 and 1925

The effects of WW2 were to be far more profound.

Soaring Membership

By July 1930, membership stood at 1,631, ie 563 Life Members plus 1,068 Ordinary and Country Members. In December 1932, this had soared to 2,435 and, by 1936, the Club was over the 3,000 target. There was a steady increase in numbers only halted by WW2.

The new school, an appeal for financial help, the continued enthusiasm of Henry John and strong Watsonian Club leadership in the form of AW Angus and GM Byres certainly helped raise awareness. The Club raised money for a new pitch and the grandstand at Myreside plus the embellishment and

Above Left: The Watsonian, *1930. Smith Ltd Advertisement.*
Above Right: The Watsonian, *1938. RW Forsyth Advertisement.*

By 1938, the blazer badge had been registered. The ubiquitous blue blazer is familiar to all, but less well known is the colourful 'Stripe Blazer' seen here in an advertisement for RW Forsyth in 1938.

furniture of the Assembly Hall, but not enough for pavilion accommodation, or the proposed boarding houses. Nevertheless, a brilliant effort, especially by the overseas branches.

The Old School Tie

Overseas members particularly pressed for this manifestation of Club Membership. Colours were agreed and available from 12 February 1923: maroon and Cambridge blue separated by a narrow strip of Oxford Blue with the Club Badge attached to the tie. Unfortunately, by 1930, there were several unofficial versions being sold and an effort was made to register the Club Tie. In 1931, the design was altered to maroon with narrow diagonal white lines with a three-masted ship at intervals. The main problem, apart from agreement on the design, was whether or not it impinged the rights of other parties. By 1933, the latest design had been abandoned. Yet another was tried: broad stripes of maroon and dark blue separated by narrow stripes of light blue with a design (necessary for registration) being the heart in flames contained in the dark blue stripes. They were to be available from only Smith Ltd, Forsyth Ltd, Aitken & Niven, or Stark Brothers. Again there was a delay while the design was checked, but it was eventually registered in December 1933 with the 'Heart-in-flame' as the registered Trade Mark. A tie and a square were made first and soon followed by a muffler, flannel blazer, cap, wrap (single and double) and binding for the neck and foot of sweaters. The tie proved very popular and soon members were clamouring for a blazer badge. The design for that was eventually registered on 1938. In the same year a longer and wider version of the tie was produced as well as a wider wrap.

Helping the School, 1919–39

Apart from the Appeal to help build the new school in Colinton Road, branches and individuals continued to help by donating money and prizes. In 1924, both Border and Glasgow Branches donated cups for sport, the latter for the 120 Yard Hurdles Competition. In 1925, New

The cup presented in memory of Harry Armour, 1930.

Zealand and South Africa generously donated monetary prizes for the Annual Games. In 1930, Sir James H Stewart-Lockhart fronted a scheme to present a cup to perpetuate the memory of Harry Armour, the first Captain of the school Rugby Team. In 1932, RG Hunter of British Columbia donated a cup for Inter-House Cricket whilst the Malaya Branch donated 10 guineas for prizes and 15 guineas for 'something' for the new school. And so the generosity went on.

Dr Alison's Retiral

When the Head retired in 1926 The Watsonian Club paid for a World Tour so he could meet as many of the overseas branches as possible. He managed to visit seven from China to India.

The Amalgamation

The Amalgamation of The Watsonian Club and the Athletics Club was agreed in Dowell's Room on 20 March 1933 and would take effect from October of that year. This proved no problem for the various branches which affiliated either sooner or later. The first President was the redoubtable AW Angus.

Annual Conference of Clubs

In 1933, the Glasgow Branch suggested a Conference of Clubs be held annually. The first was held in Edinburgh on 3 June 1933. By 1935 it had grown into a three-day event in London with golf matches, a visit to the Mint and a cruise from Tower Pier to the King George Dock.

Remembrance Day

The official Club wreath was usually laid at the War Memorial on Watsonian Day in January, but, in the spirit of the times, it was decided that from 1934 it would be laid on the 11 November by the President of the new Watsonian Club. The London Club continued to lay a wreath at the Cenotaph.

Activities

Central to Club life was the Annual Dinner celebrated on Watsonian Day, but other activities proved popular. The parent Edinburgh Watsonian Club introduced a Ball in 1931 which, by 1935, attracted an astonishing 600 people glowing with *"infectious gaiety"*. By 1938, a limit of 500 was set for the Assembly Rooms so that the 'Lambeth' could be safely walked! In 1929, the Oxford Branch packed into two huge cars to reach its Dinner destination and then went on to enjoy clock golf and bowls. The Lancashire lot began a 'love-feast' in 1921 which involved being regaled by 'Watsonian storeyettes'. Golf featured greatly in almost every branch, London being famous for its McJerrow Bowl Competition at the Neasden Golf Club. Indeed, London took the initiative in many areas such as informal dances and cricket tournaments. These produced record attendances and total membership increased in to 210 in 1923. One hundred new members joined the following year.

Speechs were always popular and famous Watsonians like Sir John Anderson and the Geddes brothers were in hot demand. On 8 March 1929, at a London Branch Dinner, Major Ian Hay Beith remarked that, *"... Scotsmen either left their footprints in the sands of time, or their fingerprints at Scotland Yard!"* Dinners could also get a bit 'loud', especially towards the end, so much so that the Glasgow Branch called it, *"The George Watson's College Whoop."* Toronto celebrated with a lethal concoction called Watsonian Punch. Indeed, the Glasgow Branch was described in 1925, with a membership of 221, as, *"... one of the most virile and progressive of Watsonian Clubs."* In April 1936, one member of the Edmonton group stated that it was great, *"... once a year to be small boys again."*

The Border Branch held a popular Tennis Tournament in the summer and regularly held Skittles Matches at the Sheip Heid Inn in Duddingston, presumably using the rail service to good effect. British Columbia wanted more fun and added fishing, hunting and boating to its already wide activities list.

The Junior Watsonian Club

One of the most exciting developments of the inter-war era was the 1919 Club. It was modelled on the 1905 and 1910 Clubs, but that is where the resemblance just about ends. This was an inspired group of youngsters, many of whom were completely bonkers, but out to have fun. It had 40–50 members and first met on 30 January 1919. A Constitution was drawn up on that date and they then got down to serious business: enjoying themselves. Songs

On 15 May 1937, AS Robertson, President of the Southern Rhodesian Branch, presented to the members a model of 'The Ship' complete with dolphins. It was made in bronze and modelled by himself. The base was of a local hardwood) with brass lettering on the front (Terraque marique) and on the reverse a plate with 'The Watsonian Club of Southern Rhodesia'. It was three feet in height and weighed a hundredweight.

This Branch was also using a teak hammer made from wood from the staircase at the Old School in Lauriston Place. It was known as 'The President's Mallet'. A wooden shield encasing the mallet had on one side the Merchant Company arms which was used as the school badge until 1906 and, on the reverse, the arms of George Watson. The anvil was made of M'wanga wood with a carved representation of the school on one side and a list of founder members on the other.

Does anyone know what happened to these items?

A typical branch Watsonian Dinner. This is the Lancashire Branch, 26 January 1929. Numbers were badly affected by epidemic influenza. AW Angus was there, but not the Headmaster.

and choruses were sung, recitations given, violin, piano and flute solos played with a repertoire ranging from Chopin to 'Down on the Farm'. The Branch met three times a year and teachers were allowed to be ordinary members. The idea was to open membership to all who would leave between 1919 and 1924. Every meeting ended with an eightsome reel.

The meeting on 28 January 1921 in the ante room of the College was reported as the "... usual hilarity and abandon." The following year as "... handshakes and laughter and cigarette ends ... the gusto of young Watsonians." Pa Lennie went to entertain in 1922 and another teacher, Ligertwood, described the audience as, "... the same old rascals". In 1923, a new-fangled "wireless concert" was arranged. In 1923, the members decided to form a Choir and chose as Choirmaster the only one who could sing soprano. He continued for years and would only answer to the name of 'Cuckoo'. Business meetings became stormy battles of wits and even an ordinary dinner menu was described as an "animal and vegetable monstrosity". This was the first Branch to organise outings to a local 'Palais de Danse' and special 'chefs' to concoct 'cocktails'. For the first time the School Song was danced as a Waltz. When, in 1925, they decided to present the school with a cup for the Under-Fifteen Quarter-Mile, they consecrated it with four bottles of beer, handed it mouth to mouth and each shouted at the end, "Vivat Watsonia!" A Miniature Rifle Club was started in 1925 and in 1926, a joint night with the 1925 Club enticed 70 couples to "trip the light fantastic" at the Palais.

A 1925 Club modelled itself on this Club and had equal success. Indeed, on 3 May 1929 both agreed to a union and, on Friday 28 April 1930, it became known as The Junior Watsonian Branch with members as far away as Australia and the Argentine. This didn't stop the fun. A Contortionist Club with three members was formed in 1930, an outing to the Christmas Panto was another 'first' in 1934 as was a 'Ping-Pong' Tournament. The end dance had now turned into an 'eightsome-reel-cum-waltz'. Strip the Willow had become popular by 1936 and it was danced to a piper accompanied by the Branch President on the piano. In 1936, a teacher (Anderson) gave a wonderful rendition of Phil the Fluter's Ball which brought the house down.

These were the halcyon days of branch membership. However, grey hairs were being noticed in most and one very perceptive member of the Indian Branch (AK Jameson) gave a speech as early as January 1923 in which he noted, "... the day of the European in all branches of government service is rapidly drawing to a close ..."

Post-WW2 (1945–50)

WW2 had much the same result on the branches as WW1, but the long-term effects were greater with the rise of Asian followed by African nationalism and the emergence of a more independent youth culture at home.

For the first few years it looked as if the branches just might revive and continue as after WW1. In 1944, membership stood at 3,844 and finances were sound. The Victory Ball held in the Assembly Hall on 18 January 1946 was a runaway success and was followed by three Balls in 1947, plus another in aid of the Craigmillar Boys' Club. The branches also began to revive. In 1947, Watsonian Day became Founder's Day which included pupils for the first time in the celebrations. By that time Edinburgh, Glasgow and the West, Dundee, Newcastle, Midlands and India (Burma and Ceylon) as well as the Junior Club were picking up. By 1948, British Columbia, Ceylon, Malaya, Australia and Hong Kong were on the go too. The Junior Club held its first post-war dance on 19 March 1948 in the Silver Slipper Ballroom, Morningside. The year 1949 saw the West of England and South Wales revive and also the creation of the first new post-war branch, Dumfries and Galloway, founded on 23 March. By 1950, Aberdeen and Dundee were sending reports to The Watsonian and East Africa restarted with its first Annual Dinner since 1939 held at the Lobster Pot, Nairobi.

On 7 July 1950, the WW2 additions to the War Memorial were unveiled by Air Chief Marshal Sir James Robb. In far away Malaya, meanwhile, the 'Emergency' was restricting the activities of the branch there.

The Fifties

A new membership high was reached in October 1952: 4,698. Branches also continued to revive and be born. Revived: Yorkshire (1951), Lancashire (1955) and Highland (1956). Born: Pakistan (1952), Natal (1954), Norfolk and East Anglia (1955), Nigeria (1955), East Province of the Cape of Good Hope (1957).

The Junior Branch continued to be innovative. In April 1952, it organised a successful joint event with the Junior Royal High Club which became an annual event. In 1957, an experimental joint Dance with the Parent Club proved so popular – 640 people attended – that another was organised for the following year.

By May 1959, there were 30 functioning Branches plus a couple of one-man bands: AS Macgregor in Germantown (NY) and WL Barton in Zanzibar!

The Watsonian Club of Ceylon – 3 October 1952.
STANDING: A Sharp Paul, RW McEntire, Dr R Maclagan Gorrie, RD Scott, Commander (S) Dunn, FRJ Baker, EN Annal
SEATED: RM Macintyre, CGC Kerr, F Fenwick, AG Mathewson (Vice-President), GM Mackay (President), DH Fraser, WB Henney, AD Morison, KIM Finlay.

The Club and its branches continued the good work of helping the school. The new library received books in abundance and career advice was doled out merrily to youngsters. In the mid-Fifties the Myreside Development Fund began to complete the venture begun with the move to Colinton Road and shelved by the onset of war. A scheme for boarding houses – the dream of so many ex-pats – was also initiated.

People still took trouble to meet for the Annual Dinner. At the 1957 Indian Dinner were Cpt. Ian Hunter of the Gurkhas who had travelled 500 miles, another who had motored 250 miles and a third who had come all the way from England! There was still humour too. The Eastern Cape sent a telegram in 1957 concerning its foundation to the parent Club which ended, *"Ex Corde Caritas stop to h.. with H...'s".* Nevertheless, there were always reports of a lack of members, too many grey heads and a lack of young blood.

The Sixties

The Newcastle Branch revived in 1960, but the only two new branches of the decade were Wigtown and Fife, where 'missionary work' was carried out. The new Road Bridge helped. The biggest casualty was the Junior Branch. By 1965, all its functions had lost money due to lack of support and it *"... lacked any club spirit".* It was on the point of disbanding. Joining an FP Club was no longer in any way fashionable during the Swinging Sixties, except for a few crazy conservative rugby players and medics.

In 1966, Calgary complained that all its members were over 70, there was no point sending *The Watsonian* as it meant nothing any more to the very elderly ones and the Club was effectively in mothballs. Edmonton had begun to co-operate with FPs from other Scottish Schools. Aberdeen was poorly attended despite the University having many Watsonian students.

The once mighty Glasgow Branch had been reduced to a paltry 12 members as was the Transvaal by 1969. Lancashire had had no Annual Dinner since 1965 while Dumfries lapsed for three years, 1966–9. It was, however, the Asian Clubs which suffered most. Pakistan reported in 1966, *"... our members are dwindling fast. ... We are living under difficult conditions nowadays and it is only a matter of time until we all leave these shores. When that happens our contacts will be limited to Birmingham and Bradford where we understand that it is now possible to be arrested by a Pakistani Constable and sentenced by a Pakistani Magistrate."* Indeed, in the summer of 1968, the Pakistan Club met at the Buccleuch Arms, St Boswells! In that year the Indian Branch reported that effectively there was no Branch any more: *"Devaluation of the Rupee in 1966 saw the departure from India of many foreigners and there are, in any case, fewer 'career' Expatriates working in this country because many of the positions previously held by them are now filled by Indian Managers."* The Ceylon Branch was virtually dead by 1966.

In 1964, the Singapore Branch began its transformation into *The Edinburgh Schools Club* and then *The Scottish Schools Club.* This was one way to survive.

The winds of change were also sweeping Africa. In Rhodesia, the Branch sided with the white supremacist Smith regime only bemoaning the fact that petrol sanctions had stopped people from getting to functions. The East Africa Branch collapsed.

Nevertheless, some branches were holding their own and a desperate attempt was made to re-launch the Junior Branch based on the newly refurbished Pavilion at Myreside.

The Seventies

1970 was Centenary Year. David Veitch was President and in the following year the *GWC: History and Record,* edited by Hector Waugh, was published. The Branches that had survived the Sixties mostly continued in the Seventies, but membership and support continued to decline. The Annual Dinner in Edinburgh in 1972 attracted 250 people. By 1978, it was down to 140. Even the Junior Branch was struggling for numbers despite skittles, beer and discos.

Some revivals took place such as Glasgow and Dumfries, but others like North America were virtually defunct. The amalgamation with the Ladies College in 1974 also resulted in a union of two Watsonian Clubs agreed at a meeting in the Upper Primary Hall on 30 October 1979. There were 19 Branches in existence, compared to over 30 between the wars, but some of those were in name only.

Two important gifts were made in this decade: the London Branch gave a Rowing Trophy in 1970 to reward the *"memorable enthusiasm"* in the team and in 1973 the Toronto Branch donated the Harry Jamieson Trophy for the Inter-House 1500 Metre Championships.

The Eighties and Nineties

This era saw steady decline in some areas such as Glasgow (which folded

The Harry Jamieson Trophy
Harry Jamieson with the Athletics Trophy presented to the School in his honour by the Toronto Club.

in the early Nineties) and London (which soon revived and continues to progress). Brave efforts were made to expand, such as Pub Nights in Aberdeen, and there was a brilliant revival in the Borders. The Junior Branch, despite much discussion, failed to get off the ground. Year Reunions, however, were becoming very popular indeed. Also, the Annual Dinner in 1990, cleverly timetabled for the eve of the Scotland v France Match at Murrayfield attracted 232 people. The Ball attracted 404 to the Sheraton on 1 December 1989 and a disco for younger members was much appreciated. The 250 Appeal reached its target by 1992.

In an attempt to grapple seriously with the lack of younger members the school agreed that it would pay for all leavers to become Club Members for five years. This was a significant breakthrough which would bring

Club and school even closer over the next few years.

Another development was the establishment of a Brussels Branch on 19 December 1994. A second Annual Dinner was held in 1995, but it has not progressed although a contact still exists there.

However, of great importance, was the establishment of a Development Office within the school.

The Way Ahead
Despite aid from the school, younger members were still not joining the Club in any great number. In 1995, another factor combined to create an exciting opportunity for both school and Club. First, a full-time Development Office had been established in the College. Secondly, the contract of The Watsonian Club's Secretary was due to run out shortly and the administrator was due to

retire. Thus a great opportunity arose for closer co-operation. A group (The Joint Development Group) was formed representing Club Office Bearers, both past and present, and representatives of the school, including the Development Office. A former Chairman of Governors was elected as Chair.

It was decided that the administration of The Watsonian Club and all its branches would pass to the Development Office. Membership would be free to anyone who was a pupil at Watson's and all staff. Reunions were to be organised as the main means of encouraging FPs to come back to school and keep in touch.

In a short time both parties have gained. The Watsonian Club has strengthened world wide through its contacts and the school has a strong relationship with many of its former pupils.

Norman Bruce: Soldier, Watsonian, Gentleman

Norman (left) with his brother Stanley.

Through the long history of the school and The Watsonian Club, there are many examples of individuals who have achieved outstanding feats in their fields, or gone on to lead corporations and organisations across the world. Norman Bruce's story is perhaps not one of these examples. It is not a particularly high profile story, nor did it bring a string of accolades. It is, nonetheless, a story of achievement,

a story of commitment and energy which made a difference, a very positive difference for many, many people. Norman represents all those marvellous Watsonians who have given so freely of their time, skills and enthusiasms over the years and from whom so many countless younger members of the Watson's community have benefited beyond measure.

Champion Rugby Player
Born on Christmas Day in 1914, the youngest of three brothers who attended Watson's, Norman left school in 1932, narrowly missing the move to Colinton Road. He was a dedicated and skilful athlete who participated in many sports. An attacking full back, he played for the outstanding Watsonians rugby team in their championship-winning side of 1934/5 and represented the Club at many of the Sevens tournaments. He played for Edinburgh, captained the Co-optimists and, by many accounts, was unfortunate not to be capped.

Watsonian joins Hearts!
Over the years, Norman combined his rugby with (among other sports) football, playing for Edinburgh City, before signing as an amateur for Hearts. This caused no little consternation in local circles – a Watsonian rugby

player joining Hearts. Such a thing had never happened before and at a time when the two sports represented fairly strict social divides, this bridge between the two was bordering on the revolutionary. Highlighting this division, he was the only player in the club – which included such big names as Tommy Walker and Jack Harkness – who had a car. Times have changed. Norman remained a devoted Hearts supporter for the rest of his life.

War Service
In 1939, Norman joined the Lothians and Border Horse regiment which was equipped with Sherman tanks and

Watsonian Football Club 1st XV, 1934/5. Scottish Champions.

fought through the North African campaign in the western desert and in Italy, including the battle at Monte Cassino. He served with distinction, rising to the rank of major. Awarded the Territorial Decoration, he was also mentioned in dispatches, but like many of his generation, he never recounted the horrors of this time, recalling to others only the positives such as the camaraderie and the humour in adversity.

He stayed in the army for a further year after VE day, managing to fit in selection for British Army select teams at both rugby and football. Again, the social divides of the time were evident when he arrived to play in a football match in Milan to find that a separate dressing room had been allocated to him because he was an officer (the only one in the team). He advised those responsible as to what they might do with this arrangement.

Farmer Bruce

Norman's total commitment to the community in which he found himself was always absolute. Following his wartime service, he became a farmer, and the south of Perthshire, where he farmed until the early 1970s, was soon to appreciate that it had inherited a new driving force whose energy and ability to get things done were impossible to deny.

In the neighbouring village of Doune, for example, Norman led the way in starting the local agricultural show (the Doune and Dunblane Show), an event which he ran successfully for several years and took

to the position of being the biggest one-day show in Scotland. He was a key figure in starting up the cricket club in Doune, which still exists today. And he created a thriving Cub and Scout movement in the area, starting new Troops in some of the villages, reviving moribund ones and, in at least one village in what was then a far from prosperous part of the country, achieving the feat of raising enough

Norman Bruce in the Hearts uniform.

money to build a new hall. He went on to become the District Commissioner for scouting in the area. He served, too, for many years on the board of the Small Industries Council for Rural Areas of Scotland, a body committed to encouraging small rural businesses – an ideal dear to Norman's heart.

Back to Watson's

Throughout this period, Norman never lost touch with his Watsonian connections, particularly the rugby club, and he regularly travelled to watch matches around the country. And when, in 1971, he moved to Carlops to manage an estate there, Norman became an active – very active, of course – member of both the Football Club and The Watsonian Club. In typical style, his energetic hands-on approach encompassed a catholic cross-section of practical work in addition to the standard tasks and support. On one occasion, for example, noticing that the volunteers who collected entrance money at the gate for the rugby matches were getting cold and wet, he built and put in place a wooden shelter. Planning permission was probably not sought.

Perhaps equally practically, and certainly more enduring, Norman also designed the Watsonian tartan, which has become an established and very popular feature of the Watson's and Watsonian brand. He was very upset, however, that it (or the 'Ancient' version) was not chosen to be the tartan for the girls' new kilts.

To his disappointment, ill health forced Norman to stand down from The Watsonian Club committee after his term as vice president and so he was unable to go on to become president.

Norman Bruce in Milan, 1945.

Reviving the Pipe Band

Now a new mission – the revival of the Pipe Band! With his usual gusto Norman set to to raise support and funds to turn his dream into reality.

No connections were left untapped, no targets missed, as he pursued individuals, companies, clans and others with a fierce and relentless enthusiasm. There was no way that this was not

going to happen and its success and the creation and subsequent development of the band brought him tremendous joy and pride.

Farewell

Norman died in Edinburgh in 1993. A piper from the Watson's band, wearing a kilt in the Watsonian tartan, played at his funeral. Norman was, in many ways, a remarkable Watsonian. One who supported and encouraged others. One whose loyalty to those around him was total. One who achieved so much, but whose principle objective was always to make things better for other people. Norman was one of many of whom the Watson's community can be proud.

The Development Office & The George Watson's Family Foundation

The George Watson's College Development Office was established in 1995 when the School's first Director of Development was appointed. The original remit for the post was to manage the School's PR, Marketing and Fundraising functions. The George Watson's Family Foundation (GWFF) was established as a registered charity in 1997 and exists to enable children from less advantaged backgrounds to enjoy the scope of education available to those more fortunate. It seeks to raise funds to support bursaries and scholarships and to help to finance the ongoing building programme required to reinforce Watson's pre-eminent position as one of the UK's great schools.

The launch of the Foundation which took place on Thursday 2 October 1997 was a splendid affair with representatives from all of the School's constituent groups in attendance. Andrew Cubie who was the then Chair of the School Governing Council chaired the proceeding in front of a packed Assembly hall of pupils and guests and the Honorary President of the Foundation, The Rt Hon Sir Malcolm Rifkind officially launched the Foundation to great applause. Primary pupils Graham Unwin(P7), Julia Graham (P5), Lyndsey McGhee (P3), Head Boy David Willis and

The launch of the George Watson's Family Foundation, 1997.

Head Girl Alixe Kilgour represented pupils at the launch.

The Government's decision in 1997 to abolish the Assisted Places Scheme (which at that stage supported 17% of pupils (around 240) in the Senior School at George Watson's College) threatened the ethos of the School which since it was founded has consistently sought to provide places to a wide social range of pupils, irrespective of their financial means. The School, which predicted this move by Government had established the GWFF, but it was in its infancy at the time of the Scheme's abolition.

By session 2005/6, the number of Foundationers being supported at Watson's through the George Watson's Family Foundation had reached 125 and in addition to the extension and refurbishment of the Jack Martin Music School, the installation of

ramping in the Junior School, ramping and a lift in the Senior School, the creation of George Square (in what previously had been known as the East Quad) the Foundation was about to embark on fundraising for Phase Three of its largest capital project, namely the redevelopment of the School PE facilities. Phase One, The Murray Family Pavilion opened on 26 January 2006, Phase Two was due to start in July 2006 and the challenge of Phase Three: a full refurbishment and development of the swimming pool and a rebuilding of the central section of the existing building to include a three-storey tower.

By 2003 the staffing in the DO had risen to four full-time and one part-time members of staff and, additionally, a Marketing Manager had been appointed to look after the School PR and Marketing function to enable the Development Office staff to focus on fundraising and relations with former pupils and other constituent groups.

The Development Office worked in close contact with The Watsonian Club from its inception. A joint Development Group was established under the Chairmanship of Geoff Ball, the former Chair of the School Governing Council, to encourage a new way of the School and Club moving forward together for the benefit of both. In 2000, the administrative function of The Club moved to the Development

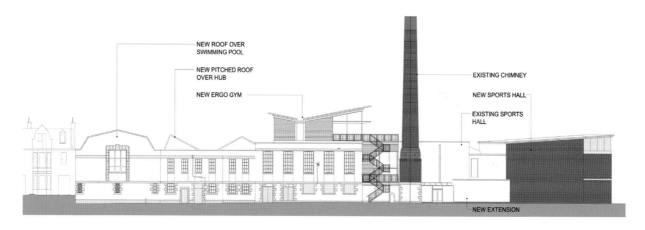

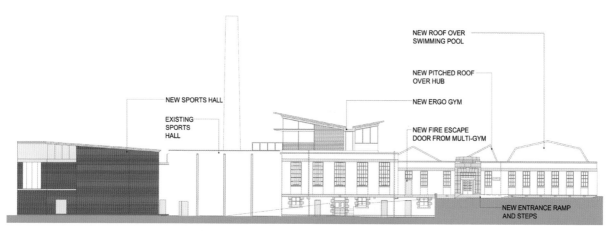

Side elevation and architects' impressions of the proposed developments.

Office and membership fees were disbanded with every former pupil automatically becoming a member of The Club. Specialist software was introduced to Watson's in 1996 to ensure that accurate records were kept so that efficient event organisation, communication and fundraising could take place. In the decade from 1995 to 2005, methods of communication with former pupils and others had dramatically changed with amongst other things, the use of email.

Issue one of *Caritas*, a magazine for former pupils and friends of the School was introduced in January 1996 with the aim of engaging the Watson's community with the School, the Foundation and the worldwide Watsonian network. This free publication helped to re-energise the Watsonian community and sparked communication from people throughout the world.

In 2004, the constitution of The Watsonian Club was amended and the objects of The Watsonian Club defined as *"to promote and maintain cooperation at home and abroad between former pupils and staff of the Schools in all matters relating to the welfare of that School: to strengthen friendships formed there: to carry on a Benevolent Fund for the benefit of Watsonians and their dependents: to promote and monitor its recognised Sections and Branches throughout the world and encourage participation in sports and other activities"*. This definition became a focus for the Watsonian Council and the Development Office for their work with former pupils.

The Development Office embarked on the route of relationship fundraising from the outset of the Foundation to ensure that former pupils, parents, staff, former parents, The Merchant Company and other friends of the school could enjoy a special relationship with the School. The three broad areas of Foundation fundraising activity introduced were the Annual Fund, Major Gifts and Legacy. In addition an active programme, to foster good relations with constituents, was implemented and considered essential if Watson's was to use its communication network to promote a fundraising culture for the future development of the School.

The Annual Fund was introduced in 1998 to try and encourage those with an interest in Watson's to support the School through annual donations. The first Annual Fund raised £74,947 and by session 2004/5 this had risen to £196,997.90. A legacy programme was introduced in 1999 and the Caritas Society was formed for all those who had pledged a legacy to the Foundation.

In addition to individual support, support for the Foundation has been received from companies and trusts. Volunteers throughout the Watsonian community have helped to fundraise and many events were introduced to raise awareness of the Foundation and also provide social opportunities for all of the School's constituent groups. The Foundation's major fundraising event of the year, the Caritas Dinner in the eight years to November 2005 had raised £212,864 and used pupil volunteers to help with the event.

Traditional former pupil events such as The Watsonian Dinner and other branch dinners continue to take place throughout the world and the introduction of more informal events are being encouraged. In 2002 the Annual reunion was introduced for the first time. This proved a success and continues to attract around 400 former pupils back to School.

In 2006 when the importance of Charitable Status is being addressed by the Office of the Scottish Charity Regulator, the importance of the Foundation and other charitable and community work undertaken by the School has never been greater. An audit of School community activity is maintained by the Development Office and is a continuation and expansion of the School's original charitable aims.

The Caritas Dinner, 2005.

The Watsonian Dinner, 2005.

Class of 1985 at the Reunion Dinner, 2005.

Development Office Staff, 2006.
BACK ROW: Carol Wood, Julie-Anne McPhee.
FRONT ROW: Ann Charman, Roy Mack, Leslie McKean.

James and Marilyn Watson and Family.

One of George Watson's signet rings.

The Watson Family

James, (wife, Marilyn, and family), and his brother Ian, (wife Michelle and son Maxwell), are the only known descendants of George Watson, but the College has only known about them since July 2002 when James and family visited us for the first time.

George was one of six children plus a step-brother John Symmer. George's younger brother, James, married Elizabeth Wilkie on 2 December 1675 and they had three children: Bethia, 1677 (who died in infancy), Elizabeth, 1679 (who is named in George's will) and George, 1678. James Watson in the photograph above descends from that George.

Most of the male Watsons were merchants and lived in the Canongate, but George's father lived on Pirrie's Close just off the Royal Mile. It is very likely that was where George and his siblings lived when their father died and he was subsequently adopted by Aunt Elizabeth (Bessie who married James Davidson).

James' great-grandfather emigrated to Canada. James modifies and tests aircraft for a living, but is also a volunteer firefighter. Marilyn is a social worker.

James Watson possesses one of three known examples of his ancestor's signet rings. Amazingly it has a ship design very similar to the one which graces the front of our school. The motto is *"We seek the far shores"*. The rings may have been used in times of poor and unsafe communication to validate family and business correspondence. James, and other members of the Watson family, including a newly adopted baby Samantha FuShu, live in Brechin, (Ontario, Canada), 60 miles north of Toronto.

Apart from a fine collection of letters, bills, notebooks and account ledgers there are two personal items of furniture in the College which once belonged to George Watson.

The first is a magnificent armoire, a cupboard or dresser, in the seventeenth century Dutch style made in oak and other woods including ebony. Jack Ferguson and Hannah Watson certainly had no idea of its value, or its connection with our Founder.

The second item is a superb fall-front bureau made in walnut. It is kept in the Principal's office.

Jack Ferguson and Hannah Watson pictured with the armoire.

Principal Gareth Edwards and his PA, Yvonne Clark, with Watson's fall-front bureau.

Gareth Edwards, Principal.

Three hundred and fifty years and more of George Watson and George Watson's College: a story involving so many over the centuries, so many ordinary and extraordinary lives but united by a common bond that is epitomised in the school motto: "*Ex Corde Caritas*".

This history records the very many 'highs' and, thankfully, the far fewer 'lows' of a tradition that has served Edinburgh, Scotland and the world. It is a record of a community that has grown, a community that has changed and adapted, but also a community which has at its core an assured purpose of developing young people to take their place in the world they inherit generation upon generation.

The world inhabited by George Watson is vastly different from our own in the twenty-first century. Yet it is remarkably similar in equal proportion. The foundations that he created remain the same, precisely because what he started has, itself, changed. In order that what is fundamental to an institution stays the same, the institution itself must change, and this is the record of such change alongside an essential continuum.

So what of the next 350 years or even the next 10? As in the past, George Watson's College will welcome challenge and it will respond and adapt to the circumstances it faces. We have

seen the amalgamation of the Boys' and the Ladies' Colleges into a confident and modern co-educational school; we have seen political and ideological influences which have moved us away from the mainstream state educational system; but in recent years we have also seen, with the advent of Scotland's new parliament, a greater understanding of the part to be played by independent schools in the future of Scotland. With a review of the status of charitable organisations in Scotland in this the early part of a new century, Watson's has to change and adapt so that its fundamental purpose, to which it is charged to remain true, can survive and flourish. The George Watson's Family Foundation, established to rise to such a challenge, and the School's vast community have a duty to preserve the legacy of its founder. The benefactors of the twenty-first century will be different; the beneficiaries too will be different but George Watson's College will remain, essentially, the same.

For those whose privilege it is to guide the school into its future, we are charged to maintain tradition alongside innovation. 'Twas ever thus', but we are sustained by a confidence based upon the quality of the relationships which are the hallmark of this successful and forward-thinking school. With such a stimulus we can continue to provide quality education that will be attractive to the coming generations of Scottish citizens. To do so we must retain confidence in ourselves and provide young people with an understanding of where they are in the continuum that is Watson's, Edinburgh and the nation. We must teach that which is relevant and in a style which reflects our knowledge of how we learn best, but we must also teach what is valuable and essential, whatever the present age might regard as relevant: that will be the practical outcome of 'changing to remain the same'.

And for our inspiration, we can do no better than to look to the wisdom of the nineteenth century.

Scottish scientist and theologian, Henry Drummond, who spoke of

the true essentials which any school can little afford to forget. He could see in the world he knew the 'white heat' of technological change as the coach was superseded by the steam age only to be confronted itself by the advent of electricity; he could see how the latest scientific research would so swiftly be consigned to the archive. In a hundred years from now, who knows what form public examinations might take at Watson's or what might be the technological assistance in the classroom, or even whether the classroom itself will be easily identifiable. Yet what Drummond believed and stated, in such a simple and straightforward manner, is as true in our time as it was then and will be in the ages to come. For he declared that: *"What we are stretches past what we do, beyond what we possess".*

What is important and what is absolute is true whatever the generation. Therefore, it is the duty of all of us who now play a part in the Watson's community to pass on those unchanging absolutes such as love of learning, commitment, integrity, a concern for others, and a sense of citizenship. For this is indeed what makes *"Ex Corde Caritas".*

Gareth Edwards
Principal

Gareth Edwards at the Loos Memorial during the 2005 Battlefields Tour where a wreath was laid on behalf of the College.

The 'Wee' Committee BACK ROW: Fiona Denyer, Liz Smith, Les Howie, David Brown, Roy Mack. FRONT ROW: Clare Mackay, Karen Tumblety, Fiona Hooper, Katrina MacIver, Graham Gibb. ABSENT: Maxi MacLaren.

Acknowledgements

So many people have helped make this book possible that it is difficult to know where to begin, but the people thanked are not in any order of precedence and if, by any horrible mischance, I have omitted someone, please forgive.

There has been nothing short of magnificent support from the Principal, Gareth Edwards, the Governors and the History Department headed until 2005 by the long-suffering Marco Longmore and now Jadzia Hind. Without two-thirds of a session free to research and write, this book would not have been possible. Above all I must thank the anonymous sponsor who had the imagination, faith and generosity to back the enterprise. I hope that person is fully gratified by the end result.

Thanks to the 'Wee' Committee for keeping the show on the road and me firmly on it. Special thanks to Fiona Denyer for her incisiveness and patience, for Graham's problem-solving abilities and Katrina's countless contacts.

Life would have been extremely difficult without the co-operation, support and advice of Fiona Hooper, Librarian and Archivist, who has a wonderful ability to solve problems easily and find material just as quickly.

I see myself as an ex-officio member of the Development Office team (Lesley McKean, Roy Mack and staff). Its enthusiasm and support for the project has been constant. Indeed, the book would be much poorer without its advice and help. Lesley and Roy have a real love for Watson's which inspires all the great work they do, day in and day out.

This is an illustrated history and, therefore, the contribution of our official school photographer, Ian MacHaffie, has been invaluable. I have never seen anyone produce photographs faster. Ask Ian to take a photograph and it is done within the day! Driven by his genuine interest in the history of Watson's, its architecture and artefacts, Ian has gone well out of his way to be supportive. His acrobatics in pursuit of the perfect image are legendary, varying from dancing on the tables at Merchants' Hall to dangling over the top of the building at Colinton Road held only by his belt grasped by the equally mad Head Janitor, Gordon Mowat. Indeed, Ian's interest in Watson's heritage is only matched by that of Gordon who has done so much over the years to preserve historical material and has supported every initiative concerned with Watson's past.

I apologise for the poor quality of some of the illustrations, usually lifted from *The Watsonian*, or other such publications. Faced with having a fuzzy picture or none, I opted for the former. May I appeal to anyone who has relevant photographs to either gift or lend them to the School Archive, or give us copies, preferably on CD.

The staff and members of the Merchant Company have always been most helpful in allowing me to burrow away in the cellar, finding bits and bobs I would otherwise have missed and allowing acrobatic Ian to take photographs.

The various Edinburgh Libraries have helped enormously. I really must thank the ever cheerful Richard Hunter of the City Archive for his heroic efforts to assist despite staff cuts and inadequate funding which make the viewing of documents quite difficult. The staff of the Edinburgh Room have been constantly patient and helpful, above all GWC parent and friend, Susan Orlowski. Edinburgh University Library (Sheila Noble, Special Collections) must be thanked for allowing us to use a photograph of Prof Simon Laurie and the Signet Library (Audrey Walker) for allowing us to photograph the first advertisements for Watson's staff and pupils. Also, thanks to Imogen Gibbon of the Scottish National Portrait Gallery for finding useful illustrative material.

A thousand thanks to Karen Tumblety for teaching me the facts of publishing and printing life. Also, to David Brown who actually prepared all of this book for the printer. The polished professional finish to this work has been David's own, as is the book's cover and format. David can be the only person to challenge Ian MacHaffie when it comes to speed of production!

Elizabeth White has poured over every word in this book to correct my errors whilst Graham Gibb has done the same to keep me on the straight and narrow historical path.

A huge debt is also owed to the many people who contributed articles, information and advice: staff, former staff, FPs, parents and friends. You are all wonderful people!

Les Howie

George Watson's Hospital and College Primary Sources

Statutes and Rules of George Watson's Hospital (Various dates)
George Watson's Hospital Minutes, 1724–1870
George Watson's College Minutes, 1870–1909
Education Board Minutes, 1909– (Edinburgh City Archive)
Merchant Company Minutes (Edinburgh City Archive)
GWC Prospectuses, 1870–1939 (Edinburgh City Archive)
GWC Quarterly Magazine, Vols 1 & 2 (1873 & 1874)
GW Literary Club Magazine, 1898
Recreation Park Joint Committee Minute Book, 1897–1938)
Watson's College Athletic Club Minute Books (1892 & 1900–8)
Minute Book of the Watsonian 1905 Clubs (Begun 1909)
The Watsonian Club Minutes, Vol 1, 1894–1921
The Watsonian Club Minutes, Vol 2, 1921–7
Reminiscences of George Heriot's Hospital, Baillie, J (Edinburgh)
Catalogue of the Pictures, Sculpture and Historical Articles belonging to the Merchants of the City of Edinburgh (Edinburgh, 1908)
Recess Studies, Grant, Sir A (ed) (Edinburgh, 1870)
Old Edinburgh Characters and Costumes, Vol 2, Howie, James (Unpublished, 1890, Edinburgh City Archive)
Report on the Burgh and Middle Class Schools in Scotland, Vols 1 & 2 (1868)
First Report of the Royal Commissioners appointed to Inquire into the Endowed Schools and Hospitals (Scotland) (Edinburgh, 1873)
Third Report with Appendix in Two Volumes (Edinburgh, 1875)
First Report of the Educational Endowments (Scotland) Commission with Evidence and Appendix (Edinburgh, 1884)
Second Report (Edinburgh, 1885)
Fifth Report with Evidence and Appendix (Edinburgh,1888)
Report of the Departmental Committee appointed in April 1927 to consider and advise regarding Educational Endowments in Scotland (Edinburgh, 1927)
The History of Edinburgh from its Foundation to the Present Time, Maitland, W (Edinburgh, 1753)
Our Bark. First Watson's School Magazine. Hand-written, 1860s.
Ben Hanson: A Story of George Watson's College, Saxby, Jessie (Edinburgh, 1886)
The Appeal: Old and New Watson's (Edinburgh, 1929?)
The Watsonian, 1904–54. A Jubilee Volume (ed H Waugh), (Oliver & Boyd, 1955)
The Watsonian Magazine (1904–present)
The Watsonian War Record, 1914–18 (War Memorial Executive, 1920)
The Watsonian War Record,1939–45 (The Watsonian Club, 1951)

George Watson's Hospital and College Secondary Sources

Education and Opportunity in Victorian Scotland, Anderson, RD (EUP, 1989)
The Royal Scots, 1914–19, Vols. 1 & 2, Ewing, Major John (Oliver & Boyd, 1925)
Fifty Years On. The History of the Watsonian Hockey Club.
William Adam, 1689–1748, Gifford, John (Mainstream, 1989)
The Company of Merchants of the City of Edinburgh and its Schools, 1694–1920, Harrison, John (Merchants' Hall, 1920)
The Rise and Progress of the Company of Merchants of the City of Edinburgh, 1681–1902, Heron, Alexander (Edinburgh, 1903)
Hospitals into Schools. The Edinburgh Merchant Company Experience. Howie, LG (Unpublished MA Dissertation, 1972) Includes references to Merchant Company Copy Letter Books disgracefully destroyed at sometime since 1972.
The Geographical Distribution of Material Wealth, Johnston, Alexander K (Peter Lawson, 1862)
Jinglin' Geordie's Legacy, Lockhart, Brian RW (Tuckwell Press, 2003)
The Life and Work of Duncan McLaren, Vols. 1 & 2, Mackie, JB (Nelson, 1888)
Makers of Scottish Education, Morgan, A (Longmans, 1929)
A History of the Royal High School, Murray, Dr J (Edinburgh, 1997)
William Adam, 1689–1748, Simpson, James (Scottish National Portrait Gallery, 1989)
History of George Heriot's Hospital, Steven, W (Edinburgh, 1859)
Supplement to Third Edition of History of George Heriot's Hospital (Edinburgh, 1878)
The Watsonian Football Club, 1875–1975
The Watsonian Cricket Club, 1875–1975
Story of a Great Hospital, Turner, AL (Thin, 1979)
The Company of Merchants of the City of Edinburgh (Merchants' Hall, 1931)
George Watson's College. History and Record, 1724–1970, Waugh, Hector (ed) (Clark, Edinburgh, 1970)

George Watson's Ladies College Primary Sources

The George Square Chronicles, 1910–74
Our Square Jessie E MacDonald (Robert Grant and Son, Edinburgh, 1925)
A Book of George Square Verse (Turnbull and Spears, Edinburgh, 1933)
George Watson's Ladies' College Prospectuses 1873–1916
The George Watson's Ladies' College Archive
George Watson's Ladies' College Register of Admissions
The Women Watsonians' Club Archive
The Watsonian Club Archive
Numerous Watsonians, Women Watsonians and former members of staff
The Perth Women Watsonians' Club
The London Watsonian Club
The Paris Watsonian Club
The Women Watsonians' Golf Club Archive
The Women Watsonians' Hockey Club Archive
Merchant Company Education Board Minutes 1871–1974
The Archive Room, Merchants' Hall
The Scotsman
The Evening News
The Evening Dispatch
The Herald
The Scottish Hockey Union
The Imperial War Museum
The Commonwealth War Graves Commission
The Red Cross Society
Madame Murzyn, Falaise, Ardennes, France
The Wagner Society, London
Gloucester Road Bookshop, South Kensington, London
Lady Hopetoun, Philipstoun House
The Archive Room, Hopetoun House
Peebles Tourist Information Office
Mr Montgomery, Grange Loan, Edinburgh
Diaries of J Melrose Smibert, Vice Convenor GWLC 1965–7
Members of the Mary Erskine Guild
The Mercators' Dramatic Club
Greyfriars' Church
George Heriot's School Archive
The Edinburgh Zoological Society
Hamilton & Inches, Ediburgh
The House of Commons Library
The Scottish National Portrait Gallery
The National Portrait Gallery
The Royal College of Surgeons
The University of Edinburgh
The University of Warwick
The University of Sheffield
Ken Lochhead, Artist
Daniel Stewart's and Melville College Archive

George Watson's Ladies College Secondary Sources

A Family Unbroken: The Mary Erskine School Tercentenary History, 1694–1994, Lydia Skinner (Tuckwell Press, 1994)
Historic South Edinburgh, Vol 1, Charles A Smith (Charles Skilton Ltd, Edinburgh 1978)
Glorious Victory: Admiral Duncan and the Battle of Camperdown 1797 (Dundee City Council Essays 1997)
The Edinburgh Directory, 1868–9
The Bank of Scotland Financial Reports 1980–90
T*he Auld Hoose: The Story of Robert Gordon's College,* Jack Webster (Edinburgh 2005)
Outdoor Adventures: the Story of Third Year Projects at George Watson's College, (eds) Sir Roger Young and Liz Smith (Edinburgh 2003)
Old and New Edinburgh Vol 1–V1, (Cassell, Petter and Galpin & Co, London 1883)
The Queen's Scotland: Edinburgh and the Lothians (ed) Theo Lang, (Hodder and Stoughton, London, 1952)